MySQL®
Administrator's
Bible

MySQL®
Administrator's
Bible

Sheeri Cabral
Keith Murphy

WILEY

Wiley Publishing, Inc.

MySQL®Administrator's Bible

Published by
Wiley Publishing, Inc.
10475 Crosspoint Boulevard
Indianapolis, IN 46256
www.wiley.com

Copyright © 2009 by Wiley Publishing, Inc., Indianapolis, Indiana

Published simultaneously in Canada

ISBN: 978-0-470-41691-4

Manufactured in the United States of America

10 9 8 7 6 5 4 3 2 1

Library of Congress Cataloging-in-Publication Data:

Cabral, Sheeri, 1978-
MySQL administrator's bible / Sheeri Cabral, Keith Murphy.
    p. cm.
Includes index.
ISBN 978-0-470-41691-4 (paper/website)
1. MySQL (Electronic resource) 2. Database management. 3. Relational databases. I. Cabral, Sheeri,
    1970- II. Title.
QA76.9.D3C3178 2009
005.75'65 — dc22

2009005633

For general information on our other products and services please contact our Customer Care Department within the United States at (877) 762-2974, outside the United States at (317) 572-3993 or fax (317) 572-4002.

About the Authors

Sheeri K. Cabral is a Database Team Lead at the Pythian Group, a remote database administration solution. She has a master's degree in computer science specializing in databases from Brandeis University and a career background in systems administration. Unstoppable as a volunteer and activist since she was 14, Sheeri founded and organizes the Boston MySQL User Group. She also produces OurSQL: The MySQL Database Podcast for the Community, By the Community and many workshop videos. These resources are freely available at www.technocation.org, the website of Technocation, Inc. Sheeri is the Treasurer of Technocation, Inc, a not-for-profit organization providing resources and educational grants for IT professionals. Sheeri currently lives in the Boston area with her husband Tony Cabral and a myriad assortment of Muppets™. When she's not working or volunteering, she reads, knits, listens to podcasts, and enjoys time with her nieces and nephews.

Keith Murphy is a MySQL database administrator who has been using MySQL server since 1998. A long-time Linux system administrator, he worked with a number of Internet companies solving systems issues. More recently he formed Paragon Consulting Services (http://www.paragon-cs.com) to provide consulting services for companies seeking training for MySQL and help with MySQL solutions ranging from everyday database administration tasks to utilizing "cloud" computing services, performance tuning, and scaling. In addition to information about the company, Keith blogs at http://blog.paragon-cs.com, which he updates as frequently as possible with tricks, tips, and general information about MySQL server.

In addition he is the editor of MySQL Magazine (http://www.mysqlzine.net), the MySQL community's digital magazine about all things MySQL. It is his pleasure to work with some of the finest people in the community in this collaborative effort to increase both the amount and quality of the available information on MySQL server.

Readers are invited to contact Keith by email at bmurphy@pargon-cs.com.

Credits

Executive Editor
Robert Elliott

Development Editor
Ed Connor

Technical Editors
Baron Schwartz
Morgan Tocker
Nicklas Westerlund

Production Editor
Liz Britten

Copy Editors
Kim Cofer
Foxxe Editorial Services

Editorial Manager
Mary Beth Wakefield

Production Manager
Tim Tate

Vice President and Executive Group Publisher
Richard Swadley

Vice President and Executive Publisher
Barry Pruett

Associate Publisher
Jim Minatel

Project Coordinator, Cover
Lynsey Stanford

Proofreader
Jen Larsen, Word One New York

Indexer
Jack Lewis

Acknowledgments

Sheeri Cabral

When I was four years old, I refused to let anyone else tie my shoes, because I wanted to do it myself. There was only one problem — I did not know how to tie my shoes yet. I went around for months with untied shoes because I made it very clear that I was going to do it. Eventually I learned to tie my shoes. I also learned that I could do anything I put my mind to.

I could not have accomplished the herculean task of writing a book had I not had the encouragement of my stubbornness. To Mom, Dad, Lymor, Noam, Josh, and Elinor, thanks for putting up with me all these years, letting me try my way so that my failures and successes were my own, and teaching me to always do a good job so I can be proud of my work. My love of databases was inspired by the man who taught me the subject at Brandeis University, Professor Mitch Cherniack. Professionally, I would not be the person I am today without the guidance and example of Tom Limoncelli, an inspirational role model, great mentor, and good friend; and Tracy Gangwer, who taught me to be a super DBA/sysadmin by confirming and triple-checking everything. A huge thank you goes to Keith for being the lead author on this project, and of course for asking me to become involved. Of course, none of this could have been done without the support of Wiley Publishing, particularly our editors Ed Connor and Bob Elliott.

I used many two-dimensional resources while writing this book, but there's a limit to how much information is in manuals and books. Special thanks are due to Brian Aker for being a constant fountain of readily available knowledge and Martin Garden for software assistance. Jay Pipes provided permission for material used in the Query Analysis chapter, Roland Bouman helped me get a firm grip on the data dictionary, and Mark Atwood answered my questions about how storage engines work. I was encouraged and supported by Carsten Turner, Ronald Bradford, Patrick Galbraith, and many fans of the OurSQL Podcast who wrote to me asking when it was coming back.

Keith Murphy

There are many people involved in any book project. Without the crew of people from Wiley we could never have finished this book. Thank you, Bob Elliott (our Executive Editor) for taking a chance on me. I hope you weren't disappointed. Without our Development Editor, Ed Connor, I suspect we would have ended up in the ditch — never to get out. And thanks to all the other people at Wiley who I didn't have the chance to meet who help make this happen.

Sheeri, I could not have done this alone. I am grateful for all the long hours and the meticulous attention to detail that you brought to the project. If I ever get the notion to write another book you will be the first person I call. Of course you don't have to answer!

And a big thanks for all those in the MySQL community. It is you who help power this crazy thing we call Open Source. Thank you for taking the time help others learn and become better.

Contents at a Glance

Contents

Part III Core MySQL Administration

Part IV Extending Your Skills

Contents

Introduction

Welcome to the MySQL Administrator's Bible. Like all books in the Bible series, you can expect to find both hands-on tutorials and real-world practical application information, as well as reference and background information that provide a context for what you are learning. This book is a comprehensive resource on MySQL database administration. It covers almost every conceivable topic of database administration from the very basics, including server installation and user management, to some fairly complex topics such as security and high availability. By the time you have completed the MySQL Administrator's Bible you will be well-prepared to perform as a database administrator.

This book fully covers MySQL 5.1 plus early features of the 6.0 release (as of the time of writing). All of the examples work in both MySQL 5.1 and MySQL 6.0, except where noted.

Who Should Read This Book

This book is designed for two groups of people. The first group of people is those who have never worked on a database server and want to learn the fundamentals of database management using the world's number one open source database server. The second group of people is those who are currently using another database server and are looking to make a transition to MySQL server. They may be experienced database administrators, but are not experienced with MySQL.

How This Book Is Organized

The MySQL Administrator's Bible is divided into four parts.

Part I makes no assumptions on the knowledge level of the reader. Chapter 1 is a brief introduction to MySQL's history. After this introduction Part I covers:

- MySQL server installation (Chapter 2)
- Accessing MySQL server (Chapter 3)

Part II covers how MySQL compares to standards and MySQL's SQL syntax:

- How MySQL extends and deviates from standard SQL (Chapter 4)
- MySQL data types (Chapter 5)
- MySQL index types (Chapter 6)

- Stored routines, triggers and events (Chapter 7)
- MySQL Views (Chapter 8)
- Transactions in MySQL (Chapter 9)

Part III is all about MySQL administration:

- Tuning the server (Chapter 10)
- MySQL storage engines (Chapter 11)
- Caching with MySQL (Chapter 12)
- Backups, recovery and disaster planning (Chapter 13)
- Managing MySQL users (Chapter 14)
- Partitioning in MySQL server (Chapter 15)
- Logging and replication (Chapter 16)
- Measuring performance (Chapter 17)

Part IV highlights intermediate topics ranging from further administrative tasks to performance tuning:

- Query analysis and index tuning (Chapter 18)
- Monitoring MySQL servers (Chapter 19)
- Securing MySQL (Chapter 20)
- The MySQL data dictionary (Chapter 21)
- Scaling MySQL server and high availability (Chapter 22)

  In addition to the two parts there are three appendixes of additional material:
- Using the MySQL Proxy (Appendix A)
- MySQL Functions reference (Appendix B)
- Additional resources for MySQL (Appendix C)

Conventions and Features

There are many different organizational and typographical features throughout this book designed to help you get the most of the information.

Tips, Notes, and Cautions

Whenever the authors want to bring something important to your attention the information will appear in a Tip, Note, Caution or On the Website.

CAUTION This information is important and is set off in a separate paragraph with a special icon. Cautions provide information about things to watch out for, whether simply inconvenient or potentially hazardous to your data or systems.

TIP Tips generally are used to provide information that can make your work easier — special shortcuts or methods for doing something easier than the norm.

NOTE Notes provide additional, ancillary information that is helpful, but somewhat outside of the current presentation of information.

ON the WEBSITE On the Website points the reader to the companion website (www.wiley.com/go/mysqladminbible). The website contains new material and up to-date information about evolving MySQL features.

What's on the Companion Website

On the companion website (www.wiley.com/go/mysqladminbible), you will find the following:

- Sample code — each chapter has its own subfolder on the website and you'll find all the code output that was discussed in each chapter organized accordingly.
- Examples that work in both MySQL 5.1 and MySQL 6.0 (as released at the time of writing), except where noted.
- Extra material such as a new SQL tutorial, information on spatial data and indexes, and up-to-date information on the new features in MySQL 6.0.
- Errata updates.

Where To Go From Here

When you finish reading MySQL Administrator's Bible you will have a solid foundation for working as a MySQL database administrator. While it takes experience to produce a quality database administrator, knowledge and understanding of foundational principals is critical. Our goal in this book is to provide those two parts of the equation.

You will definitely want to check out the companion website (www.wiley.com/go/mysqladminbible). MySQL 6.0 is still new technology at the time of publication of this book and it will continue to evolve for some time. The world of MySQL changes quickly and the information in the book is up-to-date at time of publication. However, as more changes occur, we will write about the latest changes on the website.

In addition there are many other resources available as you grow in your knowledge of MySQL server. Many of these resources are listed in Appendix C of the book but we would point out in particular Planet MySQL (http://www.planetmysql.org), a blog aggregation site, and MySQL Magazine (http://www.mysqlzine.net), a free digital magazine with which the co-authors are involved.

MySQL®
Administrator's
Bible

Part I

First Steps with MySQL

Chapter 1

Introduction to MySQL

IN THIS CHAPTER

Learning MySQL's history

Finding the MySQL community

Contributing to MySQL

Everyone who has been involved with IT for more than a few months has at least heard of MySQL. The acquisition of MySQL AB by Sun Microsystems brought a great deal of additional attention to MySQL's database management system (DBMS). Even so, there is often more to MySQL than many people realize. They simply do not realize the full capabilities of MySQL.

Recent versions of MySQL have brought a large feature set that covers just about every imaginable need. This includes partitions, scheduled events, prepared statements, triggers, and views. MySQL has long been used in dynamic websites and applications. Whether you program in Perl, PHP, ASP, .NET or Ruby you can integrate MySQL into your environment.

MySQL Mission — Speed, Reliability, and Ease of Use

The driving force behind MySQL has been to provide a reliable, high-performance server that is easy to set up and use. These qualities are why many Internet companies in the late 1990s chose MySQL to power their websites. These same qualities are why MySQL is making strong inroads into the internal database servers of Fortune 1000 companies that have traditionally used commercial databases. MySQL did not corner the existing database market; instead, MySQL allowed the database market to expand and grow to include people all over the world. MySQL created a niche by creating the opportunity for almost anyone to be able use a database. Had there not been an easy-to-use, fast, reliable database server such as MySQL, there would be a dearth of the user-provided content and collaborative efforts that are what we expect from the Internet. Without MySQL, there would be far fewer articles, podcasts, online 'zines, tutorials, photos, forums, videos, collaborative reference material, and search engines. The World (Wide Web) as we know it would be completely different.

MySQL is not the only free database management system; it also is not the only open source database management system. One of the largest differences is the user friendliness that pervades MySQL. The friendliness, starting with the cost — free unless embedded in another product — shines through the quick installation and setup, and pleases the new database user with SQL language extensions that are nearly intuitive. For example, the SHOW DATABASES command shows a list of databases you have permission to see.

Experienced database administrators can install, configure, and bring a MySQL server online in less than fifteen minutes. If the installation process is packaged it can be done in five minutes. We look at the installation process in more detail in Chapter 2.

The reliability of MySQL played a role in MySQL's rise to become, as stated at www.mysql.com, "the world's most popular open source database." In addition to this reliability, MySQL operates on a wide range of hardware and operating systems from laptops to multi-core servers. Though benchmark comparisons can be slanted to benefit one server or another, the various benchmarks available show that MySQL competes with and frequently beats competing database servers.

Company background

MySQL server has been downloaded more than 100 million times. MySQL is *open source* software. An admittedly simple definition of open source software is software that is freely available (including *source code*) with free redistribution. Source code is the source of a program — the file(s) containing the original programming language code, which can be read, discussed, and learned from, just as the words of a book can. The roots of MySQL server are found in a database system called Unireg that was developed by Michael "Monty" Widenius for a Swedish company called TcX during the 1980s. The initial release of MySQL server was created in 1995 when Monty added an SQL interface to Unireg. Shortly after, David Axmark recommended MySQL server be released under a *dual licensing* model, where it would be available for widespread free use but could also be used in situations that require a more restrictive licensing use (such as in embedded devices). David and Monty, together with Allan Larsson, founded MySQL AB in 1995. MySQL AB was the company that, until its acquisition by Sun Microsystems in January 2008, provided support and service for the MySQL database in addition to developing most of the code.

In 2001 MySQL began supporting transactions with the integration of the BDB and InnoDB engines. This allowed for safer handling of concurrent write operations, which began the trend of adding features needed by enterprise environments.

Over the years the feature set of the MySQL server has grown to cover almost any feature needed in an enterprise database server. Some might even argue that it has too many features! Innovation has continued; within months of readily accessible cloud computing environments such as Amazon Web Services (http://aws.amzon.com), hobbyists and companies alike are deploying and using MySQL in creative environments.

Table 1-1 shows an overview of MySQL server's release history, including important pre-release (Alpha and Beta) unstable versions as well as public stable releases that were determined to be *generally available* (GA). In Table 1-1, only the first release notes the new features, though all features mentioned in the pre-release Beta version were also released in the GA version.

TABLE 1-1

MySQL Server Timeline

Version	Release Date	Release Level	New Features
Internal release	May 23, 1995		
Public Release	August 31, 1996		Binaries for Solaris
Windows Release	January 8, 1998		Windows 95 & Windows NT
3.23	June 2000	Beta	BDB and InnoDB
3.23	January 2001	GA	
4.0	August 2002	Beta	Unions
4.0	March 2003	GA	
4.1	June 2004	Beta	Subqueries, prepared statements, B-tree and R-tree indexes
4.1	October 2004	GA	
5.0	March 2005	Beta	Stored procedure, cursors, views, triggers, and XA transactions.
5.0	October 2005	GA	
5.1	May 2006	Beta	Partitioning, row-based replication, plug-in storage engine API, and event scheduler
5.1	November 2008	GA	
6.0	April 2007	Alpha	Falcon and Maria storage engines and online backup

Community and Enterprise server versions

In August of 2007 MySQL AB began offering the MySQL server in two different versions: MySQL Community and MySQL Enterprise. Although the code base of the two servers is similar, there are different levels of support for the servers. With MySQL Enterprise you purchase one of four support packages in addition to receiving the MySQL server binaries and source code. Sun has a table of available options at www.mysql.com/products/enterprise/features.html.

MySQL Community offers freely downloadable binaries with no support guarantee. When a database experiences problems the user is on his or her own to resolve those problems.

MySQL Enterprise has more frequent releases than MySQL Community Server. Owners of the source code must be allowed to redistribute the source code in full — this is required under the provisions of the GPLv2 license that governs MySQL distributions.

The MySQL Community

The MySQL community is a diverse population of both users of and contributors to MySQL, spread across the world. The large user community brings many opinions about what features are needed and discussions about the best methods to implement those features. Though this can sometimes bring about somewhat heated discussions, it also allows for honest and direct feedback that many companies may not hear.

How to contribute

You can contribute to MySQL server in a number of ways:

- **Blogging:** Many people who work on MySQL either full or part time write about their experiences online. These blogs can be valuable for learning more about the ins and outs of working with MySQL. Many of these blogs are aggregated at the Planet MySQL website (www.planetmysql.org).

- **Mailing lists:** The official public MySQL mailing lists are available at http://lists.mysql.com. The mailing lists are a great way to both contribute your knowledge and learn something new. The General Discussion list, in particular, has a wide range of topics. Dive in and take a look.

- **IRC channels:** Various IRC channels are available. These can often provide instant feedback and help with problems. One of the most popular is the #mysql channel on the Freenode IRC network (irc.freenode.net, or visit http://freenode.net for more information).

- **User groups:** Many active user groups exist around the world. It is a great experience to get together with other people who share a similar passion. Each month the user groups will have someone present on a topic relating to MySQL. One month it might be backups and recovery. The next month it might be about how to scale an application effectively. The place to look for a user group near you is www.meetup.com. If there is not a user group near you, consider starting one!

- **Documentation:** MySQL has some of the best software documentation available, located at http://dev.mysql.com/doc. Working on the documentation is the easiest way to directly contribute to the MySQL project. As MySQL continues to change it is necessary to keep the documentation up to date, so this is always an ongoing project.

- **Code:** The MySQL server code is complex software. However, it is somewhat modular and there are areas where an experienced C or C++ coder can help out. For smaller projects you might want to investigate the MySQL forge (`http://forge.mysql.com`) where many projects find a home. These projects are in many coding languages including (among others) Perl, Python, PHP, bash, C, and even Ruby.

- **MySQL Magazine:** Do you like to write? Then MySQL Magazine (`www.mysqlzine.net`) might be your venue. Articles cover anything from coding to how-to articles on normal DBA activities. The audience is a large group of the best database administrators and developers in the world.

Reasons to contribute

Many people never do anything other than download MySQL server, read a tutorial or two, and install the software and use it. They never contribute in any manner. That is fine, but we think that you can have a far more positive experience by becoming part of the community and contributing what you can while learning about this fascinating server software.

Though it is beyond the scope of this book to discuss the open source software philosophy in depth, openly and freely giving and receiving knowledge is the basis of this philosophy. Both code and knowledge are free to be shared. By doing so, everyone benefits from the exchange.

Summary

MySQL server has a long history of innovation. The community that has grown around MySQL provides learning experiences and teaching opportunities for database administrators old and young, veteran and newbie alike.

This chapter covered:

- MySQL company history
- The original and continuing mission of the MySQL database
- MySQL server version and feature overview
- Where to find more information
- How you can contribute to MySQL server

The *MySQL Administrator's Bible* covers all the topics you need to understand as a beginning MySQL database administrator. If you are a more advanced administrator switching from another database system, this book offers a unique look at where MySQL is different from the ISO SQL:2003 standard. After advancing to an intermediate level of familiarity with MySQL, the material on scaling and high availability, replication, metadata, and server tuning will continue to provide guidance.

Chapter 2

Installing and Upgrading MySQL Server

The MySQL server has two installation formats, and the MySQL server itself runs on more than sixteen different operating system platforms. The top three operating system platforms for MySQL are covered in some depth: GNU/Linux, Microsoft Windows, and Sun Solaris.

> **TIP** For information on how to install the MySQL server on Mac OS X, see the MySQL manual page at `http://dev.mysql.com/doc/refman/6.0/en/mac-os-x-installation.html`.

This chapter takes you through the bare bones of what you need to get the MySQL server (also known as `mysqld`) up and running, including the initial configuration. For more complete configuration tuning, see Chapter 10. It then delves into upgrading `mysqld`, which is very similar to installation. The chapter ends with troubleshooting assistance.

IN THIS CHAPTER

Pre-installation

Installation

Initial Configuration

Upgrading

Troubleshooting Installation

Before Installation

Before installing, you must choose what to install. You have two basic installation formats to choose from when performing an installation — source code installation and binary file installation. A source code installation means that you download the actual source code and then compile the code on your server in order to actually install the software. With a binary installation the server software is precompiled and ready to install. Think of it as the difference between preparing a meal by combining ingredients and cooking them and getting takeout from the local Chinese restaurant. A binary installation is like getting takeout: when you receive the food it is already pre-cooked and ready for eating.

Source Code vs. Binary File

A binary file is a file that contains binary data. It is not readable by humans, but a machine can read binary data very efficiently. Binary data is more compact than regular text, and many programs are run in binary format.

A binary file does not start out that way, though. A software developer writes some code in a text file, and then generates a binary file from that text file. The code is called "source code" because it is the source of the binary file. Generating the binary file is called *compiling*.

To compile source code you need a special program called a compiler. If you are new to compiling files on your operating system, it is best to download the binary files and use them. Compiling MySQL from source code is an advanced technique not covered by this book.

When you cook your own food it takes longer than picking up the telephone and placing an order with a restaurant. However, you can make the food exactly as you want. The difference between source and binary installs is the same. With source code installations it will take longer and require more expertise. However, the benefit is that you can control every configuration option for the compilation process. With the binary installation you can be up and running much faster, but those compilation choices are made by someone else. This is not always optimal for your situation.

Most installations of MySQL Server are binary installations. This choice is made because it is often not worth the extra work that source code installation requires. Compiling a MySQL Server binary from source code does not necessarily result in a better, faster database. Upgrading takes more work, because compiling takes time and expertise, and you have to document how and why you compiled the binary a certain way.

If a database administrator chooses to use binary format installations there is another decision: whether to use the official binary from Sun Microsystems or a binary from the operating system vendor. Many operating systems, such as Debian and Red Hat, provide their own version of a binary for MySQL Server. Some of these packages consist of a few wrapper scripts around the Sun-provided package, whereas other packages are made from taking the source code, revising it, and compiling it. Because of this, we recommend using the binaries available for download from `http://dev.mysql.com/downloads/mysql`, unless you are specifically using a patched binary for the feature(s) it has.

Problems with Vendor-Supplied Packages

Many vendors supply MySQL packages. Some vendors simply place the official packages into their repositories. Others repackage the official binaries, and still others start with the official source code, make changes, and compile and produce their own, unique package.

Debian packages have many extras; in the version of MySQL packaged by Debian, the `my.cnf` file is placed in `/etc/mysql/my.cnf`, and a `debian-sys-maint@localhost` user is created with a password that is stored in `/etc/mysql/debian.cnf`. These types of enhancements can make administering databases on different operating systems difficult.

The documentation for specific MySQL Server versions is based on the complete source code. Some vendor-supplied packages may not include all the features and bug fixes, because the packaging process does not necessarily include all the documented changes. This can lead to behavior that is inconsistent with the expected behavior.

As an example, in May 2008, a serious bug was revealed in the Debian package for OpenSSL. The package, built in 2006, had been built without code that caused some security tools to generate warnings. This led to the side-effect that the ssl keys generated by the package could be easily compromised. This was a serious security flaw that was in the Debian package for two years without being discovered.

Though Debian was used as an example, any vendor supplying packages may be changing the expected behavior — including Red Hat, Solaris, BSD, and others. Therefore, we recommend using the official MySQL downloads from `http://dev.mysql.com` to ensure that you get the features you expect.

In addition, third-party packages are often out of date. If you are installing third-party packages, these instructions may not work; consult the third-party documentation. To ensure you have an official Sun package, download directly from `http://dev.mysql.com/downloads`.

Choosing the MySQL version

Sun Microsystems has four release levels for the MySQL Server. These levels are GA (General Availability), RC (Release Candidate), beta, and alpha.

Software that is considered to be ready for production is labeled GA. The qualification for GA is that it has very few known bugs that cause severe production issues. It does not mean that the code is bug free. When a version of the server is declared GA it is typically quite solid.

A release candidate is high enough quality that Sun thinks it is a possibility for GA. There might be some serious, severe, or critical bugs left in the code, but they do not affect all users, just those using features in an obscure way, or using a few rare features.

Beta software is a step below a release candidate in terms of quality. Known issues (documented at `http://bugs.mysql.com`) exist with the server. Beta software should not be used in production. As a database administrator, however, it can be prudent to test the beta software and follow its development. It is a good idea to be familiar with the features and bug fixes in beta software, because after even more enhancements and corrections the beta software will become a release candidate and then GA.

Alpha software is where new features are added, and thus is very much experimental. Do not run alpha-level software in production. It is strictly a test bed of server features.

32-bit vs. 64-bit Systems

The official download page offers software for 32-bit systems and 64-bit systems. We recommend using a 64-bit operating system and a 64-bit MySQL installation. 32-bit systems can only use about 2.4 Gb of RAM per process, which means that the MySQL Server daemon will not be able to use more than 2.4 Gb of RAM. Most machines can handle a 64-bit operating system.

MySQL support

Several types of support are available for MySQL Server. Many resources are freely available on the Internet including mailing lists, forums, online reference manuals from Sun/MySQL, and many websites with information. See Appendix C, "Resources," for more information. Companies exist that provide one-time or ongoing training and consulting services for MySQL. Sun also provides support through its paid Enterprise program.

Downloads

The official download location is at `http://dev.mysql.com/downloads`. Here you will find current and past versions of MySQL Community server. In addition, there is information about the Enterprise version of the server. The Enterprise binary is a part of the MySQL Enterprise program, which includes monitoring and support software in addition to the database server. It is not necessary to purchase MySQL Enterprise to have a fully functioning, production-quality database. However, many useful tools such as the MySQL Monitor and the Query Analyzer can help DBAs do their job better in less time. MySQL Enterprise also comes with support, which is also a useful resource.

Installation

GNU/Linux platforms have several installation methods. There are distribution-specific packages (`rpm`, `deb`, `tar.gz`, and so on). Distribution-specific packages can be downloaded from the official download site listed in the previous section. As another installation method, some operating systems offer MySQL packages; this is not recommended for reasons discussed in the

"Problems with Vendor-Supplied Packages" note.

The third installation method is using an official compressed archive. We cover all three installation methods in detail with an example of an rpm package installation on a CentOS distribution, an example of a pkg package installation on a Solaris distribution, and an example using the compressed archive.

On Windows are two installation packages that have wizards to assist with installation and configuration. There is also a compressed archive package available that has no wizards. We cover all three installation methods on Windows.

There is another option for installation: downloading the source code and compiling your own binary, which this book does not cover.

Regardless of operating system, mysqld is initialized with users who have insecure permissions. Make sure to refer to the installation instructions for your operating system as well as the post-install instructions to secure your database.

MySQL Server installations on Unix

Unix-based servers with MySQL installations represent the majority of current installations of MySQL Server. Unlike Windows, Unix-based servers come in a number of packaging formats and configurations. We discuss three major packages: rpm-based packaging, the Solaris pkg package, and the binary archive package.

Installing from an rpm file on GNU/Linux

In most cases, you only need to install the server and client rpm packages (MySQL-server and MySQL-client) to get a functional MySQL installation. Other packages (see Table 2-1) may or may not be required for a standard installation but may have useful libraries. For example, you may get an error such as the following:

```
Error:  removing these packages would break dependencies libmysql-
client.so.10 is needed by...
```

Installing the mysql-shared-compat package might fix this problem. The mysql-shared-compat package includes shared libraries for backward compatibility (libmysqlclient.so.12 for MySQL Server 4.0 and libmysqlclient.so.10 for MySQL Server 3.23).

> **TIP** Document which packages your environment needs, and why, to make upgrading and testing easier.

On Unix systems, the MySQL server binary is a file called mysqld. The recommended way to install mysqld on rpm-based GNU/Linux distributions is by using the rpm packages provided on the official download page at http://dev.mysql.com/downloads. These rpms should work on all versions of GNU/Linux that support rpm packages and use the glibc2.3 library.

There are platform-specific and generic rpms; the difference is that a platform-specific rpm dynamically links to libraries found on a platform and a generic rpm is linked statically with LinuxThreads.

Whether to use a dynamically linked rpm or a statically linked rpm is up to your organization's policies and your own personal preference. Using dynamically linked libraries means that when the libraries are upgraded, the database automatically uses the libraries. However, this also means that an upgrade may change or break the way mysqld works. Using a statically linked library takes away this danger; however, if the library code requires upgrading, you have to upgrade the mysqld package, not just the library code itself.

The available rpm packages are shown in Table 2-1. The source code package has the form of MySQL-VERSION.platform.src.rpm, such as MySQL-community-5.1.25-0.rhel4.src.rpm. The other packages have a name as shown in Table 2-1, and a suffix with the version, platform (such as Red Hat Enterprise version 4), and the name of the dynamically linked library (such as glibc2.3). Finally, it will have an abbreviation for the processor type for which the rpm was compiled and packaged. An example package filename is MySQL-server-community-6.0.8-0.rhel4.x86_64.rpm.

TABLE 2-1

MySQL RPM Packages

Package Name	Description
MySQL-client	MySQL client package including the mysql command-line tool.
MySQL-debuginfo	Used for debugging problems with both the client and server programs. Can be used to generate extra information with MySQL Server crashes.
MySQL-devel	The libraries needed to compile additional MySQL clients.
MySQL-embedded	The MySQL embedded server. You only need this package if you are creating an application that has MySQL embedded in it.
MySQL-ndb-management	Files used by the MySQL Cluster server.
MySQL-server	The MySQL Server files, including the mysqld binary. This is required to run a MySQL Server.
MySQL-shared	Shared libraries used by various applications and languages to communicate with MySQL.
MySQL-shared-compat	This package is a replacement for MySQL-shared if your application requires libraries from older versions of MySQL but you need to upgrade mysqld to a newer version.
MySQL-test	The MySQL test suite.
MySQL-VERSION.PLATFORM.src.rpm	Source code for all the packages.

Executing `rpm -qa` will list all rpm files installed on your system. To see if you currently have any `mysql` packages installed:

```
shell> rpm -qa | grep -i mysql
MySQL-server-6.0.8-0.glibc23
MySQL-shared-6.0.8-0.glibc23
MySQL-client-6.0.8-0.glibc23
perl-DateTime-Format-MySQL-0.04-1.el5.rf
MySQL-devel-6.0.8-0.glibc23
perl-DBD-MySQL-3.0007-1.fc6
```

In this example, four MySQL packages and two Perl libraries are installed. The Perl libraries are third-party packages for being able to connect Perl with MySQL, and are not actually a part of a MySQL installation. If you see existing MySQL installations on your system, refer to the "Upgrading mysqld" section.

To install an rpm package, run the command `rpm -i file.rpm`. You can list multiple packages separated by spaces and rpm will install them at the same time. The `-v` option gives more verbose output, which is useful in case anything goes wrong. The `-h` option shows installation progress using hash (#) marks. For a basic setup of the MySQL Server, install the server and client rpms using the `rpm` command with the `-ivh` options:

```
shell> rpm -ivh MySQL-server-VERSION.PLATFORM-PROCESSOR.rpm MySQL-
client-VERSION.PLATFORM-PROCESSOR.rpm
```

The `mysql` user is used to run `mysqld`; if the `mysql` user and group do not exist, the rpm will create them. The server rpm places the data files in the data directory, which is `/var/lib/mysql` by default. Also by default, the pid file for the `mysqld` daemon and the error logs are located in the data directory. A database is simply a directory in the data directory, so you will see directories corresponding to the `mysql` and `test` databases that the rpm creates. A startup script is created in `/etc/init.d` that can be used by the database administrator to manually start, stop, and restart the server. In addition, links are used from this script to the `/etc/rc.d/` directory structure where scripts are used to start up and shut down server programs such as `mysqld` when the operating system is started or shut down. After the installation is finished, `mysqld` will start.

Once the installation is complete you should be able to connect to the server to see if everything worked. The `MySQL-client` rpm includes the `mysql` command-line client so you can test your configuration by running the following from a command prompt:

```
shell> mysql -u root
```

The Sun-built rpms do not configure passwords for the initial user accounts. If your MySQL Server is running properly, this will log you in to the server. You should see something like this:

```
Welcome to the MySQL monitor.  Commands end with ; or \g.
Your MySQL connection id is 3
Server version: 6.0.8-alpha MySQL Community Server (GPL)
```

15

```
Type 'help;' or '\h' for help. Type '\c' to clear the buffer

mysql>
```

If an error message is returned it will be helpful to check the error log, which is by default in the data directory at /var/lib/mysql. The filename is of the format hostname-err.log. Troubleshooting installation problems is discussed in the "Troubleshooting" section later in the chapter.

Now that your server installation is complete you need to configure mysqld for your hardware and anticipated usage. Post-installation work is covered in the "Initial Configuration" section later in this chapter.

Installing from a pkg file on Solaris

You can install mysqld on Solaris using a binary package in pkg format instead of the binary tarball distribution. The mysql user is used to run mysqld; if the mysql user and group do not exist, you need to create the mysql user and group before installing the pkg file. For example:

```
shell> groupadd mysql
shell> useradd -g mysql mysql
```

Executing pkginfo will list all packages installed on your system. To see if you have any mysql packages installed:

```
shell> pkginfo | grep -i mysql
system         SUNWmysqlr                        mysql - MySQL Database
 Management System (root component)
system         SUNWmysqlt                        mysql - MySQL Database
 Management System (test component)
system         SUNWmysqlu                        mysql - MySQL Database
 Management System (usr component)
application mysql                                 MySQL Community Server
 (GPL)
```

If you need to remove old packages the command is pkgrm package_name. The official Sun packages for MySQL are available from http://dev.mysql.com/downloads. The pkg package is in a gzip format so before installing you must use the gunzip command to extract the pkg file:

```
shell> gunzip package_package_name.pkg.gz
```

When gunzip finishes execution you will be left with the package itself.

To install the pkg file you will need to run `pkgadd -d file.pkg` with root privileges. You can list multiple packages separated by spaces and rpm will install them at the same time:

```
shell> pkg -d mysql-VERSION.PLATFORM-PROCESSOR.pkg
```

The following shows an example with the start of the package installation:

```
shell> pkgadd -d mysql-6.0.8-alpha-solaris10-x86_64.pkg

The following packages are available:
  1  mysql      MySQL Community Server (GPL)
                6.0.8

Select package(s) you wish to process (or 'all' to process
all packages). (default: all) [?,??,q]: 1

Processing package instance <mysql> from
</export/home/user/mysql-6.0.8-alpha-solaris10-x86_64.pkg>

MySQL Community Server (GPL) 6.0.8
Copyright (C) 2000-2005 MySQL AB & MySQL Finland AB & TCX
 DataKonsult AB

The selected base directory </opt/mysql> must exist before
installation is attempted.

Do you want this directory created now [y,n,?,q] y
Using </opt/mysql> as the package base directory.
## Processing package information.
## Processing system information.
## Verifying disk space requirements.
## Checking for conflicts with packages already installed.
## Checking for setuid/setgid programs.

This package contains scripts which will be executed with super-user
permission during the process of installing this package.

Do you want to continue with the installation of <mysql> [y,n,?] y

Installing MySQL Community Server (GPL) as <mysql>
```

The package places the data files in the data directory, which is /var/lib/mysql by default. This can be somewhat confusing because the base directory defaults to /opt/mysql/mysql. In addition both the pid file and error log are in the data directory. Once installation is complete you will need to perform post-installation configuration, which is covered in the "Initial Configuration" section later in the chapter.

Installing from an archive package on Unix

A common installation method is to use the compressed archive distributions provided for various platforms. MySQL archive binary distributions have names of the form `mysql-VERSION-OS.tar.gz`, where *VERSION* is a number (for example, 6.0.8), and *OS* indicates the type of operating system for which the distribution is intended (for example, pc-linux-i686).

WARNING The Solaris version of tar does not work with filenames longer than 138 characters. If this is a problem, use GNU tar (`gtar`) to unpack the distribution. You can find a precompiled copy of `gtar` for Solaris at `http://dev.mysql.com/downloads/os-solaris.html`.

When installing MySQL Server on Unix using the archive package you should perform the following steps:

1. Create a backup of your installation. How to perform backups is covered in Chapter 13, "Backups and Recovery."

2. Add a `mysql` user and group `mysqld` to run the `mysqld` binary:

    ```
    shell> groupadd mysql
    shell> useradd -g mysql mysql
    ```

    The exact syntax for `useradd` and `groupadd` may vary slightly on different versions of Unix. Some versions of Unix utilize other commands such as `adduser` and `addgroup` to accomplish the same task.

3. Download the archive package from `http://dev.mysql.com` into the directory where you want to install the server files. It is common to use the `/usr/local` directory and we use this directory for the example.

4. Unpack the archive to create the distribution directory (`/usr/local/mysql-version-OS`). The following command both unzips and extracts the files from the compressed tar archive:

    ```
    shell> tar zxvf mysql-version-OS.tar.gz
    ```

    Take a few minutes to take a look at the layout of the directory that you just extracted. The MySQL Server 6.0.8 archive package contains ten directories. Table 2-2 lists these directories and briefly describes their contents.

5. Create a symbolic link from this new directory to `/usr/local/mysql`:

    ```
    shell> ln -s /usr/local/mysql-version-OS /usr/local/mysql
    ```

    This means you refer to the installation directory as `/usr/local/mysql`. If you upgrade to a newer version of the server later, you can change the symbolic link and all directory paths will still be accurate. For example, if your installation directory is `/usr/local/mysql-6.0.8-alpha-solaris10-x86_64`:

```
shell> ln -s /usr/local/mysql-6.0.8-alpha-solaris10-x86_64
/usr/local/mysql
```

You can refer to the mysql client using the path /usr/local/mysql/bin/mysql. When it is time to upgrade you can unpack a new distribution to /usr/local/mysql-6.0.9-alpha-solaris10- x86_64 and change the link as follows:

```
shell> rm /usr/local/mysql
shell> ln -s /usr/local/mysql-6.0.9-alpha-solaris10-x86_64
/usr/local/mysql
```

The mysql client binary will still be located at /usr/local/mysql/bin/mysql.

TABLE 2-2

MySQL Server Archive Package Directories

Directory Name	Description
bin	Binary files for the server binaries and client programs such as the mysql command-line client, mysqldump, and mysqladmin
data	Databases and database data and index files
include	Header files
lib	Compiled libraries
man	Man pages
mysql-test	Test suite for testing MySQL Server
scripts	Contains the script used to initialize a new installation
share	Language support for messages such as errors
sql-bench	Benchmarking test program files
support-files	Example configurations and scripts for log rotation and starting MySQL Server

6. Change to the installation directory:

```
shell> cd /usr/local/mysql
```

7. Create the data directory and initialize the system tables:

```
shell> scripts/mysql_install_db --user=mysql
```

8. Ensure that the distribution contents are accessible to the mysql user. This was done if you unpacked the distribution as the mysql user.

   If you unpacked the distribution as any user other than mysql the contents will be owned by that user. You will need to change ownership to the mysql user by executing the following commands as root in the installation directory:

   ```
   shell> chown -R mysql:mysql /usr/local/mysql
   ```

9. To configure mysqld for automatic startup when the host server is started you must copy the support-files/mysql.server file to the location where your system has its startup files. This is typically /etc/init.d. In addition you will have to create the appropriate links to run levels for automatically starting and stopping the server. This is covered in the section "Starting and stopping mysqld on System V-based Unix" later in the chapter.

10. At this point you are ready to begin the server. You can start mysqld manually using the following command:

    ```
    shell> bin/mysqld_safe --user=mysql --group=mysql &
    ```

The --user option allows you to begin the MySQL daemon running under a username other than the account you are logged in under. Files created by mysqld will be owned by the user and group specified by the --user and --group options. In the preceding example the user that the daemon runs under is the mysql user.

We recommend starting mysqld_safe as the root operating system user with the --user and --group options as in the preceding code. The mysqld_safe process will be owned by root, and the mysqld process will be owned by the mysql user. The mysqld process will inherit important limits from the mysqld_safe process such as the limit in the number of open files. The mysqld binary itself should be run as the mysql user, which is why the --user option is so important.

If the mysqld_safe command fails and prints mysqld ended there will be some information written in the error log host_name.err located in the data directory. This information is useful for troubleshooting.

MySQL Server Installation on Windows

On Windows, the MySQL server daemon is the mysqld.exe binary. We will refer to mysqld as the server binary throughout this book; if you are on Windows you can run mysqld.exe without the .exe extension — just use mysqld.

The MySQL server daemon runs on a variety of Microsoft operating systems including Windows Server 2008, Windows Server 2003, and Windows Vista, XP, and 2000. There are 32-bit and 64-bit binaries available.

MySQL for Windows is available in several distribution formats: a source code version, which we do not cover, two packages containing a setup program that installs and configures everything needed, and a compressed archive that you unpack in the installation location and manually configure. The binary packages are listed here:

- **Essentials package:** This package contains both the Installation and Configuration Wizards along with the essentials needed to install the mysqld.exe binary. We recommend using this package to install, unless you need a particular component in the Complete package.

- **Complete package:** This package contains everything in the Essentials package, and adds optional components like the embedded server and benchmark suite. For most server installations these optional components are not necessary.

- **Noinstall archive:** This package must be manually installed and configured. It does not contain the Installation and Configuration Wizards. Otherwise, it contains all the files found in the Complete install package. Only those who have unusual needs should use the Noinstall package. As an example, if you need to install multiple instances of mysqld on a single host server you will need to use the Noinstall package. Multiple instances configuration is not covered in either the Essentials or Complete package and must be manually configured.

You must install MySQL on Windows using an account that has administrator rights, or there will be problems with the installation. MySQL does not need to be started by a user with administrator privileges.

The installer packages make installation easier than the archive package. The installer packages use an Installation Wizard to install the server binary, and a Configuration Wizard to create an option file, create the initial user accounts, and start the server.

Installing MySQL from the installation packages on Windows

The wizard-driven Essentials and Complete package installations are the most common way to install MySQL on Windows. How you start the wizards depends on which installation package you download. To begin installation, double-click either the extracted setup.exe file (extracted from the Complete package .zip file) or the msi file (Essentials package).

When beginning the installation from the Essentials or Complete packages you must first determine what installation type you wish to perform.

Three installation types are available: Typical, Complete, and Custom:

- **Typical** installation will install the MySQL Server and the various command-line utilities.

- **Complete** installation installs all components in the installation package. The full package includes the embedded server library, a benchmark suite, support programs, and documentation.

■ **Custom** installation will give you complete control over the packages installed and the location of the files installed.

If you choose either the Typical or Complete installation types and click the Next button, you will advance to a verification screen and begin the installation after verifying that you want to install. If you choose the Custom installation type and click the Next button you will advance to the Custom Installation screen.

On the Custom Installation screen there is a listing of all components displayed on the left. Components not selected for installation have a red X icon beside the component name. Components selected for installation have a gray icon. To change the installation state of a component click that component's icon and choose a new option from the drop-down list that appears. Figure 2-1 shows what the Custom Installation screen looks like.

FIGURE 2-1

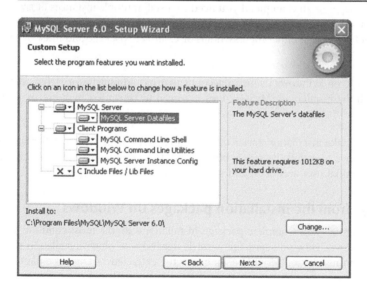

To change the installation path of the server, click the Change button on the right side of the screen across from the currently configured install path.

Once you are done choosing the components you want installed and selecting the installation path, click the Next button to advance to the Verification screen. On this screen you can review your current selections and click the Install button if everything is correct. To make changes to the settings click the Back button to return to the previous screen. The Cancel button can be used to exit the Installation Wizard without performing any installation activities.

The final screen of the Installation Wizard provides a summary of the installation and gives you the option to launch the MySQL Configuration Wizard. This wizard allows you to create a configuration file, install the MySQL service, and configure security settings.

Initial configuration of MySQL on Windows

On the Windows platform the configuration file is named my.ini and by default is placed in the installation directory. The Configuration Wizard creates a custom my.ini file by asking questions in a series of screens and creating the configuration file based on the answers you provide.

When you start the MySQL Configuration Wizard for a new MySQL installation the Configuration Type screen is shown.

Two configuration types are available: Detailed Configuration and Standard Configuration. The Standard Configuration option is for new users to get started quickly. The Detailed Configuration option is for more control over the configuration. For more information on the Detailed Configuration option, see the "Detailed Configuration" section later in this chapter.

If this is your first time installing MySQL, choose the Standard Configuration option. The MySQL Configuration Wizard will automatically configure all options except for the Service Options and Security Options.

Service Options screen

The MySQL Configuration Wizard installs mysqld as a service named MySQL by default. This service is configured to launch when the machine boots up. If you do not wish to install the service, uncheck the box next to Install As Windows Service. The service name can be changed by selecting a new one from the drop-down box or by typing a new service name into the drop-down box. If you wish to install the service but do not want it to launch when the machine boots up, uncheck the box next to "Launch the MySQL Server Automatically".

Security Options screen

By default, the MySQL Configuration Wizard requires you to set a password for the root username. You can bypass this requirement by unchecking the box next to Modify Security Settings. It is not a good idea from a security perspective to bypass this requirement. To set the root password, type the password in the New Root Password and Confirm text boxes.

To limit root logins to the local host only, check the box next to Root May Only Connect From localhost. To create an anonymous user account, check the box next to Create An Anonymous Account. We do not recommend allowing root connections from hosts other than the local host, nor do we recommend creating an anonymous user. Both decrease security.

If you are using the Configuration Wizard to reconfigure an existing machine that already has the root password set, you need to enter in the existing root password into the Current root password box.

Confirmation screen

In the Confirmation screen you can:

- Click the Execute button to save the options to a my.ini file. If applicable, the Configuration Wizard will create and start a service for MySQL, and apply the root password, root host settings, and anonymous user settings.

- Go back to a previous screen by clicking the Back button.

- Cancel configuration without making changes by clicking the Cancel button.

After the MySQL Configuration Wizard has completed everything it will display a summary. Click the Finish button to exit the MySQL Configuration Wizard.

Installing MySQL from a Noinstall Zip Archive

The Noinstall Zip Archive installation is designed to be installed manually. To install the archive you will need to do the following:

1. Make sure that you are logged in as a user with administrator privileges.

2. Extract the Zip archive to an installation location, traditionally C:\mysql.

3. Create a configuration file, if needed. When mysqld.exe starts on Windows, it looks for configuration files in %WINDIR%\my.ini and C:\my.cnf. %WINDIR% is the Windows environment variable for the Windows directory. You can figure out the Windows directory by opening a command shell with Start ➤ Run, typing **cmd** in the box that appears, clicking Run, and typing the following at the command-line prompt:

```
C:\> echo %WINDIR%
```

To set options in a configuration file, you can create a new file or use one of the sample configuration files that have been extracted to the installation directory — these sample configuration files are named my-small.ini, my-medium.ini, my-large.ini, my-huge.ini, and my-template.ini. Any text editor (Notepad, Wordpad, and so on) can be used to create and change a configuration file.

If you did not install MySQL at C:\mysql in step 2, you will need to set two variables in a my.ini configuration file under the [mysqld] section. Note that directories on Windows can be specified with either forward slashes or backslashes. If you use backslashes they must be escaped with a second backslash. For example, the directory C:\mysql could be written as C:/mysql or it could be written as C:\\mysql. If you installed MySQL at C:\customdir\mysql, your my.ini file would contain something similar to this:

```
[mysqld]
# basedir should point to the installation directory
basedir=C:/customdir/mysql

# datadir should point to the data directory.
```

```
# By default the datadir is in the "Application Data\MySQL"
# subdirectory of the home directory of the user running MySQL.
# Thus, if the user is CorpUser1, the data directory will be in
# C:\Documents and Settings\CorpUser1\Application Data\MySQL
datadir= C:\\Documents and Settings\\CorpUser1\\Application
 Data\MySQL\\data
```

4. Choose a MySQL server type. For production installations it is recommended to use the mysqld binary. It is compiled with everything necessary to run MySQL server. For development or test installations, you may want to use the mysqld-debug server type. This binary is complied with extra debugging information.

5. Start mysqld manually, to confirm a successful installation. See the next section, "Starting and Stopping MySQL from the Windows Command Line," for more information.

WARNING The accounts that are automatically created have blank passwords. To make your server more secure, set up passwords using the instructions in the section "Setting Initial Passwords" later in this chapter.

Starting and stopping MySQL from the Windows command line

Once you have installed the server from the archive it is time to start up the server for the first time.

If during installation you chose the mysqld server type, you will start the server using the mysqld.exe binary. If you chose the mysqld-debug server type, you will start the server using the mysqld-debug.exe binary. Our examples use the mysqld.exe binary, and an installation directory of C:\Program Files\MySQL\MySQL Server 6.0. If you have MySQL installed in a different location adjust the pathname accordingly.

Start the server using the following command at the command-line prompt:

```
C:\> "C:\Program Files\MySQL\MySQL Server 6.0\bin\mysqld" --console
```

The --console option forces mysqld to display status messages in the window instead of writing them to the error log. This option is just for testing purposes. If you are not testing the mysqld server, it is recommended to start it as a service, not manually from the command line. See the section "Starting and Stopping MySQL as a Windows Service" for information on how to do that.

For a server that uses InnoDB, you should see messages similar to these the first time mysqld starts (the pathnames and file sizes may differ):

```
InnoDB: The first specified data file .\ibdata1 did not exist:
InnoDB: a new database to be created!
```

```
090423 16:55:46  InnoDB: Setting file .\ibdata1 size to 10 MB
InnoDB: Database physically writes the file full: wait...
090423 16:55:47  InnoDB: Log file .\ib_logfile0 did not exist: new to
  be created
InnoDB: Setting log file .\ib_logfile0 size to 10 MB
InnoDB: Database physically writes the file full: wait...
090423 16:55:48  InnoDB: Log file .\ib_logfile1 did not exist: new to
  be created
InnoDB: Setting log file .\ib_logfile1 size to 10 MB
InnoDB: Database physically writes the file full: wait...
InnoDB: Doublewrite buffer not found: creating new
InnoDB: Doublewrite buffer created
InnoDB: Creating foreign key constraint system tables
InnoDB: Foreign key constraint system tables created
090423 16:55:50  InnoDB: Started; log sequence number 0 0
090423 16:55:55 [Note] Event Scheduler: Loaded 0 events
090423 16:55:55 [Note] C:\Program Files\MySQL\MySQL Server 6.0\bin\
mysqld: ready for connections.
Version: '6.0.8-alpha-community'  socket: ''  port: 3306  MySQL
  Community Server (GPL)
```

If this is not the first time the server has been started, a successful startup will display messages similar to the last four lines. The last two lines indicate that the server is ready for client connections.

If mysqld does not start, check the error log to see if there are any messages that indicate the cause of the problem. The error log is located in the data directory (datadir) by default, and has a filename of hostname.err, where hostname is the hostname of the machine. The error log path and filename and can be changed by setting the log-error variable in the configuration file.

Once the mysqld daemon is started you can stop the server by running the following command:

```
C:\> "C:\Program Files\MySQL\MySQL Server 6.0\bin\mysqladmin" -u root
shutdown -p
```

Type the root password followed by pressing the Enter key when prompted. If you have not yet set a root password you can just press the Enter key.

WARNING If you have not yet set a root password and disabled the anonymous user it would be a good time to do so. The section "Setting Initial Passwords" later in this chapter describes how to do this.

Starting and stopping MySQL as a Windows service

The recommended method of running mysqld on Windows is to install it as a Windows service. As a Windows service, mysqld can be controlled manually from the command line or the graphical Services utility. It can also be started and stopped automatically when Windows starts and stops. When installing MySQL as a Windows service you must use an account that has administrator privileges.

Before installing `mysqld` as a Windows service, you should first stop the current server if it is running by using the `mysqladmin shutdown` command discussed in the previous section.

Install the server as a service using this command on the Windows shell command line:

```
C:\> "C:\Program Files\MySQL\MySQL Server 6.0\bin\mysqld" --install
```

This command installs the service so that it starts and stops automatically when Windows starts or stops. By default, the service name is `MySQL`. If you want to use a different service name, specify the service name after the `--install` option. To give `mysqld` a service name of `mysql60`, run:

```
C:\> "C:\Program Files\MySQL\MySQL Server 6.0\bin\mysqld" --
install mysql60
```

After the service name, you can specify server options. However, the best way to have server options permanently saved and used every time the server is started is to use the option `--defaults-file=C:/path/to/configfile` and save a configuration file to that path.

In Windows systems starting from XP and newer, the `--local-service` option can be specified to run `mysqld.exe` as the LocalService user, which has limited system privileges. This may be desirable for security purposes.

If you want to install `mysqld` as a service but do not want it to start and stop automatically when Windows starts and stops, use the `--install-manual` option instead of `--install`. Once `mysqld` is installed as a service, you can start and stop it on the command line easily. This is true regardless of whether or not `mysqld` is set to start and stop automatically when Windows starts and stops. To start the service, run `net start servicename`, where `servicename` is the `servicename` associated with `mysqld`. For example, the following command starts a `mysqld` service installed with the default `servicename`:

```
C:\> net start MySQL
```

Similarly, to stop a running `mysqld` service, run `net stop servicename`, as in the following example:

```
C:\> net stop MySQL
```

Once `mysqld` is installed as a service, you can use the Services GUI to start and stop it manually and toggle whether it starts and stops automatically when Windows starts and stops. The graphical Services utility can be found in Control Panel ➢ Administrative Tools on Windows 2000, XP, Vista, and Server 2003.

Figure 2-2 shows the Services configuration screen.

FIGURE 2-2

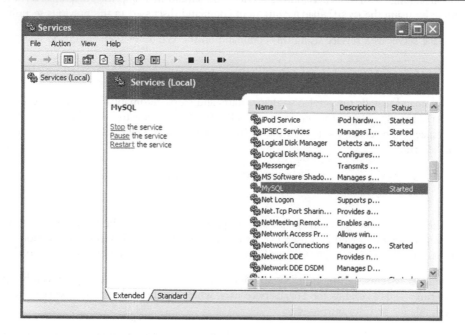

Simply left-click the service name you want to work with on the right side of the screen (scrolling up or down as needed). In this case the service is called "MySQL." You can start, stop, pause, and restart the service four different ways:

■ You can manage the service by right-clicking the service name and then left-clicking the desired action.

■ You can click the desired action in the middle area of the screen after left-clicking the service name in the list. In this case the actions displayed change depending on the state of the service.

■ On the menu bar there is a heading of Action. Click it and you can choose any action needed for the highlighted service.

■ Finally, you can use the four control buttons on the menu bar.

You can use the Properties screen to define if the service stops and starts with mysqld. To access the Properties screen you can right-click the service name and then choose Properties or choose Properties from the Action menu item. Finally, it can be reached by clicking the hand holding a card icon. Once you have opened the properties menu you can see Startup type: about halfway down the General tab. Just select Automatic, Manual, or Disabled and click OK.

To remove `mysqld` as a service, first execute `net stop servicename` to stop any running instances. Then use the `--remove` option with `mysqld as follows`:

```
C:\> "C:\Program Files\MySQL\MySQL Server 5.1\bin\mysqld" --remove
```

Initial Configuration

After installation, `mysqld` must be initialized and configured. For example, on Unix, the data directory and system tables must be set up. On all platforms, the initial accounts are set up with blank passwords, which should be changed to secure `mysqld`.

Many MySQL programs, including `mysqld`, use a central configuration file to allow a database administrator to set various parameters that will persist across reboots. Though most parameters can be set from the command line when starting the server manually, it quickly becomes very cumbersome to do this. The configuration file makes this much more efficient and less prone to errors. This configuration file can have several locations and the name varies between Windows and Unix-based systems.

> **TIP** The MySQL configuration file is used for many MySQL programs, including `mysqld`. This centralized configuration file allows control of the behavior and characteristics of MySQL. Different MySQL programs use options from different *directives* in the configuration file. For example, `mysqld` uses options under the `[mysqld]` directive. Client programs such as `mysql` and `mysqladmin` use options under the `[client]` directive. This configuration file is also known as an *option file*, because it contains options and their values.

On Unix-based servers the configuration file is called `my.cnf`. On Windows servers it can be either `my.cnf` or `my.ini`. On startup, `mysqld` looks for this configuration file in several locations. This is done in a specific order. Even if the server finds a configuration file in the first location it will still check each location for a configuration file. If more than one file is located, all option files are used by the server. If more than one file has the same option, the last option read is used with one exception — with the `user` option the first instance is always used for security purposes.

> **WARNING** The exception to the order of precedence of the configuration files on all operating systems is if the `defaults-file=/path/to/file` option is specified. In that case, *only* the file given is used, even if other configuration files exist.

On Unix-based systems the following order of precedence is used:

- `/etc/my.cnf`
- `/etc/mysql/my.cnf`

- `$MYSQL_HOME/my.cnf`
- `/path/to/file` when `defaults-extra-file=/path/to/file` is specified
- `~/.my.cnf`

`$MYSQL_HOME` refers to an operating system user environment variable. If it is not set, MySQL programs will set it to be the same as the base directory (`basedir`) by default, unless there is a `my.cnf` file in the data directory (`datadir`), in which case the data directory will be used.

The `defaults-extra-file` is used to specify an additional location of a configuration file. It is passed as an argument when beginning start-up of the `mysqld` binary. For example:

```
shell> mysqld_safe --defaults-extra-file=/etc/mysql/my_instance.cnf
```

The `~/.my.cnf` file is used on a per-user basis. The `~/` represents the home directory of the user calling the MySQL program. Note that `.my.cnf` starts with `.` and thus is a hidden file. For example, this would be a good place to configure a default character set for someone who has need of a different default than other users. You should not put server-wide configuration values in this file, even if the file is in the home directory of the `root` or `mysql` users.

With Windows servers the following order of precedence is used:

- `%WINDIR%\my.ini, %WINDIR%\my.cnf`
- `C:\my.ini, C:\my.cnf`
- `%INSTALLDIR%\my.ini, %INSTALLDIR%\my.cnf`
- `/path/to/file` when `defaults-extra-file=/path/to/file` is specified

`%WINDIR%` is the Windows environment variable for the Windows directory.

`%INSTALLDIR%` is the directory used for installation of your MySQL server. By default this would be `C:\Program Files\MySQL\MySQL version_number Server`. You should replace `version_number` with the major version number of your server (5.1 or 6.0).

To see the value of Windows environment variables, open a command shell with Start ➤ Run, type **cmd** in the box that appears, click Run, and print the variable. For example, to see the value of the Windows directory, type the following at the command-line prompt:

```
C:\> echo %WINDIR%
```

As with Unix-based servers the `defaults-extra-file` is used to specify an additional location of a configuration file. It is used as an argument when starting the `mysqld` binary. For example:

```
C:\> "C:\Program Files\MySQL\MySQL Server 6.0\bin\mysqld --defaults-
extra-file=c:\mysql\defaults.cnf"
```

TIP
Keep your installations as uniform as possible. Even if your servers are running on different operating systems, locations of data directories, log directories, and configuration files can be kept consistent. This makes it easier to administer the systems over the long term.

Unix configuration file

After your installation of the server packaging is complete you need to either use a previously created my.cnf file or use one of the configuration example files. With both the pkg and the archive packaging these examples are in the support-files directory (located under the basedir directory). With the official rpms these same files are placed under the /usr/share/mysql directory.

The files are given descriptive names such as my-small.cnf, although they are a bit dated. For example, from the beginning of the my-small.cnf file: "This is for a system with little memory (<=64M) ... " If you choose to use one of these files take the time to read through the parameters and make adjustments as needed. Many database administrators will have tuned configuration files that they use for specific hardware at their location that performs well for their specific system.

Windows configuration file

MySQL running on Windows can use a configuration with two different filenames — the traditional my.cnf and the my.ini file. The format of the files is identical. The only difference is the name of the file.

If you are setting up using a Noinstall Zip Archive (see "Installing MySQL from a Noinstall Zip Archive"), you have to create your own configuration file or use one of the sample configurations.

To set options in a configuration file, you can create a new file or use one of the sample configuration files that have been extracted to the installation directory — these sample configuration files are named my-small.ini, my-medium.ini, my-large.ini, my-huge.ini, and my-template.ini. Any text editor can be used to create and change a configuration file.

If you run the Installation Wizard but not the Configuration Wizard, no configuration file is created. You can run the Configuration Wizard later and have it create a configuration file or you can create a new configuration by hand as described earlier.

MySQL Configuration Wizard on Windows

The Configuration Wizard can be used to configure a new installation immediately after execution of the Installation Wizard and to reconfigure an existing server.

If you use the Installation Wizard to perform an installation it will continue, by default, with the Configuration Wizard. However, you do have the option of exiting at this time and not running the Configuration Wizard. You can exit the wizard at this point and either configure the server by hand or rerun the Configuration Wizard later to continue with the configuration process.

The process of reconfiguring a service is almost identical to the initial configuration process. See the section "Initial Configuration of MySQL on Windows" earlier in this chapter for more information on the initial configuration process. The following outlines what is different about the reconfiguration process.

If you have already installed the server and run the Configuration Wizard later it will discover any existing configuration files. When this happens you are given two options: reconfigure the server or remove it.

Selecting the Remove Instance option and clicking Next will stop mysqld, delete the configuration file, and remove the MySQL service.

WARNING When you remove mysqld using the Configuration Wizard, the server installation directory and data directory are not deleted. You must manually delete them if you do not want them.

The various command-line programs such as mysql and mysqladmin will not be able to utilize a configuration file that is located in the server installation directory. For these applications you can create a new my.ini file in the C:\WINDOWS directory.

If you choose the Re-configure Instance option and click the Next button your existing configuration file will be renamed with a suffix of .bak to signify it is a backup file.

Choosing the Re-configure Instance option will advance you to the Configuration Type screen. This screen and all following are identical to the screens used by the Configuration Wizard immediately after an installation is performed. We discussed everything except the Detailed Configuration type in the "Initial Configuration of MySQL on Windows" section earlier in this chapter. The Detailed Configuration screens are covered in the following section.

WARNING If you are reconfiguring a server you should not use the Standard Configuration option. There are known problems when doing so. You should use the Detailed Configuration option if you have an existing MySQL installation.

Detailed Configuration

The Detailed Configuration option goes through the following screens, in order:

- Server Type
- Database Usage
- InnoDB Tablespace

- Concurrent Connections
- Networking Options and Strict Mode Options
- Character Set
- Service Options (also in the Standard Configuration)
- Security Options (also in the Standard Configuration)
- Confirmation (also in the Standard Configuration)

The Server Type screen

The Server Type screen offers three server types, which determine how the Configuration Wizard allocates disk, CPU, and RAM:

- **Developer machine:** This server type is for an installation where mysqld is run on a desktop machine. mysqld is configured to use minimal system resources, assuming that many other desktop applications are running.

- **Server machine:** This server type is for an installation where mysqld is intended for testing or low-use purposes. mysqld is configured to use a moderate amount of system resources, assuming that other server applications such as an application server or a web server are running.

- **Dedicated MySQL server machine:** This server type is for an installation where mysqld is intended for production use. mysqld is configured to use most of the available system resources, so no other large applications (such as SFTP, e-mail, web, or application servers) should be running.

Database Usage screen

The Database Usage screen lets you select the storage engines you anticipate using when creating tables. For more information on storage engines, see Chapter 11. Your selection here determines if the InnoDB storage engine is available and the percentage of resources allocated to MyISAM and InnoDB.

- **Multifunctional database:** This option enables both the InnoDB and MyISAM storage engines. Server resources are used equally between the two storage engines.

- **Transactional database only:** This option is misnamed as it enables both the InnoDB and MyISAM storage engines. The InnoDB storage engine supports transactions, whereas MyISAM does not. The majority of the storage engine resources are allocated for use by InnoDB. This option is for users who use InnoDB tables extensively with little need for MyISAM tables.

- **Non-Transactional database only:** This option disables the InnoDB storage engine from use. All storage engine resources are allocated for use by the MyISAM storage engine.

InnoDB Tablespace screen

By default, the centralized InnoDB tablespace information, including metadata and the data dictionary, are stored inside a file named ibdata1. Sometimes you want to place the InnoDB tablespace files in a different location than the data directory. Moving the InnoDB tablespace files to a different location is useful if you need to move the InnoDB tablespace files to a larger file system partition or a RAID storage system.

To change the default location for the InnoDB tablespace files, use the drop-down menus to select both a drive and directory path for the new location. Alternatively you can browse to a custom path by clicking the " ... " button, which is immediately to the right of the drop-down menu for the directory path. If you are modifying the configuration of an existing server you must click the Modify button to make any changes to your configuration and confirm that this is the operation you want to perform. It also warns that you must move the existing tablespace file(s) to the new location before starting the server, otherwise MySQL will not be able to start with InnoDB enabled.

Concurrent Connections screen

The Concurrent Connections screen allows you to configure the value of max_connections. The max_connections system variable is used to specify the maximum number of connections at any given time to mysqld. The three options are:

- **Decision Support (DSS)/OLAP:** max_connections is set to 100.
- **Online Transaction Processing (OLTP):** max_connections is set to 500.
- **Manual Setting:** Use the drop-down box to select the value of max_connections, or type a number in the drop-down box for a custom value of max_connections.

Networking Options and Strict Mode Options screen

By default TCP/IP networking is enabled. If you want to disable TCP/IP networking and force all connections to be local, uncheck the box next to the Enable TCP/IP Networking option. The default port for TCP/IP connections to MySQL is 3306. To change the port MySQL listens on, use the drop-down box to select the new port number, or type a number in the drop-down box for a custom port number.

The Server SQL Mode can be set to enable or disable strict mode. The default is to have strict mode enabled. Among other behaviors, strict mode ensures that there are no implicit data changes, and in places where such an implicit change would happen, an error is generated instead. If strict mode is disabled, implicit data changes can happen and throw a warning. This is equivalent to setting sql_mode=STRICT_TRANS_TABLES in the my.ini file. For more information on SQL modes, see Chapter 5.

Character Set screen

The MySQL server supports multiple character sets. This screen allows you to configure the default server character set that is applied globally to all databases and tables unless explicitly overridden.

You will need to choose one of the following options:

- **Standard Character Set:** Choosing this option configures the latin1 character set as the default server character set. The latin1 character set is used frequently for English and many Western European languages. This character set only uses one byte per character.

- **Best Support For Multilingualism:** Choosing the option configures the utf8 character set as the default server character set. The utf8 character set can be used for many different languages including very complex sets such as Chinese, Japanese, and Korean. It uses four bytes per character.

- **Manual Selected Default Character Set / Collation:** This option allows you to choose any character set from the drop-down menu as the default character set.

For more information on character sets and collations, see Chapter 4.

Service Options screen

The MySQL Configuration Wizard installs the MySQL server as a service named MySQL by default. This service is configured to start automatically on system startup. Removing the check next to Install as Windows Service means the service is not installed. The service name can be changed by selecting a new service name from the drop-down box or by typing a new service name into the drop-down box. If you wish to install the service but do not want it to launch when the machine boots up, uncheck the box next to Launch the MySQL Server Automatically. There is also a check box next to Include Bin Directory in Windows PATH. This is used to include the directory where all of the client and server executables are kept in the Windows PATH variable. This allows you to run programs such as the mysql client without specifying the full path.

Security Options screen

By default, the MySQL Configuration Wizard requires you to set a password for the root username. You can bypass this requirement by unchecking the box next to Modify Security Settings. It is not secure to bypass this requirement. To set the root password, type the password in the New root password and Confirm text boxes.

To limit root logins to the local host only, check the box next to Root May Only Connect From localhost. To create an anonymous user account, check the box next to Create An Anonymous Account.

If you are using the Configuration Wizard to reconfigure an existing machine that already has the root password set, you need to enter the existing root password into the Current root password box.

WARNING We do not recommend allowing root connections from hosts other than the local host, nor do we recommend creating an anonymous user. Either one of these actions decreases security. As well, using a root password increases security and is strongly recommended.

Confirmation screen

In the Confirmation screen you can:

■ Click the Execute button to save the options to a my.ini file. If applicable, the Configuration Wizard will create and start a service for MySQL, and apply the root password, root host settings, and anonymous user settings.

■ Go back to a previous screen by clicking the Back button.

■ Cancel configuration without making changes by clicking the Cancel button.

After the MySQL Configuration Wizard has completed everything it will display a summary. Click the Finish button to exit the MySQL Configuration Wizard.

MySQL Post-Install Configuration on Unix

With Unix-based servers, just as with Windows, there is some post-installation configuration needed. This includes creating user accounts, setting initial passwords, and possibly configuring your system to start up and shut down automatically when the host server does the same.

Initializing the system tables

On Unix-based systems the grant tables, containing user accounts and permissions, are part of the system tables set up by the mysql_install_db script. For installations of rpm-based GNU/Linux distributions and the Solaris pkg this script is run during the package install process. When installing using an archive package you will need to run the mysql_install_db script manually.

WARNING For the mysql_install_db script to run properly, the MySQL server must be shut down. If not, your server may crash. If this happens, make sure mysqld is shut down and run the script again.

To run the mysql_install_db script manually, navigate to the installation directory of your MySQL installation. Then run the setup script as follows:

```
shell> scripts/mysql_install_db --user=mysql
```

This script creates the data directory, the test database, and the mysql database directory that holds all system tables. In the mysql database mysql_install_db creates several tables including user, db, host, tables_priv, columns_priv, and func. The script also creates several user accounts with usernames of root and " (the anonymous user). The accounts are initialized with blank passwords.

> **TIP** To see the system tables that the mysql_install_db script created, look in your data directory in the mysql directory:
>
> ```
> shell> ls -la /path/to/datadir/mysql
> ```
>
> Many of these system tables are used to support user permissions. You will commonly hear these tables referred to as the grant tables.

Setting initial passwords

On Windows-based servers installed using the Configuration Wizard you configured passwords for your accounts. This was covered in the "Security Options screen" section earlier in this chapter. On all other installations you will need to configure passwords for your user accounts.

With Unix-based installations, all initial accounts are created without passwords. This includes the accounts with a username of root that are allowed to execute any command on the server. This is a large security hole and should be resolved as soon as possible.

With Unix-based servers a total of five users are created by the mysql_install_db script described in the previous section. There are three root accounts: root@127.0.0.1, root@localhost, and the root@hostname user. In addition, two anonymous user accounts are created. The first account is ''@localhost and the second account has the empty string as the username and the server hostname for the host.

Root user password assignment

On a Unix server, when the mysql_install_db script finishes execution it displays several options for next steps you should take. One of these options is to run the mysqladmin program to change your root passwords. The following is from the output of the mysql_install_db script of an rpm-based installation on a host called this_host_name:

```
PLEASE REMEMBER TO SET A PASSWORD FOR THE MySQL root USER !
To do so, start the server, then issue the following commands:

/usr/bin/mysqladmin -u root password 'new-password'
/usr/bin/mysqladmin -u root -h this_host_name password 'new-password'
```

The script is telling you exactly what to run. You simply run mysqladmin with the password option specifying your new password in quotes. You should run both commands because they are modifying different user accounts. After this is done you must use the new password when logging in to the server.

In addition to the mysqladmin tool, the mysql_install_db script also describes how to run the mysql_secure_install script. Running this script and accepting the defaults will provide for an even more secure server than just running the previously described mysqladmin command. We describe this program in the "Securing Your System" section that follows.

Another way to change passwords for accounts having a username of root is to manually configure these passwords. You have two methods of doing this manually: executing the SET PASSWORD command or executing the appropriate UPDATE statement followed by a FLUSH PRIVILEGES statement.

To assign passwords to users other than yourself using the SET PASSWORD command, you must connect to the server as a user with SUPER privileges. Initially, the users with a username of root have the SUPER privilege. Connect to the server by issuing the following:

```
shell> mysql -u root
```

Then, issue the following SET PASSWORD statement — the PASSWORD() function encrypts the password appropriately, and must be used:

```
mysql> SET PASSWORD FOR 'root'@'localhost' = PASSWORD('new_
password');
```

On Unix-based servers, there is an additional user with a username of root to set a password for:

```
mysql> SET PASSWORD FOR 'root'@'host_name' = PASSWORD('new_
password');
```

The value host_name should be set to the name of the server host.

WARNING   We strongly recommend that you drop the root@'%' user because it is a security risk. The '%' host allows someone from any host to attempt to gain access to your server. The root@'%' user allows someone from any host to possibly gain SUPER privileges on your server. To remove this user log in as root@localhost and execute:

```
DROP USER 'root'@'%' command.
```

A final method of configuring your root passwords is using the UPDATE statement to update the user table directly. The following statement updates all accounts with a username of root to the same password:

```
mysql> UPDATE mysql.user SET Password = PASSWORD('new_password')
WHERE User = 'root';
mysql> FLUSH PRIVILEGES;
```

The FLUSH PRIVILEGES command is used reload the grant tables. Until this is done the changes that you made do not take effect on a running server.

To ensure that you have set a password for all users with the root username, run the following query:

```
mysql> SELECT user,host,password FROM mysql.user WHERE user='root'
 AND password='';
Empty set (0.00 sec)
```

If you see a result table instead of Empty set, you will need to set the password for those users.

Configuring the passwords for all the accounts with the root username is your first step toward securing your system.

Anonymous users

Anonymous users are user accounts with a username of an empty string (''). It is a best practice to drop the anonymous users because there is very rarely any valid reason to retain these accounts.

The easiest method to remove them on any operating system is just log in with a root user account and issue the command:

```
mysql>  DROP USER ''@localhost;
Query OK, 0 rows affected (0.00 sec)
```

On Unix machines, there is also a ''@host_name user to drop:

```
mysql>  DROP USER ''@'host_name';
Query OK, 0 rows affected (0.00 sec)
```

If you receive the following error, it means that you tried to drop a user that did not exist:

```
ERROR 1396 (HY000): Operation DROP USER failed for ''@'wrong_
host_name'
```

To ensure that you have dropped all anonymous users, run the following query:

```
mysql> SELECT user,host,password FROM mysql.user WHERE user='';
Empty set (0.00 sec)
```

If you see a result table instead of Empty set, you will need to issue a DROP command to remove any remaining anonymous users.

Securing Your System

With Unix-based systems you have the option of running the `mysql_secure_installation` script to initialize passwords and perform other security-related tasks. It manages for you much of the previous complexity described in the last few sections by assigning passwords for the accounts with the username `root` and removing the anonymous accounts.

Unlike the `mysql_install_db` script, the `mysql_secure_installation` script requires the server to be running. If you see the following error, it means `mysqld` is not running:

```
ERROR 2002 (HY000): Can't connect to local MySQL server through
socket '/tmp/mysql.sock' (2)
```

As soon as you finish the installation of your system tables with the `mysql_install_db` script you should start up `mysqld` and then immediately run the `mysql_secure_installation` script.

The script will ask you for the current password for the root account. If it is not configured just press the Enter key. The script will continue by asking you a series of questions. The most secure system will be configured by answering yes to all questions by pressing the Y key and then pressing Enter. If you answer no to a question, think carefully about why you are doing so.

The following shows the script being run:

```
shell> mysql_secure_installation


NOTE: RUNNING ALL PARTS OF THIS SCRIPT IS RECOMMENDED FOR ALL MySQL
      SERVERS IN PRODUCTION USE!  PLEASE READ EACH STEP CAREFULLY!


In order to log into MySQL to secure it, we'll need the current
password for the root user.  If you've just installed MySQL, and
you haven't set the root password yet, the password will be blank,
so you should just press enter here.

Enter current password for root (enter for none):
OK, successfully used password, moving on...

Setting the root password ensures that nobody can log into the MySQL
root user without the proper authorization.

Set root password? [Y/n] y
New password:
Re-enter new password:
```

```
Password updated successfully!
Reloading privilege tables..
 ... Success!

By default, a MySQL installation has an anonymous user, allowing
anyone to log into MySQL without having to have a user account
created for them.  This is intended only for testing, and to make the
installation go a bit smoother.  You should remove them before
moving into a production environment.

Remove anonymous users? [Y/n] y
 ... Success!

Normally, root should only be allowed to connect from
 'localhost'.  This
ensures that someone cannot guess at the root password from
 the network.

Disallow root login remotely? [Y/n] y
 ... Success!

By default, MySQL comes with a database named 'test' that anyone
 can access.  This is also intended only for testing, and should be
 removed before moving into a production environment.

Remove test database and access to it? [Y/n] y
 - Dropping test database...
 ... Success!
 - Removing privileges on test database...
 ... Success!

Reloading the privilege tables will ensure that all changes made
 so far will take effect immediately.

Reload privilege tables now? [Y/n] y
 ... Success!

Cleaning up...

All done!  If you've completed all of the above steps, your MySQL
installation should now be secure.

Thanks for using MySQL!
```

Remember the five users the Unix-based systems create when running the `mysql_install_db` script? After running the `mysql_secure_installation` script there is one user left who has a password. Congratulations, your system is now much more secure!

Windows PATH Variable Configuration

To run MySQL programs without having to type the full path to the program, add the `bin` directory to your `PATH` environment variable. To do this, begin by right-clicking your My Computer icon and then left-clicking Properties.

Now click the Advanced tab from the System Properties menu and click the Environment Variables button.

With the screen that opens up, under System Variable you must select Path and then click the Edit button. Next the Edit System Variable screen should appear.

At the end of the Variable Value field, enter a semicolon followed by the complete path of the MySQL `bin` directory (for example, `;C:\Program Files\MySQL\MySQL Server 6.0\bin`). Close up the screens by clicking OK until all of the screens that were opened have been closed. Now you can run any program in the `bin` directory by typing its name at the command prompt — there is no need to use a full path.

WARNING You should be very careful when editing `PATH` by hand. If you delete or modify any part of the `PATH` value it can break other programs.

Automated startup

Both Windows and Unix-based servers have methods that allow for `mysqld` to start automatically when the operating system boots. With Windows-based servers you can configure `mysqld` as a service (see "Starting and Stopping MySQL as a Windows Service," earlier in this chapter, for how to do that). Unix-based server startup options will vary somewhat depending on the operating system configuration. We cover the most common methods in the following section.

Starting and stopping mysqld on System V-based Unix

Solaris is a System V-based Unix operating system. All Linux variants (Red Hat, Debian, and so on) follow the POSIX standard, which uses System V run levels. In contrast, BSD-based operating systems (including Mac OS X) do not use System V run levels. We do not discuss how to set up automated startup and shutdown on BSD-based operating systems.

You have three methods of starting `mysqld`. The simplest way is to run `mysqld` directly from the command line. This method works on any operating system. Similar to executing the `mysqld` binary directly is running the `mysqld_safe` script. This script is a wrapper script that is used to call the `mysqld` binary. It will automatically attempt to restart `mysqld` if `mysqld` dies.

The third method of starting a MySQL server is by running the `mysql.server` script. This wrapper script is used primarily at system startup and shutdown on systems that use the System V-style run level directories (see next section). The script itself is located in the `support-files` subdirectory of the installation directory. It is frequently copied into `/etc/init.d/mysql`. Please note that the file does not have to be called `mysql`, it is just what most administrators do. This script starts the server by invoking `mysqld_safe` after setting some options and running some tests.

System V run levels

The System V run levels are states that the operating system is defined to be in on System V and POSIX operating systems such as Solaris, Red Hat, and Debian. Unfortunately, what each run level means varies somewhat by operating system. Table 2-2 shows the defined run levels for Red Hat distributions.

TABLE 2-3

Red Hat System Run Levels

Run Level	Description
0	Server halt (shutdown).
1	The system is configured for single user access with the minimum services needed for operation. Typically used for maintenance.
2	Custom service level that can be defined by system administrators.
3	Multi-user without X-Windows.
4	Custom service level that can be defined by system administrators.
5	Multi-user with X-Windows.
6	Server restart.

Run levels 3 and 5 are the most common states the operating system is in under normal conditions. Run levels 0 and 6 are the states used by the operating system when it is shut down and rebooted.

The control of your system services is accomplished through the use of the `rcX.d` directories. The `X` is an integer that corresponds to the run level. For example, `rc3.d` is the directory containing all the scripts to either start or shut down a service when the server enters or exits the third run level.

On Red Hat distributions the `rcX.d` directories are in `/etc/rc.d`. On Debian and Solaris distributions they are stored in `/etc`. When you list the contents of one of these `rcX.d` directories you will see links to scripts that begin with either an S or a K. The S stands for start (the service) and the K stands for kill (the service). Each link also has a number that corresponds to the order in which it is started or killed.

Often when you are performing a package install (such as with pkg or rpm) the installation program configures mysqld to automatically start and stop on system start and shutdown. For example, the official rpms copy the mysql.server script into /etc/init.d/mysql and configure the operating system for automatic startup and shutdown of mysqld. However, this is not always the case. For example, the Sun Solaris pkg package does not configure the startup and shutdown of mysqld. Manual installations such as the archive package also do not configure automatic startup and shutdown of mysqld.

Configuring the operating system to automatically start up and shut down mysqld at certain run levels typically involves copying the mysql.server support script into the /etc/init.d directory. Then, create symbolic links from files such as /etc/rc3.d/S99mysql and /etc/rc0.d/K01mysql to the startup script in the /etc/init.d directory. A symbolic link is created using the ln command with the -s option.

You will need to check the appropriate run level directories (such as rc3.d and rc0.d) to choose values for the numbers after the S and K. mysqld is usually one of the last services started and, conversely, one of the first services ended. If this is the case, use S99mysql as a link name to indicate mysqld should start last, and K01mysql to indicate that it should be killed first. You may require different numbers if you have service dependencies. For example, if the web server Apache depends on mysqld already being started, and there are links to S95apache and K05apache, you will want to make links to S94mysqld and K06mysqld. This will ensure that the dependency is met — Apache is started after mysqld and killed before mysqld.

After copying the mysql.server script to /etc/init.d/mysql the following two commands (run as the root operating system user) create the links from /etc/init.d/mysql to the rc3.d and rc0.d directories on Debian or Solaris:

```
#  ln -s /etc/init.d/mysql /etc/rc3.d/S99mysql
#  ln -s /etc/init.d/mysql /etc/rc0.d/K01mysql
```

Even if your installation is configured to start and stop automatically it is necessary sometimes to start or stop the server manually. This can be done by using the mysql.server script, invoking it with a start or stop argument. If you have already copied the mysql.server script to /etc/init.d/mysql as shown previously it can be done like this:

```
shell> /etc/init.d/mysql stop
shell> /etc/init.d/mysql start
```

And if you want to immediately restart the server upon stopping:

```
shell> /etc/init.d/mysql restart
```

You should always run the startup script as the root user, and run mysqld as a non-root user. To run mysqld as a specified user you should add an appropriate user option to the [mysqld] directive of an option file:

```
[mysqld]
user=mysql
```

Upgrading mysqld

Each MySQL release has three different numbers in the release version, which make up the release series and the minor version. For mysqld version 6.0.8, the release series is 6.0 and the minor version is 6.0.8. All MySQL releases are cumulative — that is, features in one version are included in the next (unless changed or taken out due to a bug fix). When performing minor release upgrades, it is possible to skip intermediate versions. For example, upgrading from 6.0.6 to 6.0.8 can be done without needing to upgrade to 6.0.7 first. You should not skip intermediate release series. To upgrade from 5.0 to 6.0, upgrade to 5.1 first, then upgrade to 6.0 after 5.1 is tested and working properly.

If your installation has multiple packages (that is, mysql-server and mysql-client) it is best to upgrade all the packages at the same time.

The MySQL changelog

The *changelog* is a list of all the changes from a previous version of MySQL Server software to a new version. It lists incompatible changes from previous versions, bug fixes, and new features. You will need to go through this changelog carefully and understand the changes that might affect your servers and the applications that interact with them. Because MySQL releases are cumulative, you must read all intermediate changelog pages.

As an example, to upgrade from mysqld version 6.0.6 to version 6.0.8 there are two changelog pages to read — the changelog page for 6.0.7 and the changelog page for 6.0.8 (see http://dev.mysql.com/doc/refman/6.0/en/news-6-0-x.html). While reading those, you will learn that there is an incompatible change listed for the tables for MySQL Backup logging. If your application uses MySQL Backup the upgrade could cause a problem in the way your application works.

> **TIP** Take the time to read and understand the bug fixes and new features added to each version before upgrading. This may take an hour or more, but it is well worth it to discover incompatible changes before an upgrade, instead of afterwards by upset customers.

It is a good idea to back up your old mysqld before installing a newer one. For example, if you are using version 6.0.6 and want to upgrade to 6.0.8, rename your current binary from mysqld to mysqld-6.0.6. If your new mysqld does not function properly, shut it down, move the new binary from mysqld to mysqld-6.0.8, move mysqld-6.0.6 to mysqld, and restart.

Though every effort is made to protect data during upgrades, it is always smart to back up your data before installing any new version of software. Sun Microsystems recommends that you export and import your data when doing a release series upgrade (for example, from 5.1 to 6.0).

Use the following guidelines when upgrading from one release series to the next:

■ Examine the changelogs for all intermediate versions carefully before the upgrade and determine if they will affect your setup.

- Create a logical backup (export) of your data before the upgrade. How to do so is described in Chapter 13. Once the upgrade is complete you will need to import your data from the backup.

- After the installation of the new binaries you will need to run the `mysql_upgrade` script. This script will check and repair your tables with `REPAIR TABLE FOR UPGRADE`, if needed. In addition, it updates any system tables (such as grant tables) by modifying the table structures as necessary and adding new tables if needed. This is done to support new functionality.

If problems occur, such as the new `mysqld` does not start or that you cannot connect to the server, you should verify that the server is running with the options you expect it to be running with. You can check this with the `--print-defaults` option (for example, `mysqld --print-defaults`). This option will display all options that are configured by option files. To list all the options that `mysqld` will run with, including the default options, you can also use the `my_print_defaults` program.

It is a good idea to upgrade client packages whenever you upgrade MySQL. These client packages include the Perl DBD::mysql module, the PHP mysql extension and the Python MySQLdb module. Your environment may have different client packages.

Upgrading MySQL on Windows

When upgrading `mysqld` on Windows (whether upgrading to a new minor release or to a new release), use the following steps:

1. Choose the version to upgrade to by reading the changelog pages for all intermediate versions.

2. Create a backup of your installation. How to perform backups is covered in Chapter 13.

3. Download the new installation files that you will use for the upgrade process.

4. Stop `mysqld` if it is running. If `mysqld` is installed as a service you can stop the service with the following command:

```
C:\> net stop MySQL
```

If not running as a service you must stop `mysqld` manually:

```
C:\> mysqladmin -u root -p shutdown
```

5. If you are upgrading from a previous version that was installed from a zip archive and are installing the new version using the Installation Wizard, you must manually remove the previous installation and the MySQL service if one was created.

To remove the MySQL service, use the following command:

```
C:\> mysqld --remove
```

If you do not remove an existing MySQL service the Installation Wizard may fail to install the new MySQL service.

6. When upgrading from a version older than mysqld 5.1.23 to mysqld 5.1.23 or higher, the default location of the data directory changes from a subdirectory of the MySQL installation to the AppData folder. In order for the new installation to utilize these files you must manually copy or move them from your old installation to the new location.

7. a) If you are using the Installation Wizard for the upgrade you should run the Installation Wizard as described in the section "Installing MySQL from the Installation Packages on Windows" earlier in this chapter.

   b) If you are installing MySQL from a Zip archive you must extract the archive first. You can either use the same directory as the current MySQL installation or install it into a different location. We recommend moving the current MySQL installation to a backup directory and installing to the location where the current MySQL installation was.

8. To reinstall the service, run the following from the command line:

```
C:\> mysqld --install
```

9. You are now ready to start your new server installation. If you installed MySQL as a service, use the C:\> net start MySQL command. Otherwise you must start mysqld manually as described in the "Starting and Stopping MySQL from the Windows Command Line" section earlier in this chapter.

Troubleshooting

It can be frustrating when you perform an installation of MySQL server and it does not start properly. However, after you work with MySQL server installations for a while you begin to see patterns that can be used for problem resolution. A good thing about these patterns is that they will work on any installation platform. This section will help you start to find those patterns.

The most important things to do when troubleshooting a failed installation are:

- Check the mysqld error log to see why the server does not start. This is the first and most important place for troubleshooting any problem involving mysqld. Check the error log before doing any other troubleshooting, because most often it will tell you why the server could not start.

- Verify that the server knows where to find the configuration file(s) and that your problem is not a result of one configuration file overriding the options in another. See the section "Initial Configuration" earlier in this chapter for information on configuration files.

- If you see messages such as:

```
System error 1067 has occurred.
Fatal error: Can't open privilege tables: Table 'mysql.host'
 doesn't exist
```

ensure your system tables were installed properly. On Unix-based servers the `mysql_install_db_` script can be run to install system tables. Shut down `mysqld` and run this script to install your system tables as described earlier in this chapter.

On Windows, run the MySQL Configuration Wizard as described earlier in this chapter.

If your system tables exist, check to see if `mysqld` can find them. If the base directory and data directory are not in the default locations, make sure the appropriate options (`basedir` and `datadir`) are configured in an option file, and that option file is being used by `mysqld`.

■ Make sure you specify all required options by the storage engines being used in your installation.

■ Improper permissions on the data directory can keep the server from having access. The data directory and its contents must have the proper read/write permissions for the user that runs `mysqld` (usually `mysql`).

 For the most up-to-date information on specific errors you may encounter, check the website at `www.wiley.com/go/mysqladminbible`.

Summary

Installations and upgrades are part of the duties of a database administrator. We covered the following topics in this chapter:

■ Choosing and downloading the appropriate MySQL version

■ Installing MySQL

   ▧ GNU/Linux

   ▧ Solaris

   ▧ Windows

■ Post-install configuration

   ▧ Initializing the data directory

   ▧ Initializing the system tables

   ▧ Setting user passwords

   ▧ Getting rid of unsecure users

   ▧ How to start and stop `mysqld` automatically

■ Upgrading to new minor releases and to new release series

■ Troubleshooting

Chapter 3

Accessing MySQL

You have several ways to access an instance of mysqld (the MySQL server daemon). There are command-line clients and graphical clients for interactively executing SQL commands. Some of these clients can also run files that contain multiple SQL statements for non-interactive use. A database administrator needs to be able to effectively use these tools daily in order to check data integrity, debug application issues, and gather database information to help tune the server.

Graphical User Interface (GUI) tools can perform many of the same functions plus some additional functions such as building ER (Entity Relationship) diagrams.

IN THIS CHAPTER

Accessing mysqld with Command-Line Tools

Managing the database with GUI tools

Using GUI tools for special tasks

Accessing mysqld with Command-Line Tools

Most database administrators use command-line client tools for access and for getting information. It is important to understand these tools because you will use them on a daily basis. These tools include mysql, mysqladmin, and mysqlshow.

Though each tool performs different functions, they have several common options. Often these options will have a long form and a short form — for example, to specify a username, you can use the short form -u or the long form --user. The most important common tool option is the help option, which is specified with -? or -I or --help. The help option shows a brief summary of the tool, syntax, a list of options and their meanings, and finally a list of the variables and their values after reading in all the options.

Many options can be saved in a configuration file, to reduce the amount of information on the command line. In configuration files, options are specified using their long format, without the `--` prefix. For example, instead of always typing `--user=testuser` on the command line, the option can be saved in the appropriate place in a configuration file as `user=testuser`. See the "Initial Configuration" section in Chapter 2 for more details about configuration files.

If you experience problems trying to connect to `mysqld`, we have a series of troubleshooting steps on our website at `www.wiley.com/go/mysqladminbible`.

Frequently used options

These are the most often used options for command-line tools:

- `-u user_name` or `--user=user_name`: `user_name`: This is the username to connect as. If not specified on Windows, the user ODBC is used. If not specified on other operating systems, the operating system user is used. For example, if you are logged in to a Unix account named `dba`, the default username used to connect is `dba`.

- `-p pass` or `--password=pass`: `pass`: This is the password to use when authenticating. If the password option (`-p` or `--password`) is not specified, a blank password is used. If the password option is specified and the password is omitted, you will be prompted for a password.

- The following example shows how to use the command-line `mysql` client to connect to the `mysqld` server using the `-u` and `-p` options to specify a username and password. Two connections are made: the first enters a password at a prompt and the second specifies the password on the shell command line:

```
shell> mysql -u testuser -p
Enter password:
Welcome to the MySQL monitor.  Commands end with ; or \g.
Your MySQL connection id is 8
Server version: 6.0.8-alpha MySQL Community Server (GPL)

Type 'help;' or '\h' for help. Type '\c' to clear the buffer.

mysql> exit
Bye
shell> mysql -u testuser -ptestuser_password
Welcome to the MySQL monitor.  Commands end with ; or \g.
Your MySQL connection id is 9
Server version: 6.0.8-alpha MySQL Community Server (GPL)

Type 'help;' or '\h' for help. Type '\c' to clear the buffer.

mysql> exit
Bye
shell>
```

You can find more information on the `mysql` command-line client later in this chapter.

■   `--protocol=protocol_type`: On non-Windows machines, `protocol` can be either `SOCKET` or `TCP` (`SOCKET` is the default). On Windows machines, `protocol` can be either `TCP`, `PIPE`, or `MEMORY` (`TCP` is the default). Named pipes use the `PIPE` protocol, and shared memory uses the `MEMORY` protocol. Both are turned off by default in `mysqld` on Windows.

Using both the host and port options on a Unix server will override the default protocol of `SOCKET` on Unix, when the host is not `localhost`.

■   `-S sock_location` or `--socket=sock_location`: On non-Windows machines, `sock_location` is the path to the Unix socket file. By default, command-line tools will try to connect via a socket, and the default socket on Unix is `/tmp/mysqld.sock`. This is true even if no socket option is used.

On Windows, the socket option indicates a local connection via a named pipe, with `socket_location` being the name of the named pipe to use. Named pipes are turned off by default in `mysqld`. If named pipes are not enabled (as is the default), the socket option is ignored with no warnings or errors.

Connecting to a `mysqld` server without using a socket file actually means connecting via a different protocol. To do this, you must specify both a host option and a port option, and the host option must not be `localhost`. See the host, port, and protocol options for more information.

■   `-h mysqld_host` or `--host=mysqld_host`: `mysqld_host` is the server to connect to. `mysqld_host` can be either the short hostname (say, `db1`), the fully qualified domain name (*fqdn*, such as `db1.company.com`), the IP address (as in `192.168.100.7`), or `localhost`. If no host option is specified, `localhost` is used.

The host option is used to connect to `mysqld` instances on a different machine. It can also be used to connect to a `mysqld` instance on the local machine, and is often used to connect to a local `mysqld` instance that does not have its socket in the default place.

Note that if the host is `localhost`, the port option is ignored and the socket file will be used. To connect to `mysqld` using a port on the local machine, you must specify either `--protocol=TCP` or a hostname or IP address for the local machine (such as `127.0.0.1`).

WARNING   You may run into odd behavior when trying to connect to a local `mysqld` instance on a non-Windows machine. If you seem to be having trouble connecting, check your options against your intentions. This type of odd behavior is usually seen when your intention is to connect using TCP/IP, but the connection is using a socket file instead. Note the following behaviors:

■   If there are no protocol, socket, host, or port options given, a socket file will be used for connecting.

■   If a port option is given and no host or protocol options are given, a socket file is used to connect.

■ If the protocol specified is TCP, the connection will be made via TCP/IP even if a socket option is given.

■ If the protocol specified is SOCKET and a port is given but no host is given, a socket file is used to connect.

■ If the protocol specified is SOCKET and the host option localhost is given, a socket file is used to connect. This is true regardless of whether a port option is given.

■ If the protocol specified is SOCKET and a host option other than localhost is given, an error occurs (regardless of whether a port option is given):

```
shell> mysql --protocol=SOCKET -h 127.0.0.1
ERROR 2047 (HY000): Wrong or unknown protocol
```

A socket file is used when the host and protocol options are not given, regardless of whether the port option is given.

■ If the host, port, and socket options are all given but the protocol option is not, the host and port are used.

See "Troubleshooting MySQL Connections" later in this chapter for examples showing correct and incorrect ways to use host, port, protocol, and socket options to connect to mysqld as well as how to debug connectivity issues.

Table 3-1 shows other, infrequently used common options for command-line tools.

Using the command-line mysql client

The most common way to access mysqld is through the command-line client tool simply called mysql. A DBA can log in (for example, with ssh) to the machine running mysqld and use the mysql command-line client on the server. Or, a remote database can be accessed by using a local mysql client to access a server remotely using the host option (-h or --host) as described earlier in the section "Frequently Used Options."

In addition to the common options, the most frequently used option to mysql is the database option. The database option is specified by -D dbname or --database=dbname or dbname, where dbname is the database to connect to initially. In the following example, the first three commands illustrate the three different syntaxes of the database option, and the fourth command shows typical options to mysql. All four examples connect to the test database:

```
shell> mysql -D test
shell> mysql --database=test
shell> mysql test

shell> mysql -u testuser -p test
Enter password:
Reading table information for completion of table and column names
You can turn off this feature to get a quicker startup with -A

Welcome to the MySQL monitor.  Commands end with ; or \g.
```

```
Your MySQL connection id is 44
Server version: 6.0.8-alpha MySQL Community Server (GPL)

Type 'help;' or '\h' for help. Type '\c' to clear the buffer.

mysql> exit
Bye
shell>
```

TABLE 3-1

Other Common Options for Command-Line Tools

Option	Description
`--compress`	Compresses all data between the client program and `mysqld`.
`--default-character-set=charset_name`	Uses `charset_name` as the client's default character set.
`--version` or `-V`	Displays the tool's version information.
`--verbose` or `-v`	Gives more detailed output.
`--ssl-ca=/path/to/ssl_ca_file`	Specifies the path and filename of trusted SSL CAs (Certificate Authorities).
`--ssl-capath=/path/to/ca_dir`	Specifies the directory that contains SSL CA certificates in PEM format.
`--ssl-cert=/path/to/cert_file`	Specifies the path and filename of the SSL certificate file.
`--ssl-cipher=cipher_list`	Specifies the ciphers allowed with SSL encryption in a colon (:) separated list.
`--ssl-key=/path/to/key_file`	Specifies the path and filename of the SSL key file.
`--ssl-verify-server-cert`	This option, available since `mysqld` 5.1.11, requires that the server certificate's Common Name value is the same as the host option specified by the client. Connections will be rejected if the `mysqld` certificate Common Name does not match the hostname given in the host option. This helps prevent man-in-the-middle attacks, and is off by default.

Note that `test` is the database name, not the password. The password is entered at the prompt. To specify a password for use with `-p`, there must be no space between `-p` and the password.

mysql will read options in the [client] directive of configuration files. For example:

```
[client] database=test
user=testuser
password=pass
```

Now you can just type mysql from a shell prompt and mysql will connect as if you typed mysql -u testuser -ppass test.

> **NOTE** Recall from the Chapter 2 section "Initial Configuration" that configuration files are stored as plain text. You need to make sure to secure any configuration files that contain passwords.

Non-interactive modes

One common use of mysql is to execute a non-interactive batch file of SQL queries. This can be done by redirection. The following example uses the < redirection operator to install the sakila sample database:

```
shell> mysql < sakila-schema.sql
shell> mysql < sakila-data.sql
```

For the sake of simplicity, we have eliminated options you may need to specify, such as options used for connection and authentication (the host and user options, for example). There is no restriction on the filename of a file redirected to mysql, though there is a convention of using .sql as a file extension to indicate a file of SQL queries.

> **NOTE** The sakila sample database is used throughout this book. You can download it from the official download site at http://dev.mysql.com/doc/#sampledb.

By default, if mysql encounters an error when running a batch file non-interactively it will print out the error and the line number of the statement causing the error, and exit. Any lines after the statement causing the error will not be processed. You can change this behavior to simply print the error and continue by giving the -f or --force option to mysql.

Another way to run a batch file of SQL queries is to use the source command (source or \.) within the mysql interactive shell. The syntax for the source commands is:

```
source /path/to/filename
\. /path/to/filename
```

The path and filename are relative to the directory you started mysql from. If you start mysql from your home directory and there is a file called test.sql in your home directory, you can specify:

```
mysql> source test.sql
```

Only one argument to source is allowed. You cannot specify more than one argument to source:

```
mysql> source test.sql test2.sql
ERROR: Failed to open file 'test.sql test2.sql', error: 2
mysql> source test.sql,test2.sql
ERROR: Failed to open file 'test.sql,test2.sql', error: 2
```

By default, if source encounters an error when running a batch file, it will print out the error and continue to the next statement. Lines after the statement causing the errors are processed. To make source leave the batch file where the error occurs, start mysql with the --abort-source-on-error option before calling the source command.

To execute queries non-interactively without using a file, use the -e "queries" option to mysql (or the long format, --execute="queries"). For example:

```
shell> mysql -e "SHOW DATABASES; SELECT 1+2"
+--------------------+
| Database           |
+--------------------+
| information_schema |
| sakila             |
| test               |
+--------------------+
+-----+
| 1+2 |
+-----+
|   3 |
+-----+
shell>
```

Useful features of mysql

mysql has many features — some features are used by specifying options and some features are used via a command in the mysql shell. Some features, like batch query processing, can be used by specifying an option or using a command.

The help option to mysql, as stated previously, is --help or -? or -I. The help command in the mysql shell (? or \? or help) will display all non-SQL commands specific to mysql.

Using Named Commands at the Beginning of Any Line

The mysql interactive shell has several non-SQL commands. All of these have a long format and a short format. The short format consists of the backslash (\) followed by a single character, and can be used anywhere on the mysql command line. The long format is a word that must be used as the first word of the first line by default. You can change this requirement to be the first word of any line by issuing the -G or --named-commands option to mysql. For example, the exit command will only be parsed if it is at the start of a new command, but the \q command will be parsed even if it is in the middle or at the end of a command:

```
mysql> SELECT exit;
ERROR 1064 (42000): You have an error in your SQL syntax; check the
manual that corresponds to your MySQL server version for the right syntax to
use near 'exit' at line 1

mysql> SELECT exit
    -> exit;
ERROR 1064 (42000): You have an error in your SQL syntax; check the
manual that corresponds to your MySQL server version for the right syntax to
use near 'exit exit' at line 1

mysql> SELECT ex\qit;
Bye
shell>
```

When mysql is started with -G or --named-commands, the second example actually exits:

```
mysql> select exit
    -> exit;
Bye
```

Long formats such as clear and go are functionally useless unless the -G or --named-commands options to mysql are used — at the beginning of the command, there is nothing to cancel or submit. Most database administrators are comfortable using the shorter commands and not turning named commands on.

TIP As we discuss features and how they are used, you may be confused between what is an option and what is a command. Keep in mind that an option to mysql starts with a - or --. A command within the mysql interactive shell starts with \ or is a word with no special character prefix.

The most useful features of mysql are:

■ Leave the mysql interactive shell (command only, exit, quit or \q)

■ Specify the use feature to change databases within mysql. The short form is \u, and either form looks at the first argument given and tries to change to a database with that name. For example, the sakila sample database was created by the sakila-sample.sql file executed earlier. To change to it, you can run:

```
mysql> \u sakila
Database changed
```

```
mysql> use sakila anything after the first word is ignored
Database changed
```

NOTE **Databases are stored as directories in the data directory. This means that on Windows machines, database names are case-insensitive, because the file system is case-insensitive. That means that Sakila and sakila reference the same database on Windows.**

On non-Windows machines, database names are case-sensitive, because non-Windows file systems are case-sensitive. Thus, Sakila and sakila are different databases on non-Windows machines.

■ mysql keeps an in-memory list of the commands typed in the session. You can use the up and down arrow keys to scroll through the lines of the commands. The scrolling behavior is slightly different on Windows and non-Windows machines. To illustrate this, imagine the last three commands you typed in mysql were queries involving math, time, and a string:

```
SELECT 1+2;
SELECT NOW();
SELECT "last command typed";
```

On Windows machines, the position in the list of command lines is remembered. If you press the down arrow key, nothing will happen, because there is no query after the last one you typed. If you press the up arrow key once, you will see the string query. If you press the up arrow key again, you will see the time query. If you press the Enter key, the time query will run again. Now, if you press the down arrow key, you will see the string query — mysql remembered that you were at the time query and thus the next query in the session history is the string query.

This means that if you have a multi-line query that you want to repeat, you can use the up arrow key to scroll to the first line, and then press the Enter key to accept the first line. To get the second line, press the down arrow key once, and press Enter. For example:

```
mysql> SELECT 1+2,
    -> NOW(),
    -> "last command typed";
```

To run the command line-by-line again, press the up arrow key until you see the line SELECT 1+2, and press Enter to accept the line. Then press the down arrow key once, and the NOW() line appears. Press Enter, then the down arrow key again, and "last command typed"; appears. This makes it easier to run similar queries — after the first query is run, use the scrolling feature and change part of the query, instead of re-typing the whole query.

On non-Windows machines, the behavior is different. The position in the list of commands is not remembered. Taking the same example on a non-Windows machine, press the up arrow key until you see the line SELECT 1+2, and press Enter to accept the line. If you press the down arrow key, nothing will happen, because the position is not remembered. You are always at the end of the list. To get the NOW() line to appear, you have to press the up arrow key a few times to scroll to it.

■ Some shell interpreter keys retain their function on the mysql command line. For example, on non-Windows machines:

   ▨ Ctrl-w deletes the previous word and stores it in a buffer. Using this more than once stores all the words in the buffer.

   ▨ Ctrl-y retrieves (*yanks*) the contents of buffers filled with Ctrl-u or Ctrl-w.

   ▨ Ctrl-u deletes the entire line prior to the cursor position and stores it in a buffer.

   ▨ Ctrl-a moves the cursor to the beginning of the current line.

   ▨ Ctrl-e moves the cursor to the end of the current line.

■ On non-Windows machines, mysql saves commands in a history file. The history file is ~/.mysql_history — a hidden file in the home directory of the operating system user that calls mysql.

■ On non-Windows machines, mysql has a tab completion feature. Objects such as databases, tables, columns, and functions are stored in memory, and pressing the Tab key once will complete a unique name. Pressing the Tab key twice will show a list of possible completions for non-unique names. If there is no such possible completion, there is no additional output.

For example, if you type s, then a, then k, then press the Tab key, your command line will look like this:

```
mysql> sakila
```

If you type s, then a, then press the Tab key, auto-complete does not fill anything in, and you may get a warning beep. If you press Tab again, your command line will look like this:

```
mysql> sa
sakila                                sales_by_store
sales_by_film_category                sales_by_store.manager
sales_by_film_category.category       sales_by_store.store
sales_by_film_category.total_sales    sales_by_store.total_sales
mysql> sa
```

You can continue to use tab completion. Continuing the last example where you have already typed sa, continue typing les_by_film and then press the Tab key twice. After the first time you press Tab, auto-complete has added:

```
mysql> sales_by_film_category
```

Then, after the second time you press Tab, you see:

```
sales_by_film_category              sales_by_film_category.total_sales
sales_by_film_category.category
mysql> sales_by_film_category
```

Tab completion works with SQL, too. However, SQL commands will only appear in tab completion as uppercase. There is no auto-complete if you type `sel` and then press the Tab key twice, but if you type `SEL` and press the Tab key once auto-complete will generate `SELECT`.

■ Database objects are loaded when changing to the database. The first time you connect to a database in a session, you see:

```
mysql> USE sakila;
Reading table information for completion of table and column names
You can turn off this feature to get a quicker startup with -A

Database changed
```

If it takes too long to read the information, you may want to disable the auto-completion feature. If you specify `-A` as an option to `mysql`, you will only see the `Database changed` message, and tab completion will not work at all — not even for built-in SQL commands such as `SELECT`. You can specify the `--no-auto-rehash` or `--disable-auto-rehash` longer forms instead of `-A`.

If you create a new database object, such as a table, the new name will not be part of the auto-completion list until the list is regenerated. This can be done with the `\#` or `rehash` commands on the `mysql` command line. Even though tab completion is not supported on Windows, the `\#` and `rehash` commands are valid in `mysql` on Windows.

■ Cancel a query with the clear command (`clear` or `\c`). This can be used when you have made a mistake or otherwise want to cancel what you are typing without having to delete the entire line. For example:

```
mysql> SHOW MYDATABASES\c
mysql> SHOW DATABASES;
+--------------------+
| Database           |
+--------------------+
| information_schema |
| sakila             |
| test               |
+--------------------+
3 rows in set (0.00 sec)
```

See the sidebar "Using Named Commands at the Beginning of Any Line" earlier in this chapter to be able to use `clear` at the beginning of any line, not only the beginning of the first line.

> **TIP**   Combine the cancel feature with the command history feature to easily correct mistakes when writing long queries on the command line. For example, if you are on the third line of a query when you see a mistake on the first line, cancel the query and scroll through the history to get the line on which to fix the mistake.

■ By now you have seen that ; is used to signify to mysql that the command is finished and can be sent to the server. However, this is only the default behavior, and can be changed with the \d or delimiter command followed by one character or word. The following example shows how to change the delimiter to |, how using ; after the change does not submit the query, and then changes the delimiter back to ;:

```
mysql> SELECT 1+2;
+-----+
| 1+2 |
+-----+
|   3 |
+-----+
1 row in set (0.00 sec)

mysql> delimiter |
mysql> SELECT 1+2;
    -> |
+-----+
| 1+2 |
+-----+
|   3 |
+-----+
1 row in set (0.00 sec)

mysql> \d ;
mysql> SELECT 1+2;
+-----+
| 1+2 |
+-----+
|   3 |
+-----+
1 row in set (0.00 sec)
```

■ The default delimiter can be changed by specifying the --delimiter=new_delimiter option to mysql. Changing the delimiter is required when writing stored SQL that uses multiple statements. For more information on writing stored SQL, see Chapter 7.

■ To send a command regardless of the delimiter, use \g or go:

```
mysql> \d |
mysql> SELECT 1+2;
    -> \g
+-----+
| 1+2 |
```

```
+-----+
|  3  |
+-----+
1 row in set (0.00 sec)
```

- See the sidebar "Using Named Commands at the Beginning of Any Line" earlier in this chapter to be able to use go at the beginning of any line, not only the beginning of the first line.

- By default, output is displayed horizontally. To display output vertically, send the command using the \G or ego command:

```
mysql> SELECT 'hi'\G
*************************** 1. row ***************************
hi: hi
1 row in set (0.00 sec)
```

- Like \g and go, \G and ego send the command regardless of the delimiter used. See the sidebar "Using Named Commands at the Beginning of Any Line" earlier in this chapter to be able to use ego at the beginning of any line, not only the beginning of the first line.

- To change the default output display to always be vertical, specify the -E or the --vertical option to mysql.

- One of the most user-friendly features is the --auto-vertical-output option to mysql. This option will display output horizontally by default. If the output is wider than the width of your terminal, the display will automatically output vertically. For example:

```
mysql> SELECT "Strings less than the width of my terminal window
display horizontally.";+----------------------------------------+
| Strings less than the width of my terminal window display
  horizontally. |
+--------------------------------------------------------+
| Strings less than the width of my terminal window display
  horizontally. |
+--------------------------------------------------------+
1 row in set (0.00 sec)

mysql> SELECT "This string is more than 80 characters, and my
terminal window is only 80 characters, thus it should display
vertically.";
*************************** 1. row ***************************
This string is more than 80 characters, and my terminal
window is only 80 characters, thus it should display
vertically.: This string is more than 80 characters, and my
terminal window is only 80 characters, thus it should
display vertically.
1 row in set (0.00 sec)
```

- Some commands and queries will produce many lines of output. On non-Windows machines, the pager feature can be used to change how the output is paginated. The pager feature can be specified as an option to mysql or as a command within mysql:

```
shell> mysql --pager=page_program
mysql> \P page_program
mysql> pager page_program
```

- The values of page_program are similar to values from the PAGER operating system environment variable. They include more, less, cut, and grep. For example:

```
mysql> \P more
PAGER set to 'more'
```

- Output will now be paginated as when using the operating system's more command. By default, the pager is set to the PAGER operating system environment variable. If none is set, the default is to print to stdout (the terminal window you see on your screen). To reset the pager, use the nopager or \n command, or set the pager with no value:

```
mysql> nopager
PAGER set to stdout
mysql> \P
Default pager wasn't set, using stdout.
```

- On a non-Windows machine, you can escape to a shell and run one command by using the system or \! command. This is an indispensable command when trying to debug an issue that affects the entire system. For example:

```
mysql> \! uptime
18:16  up 2 days,  4:58, 2 users, load averages: 0.51 0.45 0.36
mysql>
```

The previous list explained many useful features of mysql, but there are many more features that can be used. Spend some time reviewing the output of mysql -h to learn about features not explained here, such as changing the prompt and sending all input and output to a file.

mysqladmin – Client for administering a server

The mysqladmin program is used to perform administrative tasks. Some of the tasks include creating and dropping databases, displaying server configuration, current status information, changing a password, and stopping a server. mysqladmin can be very useful in scripting situations. The following shows the syntax for the mysqladmin command:

```
mysqladmin [option] command [arg] [command [arg]] ...
```

The options and arguments depend on what command mysqladmin uses. Table 3-2 lists all the command parameters, along with a brief description, that mysqladmin supports. Many commands require mysqladmin to be issued with authentication from a user with certain permissions. For example, the flush commands require the RELOAD privilege. See Chapter 14 for more details on user permissions. Use the common options to specify a username and password, for example mysqladmin --user=root --password flush-hosts.

TABLE 3-2

mysqladmin Command Parameters

Command	Usage	Description
create	mysqladmin create test2	Creates the test2 database.
debug	mysqladmin debug	Sends information to the error log. Includes the following, where applicable: a safemalloc memory dump, event scheduler and queue status, server status variables, current stack size, current locks, key cache status, handler status, table status, and alarm status.
drop	mysqladmin drop test2	Drops the test2 database, including all tables and data.
extended-status	mysqladmin extended-status	Displays mysqld system variables and their current values.
flush-hosts	mysqladmin flush-hosts	Clears internal information about hosts, including the DNS cache and hostnames blocked due to too many connection errors.
flush-logs	mysqladmin flush-hosts	Flushes server logs by closing current logs and reopening new log files. This rotates binary logs (if enabled) but does nothing for slow query logs (if enabled).
flush-privileges	mysqladmin flush-privileges	Reloads the grant tables, refreshing user privileges. See Chapter 14 for more details.
flush-status	mysqladmin flush-status	Resets most server status variables.
flush-tables	mysqladmin flush-tables	Closes currently open table file handles. It waits for the current thread connections to finish before releasing file handles used by those connections.
flush-threads	mysqladmin flush-threads	Resets the thread cache.
kill	mysqladmin kill 50mysqladmin kill 50.55	Kills the specified client thread(s). Do not put any whitespace in the comma-separated list of thread ids.
password	mysqladmin password pass	Changes the connection password to pass for the user account specified.

continued

TABLE 3-2	(continued)	
Command	**Usage**	**Description**
old-password	mysqladmin old-password pass	Changes the connection password to pass for the user account specified. Similar to the password command but stores the password using the password hashing format used by default through MySQL Server 4.0. The old password format is 16 characters long and less secure than the newer 41 character default format.
ping	mysqladmin ping	Determines if the server is online and available.
processlist	mysqladmin processlist	Displays all active server threads. The same as executing a SHOW PROCESSLIST from the mysql client.
reload	mysqladmin reload	See flush-privileges.
refresh	mysqladmin refresh	Closes all open tables and rotates the server log files by closing the current file and opening a new log file. Similar to issuing both flush-hosts and flush-logs.
shutdown	mysqladmin shutdown	Stops the mysqld instance (cleanly). By default, shutdown occurs immediately, but this can be changed with the --shutdown_timeout=x option, where x is the number of seconds to wait before shutdown.
start-slave	mysqladmin start-slave	Starts replication. The server must have been configured as a slave previously. See Chapter 16 for more information about replication.
status	mysqladmin status	Displays the following global status variables and values: Uptime, Threads, Questions, Slow queries, Opens, Flush tables, Open tables, Queries per second avg.
stop-slave	mysqladmin stop-slave	Stops replication.
variables	mysqladmin variables	Displays the global status variables and values.
version	mysqladmin version	Displays the version of mysqld. To get the version of mysqladmin, use mysqladmin -V.

A useful command with mysqladmin is ping. In the following example the localhost server, which is running a mysqld daemon, is pinged:

```
shell > mysqladmin ping --p --host=127.0.0.1
mysqld is alive
shell >
```

It returns positively, so you know the local server is running mysqld. Next try and ping something that is not running a mysqld daemon and see the result:

```
shell > mysqladmin ping --host=www.nosuchhost.com
mysqladmin: connect to server at 'www.nosuchhost.com' failed
error: 'Unknown MySQL server host 'www.nosuchhost.com' (0)'
Check that mysqld is running on www.nosuchhost.com and that the
 port is 3306.
You can check this by doing 'telnet www.nosuchhost.com 3306'
shell >
```

In this case the server does not appear to be running a mysqld daemon. Using the mysqladmin ping command is a great first step in troubleshooting the seeming failure of a MySQL server.

Another useful command is the status command. This is used to return some basic information from mysqld including uptime, current number of threads, and queries per second being executed. You can combine the status command with the --sleep option to have mysqladmin pause for the specified number of seconds and then display updated status information. Unless you specify the --count option (which only works in conjunction with the --sleep option) mysqladmin will continue to provide updated status information for as long as you allow it to run.

```
shell>  mysqladmin status --sleep=1 --count=2
Uptime: 177523  Threads: 1  Questions: 340  Slow queries: 0  Opens:
 64  Flush tables: 1  Open tables: 53  Queries per second avg: 0.1
Uptime: 177525  Threads: 1  Questions: 340  Slow queries: 0  Opens:
 64  Flush tables: 1  Open tables: 53  Queries per second avg: 0.1
shell>
```

As you can see mysqladmin executed twice and then stopped.

Want some more information? What about some host server statistics such as CPU and memory statistics? Add the --debug-info option and it writes this information at the end of the output:

```
shell >  mysqladmin status status --debug-info
Uptime: 34336  Threads: 1  Questions: 1494  Slow queries: 0  Opens:
 177  Flush tables: 1  Open tables: 44  Queries per second avg: 0.43

User time 0.00, System time 0.01
Maximum resident set size 0, Integral resident set size 0
Non-physical pagefaults 531, Physical pagefaults 0, Swaps 0
Blocks in 0 out 0, Messages in 0 out 0, Signals 0
Voluntary context switches 1, Involuntary context switches 8
shell >
```

All three of these options could be combined; `mysqladmin status --sleep=3 --count=5 --debug-info` would be perfectly acceptable. Other options to `mysqladmin` are used infrequently; see `mysqladmin --help` for more information.

The final example shows how to shut down the MySQL server. Because the password is not included the server will ask for you to input the password. If it is entered correctly and `testuser` has the `SHUTDOWN` the server begins the shutdown process in 60 seconds:

```
mysqladmin -u testuser -p shutdown --shutdown_timeout=60
```

To monitor your processes for some period of time because of an ongoing problem:

```
mysqladmin -u root -p processlist --sleep=30
```

This will run the `processlist` command every thirty seconds, giving you continually updated output.

GUI Tools

GUI tools are often thought to be easier to use than the command-line tools. Though this is typically true for beginners, as database administrators become more experienced with the command-line tool they find it is more powerful, faster, and more convenient to use. Even so, there are certainly situations when it makes sense to use GUI-based tools and there are some tasks (such as ER diagramming) that are impossible from the command line.

In this section we cover five different tools that can be used for database management tasks. Though there is overlap in the functionality of most of these tools, each of these tools has areas where it excels.

SQLyog

The SQLyog program is probably the most popular GUI tool for MySQL. The program has been around since August 2002 and the maturity of the product is evident when you use the tool. For people who come from a Windows desktop background this can be a very useful and practical tool. Though it only runs on Windows desktops, there is both a free community version that is somewhat limited and an enterprise version that currently costs less than 100 USD for a single user license.

 The SQLyog website at `http://www.webyog.com` has downloads and lots of information about SQLyog.

Server connections

With any of these GUI tools, first you will need to make a connection to `mysqld`. It is common to use the `ssh` protocol to establish secure connections. One of the reasons SQLyog stands out among other tools is that it is easy to create an `ssh` connection using what is called `ssh` tunneling. Creating an `ssh` tunnel is as easy as checking a box and filling in the information about the server host and the `mysqld` instance. If you experience any problems SQLyog has very thorough, context-sensitive help. Figure 3-1 shows this connection dialog.

FIGURE 3-1

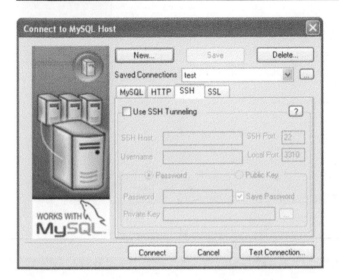

SQL query creation

SQLyog has two methods of SQL query creation. With the first method you type the query in a query building window. SQLyog provides two tools to assist you — the auto-completion feature and SQL templates. `mysql` does not have tab completion on Windows (see the previous section on `mysql` features). With SQLyog you can use the Tab key to complete table or column names or even functions, no matter what operating system you are using. SQL templates help with the proper syntax for the various SQL commands. First, right-click in the query building window. This will bring up a menu where you left-click Insert Templates to use a template. Figure 3-2 shows the list of available templates with the `CREATE TRIGGER` statement template selected.

At this point you just click the Insert button and SQLyog will create the template for you to fill in with your specific data.

The second method of query writing is using the query builder to create the query. This is a more graphical method of query building where you drag the appropriate tables from the schema objects to a blank window. You can then do the common query actions of joining tables, sorting, filtering, and grouping based on your chosen criteria. SQLyog will then build the SQL command for you to execute without actually having to type any SQL code.

Figure 3-3 shows how the query builder looks with a simple query built from the `sakila` database.

FIGURE 3-2

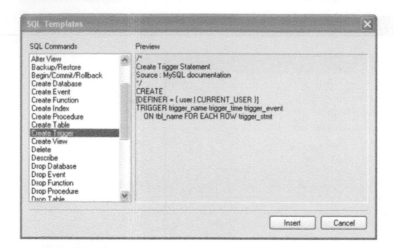

FIGURE 3-3

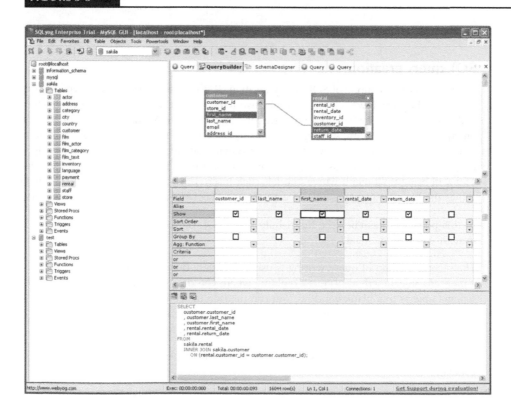

After building the query you can copy the query over to the Query tab and then execute it with just a couple of clicks.

Database management

SQLyog has numerous features designed for database management. Among the tasks you can perform are:

- Create new tables
- Manage table indexes
- Manage users
- Synchronize databases
- Back up and restore databases
- Create triggers, views, events, and stored procedures

Database synchronization

One of the best features of SQLyog is the database synchronization with its *powertool*. This tool allows you to synchronize two different databases by creating the corresponding SQL commands needed to match both the structure and data of the two database tables. There is a wizard that will guide through each step of the process. The process is simple — just select the databases and tables to synchronize and SQLyog takes care of everything else. Resolving a data synchronization problem by hand is incredibly difficult, and SQLyog reduces the complexity to a few simple clicks.

phpMyAdmin

phpMyAdmin is a free set of PHP scripts that are used to manage a MySQL server via a web interface. Because phpMyAdmin is based on these PHP scripts it does require a web server to run. Though this might be seen as a drawback, it also means that you can access your MySQL servers from any computer that has a web browser. phpMyAdmin can be used to manage an entire MySQL server or a single database.

> **NOTE**   You can find more information about phpMyAdmin, including how to download the program, at http://www.phpmyadmin.net/.

We are not going to show how to install phpMyAdmin for your server setup because it varies depending on your operating system. Typically, it is not very difficult. Once done with the installation of phpMyAdmin, access the system by simply going to the following URL in your browser: http://yourserverip/phpmyadmin. You will need to replace yourserverip with the hostname or IP address of your web server. You will be presented with a login screen where you will input your MySQL server login credentials.

Figure 3-4 shows the opening screen for phpMyAdmin once you log in.

FIGURE 3-4

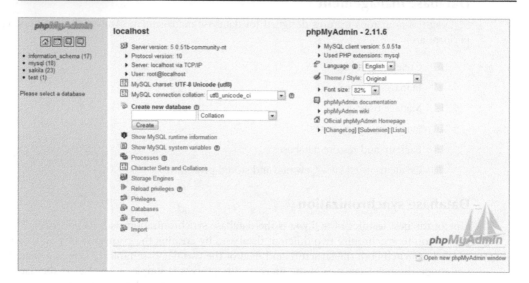

You will use the left-hand frame in phpMyAdmin for navigation. Initially you will see the databases on the server displayed in this area. Tables will also be displayed under each database as they are created. In addition to the database navigation area on the left side, a number of options are available on the right-hand side of the split screen.

Creating a database

If you need to create a database there is a Create Database option on the main screen. You simply enter the new database name and click the Create button.

Creating a table in your database

Creating a table is almost as easy as creating a database. Just click the database you created in the navigation frame and a new window will appear on the right-hand side of the split screen.

To create a table you just use the Create New Table option. You should enter the name of the new table into the Name field, and the number of expected fields for the table into Fields.

At this point, after you click Go, you just fill in the information for the columns in your new table. Once you are done with configuration, clicking the Save button will create your new table.

Data insertion into a table

Once your table is configured you can fill it with data using phpMyAdmin. On the screen that is displayed after you create a table there is an Insert tab. Click this and another screen should appear. This screen is your data entry screen. When you are done with a record just click Save and it will be saved to the table.

After you click Save, the record is saved to the testing table, and the data entry screen is shown again. You can insert more records by selecting Insert again. If you are going to be inserting multiple records it is faster if you select the Insert Another New Row radio button on the input form.

Database backup

Backing up databases is easy with phpMyAdmin. You select the database you want to back up by clicking the database name in the left-hand navigation bar. Next you click the Export button and then make sure all tables are highlighted that you want to back up.

You can then specify the options you want under Export. Make sure that you enter a filename so you can save the output. In the background phpMyAdmin is using the `mysqldump` program, which is covered in Chapter 13.

The phpMyAdmin program has a fairly user-friendly interface. Because it is used by a number of web-hosting providers, many administrators are at least somewhat familiar with it. Although it has a modest range of abilities, it does have some flexibility in that you can access the program from anywhere with a web browser. It should be pointed out, as we discuss in Chapter 20, that running both a web server and a database server on the same server increases your security risk. Sharing resources means there will be fewer available for `mysqld`. Think very carefully before installing phpMyAdmin on the same machine as `mysqld`.

MySQL Query Browser

The Query Browser is part of the GUI bundle that MySQL has available for free download from `http://dev.mysql.com/downloads/gui-tools`. Also included in this bundle are the MySQL Administrator tool (discussed in the following section) and the MySQL Migration Tool, which we will not be covering. The Query Browser and other associated tools are available for Windows, Macintosh OS X, and Linux so it allows for a good degree of cross-platform usage.

The Query Browser is a GUI tool for creating, executing, and optimizing queries.

The Query Browser includes the following components:

- **Query Toolbar:** Create small queries and execute them. Browse old queries.
- **Script Editor:** Useful for editing more complex queries.

- **Results Window:** Displays query results.
- **Database Explorer:** Navigate, create, and drop tables and fields.

The central interface of the Query Browser provides access to all of the preceding functionality. This window is also customizable by allowing you to control which toolbars are present. The Query History functionality combined with navigation buttons allows you to browse your query history and re-execute queries with or without editing them.

To begin a Query Browser session you have to establish a connection to your server. When you start Query Browser you see the screen in Figure 3-5.

FIGURE 3-5

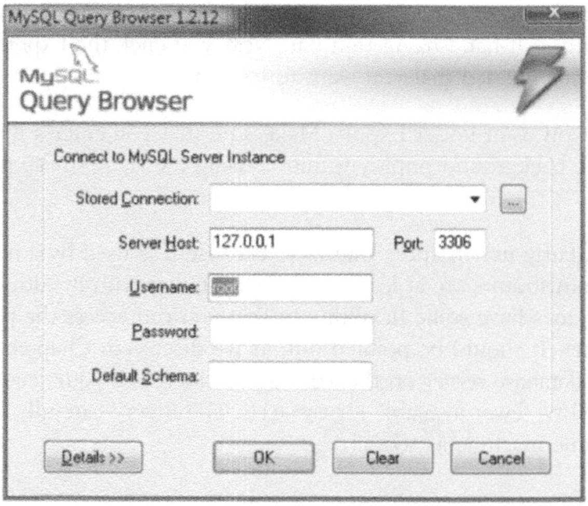

One of the biggest shortcomings of Query Browser is that it does not allow for the direct connection to a server using an ssh session. In many organizations, administrator access to mysqld is restricted to connecting only from the local server. In order to use Query Browser you must establish an ssh tunnel manually, which can be a tricky operation. It is also frustrating to have to set up an ssh tunnel every time you want to use MySQL Query Browser. In contrast, the previously discussed SQLyog program allows direct secure connections using ssh tunneling very easily.

Once you have established your connection to the server you are presented with the main Query Browser screen, which is shown in Figure 3-6.

Looking on the right-hand side of the screen you can see the databases on the connected server. In this case you can see the information_schema and mysql databases (used by the MySQL server) and a test database. Also there is the sakila database, which you will be using for the example.

FIGURE 3-6

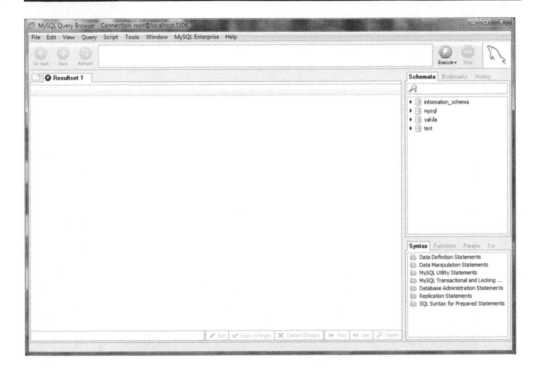

To work with the sakila database a single mouse-click on the arrow to the left of the sakila database icon will display all the tables. Just enter the query to execute and click the Execute button to the right of query entry screen. Once you enter the query and execute it the results are shown in the results pane on the bottom left of the screen, as shown in Figure 3-7.

After you have entered multiple queries you can use the Go Back and Next buttons to browse through the history of the already executed queries.

Under the Tools menu you can start MySQL Administrator, the mysql command-line client, the Windows command line (if you are on Windows), a text importer (that uses regular expressions), and the connections manager, where you can save connection information.

You can also manage stored routines very easily with Query Browser. This might be one of the best features of Query Browser because it is very difficult to manage a stored routine from the MySQL command line (see Chapter 7 for more information about stored routines). Though a procedure or function can be programmed from the command line, it is awkward at best. A graphical environment such as Query Browser makes it much easier to work with stored procedures and functions.

FIGURE 3-7

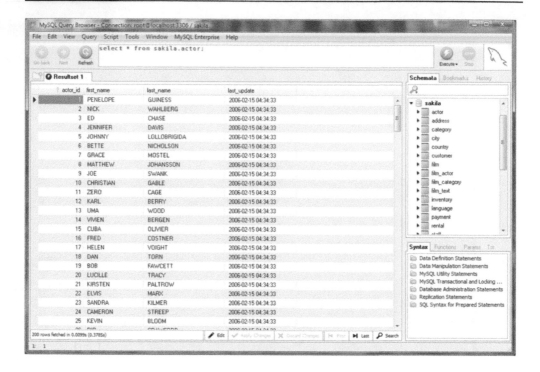

To begin a new stored procedure, make sure you have a database selected and then just click Script and then Create Stored Procedure/Function. Once you have created the stored procedure or function you will be presented with the editing screen as shown in Figure 3-8.

All of the initial setup is already done for you. Just write your query and click the Execute button to store it on the server. You can also examine and edit stored procedures and functions that are already created. To do this just click Script on the menu bar and select Edit All Stored Procedures/Functions. Figure 3-9 shows what this looks like.

Now you just edit the appropriate procedure and click Execute to reload the procedures.

The Query Browser program is well rounded with only one major weakness: Though it is more specialized than the other programs covered here, it is designed to work in tandem with the MySQL Administrator program covered in the next section.

MySQL Administrator

The MySQL Administrator is included in the same bundle with the Query Browser. It is a cross-platform tool that runs on Windows, Linux, and the Mac OS X. MySQL Administrator is a GUI console that enables you to administer a `mysqld` server instance.

FIGURE 3-8

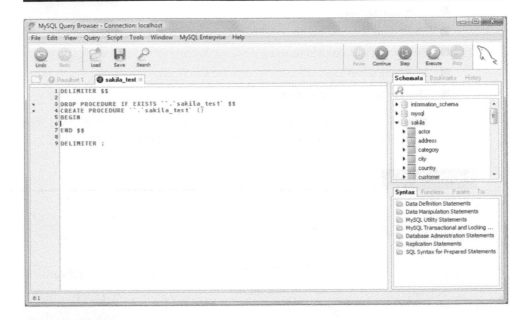

FIGURE 3-9

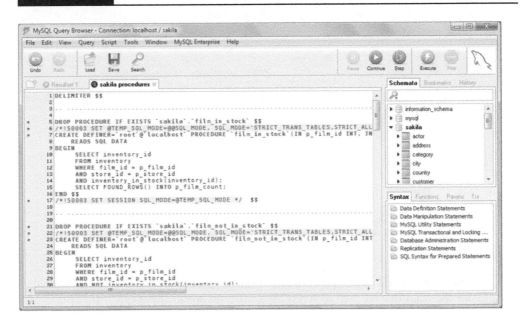

Some of the functionality that MySQL Administrator allows includes:

- User management
- Monitoring database health
- Performing backups and restores
- Managing server logs
- Monitoring server connections

The connection dialog is the same as for Query Brower. Once you have established your connection to a server the main screen will look similar to what is shown in Figure 3-10.

FIGURE 3-10

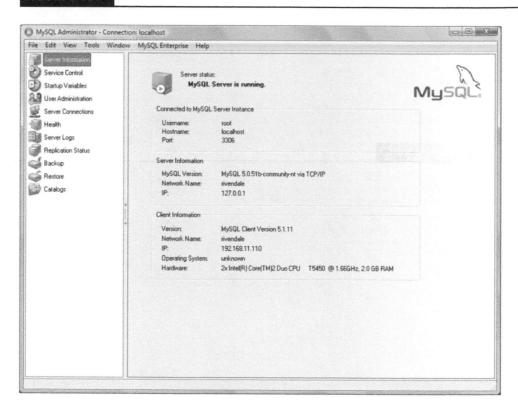

This is the central control panel used to manage your servers. On the left-hand panel you can see the icons that are used to access the screens for specific functions.

User administration

MySQL Administrator makes creating users, dropping users, granting privileges, and seeing privileges quite easy. Using an intuitive form you can add users, set passwords, and specify more information about the user. Figure 3-11 shows the user administration screen.

FIGURE 3-11

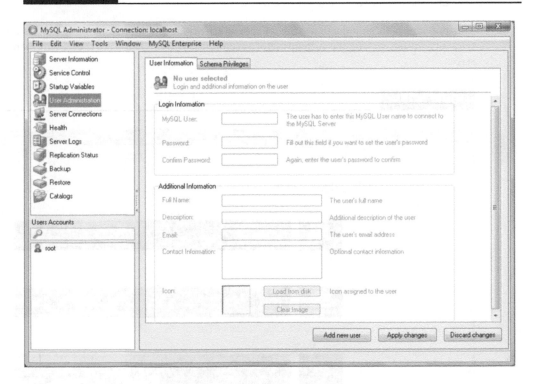

As you can see there are two tabs in the right-hand pane. The first tab (User Information) is used to enter the basic login credentials and details about the user such as name and e-mail. The Schema Privileges tab is used to both assign and remove global, database, and table/column-level privileges.

There is a list of the system users in the lower-left part of the screen. To view and edit the current information on a user just click the username. Then you will be able to edit the properties on the right-hand side of the screen. Once you are done just click Apply Changes. With a reasonable layout this screen makes it very easy to edit a user's password or schema privileges.

Health monitoring

The health monitoring screen gives you a view into the activity of your MySQL server. Very nice graphing functionality shows you:

- The percentage of memory used
- The number of current connections
- The number of SQL queries being executed

This provides both an immediate view of system activity, plus a more long-term view as it keeps track of statistics as long the Administrator is running. Figure 3-12 shows the Health monitoring screen.

FIGURE 3-12

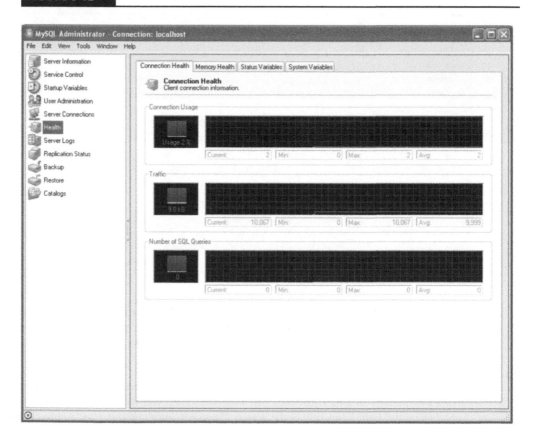

Although this is a nice feature it does require that the MySQL Administrator program be connected to the database server for extended periods of time if you want to gather long-term statistics. Chapter 19 covers various programs that can be used for monitoring your database servers.

Backup and recovery

With the backup and recovery screen, you can create backups and restore data using a graphical interface. You can choose to back up an entire database or one or more tables by clicking on check boxes. This screen looks fancy, but it is actually simply providing a nice interface to the mysqldump program, which is covered in Chapter 13. We also cover general background about why it's important to back up your servers and other topics such as how often you should back up. Figure 3-13 shows the backup screen with the sakila database chosen to backup.

FIGURE 3-13

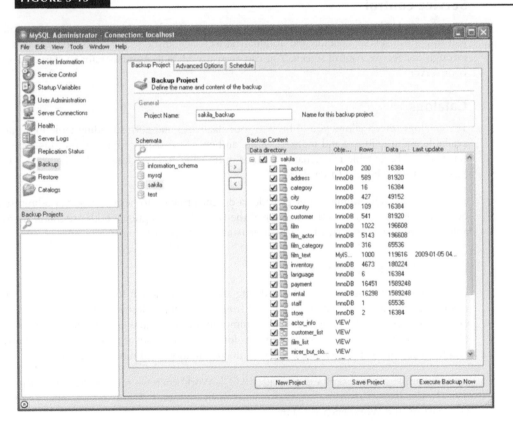

Server information

The server information screen shows basic server and client information, including status, version numbers, and host information.

Replication status

The replication status screen allows you to view the network topology of your replication master and slaves if the slaves are configured with the report-host option in the MySQL server configuration file and you are connected to the master server with the MySQL Administrator program.

Server log management

On the server log management screen, you can view all the log files — error logs, binary logs, and slow query logs. This can help you when troubleshooting server issues.

Service control

When your database servers are running on Microsoft Windows, MySQL Administrator allows you to control service creation and automatically creates, installs, and configures services through the service control screen. You can even use MySQL Administrator to start and stop your server.

Catalogs

The catalogs screen allows you to browse your databases and corresponding table information available about columns and indexes, views, and even stored procedures. From this screen you can perform basic table maintenance such as optimizing and checking tables. Figure 3-14 shows this screen for the sakila database.

Overall the MySQL Administrator provides a decent program to help with server administration. The Query Browser is the stronger of the two related programs. Both programs are available from http://dev.mysql.com/downloads/gui-tools.

MySQL Workbench

MySQL Workbench is a visual data modeling and database design tool. Schema creation and change scripts can be automatically created from the database designs. There are two versions of MySQL Workbench: an open source Community Edition and a commercial Standard Edition (SE). The SE version includes enhancements for reverse and forward engineering of databases, synchronization to and from live databases, documentation, and model validation.

As an example of what can be done with MySQL Workbench we reverse engineered the sakila database. This entire process took about five minutes. Figure 3-15 is what you see when you start up the Workbench program.

FIGURE 3-14

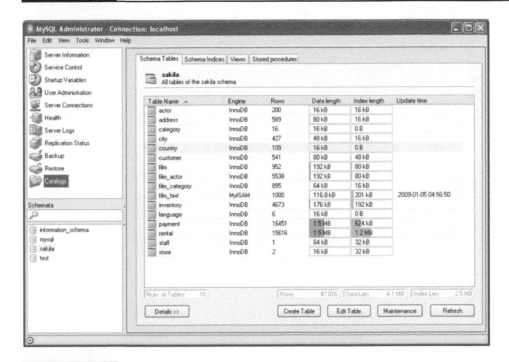

FIGURE 3-15

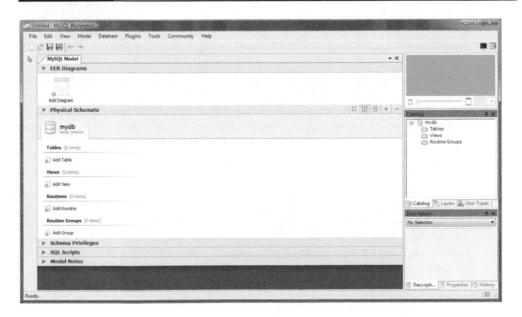

FIGURE 3-16

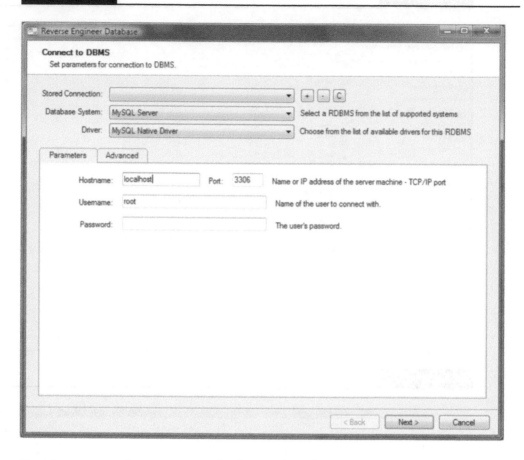

Now that you have the program started, select Database from the menu and then Reverse Engineer. This will bring up the connection screen where you have to fill in the hostname, user-name, and password used to access the server. You need to make sure that you have permission to access the server you are trying to reverse engineer. Figure 3-16 shows the connection screen.

Once you have established the connection to the server, the next screen will allow you to select (by default) all the tables or any number of individual tables.

Once you have selected the desired tables it is just a matter of having MySQL Workbench construct the Entity Relationship (ER) diagram. As the server builds the diagram it will ask if it should automatically place the tables on the diagram. We recommend that you choose this option. Once the initial diagram is built you can then rearrange them to your heart's content. You can print the ER diagram directly or export to a PDF file. Figure 3-17 shows the sakila database after being reverse engineered.

FIGURE 3-17

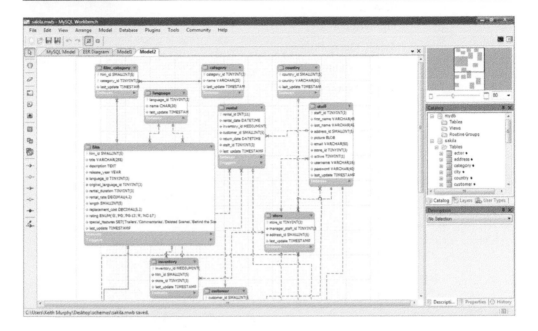

Reverse engineering a database is easy with the proper tools. If you have a significant number of tables it might take some time to arrange the tables in your ER diagram as you want, but that this is much faster than building the ER diagram by hand. In the preceding figure, the lines on the diagram represent the foreign key relationships between the tables.

Summary

Any database administrator should to take the time first to learn the `mysql` client, because it is the default access client and will always be available. The other tools, both GUI-based and command-line–oriented, certainly have a place in many environments. Some tasks can be much more difficult with command-line tools or even impossible, such as with ER diagramming.

This chapter covered:

- MySQL command-line tools including:
  - The `mysql` client
  - The `mysladmin` tool
  - The `mysqlshow` tool

- GUI tools for MySQL administration including:
  - SQLyog
  - phpMyAdmin
  - MySQL Query Browser
  - MySQL Administrator
  - MySQL Workbench

Part II

Developing with MySQL

Chapter 4

How MySQL Extends and Deviates from SQL

MySQL was originally designed with three basic ideas in mind: to be fast, reliable, and easy to use. Like every database system, MySQL does not completely follow the SQL standard and has its own extensions to SQL. Some very basic SQL standards, however, did not exist for a very long time — the data dictionary was only added in MySQL 5.0, released in October 2005.

MySQL became popular because of its relative ease of use. For example, the SQL standard way of finding out which tables are in the sakila database is:

```
SELECT TABLE_NAME
FROM INFORMATION_SCHEMA.TABLES
WHERE TABLE_SCHEMA='sakila';
```

The easiest way to find out this information in MySQL is:

```
SHOW TABLES FROM sakila;
```

Most of the differences from standard SQL and SQL extensions in MySQL come from the desire to make the database system easy to use. In the past several years, there has been more of a commitment to support the current SQL standard — as of the time of the writing of this book, that standard is the ANSI/ISO SQL:2003 standard. When we refer to "the SQL standard" or "standard SQL," we are referring to ANSI/ISO SQL:2003.

For information on the different SQL modes supported, see Chapter 5.

IN THIS CHAPTER

Learning MySQL language Structure

Understanding MySQL deviations

Using MySQL extensions

Using the Sample Database

In Chapter 3, you imported the sakila sample database. Throughout this chapter and the rest of the book, we will be using the sakila sample database to demonstrate database features. The sakila sample database was created by Mike Hillyer and contains data that might be found in a video rental store. For the purpose of our examples, we refer to a fictional video store whose data is stored in the sakila database and whose owner, Ziesel Skelley, uses a MySQL backend to store and query her company's information.

Learning MySQL Language Structure

Before getting into the extensions to SQL and deviations from SQL, there are some important rules to know about some of the language structure in MySQL, specifically relating to:

- Comments and portability
- Case-sensitivity
- Escape characters
- Naming limitations
- Quoting
- Time zones
- Character sets and collations

While some of these may be seen as SQL deviations or extensions, they are important enough to discuss before learning about the rest of MySQL's customized SQL syntax.

ON the WEBSITE   If you are new to SQL, there is an SQL Primer on the accompanying website for this book at www.wiley.com/go/mysqladminbible.

Comments and portability

One of the cleverest MySQL extensions to the SQL standard is actually a way to manage portability. In some cases, portability of the schema and queries is desired, but being able to use MySQL-specific extensions when the environment is right is also desired. MySQL has an extension that specifies a MySQL version as part of a comment. The comment will be only parsed if the mysqld server is of an appropriate version; otherwise, the comment will be left as a comment and ignored by other databases and mysqld versions.

The -- is the standard SQL simple comment introducer. Everything on a line after this is considered a comment. The SQL standard bracketed comment introducer and terminator /* */ allow partial line and multi-line commenting. Putting ! after the bracketed comment introducer indicates that this is MySQL specific code, and the `mysqld` server will parse it:

```
/*! SHOW DATABASES */;
```

The `mysqld` server will parse the `SHOW DATABASES` statement, but other database systems will not — that is, if the other database systems follow the SQL standard for comments. A five-digit number after the ! can be used to specify a minimum `mysqld` version. The first digit of the number is the major version, the next two digits are the minor version, and the last two digits are the revision number. For example, the output of `mysqldump sakila` starts with:

```
-- MySQL dump 10.13  Distrib 6.0.8-alpha
--
-- Host: localhost    Database: sakila
-- ------------------------------------------------------
-- Server version       6.0.8-alpha

/*!40101 SET @OLD_CHARACTER_SET_CLIENT=@@CHARACTER_SET_CLIENT */;
/*!40101 SET @OLD_CHARACTER_SET_RESULTS=@@CHARACTER_SET_RESULTS */;
/*!40101 SET @OLD_COLLATION_CONNECTION=@@COLLATION_CONNECTION */;
/*!40101 SET NAMES utf8 */;
/*!40103 SET @OLD_TIME_ZONE=@@TIME_ZONE */;
/*!40103 SET TIME_ZONE='+00:00' */;
/*!40014 SET @OLD_UNIQUE_CHECKS=@@UNIQUE_CHECKS, UNIQUE_CHECKS=0 */;
/*!40014 SET @OLD_FOREIGN_KEY_CHECKS=@@FOREIGN_KEY_CHECKS,
FOREIGN_KEY_CHECKS=0
*/;
/*!40101 SET @OLD_SQL_MODE=@@SQL_MODE, SQL_MODE='NO_AUTO_VALUE_
ON_ZERO' */;
/*!40111 SET @OLD_SQL_NOTES=@@SQL_NOTES, SQL_NOTES=0 */;
```

This means that `mysqld` versions 4.1.1 and higher will apply the first statement, and `mysqld` versions 4.1.11 and higher will apply the last statement. A comment that will only be applied to `mysqld` versions 6.0.8 and higher begins with /*!60008.

While this syntax makes the code portable, it does not guarantee that the code will work as expected. For example, `mysqldump` exports tables in alphabetical order. The SET `FOREIGN_KEY_CHECKS=0` statement is utilized so that a table with a foreign key constraint can be imported even if the referencing table has not yet been created. Attempting to import this on a different database server should result in an error, because a reference is being generated to a table that does not exist.

MySQL extends commenting by parsing anything after an unquoted, unescaped # as a comment, regardless of whitespace around the #:

```
mysql> SELECT#example of # as a comment
    -> 0;
```

```
+---+
| 0 |
+---+
| 0 |
+---+
1 row in set (0.00 sec)
```

See the "Escape characters" and "Naming limitations and quoting" sections in this chapter for more information on escaping and quoting characters.

Case-sensitivity

Traditionally, SQL reserved words are written in uppercase, such as SELECT, FROM, NULL, and AS. These words are case-insensitive, meaning that SELECT, select, and SeLeCt are all parsed by mysqld as the same reserved word. Throughout this book, we will format reserved words in uppercase, even though mysqld will properly parse reserved words regardless of case.

In general, mysqld is case-insensitive with respect to names of fields, indexes, stored routines and events. However, mysqld stores information on the file system and makes assumptions based on the files and directories found on the file system. For example, mysqld assumes that any directory in the data directory (datadir) is a database. This means that a directory with a path of datadir/backup will show up as a database named backup when SHOW DATABASES is run — whether or not backup was intended to be a database. All tables must have a .frm format file within the directory that represents the database they belong to; otherwise, mysqld does not recognize the table as existing.

MyISAM tables are defined by a .frm format file, a .MYD data file, and a .MYI index file (see Chapter 11 for more information on MyISAM tables). It is possible to move a MyISAM table to a different database by moving the associated files to a different directory. It is also possible to rename a MyISAM table by renaming the associated files. However, it is not recommended that you make these types of changes. To change the database of the move_me table from test to test2, issue the statement:

```
ALTER TABLE test.move_me RENAME test2.move_me;
```

To change the name of the move_me table to keep_me, issue:

```
ALTER TABLE move_me RENAME keep_me;
```

> **NOTE**   It is not necessarily harmful to have a directory appear as a database (such as a lost+found directory). However, this may lead to errors with code that automatically traverse all databases, such as a custom backup script. It is important to be extremely careful when deleting and moving directories and files within the data directory and dropping databases.

The way mysqld stores information on the file system has the consequence that some names are case-sensitive, if the file system is case-sensitive. Unix has a case-sensitive file system, and

Windows has a case-insensitive file system. Mac OS X uses a case-insensitive file system by default, although it supports other, case-sensitive file systems. Case-sensitivity for names is determined by whether or not the file system is case-sensitive for the following:

- Databases
- Tablespaces
- Tables
- Views
- Aliases
- Triggers
- Log file groups

In general, there should not be problems unless the databases are used on different file systems, for example when migrating from one file system to another. The static, global `lower_case_table_names` system variable can be set to change the default behavior of `mysqld`:

- If `lower_case_table_names=0` is set, table and database names are stored using the case specified in the CREATE statement. In queries, table names, table aliases, and database names are case-sensitive. This is the default value on Unix, where the file system is case-sensitive.

- If `lower_case_table_names=1` is set, table and database names are stored using lower-case. In queries, table names, table aliases, and database names are case-insensitive — they are actually converted to lowercase by `mysqld`. This is the default value on Windows, where the file system is case-insensitive.

- If `lower_case_table_names=2` is set, most table and database names are stored using the case specified in the CREATE statement. The exception is InnoDB table names, which are stored using lowercase. In queries, table names, table aliases, and database names are case-insensitive — they are converted to lowercase by `mysqld`, as they are when the value is set to 1. This is the default value on Mac OS X.

> **TIP** Come up with a naming convention that includes rules about case. For example, perhaps databases and tables will be all lowercase, with underscores to show different words (such as in `table_name`) and fields will use *camelCase* (such as in `fieldName`). In this way, the issue of case is resolved, no matter what platform is being used.

Escape characters

The escape character is the backslash (\). An *escape sequence* is a backslash followed by one character. Chapter 3 discussed some commands that looked like escape sequences such as \P and \u — these are actually translated into other commands by the `mysql` command line client. However, `mysqld` has actual escape sequences, which are independent of the `mysql` commands.

These escape sequences are used only within strings (the mysql ones are not within strings) and are parsed unless the NO_BACKSLASH_ESCAPES SQL mode is set. See Chapter 5 for more information on SQL modes.

The escape sequences for strings in mysqld are:

- ■ \\ to print the \ character.
- ■ \' to print the ' character, even if the string is quoted with '.
- ■ \" to print the " character, even if the string is quoted with ".
- ■ _ prints the _ character. This can be used to search for the actual value when using LIKE. If _ is not escaped, it is used as the wildcard character for one character.
- ■ \% prints the % character. This can be used to search for the actual value % when using LIKE. If % is not escaped, it is used as the wildcard character for one or more characters.
- ■ \b prints a backspace character, which actually means that it deletes the previous character. For example, SELECT "Hi!\b" returns Hi, not Hi! because of the backspace.
- ■ \r and \n print a carriage return and a new line, respectively.
- ■ \t prints a tab separator, as actually hitting the Tab key may try to use the auto-complete function of the mysql client. For more information on the auto-complete function in mysql, see Chapter 3.
- ■ \0 and \Z print ASCII 0 (NUL) and ASCII 26 (Ctrl-Z), respectively. In Windows, Ctrl-Z is a special character marking an end of a file, and on Mac OS X and Unix, Ctrl-Z is the special key sequence that will suspend the current foreground process.

These escape sequences are case-sensitive. In a string, a backslash followed by any other character will just print the character. The following queries exemplify this behavior:

```
mysql> SELECT 'Hi!';
+-----+
| Hi! |
+-----+
| Hi! |
+-----+
1 row in set (0.00 sec)

mysql> SELECT 'Hi!\b';
+------+
| Hi |
+------+
| Hi |
+------+
1 row in set (0.00 sec)
```

```
mysql> SELECT 'Hi!\B';
+------+
| Hi!B |
+------+
| Hi!B |
+------+
1 row in set (0.00 sec)
```

Naming limitations and quoting

Identifiers are names of: databases, tables, views, fields, indexes, tablespaces, stored routines, triggers, events, servers, log file groups, and aliases (specified with the AS keyword). Identifiers are all limited to 64 characters except aliases, which are limited to 255 characters. Note that characters may be one or more bytes; see Chapter 5 for a discussion of the difference between characters and bytes. Identifiers are stored using the utf8 character set.

WARNING The utf8 character set before MySQL 6.0 used up to 3 bytes to store each character. In MySQL 6.0 and up, that character set was renamed to utf8mb3, and the character set named utf8 is a true implementation of Unicode, using up to 4 bytes to store each character. When upgrading from MySQL 5.1 to MySQL 6.0, fields using utf8 follow the renaming of the character set and are shown to use utf8mb3. There is no conversion that takes place during an upgrade from MySQL 5.1 to MySQL 6.0. Therefore, to use a true implementation of Unicode, MySQL must be upgraded to version 6.0 or higher, and an explicit conversion must be done of all fields using utf8mb3. For more information about this type of upgrade, see the MySQL manual at http://dev.mysql.com/doc/refman/6.0/en/charset-unicode-upgrading.html.

Identifiers can be almost anything. However, identifiers may not end with one or more spaces:

```
mysql> CREATE TABLE `space ` (id INT);
ERROR 1103 (42000): Incorrect table name 'space '
mysql> CREATE TABLE space (`id ` INT);
ERROR 1166 (42000): Incorrect column name 'id '
```

Identifier names can be reserved words or numbers, and include punctuation. However, to be parsed correctly, such identifiers need to be quoted. When sql_mode includes ANSI_QUOTES (see "SQL Modes" in Chapter 5), the double quotation mark character (") is used to quote identifiers such as database and table names, and strings are quoted by the single quotation mark character (').When sql_mode does not include ANSI_QUOTES, as is the default, the backtick character (`) is used to quote identifiers such as database and table names, and strings are quoted by the either the double quotation mark character (") or the single quotation mark character (').

The escape string is the backslash (\) — see the "Escape characters" section earlier in this chapter for more information. This is used in conjunction with strings to escape special characters. For example, % and _ are wildcard characters as specified in the SQL standard. To find a string that contains the actual character % using the LIKE operator, escape it with \:

```
mysql> USE sakila;
Database changed
mysql> SELECT first_name FROM staff WHERE first_name LIKE 'M%';
+------------+
| first_name |
+------------+
| Mike       |
+------------+
1 row in set (0.00 sec)

mysql> SELECT first_name FROM staff WHERE first_name LIKE 'M\%';
```

The empty set (0.00 sec) in queries, strings needs to be quoted to distinguish it from an identifier. The following example shows that, when the string Mike is not quoted, mysqld parses it as the name of a field. However, when the string is quoted, mysqld parses it as a string:

```
mysql> SELECT last_name FROM staff WHERE first_name=Mike;
ERROR 1054 (42S22): Unknown column 'Mike' in 'where clause'
mysql> SELECT last_name FROM staff WHERE first_name='Mike';
+-----------+
| last_name |
+-----------+
| Hillyer   |
+-----------+
1 row in set (0.00 sec)
```

On the other hand, numbers will be parsed as numbers. In order to parse a number as an identifier, it must be quoted. The following example shows that when the number 1 is not quoted, mysqld parses it as a number. However, when the number is quoted, mysqld parses it as a field name:

```
mysql> SELECT first_name, last_name FROM staff WHERE active=1;
+------------+-----------+
| first_name | last_name |
+------------+-----------+
| Mike       | Hillyer   |
| Jon        | Stephens  |
+------------+-----------+
2 rows in set (0.00 sec)

mysql> SELECT first_name, last_name FROM staff WHERE active=`1`;
ERROR 1054 (42S22): Unknown column '1' in 'where clause'
```

Note that a number can be any of the following:

- An unsigned integer such as 12345
- A signed integer such as +12345 or -12345

- A signed or unsigned decimal such as 12.345, +12.345 or -12.345
- A signed or unsigned number in scientific notation format, such as 123.4e+5, 123.4e-5, or -123.4e5
- A number in binary format, such as 0b100 (the number 4)
- A number in hexadecimal format, such as 0x100 or 0x1F4 (the numbers 256 and 500, respectively)
- If used in a numeric context, a string beginning with a number will be parsed as a number equal to the first numeric part of the string. For example, '10q4' is parsed as 10 when used in a numeric context:

```
mysql> SELECT 1+'10q4';
+----------+
| 1+'10q4' |
+----------+
|       11 |
+----------+
1 row in set, 1 warning (0.00 sec)

mysql> SHOW WARNINGS;
+---------+------+-------------------------------------------+
| Level   | Code | Message                                   |
+---------+------+-------------------------------------------+
| Warning | 1292 | Truncated incorrect DOUBLE value: '10q4'  |
+---------+------+-------------------------------------------+
1 row in set (0.00 sec)
```

- If such a truncation occurs when storing a value in a table, by default mysqld issues a similar warning and stores the truncated value. For mysqld to issue an error and refuse to store such values, a strict SQL mode must be used. See Chapter 5 for more information on SQL modes. Errors only apply to storing values in tables; the preceding example will always issue a warning and calculate the expression with the truncated value, even if a strict SQL mode is used.
- An expression that results in a number, such as 1+1 or ABS(-1)

Like numbers, the reserved words TRUE, FALSE, and NULL do not need to be quoted. As with other reserved words, TRUE, FALSE, and NULL are case-insensitive.

Dot notation

MySQL has a special *dot notation* that can be used to specify a database when referring to a table. Simply place a dot character (.) between the database and table name. The following example shows that the TABLES table does not exist in the current working database (sakila) but prefixing the table name with the string "INFORMATION_SCHEMA." specifies the database to which the TABLES table belongs:

```
mysql> SELECT TABLE_NAME FROM TABLES LIMIT 1;
ERROR 1146 (42S02): Table 'sakila.tables' doesn't exist
```

```
mysql> SELECT TABLE_NAME FROM INFORMATION_SCHEMA.TABLES LIMIT 1;
+----------------+
| TABLE_NAME     |
+----------------+
| CHARACTER_SETS |
+----------------+
1 row in set (0.01 sec)
```

MySQL allows identifiers such as tables and fields to have any name, including reserved words, such as FROM, and function names, such as COUNT and DATE. Furthermore, table names can use any character, including punctuation such as . and ;. Reserved words and punctuation other than _ must be enclosed by the quotation mark that specifies an identifier; this is usually the backtick (`) character (see the "Naming limitations and quoting" section earlier in this chapter for more information). Function names do not need to be enclosed by quotation marks. The following example shows that mysqld returns an error if reserved words (FROM) and special punctuation (.) are not enclosed by the backtick character, but function names (DATE) do not need to be enclosed similarly to work:

```
mysql> CREATE TABLE name.test(from DATE);
ERROR 1049 (42000): Unknown database 'name'
mysql> CREATE TABLE `name.test`(from DATE);
ERROR 1064 (42000): You have an error in your SQL syntax; check
the manual that corresponds to your MySQL server version for the
right syntax to use near 'from DATE)' at line 1
mysql> CREATE TABLE `name.test`(date DATE);
Query OK, 0 rows affected (0.37 sec)

mysql> SELECT COUNT(*) FROM dot.test;
ERROR 1146 (42S02): Table 'dot.test' doesn't exist
mysql> SELECT COUNT(*) FROM test.dot.test;
ERROR 1064 (42000): You have an error in your SQL syntax; check
the manual that corresponds to your MySQL server version for the
right syntax to use near '.test' at line 1
mysql> SELECT COUNT(*) FROM test.`dot.test`;
+----------+
| COUNT(*) |
+----------+
|        0 |
+----------+
1 row in set (0.01 sec)
```

Identifier names can be a numbers, such as a table named 12345, but they must be quoted as an identifier just as reserved words and punctuation are. This dot notation also extends to fields:

```
mysql> SELECT test.`dot.test`.foo FROM test.`dot.test` limit 1;
Empty set (0.00 sec)

mysql> SELECT `dot.test`.foo FROM test.`dot.test` limit 1;
Empty set (0.00 sec)
```

Note that the table name dot.test had to be quoted with backticks. Using dot notation to specify fields is not done very often, but it can be useful when querying fields with similar names.

> **TIP**   Avoid problematic naming of your databases, tables, and fields. Do not use a number, reserved word, function name, or punctuation other than _ in your database, table, and field names. If you are getting an error because - is being parsed as the subtraction function, use _ instead. Because mysqld requires quoting for numbers, reserved words, and punctuation, those are easily avoided. It is more difficult to realize when function names such as COUNT and DATE are used.

Time zones

When mysqld starts, it determines the time zone of the operating system and sets the system_time_zone system variable accordingly. By default, mysqld sets the value of time_zone to SYSTEM, which means that it operates using the time zone in system_time_zone. Fields with a TIMESTAMP value are converted to UTC and stored. When retrieved, TIMESTAMP fields are converted to the value of time_zone. Because TIMESTAMP fields are stored as UTC values and conversion is transparent, there are no problems if the underlying operating system time zone changes.

Because of the many issues surrounding time zones, it is best to keep the time_zone variable set to a value of SYSTEM. Even when mysqld uses the operating system time zones, problems can arise in the following scenarios:

- Unlike TIMESTAMP, DATE, TIME, and DATETIME fields are not converted and stored as UTC. Furthermore, there is no time zone information in these fields. If a DATETIME value is stored as '2009-01-01 00:00:00', there is no way to specify what the time zone associated with that time is. For other differences between TIMESTAMP and other time-based data types, see Chapter 5.

- Web servers and database servers may have different time zones, and thus have different times. An order coming from an application on a web server whose time is in PST (UTC-8) and stored on a database server whose time is in EST (UTC-5) has a problem: At what time was the order made? Was it made on December 31, 2008 at 9 PM PST or January 1, 2009 at midnight EST? While both of those represent the same time, recall that DATE, TIME, and DATETIME fields do not store time zone information. For taxes, tariffs, legal purposes, and financial reports, does that order belong in 2008 or 2009?

- If the application code uses the time local to the web server as the order time, orders from web servers configured with different time zones will be stored in the database as if they occurred at different times. For example, if two different web servers are configured so that one uses PST and the other uses EST, orders coming in at the exact same time — January 1, 2009 at 5 AM UTC — and stored in a DATETIME field will appear to have been made three hours apart, because the time zone information will be lost.

■ To avoid this issue, do not have application code determine the time. Instead, use the CURRENT_TIMESTAMP() function or the NOW() alias to insert the current time into a field. These values are replication-safe (do not use the SYSDATE() function; it is not safe for replication).

NOTE If you feel up to the challenge of trying to manage time zones within MySQL and can brave adding another level of complexity to time management, the MySQL manual has information on how to specify time zones in MySQL at:

http://dev.mysql.com/doc/refman/6.0/en/time-zone-support.html

In practice, managing time zones in MySQL adds so much headache and hassle that is rarely worth it. In our experience, it is much more worthwhile to set operating systems to the same time zone (preferably UTC) and configure time synchronization software (such as ntpd) so that all servers have the same times and time zones.

Character sets and collations

MySQL supports many different *character sets* and *collations*. A character set, or *charset*, is the set of available characters that can be used — similar to an alphabet. Different languages have different alphabets, and the most often used character sets contain the letters of many alphabets (for example, the default latin1 character set includes all of the characters in Latin languages, including accented characters and characters using the cedilla. A collation specifies the lexical sort order; in English the lexical sort order begins with a, b, c, d; in Spanish the lexical sort order begins with a, b, c, ch, d; in Greek the lexical sort order begins with α, β, χ, δ. A collation can also specify if a sort order is case-sensitive or not; a *binary collation* is a collation that is case-sensitive. In MySQL, binary collations usually end in _bin, such as ascii_bin. In a binary collation, the sort order is determined by the numeric representation of the character. This has the result that sort order is case-sensitive, because the same letter in a different case has a different numeric representation.

To illustrate the difference among case-insensitive sort order, case-sensitive sort order, and binary sort order, create a table that specifies three fields, each with its own sort order, and insert some values:

```
mysql> use test;
Database changed
mysql> CREATE TABLE sort_test (
    -> ci CHAR(1) CHARACTER SET latin1 COLLATE latin1_general_ci,
    -> cs CHAR(1) CHARACTER SET latin1 COLLATE latin1_general_cs,
    -> cbin CHAR(1) CHARACTER SET latin1 COLLATE latin1_bin);
Query OK, 0 rows affected (0.39 sec)
```

```
mysql> INSERT INTO sort_test VALUES
    -> ('A','A','A'), ('a','a','a'), ('b','b','b'), ('B','B','B');
Query OK, 4 rows affected (0.00 sec)
Records: 4  Duplicates: 0  Warnings: 0
```

In case-insensitive search, first the letters a and A are displayed, and then the letters b and B are displayed:

```
mysql> SELECT ci FROM sort_test ORDER BY ci;
+------+
| ci   |
+------+
| A    |
| a    |
| b    |
| B    |
+------+
4 rows in set (0.00 sec)
```

Note that the order with regard to case does not matter — in this case, the order of the input determines the order of the output. A case-sensitive ordering, on the other hand, sorts the letters a and A before b and B, but also sorts with respect to capital letters — within a letter, the capital letter is sorted first:

```
mysql> SELECT cs FROM sort_test ORDER BY cs;
+------+
| cs   |
+------+
| A    |
| a    |
| B    |
| b    |
+------+
4 rows in set (0.00 sec)
```

In a binary collation, the order depends on the order of the numeric representation. The numeric order of the letters in the preceding example is:

```
mysql> SELECT ASCII('a'),ASCII('A'),ASCII('b'),ASCII('B');
+------------+------------+------------+------------+
| ASCII('a') | ASCII('A') | ASCII('b') | ASCII('B') |
+------------+------------+------------+------------+
|         97 |         65 |         98 |         66 |
+------------+------------+------------+------------+
1 row in set (0.00 sec)
```

Therefore, a binary collation should sort these letters as A B a b, because numerically the order is 65 66 97 98. And indeed, this is the case:

```
mysql> SELECT cbin FROM sort_test ORDER BY cbin;
+------+
| cbin |
+------+
| A    |
| B    |
| a    |
| b    |
+------+
4 rows in set (0.00 sec)
```

Many other database systems support only one character set, utf8. The default character set in MySQL is latin1, and the default collation is latin1_swedish_ci. Each character set has at least one collation, and each collation is associated with exactly one character set. Collation names are of the form *charset_description_suffix*, where *charset* is the character set (such as latin1), *description* is a brief description (such as swedish or general), and *suffix* is either ci (case insensitive), cs (case sensitive), or bin (binary).

NOTE   The exception to the collation naming rule is the binary collation, which is associated with the binary character set and is a binary collation. If it conformed to the naming algorithm, its name would be binary_binary_bin.

Each character set has a default collation and may have other collations associated with it as well. The default character set for MySQL, latin1, has a default collation of latin1_swedish_ci and seven additional collations:

```
mysql> SELECT COLLATION_NAME, IS_DEFAULT
    -> FROM INFORMATION_SCHEMA.COLLATIONS
    -> WHERE CHARACTER_SET_NAME='latin1';
+-------------------+------------+
| COLLATION_NAME    | IS_DEFAULT |
+-------------------+------------+
| latin1_german1_ci |            |
| latin1_swedish_ci | Yes        |
| latin1_danish_ci  |            |
| latin1_german2_ci |            |
| latin1_bin        |            |
| latin1_general_ci |            |
| latin1_general_cs |            |
| latin1_spanish_ci |            |
+-------------------+------------+
8 rows in set (0.00 sec)
```

For more information on the COLLATIONS system view in the INFORMATION_SCHEMA database, see Chapter 21.

All collations disregard trailing whitespace in sort ordering. Some data types automatically strip trailing whitespace; see Chapter 5 for more details.

The default character set and collation in MySQL can be set at many different levels. Changing the character set without changing the collation will result in the character set's default collation to be used. Changing the collation without changing the character set will result in the character set being changed to the character set associated with the specified collation.

Standard SQL defines the CHARACTER SET and COLLATE clauses in CREATE TABLE and ALTER TABLE statements only when adding fields. Specifying a character set and collation on a table level is not supported by standard SQL. When specifying character sets on any level in MySQL, CHARSET is an alias for CHARACTER SET.

The different levels to which character set and collation can be set are:

- **Server** — The system variables character_set_server and collation_server specify the default character set and collation for a database when a CREATE DATABASE statement does not have any CHARACTER SET or COLLATE clauses.

- **Database** — The system variables character_set_database and collation_database specify the default character set and collation for the current database. These are set with the CHARACTER SET and COLLATE clauses of the CREATE DATABASE and ALTER DATABASE statements. The database character set and collation are used by LOAD DATA INFILE and specify the default character set and collation for a table when a CREATE TABLE statement does not have any CHARACTER SET or COLLATE clauses.

- The session variables will change the current database only, and the global variables will change all databases. When checking the default character set for the current database, make sure that you are in the correct database and are looking at the correct variable scope (GLOBAL or SESSION).

WARNING The SHOW VARIABLES and SET commands default to using session-level variables. To avoid confusion, always use SHOW SESSION VARIABLES or SHOW GLOBAL VARIABLES and SET GLOBAL, SET @@global, SET SESSION, or SET @@session.

- Database options such as the default character set and collation are stored in plain text in the db.opt file in each database.

- **Table** — A CREATE TABLE or ALTER TABLE tblname ADD COLUMN statement can use a CHARACTER SET or COLLATE clause. This will set the default character set and collation for a field added with no character set or collation specified.

- **Field** — The earlier example with the sort_test table showed how to specify CHARACTER SET and COLLATE clauses to fields that are the CHAR, VARCHAR, TINYTEXT, TEXT, MEDIUMTEXT or LONGTEXT data type. For more information on data types, see Chapter 5. The syntax for the CHARACTER SET and COLLATE clauses is the same for CREATE TABLE and ALTER TABLE statements. Each field can have its own character set and collation, as shown in the example with the sort_test table.

> **NOTE**   Most of the time, individual fields are not given different character sets and collations. Make sure that your default character sets and collations are set appropriately.

- **String** — The system variables `character_set_connection` and `collation_connection` specify the default character set and collation for the strings sent via the current connection. A string such as the one in `SELECT "hi"` will be returned with the character set and collation specified by the `character_set_connection` and `collation_connection` system variables.

- Standard SQL allows the character set of a string to be specified with an *introducer*, which is simply the underscore character (_) followed by the character set name. The introducer appears before the string:

```
mysql> SELECT 'hi', CHARSET('hi');
+----+---------------+
| hi | CHARSET('hi') |
+----+---------------+
| hi | latin1        |
+----+---------------+
1 row in set (0.00 sec)

mysql> SELECT _ascii 'hi', CHARSET(_ascii 'hi');
+----+----------------------+
| hi | CHARSET(_ascii 'hi') |
+----+----------------------+
| hi | ascii                |
+----+----------------------+
1 row in set (0.00 sec)
```

- The introducer tells `mysqld` to parse the string using that character set. Similarly, the `COLLATE` clause, also standard SQL, tells `mysqld` to parse the string using the specified collation. Unlike the introducer, the `COLLATE` clause comes after the string:

```
mysql> SELECT COLLATION(_ascii 'hi'),
    -> COLLATION (_ascii 'hi' COLLATE ascii_bin)\G
*************************** 1. row ***************************
                 COLLATION(_ascii 'hi'): ascii_general_ci
COLLATION (_ascii 'hi' COLLATE ascii_bin): ascii_bin
1 row in set (0.00 sec)
```

- The introducer and the `COLLATE` clause are different from the `CAST` and `CONVERT` functions. The `CAST` and `CONVERT` functions take a string of one character set and collation and change it to another character set and collation. The introducer and `COLLATE` clause inform `mysqld` of the character set and collation of the string.

- The default collation of a result can be overridden by specifying an introducer and `COLLATE` clause for a string. For example, to override the `latin1_bin` collation on the `cbin` field of the `sort_test` table use:

```
mysql> SELECT cbin FROM sort_test
    -> ORDER BY cbin COLLATE latin1_general_ci;
+------+
| cbin |
+------+
| A    |
| a    |
| b    |
| B    |
+------+
4 rows in set (0.00 sec)
```

- This yields the same result as when the ci field was sorted using its default collation.

- The character_set_client variable specifies the character set used by the client application. Statements are converted from character_set_client to character_set_connection, unless an introducer and COLLATE clause are applied to a string. Often (and by default), the character_set_client and character_set_connection are set to the same value, so this conversion does not need to happen. However, in the event that a client uses an ASCII character set, connects to a database, and wants all statements to be converted to UTF-8, the character_set_client would be set to ascii and the character_set_connection would be set to utf8. The conversions will be done automatically by mysqld. These two variables ensure that clients using different character sets can send the same queries to mysqld and achieve the same results.

- The character_set_results variable is similar to the character_set_client variable. However, the character_set_results variable sets the character set that results should be returned as. If a retrieved field has a character set of latin1 and the character_set_results value is utf8, mysqld will convert the retrieved field to utf8 before sending the result back to the client.

> **NOTE** To summarize the confusing connection/client/results relationship, consider this: A client sends a statement in character_set_client, which is converted to character_set_connection and collation_connection by mysqld. After query execution, results are converted by mysqld to character_set_results. Almost all of the time, the character_set_client and character_set_results variables will be set with the same value — the character set of the client.

- **File system** — The character_set_filesystem system variable specifies the character set of the file system. When a filename is specified (such as in a LOAD DATA INFILE statement), mysqld converts the filename from the character set specified by character_set_client to the one specified by character_set_filesystem. The default value is binary, which means that no conversion is done and the filename is used as specified.

■ **System** — The `character_set_system` variable is always set to `utf8`, as that is the character set `mysqld` uses to store information such as identifiers.

The `SET CHARACTER SET charset_name` statement sets the value of the session variables `character_set_client` and `character_set_connection` to `charset_name` for the duration of the session, or until the system variables are changed again.

The `SET NAMES charset_name` statement sets the value of the session variables `character_set_client`, `character_set_connection`, and `character_set_results` to `charset_name` for the duration of the session, or until the system variables are changed again. `SET NAMES charset_name COLLATE collation_name` additionally sets the session variable `collation_connection` to `collation_name`.

The `charset charset_name` command is a `mysql` client command, which behaves as a `SET NAMES` command, except that values will not be lost if a reconnect (such as with `\r`) occurs.

To have the `mysql` client behave as if it connects and immediately runs a `SET NAMES charset_name` statement, use the `--default-character-set=charset_name` option to `mysql`.

> **WARNING** Converting data from one character set to another can produce unexpected results. Consult the MySQL manual for more information about how to convert fields from one character set to another.

Functions that manipulate strings will return a string in the same character set and collation as the input string. Functions do not change the character set or collation of a string unless explicitly told to do so (with `CAST`, `CONVERT`, `BINARY`, `COLLATE`, or the use of an introducer). Note that other conversions may occur, for instance, if `mysqld` changes the character set due to values of `character_set_client`, `character_set_connection` and `character_set_results`. Also, note that the `REPLACE` function always does a case-insensitive match, regardless of the collation of the strings involved.

MySQL uses the standard SQL `CONVERT(text_expr USING charset_name)` syntax. MySQL extends SQL with the `CAST(text_expr AS text_data_type CHARACTER SET charset_name)` syntax. For example:

```
mysql> SELECT CAST('hi' AS CHAR(2) CHARACTER SET ascii);
+-------------------------------------------+
| CAST('hi' AS CHAR(2) CHARACTER SET ascii) |
+-------------------------------------------+
| hi                                        |
+-------------------------------------------+
1 row in set (0.00 sec)
```

`CAST` cannot specify a collation. However, because `CAST` returns a string expression, a `COLLATE` clause can follow a `CAST` function to indicate what collation should be associated with the string. If the previous example wanted to specify that the return from the `CAST` function should be considered the `ascii_bin` collation, the following `SELECT` statement would have been issued:

```
mysql> SELECT
    -> CAST('hi' AS CHAR(2) CHARACTER SET ascii) COLLATE ascii_bin;
```

For information on how to examine the available character sets and collations, see Chapter 21.

Understanding MySQL Deviations

MySQL has worked on supporting the ODBC SQL standard and the ANSI SQL standard. However, as with all other database systems, some of the SQL commands do not function as the standard indicates. For example, there are many privilege system differences in how the `GRANT` and `REVOKE` commands work; some deviations are listed in the "Privileges and Permissions" section. For more complete information on how the privilege system works in MySQL, see Chapter 14. How MySQL handles transactions and isolation levels is discussed in Chapter 9.

While this section explains deviations from theoretical SQL standards and some of the more outstanding differences from expected behavior, it does not explain all specific deviations from other database management systems, such as Oracle, Microsoft SQL Server, Sybase, or DB2. There are many details that SQL standards do not explain, and many of these details are implementation details. For instance, materialized views are an implementation detail of how views are handled by a database management system. The SQL standard covers syntax to create and drop views, but it does not specify that views should be materialized. However, if you are experienced in a database management system that uses materialized views, you may assume that a view in MySQL is materialized. This assumption can lead to poor query performance. As much as possible, we have tried to explain how MySQL works, particularly with respect to implementation details that are radically different from other database management systems. For example, Chapter 8 discusses views and explains that MySQL does not use materialized views, showing examples of how MySQL parses and optimizes view queries.

MySQL deviates from how most database administrators expect it to behave in the following ways:

- **Storage engines** — Each table is an instantiation of a storage engine. Different tables can have different storage engines. Different storage engines function differently with regard to performance, ACID (atomicity, consistency, isolation, durability) compliance (see Chapter 9 for more information on ACID compliance), supported features, and more. Information about how different storage engines work appears throughout the book; however, Chapter 11 focuses on the major differences among the storage engines.

- **Errors** — MySQL makes attempts to make sense of what should throw an error. By default, `mysqld` automatically allows inserting invalid data, automatically truncates data that is too large for a data type, implicitly converts data and more. The `sql_mode` server variable can be set to change most of this type of behavior. See Chapter 5 for more details on SQL modes.

- **String comparison** — By default, strings are compared in the order determined by the collation (see the "Character sets and collations" section earlier in this chapter for more information). However, strings are compared in a case-insensitive manner, unless a string is cast using the BINARY() function or a string is stored in a field that specifies the BINARY attribute. See Chapter 5 for more details on specifying the BINARY attribute in a field that stores strings.

- In addition, LIKE can be used to compare numbers:

```
mysql> SELECT 0 LIKE 0;
+----------+
| 0 LIKE 0 |
+----------+
|        1 |
+----------+
1 row in set (0.00 sec)
```

MySQL deviates from the SQL standard in the following ways:

- **Data types** — See Chapter 5 for how MySQL deviates from the SQL standard data types.

- **Index types** — See Chapter 6 for how MySQL deviates from the SQL standard index types.

- MySQL has no refined concept of GLOBAL or LOCAL tables. A TEMPORARY table can be considered local, as it is an in-memory table that is only available to the session that defines it. All other tables can be considered global, as they are available to other sessions as soon as a successful CREATE TABLE statement completes.

- MySQL does not support the ON COMMIT, REF IS, UNDER and AS SUBQUERY clauses to CREATE TABLE. The LIKE clause to CREATE TABLE only takes a table name as an argument; no options (such as INCLUDING DEFAULTS and EXCLUDING DEFAULTS) are allowed.

- SCHEMA is an alias to DATABASE in the CREATE SCHEMA, ALTER SCHEMA and DROP SCHEMA statements. MySQL does not support the AUTHORIZATION clause.

- Stored code such as the stored procedures, stored functions, triggers, and events can only use SQL statements. MySQL has no equivalent to a procedural programming language such as PL/SQL. Stored code in MySQL does not contain many of the options in the SQL standard and contains a few extensions. See Chapter 7 for more information about stored procedures, stored functions, triggers, and events.

- User-defined system views (metadata) are allowed, though they can only be written only in C. See the "Custom Metadata section" in Chapter 21 for more information.

- User-defined functions are allowed, though they can only be written only in C.

ON the WEBSITE More information on how to create and use a user-defined function can be found on the accompanying website for this book at www.wiley.com/go/mysqladminbible.

- Comparison operators can be used in the result expressions of the SELECT fields. If used, these will return TRUE (1), FALSE (0), or NULL (NULL). For example:

```
mysql> use sakila;Database changed
mysql> SELECT staff_id, staff_id>1, '|',
    -> first_name, first_name LIKE 'M%'
    -> FROM staff;
+----------+------------+---+------------+----------------------+
| staff_id | staff_id>1 | | | first_name | first_name LIKE 'M%' |
+----------+------------+---+------------+----------------------+
|        1 |          0 | | | Mike       |                    1 |
|        2 |          1 | | | Jon        |                    0 |
+----------+------------+---+------------+----------------------+
2 rows in set (0.00 sec)
```

- MySQL does not support the concept of catalogs. The INFORMATION_SCHEMA database has many system views with fields relating to catalogs where the value is NULL. In addition, the SET CATALOG statement is not supported.

- **Foreign key constraints** — MySQL accepts foreign key constraints in table definitions, but only tables using transactional storage engines (such as InnoDB and Falcon) actually implement foreign key checking. All other storage engine types disregard foreign key constraint definitions without producing an error. See Chapter 6 for more details on foreign key constraints in MySQL.

- In MySQL, foreign key constraints are always checked, unless the FOREIGN_KEY_CHECKS session variable is set to OFF or 0. There is no way to disable foreign key constraints on an individual basis. Thus, MySQL does not support the REFERENCES ARE CHECKED and REFERENCES ARE NOT CHECKED clauses.

- The MATCH clause in a foreign key constraint is disregarded in all storage engines, even InnoDB and Falcon, which implement foreign keys.

- Prepared statements in MySQL have a local scope; that is, a prepared statement can only be used by the session that creates it. MySQL does not have as big a performance boost when using prepared statements, because each session has to compile each prepared statement the first time it is used in the session. In addition, the PREPARE syntax in MySQL is very basic — it only allows the name of the prepared statement and the statement itself to be specified (using a string or a user-defined variable containing a string). PREPARE in MySQL does not support the ATTRIBUTES keyword.

- MySQL does not support querying data samples using the TABLESAMPLE clause.

- CAST() and CONVERT() — According to the SQL standard, the CAST() and CONVERT() functions should be able to cast to any data type. However, in MySQL, CAST()and CONVERT() cannot be used to cast a number to the REAL or BIGINT data type.

- In standard SQL, the TRIM() function can only be used to remove a single leading character and a single trailing character. In MySQL, the TRIM() function can be used to remove multiple leading and trailing characters.

- **String concatenation** — The || string concatenation function is not supported. Use CONCAT() instead. In MySQL, || is an alias for OR.

- MySQL does not support assertions. The CREATE ASSERTION and DROP ASSERTION statements are not supported.

- MySQL does not support the SQL standard way of defining character sets and collations. The CREATE CHARACTER SET, DROP CHARACTER SET, CREATE COLLATION, and DROP COLLATION statements are not supported. For details on how to add a character set to MySQL, see the manual page at:

  http://dev.mysql.com/doc/refman/6.0/en/adding-character-set.html

- For details on how to add a collation to MySQL, see the manual page at:

  http://dev.mysql.com/doc/refman/6.0/en/adding-collation.html

- GROUP BY in MySQL does not support the CUBE or GROUPING SETS options.

- MySQL does not support the following functions: binary set functions (including CORR, COVAR_POP, COVAR_SAMP, etc.), COLLECT, FUSION, and INTERSECTION.

- MySQL does not support windowing functions such as RANK, DENSE_RANK, PERCENT_RANK, CUME_DIST.

- MySQL does not support static cursors. In MySQL, all cursors are dynamic (prepared at runtime). However, cursors are stored (cached) in temporary tables, so they are not fully dynamic. The performance of cursors in MySQL is usually worse than the performance of cursors in other database management systems. See http://forge.mysql.com/worklog/task.php?id=3433 for more details on the tasks that need to be completed in order for cursors to be fully dynamic.

- MySQL does not support domains or domain constraints. The CREATE DOMAIN, ALTER DOMAIN, and DROP DOMAIN statements are not supported, and DOMAIN permissions cannot be granted using GRANT.

- MySQL does not support sequences. The CREATE SEQUENCE, ALTER SEQUENCE, and DROP SEQUENCE statements are not supported, and SEQUENCE permissions cannot be granted using GRANT. In addition, field definitions in MySQL do not support the GENERATED, ALWAYS, BY DEFAULT, and AS IDENTITY keywords. The LIKE clause of a CREATE TABLE statement in MySQL does not support the INCLUDING IDENTITY and EXCLUDING IDENTITY options.

- MySQL does not support user-defined types nor transform functions for user-defined types. The CREATE CAST, DROP CAST, CREATE ORDERING FOR, DROP ORDERING FOR, CREATE TYPE, ALTER TYPE, DROP TYPE, CREATE TRANSFORM, ALTER TRANSFORM, and DROP TRANSFORM statements are not supported, and TYPE permissions cannot be granted using GRANT.

- MySQL does not support transliterations. The CREATE TRANSLATION and DROP TRANSLATION statements are not supported, and TRANSLATION permissions cannot be granted using GRANT.

- MySQL does not support any embedded declarations. DECLARE is supported for cursors but not for embedded SQL, embedded authorization declarations, and temporary table declarations. Temporary tables can be created by specifying `CREATE TEMPORARY TABLE` instead of `CREATE TABLE` and dropped with `DROP TEMPORARY TABLE`. MySQL extends `DECLARE` to be able to specify variables, conditions, and handlers. See Chapter 7 for more details on the `DECLARE` extensions.

■ Updatable cursors and the `WHERE CURRENT OF` clauses in `UPDATE` and `DELETE` statements are not supported in MySQL.

■ MySQL does not support recursive queries or the `SEARCH DEPTH FIRST BY`, `SEARCH BREADTH FIRST BY`, and `CYCLE` clauses.

■ In the SQL standard, `DESCRIBE` is used to obtain information about prepared statement input and output parameters. In MySQL, `DESCRIBE` is an alias for `SHOW COLUMNS`. Table 4-1 shows the `DESCRIBE` syntax and how it is translated into `SHOW COLUMNS` statements.

TABLE 4-1

Translating DESCRIBE into SHOW COLUMNS

DESCRIBE Statement	Corresponding SHOW COLUMS Statement
`DESCRIBE tblname;`	`SHOW COLUMNS FROM tblname;`
`DESCRIBE tblname fldname;`	`SHOW COLUMNS FROM tblname WHERE Field='fldname';`
`DESCRIBE tblname 'fldname';`	`SHOW COLUMNS FROM fldname WHERE Field LIKE 'fldname';`

■ The third syntax can be used with the % and _ wildcard characters. `DESC` can be used in place of `DESCRIBE`, if desired. For more information on `SHOW COLUMNS`, see Chapter 21.

■ MySQL does not support descriptor areas. The `ALLOCATE DESCRIPTOR`, `DEALLOCATE DESCRIPTOR`, `GET DESCRIPTOR`, and `SET DESCRIPTOR` statements are not supported.

■ MySQL does not support connection management with the `CONNECT TO`, `SET CON-NECTION`, and `DISCONNECT` statements. In addition, session management is not supported — the `SET ROLE` and `SET TIME ZONE` statements are not supported by MySQL. The SQL standard `SET SESSION` statement is not supported by MySQL. However, MySQL has a conflicting syntax — the `SET` statement takes an optional keyword of `GLOBAL` or `SESSION` when setting a system variable. Therefore, even though SQL standard `SET SESSION` commands such as `SET SESSION AUTHORIZATION`, and `SET SESSION CHARACTERISTICS` are not valid, there are valid nonstandard `SET SESSION` commands, such as:

`SET SESSION character_set_client=latin1;`

■ MySQL does not support the `SET SCHEMA` statement. The default database can be set by specifying a default database as a client option when connecting, and it can be changed in the `mysql` client program with the `\u` or `use` command.

- MySQL does not support dynamically prepared statements using EXECUTE IMMEDI-ATE. Regular prepared statements are supported, as is the EXECUTE statement without the IMMEDIATE qualifier.

- MySQL does not support diagnostics management with the GET DIAGNOSTICS statement. The SHOW ERRORS and SHOW WARNINGS statements can be used to see errors and warnings from the previous statement, and the error log can be monitored for errors (and warnings if the log_warnings system variable is set). More information on SHOW ERRORS and SHOW WARNINGS can be seen later in this chapter in The "SHOW extension" section.

Privileges and permissions

MySQL uses the GRANT and REVOKE syntax as specified in the SQL standard, with some changes already mentioned (such as lack of domains and thus a lack of DOMAIN privileges) in addition to the following deviations:

- There is no WITH ADMIN OPTION; instead the SUPER privilege exists, and the WITH GRANT OPTION can be specified to allow a user to GRANT any subset of privileges that user has to another user.

- MySQL does not support the GRANTED BY or WITH HIERARCHY OPTION clauses.

- MySQL has a limited concept of users; a user is unique with respect to its user-name@host value. However, because of wildcards, localhost, and multiple hostname support, it is possible that a user connecting from a particular host may not receive the expected permissions. Fields cannot be associated with a user, role or path.

- MySQL does not support the concept of roles. The DROP ROLE statement is not supported.

- One or more users can be renamed using the RENAME USER statement:

```
RENAME USER user1@host1 TO user2@host2;
RENAME USER user1@host1 TO user2@host2, userA@hostA TO userB@hostB;
```

- A user can be created without having any privileges explicitly granted via a CREATE USER user@host [IDENTIFIED BY 'password_string'] statement. The USAGE ON *.* privilege is implicitly granted by this statement.

- DROP USER user@host will revoke all privileges, including USAGE, from user@host.

- There are no CHARACTER SET or COLLATION privileges.

For more information about privileges and permissions, see Chapter 14.

Transaction management

Transaction management is partially supported in MySQL. Transactions are only supported when using tables defined with transactional storage engines, such as InnoDB and Falcon.

For more information on storage engines, see Chapter 11; for more information on transactions in MySQL, see Chapter 9.

MySQL supports the START TRANSACTION command to note the beginning of a transaction. However, START TRANSACTION in MySQL does not allow any optional arguments to specify transaction modes. Table 4-2 shows the SQL standard transaction modes and how those transaction modes can be set in MySQL.

TABLE 4-2

Setting Transaction Modes in MySQL

SQL Standard	MySQL Equivalent
ISOLATION LEVEL iso_level	See Chapter 9 for how to set isolation levels.
READ ONLY	Change permissions for the user. See Chapter 14 for more information on granting privileges. Set the server to read_only. See the "Promoting a new master" section in Chapter 22 for more information on the read_only server variable.
READ WRITE	Change permissions for the user; see Chapter 14 for more information on granting privileges.
DIAGNOSTICS SIZE	N/A (MySQL does not support this feature with an alternative syntax)

SET TRANSACTION and SET LOCAL TRANSACTION commands are not supported by MySQL.

Check constraints

MySQL does not support check constraints, other than those implemented by specifying data types, foreign key constraints, and unique key constraints (for more information about key constraints, see Chapter 6). The SET CONSTRAINTS statement is not supported.

Check constraints defined with the CONSTRAINT...CHECK clause in the CREATE TABLE or ALTER TABLE statements are allowed but ignored, no matter what storage engine is used. The following example defines a check constraint where the id field must only have a value of 0, and shows how the check constraint is ignored:

```
mysql> CREATE TABLE check_test (id INT PRIMARY KEY) ENGINE=InnoDB;
Query OK, 0 rows affected (0.37 sec)

mysql> ALTER TABLE check_test
    -> ADD CONSTRAINT is_ignored CHECK (id=0);
Query OK, 0 rows affected (0.39 sec)
Records: 0  Duplicates: 0  Warnings: 0
```

```
mysql> SHOW CREATE TABLE check_test\G
*************************** 1. row ***************************
       Table: check_test
Create Table: CREATE TABLE `check_test` (
  `id` int(11) NOT NULL,
  PRIMARY KEY (`id`)
) ENGINE=InnoDB DEFAULT CHARSET=latin1
1 row in set (0.00 sec)

mysql> INSERT INTO check_test (id) VALUES (0),(1);
Query OK, 2 rows affected (0.00 sec)
Records: 2  Duplicates: 0  Warnings: 0

mysql> SELECT id FROM check_test;
+----+
| id |
+----+
|  0 |
|  1 |
+----+
2 rows in set (0.00 sec)
```

Upsert statements

MySQL does not support *upsert* statements with the standard SQL MERGE statement. An upsert statement either inserts a new record or, if a certain condition is met, updates existing records. MySQL supports limited upsert statements with the ON DUPLICATE KEY UPDATE clause to an INSERT statement. The SQL standard MERGE statement supports any condition, but the ON DUPLICATE KEY UPDATE clause in MySQL only supports the condition where a unique or primary key already exists.

To test this, first find a suitable key constraint on the store table in the sakila database, and some data to work with:

```
mysql> SELECT INDEX_NAME, SEQ_IN_INDEX, COLUMN_NAME
    -> FROM INFORMATION_SCHEMA.STATISTICS
    -> WHERE NON_UNIQUE=0 AND TABLE_SCHEMA='sakila'
    -> AND TABLE_NAME='store';
+--------------------+--------------+-----------------+
| INDEX_NAME         | SEQ_IN_INDEX | COLUMN_NAME     |
+--------------------+--------------+-----------------+
| PRIMARY            |            1 | store_id        |
| idx_unique_manager |            1 | manager_staff_id |
+--------------------+--------------+-----------------+
2 rows in set (0.00 sec)

mysql> use sakila
Database changed
mysql> SELECT store_id, manager_staff_id, address_id, last_update
```

```
    -> FROM store;
+----------+-----------------+------------+---------------------+
| store_id | manager_staff_id | address_id | last_update         |
+----------+-----------------+------------+---------------------+
|        1 |               1 |          1 | 2006-02-15 04:57:12 |
|        2 |               2 |          2 | 2006-02-15 04:57:12 |
+----------+-----------------+------------+---------------------+
2 rows in set (0.00 sec)
```

Ziesel (the store owner of our fictional video store rental company that utilizes the sakila database) wants to make sure that all of her stores are in the database. The data to upsert (insert or update records) is shown in Table 4-3.

TABLE 4-3

Data to Upsert to Store

Store_id	Manager_staff_id	Address_id
1	1	1
2	2	3

As Ziesel feared, the data in the store table is not correct. Specifically, the address_id for store 2 is incorrect. Table 4-3 corresponds with the following upsert statement, which should update the address id for the record with a store_id of 2:

```
mysql> INSERT INTO store (store_id, manager_staff_id, address_id)
    -> VALUES (1,1,1),(2,2,3)
    -> ON DUPLICATE KEY UPDATE address_id=VALUES(address_id);
Query OK, 2 rows affected (0.00 sec)
Records: 2  Duplicates: 1  Warnings: 0

mysql> SELECT store_id, manager_staff_id, address_id, last_update
 FROM store;
+----------+-----------------+------------+---------------------+
| store_id | manager_staff_id | address_id | last_update         |
+----------+-----------------+------------+---------------------+
|        1 |               1 |          1 | 2006-02-15 04:57:12 |
|        2 |               2 |          3 | 2009-01-25 04:35:18 |
+----------+-----------------+------------+---------------------+
2 rows in set (0.00 sec)
```

As desired, the record with a store_id of 2 was updated.

Similar upsert behavior can be accomplished with the REPLACE statement. A REPLACE statement, like the ON DUPLICATE KEY UPDATE statement, will insert a record if there is no existing record with a duplicate PRIMARY or UNIQUE KEY constraint. However, if there is a duplicate key constraint, REPLACE will DELETE the existing record and INSERT a new one. This has many consequences — two actions are performed (DELETE and INSERT) instead of one (UPDATE, as with ON DUPLICATE KEY UPDATE). In an ON DUPLICATE KEY UPDATE statement, any INSERT or any UPDATE trigger may fire, depending on whether data was inserted or updated. In a REPLACE statement, either the INSERT trigger(s) or the INSERT and DELETE triggers will fire — either the record is inserted, in which case the INSERT trigger(s) will fire, or the record is replaced via DELETE and INSERT statements, in which case those triggers will fire.

WARNING REPLACE can be useful, but keep in mind that performance may suffer because there are two actions being performed.

The REPLACE statement has almost the same syntax as the INSERT statement, including the LOW_PRIORITY and DELAYED extensions (see the "DML extensions" section later in this chapter). However, the IGNORE and ON DUPLICATE KEY UPDATE extensions are not part of REPLACE syntax. This is acceptable, as the desired behavior when a duplicate key is found is either:

- Delete the existing record and insert a new record (as with REPLACE)
- Update the existing record (as with ON DUPLICATE KEY UPDATE)
- Do nothing (as with IGNORE)

Thus, the REPLACE, ON DUPLICATE KEY UPDATE, and IGNORE clauses are mutually exclusive.

Using MySQL Extensions

Many of the extensions to MySQL have been developed to make MySQL easier to use. Many of the MySQL SHOW statements, for example, are much easier to use for a beginner than having to query the INFORMATION_SCHEMA database. Some of the extensions to SQL are actually commands in the client, such as use (\u) and source (\.) and have been discussed in Chapter 3. Many of the extensions are in mysqld. The following extensions are explained throughout the rest of this chapter:

- Aliases
- ALTER TABLE extensions
- CREATE extensions
- DML extensions (INSERT, UPDATE, DELETE)
- DROP extensions
- The LIMIT extension
- SELECT extensions

- Server maintenance extensions
- The SET extension
- The SHOW extension
- Table definition extensions
- Table maintenance extensions
- Transactional statement extensions

ON the WEBSITE MySQL has added numerous new functions and extensions to existing functions. Appendix B contains a reference of all of the functions and their syntaxes. On the accompanying website for this book at www.wiley.com/go/mysqladminbible, you will find examples and uses for the functions with nonstandard behaviors, and the more frequently used nonstandard functions.

Aliases

The following MySQL extensions are aliases to standard SQL statements:

- BEGIN and BEGIN WORK are aliases for START TRANSACTION.
- DROP PREPARE stmt_prep is a synonym for DEALLOCATE PREPARE stmt_prep.
- EXPLAIN tbl_name is an alias for SHOW COLUMNS FROM tbl_name.
- num1 % num2 is the same as MOD(num1,num2).

ALTER TABLE extensions

The ALTER TABLE statement has a number of extensions in MySQL that add features to allow an ALTER TABLE statement to do almost everything a CREATE TABLE statement can do. Many ALTER TABLE statements are *offline* statements — to change the table, the statements copy the table, blocking access to the table, as if the table itself were offline. The largest performance enhancement is that many ALTER TABLE statements are *online* statements — ALTER TABLE statements that do not copy the table. Online statements are done in the background.

The following statements are online statements:

- ADD INDEX and DROP INDEX for variable-width indexed fields.
- Renaming a field using CHANGE COLUMN and specifying the same data type.
- Using CHANGE COLUMN or MODIFY COLUMN to modify the default value for a field.
- Adding items to the end of an ENUM or SET value data type (with CHANGE COLUMN or MOD-IFY COLUMN). See Chapter 5 for more information about data types, including the ENUM and SET data types.

Unfortunately, that still leaves many operations as offline operations. However, a MySQL extension to ALTER TABLE that can help that is the ability to specify more than one operation at a time on a table, using a comma-separated list of ALTER TABLE options. For example, Ziesel uses the following query on the film table in the sakila database to perform three offline operations at the same time: adding a new field for the film's country of origin with a default country of the United States (country_id 103), creating an index on that field, and creating a foreign key constraint on that field to the country_id field of the country table.

```
mysql> use sakila;
Database changed
mysql> ALTER TABLE film
    -> ADD COLUMN origin_country SMALLINT(5) UNSIGNED
    ->    NOT NULL DEFAULT 103,
    -> ADD INDEX idx_fk_origin_country (origin_country),
    -> ADD CONSTRAINT fk_film_country FOREIGN KEY (origin_country)
    -> REFERENCES country(country_id);
Query OK, 1000 rows affected (1.12 sec)
Records: 1000   Duplicates: 0  Warnings: 0
```

Other than check constraints, which MySQL does not handle (see the "Understanding MySQL Deviations" section earlier in this chapter), the SQL standard defines the following actions an ALTER TABLE can perform:

- ADD/ALTER/DROP COLUMN
- ADD/DROP PRIMARY/UNIQUE/FOREIGN KEY

MySQL has added many extensions that add functionality to ALTER TABLE and provide methods to control the performance of ALTER TABLE:

- ADD FULLTEXT INDEX — Add a fulltext index. See Chapter 6 for more details on fulltext indexes.
- ADD INDEX — Add an index. See Chapter 6 for more details on indexes.
- ADD SPATIAL INDEX — Add a spatial index.

ON the WEBSITE   For more information about spatial indexes, see the companion website for this book at www.wiley.com/go/mysqladminbible.

- CHANGE COLUMN old_fld_name new_fld_name new_fld_definition — Change the field name and definition. Note that there is no way to change the field name without specifying the field definition as well. In addition, the field definition can end with either FIRST or AFTER other_fld_name to specify the position the field should be put in.
- CONVERT TO CHARACTER SET charset_name
- CONVERT TO CHARACTER SET charset_name COLLATION collation_name
- DISABLE KEYS — Disables any indexes so that they are not updated when records are inserted, deleted, or updated. Speeds up large data imports in conjunction with ENABLE KEYS.

- ENABLE KEYS — Enables automatic index updating and rebuilds all indexes on the table. Speeds up large data imports in conjunction with DISABLE KEYS.

- IGNORE — If an ALTER TABLE statement results in a duplicate key error, the table copy is stopped and the table is reverted to its original schema. All of the changes in the ALTER TABLE are lost, even if the change did not cause the duplicate key error. When you specify IGNORE between ALTER and TABLE, duplicate records that would cause such errors are deleted from the table.

To see this behavior, Ziesel copies her customer table:

```
mysql> use sakila;
Database changed
mysql> CREATE TABLE customer_test LIKE customer;
Query OK, 0 rows affected (0.04 sec)

mysql> INSERT INTO customer_test SELECT * FROM customer;
Query OK, 599 rows affected (0.17 sec)
Records: 599  Duplicates: 0  Warnings: 0
```

Now that she has a table with all 599 customers that she can test without destroying her production data, Ziesel purposefully causes a duplicate key error, so that she can later compare ALTER TABLE to ALTER IGNORE TABLE:

```
mysql> SELECT COUNT(*), active
    -> FROM customer_test
    -> GROUP BY active;
+----------+--------+
| COUNT(*) | active |
+----------+--------+
|       15 |      0 |
|      584 |      1 |
+----------+--------+
2 rows in set (0.02 sec)

mysql> ALTER TABLE customer_test ADD UNIQUE KEY(active);
ERROR 1062 (23000): Duplicate entry '1' for key 'active'
```

Now that she has caused a duplicate key error, she compares the behavior of using the IGNORE keyword:

```
mysql> ALTER IGNORE TABLE customer_test ADD UNIQUE KEY(active);
Query OK, 599 rows affected (0.40 sec)
Records: 599  Duplicates: 597  Warnings: 0

mysql> SELECT COUNT(*), active
    -> FROM customer_test
    -> GROUP BY active;
```

```
+----------+--------+
| COUNT(*) | active |
+----------+--------+
|        1 |      0 |
|        1 |      1 |
+----------+--------+
2 rows in set (0.00 sec)

mysql> SELECT COUNT(*) from customer_test;
+----------+
| COUNT(*) |
+----------+
|        2 |
+----------+
1 row in set (0.00 sec)
```

There were 597 duplicate keys that were deleted because of the ALTER IGNORE. Only two records are left in the table — one record with an active value of 0, and the other with an active value of 1. Take care not to lose important data when using ALTER IGNORE TABLE.

- MODIFY COLUMN fld_name new_fld_definition — Note that there is no way to change a part of the field definition without specifying the whole field definition. For example, to change an INT NOT NULL to an UNSIGNED INT NOT NULL, the entire field definition UNSIGNED INT NOT NULL must be used. In addition, the field definition can end with either FIRST or AFTER other_fld_name to specify the position the field should be put in.

- ORDER BY fld_list — Performs a one-time sort of the data records, sorting each row in order of the comma-separated field list (just as if it was the result of a SELECT query with the same ORDER BY clause).

- RENAME new_tblname or RENAME TO new_tblname will change the name of a table and associated objects such as triggers and foreign key constraints.

Other table-level extensions are listed in the "Table definition extensions" section later in this chapter. Table extensions are valid for both CREATE TABLE and ALTER TABLE statements. For example, ENGINE=MyISAM is valid for both CREATE TABLE and ALTER TABLE:

```
CREATE TABLE foo (id int) ENGINE=MyISAM
ALTER TABLE foo ENGINE=MyISAM
```

CREATE extensions

Many MySQL CREATE statements contain an IF NOT EXISTS extension. This specifies that a warning, not an error, should be issued if mysqld cannot complete the CREATE statement because of an existing identifier conflict. For example:

```
mysql> CREATE DATABASE IF NOT EXISTS test;
Query OK, 0 rows affected, 1 warning (0.00 sec)

mysql> SHOW WARNINGS;
+-------+------+-----------------------------------------------+
| Level | Code | Message                                       |
+-------+------+-----------------------------------------------+
| Note  | 1007 | Can't create database 'test'; database exists |
+-------+------+-----------------------------------------------+
1 row in set (0.00 sec)
```

■ Creating an index in a CREATE TABLE statement is a MySQL extension to standard SQL. In addition, creating a named index, specifying an index storage method (such as USING HASH) and creating an index that uses a column prefix are also nonstandard SQL — whether the index is created with CREATE INDEX or ALTER TABLE ADD INDEX. See Chapter 6 for more details on all of the standard and nonstandard features of indexes in MySQL.

■ CREATE VIEW can be specified as CREATE OR REPLACE VIEW view_name to create a view if a view with view_name does not exist, or delete the existing view and replace it with the new view being defined if it does exist.

■ Other table-level extensions are listed in the "Table definition extensions" section later in this chapter. Table extensions are valid for both CREATE TABLE and ALTER TABLE statements. For example, the ENGINE=MyISAM is valid for both of these:

```
CREATE TABLE foo (id int) ENGINE=MyISAM
ALTER TABLE foo ENGINE=MyISAM
```

DML extensions

MySQL extends DML (Data Manipulation Language — INSERT, REPLACE, UPDATE, and DELETE statements) with the following:

■ IGNORE — Any errors caused by executing the specified DML are issued as warnings. This will cause the statement to continue instead of stopping at the first error. All errors appear as warnings and can be seen by issuing SHOW WARNINGS after the DML finishes.

■ LOW_PRIORITY — Does not receive a write lock and execute the specified DML (INSERT/REPLACE/UPDATE/DELETE) until all read locks have been granted and there are no locks waiting in the read lock queue. (The default behavior is for all write locks to be granted before any read locks). The LOW_PRIORITY option is specified just after the first word of the statement — for example, INSERT LOW_PRIORITY INTO tblname.

The low-priority-updates option to mysqld changes the default behavior so that all DML acts as if it were specified with LOW_PRIORITY. In other words, the `low-priority-updates` option changes the default behavior to grant all read locks before granting a write lock.

If the `low-priority-updates` option is specified, the `INSERT` statement can take a `HIGH_PRIORITY` option to prioritize the write lock for specific `INSERT` statements. The `HIGH_PRIORITY` option is specified in the same position the `LOW_PRIORITY` option is. However, the `HIGH_PRIORITY` option is only valid with the `INSERT` statement — the `LOW_PRIORITY` statement is valid with all DML. Both `LOW_PRIORITY` and `HIGH_PRIORITY` only affect storage engines with table-level locks as their most granular lock.

See the "Table-level locks" section in Chapter 9 for more information on read and write lock queues.

- `LIMIT` — `UPDATE` and `DELETE` statements can change or delete a subset of matching rows. See "The LIMIT extension" section earlier in this chapter for details.

- `ORDER BY` — `UPDATE` and `DELETE` statements can specify a particular order. This is usually used with the `LIMIT` clause to change or delete only some rows — for example, `ORDER BY` and `LIMIT` can be used together in a `SELECT` statement to retrieve the oldest five records in a table. In the same way, `ORDER BY` and `LIMIT` can be used with `UPDATE` or `DELETE` to change or remove the oldest five records in a table.

- Upsert — MySQL has extended the `INSERT` statement to include upsert (insert/update) functionality. See the Upsert statements subsection (under the "Understanding MySQL deviations" section) earlier in this chapter for more information about upsert statements in MySQL, including the `ON DUPLICATE KEY` option to `INSERT` and the new `REPLACE` statement.

- `DELETE QUICK` — The `QUICK` option to `DELETE` may speed up some deletes by not merging index leaves when it changes the index to reflect that records have been removed. This can lead to more fragmentation in the index.

- `TRUNCATE` — Issue `TRUNCATE tbl_name` (or `TRUNCATE TABLE tbl_name`) to very quickly remove all the rows from a table. This does not actually issue any `DELETE` statements, so no `DELETE` triggers are invoked. Most storage engines drop and re-create the table; in addition to being faster than a `DELETE` statement, this will reset the `AUTO_INCREMENT` value to 0.

  InnoDB will drop and re-create the table unless there are foreign key constraints, in which case it will act exactly as `DELETE FROM tbl_name`, with no filter specified in a `WHERE` clause so all rows are deleted. If foreign keys are present, rows are deleted one at a time and foreign key `ON DELETE` clauses are processed as usual.

  Aside from the speed, another reason to use `TRUNCATE` instead of `DELETE` is if a `DELETE` cannot be used, for example when a table has a corrupt index or the data itself is corrupt. In addition, a `DELETE` statement requires the `DELETE` privilege, and a `TRUNCATE` statement requires the `DROP` privilege. Therefore, `TRUNCATE` can be used to remove all rows from a table if a user has the `DROP` privilege but not the `DELETE` privilege.

■ INSERT readability — The INSERT statement has an alternate syntax for better readability when inserting many fields. This alternate syntax uses one or more SET fld=value clauses, like the standard syntax for UPDATE. The following two queries illustrate the difference between the SQL standard for INSERT statements (first query) and the alternative INSERT syntax allowed by MySQL (second query):

```
INSERT INTO address (address, address2, district, city_id,
postal_code, phone) VALUES
('44 Massachusetts Avenue', 'Apt. 102', 'Bergen County', 5,
'07742', '867-5309');

INSERT INTO address SET address='44 Massachusetts Avenue',
address2='Apt. 102', district='Bergen County', city_id=5,
postal_code='07742', phone='867-5309';
```

Both queries are valid in MySQL and would insert the exact same row into the address table. Although it is longer, the second syntax makes it easier to correspond field names and the values being inserted. This also makes it very difficult to specify a different number of field names and values, such as in the following query (there is no value for the phone field):

```
INSERT INTO address (address, address2, district, city_id,
postal_code, phone) VALUES
('44 Massachusetts Avenue','Apt. 102', 'Bergen County', 5,
'07742');
ERROR 1136 (21S01): Column count doesn't match value count at row 1
```

■ DELETE using more than one table — Alternate syntaxes for DELETE allow rows from multiple tables to be used in the deletion criteria, or allow rows from multiple tables to be deleted, or both. ORDER BY and LIMIT cannot be used when more than one table is specified, but the LOW_PRIORITY, QUICK and IGNORE options can be used.

The syntaxes that allow DELETE to reference and/or delete from more than one table are:

```
DELETE tbl_list FROM tbl_expr [ WHERE condition ]
DELETE FROM tbl_list USING tbl_expr [ WHERE condition ]
```

In both syntaxes, tbl_list is a comma-separated list of tables whose rows should be deleted based on the tbl_expr and the optional WHERE clause. The expression tbl_expr can be any expression that returns a table, including any type of JOIN clause and subqueries. Any tables that are in tbl_expr that are not in tbl_list will not have rows deleted.

■ INSERT DELAYED — The DELAYED option to INSERT specifies that the data should be queued for a later batch insertion. When an INSERT DELAYED is issued, mysqld puts the information into a queue and returns successfully. The session can continue without waiting for the INSERT to finish. Many INSERT DELAYED statements are batched together and written at the same time, which is faster than many individual writes when there is a lot of activity on the table. INSERT DELAYED will wait until there is no activity on the table and then insert a batch of records.

If there is not a lot of activity on a table, INSERT DELAYED will not perform better than individual INSERT statements. If there is not a lot of activity on a table when an INSERT DELAYED is issued, mysqld still puts the INSERT DELAYED information into a queue and returns successfully. However, the queue can immediately insert the batch in the queue. If the table has little activity, mysqld will be doing batch inserts where the batch size is 1 record. Regular INSERT statements would be faster in this case, because INSERT DELAYED has the additional overhead of enqueuing and dequeuing the information and the extra thread per table used to insert the batch. The MySQL manual has a detailed account of what takes place in an INSERT DELAYED statement at http://dev.mysql.com/doc/refman/6.0/en/insert-delayed.html.

INSERT DELAYED is not appropriate for data that needs to be stored in the database immediately. The batch queue is stored in memory, and in the event of a crash or a schema change from a higher priority ALTER TABLE statement, the information in the batch queue will be lost and *not* inserted. In addition, LAST_INSERT_ID() will not function as expected, because it reflects the most recent value actually inserted.

INSERT DELAYED can only be used on tables using the MyISAM, ARCHIVE, BLACK-HOLE, and MEMORY storage engines and cannot be used on views or partitioned tables. The DELAYED option is ignored if an upsert is specified with ON DUPLICATE KEY, and when the SQL standard INSERT INTO...SELECT syntax is used.

■ LOAD DATA INFILE — The LOAD DATA INFILE command is used to load data from a text file created by the SELECT INTO OUTFILE command. See the section on SELECT extensions for more information about SELECT INTO OUTFILE.

To show an example of LOAD DATA INFILE first export the rental table from the sakila database, using SELECT ... INTO OUTFILE. By default, this puts the file in the directory of the database, but a location for the file can be specified optionally.

```
mysql> SELECT * FROM rental INTO OUTFILE 'rental.sql';
Query OK, 16044 rows affected (0.05 sec)
```

There is no table definition included in the SELECT ... INTO OUTFILE so you should always ensure that you have a copy of the table definition for restoration of the file:

```
shell> mysqldump --no-data sakila rental > /tmp/rental-schema.sql
```

To create a new database sakila2 and load the rental table definition into it:

```
shell> mysqladmin create sakila2
shell> mysql sakila2 < /tmp/rental-schema.sql
```

Then, load the data into the sakila2.rental table:

```
mysql> use sakila2;
Database changed
```

```
mysql> LOAD DATA INFILE '/tmp/rental.sql' INTO TABLE rental;
Query OK, 16044 rows affected (1.24 sec)
Records: 16044  Deleted: 0  Skipped: 0  Warnings: 0
```

The default options for both SELECT ... INTO OUTFILE and LOAD DATA INFILE are quite reasonable and will work in most cases. There are two optional clauses FIELDS and LINES that can be used for specific cases where it is necessary to change the options such as quoting, field boundaries (to separate fields by a custom character such as the tab character or comma) and line boundaries.

For more information on the FIELDS and LINES options for both LOAD DATA INFILE and SELECT ... INTO OUTFILE, see the MySQL manual at http://dev.mysql. com/doc/refman/6.0/en/load-data.html.

■ LOAD XML INFILE — The LOAD XML INFILE command can be used to load XML data into tables. The text file for input can be any XML file. To generate XML output by using the mysql client, use the --xml option, as shown here:

```
shell> mysql --xml -e 'SELECT * FROM sakila.film' > /tmp/film.xml
```

Remember, the output file does not contain the table structure! Use mysqldump to save the structure:

```
shell> mysqldump --no-data sakila film > /tmp/film-schema.sql
```

Here is a sample of the output generated by the command executed previously:

```
<?xml version="1.0"?>

<resultset statement="SELECT * FROM sakila.film
" xmlns:xsi="http://www.w3.org/2001/XMLSchema-instance">
  <row>
 <field name="film_id">1</field>
 <field name="title">ACADEMY DINOSAUR</field>
 <field name="description">A Epic Drama of a Feminist And a Mad
Scientist who must Battle a Teacher in The Canadian Rockies</field>
 <field name="release_year">2006</field>
 <field name="language_id">1</field>
 <field name="original_language_id" xsi:nil="true" />
 <field name="rental_duration">6</field>
 <field name="rental_rate">0.99</field>
 <field name="length">86</field>
 <field name="replacement_cost">20.99</field>
 <field name="rating">PG</field>
 <field name="special_features">Deleted Scenes,Behind the
  Scenes</field>
 <field name="last_update">2006-02-15 05:03:42</field>
  </row>
```

The <row> and </row> tags are used to reference the start and end of a row in the output file. The <field name> and </field> tags are used to represent the columns in the row. The name attribute of the <field> tag specifies the name of the column.

In the following example the film table that was exported previously is loaded into an existing sakila2 database. First, the empty table with the proper schema must be created:

```
shell> mysql sakila2 < /tmp/film-schema.sql
```

Then, the data can be loaded with LOAD XML INFILE:

```
mysql> load xml infile '/tmp/film.xml' into table film;
Query OK, 1000 rows affected, 3 warnings (0.18 sec)
Records: 1000  Deleted: 0  Skipped: 0  Warnings: 3
```

The LOAD XML INFILE command was added in MySQL 6.0. More information about the available options for LOAD XML INFILE is available in the MySQL Manual at http://dev.mysql.com/doc/refman/6.0/en/load-xml.html.

DROP extensions

Similar to the IF NOT EXISTS extension to many CREATE statements, MySQL has the IF EXISTS extension to many DROP statements. For example:

```
mysql> DROP DATABASE IF EXISTS db_does_not_exist;
Query OK, 0 rows affected, 1 warning (0.00 sec)

mysql> SHOW WARNINGS\G
*************************** 1. row ***************************
  Level: Note
   Code: 1008
Message: Can't drop database 'db_does_not_exist'; database
 doesn't exist
1 row in set (0.00 sec)
```

In addition to the IF EXISTS extension to many DROP statements, MySQL extends other DROP statements:

■ DROP TABLE can delete one or more tables in a comma-separated list. For example:

```
mysql> use test;
Database changed
mysql> CREATE TABLE drop_me1 (id int);
Query OK, 0 rows affected (0.35 sec)

mysql> CREATE TABLE drop_me2 (id int);
Query OK, 0 rows affected (0.36 sec)

mysql> SHOW TABLES LIKE 'drop%';
```

```
+------------------------+
| Tables_in_test (drop%) |
+------------------------+
| drop_me1               |
| drop_me2               |
+------------------------+
2 rows in set (0.00 sec)

mysql> DROP TABLE drop_me1, drop_me2;
Query OK, 0 rows affected (0.00 sec)

mysql> SHOW TABLES LIKE 'drop%';
Empty set (0.00 sec)
```

■ Dropping an index with the DROP INDEX statement is nonstandard SQL. MySQL's DROP INDEX extension may take an ONLINE or OFFLINE option. Currently DROP OFFLINE INDEX has no function, as all DROP INDEX commands behave as if specified as DROP ONLINE INDEX.

The LIMIT extension

The LIMIT extension applies mostly to SELECT statements, although other statements may use the same syntax (such as UPDATE, DELETE, and SHOW ERRORS). It is a clause that begins with the reserved word LIMIT and takes one or two numeric arguments. If only one argument is present, it is the number of rows to constrain the output to. For example:

```
mysql> SELECT TABLE_SCHEMA, TABLE_NAME
    -> FROM INFORMATION_SCHEMA.TABLES
    -> WHERE ENGINE='InnoDB'
    -> LIMIT 5;
+--------------+------------+
| TABLE_SCHEMA | TABLE_NAME |
+--------------+------------+
| sakila       | actor      |
| sakila       | actor2     |
| sakila       | address    |
| sakila       | category   |
| sakila       | city       |
+--------------+------------+
5 rows in set (0.03 sec)
```

If the LIMIT clause has two arguments, the first value is the offset and the second value is the number of rows to constrain the output to. The offset starts at 0 (no offset) — thus, a single argument to LIMIT such as LIMIT 5 acts as LIMIT 0,5. To get the middle three records from the previous example, use:

```
mysql> SELECT TABLE_SCHEMA, TABLE_NAME
    -> FROM INFORMATION_SCHEMA.TABLES
    -> WHERE ENGINE='InnoDB'
```

125

```
    -> LIMIT 1,3;
+---------------+------------+
| TABLE_SCHEMA  | TABLE_NAME |
+---------------+------------+
| sakila        | actor2     |
| sakila        | address    |
| sakila        | category   |
+---------------+------------+
3 rows in set (0.03 sec)
```

The syntax for two arguments to LIMIT can be comma separated, as in the example above
(LIMIT 1,3) or it can be specified as LIMIT 3 OFFSET 1.

Although the LIMIT clause can be useful, its implementation is very basic. In order to retrieve
the information, mysqld processes a query as if there were no LIMIT, and stops when it
reaches the row count it needs to. This means that a query, including an ORDER BY or GROUP
BY with a LIMIT, still has to sort all the data. Additionally, a query that has a LIMIT and
specifies an offset will have to process all the rows in the offset first — to retrieve the results
of a query containing the clause LIMIT 99,20, the mysqld server will process 120 rows and
return 20.

The LIMIT clause is the very last clause in a query or subquery.

SELECT extensions

The SELECT statement is one of the most frequently used SQL statements. In standard SQL,
SELECT is a versatile tool for a wide variety of record retrieval and reporting activities. MySQL
has extended the functionality of SELECT with many new nonstandard options and clauses,
some of which relate to performance and backup.

ON the WEBSITE MySQL has extended how the GROUP BY clause interacts with the SELECT
fields by adding more aggregating functions, the WITH ROLLUP clause,
ASC and DESC sort orders, and more. See the accompanying website for this book at
www.wiley.com/go/mysqladminbible for explanations and examples of the GROUP BY
extensions.

The SELECT extensions SQL_CACHE and SQL_NO_CACHE control query interaction with the
mysqld internal query cache. For information about the query cache and how to use these
extensions, see Chapter 12.

SELECT . . . INTO OUTFILE/SELECT . . . INTO DUMPFILE

The SELECT...INTO OUTFILE command is used to create a text file of the contents of database
table. This can be used to logically export an entire table or a subset of the table data. The
mysqldump tool for logical export (See Chapter 13 for more information on mysqldump) can

support filters with its --where option; however it will always export all fields in a table. SELECT...INTO OUTFILE allows you to export only some fields.

By default, SELECT...INTO OUTFILE writes to a the file in datadir, but a location for the file can be specified optionally. The following shows how to export part of sakila.rental:

```
mysql> SELECT rental_id INTO OUTFILE '/tmp/rental-data.sql'
    -> FROM rental WHERE staff_id=1;
Query OK, 8042 rows affected (0.05 sec)
```

SELECT...INTO OUTFILE will not overwrite existing files. If the file specified already exists, mysqld throws an error:

```
ERROR 1086 (HY000): File '/tmp/rental-data.sql' already exists
```

There is no table definition included in the SELECT...INTO OUTFILE so you should make sure to save a copy of the table definition for restoration of the file.

The SELECT INTO DUMPFILE command works similarly to the SELECT...INTO OUTFILE command. However, it will only write one row with no processing of any kind. If you want to dump a BLOB object this would be a good option.

SQL_SMALL_RESULT/SQL_BIG_RESULT

With the SELECT statement the SQL_SMALL_RESULT option can be used in conjunction with the GROUP BY or DISTINCT clauses to specify that the result set of the query will be small enough that the server can use in-memory temporary tables. This could potentially result in faster execution.

The SQL_BIG_RESULT option is used in conjunction with the GROUP BY or DISTINCT clauses to specify that the result set of the query will be too large to fit an in-memory temporary table. Instead, a disk-based temporary table will be constructed.

UNION . . . ORDER BY

The ORDER BY clause can be used with the UNION statement joining two or more SELECT statements to specify a sort order to the returned results. Any column references in the ORDER BY clause are not allowed to include the table name. You should use an alias in the SELECT statement and then use this alias in the ORDER BY clause.

SELECT . . . FOR UPDATE

When using the FOR UPDATE clause a write lock is placed on any rows the SELECT statement processes. This lock is held for the duration of the transaction and released at the end of the transaction. For more information about transaction and locking, see Chapter 9.

SELECT . . . LOCK IN SHARE MODE

When using the LOCK IN SHARE MODE clause a read lock is placed on the rows the SELECT statement processes. Other transactions are allowed to read the locked rows, but they are not allowed to either update or delete any of the locked rows. This lock is released at the end of the transaction. See the "Row level lock" section of Chapter 9 for details on the LOCK IN SHARE MODE extension to SELECT.

DISTINCTROW

The DISTINCTROW option specifies that only distinct rows are returned in the result set of a SELECT statement. DISTINCTROW is a synonym of the SQL standard DISTINCT.

SQL_CALC_FOUND_ROWS

The SQL_CALC_FOUND_ROWS option is used to force mysqld to calculate how many rows are in the result set. After the SELECT with the SQL_CALC_FOUND_ROWS option finishes executing, the row count can be returned with the SELECT FOUND_ROWS() query. The following example demonstrates that using the LIMIT clause does not change the result of this calculation:

```
mysql> SELECT SQL_CALC_FOUND_ROWS rental_date, inventory_id,
    -> customer_id, return_date FROM RENTAL LIMIT 1\G
*************************** 1. row ***************************
rental_date: 2005-05-24 22:53:30
inventory_id: 367
 customer_id: 130
 return_date: 2005-05-26 22:04:30
1 row in set (0.01 sec)
```

In this case the LIMIT clause caused the SELECT to return data from one record. Now to see what the row count was:

```
mysql> SELECT FOUND_ROWS();
+-------------+
| found_rows() |
+-------------+
|       16044 |
+-------------+
1 row in set (0.00 sec)
```

Then to verify that the row count is accurate:

```
mysql> SELECT COUNT(*) FROM RENTAL;
+----------+
| count(*) |
+----------+
|    16044 |
+----------+
1 row in set (0.00 sec)
```

SQL_BUFFER_RESULT

Specifying `SQL_BUFFER_RESULT` in a `SELECT` means that the result sets of `SELECT` statements are placed into temporary tables. With storage engines that use table-level locking this can speed up the release of the table lock. There is a corresponding global system variable, `sql_buffer_result`, which controls this behavior for all `SELECT` statements. By default this system variable is set to 0 (off). Setting this system variable to 1 will enable it, and cause all `SELECT` statements to act as if they were `SELECT SQL_BUFFER_RESULT` statements.

HIGH_PRIORITY/LOW_PRIORITY

See the "Table-level locks" section in Chapter 9 for more information on using `SELECT HIGH_PRIORITY` and `SELECT LOW_PRIORITY` to change the behavior of how `mysqld` chooses the next lock to grant from the read and write lock queues.

■ `DO` — Though not actually a `SELECT` extension, `DO` is a separate statement that can be used instead of `SELECT` to execute a statement and ignore the results. The syntax for `DO` is the same as for `SELECT`. Use `DO` when the query execution is the important part, not the results from the query execution (such as when running queries for the purpose of preloading the query cache). The `SLEEP()` function is a good example of a function whose execution is more important than its results:

```
mysql> SELECT SLEEP(1);
+----------+
| SLEEP(1) |
+----------+
|        0 |
+----------+
1 row in set (1.00 sec)

mysql> DO SLEEP(1);
Query OK, 0 rows affected (1.00 sec)
```

■ `LIMIT` — See the section "The LIMIT extension" in this chapter for details.

■ `PROCEDURE ANALYSE()` — See Chapter 5 for how to use `PROCEDURE ANALYSE()` to determine the optimal data type for fields already populated with data.

■ `EXPLAIN SELECT` — See Chapter 18 for how to use `EXPLAIN SELECT` to analyze query performance.

Server maintenance extensions

MySQL has extended SQL to include server maintenance extensions. Most of these server maintenance extensions are described in other parts of this book; however, for the sake of completeness, they are listed here and the relevant chapter(s) are referenced.

All of the FLUSH statements are written to the binary log by default and will be replicated to any slaves. To change this default behavior, specify NO_WRITE_TO_BINLOG TABLE right after FLUSH, for example:

```
FLUSH NO_WRITE_TO_BINLOG TABLE TABLES;
```

 TIP   LOCAL is a shorter alias for NO_WRITE_TO_BINLOG.

The server maintenance statements are:

- KILL — KILL QUERY thread_id kills the query currently running from the thread_id thread. The values of thread_id for all connections to mysqld are shown in the output of SHOW PROCESSLIST and can be queried in the PROCESSLIST system view in the INFORMATION_SCHEMA database.

- KILL CONNECTION thread_id kills the query and the connection from the thread_id thread. KILL thread_id is an alias for KILL CONNECTION thread_id.

WARNING   The KILL CONNECTION and KILL QUERY statements both kill the query associated with the specified thread_id. However, if a connection is interrupted in any other way, the query will continue until it finishes or mysqld knows the connection has been broken. This means that pressing Ctrl-C to abort a long-running query may only abort the connection, not the query itself!

It is important to always double-check that your expectations match reality. After using the KILL command, run a SHOW PROCESSLIST to ensure that the command is gone or has the status Killed, which means that mysqld is killing the process. After aborting a connection in any other way, reconnect to the database and check SHOW PROCESSLIST to make sure that there are no unwanted queries. This includes connections that were accidentally aborted, such as a network interruption, and programs aborted by external kill commands, such as Ctrl-C or an operating-system-level kill.

- FLUSH HOSTS, FLUSH TABLES, and FLUSH STATUS — These server maintenance extensions can be run as SQL statements in a client. They can also be run via the mysqladmin command line client, specifying flush-hosts, flush-tables, and flush-status. See the "mysqladmin" section of Chapter 3 for the description of what these statements do.

- FLUSH DES_KEY_FILE — Disregard the DES keys currently in memory and reload them from the file specified in the --des_key_file option to mysqld.

- FLUSH LOGS and FLUSH BACKUP LOGS — See Chapter 16 for more information about logs and the FLUSH LOGS and FLUSH BACKUP LOGS statements. FLUSH LOGS can also be run via mysqladmin; see the "mysqladmin" section of Chapter 3 for the description of what the flush-logs option does.

- FLUSH PRIVILEGES and FLUSH USER_RESOURCES — See Chapter 14 for more information about managing permissions and privileges, and the FLUSH PRIVILEGES and FLUSH USER_RESOURCES statements. FLUSH PRIVILEGES can also be run via mysqladmin; see the "mysqladmin" section of Chapter 3 for the description of what the flush-privileges option does.

- FLUSH TABLES WITH READ LOCK — This will lock the tables, preventing modifications from happening until the lock is released, flush MyISAM buffers to disk, and close any open file descriptors. The read lock can be released explicitly by issuing an UNLOCK TABLES command or by issuing a command that implicitly releases the lock.

- FLUSH QUERY CACHE and RESET QUERY CACHE — See Chapter 12 for the query cache and information about the FLUSH QUERY CACHE and RESET QUERY CACHE statements.

- RESET MASTER and RESET SLAVE — See Chapter 22 for information about how RESET MASTER and RESET SLAVE commands are used in replication setups.

- CACHE INDEX...IN — The CACHE INDEX statement is used to configure MyISAM tables to utilize a named key cache. The following command would configure table_one and table_two to use the key cache small_cache instead of the global key cache.

  ```
  mysql> CACHE INDEX table_one, table_two IN small_cache
  ```

  The named key cache must be created before the CACHE INDEX statement is run. To create a key cache called small_cache, you could include the following in your configuration file in the [mysqld] directive:

  ```
  small_cache.key_buffer_size=128M
  ```

- LOAD INDEX INTO CACHE — The LOAD INDEX INTO CACHE statement can be used to preload one ore more tables into a key cache. The key cache can be the default key cache or an explicitly named key cache. To preload the two tables used in the previous example:

  ```
  mysql> LOAD INDEX INTO CACHE table_one, table_two;
  ```

The SET extension and user-defined variables

The SET extension in mysqld is used to assign values to variables. Values can be assigned to user-defined variables, using either of the following syntaxes, which differ only in the assignment operator:

```
SET @varname:=value
SET @varname=value commands
```

In the first example, the assignment operator is := and the second syntax just uses = as the assignment operator. To use a user-defined variable, simply replace any number or string with the variable itself. For example:

```
mysql> SELECT 100+100;
+---------+
| 100+100 |
+---------+
|     200 |
+---------+
1 row in set (0.00 sec)

mysql> SET @num:=100;
Query OK, 0 rows affected (0.05 sec)
```

```
mysql> SELECT @num+100;
+----------+
| @num+100 |
+----------+
|      200 |
+----------+
1 row in set (0.00 sec)

mysql> SELECT @num+@num;
+-----------+
| @num+@num |
+-----------+
|       200 |
+-----------+
1 row in set (0.00 sec)
```

Changing the value of a number is as easy as setting the value:

```
mysql> SET @num:=100+@num;
Query OK, 0 rows affected (0.00 sec)

mysql> SELECT @num;
+------+
| @num |
+------+
|  200 |
+------+
1 row in set (0.00 sec)
```

User-defined variables are local in scope. They cannot be seen by other sessions, and if you exit the session, the user-defined variables are lost. User-defined variables are case-insensitive:

```
mysql> SELECT @NUM;
+------+
| @NUM |
+------+
|  200 |
+------+
1 row in set (0.01 sec)
```

In a SELECT statement, the := assignment operator sets the value of a user-defined variable and returns the new value. For example:

```
mysql> SELECT @num, @num:=@num+100, @num;
+------+----------------+------+
| @num | @num:=@num+100 | @num |
+------+----------------+------+
|  200 |            300 |  300 |
+------+----------------+------+
```

```
1 row in set (0.01 sec)
mysql> SELECT @num, @num:=@num+100, @num;
+--------+----------------+--------+
| @num   | @num:=@num+100 | @num   |
+--------+----------------+--------+
|   300  |            400 |   400  |
+--------+----------------+--------+
1 row in set (0.00 sec)
```

Note how mysqld processes the query from left to right. This is an implementation detail that has been used for many purposes, including row numbering and running totals. For example, Ziesel wants to show a running total of rental fees and the average fee collected. She uses the payment table in the sakila database and two user-defined variables to keep track of the total count (@count) and the total amount of fees collected (@payments):

```
mysql> use sakila;
Database changed
mysql> SET @payments:=0, @count:=0;
Query OK, 0 rows affected (0.00 sec)

mysql> SELECT @count:=@count+1 AS '#', amount,
    -> @payments:=@payments+amount AS running_total,
    -> @payments/@count AS running_avg
    -> FROM payment LIMIT 5;
+------+--------+---------------+-------------+
| #    | amount | running_total | running_avg |
+------+--------+---------------+-------------+
|    1 |   2.99 |          2.99 | 2.990000000 |
|    2 |   0.99 |          3.98 | 1.990000000 |
|    3 |   5.99 |          9.97 | 3.323333333 |
|    4 |   0.99 |         10.96 | 2.740000000 |
|    5 |   9.99 |         20.95 | 4.190000000 |
+------+--------+---------------+-------------+
5 rows in set (0.01 sec)
```

To be able to use the running average after the query is complete, Ziesel initializes a third variable, @run_avg, and changes the query to:

```
SELECT @count:=@count+1 AS '#', amount,
@payments:=@payments+amount AS running_total,
@run_avg:=@payments/@count AS running_avg
FROM payment LIMIT 5;
```

After the query is run, each variable retains its most current value. Ziesel can now use @run_avg in her next reporting query, if she so desires. Or, she can disconnect, and the values of @count, @payments and @run_avg will be NULL.

Local variables in stored code

Setting and manipulating local variables in stored code (such as stored procedures) is also done with SET and SELECT. However, in stored code, variables do not need @ in front of their names. See the sections on local variables in Chapter 7 for examples of how local variables are used in stored code.

Assigning values to dynamic server variables

Dynamic server variables can be changed while mysqld is running — there is no need to restart mysqld for the variable to be set. Server variables can be viewed at a GLOBAL or SESSION scope using SHOW GLOBAL VARIABLES and SHOW SESSION VARIABLES, respectively (see the SHOW extension later in this chapter). Similarly, dynamic server variables can be set on a GLOBAL or SESSION level as in the following:

```
mysql> SET GLOBAL max_allowed_packet=2*1024*1024;
Query OK, 0 rows affected (0.00 sec)

mysql> SET SESSION max_allowed_packet=4*1024*1024;
Query OK, 0 rows affected (0.00 sec)
```

Just as user-defined variables are accessible via a special prefix (@), server variables are similarly accessible, with the (@@) prefix:

```
mysql> SELECT @@global.max_allowed_packet,
    -> @@session.max_allowed_packet\G
*************************** 1. row ***************************
 @@global.max_allowed_packet: 2097152
@@session.max_allowed_packet: 4194304
1 row in set (0.00 sec)

mysql> SET @@session.max_allowed_packet = @@global.max_
 allowed_packet;
Query OK, 0 rows affected (0.00 sec)

mysql> SELECT @@global.max_allowed_packet,  @@session.max_allowed_
 packet\G
*************************** 1. row ***************************
 @@global.max_allowed_packet: 2097152
@@session.max_allowed_packet: 2097152
1 row in set (0.00 sec)
```

> **TIP**   As with SHOW VARIABLES, and SHOW STATUS, the SET server_variable command without a GLOBAL or SESSION scope setting will default to SESSION. To avoid confusion, always specify GLOBAL or SESSION. Similarly, always specify @@global.server_variable or @@session.server_variable in SELECT and SET statements.

The LOCAL and @@local specifiers are aliases for SESSION and @@session, respectively. We recommend using SESSION and @@session so there is no question about the difference between a "local" server variable and a user-defined variable.

The SHOW extension

Metadata is available in the INFORMATION_SCHEMA database (See Chapter 21 for more details). Much of the information in the INFORMATION_SCHEMA database can be retrieved by using the SHOW extension. Although the SHOW syntax is less flexible than querying the INFORMA-TION_SCHEMA database, it is simpler than using a standard SQL query. SHOW statements are usually shorter than a standard SQL query, and thus faster to type. There are some SHOW commands that do not have INFORMATION_SCHEMA equivalents, such as the SHOW CREATE statements, which return CREATE statements.

The sql_quote_show_create system variable is a session-level variable settable via an option file such as my.cnf or via command line. This system variable takes a value of 0 or 1, with 1 being the default. When set to 0, identifiers (such as table, database, and field names) are not quoted:

```
mysql> select @@sql_quote_show_create;
+-------------------------+
| @@sql_quote_show_create |
+-------------------------+
|                       1 |
+-------------------------+
1 row in set (0.00 sec)

mysql> SHOW CREATE DATABASE sakila;
+----------+-----------------------------------------------------+
| Database | Create Database                                     |
+----------+-----------------------------------------------------+
| sakila   | CREATE DATABASE `sakila` /*!40100 DEFAULT           |
|          |      CHARACTER SET latin1 */                         |
+----------+-----------------------------------------------------+
1 row in set (0.41 sec)


mysql> set @@sql_quote_show_create=0;
Query OK, 0 rows affected (0.00 sec)

mysql> SHOW CREATE DATABASE sakila;
+----------+-----------------------------------------------------+
| Database | Create Database                                     |
+----------+-----------------------------------------------------+
| sakila   | CREATE DATABASE sakila /*!40100 DEFAULT             |
|          |      CHARACTER SET latin1 */                         |
+----------+-----------------------------------------------------+
1 row in set (0.00 sec)
```

Many SHOW commands support a LIKE clause, which will return all values where a specific field matches the pattern in the LIKE clause. For example, SHOW CHARACTER SET matches a LIKE pattern to the Charset field:

```
mysql> SHOW CHARACTER SET LIKE 'utf%';
+---------+----------------+--------------------+---------+
| Charset | Description    | Default collation  | Maxlen  |
+---------+----------------+--------------------+---------+
| utf8mb3 | UTF-8 Unicode  | utf8mb3_general_ci |       3 |
| utf8    | UTF-8 Unicode  | utf8_general_ci    |       4 |
| utf16   | UTF-16 Unicode | utf16_general_ci   |       4 |
| utf32   | UTF-32 Unicode | utf32_general_ci   |       4 |
+---------+----------------+--------------------+---------+
4 rows in set (0.00 sec)
```

Some will also support a WHERE clause, which is more flexible than a LIKE clause:

```
mysql> SHOW CHARACTER SET WHERE Maxlen=4;
+---------+----------------+--------------------+---------+
| Charset | Description    | Default collation  | Maxlen  |
+---------+----------------+--------------------+---------+
| utf8    | UTF-8 Unicode  | utf8_general_ci    |       4 |
| utf16   | UTF-16 Unicode | utf16_general_ci   |       4 |
| utf32   | UTF-32 Unicode | utf32_general_ci   |       4 |
+---------+----------------+--------------------+---------+
3 rows in set (0.00 sec)
```

These WHERE clauses can support multiple conditions:

```
mysql> SHOW CHARACTER SET WHERE Maxlen=4 AND Charset LIKE '%8';
+---------+----------------+--------------------+---------+
| Charset | Description    | Default collation  | Maxlen  |
+---------+----------------+--------------------+---------+
| utf8    | UTF-8 Unicode  | utf8_general_ci    |       4 |
+---------+----------------+--------------------+---------+
1 row in set (0.00 sec)
```

The SHOW commands are:

- SHOW AUTHORS — Takes no input. Displays Name, Location and a Comment about the various authors of the MySQL codebase.
- SHOW BINLOG EVENTS — See "Replication and Logging," Chapter 16.
- SHOW BINARY LOGS — See "Replication and Logging," Chapter 16.
- SHOW CHARACTER SET — Displays the name (Charset), Description, Default collation and maximum number of bytes required to store one character (Maxlen) for the character sets supported by the mysqld server. This does not require input, although both LIKE and WHERE clauses are supported. LIKE matches against the Charset field.

- The CHARACTER_SETS system view in the INFORMATION_SCHEMA database contains the same information as the SHOW CHARACTER SET statement. The corresponding fields are CHARACTER_SET_NAME, DEFAULT_COLLATE_NAME, DESCRIPTION, and MAXLEN.

- SHOW COLLATION — Displays the name (Collation), character set (Charset), Id, whether or not it is the default collation for its character set (Default), whether it is compiled into the server (Compiled), and the amount of memory in bytes that is required to sort using this collation (Sortlen). This does not require input, although both LIKE and WHERE clauses are supported. LIKE matches against the Collation field.

- The COLLATIONS system view in the INFORMATION_SCHEMA database contains the same information as the SHOW COLLATION statement. The corresponding fields are COLLATION_NAME, CHARACTER_SET_NAME, ID, IS_COMPILED, and IS_DEFAULT and SORTLEN.

- SHOW COLUMNS — See the information for the COLUMNS system view in Chapter 21, "MySQL Data Dictionary."

- SHOW CONTRIBUTORS — Takes no input. Displays Name, Location, and a Comment about a few contributors to causes supported by the former company MySQL AB.

- SHOW COUNT(*) ERRORS — Displays the value of the error_count session variable:

```
mysql> SHOW COUNT(*) ERRORS;
+----------------------+
| @@session.error_count |
+----------------------+
|                    0 |
+----------------------+
1 row in set (0.00 sec)
```

SHOW ERRORS provides more information about the error(s) from the previous command that generated errors. Supports the LIMIT clause (see the section "The LIMIT extension" earlier in this chapter).

- SHOW COUNT(*) WARNINGS — Displays the value of the warning_count session variable. SHOW WARNINGS provides more information about the error(s) from the previous command that generated errors, warnings or notes.

- SHOW CREATE DATABASE — Requires a database name as an input. Displays the name of the database (Database) and a CREATE statement that can be used to create the database (Create Database). For example:

```
mysql> SHOW CREATE DATABASE sakila;
+----------+-------------------------------------------------------------+
| Database | Create Database                                             |
+----------+-------------------------------------------------------------+
| sakila   | CREATE DATABASE `sakila` /*!40100 DEFAULT
  CHARACTER SET latin1 */                                      |
+----------+-------------------------------------------------------------+
1 row in set (0.41 sec)
```

A synonym for SHOW CREATE DATABASE is SHOW CREATE SCHEMA. See Chapter 21 for information on the SCHEMATA system view in the INFORMATION_SCHEMA database.

- SHOW CREATE EVENT — Requires an event name as an input. Displays the name of the event (Event), a CREATE statement that can be used to create the event (Create Event), the character set of the session in which the event was created (character_set_client), the collation of the session in which the event was created (collation_connection), and the collation of the database that the event is associated with (Database Collation). See Chapter 7 for more information on events, and Chapter 21 for information on the EVENTS system view in the INFORMATION_SCHEMA database.

- SHOW CREATE FUNCTION — Requires a function name as an input. Displays the name of the function (Function), a CREATE statement that can be used to create the function (Create Function), the character set of the session in which the function was created (character_set_client), the collation of the session in which the function was created (collation_connection), and the collation of the database that the function is associated with (Database Collation). See Chapter 7 for more information on stored functions, and Chapter 21 for information on the ROUTINES system view in the INFORMATION_SCHEMA database.

- SHOW CREATE PROCEDURE — Requires a procedure name as an input. Displays the name of the procedure (Procedure), a CREATE statement that can be used to create the procedure (Create Procedure), the character set of the session in which the procedure was created (character_set_client), the collation of the session in which the procedure was created (collation_connection), and the collation of the database that the procedure is associated with (Database Collation). See Chapter 7 for more information on stored procedures, and Chapter 21 for information on the ROUTINES system view in the INFORMATION_SCHEMA database.

- SHOW CREATE SCHEMA — See SHOW CREATE DATABASE.

- SHOW CREATE TABLE — Requires a table name as an input. Displays the name of the table (Table) and a CREATE statement that can be used to create the table (Create Table). See Chapter 21 for information on the TABLES system view in the INFORMATION_SCHEMA database.

- SHOW CREATE TRIGGER — Requires a trigger name as an input. Displays the name of the trigger (Trigger), the sql_mode of the session in which the trigger was created (sql_mode), a CREATE statement that can be used to create the trigger (SQL Original Statement), the character set of the session in which the trigger was created (character_set_client), the collation of the session in which the trigger was created (collation_connection), and the collation of the database that the trigger is associated with (Database Collation). See Chapter 7 for more information on triggers, and Chapter 21 for information on the TRIGGERS system view in the INFORMATION_SCHEMA database.

- SHOW CREATE VIEW — Requires a view name as an input. Displays the name of the view (View), a CREATE statement that can be used to create the view (Create View), the character set of the session in which the view was created (character_set_client), and the collation of the session in which the view was created (collation_connection). See Chapter 8 for more information on views, and Chapter 21 for information on the VIEWS system view in the INFORMATION_SCHEMA database.

- SHOW DATABASES — Displays the database name (Database). Does not require input, although both LIKE and WHERE clauses are supported. LIKE matches against the Database field.

  The SCHEMATA system view in the INFORMATION_SCHEMA database contains the same information as the SHOW DATABASES statement. The corresponding field is SCHEMA_NAME. The SCHEMATA system view also contains the DEFAULT_CHARACTER_SET_NAME and DEFAULT_COLLATION for the database, which the SHOW command does not contain.

- SHOW ENGINE — Requires an engine name and what type of information to see. Supported statements are:

  - SHOW ENGINE INNODB STATUS — Displays information about semaphores, foreign key errors, transactions, file I/O, the insert buffer, the adaptive hash index, logs, buffers and buffer pool, and row operations.

  - SHOW ENGINE INNODB MUTEX — Displays information about mutexes: Type (always Innodb), the source file where the mutex was created (Name) and Status, which contains a comma-separated set or subset of the following values:

  - count — How many times the mutex was requested.

  - spin_waits — How many times the spinlock ran.

  - spin_rounds — How many spinlock rounds.

  - os_waits — How many times the operating system had to wait due to a spinlock failing to acquire a mutex lock.

  - os_wait_times — If the timed_mutexes variable is set to 1, how much time, in ms, was spent on waiting for the operating system. This value is 0 if the timed_mutexes system variable is set to 0 or OFF, which it is by default.

  - os_yields — How many times the thread acquiring a mutex lock yielded to the operating system, giving up its time slice, in the hope that yielding will remove the barriers to acquiring the mutex lock.

  For example:

```
mysql> SHOW ENGINE INNODB MUTEX;
+---------+------------------------+------------+
| Type    | Name                   | Status     |
+---------+------------------------+------------+
| InnoDB  | trx/trx0trx.c:143      | os_waits=0 |
| InnoDB  | dict/dict0dict.c:1365  | os_waits=0 |
```

```
| InnoDB | dict/dict0mem.c:90   | os_waits=0 |
| InnoDB | dict/dict0dict.c:1365 | os_waits=0 |
| InnoDB | dict/dict0dict.c:1365 | os_waits=0 |
| InnoDB | dict/dict0dict.c:1365 | os_waits=0 |
| InnoDB | dict/dict0mem.c:90   | os_waits=0 |
...
```

Debugging InnoDB mutexes is beyond the scope of this book.

If mysqld supports the NDB cluster storage engine, SHOW ENGINE NDB STATUS and SHOW ENGINE NDBCLUSTER STATUS are supported. Either command will show information about the NDB storage engine.

■   SHOW ENGINES — Takes no input. Displays information about storage engines, including name (Engine), how mysqld supports it (Support), Comment, and whether the storage engine supports transactions, XA, and savepoints. See Chapter 11 for more information on storage engines, and Chapter 21 for information on the ENGINES system view in the INFORMATION_SCHEMA database.

Values for Support include DEFAULT (for the default storage engine), YES (for usable supported storage engines), and DISABLED (for supported storage engines that cannot be used). The NO value is not applicable, because storage engines can be runtime plugins.

■   SHOW ERRORS — Displays the error number(s) and description(s) from the last command that generated an error. Supports the LIMIT clause (see the section "The LIMIT extension" earlier in this chapter).

■   SHOW EVENTS — Displays the database the event is associated with (Db), Name, Definer, Time zone, Type (ONE TIME or RECURRING), Execute at (non-NULL for a ONE TIME event), Interval_value (non-NULL for a RECURRING event), Interval_Field (non-NULL for a RECURRING event), Starts (non-NULL for a RECURRING event), Ends (non-NULL for a RECURRING event), Status (ENABLED, DISABLED or SLAVESIDE_DISABLED), the server-id of the mysqld instance that created the event (Originator), the character set of the session in which the event was created (character_set_client), the collation of the session in which the event was created (collation_connection), and the collation of the database that the event is associated with (Database Collation).

SHOW EVENTS does not require input. Without input, SHOW EVENTS will show all events associated with the current database. If there is no current database, error 1046 occurs:

```
mysql> SHOW EVENTS;
ERROR 1046 (3D000): No database selected
```

To show events from a particular database, specify SHOW EVENTS FROM db_name. Both the LIKE and WHERE clauses are supported, and either can occur alone or with a FROM clause. LIKE matches against the Name field.

The EVENTS system view in the INFORMATION_SCHEMA database contains the same information as the SHOW EVENTS statement. The corresponding fields are EVENT_SCHEMA, EVENT_NAME, DEFINER, TIME_ZONE, EVENT_TYPE, EXECUTE_AT. The EVENTS system view also contains the EVENT_BODY (always SQL), EVENT_DEFINITION, SQL_MODE,

ON_COMPLETION, CREATED, LAST_ALTERED, LAST_EXECUTED, and EVENT_COMMENT for the event, which the SHOW command does not contain. See Chapter 7 for more information on events, and Chapter 21 for more information about the EVENTS system view in the INFORMATION_SCHEMA database.

- SHOW FULL TABLES — See SHOW TABLES.

- SHOW FUNCTION CODE — Displays the ordinal position (Pos) and Instruction for each step in a stored function. This is only valid if mysqld was compiled with --with-debug:

```
mysql> SHOW FUNCTION CODE sakila.inventory_in_stock;
ERROR 1289 (HY000): The 'SHOW PROCEDURE|FUNCTION CODE'
feature is disabled; you need MySQL built with '--with-
debug' to have it working
```

This is useful for debugging stored functions.

- SHOW FUNCTION STATUS — Displays the database the function is associated with (Db), Name, Type (FUNCTION), Definer, Modified, Created, Security_type (DEFINER or INVOKER), Comment, the character set of the session in which the event was created (character_set_client), the collation of the session in which the event was created (collation_connection), and the collation of the database that the event is associated with (Database Collation). See Chapter 7 for more information on stored functions, and Chapter 21 for information on the ROUTINES system view in the INFORMATION_SCHEMA database.

Without input, SHOW FUNCTION STATUS will show all functions associated with all databases. Both the LIKE and WHERE clauses are supported, and either can occur alone or with a FROM clause. LIKE matches against the Name field.

- SHOW GRANTS — Displays the GRANT statement(s) that can be used to re-create the privileges for a particular user@host. With no input, SHOW GRANTS displays grant statements for the current user@host, which can be seen in the output of SELECT CURRENT_USER(). A different user@host, is specified with a FOR clause, for example:

```
SHOW GRANTS FOR guest@localhost;
```

- SHOW INDEX — Displays the index information for a table. For the meaning of the fields, see the information about the STATISTICS system view in the INFORMATION_SCHEMA database, in Chapter 21.

A table name is required as part of a FROM clause. A database may be specified by using a second FROM clause. The following are all equivalent and will produce the output shown here:

```
SHOW INDEX FROM sakila.country\G
SHOW INDEX FROM country FROM sakila\G
USE sakila; SHOW INDEX FROM COUNTRY\G
*************************** 1. row ***************************
        Table: country
    Non_unique: 0
```

```
         Key_name: PRIMARY
     Seq_in_index: 1
      Column_name: country_id
        Collation: A
      Cardinality: 109
         Sub_part: NULL
           Packed: NULL
             Null:
       Index_type: BTREE
          Comment:
    Index_Comment:
1 row in set (0.00 sec)
```

SHOW INDEXES and SHOW KEYS are aliases for SHOW INDEX.

■ SHOW INDEXES — See SHOW INDEX.

■ SHOW KEYS — See SHOW INDEX.

■ SHOW MASTER STATUS — "See Replication and Logging" in Chapter 16.

■ SHOW OPEN TABLES — Displays information about currently open tables. A table is open if a thread is using it, and the number of open tables depends on how many threads have opened a table. If two different threads use the same table, there are two open tables — because each thread opens the table. The table_open_cache server variable can be used to cache open tables to reduce the overhead of opening and closing the same table.

■ SHOW OPEN TABLES — For each currently open non-temporary table, SHOW OPEN TABLES displays the Database, Table, whether or not the open table is being used (In_use), and whether the table name is locked (Name_locked, value is 1 when renaming and dropping tables). Without input, SHOW OPEN TABLES will show all open tables from all databases. To show open tables from a particular database, specify SHOW OPEN TABLES FROM db_name. Both the LIKE and WHERE clauses are supported, and either can occur alone or with a FROM clause. LIKE matches against the Table field:

```
mysql> SHOW OPEN TABLES from mysql LIKE 't%';
+----------+----------------------------+--------+-------------+
| Database | Table                      | In_use | Name_locked |
+----------+----------------------------+--------+-------------+
| mysql    | time_zone                  |      0 |           0 |
| mysql    | time_zone_name             |      0 |           0 |
| mysql    | time_zone_transition_type  |      0 |           0 |
| mysql    | time_zone_leap_second      |      0 |           0 |
| mysql    | time_zone_transition       |      0 |           0 |
| mysql    | tables_priv                |      0 |           0 |
+----------+----------------------------+--------+-------------+
6 rows in set (0.00 sec)
```

- SHOW PLUGINS — Displays the Name, Status, Type, filename of the plugin (Library, NULL for built-in plugins such as storage engines) and License. For the meaning of the fields, see the information about the PLUGINS system view in the INFORMATION_SCHEMA database, in Chapter 21. The PLUGINS system view also contains additional information, including the PLUGIN_VERSION, PLUGIN_TYPE_VERSION (specifies which version of mysqld the plugin supports), IN_LIBRARY_VERSION, PLUGIN_AUTHOR, and PLUGIN_DESCRIPTION.

- SHOW PRIVILEGES — Display the name (Privilege), Context and Comment about each type of privilege that can be used in a GRANT statement. See the "Permissions" section of Chapter 21, "The MySQL Data Dictionary", for more information.

- SHOW PROCEDURE CODE — Displays the ordinal position (Pos) and Instruction for each step in a stored procedure. This is only valid if mysqld was compiled with --with-debug:

```
mysql> SHOW PROCEDURE CODE sakila.rewards_report;
ERROR 1289 (HY000): The 'SHOW PROCEDURE|FUNCTION CODE'
feature is disabled; you need MySQL built with '--with-
debug' to have it working
```

This is useful for debugging stored procedures.

- SHOW PROCEDURE STATUS — Displays the database that the procedure is associated with (Db), Name, Type (PROCEDURE), Definer, Modified, Created, Security_type (DEFINER or INVOKER), Comment, the character set of the session in which the event was created (character_set_client), the collation of the session in which the event was created (collation_connection), and the collation of the database that the event is associated with (Database Collation). See Chapter 7 for more information on stored procedures, and Chapter 21 for information on the ROUTINES system view in the INFORMATION_SCHEMA database.

- Without input, SHOW PROCEDURE STATUS will show all procedures associated with all databases. Both the LIKE and WHERE clauses are supported, and either can occur alone or with a FROM clause. LIKE matches against the Name field.

- SHOW PROCESSLIST — See the information in Chapter 21, The MySQL Data Dictionary, for the PROCESSLIST system view in the INFORMATION_SCHEMA database.

- SHOW PROFILE — As of MySQL version 6.0.5, query profiling can be done on a session-level basis. By default, the profiling session variable is set to 0 and the PROFILING system view has no rows. If it is set to 1, queries can be profiled. The output of SHOW PROFILE is the Status and Duration of each step:

```
mysql> SHOW PROFILE;
Empty set (0.00 sec)

mysql> SET profiling=1;
Query OK, 0 rows affected (0.00 sec)
```

```
mysql> SELECT COUNT(*) FROM sakila.film;
+----------+
| COUNT(*) |
+----------+
|     1000 |
+----------+
1 row in set (0.00 sec)

mysql> SHOW PROFILE;
+--------------------+----------+
| Status             | Duration |
+--------------------+----------+
| starting           | 0.000126 |
| Opening tables     | 0.000057 |
| System lock        | 0.000016 |
| Table lock         | 0.000013 |
| init               | 0.000018 |
| optimizing         | 0.000009 |
| statistics         | 0.000018 |
| preparing          | 0.000014 |
| executing          | 0.000008 |
| Sending data       | 0.000634 |
| end                | 0.000010 |
| query end          | 0.000007 |
| freeing items      | 0.000054 |
| logging slow query | 0.000006 |
| cleaning up        | 0.000020 |
+--------------------+----------+
15 rows in set (0.00 sec)
```

This is very useful for debugging exactly why a query takes a long time.

Without input, SHOW PROFILE displays profiling information for the most recent query. With a FOR QUERY n clause, profiling information will be shown for the query with a Query_ID of n. The Query_ID value is obtained from the SHOW PROFILES statement. SHOW PROFILE accepts the LIMIT clause (see The LIMIT Extension earlier in this chapter).

The SHOW PROFILE statement also accepts an optional comma-separated list of extra information to show in addition to Status and Duration. Table 4-4 shows the values and the information returned (for the description of the fields, please refer to the information in Chapter 21 about the PROFILING system view.

To show partial output with the CPU and Source information for our sample query (SELECT COUNT(*) FROM sakila.film):

```
mysql> SHOW PROFILE CPU, SOURCE FOR QUERY 1 LIMIT 2 OFFSET 0\G
*************************** 1. row ***************************
   Status: starting
 Duration: 0.000126
```

```
          CPU_user: 0.000109
        CPU_system: 0.000016
   Source_function: NULL
       Source_file: NULL
       Source_line: NULL
*************************** 2. row ***************************
            Status: Opening tables
          Duration: 0.000057
          CPU_user: 0.000033
        CPU_system: 0.000023
   Source_function: open_tables
       Source_file: sql_base.cc
       Source_line: 3588
2 rows in set (0.00 sec)
```

TABLE 4-4

SHOW PROFILE Extra Field Information

Extra Name in SHOW PROFILE Statement	Fields Shown
ALL	Status, Duration, CPU_user, CPU_system, Context_voluntary, Context_involuntary, Block_ops_in, Block_ops_out, Messages_sent, Messages_received, Page_faults_major, Page_faults_minor, Swaps, Source_function, Source_file, Source_line
BLOCK IO	Status, Duration, Block_ops_in, Block_ops_out
CONTEXT SWITCHES	Status, Duration, Context_voluntary, Context_involuntary
CPU	Status, Duration, CPU_user, CPU_system
IPC	Status, Duration, Messages_sent, Messages_received
MEMORY	Status, Duration
PAGE FAULTS	Status, Duration, Page_faults_major, Page_faults_minor
SOURCE	Status, Duration, Source_function, Source_file, Source_line
SWAPS	Status, Duration, Swaps

■ SHOW PROFILES — As of MySQL version 6.0.5, query profiling can be done on a session-level basis. By default, the profiling session variable is set to 0 and the

PROFILING system view has no rows. If it is set to 1, queries can be profiled. The SHOW PROFILES statement is related to, but very different from, the SHOW PROFILE statement. SHOW PROFILES outputs profiling information for the most recent queries. There is one query per row, and the maximum number of queries shown is determined by the profiling_history_size session variable. This session variable also restricts the number of queries that are saved in the PROFILING system view.

```
mysql> SHOW PROFILES;
+----------+------------+-----------------------------------+
| Query_ID | Duration   | Query                             |
+----------+------------+-----------------------------------+
|        1 | 0.00101000 | SELECT COUNT(*) FROM sakila.film  |
+----------+------------+-----------------------------------+
1 row in set (0.00 sec)
```

- SHOW SCHEMAS — See SHOW DATABASES.
- SHOW SLAVE HOSTS — See "Replication and Logging," Chapter 16.
- SHOW SLAVE STATUS — See "Replication and Logging," Chapter 16.
- SHOW STATUS — See the information in Chapter 21 on the GLOBAL_STATUS and SESSION_STATUS system views in the INFORMATION_SCHEMA database.

> **WARNING** SHOW STATUS **shows session variables by default. To avoid confusion, always specify either** SHOW GLOBAL STATUS **or** SHOW SESSION STATUS**.**

- SHOW TABLE STATUS — See the information in Chapter 21 on the TABLES system view in the INFORMATION_SCHEMA database.
- SHOW STORAGE ENGINES — See SHOW ENGINES.
- SHOW TABLES — Displays table names in an output field beginning with Tables_in_. Without input, SHOW TABLES will show all tables and views associated with the current database. If there is no current database, error 1046 occurs:

```
mysql> SHOW TABLES;
ERROR 1046 (3D000): No database selected
```

To show tables and views from a particular database, specify SHOW TABLES FROM db_name. Both the LIKE and WHERE clauses are supported, and either can occur alone or with a FROM clause. LIKE matches against the Tables_in_ field:

```
mysql> SHOW TABLES LIKE 'f%';
+-----------------------+
| Tables_in_sakila (f%) |
+-----------------------+
| film                  |
| film_actor            |
| film_category         |
| film_list             |
| film_text             |
+-----------------------+
5 rows in set (0.00 sec)
```

SHOW FULL TABLES adds one field to the information in SHOW TABLES. Table_type, specifies whether the table is a base table, view or system view:

```
mysql> SHOW FULL TABLES LIKE 'f%';
+-----------------------+------------+
| Tables_in_sakila (f%) | Table_type |
+-----------------------+------------+
| film                  | BASE TABLE |
| film_actor            | BASE TABLE |
| film_category         | BASE TABLE |
| film_list             | VIEW       |
| film_text             | BASE TABLE |
+-----------------------+------------+
5 rows in set (0.01 sec)
```

Only the INFORMATION_SCHEMA views are system views. See Chapter 8 for more information on views, and Chapter 21 for detailed information about the INFORMATION_SCHEMA database.

- SHOW TRIGGERS — See the information in Chapter 21 on the TRIGGERS system view in the INFORMATION_SCHEMA database.

- SHOW VARIABLES–See the information in Chapter 21 on the GLOBAL_VARIABLES and SESSION_VARIABLES system views in the INFORMATION_SCHEMA database.

WARNING SHOW VARIABLES shows session variables by default. To avoid confusion, always specify either SHOW GLOBAL VARIABLES or SHOW SESSION VARIABLES.

- SHOW WARNINGS — Displays the error, warning and note number(s) and description(s) from the last command that generated an error, warning, or note. Supports the LIMIT clause (see "The LIMIT extension" earlier in this chapter).

Table definition extensions

MySQL has added features to tables, which require extended SQL syntax in order to specify. The following SQL extensions are related to nonstandard table features in MySQL:

- AUTO_INCREMENT=num — Set the AUTO_INCREMENT value for the table. See Chapter 5 for more details on AUTO_INCREMENT.

- AVG_ROW_LENGTH=num — Set the average row length. This helps mysqld allocate proper space for records and is only applicable for very large MyISAM tables (over 256 Tb). See the MySQL manual at http://dev.mysql.com/doc/refman/6.0/en/create-table.html for more details on when and how to set this parameter, and how other variables interact.

- CHARACTER SET charset_name — Specify the default character set for fields created in this table. See the "Character sets and collations" section earlier in this chapter for more information.

- CHECKSUM=1 — This will enable a *live* checksum of a table. Every time a record is changed, the checksum is updated. Tables with CHECKSUM=1 keep the current value of CHECKSUM TABLE tblname stored in their metadata, using very little overhead. Setting

CHECKSUM=0 will disable this feature. This feature only works on MyISAM tables and is set to 0 by default.

- COLLATE collation_name — Specify the default collation for fields created in this table. See the "Character sets and collations" section earlier in this chapter for more information.

- COMMENT='comment string' — Give the table a descriptive comment, that can be seen in the TABLES system view of the INFORMATION_SCHEMA database and in the output of SHOW TABLE STATUS and SHOW CREATE TABLE.

   Fields and indexes can also be given a comment within a definition in a CREATE TABLE or ALTER TABLE statement. The COMMENT 'comment string' syntax gives the field or index a descriptive comment that can be seen in the COLUMNS (for fields) or STATISTICS (for indexes) system views of the INFORMATION_SCHEMA database and in the output of SHOW CREATE TABLE. Note that unlike the COMMENT option for a table, for fields and indexes the COMMENT keyword is separated from the comment string by a space, not an equals sign (=).

- CONNECTION='connection string' — For tables using the FEDERATED storage engine, this specifies the connection information. See Chapter 11 for more information on the FEDERATED storage engine and how to specify a connection string.

- DATA DIRECTORY='path_to_dir' — MyISAM tables will store their .MYD files in the path_to_dir directory. This option is ignored for ALTER TABLE statements but is honored in most CREATE TABLE statements — the exception is when a table is created with partitioning, the table-level DATA DIRECTORY option is ignored.

- DELAY_KEY_WRITE=1 — This will delay index buffer updates until a table is closed and then update an index buffer all at once. This makes writes faster, as index updates are batched, but can lead to corruption. DELAY_KEY_WRITE=0 will flush the index buffer every time the index is updated. This option is only for MyISAM tables. In addition, this option depends on the value of the system variable delay_key_write. By default, delay_key_write is set to ON, which means that MyISAM tables default to a DELAY_KEY_WRITE value of 0. If the delay_key_write server variable is set to OFF, no MyISAM tables delay key writes even if DELAY_KEY_WRITE is set to 1. If the delay_key_write server variable is set to ALL, the default setting for DELAY_KEY_WRITE is 1.

- ENGINE=storage_engine_name — This sets the storage engine of the table. For more information about storage engines, see Chapter 11.

- INDEX DIRECTORY='path_to_dir' — MyISAM tables will store their .MYI files in the path_to_dir directory. This option is ignored for ALTER TABLE statements but is honored in most CREATE TABLE statements — the exception is when a table is created with partitioning, the table-level INDEX DIRECTORY option is ignored.

- INSERT_METHOD=method_name — Sets how an INSERT to a MERGE table should behave. If method_name is set to FIRST, records will be inserted into the first table in the UNION definition. If method_name is set to LAST, records will be inserted into the last table in the UNION definition. If method_name is set to NO, the table will be marked as read-only and an insert into the merge table will result in an error:

```
ERROR 1036 (HY000): Table 'merge_test' is read only
```

■ KEY_BLOCK_SIZE=num — The value of num is given to the storage engine as a suggested index block size. The storage engine may or may not use the value of num. The default is 0, which indicates that the storage engine should use its default index block size.

■ MAX_ROWS=num — This helps mysqld allocate proper space for records and is only applicable for very large MyISAM tables (over 256 Tb). See the MySQL manual at http://dev.mysql.com/doc/refman/6.0/en/create-table.html for more details on when and how to set this parameter, and how other variables interact.

■ MIN_ROWS=num — The minimum number of rows expected to be stored in this table.

■ PACK_KEYS=value — The default value is DEFAULT, which specifies that for MyISAM tables, long indexes for CHAR, VARCHAR, BINARY, and VARBINARY fields are compressed. If value is set to 1, number fields are also compressed. If value is set to 0, no indexes are compressed.

Partitioning-related extensions include defining partitions and subpartitions with PARTITION BY, and changing partitioning with ADD PARTITION, DROP PARTITION, COALESCE PARTITION, REORGANIZE PARTITION, ANALYZE PARTITION, CHECK PARTITION, OPTIMIZE PARTITION, REBUILD PARTITION, REPAIR PARTITION, and REMOVE PARTITIONING. These are discussed in Chapter 15.

■ PASSWORD='password_string' — This option provides no functionality.

■ ROW_FORMAT='row_format_name' — Currently there are six different row format types. Each storage engine uses one or more of the following row format types:

  ■ Default — Uses the default row format for the storage engine.

  ■ Compact — The default InnoDB row format. Uses more processing power, storing less data.

  ■ Redundant — An older InnoDB row format. Requires less processing power but stores redundant data.

  ■ Fixed — Rows are a fixed-width, minimizing fragmentation. Fixed is the default for MyISAM, Falcon, BLACKHOLE, CSV, and MEMORY storage engines, and is used unless the table contains a variable-width field.

  ■ Dynamic — Rows are variable-width, containing one or more variable-width fields, such as VARCHAR, TEXT or BLOB. Used by the MyISAM, Falcon, BLACKHOLE, and CSV storage engines.

  ■ Page — The Maria storage engine uses the Page row format by default. No other storage engine uses this row format.

  ■ Compressed — Rows are compressed and read-only. Compressed is the default and only row format for the ARCHIVE storage engine and MyISAM tables when compressed with myisampack.

- UNION=(tbl_list) — In a MERGE table, the UNION clause specifies a comma-separated list of tables that the MERGE table is a wrapper for. The first and last table names in this list are the tables used when INSERT_METHOD is set to FIRST and LAST, respectively. See Chapter 11 for more information on MERGE tables.

Table maintenance extensions

Indexes stay up to date with regard to the data within the index data structure. However, indexes require periodic maintenance for stability, speed and metadata updates. Table maintenance solves the following problems:

- Out-of-date table structure
- Index and data corruption
- Index and data fragmentation
- Out-of-date index and data statistics

MySQL has several commands to maintain index and table data:

- CHECK TABLE
- REPAIR TABLE
- CHECKSUM TABLE
- ANALYZE TABLE
- OPTIMIZE TABLE

Index and data corruption

Corruption can occur to both the data and the indexes belonging to a table, and may occur for several reasons. The most common cause of corruption is when data and index files are changed at the file system level, or when mysqld crashes, such as when there is not enough RAM or the host machine is turned off abruptly without shutting down mysqld properly. Other, more infrequent causes of table corruption are hardware problems, such as a malfunctioning RAID controller or corrupted RAM, and bugs in the client code, mysqld code, or storage engine code.

To determine if a table has corruption, use the CHECK TABLE command:

```
mysql> USE sakila;
Database changed
mysql> CHECK TABLE film\G
*************************** 1. row ***************************
   Table: sakila.film
      Op: check
Msg_type: status
Msg_text: OK
1 row in set (0.02 sec)
```

CHECK TABLE is only supported by tables using the MyISAM, InnoDB, ARCHIVE, and CSV storage engines. If you try to use CHECK TABLE on a table that does not support it, the Msg_text field of the output contains:

```
The storage engine for the table doesn't support check
```

Other storage engines such as Falcon, PBXT, and Maria implement their own methods of checking for table corruption and performing repairs; See Chapter 11 for more details. When table corruption does occur, the output from CHECK TABLE will include a Msg_type of error and the Msg_text field will describe the problem:

```
mysql> CHECK TABLE film_text\G
*************************** 1. row ***************************
   Table: sakila.film_text
      Op: check
Msg_type: error
Msg_text: Unexpected byte: 5 at link: 1065187756
*************************** 2. row ***************************
   Table: sakila.film_text
      Op: check
Msg_type: error
Msg_text: Corrupt
2 rows in set (54.18 sec)
```

CHECK TABLE takes a comma-separated list of one or more tables and supports the following options:

- EXTENDED — As the name implies, this takes a longer time to run than any other option. However, this option will perform a full lookup on all keys and indexes, checking for 100% data consistency.

- MEDIUM — This is the default option used if no option is specified. For every table, calculate a checksum for the indexes on each data row, comparing the final result to the checksum of the index rows. Also verify that deleted links are valid.

- CHANGED — Only check a table if it was changed since the last time it was checked, or if the table was not closed properly. If a table is checked, the checks that are done are the same as the MEDIUM option.

- FAST — Only check a table if it was not closed properly. If a table is checked, the checks that are done are the same as the MEDIUM option.

- QUICK — Calculate a checksum for the indexes on each data row, comparing the final result to the checksum of the index rows. Same as MEDIUM, without the verification for deleted links.

- FOR UPGRADE — Checks to see if the table is out of date due to a server upgrade. Although this is a quick check, if the table is found to be out of date, a MEDIUM check will be run automatically, which can take some time.

Options are specified after the list of tables:

```
mysql> CHECK TABLE film_text, film FAST;
+------------------+-------+-----------+------------------------------+
| Table            | Op    | Msg_type  | Msg_text                     |
+------------------+-------+-----------+------------------------------+
| sakila.film_text | check | status    | Table is already up to date  |
| sakila.film      | check | status    | OK                           |
+------------------+-------+-----------+------------------------------+
2 rows in set (0.01 sec)
```

Other common warnings and errors are described in the following list. Note that these are actual errors we have encountered, but the table names have been changed to sakila.film_text to protect privacy:

- Table './sakila/film_text' is marked as crashed and should be repaired
- 1 client is using or hasn't closed the table properly
- Incorrect information in file: './sakila/film_text.frm'
- Table './sakila/film_text' is marked as crashed and last (automatic?) repair failed
- Invalid key block position: 284290829344833891 key block size: 1024 file_length: 4453643264
- key delete-link-chain corrupted
- Table 'sakila.film_text' doesn't exist
- Record-count is not ok; is 330426316 Should be: 330426389
- Size of datafile is: 0 Should be: 172
- Found 1533 deleted space. Should be 0
- Found 73 deleted blocks Should be: 0

If CHECK TABLE returns a Msg_type of error, you will need to attempt to fix the problem. The first step to try when fixing a corrupt table is REPAIR TABLE. Only the MyISAM, ARCHIVE, and CSV storage engines support REPAIR TABLE, and you must have the INSERT and SELECT privileges on the tables you want to repair. The following example shows a successful REPAIR TABLE command, followed by a CHECK TABLE command as a sanity check to ensure that the table is actually not corrupt anymore:

```
mysql> REPAIR TABLE film_text\G
*************************** 1. row ***************************
   Table: sakila.film_text
      Op: repair
Msg_type: warning
Msg_text: Number of rows changed from 4733691 to 4733690
*************************** 2. row ***************************
   Table: sakila.film_text
      Op: repair
```

```
    Msg_type: status
    Msg_text: OK
2 rows in set (5min 24.40 sec)

mysql> CHECK TABLE film_text\G
*************************** 1. row ***************************
    Table: sakila.film_text
       Op: check
 Msg_type: status
 Msg_text: OK
1 row in set (36.08 sec)
```

Note that the REPAIR TABLE in this case took almost five and a half minutes. REPAIR TABLE makes all the data and indexes for that table unavailable for the duration of the repair. Canceling the repair before it is complete is a bad idea as it will only add to the current corruption.

REPAIR TABLE optionally takes one of three options after the table name is specified:

- ■ QUICK — Only a repair of the index tree is attempted.
- ■ EXTENDED — Instead of attempting to fix indexes by doing a REPAIR BY SORT on one entire index at a time, the index is rebuilt one row at a time.
- ■ USE_FRM — Uses the .frm file to rebuild the index, disregarding the existing .MYI index file. This option should be used only as a last resort, as the .MYI file has important information that will be lost, such as the AUTO_INCREMENT value. Also, using USE_FRM can cause fragmentation in the table records.

NOTE   **If a table needs to be repaired because of a** mysqld **upgrade, do not use the** USE_FRM **option. Before** mysqld **version 6.0.6, the table may be truncated, removing of all data, if the** USE_FRM **option was used when the table needed to be repaired because of an upgrade. In versions 6.0.6 and higher, attempting to specify** USE_FRM **when a table needed to be repaired because of an upgrade returns a** Msg_type **of** error **and a** Msg_text **of** Failed repairing incompatible .FRM file. **In this situation, try a simple** REPAIR TABLE tblname **with no options first.**

Should you need to use USE_FRM, a successful REPAIR TABLE will likely return at least two rows, one of which issues a warning that the Number of rows changed from 0 to a greater number. This is because at the start of the REPAIR TABLE, the existing .MYI file was disregarded, so the number of rows in the index at the start of the repair process was 0. Sample output is shown here:

```
mysql> REPAIR TABLE film_text USE_FRM\G
*************************** 1. row ***************************
    Table: sakila.film_text
       Op: repair
 Msg_type: warning
 Msg_text: Number of rows changed from 0 to 1000
*************************** 2. row ***************************
```

```
      Table: sakila.film_text
         Op: repair
   Msg_type: status
   Msg_text: OK
2 rows in set (0.08 sec)
```

There are some command-line tools available that can be used for table repair. For example the Maria storage engine has command-line tool called maria_chk that can be used to check, repair, and optimize Maria tables. MyISAM can be managed with the myisamchk utility. Both of these tools must be used while mysqld is shut down, or you risk causing further corruption by changing the files on the file system when mysqld is still using them.

For tables created using storage engines that do not support the REPAIR TABLE command, you can try rebuilding the table using an ALTER TABLE table_name ENGINE = storage_engine command, which will force a rebuild of the data and indexes. Like REPAIR TABLE, rebuilding the data and indexes with this type of ALTER TABLE command will make all the data and indexes for the table unusable for the duration of the rebuild. Again, canceling the ALTER TABLE before it is complete may add to the current corruption.

TIP It is best to fix table corruption when the table does not need to be used immediately. Chapter 22 has scaling and high availability architectures that you may want to implement. If table corruption happens on one of a few slave servers, the slave server can be taken out of production while the corruption is fixed. In the meantime, the other slave servers can split the extra load. If the table corruption happens on a master server, but the slave servers have no corruption, promote a slave to be the new master (as discussed in Chapter 22), and take the old master out of production service while the corruption is being fixed. In this way, taking a database offline for maintenance does not require noticeable downtime for your application. This tip is extremely useful for proactive maintenance such as upgrading mysqld.

Using the methods previously outlined should resolve any problems if the table corruption is in the index data. If the indexes are still corrupt, or if the corruption is in the row data itself, your only choice may be to restore a previous version from backup. Backups and restoration of data are covered in Chapter 13.

Fragmentation

Fragmentation of the data and indexes can occur when the ordering of the index pages on the disk are not similar to the index ordering of the records on the pages. Fragmentation also occurs when there are a large number of unused pages in the blocks allocated for the index. Fragmentation is most often caused when data is deleted, leaving gaps in the index and data files that may not be filled even when a new row is inserted.

Resolving fragmentation can be difficult. With some storage engines such as MyISAM you can use the OPTIMIZE TABLE command. This will resolve data and index fragmentation issues. As with a REPAIR TABLE command, the data and indexes will be unavailable for the duration of the OPTIMIZE TABLE.

Here is an example of a successful OPTIMIZE TABLE command:

```
mysql> OPTIMIZE TABLE film_text;
+-------------------+----------+----------+----------+
| Table             | Op       | Msg_type | Msg_text |
+-------------------+----------+----------+----------+
| sakila.film_text  | optimize | status   | OK       |
+-------------------+----------+----------+----------+
1 row in set (0.11 sec)
```

Tables using the InnoDB storage engine map the OPTIMIZE TABLE command to an ALTER TABLE command. While this will defragment the row data, it will not always defragment the index data. If the index data is not defragmented by an OPTIMIZE TABLE, only a logical data export and reimport will resolve index fragmentation. See Chapter 13 for how to export and reimport data.

Reclaiming disk space

When a table that stores its data and indexes directly on the file system is defragmented, the size of the files decrease. For example, a fragmented MyISAM table will have smaller .MYD and .MYI files after defragmentation. The disk space is automatically reclaimed.

When InnoDB is used and mysqld is set to use innodb_file_per_table, table data and indexes are stored in a .ibd file in the data directory. All table metadata is stored together in a centralized ibdata file. When an InnoDB table is defragmented, its .ibd file will shrink and disk space will automatically be reclaimed.

However, by default, mysqld is *not* set to use innodb_file_per_table, and InnoDB puts all of the metadata, data and indexes for all tables into a centralized ibdata file. When an InnoDB table is defragmented on this configuration, the ibdata file will not shrink, even though the data is successfully defragmented. The good news is that the space is not lost — InnoDB will add that space to its pool of free space and put new rows in it. The amount of InnoDB free space reported in the TABLE_COMMENT field of the INFORMATION_SCHEMA.TABLES system view and the Comment field of SHOW TABLE STATUS for an InnoDB table will increase. The bad news is that the operating system cannot reclaim that disk space.

> **TIP** If the size of your data is more than a few hundred gigabytes, consider utilizing innodb_file_per_table so that defragmentation can reclaim disk space. Many organizations actually see a performance improvement when switching to innodb_file_per_table because writes and reads are happening from several different .ibd files instead of one or two centralized ibdata files!

Maintaining table statistics

The maintenance of data and indexes should include maintaining the metadata that the server stores about table statistics. This is important because the query optimizer uses this information in choosing which indexes, if any, to use when executing a query. To recalculate statistics, use the ANALYZE TABLE command as shown here:

```
mysql> ANALYZE TABLE film;
+-------------+---------+----------+----------+
| Table       | Op      | Msg_type | Msg_text |
+-------------+---------+----------+----------+
| sakila.film | analyze | status   | OK       |
+-------------+---------+----------+----------+
1 row in set (0.15 sec)
```

ANALYZE, REPAIR, and OPTIMIZE TABLE statements are written to the binary log by default, and will be replicated to any slaves. To change this default behavior, specify NO_WRITE_TO_BINLOG TABLE between the first word and the word TABLE — for example:

```
REPAIR NO_WRITE_TO_BINLOG TABLE film;
```

LOCAL is a shorter alias for NO_WRITE_TO_BINLOG and can be used with any of the three statements.

Getting a table checksum

To get a checksum of the entire table, use the CHECKSUM TABLE tblname command. By default, mysqld will return a live checksum if this is supported by the table (see the "Table definition extensions" section earlier in this chapter for more information). If the table does not support a live checksum, mysqld will calculate a checksum of the table. This requires a full table scan and can be very slow.

CHECKSUM TABLE tblname optionally takes one of two options at the end of the statement:

- QUICK — Returns the live checksum if supported by the table, otherwise returns NULL.
- EXTENDED — Calculates a checksum of the table, even if live checksum is supported.

Transactional statement extensions

In MySQL, several statements cause an *implicit transaction* — that is, they will perform an *implicit commit* before and after executing the actual statement. The commits, and thus the transaction caused by a COMMIT before and a COMMIT after the statement, are done without your approval and without informing you. These commands include commands that start transactions, change the mysql system database, DDL (Data Definition Language) commands that change the schema and some server maintenance commands:

- ANALYZE TABLE
- ALTER -- DATABASE, EVENT, FUNCTION, PROCEDURE, TABLE, VIEW
- BACKUP DATABASE
- BEGIN, BEGIN WORK

- CACHE INDEX
- CHECK TABLE
- CREATE -- DATABASE, EVENT, FUNCTION, INDEX, PROCEDURE, TABLE, TRIGGER, USER, VIEW
- DROP -- DATABASE, EVENT, FUNCTION, INDEX, PROCEDURE, TABLE, TRIGGER, USER, VIEW
- FLUSH
- GRANT
- LOAD INDEX INTO CACHE
- LOCK TABLES
- RENAME -- TABLE, USER
- OPTIMIZE TABLE
- REPAIR TABLE
- RESTORE
- REVOKE
- SET -- PASSWORD, autocommit=1
- START TRANSACTION
- TRUNCATE TABLE
- UNLOCK TABLES

Implicit commits are not performed if there is no change. For example, SET autocommit=1 only performs an implicit commit if the value was previously 0. Implicit commits are also not performed before or after the ALTER TEMPORARY TABLE, CREATE TEMPORARY TABLE, and DROP TEMPORARY TABLE statements.

MySQL extends the SQL standard transactional statements with the following:

- By default, mysqld runs in *autocommit* mode. This means that every SQL statement is its own transaction, and an atomic transaction with more than one SQL statement does not occur. The system variable autocommit controls autocommit mode, and is set to 1 (ON) by default. To use transactions, SET autocommit=0 in the client or start mysqld with the autocommit system variable set to 0 (OFF).

- Alternatively, explicitly starting a transaction with START TRANSACTION will turn off autocommit mode for the duration of the transaction.

- START TRANSACTION can be specified with an optional WITH CONSISTENT SNAPSHOT statement. This will attempt, but not guarantee, to make transactions have consistent reads. If the transactional tables used in the transaction are InnoDB, a consistent snapshot will occur if the isolation level is REPEATABLE READ or SERIALIZABLE. The default isolation level for mysqld is REPEATABLE READ; for more information about transactions and isolation levels, see Chapter 9.

■ When a transaction completes with either COMMIT or ROLLBACK, the default mysqld behavior (specified by a completion_type system variable with a value of 0) is to finish working with the transaction but not begin a new transaction. This default behavior can be changed in a few ways:

  ▪ To immediately start a new transaction, specify COMMIT CHAIN or ROLLBACK CHAIN. This will *chain* transactions, so they occur back to back without needing to explicitly start a new transaction when the previous transaction is finished. To change the default mysqld behavior to always chain transactions, set the completion_type server variable to 1.

  ▪ To have mysqld disconnect the client immediately after a transaction completes, specify COMMIT RELEASE or ROLLBACK RELEASE. This will *release* the client connection after the transaction is finished. To change the default mysqld behavior to always release connections after a transaction completes, set the completion_type server variable to 2.

  ▪ To override the behavior of the completion_type server variable when it is set to 1 or 2, specify NO RELEASE or NO CHAIN after COMMIT or ROLLBACK. For example, if the completion_type server variable was set to 1 (always chain transactions), specifying ROLLBACK NO CHAIN would override the chain behavior specified by completion_type.

Summary

This chapter has shown the nonstandard SQL that MySQL supports, and the ways in which MySQL deviates from the SQL standard. You should have learned the following topics from this chapter:

■ MySQL language structure

■ MySQL deviations

■ DML and SELECT command extensions

■ The SET extension

■ Table maintenance extensions

## Chapter 5

MySQL Data Types

C hoosing optimal data types is an extremely important part of having a database system that runs smoothly and efficiently. For example, comparing numeric types takes less time than comparing character string types, because character string types have character set and collation considerations. In addition, smaller data is faster to process than larger data. If the data is compact enough to fit entirely in memory, there is a huge reduction in disk I/O, making queries perform even better.

In this chapter you find how to define the standard and nonstandard data types that MySQL offers, as well as advice on the best ways to use them.

Looking at MySQL Data Types

In order to store, retrieve, or process data, the data must be assigned a data type. MySQL includes many of the ISO SQL:2003 standard data types, and adds in more data types. The ISO SQL:2003 standard defines seven categories of data types:

- Character String Types
- National Character String Types
- Binary Large Object String Types
- Numeric Types
- Boolean Types
- Datetime Types
- Interval Types

Character String Types

The ISO SQL:2003 standard defines three character string types. Each string type has more than one keyword associated with it; for example, CHARACTER can be abbreviated as CHAR. The standard character string types and their associated keywords are:

- Fixed-width strings:
    - CHARACTER(length)
    - CHAR(length)
- Variable-length strings:
    - CHARACTER VARYING(length)
    - CHAR VARYING(length)
    - VARCHAR(length)
- Character objects:
    - CHARACTER LARGE OBJECT
    - CHAR LARGE OBJECT
    - CLOB

MySQL supports the SQL standard data types for fixed- and variable-length strings, but not for character objects. MySQL stores fixed-width strings as CHAR and variable-length strings as VARCHAR:

```
mysql> USE test;
Database changed
mysql> CREATE TABLE string_type (
    -> fw1 CHARACTER(10) NOT NULL DEFAULT '',
    -> fw2 CHAR(10) NOT NULL DEFAULT '',
    -> vl1 CHARACTER VARYING(10) NOT NULL DEFAULT '',
    -> vl2 CHAR VARYING(10) NOT NULL DEFAULT '',
    -> vl3 VARCHAR(10) NOT NULL DEFAULT ''
    -> );
Query OK, 0 rows affected (0.13 sec)

mysql> EXPLAIN string_type;
+-------+-------------+------+-----+------------+-------+
| Field | Type        | Null | Key | Default    | Extra |
+-------+-------------+------+-----+------------+-------+
| fw1   | char(10)    | NO   |     |            |       |
| fw2   | char(10)    | NO   |     |            |       |
| vl1   | varchar(10) | NO   |     |            |       |
| vl2   | varchar(10) | NO   |     |            |       |
| vl3   | varchar(10) | NO   |     |            |       |
+-------+-------------+------+-----+------------+-------+
5 rows in set (0.02 sec)
```

MySQL also supports the following nonstandard string types:

- Variable-length strings:
  - TINYTEXT
  - TEXT
  - MEDIUMTEXT
  - LONGTEXT

The four nonstandard variable-length strings that MySQL offers are known as the TEXT data types, because they share the same properties aside from size. Unlike most data types, the four TEXT data type fields are objects separate from the containing table or result set. They are queried as regular fields are, but behind the scenes they are not actually stored in the table, they are stored as separate objects.

Any character can be stored in a character string type, though some character sets may support more characters than others. It may be necessary to escape some strings in order to process them, as shown by the strings submitted and returned in the following:

```
mysql> SELECT "Single quotes (') within double quotes do not need
    to be escaped" AS text;
+------------------------------------------------------------------+
| text                                                             |
+------------------------------------------------------------------+
| Single quotes (') within double quotes do not need to be escaped |
+------------------------------------------------------------------+
1 row in set (0.00 sec)

mysql> SELECT 'Double quotes (") within single quotes do not need
    to be escaped' AS text;
+------------------------------------------------------------------+
| text                                                             |
+------------------------------------------------------------------+
| Double quotes (") within single quotes do not need to be escaped |
+------------------------------------------------------------------+
1 row in set (0.00 sec)

mysql> SELECT 'Escape ''quotes\' by using two of them together or
    with \\' AS text;
+-------------------------------------------------------------+
| text                                                        |
+-------------------------------------------------------------+
| Escape 'quotes' by using two of them together or with \ |
+-------------------------------------------------------------+
1 row in set (0.00 sec)

mysql> SELECT "Escape ""quotes\" by using two of them together or
    with \" AS text;
+-------------------------------------------------------------+
```

```
| text                                                       |
+------------------------------------------------------------+
| Escape "quotes" by using two of them together or with \ |
+------------------------------------------------------------+
1 row in set (0.00 sec)
```

Length

The CHAR and VARCHAR data types require a length argument. A data type of CHAR or VARCHAR with a length of 0 is valid, but can hold only two values: the empty string and NULL. For CHAR and VARCHAR data types, the length is an integer representing the number of characters in a string, which may be different from the number of bytes in a string. This is due to different character sets having different character lengths. For example, the latin1 character set uses one byte to store each character, whereas the utf8 character set uses up to four bytes per character. For more information on character sets, see Chapter 4.

 In MySQL 5.1, the support for the utf8 character set was limited, and utf8 characters used 3 bytes per string, not 4 bytes per string as it does in MySQL 6.0.

CHAR length

The length of CHAR is an integer from 0–255. If a string is stored as a CHAR and is smaller than the allowed length, spaces are appended to the string. When retrieving a CHAR from a table, all trailing spaces are removed. This means that if a string stored in a fixed-width field has trailing spaces in it, they will be removed upon retrieval:

```
mysql> INSERT INTO string_type (fw1)
    -> VALUES ('a'),('a '),(' '),(' a'),(' a ');
Query OK, 5 rows affected (0.52 sec)
Records: 5  Duplicates: 0  Warnings: 0

mysql> SELECT CONCAT('/',fw1,'/'), CHAR_LENGTH(fw1) FROM string_type;
+---------------------+--------------+
| CONCAT('/',fw1,'/') | LENGTH(fw1) |
+---------------------+--------------+
| /a/                 |            1 |
| /a/                 |            1 |
| //                  |            0 |
| / a/                |            2 |
| / a/                |            2 |
+---------------------+--------------+
5 rows in set (0.02 sec)
```

 The SQL mode PAD_CHAR_TO_FULL_LENGTH changes the behavior of retrieving a fixed-width string from a table. If the SQL mode PAD_CHAR_TO_FULL_LENGTH is set, the string retrieved is the full length of the field:

```
mysql> SELECT @@session.sql_mode;
+-------------------------------------------------------------------+
| @@session.sql_mode                                                |
+-------------------------------------------------------------------+
| STRICT_TRANS_TABLES,NO_AUTO_CREATE_USER,NO_ENGINE_SUBSTITUTION |
+-------------------------------------------------------------------+
1 row in set (0.02 sec)

mysql> SET SESSION sql_mode = 'PAD_CHAR_TO_FULL_LENGTH,STRICT_TRANS_
    TABLES,NO_AUTO_CREATE_USER,NO_ENGINE_SUBSTITUTION';
Query OK, 0 rows affected (0.00 sec)

mysql> SELECT CONCAT('/',fw1,'/'), LENGTH(fw1)
    -> FROM string_type;
+---------------------+-------------+
| CONCAT('/',fw1,'/') | LENGTH(fw1) |
+---------------------+-------------+
| /a        /         |          10 |
| /a        /         |          10 |
| /         /         |          10 |
| / a       /         |          10 |
| / a       /         |          10 |
+---------------------+-------------+
5 rows in set (0.03 sec)
```

This also means that a unique constraint on a CHAR field will not allow both 'a' and 'a ' because they are not different values. For more on unique constraints, see Chapter 6.

Be cautious when storing a value that may have trailing spaces in a CHAR field! One unexpected issue occurs when a user enters one or more spaces into a string field. The user input is success-fully declared as non-blank, but when it gets retrieved from the database, the field is now blank. To avoid this issue, use the VARCHAR type.

VARCHAR length

The maximum length of a VARCHAR in MySQL is restricted by the maximum row length of a table. The maximum row length allowed by MySQL is 65,535 bytes for most storage engines (the NDB storage engine has a different maximum value). Therefore, in theory, the maximum length of a VARCHAR is 65,535 bytes.

In practice, there is some overhead in storing the VARCHAR data type, which further limits the actual possible size of a VARCHAR. If the length of VARCHAR is less than 255 bytes, one byte per row is used to store the actual length of the string. If the length of VARCHAR is greater than 255 bytes, the overhead cost of storing the string length is two bytes per row. There is also per-table overhead — every table allocates one byte for every set of eight potentially nullable fields, regardless of field types.

Thus, the maximum length of a VARCHAR stored in a table is 65,532 bytes, and that is only if the VARCHAR field is the only field in the table. For example, consider a table that has only one other field, an INT field using 4 bytes — the maximum length of a VARCHAR in that table would be 65,528 bytes.

If you need to store variable-length strings larger than the maximum allowed for VARCHAR, use the MEDIUMTEXT or LONGTEXT data types. If you try to define a table that exceeds the maximum row length, you will get one of the following errors:

```
mysql> CREATE TABLE max_len_varchar(
    -> fld VARCHAR(65533) CHARSET latin1);
ERROR 1118 (42000): Row size too large. The maximum row size for the
    used table type, not counting BLOBs, is 65535. You have to change
    some columns to TEXT or BLOBs

mysql> CREATE TABLE max_len_varchar(
    -> fld VARCHAR(16384) CHARSET utf8);
ERROR 1074 (42000): Column length too big for column 'fld' (max =
16383); use BLOB or TEXT instead
```

TEXT sizes

The only differences among the four different TEXT types are the maximum amount of data each can store and the overhead involved:

- TINYTEXT — Up to 255 bytes, 1 byte overhead
- TEXT — Up to 64 Kb, 2 bytes overhead
- MEDIUMTEXT — Up to 16 Mb, 3 bytes overhead
- LONGTEXT — Up to 4 Gb, 4 bytes overhead

The separately allocated object property is one of the few differences between a VARCHAR field and a TINYTEXT or TEXT field; the other differences involve the allowed attributes for each data type.

Character string type attributes

Character string types can be defined with attributes that affect the storage, sorting, and comparison behaviors:

- NOT NULL — By default, NULL values are allowed. To disallow NULL values, use the NOT NULL attribute. See the "Using NULL Values" section later in this chapter for an explanation of problems NULL values can cause.
- NULL — The NULL attribute is shorthand for DEFAULT NULL. See the "Using NULL Values" section later in this chapter for an explanation of problems NULL values can cause.

- DEFAULT — The DEFAULT attribute is valid for CHAR and VARCHAR only; it is not valid for any of the TEXT data types. The DEFAULT attribute causes a character string to have a default value when a value is not specified. This means that an INSERT statement does not have to include a value for this field; if it does not, the value following DEFAULT will be inserted. Valid DEFAULT values include NULL and strings. Functions are not allowed in a DEFAULT expression.

- If no DEFAULT value is specified, MySQL will create character string type fields as DEFAULT NULL. If a field does not have a DEFAULT value and NOT NULL is also specified, there is no DEFAULT value, and INSERT statements must supply a value for that field.

- BINARY — The default behavior of a character string is to be case-insensitive when it is sorted and searched. The BINARY attribute causes a character string, its indexing, and its sorting to be case-sensitive. This means that character string fields not defined as BINARY have case-insensitive unique constraints:

```
mysql> CREATE TABLE unique_char (bry VARCHAR(10) PRIMARY KEY);
Query OK, 0 rows affected (0.09 sec)

mysql> INSERT INTO unique_char VALUES('A');
Query OK, 1 row affected (0.11 sec)

mysql> INSERT INTO unique_char VALUES('a');
ERROR 1062 (23000): Duplicate entry 'a' for key 'PRIMARY'
```

The BINARY attribute is actually an alias for using a binary collation. For example, if the BINARY attribute is used on a field with a character set of latin1, the effective collation is latin1_bin:

```
mysql> CREATE TABLE unique_binary_char (
    -> bry VARCHAR(10) BINARY PRIMARY KEY);
Query OK, 0 rows affected (0.11 sec)

mysql> SHOW CREATE TABLE unique_binary_char\G
*************************** 1. row ***************************
       Table: unique_binary_char
Create Table: CREATE TABLE `unique_binary_char` (
  `bry` varchar(10) CHARACTER SET latin1 COLLATE latin1_bin NOT NULL,
  PRIMARY KEY (`bry`)
) ENGINE=InnoDB DEFAULT CHARSET=latin1
1 row in set (0.00 sec)
```

- CHARACTER SET — The CHARACTER SET attribute causes a character string to be stored in the specified character set. If no value is specified, the default character set is used. For more on character sets, see Chapter 4.

  - ASCII — An alias for CHARACTER SET latin1
  - UNICODE — An alias for CHARACTER SET ucs2

```
mysql> CREATE TABLE alias_test (char_ascii VARCHAR(10) ASCII,
    -> char_unicode VARCHAR(10) UNICODE);
Query OK, 0 rows affected (0.55 sec)

mysql> SHOW CREATE TABLE alias_test\G
*************************** 1. row ***************************
       Table: alias_test
Create Table: CREATE TABLE `alias_test` (
  `char_ascii` varchar(10) DEFAULT NULL,
  `char_unicode` varchar(10) CHARACTER SET ucs2 DEFAULT NULL
) ENGINE=InnoDB DEFAULT CHARSET=latin1
1 row in set (0.00 sec)
```

■ COLLATION — The COLLATION attribute causes a character string to be stored, indexed, and ordered according to the specified collation. If no value is specified, the default collation is used. For more on collations, see Chapter 4.

Table 5-1 summarizes the character string types.

The numbers given in Table 5-1 are the basic storage requirements of MySQL. The storage engine used may add additional overhead or provide data compression that reduces the storage required. See Chapter 11 for more details about storage engines.

National Character String Types

Three national character string types are defined by the ISO SQL:2003 standard. Each string type has more than one keyword associated with it; for example, CHARACTER can be abbreviated as CHAR. The standard character string types and their associated keywords are:

■ Fixed-width strings:
- NATIONAL CHARACTER(length)
- NATIONAL CHAR(length)
- NCHAR(length)

■ Variable-length strings:
- NATIONAL CHARACTER VARYING(length)
- NATIONAL CHAR VARYING(length)
- NCHAR VARYING(length)

■ Character objects:
- NATIONAL CHARACTER LARGE OBJECT
- NCHAR LARGE OBJECT
- NCLOB

TABLE 5-1

Summary of MySQL Character String Types

Data Type Name	SQL Standard?	Fixed/Variable Length	Range	Size	Attributes
CHAR	Yes	Fixed	Length of 0–255, depends on character set	M*x bytes	ASCII BINARY CHARACTER SETCOLLATION DEFAULT UNICODE
VARCHAR	Yes	Variable	Length of 0–255, depends on character set	L*x+1 if L<255 L*x+2 if L>255	ASCII BINARY CHARACTER SETCOLLATION DEFAULT UNICODE
TINYTEXT	No	Variable	Max length of 255 bytes	L+1 bytes 1 byte stores length	ASCII BINARY CHARACTER SETCOLLATION UNICODE
TEXT	No	Variable	Max length of 65,535 bytes (64 Kb)	L+2 bytes 2 bytes store length	ASCII BINARY CHARACTER SETCOLLATION UNICODE
MEDIUMTEXT	No	Variable	Max length of 16,777,215 bytes (16 Mb)	L+3 bytes 3 bytes store length	ASCII BINARY CHARACTER SETCOLLATION UNICODE
LONGTEXT	No	Variable	Max length of 4,294,967,295 bytes (4 Gb)	L+4 bytes 2 bytes store length	ASCII BINARY CHARACTER SETCOLLATION NOT NULL NULL UNICODE

Like character string types, MySQL supports the SQL standard for fixed- and variable-length strings, but not for character objects.

The SQL standard states that the NATIONAL equivalents of character string types are the same as the character string types, except that a specific character set is used. In MySQL, this character set is utf8:

```
mysql> CREATE TABLE nchar_test (nchar_fld NCHAR(10));
Query OK, 0 rows affected (0.55 sec)

mysql> SHOW CREATE TABLE nchar_test\G
*************************** 1. row ***************************
       Table: nchar_test
Create Table: CREATE TABLE `nchar_test` (
  `nchar_fld` char(10) CHARACTER SET utf8 DEFAULT NULL
) ENGINE=InnoDB DEFAULT CHARSET=latin1
1 row in set (0.00 sec)
```

The characteristics and usage of national character string types is exactly the same as character string types, with one exception: the ASCII and UNICODE attributes are not proper syntax. This is because the ASCII and UNICODE attributes set the character set, which conflicts with the NATIONAL keyword.

For details on character string types, see the section "Character String Types" earlier in this chapter.

Binary Large Object String Types

A binary string type is the least restrictive data type. There is one binary large object type in the ISO SQL:2003 standard, with two aliases:

- BINARY LARGE OBJECT(length)
- BLOB(length)

MySQL supports only the second standard syntax, BLOB(length). However, MySQL extends the SQL standard for binary large object string types with five additional binary types:

- TINYBLOB
- MEDIUMBLOB
- LONGBLOB
- BINARY(length)
- VARBINARY(length)

Binary string types are byte strings. Character strings are ordered lexically; binary strings are ordered by each byte's value. The standard does not specify what makes an object "large," and there is no standard equivalent for smaller binary strings, so we have included the smaller BINARY and VARBINARY byte string types into this category.

BLOB values

The four BLOB types are very similar to each other — the only differences are the maximum amount of data each can store and the overhead involved in storing the size of each record:

- TINYBLOB — Up to 255 bytes, 1 byte overhead
- BLOB — Up to 64 Kb, 2 bytes overhead
- MEDIUMBLOB — Up to 16 Mb, 3 bytes overhead
- LONGBLOB — Up to 4 Gb, 4 bytes overhead

A BLOB data type field is a separately allocated object than the table that contains it, like the TEXT data type fields.

BINARY values

BINARY and VARBINARY are similar to the CHAR and VARCHAR data types, respectively. For the BINARY and VARBINARY data types, the length is an integer representing the length, in bytes, of a string. A data type of BINARY or VARBINARY with a length of 0 is valid, but can hold only two strings: the empty string and NULL. Note that BINARY and VARBINARY are different from CHAR BINARY and VARCHAR BINARY — BINARY and VARBINARY are byte strings, and CHAR BINARY and VARCHAR BINARY are case-sensitive character strings.

BINARY length

The length of BINARY is an integer from 0–255. If a string is stored as a BINARY and is smaller than the length, binary spaces (represented by \0) are appended to the string. A binary space is different from a regular space character; a binary space has an ASCII value of 0 and the regular space character has an ASCII value of 32:

```
mysql> SELECT ' ',ASCII(' '), '\0', ASCII('\0');
+---+------------+---+------------+
|   | ASCII(' ') |   | ASCII('\0') |
+---+------------+---+------------+
|   |         32 |   |          0 |
+---+------------+---+------------+
1 row in set (0.02 sec)
```

Because of this, a value of 'a' appears before a value of 'a ' in an ascending sort. This also means that the BINARY value 'a' is the same as the BINARY value 'a\0' for the purpose of unique constraints. There is no removal of trailing spaces when a BINARY string is retrieved from a table.

VARBINARY length

The maximum length of a VARBINARY is restricted only by the maximum row length. In most storage engines, the maximum row length is the maximum allowed by MySQL, which is 65,535 bytes. Only the NDB storage engine has a different maximum value. Like a VARCHAR, in theory, the maximum length of a VARBINARY is 65,535 bytes.

In practice, there is some overhead in storing the VARBINARY data type, which further limits the actual possible size of a VARBINARY. If the length of VARBINARY is less than 255 bytes, one byte per row is used to store the actual length of the string. If the length of VARBINARY is greater than 255 bytes, the overhead cost of storing the string length is two bytes per row. There is also per-table overhead — every table allocates one byte for every set of eight potentially nullable fields, regardless of field types.

Thus, the maximum length of a VARBINARY is 65,532 bytes, and that is only if the VARBINARY field is the only field in the table. For example, another field with a type of INT uses 4 bytes, so the maximum length of a VARBINARY in that table would be 65,528 bytes.

For VARBINARY strings larger than the maximum allowed, use the BLOB data type. If you try to define a table that exceeds the maximum row length, you will get the following error:

```
mysql> CREATE TABLE max_len_varbin(fld VARBINARY(65533));
ERROR 1118 (42000): Row size too large. The maximum row size for the
    used table type, not counting BLOBs, is 65535. You have to change
    some columns to TEXT or BLOBs
```

Table 5-2 shows a summary of the MySQL binary data types.

As with the character string data types, the numbers given in Table 5-2 are the basic storage requirements of MySQL. The storage engine used may add additional overhead or provide data compression that reduces the storage required. See Chapter 11 for more details about storage engines.

Numeric Types

The ISO SQL:2003 standard defines two numeric types. Each numeric type has a few different data types. The standard numeric types and their associated keywords are:

- Exact numeric type:
    - NUMERIC(g,f)
    - DECIMAL(g,f) can be abbreviated as DEC
    - SMALLINT
    - INTEGER can be abbreviated as INT
    - BIGINT

TABLE 5-2

Summary of MySQL Binary Data Types

Data Type Name	SQL Standard?	Fixed/Variable Length	Range	Size	Attributes
BINARY	No	Fixed	Length of 0–255 bytes	M bytes	DEFAULT NOT NULL NULL
VARBINARY	No	Variable	Length of 0–65,532 bytes	L*x+1 if L<255 L*x+2 if L>255	DEFAULT NOT NULL NULL
TINYBLOB	No	Variable	Max length of 255 bytes	L+1 bytes 1 byte stores length	NOT NULL NULL
BLOB	No	Variable	Max length of 65,535 bytes (64 Kb)	L+2 bytes 2 bytes store length	NOT NULL NULL
MEDIUMBLOB	No	Variable	Max length of 16,777,215 bytes (16 Mb)	L+3 bytes 3 bytes store length	NOT NULL NULL
LONGBLOB	No	Variable	Max length of 4,294,967,295 bytes (4 Gb)	L+4 bytes 2 bytes store length	NOT NULL NULL

- Approximate numeric type:
  - FLOAT(p)
  - REAL
  - DOUBLE PRECISION

MySQL supports these data types with one exception — the DOUBLE PRECISION data type is simply named DOUBLE. In addition, the NUMERIC data type is an alias for the DECIMAL data type. The standard SQL has been extended to add these additional numeric data types:

- Exact numeric types:
  - TINYINT
  - MEDIUMINT
  - BIT(x)
  - SERIAL

In MySQL, the SERIAL numeric data type is an alias for BIGINT UNSIGNED NOT NULL AUTO_INCREMENT UNIQUE KEY.

By default, the REAL numeric data type is an alias for DOUBLE. However, you can change that behavior by changing the sql_mode to include REAL_AS_FLOAT, which causes the REAL numeric data type to be an alias for FLOAT. See "Choosing SQL Modes" later in this chapter for more detail.

Numeric data sizes and ranges

Each numeric data type can store a limited range of values, and each numeric data type stores its values in a certain size.

DECIMAL size and range

A DECIMAL field is defined using the syntax DECIMAL(g,f). The first argument (g) is the total number of digits, and the second argument (f) is the number of digits after the decimal point. For example, the data type DECIMAL(5,2) can store values between −999.99 and 999.99. The default value for g is 10 and the default value for f is 0; the maximum value for g is 65 and the maximum value for f is 30.

The size of a DECIMAL field is variable. MySQL stores DECIMAL in a binary format, where each group of 9 digits is stored in 4 bytes. The size of a DECIMAL field is determined by the number of digits in the integer part (the value of p-s) and the number of digits in the fractional part (the value of s). The integer and fractional parts are stored separately in 4-byte, 9-digit groups. If the number of digits in each group is not divisible by nine, the remaining digits are stored in CEILING(digits/2) bytes.

As an example, the size of DECIMAL(12,2) can be calculated as follows:

```
Integer part = (12-2) digits = 10 digits = 9 digits + 1 digit
9 digits = 4 bytes
1 digit left over
CEILING(1/2) = 1 byte
Total integer part = 5 bytes

Fractional part = 2 digits
CEILING(2/2) = 1 byte

Total size = 6 bytes
```

Integer sizes and ranges

The integer data types are TINYINT, SMALLINT, INT, MEDIUMINT, and BIGINT. Table 5-3 shows the data sizes and ranges for the integer data types:

Note that the size of the field is the size of the data type, not the size of the value stored. For example, the value 123 stored in a BIGINT field is stored in 8 bytes. The same value 123 stored in a TINYINT field is stored in 1 byte.

TABLE 5-3

Data Sizes and Ranges for Integer Data Types

Data Type	SIGNED Range	UNSIGNED Range	Size
TINYINT	−128 to 127	0 to 255	1 byte
SMALLINT	−32,768 to 32,767	0 to 65,535	2 bytes
MEDIUMINT	−8,388,608 to 8,388,607	0 to 16,777,215	3 bytes
INT	−2,147,483,648 to 2,147,483,647	0 to 4,294,967,295	4 bytes
BIGINT	−9,223,372,036,854,775,808 to 9,223,372,036,854,775,807	0 to 18,446,744,073,709,551,615	8 bytes

MySQL allows a minimum display width to be set for integer types. If an integer value is less than this width, the value will be left-padded with enough spaces so the value is displayed as this width. This is only for the display and does not change the actual value returned. This can be specified by giving the width as an argument to the integer data type, for example INT(4). This does not change the range nor the size of the data type, just the minimum display width.

> **NOTE** MySQL performs calculations and comparisons using double-precision floating-point numbers. Calculations using unsigned BIGINT values larger than 63 bits (9,223,372,036,854,775,807) should only be done via bit functions.

BIT size and range

The BIT data type stores integers as a series of bits. The range of a BIT field is determined by the argument to BIT(x). The default range is 1 bit and the range can be set from 1 to 64 bits. The BIT values are stored in binary format (that is, it is stored in base 2, as opposed to decimal format, which is stored in base 10). Unlike other data types, a BIT value needs to be converted upon retrieval to produce a human-readable result. How to retrieve BIT values depends on whether you want to retrieve integers or bit strings:

```
mysql> USE test;
Database changed
mysql> CREATE TABLE bit_test (bt BIT(10));
Query OK, 0 rows affected (0.64 sec)

mysql> INSERT INTO bit_test (bt) VALUES (0),(1),(2),(3),(4);
Query OK, 5 rows affected (11.78 sec)
Records: 5  Duplicates: 0  Warnings: 0
```

```
mysql> SELECT bt,bt+0,BIN(bt) FROM bit_test;
+------+------+---------+
| bt   | bt+0 | BIN(bt) |
+------+------+---------+
|      |    0 | 0       |
| ☺    |    1 | 1       |
| ●    |    2 | 10      |
| ♥    |    3 | 11      |
| ♦    |    4 | 100     |
+------+------+---------+
5 rows in set (0.09 sec)
```

The BIT value, as it is stored, is shown in the first field of the result. As you can see, it is not in human-readable format. The second field of the result casts the result as an integer, and the third field casts the result as a bit string.

FLOAT size and range

The FLOAT data type is a single-precision floating-point number. *Floating-point* means that unlike the DECIMAL data type, the decimal point can be anywhere in the number — the decimal point *floats*. A FLOAT is limited in how many significant digits it can store. In the SQL standard, this limitation can be specified as the argument p (p stands for *precision*). In MySQL, this limitation depends on the hardware and operating system, but is usually a precision of 24 bits. This translates to 6 or 7 significant digits, and a storage cost of 4 bytes per FLOAT. If a FLOAT field is defined with a larger value of p, it is changed into a DOUBLE field:

```
mysql> USE test;
Database changed
mysql> CREATE TABLE float_double_test (
    -> f1 FLOAT(1), f2 FLOAT(10), f3 FLOAT(23),
    -> f4 FLOAT(24), f5 FLOAT(53));
Query OK, 0 rows affected (0.16 sec)

mysql> SHOW CREATE TABLE float_double_test\G
*************************** 1. row ***************************
       Table: float_double_test
Create Table: CREATE TABLE `float_double_test` (
  `f1` float DEFAULT NULL,
  `f2` float DEFAULT NULL,
  `f3` float DEFAULT NULL,
  `f4` float DEFAULT NULL,
  `f5` double DEFAULT NULL
) ENGINE=InnoDB DEFAULT CHARSET=latin1
1 row in set (0.06 sec)

mysql> ALTER TABLE float_double_test ADD COLUMN f6 FLOAT(54);
ERROR 1063 (42000): Incorrect column specifier for column 'f6'
```

A significant digit is a digit that signifies precision, and not a power of ten. The following example was done on a system where the number of significant digits is six:

```
mysql> CREATE TABLE float_test (ft float, ft_text varchar(10));
Query OK, 0 rows affected (0.59 sec)

mysql> INSERT INTO float_test (ft,ft_text) VALUES
    -> (1234567,'1234567'), (123456,'123456'), (12345.6,'12345.6'),
    -> (123.456,'123.456'), (1.23456,'1.23456'),
    -> (0.00123456,'0.00123456'),
    -> (1.23456e-3,'1.23456e-3'), (123456000,'123456000'),
    -> (1.23456e8,'1.23456e8'), (123456e3,'123456e3');
Query OK, 10 rows affected (0.08 sec)
Records: 10  Duplicates: 0  Warnings: 0

mysql> SELECT ft, ft_text FROM float_test ORDER BY ft;
+------------+------------+
| ft         | ft_text    |
+------------+------------+
| 0.00123456 | 0.00123456 |
| 0.00123456 | 1.23456e-3 |
|    1.23456 | 1.23456    |
|    123.456 | 123.456    |
|    12345.6 | 12345.6    |
|     123456 | 123456     |
|    1234570 | 1234567    |
|  123456000 | 123456000  |
|  123456000 | 1.23456e8  |
|  123456000 | 123456e3   |
+------------+------------+
10 rows in set (0.06 sec)
```

Note that the values 123456000, 1.23456e8 and 123456e3 are all the same floating-point number. The numbers including e indicate scientific notation, replacing e with *10^. Indeed, 123456000, 1.23456*10^8 and 123456*10^3 all signify the same number.

MySQL automatically rounded the value with more than six significant digits to have exactly six significant digits — the value 1234567 was rounded to 1234570.

As mentioned previously, MySQL supports the SQL standard FLOAT(p) syntax. It also supports a syntax similar to the DECIMAL syntax. A FLOAT field can be defined as in the preceding example, or it can be defined as FLOAT(g,f). The first argument (g) is the total number of digits, and the second argument (f) is the number of digits after the decimal point.

The FLOAT(g,f) syntax can be used to override the default amount of significant digits. Therefore, higher or lower precision can be specified using the two-argument syntax. It should be noted that this is not an exact substitute for defining precision, because the number of digits after the decimal point is fixed.

> **NOTE** MySQL performs calculations and comparisons using double-precision floating-point numbers. Queries involving a FLOAT field may return unexpected results; rounding an (internal) DOUBLE number often does not yield the same result as rounding a FLOAT number. Therefore, comparing a FLOAT field to a calculated number will often produce incorrect results, because the calculated number is a DOUBLE. The following example shows that calculating a FLOAT value (by adding 0) changes it to a DOUBLE value, which can produce a very different value from the original FLOAT:

```
mysql> SELECT ft_text, ft, ft+0 FROM float_test;
+------------+------------+----------------------+
| ft_text    | ft         | ft+0                 |
+------------+------------+----------------------+
| 1234567    |    1234570 |              1234567 |
| 123456     |     123456 |               123456 |
| 12345.6    |    12345.6 |      12345.599609375 |
| 123.456    |    123.456 |    123.45600128173828 |
| 1.23456    |    1.23456 |    1.2345600128173828 |
| 0.00123456 | 0.00123456 | 0.00123456004075706  |
| 1.23456e-3 | 0.00123456 | 0.00123456004075706  |
| 123456000  |  123456000 |            123456000 |
| 1.23456e8  |  123456000 |            123456000 |
| 123456e3   |  123456000 |            123456000 |
+------------+------------+----------------------+
10 rows in set (0.04 sec)
```

DOUBLE size and range

The DOUBLE data type is a double-precision floating-point number. Like a FLOAT, a DOUBLE is limited in how many significant digits it can store. See previous subsection "FLOAT Size and Range" for an explanation of floating-point numbers and significant digits. The data type is named DOUBLE because the limitation is approximately double the limitation of a single-precision FLOAT.

As with FLOAT, this limitation depends on the hardware and operating system, but is usually a precision of 53 bits. This translates to 14 or 15 significant digits, and a storage cost of 8 bytes per DOUBLE.

As with FLOAT, MySQL supports a syntax similar to the DECIMAL syntax. A DOUBLE field can be defined with no parameters as DOUBLE, or it can be defined as DOUBLE(g,f). The first argument (g) is the total number of digits, and the second argument (f) is the number of digits after the decimal point.

The DOUBLE(g,f) syntax can be used to override the default number of significant digits. It should be noted that this is not an exact substitute for defining precision, because the number of digits after the decimal point is fixed.

Numeric data type attributes

Numeric types can be defined with attributes that affect the data range and how the data is stored and displayed:

- NOT NULL — By default, NULL values are allowed. To disallow NULL values, use the NOT NULL attribute. See the "Using NULL Values" section later in this chapter for an explanation of problems NULL values can cause.

- NULL — The NULL attribute is shorthand for DEFAULT NULL. See the "Using NULL Values" section later in this chapter for an explanation of problems NULL values can cause.

- DEFAULT — The DEFAULT attribute is valid for all numeric data types. The DEFAULT attribute causes a numeric data type to have a default value when a value is not specified. This means that an INSERT statement does not have to include a value for this field; if it does not, the value following DEFAULT will be inserted. Valid DEFAULT values include NULL and valid numerical values for the field (that is, a field specified as INT DEFAULT 1.9 will be converted to INT DEFAULT 2). Functions are not allowed in a DEFAULT expression.

- If no DEFAULT value is specified, MySQL will create numeric data type fields as DEFAULT NULL. If a field does not have a DEFAULT value and NOT NULL is also specified, there is no DEFAULT value, and INSERT statements must supply a value for that field.

- AUTO_INCREMENT — The AUTO_INCREMENT attribute is used to define a sequence as a default value for a field. All numeric data types support the AUTO_INCREMENT attribute except for BIT and DECIMAL. The AUTO_INCREMENT attribute requires that a UNIQUE index exists on the field to ensure the sequence has no duplicates. If AUTO_INCREMENT is specified on a field, the field is converted to use the NOT NULL attribute. There can only be one AUTO_INCREMENT field per table, and the sequence generated by an AUTO_INCREMENT field in one table cannot be used in any other table.

  By default, the sequence starts at 1 and increases by 1 for every insert. To change the number the sequence starts at, set the auto_increment_offset variable in the configuration file or set the dynamic session or global variable of the same name. To change the amount the sequence increases by, set the auto_increment_increment variable in the configuration file or set the dynamic session or global variable of the same name.

  To see the next AUTO_INCREMENT value for an existing table, query the TABLES table in the INFORMATION_SCHEMA database, or use SHOW CREATE TABLE:

```
mysql> USE INFORMATION_SCHEMA;
Database changed
mysql> SELECT AUTO_INCREMENT
    -> FROM TABLES
    -> WHERE TABLE_SCHEMA='sakila' AND TABLE_NAME='category'\G
*************************** 1. row ***************************
AUTO_INCREMENT: 17
1 row in set (0.00 sec)
```

```
mysql> USE sakila;
Database changed
mysql> SHOW CREATE TABLE category\G
*************************** 1. row ***************************
       Table: category
Create Table: CREATE TABLE `category` (
  `category_id` tinyint(3) unsigned NOT NULL AUTO_INCREMENT,
  `name` varchar(25) NOT NULL,
  `last_update` timestamp NOT NULL DEFAULT CURRENT_TIMESTAMP ON
  UPDATE CURRENT_TIMESTAMP,
  PRIMARY KEY (`category_id`)
) ENGINE=InnoDB AUTO_INCREMENT=17 DEFAULT CHARSET=utf8
1 row in set (0.00 sec)

mysql> SELECT MAX(category_id) FROM category;
+------------------+
| MAX(category_id) |
+------------------+
|               16 |
+------------------+
1 row in set (0.00 sec)
```

To change the next AUTO_INCREMENT value for an existing table, use the following ALTER TABLE syntax:

```
mysql> ALTER TABLE category AUTO_INCREMENT=20;
Query OK, 16 rows affected (0.34 sec)
Records: 16  Duplicates: 0  Warnings: 0

mysql> SELECT AUTO_INCREMENT
    -> FROM INFORMATION_SCHEMA.TABLES
    -> WHERE TABLE_SCHEMA='sakila' AND TABLE_NAME='CATEGORY'\G
*************************** 1. row ***************************
AUTO_INCREMENT: 20
1 row in set (0.00 sec)
```

AUTO_INCREMENT values can only be 0 or positive. If a table does not contain a field with the AUTO_INCREMENT attribute, the AUTO_INCREMENT field for that table is NULL.

- UNSIGNED — The default range of numeric types includes 0, negative numbers, and positive numbers. To change the range to include only 0 and positive numbers, use the UNSIGNED attribute. Integer data types are limited by the amount of storage space, so if the UNSIGNED attribute is specified, an integer data type can actually hold larger numbers than when negative numbers are allowed (see Table 5-1).

Any field that allows the UNSIGNED attribute also allows the SIGNED attribute to be specified. However, because that is a default attribute, there is no need to specify SIGNED. In fact, the SIGNED attribute will not appear in the table schema even if it is explicitly specified in the field definition.

The only numeric data type that does not allow UNSIGNED is the BIT numeric data type.

- ZEROFILL — The ZEROFILL attribute is used to change the padding of numeric data types from spaces to zeros. It only changes this padding when displaying numbers. The number is still stored in the field as usual, and requires no extra bytes to store. The only numeric data type that does not allow ZEROFILL is the BIT numeric data type. If the ZEROFILL attribute is specified the field is automatically converted to use the UNSIGNED attribute.

  For integer data types, ZEROFILL pads to the display width, if set. For other numeric data types, the display width is implicit in the field definition. For example, a field defined as DOUBLE(8,4) has an implicit display width of three digits to the left of the decimal point and four digits to the right of the decimal point:

  ```
  mysql> USE test;
  Database changed
  mysql> CREATE TABLE double_zerofill (
      -> db DOUBLE(8,4) NOT NULL DEFAULT 0,
      -> dz DOUBLE(8,4) ZEROFILL NOT NULL DEFAULT 0);
  Query OK, 0 rows affected (0.11 sec)

  mysql> SHOW CREATE TABLE double_zerofill\G
  *************************** 1. row ***************************
          Table: double_zerofill
  Create Table: CREATE TABLE `double_zerofill` (
    `db` double(8,4) NOT NULL DEFAULT '0.0000',
    `dz` double(8,4) unsigned zerofill NOT NULL DEFAULT '000.0000'
  ) ENGINE=InnoDB DEFAULT CHARSET=latin1
  1 row in set (0.00 sec)

  mysql> INSERT INTO double_zerofill (db,dz) VALUES (1,1),(10,10),
      (100,100),(1000,1000);
  Query OK, 4 rows affected (0.06 sec)
  Records: 4  Duplicates: 0  Warnings: 0

  mysql> select db,dz FROM double_zerofill;
  +-----------+-----------+
  | db        | dz        |
  +-----------+-----------+
  |    1.0000 | 001.0000  |
  |   10.0000 | 010.0000  |
  |  100.0000 | 100.0000  |
  | 1000.0000 | 1000.0000 |
  +-----------+-----------+
  4 rows in set (0.01 sec)
  ```

- SERIAL DEFAULT VALUE — The integer numeric types (TINYINT, SMALLINT, MEDIUM-INT, INT, BIGINT) allow the SERIAL DEFAULT VALUE keyword. This is shorthand for NOT NULL AUTO_INCREMENT UNIQUE KEY. Note that this is different from the SERIAL data type:

  ```
  mysql> CREATE TABLE serial_datatype (st1 SERIAL);
  ```

179

```
Query OK, 0 rows affected (0.09 sec)

mysql> SHOW CREATE TABLE serial_datatype\G
*************************** 1. row ***************************
       Table: serial_datatype
Create Table: CREATE TABLE `serial_datatype` (
  `st1` bigint(20) unsigned NOT NULL AUTO_INCREMENT,
  UNIQUE KEY `st1` (`st1`)
) ENGINE=InnoDB DEFAULT CHARSET=latin1
1 row in set (0.00 sec)

mysql> CREATE TABLE serial_keyword (st2 INT SERIAL DEFAULT VALUE);
Query OK, 0 rows affected (0.13 sec)

mysql> SHOW CREATE TABLE serial_keyword\G
*************************** 1. row ***************************
       Table: serial_keyword
Create Table: CREATE TABLE `serial_keyword` (
  `st2` int(11) NOT NULL AUTO_INCREMENT,
  UNIQUE KEY `st2` (`st2`)
) ENGINE=InnoDB DEFAULT CHARSET=latin1
1 row in set (0.00 sec)
```

Table 5-4 (on opposite page) shows a summary of the MySQL numeric data types.

Boolean Types

The ISO SQL:2003 standard defines a boolean data type of BOOLEAN. MySQL supports the standard and adds a nonstandard abbreviation of BOOL. However, MySQL implements BOOLEAN as an alias for TINYINT(1):

```
mysql> CREATE TABLE boolean_test (
    -> bt1 BOOLEAN, bt2 BOOL, bt3 TINYINT(1));
Query OK, 0 rows affected (0.19 sec)

mysql> SHOW CREATE TABLE boolean_test\G
*************************** 1. row ***************************
       Table: boolean_test
Create Table: CREATE TABLE `boolean_test` (
  `bt1` tinyint(1) DEFAULT NULL,
  `bt2` tinyint(1) DEFAULT NULL,
  `bt3` tinyint(1) DEFAULT NULL
) ENGINE=InnoDB DEFAULT CHARSET=latin1
1 row in set (0.01 sec)
mysql> INSERT INTO boolean_test (bt1, bt2, bt3)
    -> VALUES (true, 0, NULL);
Query OK, 1 row affected (0.31 sec)
```

TABLE 5-4

Summary of MySQL Numeric Data Types

Data Type Name	SQL Standard?	Fixed/Variable Length	Size	Attributes
NUMERIC	Yes	Different definitions will have different lengths; however, these lengths are fixed once the field is defined.	See the "DECIMAL Size and Range" subsection in this chapter	AUTO_INCREMENT DEFAULT NOT NULL NULL SIGNED UNSIGNED ZEROFILL
DECIMAL	Yes	Different definitions will have different lengths; however, these lengths are fixed once the field is defined.	See the "DECIMAL Size and Range" subsection in this chapter	DEFAULT NOT NULL NULL SIGNED UNSIGNED ZEROFILL
TINYINT	No	Fixed	1 byte	AUTO_INCREMENT DEFAULT NOT NULL NULL SERIAL DEFAULT VALUE SIGNED UNSIGNED ZEROFILL
SMALLINT	Yes	Fixed	2 bytes	AUTO_INCREMENT DEFAULT NOT NULL NULL SERIAL DEFAULT VALUE SIGNED UNSIGNED ZEROFILL
INT	Yes	Fixed	3 bytes	AUTO_INCREMENT DEFAULT NOT NULL NULL SERIAL DEFAULT VALUE SIGNED UNSIGNED ZEROFILL

continued

	TABLE 5-4	*(continued)*		
Data Type Name	**SQL Standard?**	**Fixed/Variable Length**	**Size**	**Attributes**
MEDIUMINT	No	Fixed	4 bytes	AUTO_INCREMENT DEFAULT NOT NULL NULL SERIAL DEFAULT VALUE SIGNED UNSIGNED ZEROFILL
BIGINT	Yes	Fixed	8 bytes	AUTO_INCREMENT DEFAULT NOT NULL NULL SERIAL DEFAULT VALUE SIGNED UNSIGNED ZEROFILL
FLOAT	Yes	Fixed	4 bytes	AUTO_INCREMENT DEFAULT NOT NULL NULL SIGNED UNSIGNED ZEROFILL
DOUBLE	Yes	Fixed	8 bytes	AUTO_INCREMENT DEFAULT NOT NULL NULL SIGNED UNSIGNED ZEROFILL
BIT	No	Variable	See the "BIT Size and Range" subsection	DEFAULT NOT NULL NULL
REAL	Yes	REAL is an alias for DOUBLE or FLOAT, depending on sql_mode.		
SERIAL	No	SERIAL is an alias for BIGINT UNSIGNED NOT NULL AUTO_INCREMENT UNIQUE KEY.		

A value of 0 is false; non-zero values are true.

```
mysql> INSERT INTO boolean_test (bt1, bt2, bt3)
    -> VALUES (true, 0, 5);
Query OK, 1 row affected (0.20 sec)

mysql> SELECT bt1, bt2, bt3 FROM boolean_test;
+------+------+------+
| bt1  | bt2  | bt3  |
+------+------+------+
|    1 |    0 |    5 |
+------+------+------+
1 row in set (0.00 sec)
```

Recall that TINYINT(1) indicates a default width of 1, even though the field itself will allow values ranging from −128 to 127.

Datetime Types

The ISO SQL:2003 standard defines the following three datetime types:

- DATE
- TIME(p)
- TIMESTAMP(p)

It also specifies the following attributes:

- WITH TIME ZONE
- WITHOUT TIME ZONE

MySQL supports these datetime types, although it does not support the two attributes nor the TIME and TIMESTAMP precision arguments. MySQL adds the following datetime data types:

- YEAR
- DATETIME

The YEAR data type can be specified as YEAR(2) or YEAR(4). MySQL converts other values specified, including no value, as YEAR(4):

```
mysql> create table year_test (
    -> yt1 YEAR, yt2 YEAR(2), yt3 YEAR(1),
    ->  yt4 YEAR(3), yt5 YEAR(7), yt6 YEAR(100));
Query OK, 0 rows affected (0.53 sec)

mysql> SHOW CREATE TABLE year_test\G
```

```
*************************** 1. row ***************************
       Table: year_test
Create Table: CREATE TABLE `year_test` (
  `yt1` year(4) DEFAULT NULL,
  `yt2` year(2) DEFAULT NULL,
  `yt3` year(4) DEFAULT NULL,
  `yt4` year(4) DEFAULT NULL,
  `yt5` year(4) DEFAULT NULL,
  `yt6` year(4) DEFAULT NULL
) ENGINE=InnoDB DEFAULT CHARSET=latin1
1 row in set (0.00 sec)
```

The DATETIME data type contains the date in the format YYYY-mm-dd HH:ii:ss, the same as the TIMESTAMP format. However, DATETIME has a much larger range than TIMESTAMP does. See Table 5-5 for a summary of the datetime types, their ranges, sizes, and zero values.

TABLE 5-5

Datetime Data Types

	Supported Range (Guaranteed to Work)	Size	Zero Value
DATE	'1000-01-01' to '9999-12-31'	3 bytes	'0000-00-00'
DATETIME	'1000-'01-01 00:00:01' to '9999-12-31 23:59:59'	8 bytes	'0000-00-00 00:00:00'
TIMESTAMP	'1970-01-01 00:00:00' to '2038-01-18 22:14:07'	4 bytes	'0000-00-00 00:00:00'
TIME	'−838:59:59' to '838:59:58'	3 bytes	'00:00:00'
YEAR(2)	00 to 99	1 byte	'00"
YEAR(4)	1901 to 2155	1 byte	'0000'

Note that DATE and TIME each have 3 bytes, and together they can represent the same values using 6 bytes a DATETIME value can using 8 bytes.

If mysqld is running with an sql_mode of MAXDB, then TIMESTAMP is an alias for DATETIME, and the range and size are the same.

The YEAR(2) type allows any two-digit unsigned integer. When using this type the year represented depends on the value. For values between 00 and 69, the year represented is 2000 through 2069. For values between 70 and 99, the year represented is 1970 through 1999. In this way, all of the years from 1970 through 2069 can be represented in 2 bytes.

Unlike the other DATETIME data types, TIME can specify a time of day or an interval of time.

Allowed input values

The DATETIME, TIMESTAMP, and DATE values can be inputted in several different ways. The year part always comes first, thus getting rid of the need to worry about whether a locale specifies the date as month-day-year or day-month-year. Note that this is for data input only; the display of data can be formatted in many different ways, including showing the day or month first. See Appendix B for how to use the DATE_FORMAT() function.

The following formats are accepted, assuming they represent valid dates (for example, 99 is not a valid month):

- YYYY-mm-dd HH:ii:ss
- yy-mm-dd HH:ii:ss
- YYYYmmdd
- yymmdd — As a string or as a number, that is, '20090508' or 20090508
- YYYYmmddHHiiss — As a string or as a number
- yymmddHHiiss — As a string or as a number
- Actual datetime type values, such as the return from CURRENT_TIMESTAMP and CURRENT_DATE()

If an input value contains an invalid DATETIME, TIMESTAMP, or DATE value, the zero value will be used instead. The many different types of allowed input can lead to some confusion. The briefest way to specify May 2009 is 090500, which corresponds to 2009-05-00. It is not possible for mysqld to interpret 0905 as a date, because there are not enough digits to represent a year, month, and day — this example could be May 2009 or September 5th. In practice, it is best to use one of the delimited formats for clarification.

A string containing delimiters can use any punctuation in place of any other punctuation. For example, the date 2009-05-08 can be represented with any of the following:

```
mysql> SELECT DATE('2009-05-08'), DATE('2009.05.08'),
    -> DATE('2009!05@08'), DATE('2009#05$08'), DATE('2009%05^08'),
    -> DATE('2009&05*08'), DATE('2009(05)08'), DATE('2009`05~08'),
    -> DATE('2009;05"08'), DATE('2009|05/08'), DATE('2009?05>08'),
    -> DATE("2009'05<08"), DATE('2009\\05_08'), DATE('2009=05+08')\G
*************************** 1. row ***************************
 DATE('2009-05-08'): 2009-05-08
 DATE('2009.05.08'): 2009-05-08
 DATE('2009!05@08'): 2009-05-08
 DATE('2009#05$08'): 2009-05-08
 DATE('2009%05^08'): 2009-05-08
 DATE('2009&05*08'): 2009-05-08
 DATE('2009(05)08'): 2009-05-08
 DATE('2009`05~08'): 2009-05-08
 DATE('2009;05"08'): 2009-05-08
```

```
DATE('2009|05/08'): 2009-05-08
DATE('2009?05>08'): 2009-05-08
DATE("2009'05<08"): 2009-05-08
DATE('2009\\05_08'): 2009-05-08
DATE('2009=05+08'): 2009-05-08
1 row in set (0.00 sec)
```

When using delimiters, values for month, day, hour, minute, and second do not need to have a leading zero if the value is less than ten.

For TIME, the following input formats are supported, assuming the value is a valid time:

- dd HH:ii:ss
- dd HH
- dd HH:ii
- HH:ii:ss
- HH:ii
- ss — As a string or as a number
- HHiiss — As a string or as a number
- iiss — As a string or as a number
- Actual TIME values, such as the return from CURRENT_TIME()

These allowed input values mean that if a TIME value is given a single 2-digit number, it will interpret it as seconds, not days. A more common error is inputting a value such as 11:00, to indicate 11 hours and 0 minutes — but mysqld interprets this as 11 minutes and 0 seconds. When using delimiters, values for day, hour, minute, and second do not need to have a leading zero if the value is less than ten. The valid range of the days value (dd) is an integer from 0 to 34.

Microsecond input

Although functions exist that will use microseconds in their input or output, such as the MICROSECOND() function, there is currently no datetime data type that will store microseconds. To store microseconds, use a numeric data type or a string data type.

The following input values involving microseconds are allowed for the TIME data type:

- dd HH:ii:ss.uuuuuu
- HH:ii:ss.uuuuuu
- HHiiss.uuuuuu — As a string or as a number

The following input values involving microseconds are allowed for the DATETIME and TIME STAMP data types:

- YYYY-mm-dd HH:ii:ss.uuuuuu

- `yy-mm-dd HH:ii:ss.uuuuuu`

- `YYYYmmddHHiiss.uuuuuu` — As a string or as a number

- `yymmddHHiiss.uuuuuu` — As a string or as a number

Note that these values are valid, but microseconds are not stored in any fields. MySQL will truncate microseconds from all datetime data types. The preceding lists are provided to avoid errors due to incorrect formatting of microseconds.

Automatic updates

The `TIMESTAMP` data type allows for automatic updating via the attributes `DEFAULT CURRENT_TIMESTAMP` and `ON UPDATE CURRENT TIMESTAMP`. There can be only one automatically updating `TIMESTAMP` field per table. That is, there can be only one `TIMESTAMP` field that is specified with `DEFAULT CURRENT_TIMESTAMP` or `ON UPDATE CURRENT_TIMESTAMP`. Either or both attributes can be specified on one field. This example shows that only one automatically updating `TIMESTAMP` field is allowed:

```
mysql> CREATE TABLE ts_test (def TIMESTAMP DEFAULT CURRENT_TIMESTAMP,
    -> upd TIMESTAMP ON UPDATE CURRENT_TIMESTAMP);
ERROR 1293 (HY000): Incorrect table definition; there can be only one
    TIMESTAMP column with CURRENT_TIMESTAMP in DEFAULT or ON
    UPDATE clause
mysql> CREATE TABLE ts_test (
    -> ts1 TIMESTAMP DEFAULT CURRENT_TIMESTAMP
    -> ON UPDATE CURRENT_TIMESTAMP,
    -> ts_note varchar(10) NOT NULL DEFAULT '');
Query OK, 0 rows affected (0.19 sec)
```

When a row is inserted, `ts1` is updated with the current time by the `DEFAULT CURRENT_TIMESTAMP` attribute. When a row is updated, `ts1` is updated with the current time by the `ON UPDATE CURRENT_TIMESTAMP` attribute:

```
mysql> SELECT CURRENT_TIMESTAMP(); INSERT INTO ts_test (ts_note) VAL-
UES ('test');
+---------------------+
| CURRENT_TIMESTAMP() |
+---------------------+
| 2008-11-20 07:45:15 |
+---------------------+
1 row in set (0.00 sec)

Query OK, 1 row affected (0.08 sec)

mysql> SELECT CURRENT_TIMESTAMP(); INSERT INTO ts_test (ts_note) VAL-
UES ('later test');
+---------------------+
| CURRENT_TIMESTAMP() |
```

```
+---------------------+
| 2008-11-20 07:45:55 |
+---------------------+
1 row in set (0.00 sec)

Query OK, 1 row affected (0.45 sec)

mysql> SELECT ts1, ts_note FROM ts_test;
+---------------------+------------+
| ts1                 | ts_note    |
+---------------------+------------+
| 2008-11-20 07:45:15 | test       |
| 2008-11-20 07:45:55 | later test |
+---------------------+------------+
2 rows in set (0.00 sec)

mysql> UPDATE ts_test SET ts_note='early test' where ts_note='test';
Query OK, 1 row affected (0.11 sec)
Rows matched: 1  Changed: 1  Warnings: 0

mysql> SELECT ts1, ts_note FROM ts_test;
+---------------------+------------+
| ts1                 | ts_note    |
+---------------------+------------+
| 2008-11-20 07:46:30 | early test |
| 2008-11-20 07:45:55 | later test |
+---------------------+------------+
2 rows in set (0.00 sec)
```

If a TIMESTAMP field is specified with ON UPDATE CURRENT_TIMESTAMP but no DEFAULT is specified, the DEFAULT will be set to the zero value of 0000-00-00 00:00:00.

Conversion issues

One of the features of MySQL that makes it so easy to use is implicit type conversion. This can cause many problems, though, because you may not realize that this is occurring.

Numeric functions and DATETIME types

DATETIME data types are usually formatted as strings, and can be inputted as strings. However, they also have numerical representations, which can be seen by casting the value into a numeric data type. The following example shows the numerical representation of the zero value and a sample value:

```
mysql> CREATE TABLE date_test (dt1 DATE, dt2 DATETIME,
    -> dt3 TIMESTAMP, dt4 TIME, dt5 YEAR(2), dt6 YEAR);
Query OK, 0 rows affected (0.11 sec)
```

```
mysql> show create table date_test\G
*************************** 1. row ***************************
       Table: date_test
Create Table: CREATE TABLE `date_test` (
  `dt1` date DEFAULT NULL,
  `dt2` datetime DEFAULT NULL,
  `dt3` timestamp NOT NULL DEFAULT CURRENT_TIMESTAMP ON UPDATE CUR-
RENT_TIMESTAMP,
  `dt4` time DEFAULT NULL,
  `dt5` year(2) DEFAULT NULL,
  `dt6` year(4) DEFAULT NULL
) ENGINE=InnoDB DEFAULT CHARSET=latin1
1 row in set (0.00 sec)

mysql> INSERT INTO date_test (dt1, dt2, dt3, dt4, dt5, dt6)
    -> VALUES (0,0,0,0,0,0), (CURRENT_DATE, NOW(), NOW(), NOW(),
    YEAR(NOW()), YEAR(NOW()));
Query OK, 2 rows affected (0.17 sec)
Records: 2  Duplicates: 0  Warnings: 0

mysql> SELECT dt1, dt2, dt3, dt4, dt5, dt6 FROM date_test\G
*************************** 1. row ***************************
dt1: 0000-00-00
dt2: 0000-00-00 00:00:00
dt3: 0000-00-00 00:00:00
dt4: 00:00:00
dt5: 00
dt6: 0000
*************************** 2. row ***************************
dt1: 2008-12-17
dt2: 2008-12-17 04:06:11
dt3: 2008-12-17 04:06:11
dt4: 04:06:11
dt5: 08
dt6: 2008
2 rows in set (0.00 sec)

mysql> SELECT dt1+0, dt2+0, dt3+0, dt4+0, dt5+0, dt6+0
    -> FROM date_test\G
*************************** 1. row ***************************
dt1+0: 0
dt2+0: 0.000000
dt3+0: 0
dt4+0: 0
dt5+0: 0
dt6+0: 0
*************************** 2. row ***************************
dt1+0: 20081217
```

```
dt2+0: 20081217040611.000000
dt3+0: 20081217040611
dt4+0: 40611
dt5+0: 8
dt6+0: 2008
2 rows in set (0.01 sec)
```

Some functions, such as SUM( ) and AVG( ), will convert datetime values into numeric values. Using numeric functions on datetime types may not have the desired results. Instead, convert the DATETIME data type to a more appropriate numeric type:

```
mysql> SELECT dt4, dt4+0 FROM date_test;
+----------+-------+
| dt4      | dt4+0 |
+----------+-------+
| 00:00:00 |     0 |
| 06:13:41 | 61341 |
+----------+-------+
2 rows in set (0.00 sec)

mysql> SELECT AVG(dt4), AVG(dt4+0),
    -> SEC_TO_TIME(AVG(TIME_TO_SEC(dt4))) AS date_avg,
    -> SEC_TO_TIME(AVG(TIME_TO_SEC(dt4)))+0 AS date_avg_converted
    -> FROM date_test;
+----------+------------+----------+--------------------+
| AVG(dt4) | AVG(dt4+0) | date_avg | date_avg_converted |
+----------+------------+----------+--------------------+
|  30670.5 |    30670.5 | 03:06:50 |       30650.000000 |
+----------+------------+----------+--------------------+
1 row in set (0.41 sec)
```

The average of 0 and 61341 is 30670.5, but the desired result is the average of the lengths of time — 00:00:00 and 06:13:41 (0 and 6 hours, 13 minutes, and 41 seconds). So the time itself is converted to seconds, the number of seconds is averaged, and the result is converted back to time. To show that the average is actually different, the last field of the result (date_avg_converted) is the proper average converted to a NUMERIC data type. Using numerical functions on non-numerical formats can lead to problems!

Other conversion issues

During implicit conversions, the DATE value is changed into a DATETIME value by appending the zero time 00:00:00 to the date. However, usually when comparing a DATE to a DATETIME or TIMESTAMP field, a comparison of only the date part of the field is desired. The following example shows the difference between implicit conversion of DATE and explicitly casting NOW( ) as a DATE data type:

```
mysql> SELECT IF(CURRENT_DATE=NOW(),1,0);
+----------------------------+
| IF(CURRENT_DATE=NOW(),1,0) |
```

```
+---------------------------+
|                         0 |
+---------------------------+
1 row in set (0.03 sec)

mysql> SELECT IF(CURRENT_DATE=CAST(NOW() AS DATE),1,0);
+------------------------------------------+
| IF(CURRENT_DATE=CAST(NOW() AS DATE),1,0) |
+------------------------------------------+
|                                        1 |
+------------------------------------------+
1 row in set (0.00 sec)
```

Only when the explicit conversion occurs do you receive the functionality you desire — comparing the dates of CURRENT_DATE and NOW() and receiving the answer that they are the same. The reason for this is that NOW() returns the exact date and time, and comparing CURRENT_DATE() to NOW() will convert CURRENT_DATE() to a DATETIME that represents midnight of the current date.

This behavior also shows up when comparing a DATETIME or TIMESTAMP field to a DATE using BETWEEN. The filter:

```
WHERE date_and_time BETWEEN '
    2009-01-01' AND '2009-12-31'
```

acts the same as

```
WHERE date_and_time BETWEEN '
    2009-01-01 00:00:00' AND '2009-12-31 00:00:00'
```

even though the desired behavior is most likely

```
WHERE date_and_time BETWEEN '2009-01-01 00:00:00' AND
    '2009-12-31 23:59:59'
```

Datetime data type attributes

- NOT NULL — NULL values are allowed for all datetime data types. To disallow NULL values, use the NOT NULL attribute. See the "Using NULL Values" section later in this chapter for an explanation of problems NULL values can cause.

- NULL — For the TIMESTAMP data type, allow NULL values. If the NULL attribute is applied to a TIMESTAMP, the DEFAULT value is NULL unless otherwise specified by the DEFAULT attribute:

```
mysql> CREATE TABLE null_ts_test (nt1 TIMESTAMP NULL,
    -> nt2 TIMESTAMP NULL DEFAULT '2009-05-08 12:30:00');
Query OK, 0 rows affected (0.53 sec)

mysql> SHOW CREATE TABLE null_ts_test\G
```

```
*************************** 1. row ***************************
       Table: null_ts_test
Create Table: CREATE TABLE `null_ts_test` (
  `nt1` timestamp NULL DEFAULT NULL,
  `nt2` timestamp NULL DEFAULT '2009-05-08 12:30:00'
) ENGINE=InnoDB DEFAULT CHARSET=latin1
1 row in set (0.00 sec)
```

For all other data types, the NULL attribute is shorthand for DEFAULT NULL. See the "Using NULL Values" section later in this chapter for an explanation of problems NULL values can cause.

■ DEFAULT — The DEFAULT attribute is valid for all datetime data types. The DEFAULT attribute causes a datetime data type to have a default value when a value is not specified. This means that an INSERT statement does not have to include a value for this field; if it does not, the value following DEFAULT will be inserted. Valid DEFAULT values include NULL and valid datetime values for the field, including zero values. Both the actual zero value and 0 will work to specify the zero value:

```
mysql> CREATE TABLE zero_test (
    -> dt1 DATE DEFAULT '0000-00-00', dt2 DATE DEFAULT 0);
Query OK, 0 rows affected (0.13 sec)

mysql> SHOW CREATE TABLE zero_test\G
*************************** 1. row ***************************
       Table: zero_test
Create Table: CREATE TABLE `zero_test` (
  `dt1` date DEFAULT '0000-00-00',
  `dt2` date DEFAULT '0000-00-00'
) ENGINE=InnoDB DEFAULT CHARSET=latin1
1 row in set (0.00 sec)
```

If there is no DEFAULT attribute specified for TIMESTAMP, it is created with the attributes NOT NULL DEFAULT CURRENT_TIMESTAMP ON UPDATE CURRENT_TIMESTAMP (see the section "Automatic Updates" earlier in the chapter). For other datetime data types, if there is no DEFAULT attribute specified, the field will be created with the attribute DEFAULT NULL.

The effect of time zones

The TIMESTAMP field is stored in UTC. When the value is stored, it is converted to UTC, using the mysqld system variable time_zone to figure out the proper value. When a TIMESTAMP value is retrieved, it is converted to the current time_zone of the mysqld server. In this way, if the time zone is changed, the time is the same moment in time. At 5 pm EST, it is 10 pm UTC. If the value '2009-05-2008 17:00:00' is stored when mysqld has a time_zone of EST, and the time_zone is changed to CST (UTC-6), the value retrieved will be '2009-05-2008 16:00:00'. For more on time zones, see Chapter 4.

Note that the default value of time_zone is SYSTEM, and the conversions stated in the preceding paragraph do not occur when the value of time_zone is SYSTEM. Thus, if you try the example using a time_zone of SYSTEM, and change the operating system's time zone, the values are not converted as indicated in the example. The actual time_zone variable of mysqld must be changed for the display conversion to occur.

Interval Types

The ISO SQL:2003 standard defines the following two interval types:

- year-month — The 4-digit year and 2-digit month values (YYYY-mm)
- day-time — The 2-digit values for day, hour, minutes, and seconds (dd HH:ii:ss)

Unlike the other data types discussed in this chapter, the interval data types are not data types that can be stored in a table. Interval data types are used as a part of interval expressions in time-based calculations. The standard usage is the keyword INTERVAL followed by an expression and the interval type, for example, INTERVAL '3-5' year-month to specify 3 years and 5 months, or INTERVAL '1 2:3:4' day-time to specify 1 day, 2 hours, 3 minutes, and 4 seconds.

Table 5-6 shows the interval data types supported by MySQL, along with the expected formatting and a sample interval expression.

As with DATETIME, TIMESTAMP, and TIME data types, the interval data types allow any punctuation. The sample interval expressions in Table 5-6 are suggested by the MySQL 6.0 Reference Manual. If an interval expression contains fewer numbers than expected, zero values are appended to the left-hand side. For example, INTERVAL 1 YEAR_MONTH translates to "0 years + 1 month":

```
mysql> SELECT DATE_ADD('2009-01-01',INTERVAL 1 YEAR_MONTH) as Test;
+------------+
| Test       |
+------------+
| 2009-02-01 |
+------------+
1 row in set (0.05 sec)
```

Interval expressions with more than one number are treated as strings, so INTERVAL '5-4' YEAR_MONTH means "5 years and 4 months." This is different from calculating 5-4 as a numeric expression, yielding the equivalent of INTERVAL 1 YEAR_MONTH. Be careful when using arithmetic inside of a string:

```
mysql> SELECT DATE_ADD('2009-01-01',INTERVAL '5-4' YEAR_MONTH)
    as Test;
+------------+
| Test       |
+------------+
| 2014-05-01 |
+------------+
1 row in set (0.00 sec)
```

TABLE 5-6

Interval Data Types

Name	Standard Type	Format	Sample Interval Expression
MICROSECOND		n	INTERVAL 5 MICROSECOND
SECOND		n	INTERVAL 5 SECOND
MINUTE		n	INTERVAL 5 MINUTE
HOUR		n	INTERVAL 5 HOUR
DAY		n	INTERVAL 5 DAY
WEEK		n	INTERVAL 5 WEEK
MONTH		n	INTERVAL 5 MONTH
QUARTER		n	INTERVAL 5 QUARTER
YEAR		n	INTERVAL 5 YEAR
SECOND_MICROSECOND		'n.n'	INTERVAL `5.4 SECOND_MICROSECOND
MINUTE_MICROSECOND		'n.n'	INTERVAL `5.4 MINUTE_MICROSECOND
MINUTE_SECOND		'n:n'	INTERVAL `5:4 MINUTE_SECOND
HOUR_MICROSECOND		'n.n'	INTERVAL `5.4 HOUR_MICROSECOND
HOUR_SECOND		'n:n:n' (hour:minute:second)	INTERVAL `5:4:3 HOUR_SECOND
HOUR_MINUTE		'n:n'	INTERVAL `5:4 HOUR_MINUTE
DAY_MICROSECOND		'n.n'	INTERVAL `5.4 DAY_MICROSECOND
DAY_SECOND	Day-time	'n n:n:n' (day hour:minute:second)	INTERVAL `5 4:3:2` DAY_SECOND
DAY_MINUTE		'n n:n' (day hour:minute)	INTERVAL `5 4:3` DAY_MINUTE
DAY_HOUR		'n n'	INTERVAL `5 4` DAY_HOUR
YEAR_MONTH	year-month	'n-n'	INTERVAL `5-4` YEAR_MONTH

ENUM and SET Types

MySQL adds in two data types that are very different from standard data types. The ENUM data type is an enumerated list of 1 to 65,535 strings, which indicate the allowed values for the field. Only one of the allowed values can be stored in an ENUM field. The SET data type is an enumerated list of 1 to 64 strings, which indicate the allowed values for the field. In the SET data type, any combination of the strings in the enumerated list can be stored as a comma-delimited list.

The strings for ENUM and SET will have trailing spaces removed. If sql_mode contains TRADI-TIONAL, STRICT_ALL_TABLES, or if the table is a transactional table and sql_mode contains STRICT_TRANS_TABLE, creation of an ENUM or SET field with a duplicate will issue an error. Otherwise, it will issue a warning and allow the field creation. See the section "Choosing SQL Modes" later in this chapter. Because ENUM and SET values are strings, an unexpected duplicate value may occur if the collation of the field is case-insensitive. See Chapter 4 for more information on collations. The sort order of ENUM and SET data types is the order of the strings in the field definition.

Enumerations

Both ENUM and SET are enumerated lists; that is, each possible value is actually a number. The values can be inputted as strings or by their position in the enumerated list (known as the *index number*). If the sql_mode does not include TRADITIONAL, STRICT_TRANS_TABLES, or STRICT_ALL_TABLES, invalid ENUM and SET values are stored as the empty string (""). Otherwise, invalid ENUM and SET values cause mysqld to throw an error, and no values are stored. The index of the empty string is 0:

```
mysql> SET SESSION sql_mode='';
Query OK, 0 rows affected (0.00 sec)
mysql> CREATE TABLE enum_set_index (
    -> et ENUM('a','','1'), st SET('a','1'));
Query OK, 0 rows affected (0.17 sec)

mysql> INSERT INTO enum_set_index (et, st) VALUES
    -> ('a','a'), ('1','1'), ('',''), ('q','q'), (1,1), (NULL,NULL);
Query OK, 6 rows affected, 2 warnings (0.08 sec)
Records: 6  Duplicates: 0  Warnings: 2

mysql> SHOW WARNINGS;
+---------+------+----------------------------------------+
| Level   | Code | Message                                |
+---------+------+----------------------------------------+
| Warning | 1265 | Data truncated for column 'et' at row 4 |
| Warning | 1265 | Data truncated for column 'st' at row 4 |
+---------+------+----------------------------------------+
2 rows in set (0.00 sec)

mysql> SELECT et, et+0 AS enum_index,
```

```
    -> st, st+0 AS st_index
    -> FROM enum_set_index;
+------+------------+------+----------+
| et   | enum_index | st   | st_index |
+------+------------+------+----------+
| a    |          1 | a    |        1 |
| 1    |          3 | 1    |        2 |
|      |          2 |      |        0 |
|      |          0 |      |        0 |
| a    |          1 | a    |        1 |
| NULL |       NULL | NULL |     NULL |
+------+------------+------+----------+
6 rows in set (0.00 sec)
```

Note that inserting string values ('1','1') inserts the enumerated string '1', but inserting numeric values (1,1) inserts the value of the first enumerated string. Also note that in this example, inserting invalid values ('q','q') inserted the enumerated string at position 0, which is always the empty string (''). However, directly inserting the empty string into et, which explicitly enumerates the empty string, inserts the empty string with the index value as determined by the position in the enumerated list.

Using the numeric index to insert values into ENUM and SET fields is not recommended, because there are some quirks:

```
mysql> TRUNCATE enum_set_index;
Query OK, 0 rows affected (0.44 sec)

mysql> INSERT INTO enum_set_index (et, st) VALUES
    -> (0,0), (1,1), (2,2), (3,3), (4,4), (5,5);
Query OK, 6 rows affected, 5 warnings (0.11 sec)
Records: 6  Duplicates: 0  Warnings: 5

mysql> SHOW WARNINGS;
+---------+------+--------------------------------------------+
| Level   | Code | Message                                    |
+---------+------+--------------------------------------------+
| Warning | 1265 | Data truncated for column 'et' at row 1 |
| Warning | 1265 | Data truncated for column 'et' at row 5 |
| Warning | 1265 | Data truncated for column 'st' at row 5 |
| Warning | 1265 | Data truncated for column 'et' at row 6 |
| Warning | 1265 | Data truncated for column 'st' at row 6 |
+---------+------+--------------------------------------------+
5 rows in set (0.00 sec)

mysql> SELECT et, et+0 AS enum_index,
    -> st, st+0 AS st_index
    -> FROM enum_set_index;
```

```
+------+------------+------+----------+
| et   | enum_index | st   | st_index |
+------+------------+------+----------+
|      |          0 |      |        0 |
| a    |          1 | a    |        1 |
|      |          2 | 1    |        2 |
| 1    |          3 | a,1  |        3 |
|      |          0 |      |        0 |
|      |          0 | a    |        1 |
+------+------------+------+----------+
6 rows in set (0.00 sec)
```

From this result, the behavior of ENUM and SET fields is:

- ENUM and SET fields are defined with a limited set of strings. The index values of these strings start at 1 for the first string. Inserting a number that directly corresponds to the index value of the defined strings into an ENUM or SET field has the same result as inserting that string into a field.

- The ENUM data type indexes its string values sequentially. The fifth value in the ENUM definition has an index value of 5. Inserting a number into an ENUM field that is greater than the largest index value of the defined strings is the same as inserting invalid data.

- The SET data type treats its string values as digits in a 64-bit binary value. The index value of the first string is 1, the index value of the second string is 2 (10 in binary), and the index value of the third string is 4 (100 in binary). An index value of 3 (11 in binary) indicates both the first and second strings — in binary, 1+10=11. This property means that order does not matter, because the SET value a,1 is the same as the SET value 1,a. Both will be displayed as a,1 upon retrieval from the table and have the same index value.

- To compare SET values, a bitwise comparison can be done. To find exact matches, use bitwise and (&). To find if one set is a subset of another, use bitwise or (|). Alternatively, the string function FIND_IN_SET() and string comparison LIKE can be used to find exact matches and subsets. See Appendix B for how to use FIND_IN_SET() and LIKE.

- Due to the binary nature described in the previous items, the SET data type accounts for (2^n)-1 index values, where n is the number of strings listed. In our example, the number of strings listed was 2 (a and 1) so the number of index values accounted for is (2^2)-1=3.

- Any index values greater than the number accounted for by (2^n)-1 are converted to accounted numbers by calculating the remainder modulo t, where t is 2^n. In our example, t is 2^2=4, so inserting an index value of 4 corresponds to 4%4=0, and thus index 0, the empty string, is inserted. Inserting an index value of 5 corresponds to 5%4=1, and thus index 1, the value a, is inserted.

Note that these index values refer only to the enumerated value of the string, and has no relation to table indexes.

ENUM and SET data type attributes

The ENUM and SET types can be defined with attributes that affect the allowed values:

- NOT NULL — By default, NULL values are allowed. To disallow NULL values, use the NOT NULL attribute. See the "Using NULL Values" section later in this chapter for an explanation of problems NULL values can cause.

- NULL — The NULL attribute is shorthand for DEFAULT NULL. See the "Using NULL Values" section later in this chapter for an explanation of problems NULL values can cause. The index of NULL is NULL:

```
mysql> CREATE TABLE enum_test (et ENUM('a'));
Query OK, 0 rows affected (0.11 sec)

mysql> INSERT INTO enum_test (et) VALUES('a'),('b'),(''),(NULL);
Query OK, 4 rows affected, 2 warnings (0.09 sec)
Records: 4  Duplicates: 0  Warnings: 2

mysql> SHOW WARNINGS;
+---------+------+------------------------------------------+
| Level   | Code | Message                                  |
+---------+------+------------------------------------------+
| Warning | 1265 | Data truncated for column 'et' at row 2 |
| Warning | 1265 | Data truncated for column 'et' at row 3 |
+---------+------+------------------------------------------+
2 rows in set (0.00 sec)

mysql> SELECT et, et+0 AS Enum_index FROM enum_test;
+------+------------+
| et   | Enum_index |
+------+------------+
| a    |          1 |
|      |          0 |
|      |          0 |
| NULL |       NULL |
+------+------------+
4 rows in set (0.00 sec)
```

- DEFAULT — The DEFAULT attribute causes an ENUM or SET data type to have a default value when a value is not specified. This means that an INSERT statement does not have to include a value for this field; if it does not, the value following DEFAULT will be inserted. Valid DEFAULT values include NULL and valid string values for the field, including the empty string (""). Functions are not allowed in a DEFAULT expression.

  If no DEFAULT value is specified, MySQL will create ENUM and SET fields as DEFAULT NULL. If no DEFAULT value is specified and NOT NULL is specified, the DEFAULT value is the first item in the enumerated list.

  Because of the special treatment of NULL and empty string values, the only way to store a default value is not to specify a value for this field:

```
mysql> SET SESSION sql_mode='';
Query OK, 0 rows affected (0.00 sec)

mysql> CREATE TABLE enum_set_test (
    -> et ENUM('a','1') NOT NULL DEFAULT '1',
    -> st SET('a','1') NOT NULL DEFAULT 'a,1',
    -> id TINYINT NOT NULL);
Query OK, 0 rows affected (0.16 sec)

mysql> INSERT INTO enum_set_test (et, st, id)
    -> VALUES ('1','1',1), ('','',2), (NULL,NULL,3), ('q','q',4);
Query OK, 4 rows affected, 5 warnings (0.11 sec)
Records: 4  Duplicates: 0  Warnings: 5

mysql> SHOW WARNINGS;
+---------+------+----------------------------------------------+
| Level   | Code | Message                                      |
+---------+------+----------------------------------------------+
| Warning | 1265 | Data truncated for column 'et' at row 2      |
| Warning | 1048 | Column 'et' cannot be null                   |
| Warning | 1048 | Column 'st' cannot be null                   |
| Warning | 1265 | Data truncated for column 'et' at row 4      |
| Warning | 1265 | Data truncated for column 'st' at row 4      |
+---------+------+----------------------------------------------+
5 rows in set (0.00 sec)

mysql> SELECT et, st, id FROM enum_set_test;
+----+----+----+
| et | st | id |
+----+----+----+
| 1  | 1  |  1 |
|    |    |  2 |
|    |    |  3 |
|    |    |  4 |
+----+----+----+
4 rows in set (0.01 sec)

mysql> INSERT INTO enum_set_test (id) VALUES (5);
Query OK, 1 row affected (0.11 sec)

mysql> SELECT et, et+0 AS enum_index,
    -> st, st+0 AS set_index, id FROM
    -> enum_set_test;
+----+------------+-----+-----------+----+
| et | enum_index | st  | set_index | id |
+----+------------+-----+-----------+----+
| 1  |          2 | 1   |         2 |  1 |
|    |          0 |     |         0 |  2 |
|    |          0 |     |         0 |  3 |
```

```
|    |           0 |    |         0 | 4 |
| 1  |           2 | a,1 |         3 | 5 |
+----+-----------+-----+-----------+----+
5 rows in set (0.02 sec)
```

Table 5-7 shows a summary of the ENUM and SET data types.

TABLE 5-7

Summary of MySQL ENUM and SET Data Types

Data Type Name	Fixed/Variable Length	Size	Attributes
ENUM	Different definitions will have different lengths; however, these lengths are fixed once the field is defined.	1–255 enumerated strings, 1 byte 256–65,535 enumerated strings, 2 bytes	DEFAULT NOT NULL NULL
SET	Different definitions will have different lengths; however these lengths are fixed once the field is defined.	1 enumerated string, 1 byte 2–9 enumerated strings, 2 bytes 10–17 enumerated strings, 3 bytes 18–25 enumerated strings, 4 bytes 26–64 enumerated strings, 8 bytes	DEFAULT NOT NULL NULL

The numbers given in the preceding table are for basic storage requirements of MySQL. The storage engine used may add additional overhead or provide data compression that reduces the storage required. See Chapter 11 for more details about storage engines.

WARNING When changing the list of allowed values in ENUM and SET fields, the entire table may need to be rebuilt, which will lock the table such that neither reads nor writes can occur. There is no need to rebuild a table when adding one or more allowed value(s) to an ENUM or SET field at the end of the existing list. Adding allowed values in this manner is an online operation, requiring no locks.

ON the WEBSITE MySQL has implemented special data types for spatial data, including GEOMETRY, POINT, LINESTRING, POLYGON, MULTIPOINT, MULTILINESTRING, MULTIPOLYGON, and GEOMETRYCOLLECTION. For information on how to use spatial data in MySQL, please see this book's companion website at www.wiley.com/go/mysqladminbible.

Rebuilding the table occurs when you remove one or more allowed value(s) from an ENUM or SET field and when you add one or more new allowed value(s) and change the index number of existing allowed value(s). For more information on the ALTER TABLE operations that cause locking, see Chapter 4.

Choosing SQL Modes

For a long time, mysqld had automatically allowed inserting invalid data, truncating data, and more. Implicit data conversions were done by mysqld, often leading to unexpected data and data integrity problems. The sql_mode server variable can be set to change the default behavior of data validation and allowed SQL syntax. The value of the sql_mode server variable can be set on a global level with the sql_mode option to mysqld or the SET GLOBAL sql_mode=string command. The sql_mode server variable can be set per session with the SET SESSION sql_mode=string command. The string argument can be the empty string (''), or a comma-separated list of one or more of the valid values. The list may not have any spaces between values. DB2,IGNORE_SPACE is a valid sql_mode, but DB2, IGNORE_SPACE is not valid because there is a space after the comma.

Throughout this chapter and the MySQL manual, referring to a *strict* sql_mode means the sql_mode variable contains one or more of TRADITIONAL, STRICT_TRANS_TABLES, or STRICT_ALL_TABLES.

To see the value of the global server variable, use one of the following methods:

```
SHOW GLOBAL VARIABLES LIKE 'sql_mode';

SELECT @@global.sql_mode;

SELECT Variable_name, Variable_value
FROM INFORMATION_SCHEMA.GLOBAL_VARIABLES
WHERE Variable_name='sql_mode';
```

To see the value of the session server variable, use one of the following methods:

```
SHOW SESSION VARIABLES LIKE 'sql_mode';

SELECT @@session.sql_mode;

SELECT Variable_name, Variable_value
FROM INFORMATION_SCHEMA.SESSION_VARIABLES
WHERE Variable_name='sql_mode';
```

The default global sql_mode is ''. The default session sql_mode is the global sql_mode.

Invalid data

The most desired behavior of an sql_mode is the ability to change whether invalid data throws an error or simply a warning. The following is an example of the permissive default behavior, when sql_mode is set to '':

```
mysql> SET SESSION sql_mode='';
Query OK, 0 rows affected (0.00 sec)
```

```
mysql> USE test;
Database changed
mysql> CREATE TABLE sql_mode_test (sm1 tinyint not null);
Query OK, 0 rows affected (0.20 sec)

mysql> INSERT INTO sql_mode_test (sm1) VALUES (126);
Query OK, 1 row affected (0.13 sec)

mysql> INSERT INTO sql_mode_test (sm1) VALUES (127);
Query OK, 1 row affected (0.09 sec)

mysql> INSERT INTO sql_mode_test (sm1) VALUES (128);
Query OK, 1 row affected, 1 warning (0.13 sec)

mysql> SHOW WARNINGS;
+---------+------+----------------------------------------------------+
| Level   | Code | Message                                            |
+---------+------+----------------------------------------------------+
| Warning | 1264 | Out of range value for column 'sm1' at row 1       |
+---------+------+----------------------------------------------------+
1 row in set (0.00 sec)

mysql> SELECT sm1 FROM sql_mode_test;
+-----+
| sm1 |
+-----+
| 126 |
| 127 |
| 127 |
+-----+
3 rows in set (0.00 sec)
```

The inserted value that was too large for the field was truncated to the closest value that did fit in the field. Similarly, for string data, strings get truncated if they are too large. This behavior may or may not be desired; if it is not desired, set the appropriate sql_mode to throw an error:

```
mysql> SET SESSION sql_mode='TRADITIONAL';
Query OK, 0 rows affected (0.00 sec)

mysql> TRUNCATE sql_mode_test;
Query OK, 0 rows affected (0.42 sec)

mysql> INSERT INTO sql_mode_test (sm1) VALUES (126);
Query OK, 1 row affected (0.08 sec)

mysql> INSERT INTO sql_mode_test (sm1) VALUES (127);
Query OK, 1 row affected (0.09 sec)
```

```
mysql> INSERT INTO sql_mode_test (sm1) VALUES (128);
ERROR 1264 (22003): Out of range value for column 'sm1' at row 1
mysql> SELECT sm1 FROM sql_mode_test;
+-----+
| sm1 |
+-----+
| 126 |
| 127 |
+-----+
2 rows in set (0.00 sec)
```

SQL modes

Some values of sql_mode perform similar functions to each other, such as STRICT_ALL_TABLES and STRICT_TRANS_TABLES. Others can interact differently, for example ERROR_FOR_DIVISION_BY_ZERO causes division (or modulus) by zero to result in invalid data — if this data is used as an input value to a table and a strict sql_mode is used, an error will arise. If this data is used as an input value to a table and there is no strict sql_mode used, a warning will arise and truncation will occur with a warning. Some values of sql_mode are shorter ways to specify a certain set of sql_mode values.

SQL mode functionality

The values of sql_mode can be grouped into their approximate functions:

- Getting rid of silent failures, silent conversions, and silently allowing invalid data:
    - ALLOW_INVALID_DATES
    - ERROR_FOR_DIVISION_BY_ZERO
    - NO_AUTO_CREATE_USER
    - NO_AUTO_VALUE_ON_ZERO
    - NO_ENGINE_SUBSTITUTION
    - NO_ZERO_DATE
    - NO_ZERO_IN_DATE
    - STRICT_ALL_TABLES
    - STRICT_TRANS_TABLES
- Other changes to default behavior:
    - HIGH_NOT_PRECEDENCE
    - IGNORE_SPACE
    - NO_BACKSLASH_ESCAPES
    - NO_DIR_IN_CREATE
    - PAD_CHAR_TO_FULL_LENGTH

- Portability:
  - ANSI QUOTES
  - NO_FIELD_OPTIONS
  - NO_KEY_OPTIONS
  - NO_TABLE_OPTIONS
  - NO_UNSIGNED_SUBTRACTION
  - ONLY_FULL_GROUP_BY
  - PIPES_AS_CONCAT
  - REAL_AS_FLOAT
- Act like other database systems:
  - ANSI
  - DB2
  - MAXDB
  - MSSQL
  - MYSQL323
  - MYSQL40
  - ORACLE
  - POSTGRESQL
  - TRADITIONAL

SQL mode definitions

- ALLOW_INVALID_DATES — Any date in a DATETIME or DATE data type is allowed, provided the month is between 1 and 12 and the day is between 1 and 31. Invalid dates such as February 30th and September 31st are allowed — recall that invalid date insertion will throw an error if a strict sql_mode is used, otherwise it will insert a zero date.

- ANSI — Syntax and behavior closely match the SQL standard. Equivalent to setting the sql_mode to 'REAL_AS_FLOAT,PIPES_AS_CONCAT,ANSI_QUOTES,IGNORE_SPACE'. The --ansi option to mysqld sets the global sql_mode to ANSI and changes the transaction isolation level to SERIALIZABLE.

- ANSI QUOTES — A double quote (") is now treated as an identifier quote (`). Strings can only be quoted with a single quote (').

- DB2 — Syntax and behavior closely match that of IBM's DB2 database. Equivalent to setting the sql_mode to 'PIPES_AS_CONCAT,ANSI_QUOTES,IGNORE_SPACE,NO_KEY_OPTIONS,NO_TABLE_OPTIONS,NO_FIELD_OPTIONS'.

- ERROR_FOR_DIVISION_BY_ZERO — Division or modulo 0 functions return NULL with no warning if this sql_mode is not set. If this sql_mode is set, the return value is NULL with a warning:

```
mysql> SET SESSION sql_mode='';
Query OK, 0 rows affected (0.00 sec)

mysql> select 1/0;
+------+
| 1/0  |
+------+
| NULL |
+------+
1 row in set (0.05 sec)

mysql> SET SESSION sql_mode='ERROR_FOR_DIVISION_BY_ZERO';
Query OK, 0 rows affected (0.00 sec)

mysql> select 1/0;
+------+
| 1/0  |
+------+
| NULL |
+------+
1 row in set, 1 warning (0.00 sec)

mysql> SHOW WARNINGS;
+-------+------+---------------+
| Level | Code | Message       |
+-------+------+---------------+
| Error | 1365 | Division by 0 |
+-------+------+---------------+
1 row in set (0.00 sec)
```

Combined with a strict sql_mode, the INSERT and UPDATE operations will throw an error when trying to update data with this type of expression. Note that INSERT IGNORE and UPDATE IGNORE will ignore an update with this type of expression and merely issue a warning, even with a strict sql_mode enabled.

■ HIGH_NOT_PRECEDENCE — Without this sql_mode set, the NOT operator has a higher precedence than some operators, such as AND and OR, but has a lower precedence than other operators, such as BETWEEN and LIKE. You can see the complete precedence list in Appendix B.

■ When HIGH_NOT_PRECEDENCE is set in the sql_mode, the NOT operator takes a higher precedence. For example, the expression NOT 1 BETWEEN -5 AND 5 is parsed using regular precedence rules as NOT (1 BETWEEN -5 AND 5). This is equivalent to NOT (true), which evaluates to 0.

■ With the sql_mode of HIGH_NOT_PRECEDENCE set, the expression NOT 1 BETWEEN -5 AND 5 is parsed as (NOT 1) BETWEEN -5 AND 5. This is equivalent to 0 BETWEEN -5 AND 5, which evaluates to 1.

- IGNORE_SPACE — This sql_mode allows a space between a built-in function and the open parenthesis. For example, with this sql_mode, both COUNT (*) and COUNT(*) are valid. This means that built-in functions are now treated as reserved words, and must be escaped with an identifier quote (the backtick ['] character, or double quotes ["] if an sql_mode of ANSI_QUOTES is also set).

  User-defined functions or stored functions are not affected by IGNORE_SPACE; they do not need to be, because they always ignore spaces between the function name and the open parenthesis.

- MAXDB — Syntax and behavior closely matches SAP's MaxDB. Equivalent to setting the sql_mode to 'PIPES_AS_CONCAT, ANSI_QUOTES, IGNORE_SPACE, NO_KEY_OPTIONS, NO_TABLE_OPTIONS, NO_FIELD_OPTIONS, NO_AUTO_CREATE_USER', and makes TIMESTAMP an alias for DATETIME.

- MSSQL — Syntax and behavior closely matches Microsoft's SQL Server. Equivalent to setting the sql_mode to 'PIPES_AS_CONCAT, ANSI_QUOTES, IGNORE_SPACE, NO_KEY_OPTIONS, NO_TABLE_OPTIONS, NO_FIELD_OPTIONS'.

- MYSQL323 — Syntax and behavior closely matches MySQL version 3.23. Equivalent to setting the sql_mode to 'NO_FIELD_OPTIONS, HIGH_NOT_PRECEDENCE'.

- MYSQL40 — Syntax and behavior closely matches MySQL version 4.0. Equivalent to setting the sql_mode to 'NO_FIELD_OPTIONS, HIGH_NOT_PRECEDENCE'.

- NO_AUTO_CREATE_USER — With this sql_mode set, a GRANT statement only creates a new user automatically if a non-empty password is specified. If this sql_mode is not set, a GRANT statement will create a new user if the specified user does not exist, and allow passwordless login for that user (effectively gives that user a password of ").

- NO_AUTO_VALUE_ON_ZERO — A numeric data type field with the AUTO_INCREMENT property will issue the next number in the sequence if 0 or NULL is inserted. With this sql_mode set, inserting a value of 0 will actually insert 0 into the field, and only a NULL value will result in the next sequential number being inserted into the field.

- NO_BACKSLASH_ESCAPES — If this sql_mode is set, the backslash (\) becomes an ordinary character, instead of a character that can be used to escape other characters.

- NO_DIR_IN_CREATE — The directories for the data and index files for a non-partitioned MyISAM table can be specified during table creation time with the DATA DIRECTORY and INDEX DIRECTORY options to CREATE TABLE. This sql_mode ignores those options, which may be desired on a slave server.

- NO_ENGINE_SUBSTITUTION — If this sql_mode is set, an ALTER TABLE or CREATE TABLE statement that specifies a disabled or unavailable storage engine throws an error. If this sql_mode is not set, such an ALTER TABLE statement would not change the table and a warning would be thrown; a similar CREATE TABLE statement would create a table with the default storage engine type and throw a warning.

- NO_FIELD_OPTIONS — If this sql_mode is set, the output of SHOW CREATE TABLE will not show MySQL-specific field definition options and properties.

- NO_KEY_OPTIONS — If this sql_mode is set, the output of SHOW CREATE TABLE will not show MySQL-specific index options and properties.

- NO_TABLE_OPTIONS — If this sql_mode is set, the output of SHOW CREATE TABLE will not show MySQL-specific table options and properties.

- NO_UNSIGNED_SUBTRACTION — If this sql_mode is set, the result of a subtraction is always a signed numeric value. If this sql_mode is not set, the result of a subtraction is an unsigned numeric value if one of the operands is unsigned. Due to the different ranges of SIGNED and UNSIGNED integer data types (see Table 5-3), subtraction with an UNSIGNED BIGINT operand may not obtain the desired results:

```
mysql> SET SESSION SQL_MODE='';
Query OK, 0 rows affected (0.00 sec)
mysql> SELECT CAST(0 AS UNSIGNED) - 1;
+------------------------+
| CAST(0 AS UNSIGNED) - 1 |
+------------------------+
|   18446744073709551615 |
+------------------------+
1 row in set (0.00 sec)

mysql> SET SESSION SQL_MODE='NO_UNSIGNED_SUBTRACTION';
Query OK, 0 rows affected (0.00 sec)

mysql> SELECT CAST(0 AS UNSIGNED) - 1;
+------------------------+
| CAST(0 AS UNSIGNED) - 1 |
+------------------------+
|                     -1 |
+------------------------+
1 row in set (0.00 sec)
```

- NO_ZERO_DATE — If this sql_mode is not set, a warning is generated if a date field has a zero date ('0000-00-00') inserted or updated. A warning will also be issued if this sql_mode is set and a strict sql_mode is also set, and INSERT IGNORE or UPDATE IGNORE is used to change the date field to a zero date. Otherwise, if this sql_mode is set and a strict sql_mode is also set, a zero date insertion or update will be rejected with an error.

- NO_ZERO_IN_DATE — If this sql_mode is not set, partial or total zero dates are allowed:

```
mysql> USE test;
Database changed
mysql> SET SESSION SQL_MODE='';
Query OK, 0 rows affected (0.00 sec)
mysql> CREATE TABLE date_zero_test (dt1 char(10) DEFAULT NULL,
    -> dt2 date DEFAULT NULL);
Query OK, 0 rows affected (0.00 sec)
```

207

```
mysql> INSERT INTO date_zero_test (dt1, dt2) VALUES
    -> ('2012-11-25','2012-11-25'),('2012-11-00','2012-11-00'),
    -> ('2012-00-25','2012-00-25'),('2012-00-00','2012-00-00'),
    -> ('0000-11-25','0000-11-25'),('0000-11-00','0000-11-00'),
    -> ('0000-00-25','0000-00-25'),('0000-00-00','0000-00-00');
Records: 8  Duplicates: 0  Warnings: 0

mysql> SELECT dt1, dt2 FROM date_zero_test;
+------------+------------+
| dt1        | dt2        |
+------------+------------+
| 2012-11-25 | 2012-11-25 |
| 2012-11-00 | 2012-11-00 |
| 2012-00-25 | 2012-00-25 |
| 2012-00-00 | 2012-00-00 |
| 0000-11-25 | 0000-11-25 |
| 0000-11-00 | 0000-11-00 |
| 0000-00-25 | 0000-00-25 |
| 0000-00-00 | 0000-00-00 |
+------------+------------+
8 rows in set (0.00 sec)
```

If this sql_mode is set, a warning is generated and a zero date is inserted if an INSERT or UPDATE on a date field tries to use a date with a non-zero year part and a zero month or a zero day part (that is, '2009-11-00' or '2009-00-20').

```
mysql> TRUNCATE date_zero_test;
Query OK, 0 rows affected (0.00 sec)
mysql> SET SESSION sql_mode='NO_ZERO_IN_DATE';
Query OK, 0 rows affected (0.00 sec)
mysql> INSERT INTO date_zero_test (dt1, dt2) VALUES
    -> ('2012-11-25','2012-11-25'),('2012-11-00','2012-11-00'),
    -> ('2012-00-25','2012-00-25'),('2012-00-00','2012-00-00'),
    -> ('0000-11-25','0000-11-25'),('0000-11-00','0000-11-00'),
    -> ('0000-00-25','0000-00-25'),('0000-00-00','0000-00-00');
Query OK, 8 rows affected, 5 warnings (0.00 sec)
Records: 8  Duplicates: 0  Warnings: 5
mysql> SHOW WARNINGS;
+---------+------+------------------------------------------------+
| Level   | Code | Message                                        |
+---------+------+------------------------------------------------+
| Warning | 1265 | Data truncated for column 'dt2' at row 2 |
| Warning | 1265 | Data truncated for column 'dt2' at row 3 |
| Warning | 1265 | Data truncated for column 'dt2' at row 4 |
| Warning | 1265 | Data truncated for column 'dt2' at row 6 |
| Warning | 1265 | Data truncated for column 'dt2' at row 7 |
+---------+------+------------------------------------------------+
5 rows in set (0.00 sec)
```

```
mysql> SELECT dt1, dt2 FROM date_zero_test;
+------------+------------+
| dt1        | dt2        |
+------------+------------+
| 2012-11-25 | 2012-11-25 |
| 2012-11-00 | 0000-00-00 |
| 2012-00-25 | 0000-00-00 |
| 2012-00-00 | 0000-00-00 |
| 0000-11-25 | 0000-11-25 |
| 0000-11-00 | 0000-00-00 |
| 0000-00-25 | 0000-00-00 |
| 0000-00-00 | 0000-00-00 |
+------------+------------+
8 rows in set (0.00 sec)
```

A warning will also be issued and a zero date (0000-00-00) is used if this sql_mode is set and a strict sql_mode is also set, and INSERT IGNORE or UPDATE IGNORE is used to change the date field to a date with a non-zero part. Otherwise, if this sql_mode is set and a strict sql_mode is also set, a zero date insertion or update will be rejected with an error:

```
mysql> TRUNCATE date_zero_test;
Query OK, 0 rows affected (0.00 sec)

mysql> SET SESSION sql_mode='NO_ZERO_IN_DATE,STRICT_ALL_TABLES';
Query OK, 0 rows affected (0.00 sec)

mysql> INSERT INTO date_zero_test (dt1, dt2) VALUES
    -> ('2012-11-25','2012-11-25'),('2012-11-00','2012-11-00'),
    -> ('2012-00-25','2012-00-25'),('2012-00-00','2012-00-00'),
    -> ('0000-11-25','0000-11-25'),('0000-11-00','0000-11-00'),
    -> ('0000-00-25','0000-00-25'),('0000-00-00','0000-00-00');ERROR
  1292 (22007): Incorrect date value: '2012-11-00' for column
  'dt2' at row 2
mysql> SELECT dt1, dt2 FROM date_zero_test;
+------------+------------+
| dt1        | dt2        |
+------------+------------+
| 2012-11-25 | 2012-11-25 |
+------------+------------+
1 row in set (0.00 sec)
```

■ ONLY_FULL_GROUP_BY — When this sql_mode is set, a GROUP BY query requires the fields in the SELECT and HAVING clauses to contain only aggregated fields and the fields in the GROUP BY clause. That is, no fields can appear in the SELECT or HAVING clauses unless they are either in the GROUP BY clause or an aggregation of fields.

```
mysql> SET SESSION sql_mode='';
Query OK, 0 rows affected (0.00 sec)
```

```
mysql> USE sakila;
Database changed
mysql> SELECT AVG(length),rental_duration,title FROM film GROUP BY
    rental_duration;
+-------------+-----------------+-----------------+
| AVG(length) | rental_duration | title           |
+-------------+-----------------+-----------------+
|    112.9113 |               3 | ACE GOLDFINGER  |
|    111.2315 |               4 | ALI FOREVER     |
|    116.5602 |               5 | AFFAIR PREJUDICE|
|    117.0377 |               6 | ACADEMY DINOSAUR|
|    118.8272 |               7 | ADAPTATION HOLES|
+-------------+-----------------+-----------------+
5 rows in set (0.00 sec)

mysql> SET SESSION sql_mode='ONLY_FULL_GROUP_BY';
Query OK, 0 rows affected (0.03 sec)

mysql> SELECT AVG(length),rental_duration,title FROM film GROUP BY
    rental_duration;
ERROR 1055 (42000): 'sakila.film.title' isn't in GROUP BY
```

- ORACLE — Syntax and behavior closely matches Oracle. Equivalent to setting the sql_mode to 'PIPES_AS_CONCAT,ANSI_QUOTES,IGNORE_SPACE,NO_KEY_OPTIONS, NO_TABLE_OPTIONS,NO_FIELD_OPTIONS,NO_AUTO_CREATE_USER'.

- PAD_CHAR_TO_FULL_LENGTH — If this sql_mode is set, the behavior of retrieving a fixed-width string from a table is changed. See the note in the subsection on CHAR length earlier in this chapter.

- PIPES_AS_CONCAT — When this sql_mode is not set, || is an alias for OR. When this sql_mode is set, || is a string concatenation operator.

- POSTGRESQL — Syntax and behavior closely matches Postgresql. Equivalent to setting the sql_mode to 'PIPES_AS_CONCAT, ANSI_QUOTES, IGNORE_SPACE, NO_KEY_OPTIONS, NO_TABLE_OPTIONS, NO_FIELD_OPTIONS'.

- REAL_AS_FLOAT — When this sql_mode is not set, REAL is an alias for DOUBLE. When this sql_mode is set, REAL is an alias for FLOAT.

- STRICT_ALL_TABLES — When this sql_mode is not set, invalid data values are allowed, usually converted to valid data by using zero values or truncating the value. When this sql_mode is set, invalid data values are rejected, and an error is thrown. If there are multiple values in an insert or update to a non-transactional table, the updates prior to the error are completed even though the statement itself throws an error.

  If the sql_mode of STRICT_ALL_TABLES is set, the behavior of allowing invalid data and throwing a warning can be accomplished by using INSERT IGNORE and UPDATE IGNORE.

- STRICT_TRANS_TABLES — When this sql_mode is not set, invalid data values are allowed, usually converted to valid data by using zero values or truncating the value.

When this `sql_mode` is set, invalid data values in a transactional table are rejected, and an error is thrown. For invalid data inserted or updated to non-transactional tables, invalid data values are truncated or converted to zero values.

If the `sql_mode` of `STRICT_TRANS_TABLES` is set, the behavior of allowing invalid data in transactional tables and throwing a warning can be accomplished by using `INSERT IGNORE` and `UPDATE IGNORE`.

- `TRADITIONAL` — Syntax and behavior closely match traditional expectations. Equivalent to setting the `sql_mode` to `'STRICT_TRANS_TABLES, STRICT_ALL_TABLES, NO_ZERO_IN_DATE, NO_ZERO_DATE, ERROR_FOR_DIVISION_BY_ZERO, NO_AUTO_CREATE_USER'`.

Using NULL Values

Allowing `NULL` values in data types should be done only with some forethought. Many properties of `NULL` make it undesirable:

- A field that allows `NULL` values (that is, is not specified with `NOT NULL`) uses more storage space and more resources to process storage, retrieval, comparisons, and calculations. The empty string (''), and zero values such as 0 and 0000-00-00 use less space than `NULL`.

- Most operators and functions are not `NULL`-safe, and will return `NULL` if there is at least one `NULL` value used. For example, the following all return `NULL`:

```
SELECT 1+NULL;
SELECT CONCAT('foo',NULL);
SELECT NULL=NULL;
SELECT NULL<1;
SELECT NULL!=NULL;
```

This means that any number field that may be used in a calculation and allows `NULL` values either must use `NULL`-safe tests and operators, or risk returning `NULL`.

- Aggregate functions such as `SUM()`, `COUNT()`, `MIN()`, `MAX()`, and `AVG()` ignore `NULL` values. This may or may not be desired behavior — on the one hand, `SUM(fld)` should return a number and ignore `NULL` values. On the other hand, `COUNT(fld)` should return the same result as `COUNT(*)`, and if `fld` has `NULL` values, the results will be different. In a `GROUP BY`, `NULL` values are seen as equivalent and grouped together.

- `NULL` values make field and index statistics more time-consuming to calculate.

- Only the MyISAM, InnoDB, and MEMORY storage engines support `NULL` values on an indexed field. In addition, each record in an indexed field that allows `NULL` values uses an extra byte.

- `NULL` values appear first in an ascending sort, and last in a descending sort.

However, the original purpose of NULL values should not be overlooked — a NULL value means "no value has been determined." This is very different from an empty or zero value. An income of 0 is very different from a NULL income — with an income of 0, it is known that the amount of money brought in was 0. With a NULL income, the amount of money brought in is not known.

Finding an Optimal Data Type for Existing Data

For some database administrators, there is an existing database with many fields of unknown optimization. Does a name field need to be VARCHAR(255)? Does an id field need to be BIGINT? In almost all cases, the answer to these questions is "no." However, answering "how many characters should a name field be?" is a much more difficult question.

The PROCEDURE ANALYSE() function analyzes the fields returned by a SELECT query to see what an optimal data type is. There are two optional arguments to PROCEDURE ANALYSE():

- The first argument is the maximum number of values to consider for an ENUM data type (enumerated list). The default is 256; in practice, a lower value is usually preferred. Maintaining an ENUM data type can become unwieldy after a few dozen values.

- The second argument is the amount of memory in bytes to use per field to determine an optimal data type. The default is 8192.

The film table in the sakila sample database defines title field as:

```
`title` varchar(255) NOT NULL
```

Right away, notice that such a big value for title is probably not necessary. Even though VARCHAR only stores the actual amount of data plus some overhead, when fields are stored in memory (such as in buffers, caches, during joins and sorts, or in MEMORY tables) the total size of the VARCHAR is allocated as a fixed-width field. Thus, it is actually better to have a smaller VARCHAR if possible.

There are already many representative values inside the sakila.film table, so instead of estimating what an appropriate size might be, use the PROCEDURE ANALYSE() function:

```
mysql> SELECT count(title) FROM film;
+--------------+
| count(title) |
+--------------+
|         1000 |
+--------------+
1 row in set (0.00 sec)
```

```
mysql> SELECT title FROM film PROCEDURE ANALYSE(16,256)\G
*************************** 1. row ***************************
            Field_name: sakila.film.title
             Min_value: ACADEMY DINOSAUR
             Max_value: ZORRO ARK
            Min_length: 8
            Max_length: 27
     Empties_or_zeros: 0
                 Nulls: 0
 Avg_value_or_avg_length: 14.2350
                   Std: NULL
     Optimal_fieldtype: VARCHAR(27) NOT NULL
1 row in set (0.00 sec)
```

The first field returned, Field_name, is the name of the field that this row is analyzing. The next four fields give the minimum and maximum values and lengths. The Empties_or_zeros field reports on how many records have an empty value (") or a zero value for this field, and the Nulls field reports on how many records have a NULL value for this field. The Avg_value_or_avg_length field is self-explanatory, providing the average value for a numeric data type and the average length for a character or string data type. The Std field gives the standard deviation, which is the same as running SELECT STDDEV(fld), and is NULL for non-numeric types.

The Optimal_fieldtype field reveals the optimal data type for the field according to the analysis. In this case, because there are no NULL values, and the maximum length is 27, the Optimal_fieldtype is VARCHAR(27) NOT NULL.

This is a good starting point for a discussion about what the field should be — there are 1,000 titles, and the longest among them is 27, with the average length being slightly more than half the maximum length. The recommendation of VARCHAR(27) NOT NULL will fit the current data exactly. Knowing that the longest value so far is 27 helps to limit the possible range; however, there may be a longer film title in the future — maybe 28 characters, or 30 characters. Take a look at the longest title:

```
mysql> SELECT title FROM film WHERE LENGTH(title)=27;
+---------------------------+
| title                     |
+---------------------------+
| ARACHNOPHOBIA ROLLERCOASTER |
+---------------------------+
1 row in set (0.01 sec)
```

Given the title of the longest film, you may want to at least add two characters so that a sequel can be made entitled ARACHNOPHOBIA ROLLERCOASTER 2. Based on reasoning such as this, you may decide to change the data type of title to VARCHAR(35) NOT NULL. This does not have to be exact; recall that title started out as VARCHAR(255) NOT NULL, so even changing it to VARCHAR(50) NOT NULL saves a lot of space. Changing the data type of a field requires doing an ALTER TABLE statement, which locks the whole table for the duration of the change, so it is better to start with a good estimate, and re-evaluate once the real data set gets large enough to be useful, but not so large that changing a data type will take an unacceptably long time.

In the sakila.payment table, the amount field is defined as:

```
`amount` decimal(5,2) NOT NULL
```

This is a sensible amount, because it is not likely that a payment to a video store will be more than 999.99, and it is also unlikely that a refund will result in a payment amount less than −999.99. In this case, PROCEDURE ANALYSE() shows us:

```
mysql> SELECT COUNT(amount) FROM payment;
+---------------+
| COUNT(amount) |
+---------------+
|         16049 |
+---------------+
1 row in set (0.01 sec)

mysql> SELECT amount FROM payment PROCEDURE ANALYSE(16)\G
*************************** 1. row ***************************
            Field_name: sakila.payment.amount
             Min_value: 0.99
             Max_value: 11.99
            Min_length: 6
            Max_length: 14
     Empties_or_zeros: 24
                 Nulls: 0
Avg_value_or_avg_length: 4.200667
                   Std: 2.362920
      Optimal_fieldtype: DECIMAL(13, 2) NOT NULL
1 row in set (0.01 sec)
```

This output is somewhat misleading, because the Min_length and Max_length fields do not seem to have any relation to either the size or length of the field. The Optimal_fieldtype seems to be using the Max_length value when determining its recommendation. This is actually an artifact; the internal storage format of DECIMAL changed in MySQL 5.0, and the PROCEDURE ANALYSE() function was never updated, so the calculations are off. You can avoid problems by thinking about whether the output makes sense, and not necessarily depending on only the Optimal_fieldtype field for the recommended data type. Examine all the information before making a conclusion.

In this case, concentrate on the maximum and minimum amounts, and note that the actual payment amounts are much smaller than the maximum allowed value of 999.99. There are more than 16,000 payments, so this data is a good sample size. It is also notable that there are no negative values in the payments table. This suggests that refunds are handled separately, suggesting an UNSIGNED data type might be appropriate.

Looking at the schema for the payment table, each amount is associated with a rental_id, which is a foreign key to the rental table. The rental table associates a rental_id with a single inventory_id. This means that each payment is based on the amount paid for one movie rental.

Given this information, an optimal field might be DECIMAL(4,2) UNSIGNED NOT NULL, corresponding to the facts that the payment table only holds payments (not refunds), movie rentals cost anywhere from 0 (free) to 99.99, a payment (really, a record in the payment table) will always have a known value for the amount field, and that the maximum required precision of currency is 0.01.

Small data samples and PROCEDURE ANALYSE()

The PROCEDURE ANALYSE() function needs a good sample size in order to present a good optimal data type. For example, the sakila.staff table defines the first_name and last_name fields as:

```
`first_name` varchar(45) NOT NULL
`last_name` varchar(45) NOT NULL
```

What does PROCEDURE ANALYSE() believe is the optimal data type for these fields?

```
mysql> SELECT COUNT(first_name),COUNT(last_name) FROM staff;
+-------------------+------------------+
| COUNT(first_name) | COUNT(last_name) |
+-------------------+------------------+
|                 2 |                2 |
+-------------------+------------------+
1 row in set (0.00 sec)

mysql> SELECT first_name, last_name
    -> FROM staff PROCEDURE ANALYSE(16)\G
*************************** 1. row ***************************
            Field_name: sakila.staff.first_name
             Min_value: Jon
             Max_value: Mike
            Min_length: 3
            Max_length: 4
      Empties_or_zeros: 0
                 Nulls: 0
Avg_value_or_avg_length: 3.5000
                   Std: NULL
       Optimal_fieldtype: ENUM('Jon','Mike') NOT NULL
*************************** 2. row ***************************
            Field_name: sakila.staff.last_name
             Min_value: Hillyer
             Max_value: Stephens
            Min_length: 7
```

```
              Max_length: 8
       Empties_or_zeros: 0
                  Nulls: 0
  Avg_value_or_avg_length: 7.5000
                    Std: NULL
       Optimal_fieldtype: ENUM('Hillyer','Stephens') NOT NULL
2 rows in set (0.00 sec)
```

Because there are only two records to choose from, and an ENUM field can be the optimal data type so long as there are fewer than 16 strings in the enumerated list, an ENUM field was shown as the optimal data type for both first_name and last_name. Obviously, this is a poor idea for fields with first and last names.

What happens when an ENUM field cannot be used at all?

```
mysql> SELECT first_name, last_name FROM staff PROCEDURE ANALYSE(0)\G
*************************** 1. row ***************************
              Field_name: sakila.staff.first_name
               Min_value: Jon
               Max_value: Mike
              Min_length: 3
              Max_length: 4
       Empties_or_zeros: 0
                  Nulls: 0
  Avg_value_or_avg_length: 3.5000
                    Std: NULL
       Optimal_fieldtype: CHAR(4) NOT NULL
*************************** 2. row ***************************
              Field_name: sakila.staff.last_name
               Min_value: Hillyer
               Max_value: Stephens
              Min_length: 7
              Max_length: 8
       Empties_or_zeros: 0
                  Nulls: 0
  Avg_value_or_avg_length: 7.5000
                    Std: NULL
       Optimal_fieldtype: CHAR(8) NOT NULL
2 rows in set (0.00 sec)
```

Again, the sample set is too small to get a reasonable data type. The data type CHAR(4) for a first name is way too small; neither of the authors of this book ("Keith" has a length of 5 and "Sheeri" has a length of 6) would have their first name able to fit in such a field!

PROCEDURE ANALYSE() is an excellent tool to pare down existing data; however, care should be taken so that an ENUM field is not always listed, and that there is a big enough sample data size to justify an optimal data type returned. Even then, the information returned by PROCEDURE ANALYSE() should be used to make an informed decision on an optimal data type for a field.

Summary

This chapter has discussed:

- The standard data types as defined by the ISO SQL:2003 standard, and which standard data types MySQL supports
- The non-standard data types MySQL adds
- The storage requirements, allowed values (data range), and definable attributes for each possible data type
- How MySQL handles invalid data, and how you can change that behavior
- All of the possible values for sql_mode and what each sql_mode does
- Benefits and consequences of using NULL values
- How to use PROCEDURE ANALYSE() to find an optimal data type for existing data

Chapter 6

MySQL Index Types

I n SQL theory, a *key* is a data constraint, such as a unique key or foreign key. On the other hand, an *index* is an implementation detail, provided to be able access a limited set of data more quickly. MySQL has keys that act as data constraints, and indexes that make a small amount of table data readily accessible in a certain order. MySQL allows key constraints and indexes to be applied to a single data field or to more than one data field. A key constraint or index applied to one data field is a *simple* key constraint or index; on more than one data field is a *composite* key constraint or index.

Looking at Keys and Indexes

Unique key constraints in MySQL (UNIQUE KEY and PRIMARY KEY) limit the data in a table by allowing only one set of values for the indexed data. A foreign key constraint (FOREIGN KEY) limits the data in a table by requiring that the set of values for the indexed data match data from outside the table.

Regular indexes (INDEX, FULLTEXT INDEX, SPATIAL INDEX) and unique indexes (UNIQUE KEY and PRIMARY KEY) create an object separate from a table, with its own data structure, using data from the table. This allows looking up those values to be simpler.

Because UNIQUE KEY and PRIMARY KEY function as both keys and indexes, the term *key* is sometimes used interchangeably with the term *index*. We use the term *key* when we refer to a constraint, and *index* when we refer to a separate structure primarily used for faster lookups. For UNIQUE KEY and PRIMARY KEY, we may use either *index* or *key*.

The following keys can be used to constrain data:

- UNIQUE KEY
- PRIMARY KEY
- FOREIGN KEY

Data constraints are checked when an INSERT or UPDATE statement changes data. In database theory, both UNIQUE KEY and PRIMARY KEY specify that for a set of fields, duplicate values are not allowed. One difference between UNIQUE KEY and PRIMARY KEY is that there can be only one PRIMARY KEY per table, whereas there can be more than one UNIQUE KEY. In MySQL, another difference is that a UNIQUE KEY is allowed to contain a NULL value, but a PRIMARY KEY does not allow a NULL value. A FOREIGN KEY requires a set of fields in one table to correspond to another set of fields in another table. The rental table in the sakila database has UNIQUE KEY, PRIMARY KEY, and FOREIGN KEY definitions:

```
mysql> USE sakila;
Database changed
mysql> SHOW CREATE TABLE rental\G
*************************** 1. row ***************************
       Table: rental
Create Table: CREATE TABLE `rental` (
  `rental_id` int(11) NOT NULL auto_increment,
  `rental_date` datetime NOT NULL,
  `inventory_id` mediumint(8) unsigned NOT NULL,
  `customer_id` smallint(5) unsigned NOT NULL,
  `return_date` datetime default NULL,
  `staff_id` tinyint(3) unsigned NOT NULL,
  `last_update` timestamp NOT NULL default CURRENT_TIMESTAMP on
update CURRENT_TIMESTAMP,
  PRIMARY KEY  (`rental_id`),
  UNIQUE KEY `rental_date` (`rental_date`,`inventory_id`,
`customer_id`),
  KEY `idx_fk_inventory_id` (`inventory_id`),
  KEY `idx_fk_customer_id` (`customer_id`),
  KEY `idx_fk_staff_id` (`staff_id`),
  CONSTRAINT `fk_rental_customer` FOREIGN KEY (`customer_id`) REFER-
ENCES `customer` (`customer_id`) ON UPDATE CASCADE,
  CONSTRAINT `fk_rental_inventory` FOREIGN KEY (`inventory_id`) REF-
ERENCES `inventory` (`inventory_id`) ON UPDATE CASCADE,
  CONSTRAINT `fk_rental_staff` FOREIGN KEY (`staff_id`) REFER-
ENCES `staff` (`staff_id`) ON UPDATE CASCADE
) ENGINE=InnoDB AUTO_INCREMENT=16050 DEFAULT CHARSET=utf8
1 row in set (0.11 sec)
```

The UNIQUE KEY named rental_date is a *composite key* — it has more than one field. The PRIMARY KEY is on rental_id, which is also an auto_increment field. This is what is known as a *surrogate key* — a unique key that is a meaningless number.

Surrogate keys are common in databases, though they should be used only when there is not a suitable unique key. Some database administrators and schema creation tools automatically make a surrogate key for every table they create. This is not good practice — first, a natural key should be looked for, and if a natural key cannot be determined, then a surrogate key may be appropriate.

Storage engines differ in how they use the PRIMARY KEY; InnoDB stores the PRIMARY KEY with each record in each index, even if the fields in the PRIMARY KEY are not defined as part of the index. InnoDB will make a surrogate key if there is no existing PRIMARY KEY on the table. For more information on how storage engines use indexes, see Chapter 11.

In cases such as these where a small PRIMARY KEY is desired, a surrogate key might be used. For example, the rental table has a UNIQUE KEY on (rental_date, inventory_id, customer_id). This means that each record in the rental table is defined by a set of fields that is different — the date and time of the rental, what was rented, and the customer who rented it. In a real-world scenario, it is not possible for the same customer to rent the same physical copy of the movie at the same time. This set of three fields is the natural primary key for the table. However, a surrogate primary key is used, most likely to make the primary key smaller.

Three FOREIGN KEY constraints are defined on the rental table. All three are simple — that is, containing only one field. The FOREIGN KEY constraint named fk_rental_customer requires that the value of the rental table field customer_id must correspond to a value in the customer_id field of the customer table. In addition, ON UPDATE CASCADE specifies that if the customer_id field of the customer table should change its value, that change should propagate back to the customer_id field of the rental table. For more information, see the section "Creating and Dropping Foreign Key Constraints," later in the chapter.

Using Indexes to Speed Up Lookups

The following can be used to create indexes that can speed up queries that look up data:

- PRIMARY KEY
- UNIQUE KEY
- INDEX
- FULLTEXT INDEX
- SPATIAL INDEX

ON the WEBSITE Note that this book does not discuss SPATIAL INDEX. Please see this book's companion website at www.wiley.com/go/mysqladminbible for information on the SPATIAL INDEX type and its accompanying R-tree data structure.

Indexes are data structures; they can be either B-tree, R-tree, or hash data structures. The R-tree data structure is designed for searching proximity data. The RTREE index type is available only for indexes on SPATIAL data (which is only allowed for MyISAM tables). A B-tree data structure for an index is the most common, and is available for all storage engines except NDB. B-trees are optimal when searching for a range of data; it takes very little time to go from the current record in the B-tree to the next record. A hash data structure for an index is allowed for the MEMORY and NDB storage engines. Hashes are designed for exact matches or a series of exact matches; each record takes approximately the same amount of time to find. This means that searching an index looking for sequential data (for example, records with a timestamp during a certain date) is much faster using a B-tree data structure than a hash data structure.

> **NOTE**   Technically, the InnoDB storage engine uses a B+tree, and MyISAM uses a red-black B-tree. In the MySQL materials, this is simplified to "tree-based Index (including B-tree, B+tree, T-tree)". T-tree is used in the NDB storage engine, and the differences among the three are out of scope for the point of giving an overview of indexes.

One of the basic rules of query optimization is to have indexes on the sets of fields that are most often looked for. To find data without the help of an index, a full table scan must be performed. In a full table scan, the first record of the table is examined, then the next record, then the next, until either the last record of the table or the query has been satisfied (for example, a LIMIT has been reached). With an index, data can be looked up easily, without having to go through each record of the table.

Imagine having to look up an article on Wikipedia (http://www.wikipidia.org) by going to the list of all pages, starting with the very first page, and having to read the title of each article until you find the one you want. This is analogous to not having an index. Having an index on data is like Wikipedia offering search, browse by topic, or browse by letter functionality. You may be thinking, "There are so many articles on Wikipedia that it would be impossible to find anything by starting with the first article and scanning each one until I find the one I want!" You are exactly correct. Similarly, when a table has a large number of rows, it gets cumbersome and time-consuming to scan each row of data, and indexes are needed.

Data constraints are very good candidates for indexes; being able to quickly look up whether or not a certain value already exists means that checking PRIMARY KEY and UNIQUE KEY values is faster. It also means that unique key constraints can easily be compared. Indexes are automatically created by mysqld when PRIMARY KEY and UNIQUE KEY constraints are defined. Foreign key constraints need to be looked up in order to ensure that the referencing values exist; for this reason, mysqld requires indexes on a set of fields before a foreign key constraint can be defined.

Key constraints and indexes are very different; however, it is desirable to be able to speed up lookups of key constraints. This is why some MySQL database administrators — and MySQL's extended SQL syntax — use key and index interchangeably when discussing constraints and indexes. To add to the confusion, a non-unique index may be defined using either INDEX or KEY, even though using KEY is inaccurate because a non-unique index is not a constraint.

FULLTEXT INDEX and SPATIAL INDEX create special data structures designed to easily perform text matching and spatial data searching, respectively. For more information on FULLTEXT INDEX, see "Using FULLTEXT Indexes," later in this chapter. For more information on SPATIAL INDEX, see the companion website at www.wiley.com/go/mysqladminbible.

Indexes are always kept current by mysqld. When an UPDATE, DELETE, or INSERT statement changes a field involved in an index, that index must change too. This means that the tradeoff for faster data lookups is slower data updates. When updating data, key constraints are checked first, and after the constraints are met, the indexes are updated. Even though indexes are always current, there are times when maintenance is necessary and provides performance benefits. For more information, refer to the table maintenance commands in Chapter 4.

If you already have a PRIMARY KEY defined, there is no need to create a UNIQUE KEY on the same set of fields. Creating a UNIQUE KEY on the same fields in a PRIMARY KEY field adds no value, but does add overhead on INSERT, UPDATE, and DELETE statements. Similarly, there is usually no need to create a PRIMARY KEY on the same set of fields as a UNIQUE KEY unless you specifically want to take advantage of a storage-engine–specific feature that uses the PRIMARY KEY. In this case, create the PRIMARY KEY and drop the UNIQUE KEY to avoid redundancy.

Creating and dropping indexes

Indexes and key constraints can be created in a few ways: in a CREATE TABLE statement when a table is defined, in an ALTER TABLE statement, and in a CREATE INDEX statement. A CREATE INDEX statement can only be used to define a UNIQUE, FULLTEXT, or SPATIAL INDEX, and the mysqld server parses it into an ALTER TABLE statement. Like an ALTER TABLE statement, a CREATE INDEX statement is used to change an existing table.

The simplest CREATE INDEX statement adds a non-unique index to a table. The following example adds a non-unique index named idx_actor_first_name on the on the first_name field of the actor table in the sakila database:

```
mysql> USE sakila;
Database changed
mysql> CREATE INDEX idx_actor_first_name ON actor (first_name);
Query OK, 200 rows affected (1.30 sec)
Records: 200  Duplicates: 0  Warnings: 0
```

Because an index is simply a data structure, there is nothing invalid about having redundant indexes. However, there is no benefit to having a redundant index. All indexes are automatically kept current, so changing a field that is involved in a redundant index results in more overhead, because there are more indexes to update. For example, let's create a duplicate index, this time using the ALTER TABLE syntax, which is very similar:

```
mysql> ALTER TABLE actor ADD INDEX idx_actor_first_name (first_name);
ERROR 1061 (42000): Duplicate key name 'idx_actor_first_name'
```

Two indexes cannot have the same name. The name of the index must be changed. Note that redundant indexes are allowed, as long as the index name is different:

```
mysql> CREATE INDEX idx_actor_fname ON actor (first_name);
Query OK, 200 rows affected (0.45 sec)
Records: 200  Duplicates: 0  Warnings: 0
```

Now, whenever an INSERT, DELETE, or UPDATE statement changes the value of a first_name field, two index structures need to be updated. This is redundant and gives no benefits, only more overhead.

To drop an index, the syntax is simple:

```
DROP INDEX indexname ON tblname
```

For example:

```
mysql> DROP INDEX idx_actor_fname ON actor;
Query OK, 200 rows affected (0.67 sec)
Records: 200  Duplicates: 0  Warnings: 0
```

The ALTER TABLE syntax to drop an index is similar:

```
mysql> ALTER TABLE actor DROP INDEX idx_actor_fname;
Query OK, 200 rows affected (0.20 sec)
Records: 200  Duplicates: 0  Warnings: 0
```

Creating an index on table creation can be done by specifying the following:

```
KEY indexname (field_list)
```

As an example, running SHOW CREATE TABLE on the actor table shows how the indexes defined on the table could be defined if they were part of the CREATE TABLE statement:

```
mysql> SHOW CREATE TABLE actor\G
*************************** 1. row ***************************
       Table: actor
Create Table: CREATE TABLE `actor` (
  `actor_id` smallint(5) unsigned NOT NULL AUTO_INCREMENT,
  `first_name` char(45) DEFAULT NULL,
  `last_name` varchar(45) CHARACTER SET latin1 NOT NULL,
  `last_update` timestamp NOT NULL DEFAULT CURRENT_TIMESTAMP ON
UPDATE CURRENT_TIMESTAMP,
  PRIMARY KEY (`actor_id`),
  KEY `idx_actor_last_name` (`last_name`),
) ENGINE=InnoDB AUTO_INCREMENT=201 DEFAULT CHARSET=utf8
1 row in set (0.00 sec)
```

An index name is required for CREATE INDEX, otherwise mysqld issues a syntax error:

```
mysql> CREATE INDEX ON actor (first_name);
ERROR 1064 (42000): You have an error in your SQL syntax; check
the manual that corresponds to your MySQL server version for the
right syntax to use near 'ON actor (first_name)' at line 1
```

Adding an index via ALTER TABLE does not require an index name. If no index name is specified, the server will name one automatically:

```
mysql> ALTER TABLE actor ADD INDEX (first_name);
Query OK, 200 rows affected (0.57 sec)
Records: 200  Duplicates: 0  Warnings: 0

mysql> ALTER TABLE actor ADD INDEX (first_name);
Query OK, 200 rows affected (0.22 sec)
Records: 200  Duplicates: 0  Warnings: 0

mysql> SHOW CREATE TABLE actor\G
*************************** 1. row ***************************
        Table: actor
Create Table: CREATE TABLE `actor` (
  `actor_id` smallint(5) unsigned NOT NULL AUTO_INCREMENT,
  `first_name` char(45) DEFAULT NULL,
  `last_name` varchar(45) CHARACTER SET latin1 NOT NULL,
  `last_update` timestamp NOT NULL DEFAULT CURRENT_TIMESTAMP ON
UPDATE CURRENT_TIMESTAMP,
  PRIMARY KEY (`actor_id`),
  KEY `idx_actor_last_name` (`last_name`),
  KEY `first_name` (`first_name`),
  KEY `first_name_2` (`first_name`)
) ENGINE=InnoDB AUTO_INCREMENT=201 DEFAULT CHARSET=utf8
1 row in set (0.00 sec)
```

Note that the server gave no warnings or errors about creating a redundant index, because the automatic naming did not try to use the same index name. Regardless of how the indexes were created, DROP INDEX requires an index name:

```
mysql> ALTER TABLE actor DROP INDEX first_name,
    -> DROP INDEX first_name_2;
Query OK, 200 rows affected (0.48 sec)
Records: 200  Duplicates: 0  Warnings: 0
```

Note that many ALTER TABLE statements will obtain a write-lock on the entire table, rendering it unable to be updated for the duration of the ALTER TABLE statement. This may be a long time for large tables. For information about how creating and dropping indexes locks tables, see Chapter 4.

Index order

All BTREE indexes are stored in ascending order. Numbers are stored in numerical order and strings are stored in lexical order, according to the string collation being used. See Chapter 4 for more information on collations.

The ordering of an index is critical in a BTREE index type because it is optimized for scanning sequentially. This sequential scan can only be used to find the *next* value, not the *previous* value. Unfortunately, mysqld only stores indexes in ascending order. The syntax used to create indexes is misleading — it is valid syntax to create an index specifying the DESC keyword after an index field name, but mysqld ignores the keyword and does not issue a warning or an error:

```
mysql> ALTER TABLE actor ADD INDEX (first_name DESC);
Query OK, 0 rows affected (0.21 sec)
Records: 0  Duplicates: 0  Warnings: 0

mysql> SHOW CREATE TABLE actor\G
*************************** 1. row ***************************
       Table: actor
Create Table: CREATE TABLE `actor` (
  `actor_id` smallint(5) unsigned NOT NULL AUTO_INCREMENT,
  `first_name` char(45) DEFAULT NULL,
  `last_name` varchar(45) CHARACTER SET latin1 NOT NULL,
  `last_update` timestamp NOT NULL DEFAULT CURRENT_TIMESTAMP ON
UPDATE CURRENT_TIMESTAMP,
  PRIMARY KEY (`actor_id`),
  KEY `idx_actor_last_name` (`last_name`),
  KEY `first_name` (`first_name`)
) ENGINE=InnoDB DEFAULT CHARSET=utf8
1 row in set (0.00 sec)
```

From the successful return of the first statement, it looks like the index was created successfully, in descending order. However, the SHOW CREATE TABLE statement shows a lack of DESC keyword.

Unfortunately, this means that any queries that search or order data in descending order cannot use an index to do so efficiently.

Index length

String indexes allow you to specify a length for the index value. This is known as an *index prefix*, and may be used with any string type. An index prefix is required for indexing any BLOB or TEXT data type (the BLOB and TEXT data types include TINYTEXT, LONGBLOB, and so on). The index length is based on characters:

```
mysql> ALTER TABLE actor ADD INDEX idx_actor_fname (first_name(46));
ERROR 1089 (HY000): Incorrect prefix key; the used key part isn't
a string, the used length is longer than the key part, or the
storage engine doesn't support unique prefix keys
```

If the length of the index were in bytes, the maximum valid length is 182 bytes. However, the length of the index is in characters, so the maximum valid length 45 characters:

```
mysql> ALTER TABLE actor
    -> ADD INDEX idx_actor_fname_small (first_name(10));
Query OK, 200 rows affected (0.15 sec)
Records: 200  Duplicates: 0  Warnings: 0
```

For a string index that does not contain any BLOB and TEXT data types, if a length is not specified, the length of all the data in the index is used. Of course, some limitations are involved. For example, InnoDB has a limitation that indexes cannot be more than 767 bytes in length.

The length of the first_name field of the actor table can be determined by querying the INFORMATION_SCHEMA database. For more information on the INFORMATION_SCHEMA database, see Chapter 21.

```
mysql> SELECT COLUMN_TYPE,CHARACTER_SET_NAME
    -> FROM INFORMATION_SCHEMA.COLUMNS
    -> WHERE TABLE_SCHEMA='sakila' AND TABLE_NAME='actor'
    -> AND COLUMN_NAME='first_name';
+-------------+--------------------+
| COLUMN_TYPE | CHARACTER_SET_NAME |
+-------------+--------------------+
| varchar(45) | utf8               |
+-------------+--------------------+
1 row in set (0.00 sec)
```

The utf8 character set means that each character is represented by 4 bytes. The maximum length of the first_name field is 45*4=180 bytes.

NOTE In MySQL 5.1, the support for the utf8 character set was limited, and utf8 characters used 3 bytes per string, not 4 bytes per string as in MySQL 6.0. Examples in this book use MySQL 6.0.

The EXPLAIN syntax shows the length of an index used (for more information on EXPLAIN, see Chapter 18):

```
mysql> EXPLAIN SELECT first_name FROM actor\G
*************************** 1. row ***************************
           id: 1
  select_type: SIMPLE
        table: actor
         type: index
possible_keys: NULL
          key: idx_actor_fname
      key_len: 182
          ref: NULL
         rows: 200
        Extra: Using index
1 row in set (0.00 sec)
```

The key_len field shows the length of the index used. But the length is 182, not 180 bytes as calculated. The reason for this is that there are 2 bytes of overhead in the index because the data is variable length. If the data type is a CHAR instead of a VARCHAR, the index length changes to the expected 180 bytes:

```
mysql> ALTER TABLE actor MODIFY first_name CHAR(45) NOT NULL;
Query OK, 200 rows affected (0.18 sec)
```

```
Records: 200  Duplicates: 0  Warnings: 0

mysql> EXPLAIN SELECT first_name FROM actor\G
*************************** 1. row ***************************
           id: 1
  select_type: SIMPLE
        table: actor
         type: index
possible_keys: NULL
          key: idx_actor_fname
      key_len: 180
          ref: NULL
         rows: 200
        Extra: Using index
1 row in set (0.00 sec)
```

Another definition parameter that can cause a change in index length is whether or not the field is nullable. In the example, the first_name field was defined as NOT NULL. What if it were nullable?

```
mysql> ALTER TABLE actor MODIFY first_name CHAR(45);
Query OK, 200 rows affected (0.14 sec)
Records: 200  Duplicates: 0  Warnings: 0

mysql> EXPLAIN SELECT first_name FROM actor\G
*************************** 1. row ***************************
           id: 1
  select_type: SIMPLE
        table: actor
         type: index
possible_keys: NULL
          key: idx_actor_fname
      key_len: 181
          ref: NULL
         rows: 200
        Extra: Using index
1 row in set (0.00 sec)
```

There is extra overhead of 1 byte for an index on a nullable field. Now, change the field back to its original definition to clean up from testing:

```
mysql> ALTER TABLE actor MODIFY first_name VARCHAR(45) NOT NULL;
Query OK, 200 rows affected (0.14 sec)
Records: 200  Duplicates: 0  Warnings: 0
```

Index types

MySQL stores indexes in data structures. B-tree data structures are optimal when searching for a range of data; it takes very little time to go from the current record in a B-tree to the next record. A hash data structure for an index is allowed for the MEMORY and NDB storage engines.

Hashes are ideal for exact matches or a series of exact matches; each record takes approximately the same amount of time to find.

BTREE indexes are stored in the order of the index — for example, the order of strings is determined by the collation of the string. When an index is being updated, it is these data structures (B-trees and hashes) that are actually updated.

Each storage engine handles different data structures for their indexes — these data structures are known as the *index type*. The default index type for MyISAM and InnoDB tables is BTREE, which stores the index data into a B-tree structure. MyISAM can store indexes into an R-tree data structure, and RTREE is an index type used only on SPATIAL data. The FULLTEXT indexing in MyISAM is a FULLTEXT index type.

The other major index type is the HASH index type, which stores index information in a hash table. The HASH index type is used by default in memory-based storage engines, such as MEMORY and NDB. The MEMORY storage engine can also have BTREE index types. InnoDB tables can only use BTREE index types. MERGE tables do not support FULLTEXT, though the underlying MyISAM tables do. Partitioned tables also do not support FULLTEXT indexes.

B-trees are optimal when searching for a range of data; it takes very little time to go from the current record in the B-tree to the next record. A hash data structure for an index is allowed for the MEMORY and NDB storage engines. Hashes are ideal for exact matches or a series of exact matches; each record takes approximately the same amount of time to find. R-trees are ideal for proximity searches, such as finding nearby geographical locations.

To create an index using an index type other than the default for the storage engine, specify USING [indextype] when creating the index. For example:

```
mysql> CREATE TABLE temp_index (
    -> first_name CHAR(45) NOT NULL,
    -> last_name CHAR(45) NOT NULL
    -> ) ENGINE=MEMORY;
Query OK, 0 rows affected (0.75 sec)

mysql> ALTER TABLE temp_index
    -> ADD INDEX (first_name),
    -> ADD INDEX lname (last_name) USING BTREE;
Query OK, 0 rows affected (0.44 sec)
Records: 0  Duplicates: 0  Warnings: 0

mysql> SELECT INDEX_NAME,INDEX_TYPE
    -> FROM INFORMATION_SCHEMA.STATISTICS
    -> WHERE TABLE_NAME='temp_index';
+------------+------------+
| INDEX_NAME | INDEX_TYPE |
+------------+------------+
| first_name | HASH       |
| lname      | BTREE      |
+------------+------------+
2 rows in set (0.00 sec)
```

The USING keyword is not necessary, nor is it allowed, when defining the FULLTEXT and SPA-TIAL index types. For more information on defining FULLTEXT index types, see "Using FULL-TEXT Indexes," later in this chapter. For more information on defining SPATIAL index types, see the companion website at www.wiley.com/go/mysqladminbible.

Redundant indexes

An index is redundant if another index exists on the same table that provides the same indexing information. Earlier we used the example of two indexes on the first_name fields. Obviously, the exact same data in a second index is redundant.

However, there are less obvious redundant indexes, which involve compound indexes and the ordering of index fields. Index redundancy is based on the index type:

■ A SPATIAL index type can only be a simple index, not a compound index. Because there is only one field indexed in a SPATIAL index, the only type of redundant SPATIAL index is where the index is on the same field. There is no other redundant index possible, as there is with other index types.

■ A FULLTEXT index is redundant if it is a subset of another FULLTEXT index, regardless of the field order. If there is a FULLTEXT index already specified on (field2, field1, field3), the following FULLTEXT indexes are redundant:

  ▨ (field1)

  ▨ (field2)

  ▨ (field3)

  ▨ (field1, field2)

  ▨ (field2, field1)

  ▨ (field1, field2, field3)

  ▨ (field1, field3, field2)

  ▨ (field2, field3, field1)

  ▨ (field3, field2, field1)

  ▨ (field3, field1, field2)

■ A HASH index is redundant if it contains the same fields as an index, regardless of the field order. If there is a HASH index already specified on (field2, field1, field3), the following HASH indexes are redundant:

  ▨ (field1, field2, field3)

  ▨ (field1, field3, field2)

  ▨ (field2, field3, field1)

  ▨ (field3, field2, field1)

  ▨ (field3, field1, field2)

- A BTREE index is redundant if it is a subset of another BTREE index, with respect to the field order of the first field(s). If there is a BTREE index already specified on (field2, field1, field3), the following BTREE indexes are redundant:
  - (field2)
  - (field2, field1)

- Indexes that index the same fields in the same order but have different index types are not redundant, because each index type adds its own value. A BTREE index on a set of fields makes sequential index reads optimal, and a HASH index on the same set of fields makes random reads optimal.

Creating and Dropping Key Constraints

PRIMARY KEY and UNIQUE KEY in MySQL are unique key constraints. There is only one way to specify a foreign key constraint, using FOREIGN KEY. Other databases allow check constraints to be defined; MySQL has not yet implemented check constraints. Unique and foreign keys are the only key constraints MySQL supports.

Creating and dropping unique key constraints

Creating and dropping a unique key constraint is very similar to creating and dropping an index. To create a unique index, simply replace INDEX with PRIMARY KEY or UNIQUE KEY. Dropping a unique index is not different:

```
mysql> ALTER TABLE actor
    -> ADD UNIQUE KEY fname_actor (first_name,actor_id);
Query OK, 200 rows affected (0.20 sec)
Records: 200  Duplicates: 0  Warnings: 0

mysql> ALTER TABLE actor DROP KEY fname_actor;
Query OK, 200 rows affected (0.16 sec)
Records: 200  Duplicates: 0  Warnings: 0
```

Many database administrators prefer the ALTER TABLE syntax to create and drop indexes, because an ALTER TABLE can perform many different changes to a table in one statement. However, the CREATE INDEX and DROP INDEX statements are also very similar when dealing with unique keys:

```
mysql> CREATE UNIQUE INDEX
    -> fname_actor ON actor (first_name,actor_id);
Query OK, 200 rows affected (0.34 sec)
Records: 200  Duplicates: 0  Warnings: 0

mysql> DROP INDEX fname_actor ON actor;
Query OK, 200 rows affected (0.20 sec)
Records: 200  Duplicates: 0  Warnings: 0
```

Like regular indexes, there can be more than one UNIQUE KEY per table, and redundant UNIQUE KEYs can be specified. In fact, the previous example showed a unique key where the index was not redundant, but the uniqueness was. The actor_id field is already unique, due to the PRIMARY KEY designation it has, so specifying that (first_name, actor_id) is unique is redundant. However, having indexes on (actor_id) and (first_name, actor_id) is not redundant, as seen in the previous section on redundant indexes.

Creating and dropping a PRIMARY KEY using the ALTER TABLE syntax is the same as a UNIQUE KEY — just change the keyword UNIQUE to PRIMARY. The only difference is that there can be at most one PRIMARY KEY defined for a table:

```
mysql> ALTER TABLE actor ADD PRIMARY KEY (first_name,last_name);
ERROR 1068 (42000): Multiple primary key defined
```

The CREATE INDEX syntax cannot be used to create a PRIMARY KEY. A PRIMARY KEY can only be defined with a CREATE TABLE or ALTER TABLE statement.

Unique key constraints cannot be either FULLTEXT or SPATIAL index types.

Creating and dropping foreign key constraints

Foreign key constraints are only supported by the InnoDB storage engine. Other storage engines may allow foreign key definitions, but the constraints are not enforced.

A foreign key constraint can be defined within a CREATE TABLE or ALTER TABLE statement. The definition is the same for either case, and requires the fields in the current table, the referenced tables, and the referenced table fields:

```
FOREIGN KEY (field1) REFERENCES other_table (fieldA)
```

The syntax to define a foreign key constraint supports simple or compound foreign key constraints; compound foreign keys, however, can only reference fields from one table. For example, the following syntax is not valid:

```
FOREIGN KEY (field1, field2) REFERENCES
other_table (fieldA), other_table_2 (fieldB)
```

Only compound foreign key constraints that reference one table are allowed, such as:

```
FOREIGN KEY (field1, field2) REFERENCES other_table (fieldA, fieldB)
```

If you want to specify the name for the foreign key, you can optionally prepend CONSTRAINT name to the preceding syntax:

```
CONSTRAINT fk_name FOREIGN KEY (field1, field2)
REFERENCES other_table (fieldA, fieldB)
```

The foreign key name is used when removing a foreign key constraint:

```
ALTER TABLE tblname DROP FOREIGN KEY fk_name
```

If no name is assigned at create time, mysqld assigns an automatic name to it, similar to if a regular index does not have a name assigned to it.

A table can have a foreign key that references itself — that is:

```
ALTER TABLE this_table ADD FOREIGN KEY (field1)
REFERENCES this_table (fieldA);
```

In the most extreme case, it is valid syntax to have a foreign key constraint reference itself — the exact table and fields are the referring fields and the referred to fields. This is not advised, and will cause problems:

```
mysql> ALTER TABLE sakila.actor
    -> ADD CONSTRAINT fk_lastname FOREIGN KEY (last_name)
    -> REFERENCES actor (last_name);
Query OK, 0 rows affected (0.16 sec)
Records: 0  Duplicates: 0  Warnings: 0

mysql> INSERT INTO sakila.actor (last_name) VALUES ('Cabral');
ERROR 1452 (23000): Cannot add or update a child row: a foreign
key constraint fails (`sakila`.`actor`, CONSTRAINT `fk_lastname`
FOREIGN KEY (`last_name`) REFERENCES `actor` (`last_name`))
As this foreign key is highly unadvisable, drop it immediately:
mysql> ALTER TABLE sakila.actor DROP FOREIGN KEY fk_lastname;
Query OK, 0 rows affected (0.15 sec)
Records: 0  Duplicates: 0  Warnings: 0
```

As an example of how to define a foreign key within a CREATE TABLE statement, here is the foreign key constraint definition from the city table in the sakila sample database (note that setting the pager with \P and the grep command do not work on Windows):

```
mysql> \P grep CONSTRAINT
PAGER set to 'grep CONSTRAINT'
mysql> SHOW CREATE TABLE city\G
  CONSTRAINT `fk_city_country` FOREIGN KEY (`country_id`) REFER-
ENCES `country` (`country_id`) ON UPDATE CASCADE
1 row in set (0.00 sec)

mysql> \P
Default pager wasn't set, using stdout.
```

The name of the constraint is fk_city_country, and it specifies that the country_id field of the city table should match a value in the country_id field of the country table. The full details of the constraint can be seen in the REFERENTIAL_CONSTRAINTS system view in the INFORMATION_SCHEMA database:

```
mysql> SELECT * FROM INFORMATION_SCHEMA.REFERENTIAL_CONSTRAINTS
    -> WHERE CONSTRAINT_NAME='fk_city_country'\G
*************************** 1. row ***************************
       CONSTRAINT_CATALOG: NULL
        CONSTRAINT_SCHEMA: sakila
          CONSTRAINT_NAME: fk_city_country
UNIQUE_CONSTRAINT_CATALOG: NULL
 UNIQUE_CONSTRAINT_SCHEMA: sakila
   UNIQUE_CONSTRAINT_NAME: PRIMARY
             MATCH_OPTION: NONE
              UPDATE_RULE: CASCADE
              DELETE_RULE: RESTRICT
               TABLE_NAME: city
     REFERENCED_TABLE_NAME: country
1 row in set (0.05 sec)
```

For more information on the REFERENTIAL_CONSTRAINTS system view in the INFORMATION_SCHEMA database, see Chapter 21.

Foreign key constraints and data changes

If a foreign key is defined on a table and an INSERT attempts to set the foreign key fields to invalid values, mysqld will return this error:

```
ERROR 1452 (23000): Cannot add or update a child row: a foreign
key constraint fails
```

The behavior of changes on the referenced (*parent*) table is settable in the foreign key definition. If an UPDATE or DELETE statement tries to change existing data on the parent table, the server can cascade the change to the corresponding record(s) in the referencing (*child*) table, or the server can reject the change. Possible ON DELETE and ON UPDATE options are:

- RESTRICT — Changes to data that reference existing foreign keys will be rejected and will not occur in both the parent and the child table. A sample use case of this is when deleting a user who has billing records that you are required to keep for compliance. You need to keep the billing records and the user information to refer to who the user was, so an attempt to delete the user information should fail.

- CASCADE — Changes to data that reference existing foreign keys will be cascaded. If the parent table data is updated, the child table data is also updated. If the parent table data is deleted, the child table data is also deleted. A sample use case of this is when someone changes their name — you want the name change to propagate to any child tables that may also reference the name.

- SET NULL — This is similar to CASCADE except that when a DELETE occurs, records in the child table will not be removed; they will be set to NULL instead.

- NO ACTION — This is the same as RESTRICT.

Both ON DELETE and ON UPDATE are optional. If no option is given, RESTRICT is used.

Requirements for foreign key constraints

One of the most common and frustrating errors is having a foreign key constraint definition fail. Both CREATE TABLE and ALTER TABLE statements will fail with an ERROR 1005 referencing errno: 150. For example:

```
mysql> CREATE TABLE test.actor2 (
    -> first_name INT, last_name VARCHAR(50),
    -> FOREIGN KEY (first_name, last_name)
    -> REFERENCES sakila.actor (first_name, last_name)
    -> ) ENGINE=InnoDB DEFAULT CHARSET=ucs2;
ERROR 1005 (HY000): Can't create table 'test.actor2' (errno: 150)
```

The ERROR 1005 refers to the fact that a table cannot be created. If this had been an ALTER TABLE statement, the same error would occur, except the table name would start with test.#sql. The reason the table could not be created is because of errno 150. Use the perror tool that ships with mysqld to see what that error is:

```
shell> perror 150
MySQL error code 150: Foreign key constraint is incorrectly formed
```

On the mysql client command line, you can use the first part of SHOW ENGINE INNODB STATUS to help figure out what the error is:

```
mysql> SHOW ENGINE INNODB STATUS\G
*************************** 1. row ***************************
  Type: InnoDB
  Name:
Status:
=====================================
081212 13:54:06 INNODB MONITOR OUTPUT
=====================================
Per second averages calculated from the last 54 seconds
----------
SEMAPHORES
----------
OS WAIT ARRAY INFO: reservation count 9, signal count 9
Mutex spin waits 0, rounds 67, OS waits 3
RW-shared spins 10, OS waits 5; RW-excl spins 1, OS waits 1
------------------------
LATEST FOREIGN KEY ERROR
------------------------
081212 13:50:01 Error in foreign key constraint of table test/actor2:
FOREIGN KEY (first_name, last_name)
REFERENCES sakila.actor (first_name, last_name)
) ENGINE=InnoDB DEFAULT CHARSET=ucs2:
Cannot find an index in the referenced table where the
referenced columns appear as the first columns, or column types
in the table and the referenced table do not match for constraint.
Note that the internal storage type of ENUM and SET changed in
tables created with >= InnoDB-4.1.12, and such columns in old tables
cannot be referenced by such columns in new tables.
```

See http://dev.mysql.com/doc/refman/5.1/en/innodb-foreign-key-constraints.html for correct foreign key definition.

Two possible errors are described here — the first is that there is no index in the sakila.actor table that starts with (first_name, last_name). The second possibility is that the fields in test.actor2 are not similar enough to the referenced fields in sakila.actor; they do not have to match definitions exactly, but they must be similar in type. To debug the latter error, use SHOW CREATE TABLE to look at the referenced table to see the data types and indexes for the foreign key constraint you are trying to make.

For our purposes, take out the first_name field so the creation issues go away:

```
mysql> CREATE TABLE test.actor2 (last_name VARCHAR(50),
    -> FOREIGN KEY (last_name) REFERENCES sakila.actor (last_name)
    -> ) ENGINE=InnoDB;
Query OK, 0 rows affected (0.39 sec)

mysql> SHOW CREATE TABLE test.actor2\G
*************************** 1. row ***************************
       Table: actor2
Create Table: CREATE TABLE `actor2` (
  `last_name` varchar(50) DEFAULT NULL,
  KEY `last_name` (`last_name`),
  CONSTRAINT `actor2_ibfk_1` FOREIGN KEY (`last_name`) REFER-
ENCES `sakila`.`actor` (`last_name`)
) ENGINE=InnoDB DEFAULT CHARSET=utf8
1 row in set (0.00 sec)
```

Note that mysqld automatically made an index on last_name, even though one was not specified in the table creation definition. Foreign key constraints in MySQL must be indexed in both the referencing (child) table and the referenced (parent) table. Also note that the length and character set for last_name are different. That is acceptable because they are of similar data types. The error message shown earlier said there is a problem if the field types in both tables "do not match for constraint." What that means is the data types are not similar enough. The INT data type puts a constraint on the data that it can contain integers only within a certain range; the VARCHAR data type does not constrain the data in the same way.

When troubleshooting why a foreign key constraint cannot be created, check to make sure the following requirements are met:

- The referenced table must exist. If not, SHOW ENGINE INNODB STATUS will contain Cannot resolve table name close to: referenced_table_name.

- The referenced fields must exist. If not, SHOW ENGINE INNODB STATUS will contain Cannot resolve column name close to: referenced_column_name.

- Both tables must be InnoDB tables. Some tables may accept foreign key definitions with no warnings or errors; however, foreign key constraints will not be enforced unless both tables are InnoDB.

- Both tables must not be TEMPORARY tables.

- The fields in both tables must have similar data types. For numeric types, the sizes and signs (that is, UNSIGNED vs. SIGNED) must be the same. For strings, the character sets and collations must be the same, though length differences are allowed.

- The referenced fields must be the first fields in an index on the referenced table. This index must not contain index prefixes — that is, the index must contain the full data in the index. Because BLOB and TEXT fields require index prefixes, they cannot be references in a foreign key constraint.

- The referencing fields must be the first fields in an index on the referencing table; if they are not, an index will automatically be created.

Using FULLTEXT Indexes

To find all movie titles that contain DINOSAUR in their title or description, Ziesel ran the following query:

```
mysql> SELECT film_id, title, description FROM film_text
    -> WHERE title LIKE '%DINOSAUR%'
    -> OR description LIKE '%DINOSAUR%'\G
*************************** 1. row ***************************
   film_id: 1
     title: ACADEMY DINOSAUR
description: A Epic Drama of a Feminist And a Mad Scientist who
must Battle a Teacher in The Canadian Rockies
*************************** 2. row ***************************
   film_id: 131
     title: CENTER DINOSAUR
description: A Beautiful Character Study of a Sumo Wrestler And
a Dentist who must Find a Dog in California
*************************** 3. row ***************************
   film_id: 231
     title: DINOSAUR SECRETARY
description: A Action-Packed Drama of a Feminist And a Girl who
must Reach a Robot in The Canadian Rockies
3 rows in set (0.01 sec)
```

However, when she ran an EXPLAIN on the query, she noticed that it was not using any indexes:

```
mysql> EXPLAIN SELECT film_id, title, description FROM film_text
    -> WHERE title LIKE '%DINOSAUR%'
    -> OR description LIKE '%DINOSAUR%'\G
*************************** 1. row ***************************
           id: 1
  select_type: SIMPLE
        table: film_text
         type: ALL
possible_keys: NULL
          key: NULL
      key_len: NULL
          ref: NULL
         rows: 1000
        Extra: Using where
1 row in set (0.00 sec)
```

This is very inefficient (for more information on how to use EXPLAIN, see Chapter 18). Even if there were indexes on the title and description fields, they would not be used, because indexes on text fields work by comparing the beginnings of strings. This is similar to looking up a word in a dictionary — the section containing the first letter is located first, then the section containing the first two letters, then the first three, until either the word is found or the space where the word should be located is found. For example, looking up the word dinosaur in a dictionary, first the d section is found. Then the section with di is found, then din, dino, up until the word dinosaur is found.

In a dictionary, it is very easy to look up words beginning with dino — simply go to that section of the dictionary. It is much more difficult to find all words ending with saur — in fact the only way to do that is to look at every single entry and see if it ends in saur. Similarly, a BTREE index on a string can be used to find strings beginning with dino, but cannot be used to find strings that end in saur.

For finding words and phrases within a string, a FULLTEXT index is much more efficient than using LIKE with wildcards. Only the MyISAM storage engine supports the FULLTEXT index, which can only be used on fields defined as one of the CHAR, VARCHAR, or TEXT data types (the TEXT data types include TINYTEXT, LONGTEXT, and so on). Most character sets are supported, but a field defined with the ucs2 character set cannot have a FULLTEXT index defined on it.

A FULLTEXT index can be defined using CREATE INDEX, ALTER TABLE, or in a CREATE TABLE statement. The FULLTEXT index definition is created exactly like a regular index, except the FULLTEXT keyword is used, and the USING option may not be specified. The film_text table has a FULLTEXT index defined:

```
mysql> SHOW CREATE TABLE film_text\G
*************************** 1. row ***************************
       Table: film_text
Create Table: CREATE TABLE `film_text` (
```

```
  `film_id` smallint(6) NOT NULL,
  `title` varchar(255) NOT NULL,
  `description` text,
  PRIMARY KEY (`film_id`),
  FULLTEXT KEY `idx_title_description` (`title`,`description`)
) ENGINE=MyISAM DEFAULT CHARSET=utf8
1 row in set (0.00 sec)
```

FULLTEXT queries use an internal parser to determine word boundaries and extract words from strings. The WITH PARSER parser_plugin_name option can be specified after the list of fields to indicate mysqld should use the parser found in the plugin parser_plugin_name. For information on the MySQL plugin interface and how to query a FULLTEXT index, see Chapter 4.

Unlike regular indexes, a FULLTEXT index is on the entire length of the field, for all fields in the index. Up to 16 fields are allowed in one FULLTEXT index. There is no support for index length specification as there is with other indexes. If an index length is given to a FULLTEXT index, it is ignored.

The FULLTEXT index is more complicated than other index types. In essence the index is a structure where each record consists of a word (such as dinosaur) and one or more pointers to records that have those words. Changing data in a field that is part of a FULLTEXT index has a lot of overhead. When data is changed, the FULLTEXT index is automatically kept current by doing the following:

- The FULLTEXT parser finds and extracts all the words within the field(s) that are part of the FULLTEXT index.

- For each word found, the FULLTEXT index is updated with a pointer to the new record.

When a regular index is updated, it only needs to change one index record for each new set of data fields. When a FULLTEXT index is updated, it needs to change one index record for each word in the new set of data fields. Because of this, using FULLTEXT search on voluminous amounts of text may not be the best solution.

If you need to do a significant amount of searching of text it would probably be best to investigate search engines that work directly with mysqld such as Sphinx (www.sphinxsearch.com), or tools external to the database such as Lucene (http://lucene.apache.org). Both types of tools are specialized to work with textual indexes.

Summary

This chapter has gone through the difference between a key constraint and an index, and shown how to define, use, and remove constraints and indexes including:

- Primary keys
  - Natural primary keys
  - Surrogate primary keys

- Unique keys
- Foreign keys
- Simple indexes
- Composite indexes
- Index types
    - B-tree
    - Hash
    - Fulltext

How indexes are used in MySQL was discussed, including the affects of sort order and index prefix length.

Chapter 7

Stored Routines, Triggers, and Events

stored routines, triggers, and events are all ways to store SQL commands as part of the database server. These types of stored SQL enable different applications to easily use the same set of queries. Many database developers use stored SQL to build a library to give to application developers. Stored routines, triggers, and events can make the schema transparent to an application developer, which is very convenient when the schema needs to change.

Comparing Stored Routines, Triggers, and Events

MySQL has four different types of stored SQL: triggers, events, stored procedures, and stored functions. A trigger is invoked automatically when an SQL statement changes rows on a specified table. An event is invoked automatically at a predetermined time, and can be a one-time occurrence or a regular occurrence. A stored procedure is invoked manually with the CALL statement, taking zero or more arguments, and can pass back values through output variables. A stored function is invoked manually by directly using its name, taking zero or more arguments and outputting a scalar value.

A user-defined function (UDF) is another way to extend MySQL by adding a function using a different programming language. How to create and add UDFs are discussed in Chapter 4. Table 7-1 summarizes the differences among triggers, events, stored procedures, stored functions, and UDFs.

241

TABLE 7-1

Comparison of Stored Routines and UDFs

	Triggers	Stored Procedures	Stored Functions	Events	UDFs
Language	SQL	SQL	SQL	SQL	Compiled Object (C/C++)
Created, changed, and removed by	SQL statements	SQL statements	SQL statements	SQL statements	Change object code, recompile, reinstall
Invoked	Automatically when a table's data changes	Manually via CALL proc_name()	Manually via func_name()	Automatically when the scheduled time arrives	Manually via func_name()
Arguments	None	Yes	Yes	None	Yes
Output	None	One or more result sets	Limited to one scalar value	None	Limited to one scalar value
Associated with	Table	Database	Database	Database	mysqld
Unique name-space	Database	Database	Database	Database	mysqld

Using Triggers

A trigger is a set of commands invoked automatically when an SQL statement changes data on the associated table. Using a trigger you have three different ways to change table data — via the INSERT, UPDATE, and DELETE statements. A trigger can be defined to occur BEFORE the table data is changed or AFTER. MySQL allows a maximum of six triggers per table:

- BEFORE INSERT
- AFTER INSERT
- BEFORE UPDATE
- AFTER UPDATE
- BEFORE DELETE
- AFTER DELETE

SQL statements that do not use INSERT, UPDATE, or DELETE but change data will not invoke triggers. For example, both the TRUNCATE and DROP TABLE statements remove rows from a table, but do not use a DELETE statement to do so. Thus, they do not invoke a DELETE trigger. Statements that use INSERT, UPDATE, or DELETE will invoke the appropriate trigger.

For example, LOAD DATA uses an INSERT statement and therefore invokes an INSERT trigger. INSERT ... ON DUPLICATE KEY UPDATE invokes an INSERT trigger if it inserts a row, and will invoke an UPDATE trigger if a duplicate key is found and an update is made. REPLACE uses an INSERT statement to add a row, and optionally DELETE if there was an existing row with a duplicate key. Thus, REPLACE will invoke an INSERT trigger and may invoke a DELETE trigger, if there was an entry to delete.

Foreign key cascading actions (ON DELETE CASCADE and ON UPDATE CASCADE) do not invoke triggers. This is a known limitation in mysqld 6.0 that will be resolved when foreign keys are implemented across all storage keys. The fix is scheduled for mysqld 6.1.

Creating a trigger

Creating a trigger requires the TRIGGER privilege. See Chapter 14 for more information about managing privileges.

NOTE   Before mysqld 5.1.6, creating a trigger required the SUPER privilege.

The simplest CREATE TRIGGER statement has the following syntax:

```
CREATE TRIGGER triggername
[BEFORE|AFTER] [INSERT|UPDATE|DELETE] ON tablename
FOR EACH ROW {statement}
```

CREATE TRIGGER attempts to create a trigger. In this example, Ziesel creates a trigger that will change the last_update column of the staff table when a new staff member is inserted:

```
mysql> CREATE TRIGGER staff_update_date
    -> BEFORE INSERT ON staff
    -> FOR EACH ROW SET NEW.last_update = NOW();
Query OK, 0 rows affected (0.05 sec)
```

If there is already a trigger with the same name an error is thrown, even if the change type (INSERT/UPDATE/DELETE) is different:

```
mysql> CREATE TRIGGER staff_update_date
    -> BEFORE UPDATE ON staff
    -> FOR EACH ROW SET NEW.last_update = NOW();
ERROR 1359 (HY000): Trigger already exists
```

If there is already a trigger with the same combination of time (BEFORE/AFTER) and change type (INSERT/UPDATE/DELETE), an error is thrown:

```
mysql> CREATE TRIGGER staff_insert_update_date
    -> BEFORE INSERT ON staff
    -> FOR EACH ROW SET NEW.last_update = NOW();
ERROR 1235 (42000): This version of MySQL doesn't yet support 'multi-
ple triggers with the same action time and event for one table'
```

NEW.create_date is an alias for the create_date field of all rows that were just inserted in the table. In the context of an AFTER UPDATE trigger, NEW.field is an alias for the field of all rows that were just changed. There is a similar alias named OLD.field, which is a reference to the field of all rows that were just changed, in the context of AFTER DELETE and AFTER UPDATE triggers.

There is no such concept of an OLD.field alias in the context of a BEFORE trigger. Before an action is taken, there is no "old" value. Similarly, the concept of NEW.field does not exist in the context of an AFTER trigger, because after an action there is not a new value, just a current value and an old value. Logically, after an insert there is no concept of OLD.field, because an INSERT by definition inserts a new row into a table. As well, there is no concept of NEW.field in the context of an AFTER DELETE trigger, because a DELETE by definition gets rid of the old row.

Table 7-2 illustrates the uses based on context of these aliases.

TABLE 7-2

Trigger Alias Usage

Context	NEW.field alias	OLD.field alias
BEFORE INSERT	Field of all rows about to be inserted	BEFORE does not support OLD
AFTER INSERT	AFTER does not support NEW	No "old" row after an insert
BEFORE UPDATE	Field of all rows just updated	BEFORE does not support OLD
AFTER UPDATE	AFTER does not support NEW	Previous value of field of all rows just updated
BEFORE DELETE	No "new" row before a delete	BEFORE does not support OLD
AFTER DELETE	AFTER does not support NEW	Previous value of field of all rows just deleted

Dropping a trigger

To drop a trigger, use the DROP TRIGGER statement. An error is thrown if the trigger does not exist, but this can be changed to a warning by using the IF EXISTS phrase:

```
mysql> DROP TRIGGER staff_update_date;
Query OK, 0 rows affected (0.00 sec)

mysql> DROP TRIGGER staff_update_date;
ERROR 1360 (HY000): Trigger does not exist
mysql> DROP TRIGGER IF EXISTS staff_update_date;
Query OK, 0 rows affected, 1 warning (0.00 sec)
```

```
mysql> SHOW WARNINGS;
+-------+------+----------------------+
| Level | Code | Message              |
+-------+------+----------------------+
| Note  | 1360 | Trigger does not exist |
+-------+------+----------------------+
1 row in set (0.00 sec)
```

Multiple SQL statements in triggers

A trigger can be defined as a set of SQL statements by using the BEGIN ... END compound statement syntax. A trigger issuing more than one SQL statement makes the limitation of only one trigger for each time and type of event less of a problem. To define a trigger with more than one SQL statement, use MySQL's DELIMITER SQL extension (see Chapter 4) to change the client delimiter while defining the trigger. If you do not, the first semicolon used to end the first SQL statement in the trigger will be interpreted as the end of the trigger definition, and an error will be raised.

As an example, Ziesel extends the BEFORE INSERT trigger on the staff table to do some simple logging of when a staff record was inserted in addition to updating the last_update field of the row:

```
mysql> USE sakila;
Database changed
mysql> CREATE TABLE staff_creation_log (
    -> username VARCHAR(16) NOT NULL,
    -> when_created TIMESTAMP DEFAULT CURRENT_TIMESTAMP
    -> ) DEFAULT CHARSET=UTF8 ENGINE=MYISAM;
Query OK, 0 rows affected (0.05 sec)

mysql> DELIMITER |
mysql> CREATE TRIGGER before_staff_insert
    -> BEFORE INSERT ON staff
    -> FOR EACH ROW BEGIN
    -> INSERT INTO staff_creation_log (username, when_created)
    -> VALUES (NEW.username, NOW());
    -> SET NEW.last_update = NOW();
    -> END
    -> |
Query OK, 0 rows affected (0.00 sec)

mysql> DELIMITER ;
mysql> INSERT INTO staff (first_name, last_name, address_id, email,
    store_id, active, username)
    -> VALUES ('Hudson', 'Kramer', 1, 'hkramer@sakilastore.com', 1,
        1, 'hkramer');
Query OK, 1 row affected (0.06 sec)
```

```
mysql> SELECT username, when_created FROM staff_creation_log;
+----------+---------------------+
| username | when_created        |
+----------+---------------------+
| hkramer  | 2008-07-03 12:22:15 |
+----------+---------------------+
1 row in set (0.00 sec)

mysql> SELECT * FROM staff where username='hkramer'\G
*************************** 1. row ***************************
    staff_id: 3
  first_name: Hudson
   last_name: Kramer
  address_id: 1
     picture: NULL
       email: hkramer@sakilastore.com
    store_id: 1
      active: 1
    username: hkramer
    password: NULL
 last_update: 2008-07-03 12:22:15
1 row in set (0.00 sec)

mysql>
```

This example shows that the BEFORE INSERT trigger on the staff table will run two SQL queries — one to log the username and created date and time to a table, and another to update the last_update field with the current timestamp.

Note that the BEGIN and END syntax used here does not start a new transaction, nor does it have any effect on an existing transaction.

Changing a trigger

MySQL does not have a command to change an existing trigger. The only way to change a trigger is to drop the trigger and re-create it. The SHOW CREATE TRIGGER command shows the original SQL command used to create the trigger:

```
mysql> SHOW CREATE TRIGGER before_staff_insert\G
*************************** 1. row ***************************
               Trigger: before_staff_insert
              sql_mode: STRICT_TRANS_TABLES,NO_AUTO_CREATE_USER,
                NO_ENGINE_SUBSTITUTION
SQL Original Statement: CREATE DEFINER=`root`@`localhost` TRIG-
GER before_staff_insert
BEFORE INSERT ON staff
FOR EACH ROW BEGIN
INSERT INTO staff_creation_log (username, when_created)
```

```
        VALUES (NEW.username, NOW());
        SET NEW.last_update = NOW();
        END
          character_set_client: latin1
          collation_connection: latin1_swedish_ci
            Database Collation: latin1_swedish_ci
        1 row in set (0.00 sec)
```

To change this trigger, drop and re-create the trigger:

```
        mysql> DROP TRIGGER IF EXISTS before_staff_insert;
        Query OK, 0 rows affected (0.00 sec)

        mysql> CREATE DEFINER=`root`@`localhost` TRIGGER before_staff_insert
            -> BEFORE INSERT ON staff
            -> FOR EACH ROW
            -> SET NEW.last_update = NOW();
        Query OK, 0 rows affected (0.00 sec)

        mysql> SHOW CREATE TRIGGER before_staff_insert\G
        *************************** 1. row ***************************
                        Trigger: before_staff_insert
                       sql_mode: STRICT_TRANS_TABLES,NO_AUTO_CREATE_USER,
                           NO_ENGINE_SUBSTITUTION
        SQL Original Statement: CREATE DEFINER=`root`@`localhost`
        TRIGGER before_staff_insert
        BEFORE INSERT ON staff
        FOR EACH ROW
        SET NEW.last_update = NOW()
          character_set_client: latin1
          collation_connection: latin1_swedish_ci
            Database Collation: latin1_swedish_ci
        1 row in set (0.00 sec)
```

Triggers on views and temporary tables

Views and temporary tables do not support triggers, as the following example shows:

```
        mysql> USE test;
        Database changed
        mysql>  CREATE TEMPORARY TABLE staff_name (staff_name varchar(50),
           staff_created datetime);
        Query OK, 0 rows affected (0.05 sec)

        mysql> INSERT INTO staff_name (staff_name) SELECT CONCAT(first_name,
           ' ', last_name)
            ->  FROM sakila.staff;
        Query OK, 2 rows affected (0.05 sec)
        Records: 2  Duplicates: 0  Warnings: 0
```

```
mysql> SELECT staff_name, staff_created FROM staff_name;
+--------------+---------------+
| staff_name   | staff_created |
+--------------+---------------+
| Mike Hillyer | NULL          |
| Jon Stephens | NULL          |
+--------------+---------------+
2 rows in set (0.00 sec)

mysql> CREATE TRIGGER staff_created
    -> BEFORE INSERT ON staff_name
    -> FOR EACH ROW SET NEW.staff_created=NOW();
ERROR 1361 (HY000): Trigger's 'staff_name' is view or temporary table
mysql> DROP TEMPORARY TABLE staff_name
Query OK, 0 rows affected (0.45 sec)
mysql> CREATE VIEW staff_name
    -> AS SELECT CONCAT(first_name, ' ', last_name) AS full_name
    -> FROM sakila.staff;
Query OK, 0 rows affected (0.00 sec)

mysql> SELECT full_name FROM staff_name;
+--------------+
| full_name    |
+--------------+
| Mike Hillyer |
| Jon Stephens |
+--------------+
2 rows in set (0.03 sec)

mysql> CREATE TRIGGER staff_created
    -> BEFORE INSERT ON staff_name
    -> FOR EACH ROW SET NEW.staff_created=NOW();
ERROR 1347 (HY000): 'test.staff_name' is not BASE TABLE
mysql> DROP VIEW staff_name;
Query OK, 0 rows affected (0.00 sec)
```

Trigger runtime behavior

Triggers are defined by one user in one environment, and may be invoked by an action from another user in another environment. This can lead to questions as to how the trigger behaves with respect to sql_mode, collation, and whom the trigger is invoked as.

Changing the sql_mode of a trigger

By default, a trigger is saved with the sql_mode of the user defining the trigger. This may lead to problems if the execution environment has a very different sql_mode than the definition environment. If a trigger is not acting as expected, check the sql_mode of the trigger.

Both the SHOW CREATE TRIGGER and SHOW TRIGGERS commands output the sql_mode associated with a trigger. There is no way to set the sql_mode as different from the defining environment. To change the sql_mode of a trigger:

- Drop the trigger
- Set the desired sql_mode with SET @@sql_mode={string}
- Re-create the trigger
- Reset the sql_mode back to what the client was originally running

For more information on sql_mode, see Chapter 5.

Character set and collation

Similar to sql_mode, a trigger is saved with the current character set and collation stored in the character_set_client and collation_connection system variables. As with sql_mode, changing these values in a trigger involves dropping the trigger, setting the character set and collation, re-creating the trigger, and resetting the character set and collation:

```
mysql> CREATE DEFINER=`root`@`localhost` TRIGGER rental_date
    -> BEFORE INSERT ON rental
    -> FOR EACH ROW SET NEW.rental_date = NOW();
Query OK, 0 rows affected (0.00 sec)

mysql> SHOW CREATE TRIGGER rental_date\G
*************************** 1. row ***************************
               Trigger: rental_date
              sql_mode: STRICT_TRANS_TABLES,NO_AUTO_CREATE_USER,
                 NO_ENGINE_SUBSTITUTION
SQL Original Statement: CREATE DEFINER=`root`@`localhost`
TRIGGER rental_date BEFORE INSERT ON rental
        FOR EACH ROW SET NEW.rental_date = NOW()
  character_set_client: latin1
  collation_connection: latin1_swedish_ci
    Database Collation: latin1_swedish_ci
1 row in set (0.00 sec)

mysql> DROP TRIGGER IF EXISTS rental_date;
Query OK, 0 rows affected (0.00 sec)

mysql> SET CHARACTER SET ascii;
Query OK, 0 rows affected (0.00 sec)

mysql> SET COLLATION_CONNECTION=binary;
Query OK, 0 rows affected (0.00 sec)

mysql> CREATE DEFINER=`root`@`localhost` TRIGGER rental_date
    -> BEFORE INSERT ON rental
```

```
        -> FOR EACH ROW SET NEW.rental_date = NOW();
Query OK, 0 rows affected (0.00 sec)

mysql> show create trigger rental_date\G
*************************** 1. row ***************************
                Trigger: rental_date
               sql_mode: STRICT_TRANS_TABLES,NO_AUTO_CREATE_USER,
                  NO_ENGINE_SUBSTITUTION
SQL Original Statement: CREATE DEFINER=`root`@`localhost`
TRIGGER rental_date BEFORE INSERT ON rental
         FOR EACH ROW SET NEW.rental_date = NOW()
  character_set_client: ascii
  collation_connection: binary
    Database Collation: latin1_swedish_ci
1 row in set (0.00 sec)

mysql> SET CHARACTER SET latin1;
Query OK, 0 rows affected (0.00 sec)

mysql> SET COLLATION_CONNECTION=latin1_swedish_ci;
Query OK, 0 rows affected (0.02 sec)
```

For a further discussion of character sets and collations, see Chapter 4.

Changing whom a trigger is invoked as

By default, the trigger is invoked as the user who defined the trigger. However, the trigger definer can be set by using a DEFINER clause in the CREATE TRIGGER statement:

```
CREATE
DEFINER = { user | CURRENT_USER() }
TRIGGER triggername
[BEFORE|AFTER] [INSERT|UPDATE|DELETE] ON tablename
FOR EACH ROW {statement}
```

CURRENT_USER() is the default value for DEFINER. If the trigger creator is not a SUPER user, only CURRENT_USER() or the user@host string that represents the current user is allowed.

```
mysql> DROP TRIGGER IF EXISTS before_staff_insert;
Query OK, 0 rows affected (0.00 sec)
mysql> SHOW GRANTS\G
*************************** 1. row ***************************
Grants for sakila@localhost: GRANT USAGE ON *.* TO
    'sakila'@'localhost' IDENTIFIED BY PASSWORD
    '*88143446A216B9EE92DEA6C1A33F9598C83F1B8C'
*************************** 2. row ***************************
Grants for sakila@localhost: GRANT SELECT, INSERT, UPDATE, DELETE,
    TRIGGER ON `sakila`.* TO 'sakila'@'localhost'
2 rows in set (0.00 sec)
```

```
mysql> CREATE
    -> DEFINER=root@localhost
    -> TRIGGER before_staff_insert
    -> BEFORE INSERT ON staff
    -> FOR EACH ROW SET NEW.last_update = NOW();
ERROR 1227 (42000): Access denied; you need the SUPER privilege for
   this operation
mysql> CREATE
    -> DEFINER=sakila@localhost
    -> TRIGGER before_staff_insert
    -> BEFORE INSERT ON staff
    -> FOR EACH ROW SET NEW.last_update = NOW();
Query OK, 0 rows affected (0.23 sec)
```

The sakila@localhost user is allowed to create a trigger, but not allowed to specify that the trigger runs as a user other than sakila@localhost. This is for security purposes; otherwise a user with minimal privileges could define a trigger that performs queries that user does not have permission to perform.

A user with SUPER privileges can change the DEFINER to any valid user@host user string. If the user does not exist in the grant tables, a warning will be issued. It is generally a bad idea to create a trigger for a user that does not exist.

```
mysql> SHOW GRANTS\G
*************************** 1. row ***************************
Grants for root@localhost: GRANT ALL PRIVILEGES ON *.* TO
   'root'@'localhost' IDENTIFIED BY PASSWORD
   '*3800D13EE735ED411CBC3F23B2A2E19C63CE0BEC' WITH GRANT OPTION
1 row in set (0.00 sec)

mysql> DROP TRIGGER IF EXISTS before_staff_insert;
ERROR 1046 (3D000): No database selected
mysql> use sakila;
Database changed
mysql> DROP TRIGGER IF EXISTS before_staff_insert;
Query OK, 0 rows affected (0.00 sec)

mysql> SELECT user, host FROM mysql.user where user='DoesNotExist'
   and host='localhost';
Empty set (0.05 sec)

mysql> CREATE
    -> DEFINER=DoesNotExist@localhost
    -> TRIGGER before_staff_insert
    -> BEFORE INSERT ON staff
    -> FOR EACH ROW SET NEW.last_update = NOW();
Query OK, 0 rows affected, 1 warning (0.03 sec)

mysql> SHOW WARNINGS;
```

```
+-------+------+------------------------------------------------+
| Level | Code | Message                                        |
+-------+------+------------------------------------------------+
| Note  | 1449 | There is no 'DoesNotExist'@'localhost' registered |
+-------+------+------------------------------------------------+
1 row in set (0.01 sec)

mysql> INSERT INTO staff (first_name, last_name, address_id, email,
    -> store_id, active, username)
    -> VALUES ('Joshua', 'Wasserman', 1,
    -> 'jwasserman@sakilastore.com', 1, 1, 'jwasserman');
ERROR 1449 (HY000): There is no 'DoesNotExist'@'localhost' registered
```

Finding all triggers

To view all the triggers in a database, use the SHOW TRIGGERS command. To view all the triggers associated with a table, use the LIKE extension to SHOW TRIGGERS:

```
mysql> SHOW TRIGGERS LIKE 'customer'\G
*************************** 1. row ***************************
            Trigger: customer_create_date
              Event: INSERT
              Table: customer
          Statement: SET NEW.create_date = NOW()
             Timing: BEFORE
            Created: NULL
           sql_mode:
STRICT_TRANS_TABLES,STRICT_ALL_TABLES,NO_ZERO_IN_DATE,NO_Z
ERO_DATE,ERROR_FOR_DIVISION_BY_ZERO,TRADITIONAL,NO_AUTO_CREATE_USER
            Definer: root@localhost
character_set_client: utf8
collation_connection: utf8_general_ci
  Database Collation: latin1_swedish_ci
1 row in set (0.00 sec)
```

You can also query the INFORMATION_SCHEMA.TRIGGERS table. For more about the INFORMA-TION_SCHEMA database, see Chapter 21.

Trigger storage and backup

Triggers are stored in the data directory (datadir) in files named tblname.TRG and triggername.TRN. The .TRG files map triggers to tables, and the .TRN files contain the trigger definition. The sample sakila database creates the following .TRG files:

- customer.TRG
- film.TRG
- payment.TRG
- rental.TRG

The sample schema creates six different triggers. There are only four .TRG files because there are only four tables that contain triggers:

```
mysql> SELECT TRIGGER_NAME, EVENT_OBJECT_TABLE
    -> FROM INFORMATION_SCHEMA.TRIGGERS;
+----------------------+--------------------+
| TRIGGER_NAME         | EVENT_OBJECT_TABLE |
+----------------------+--------------------+
| customer_create_date | customer           |
| ins_film             | film               |
| upd_film             | film               |
| del_film             | film               |
| payment_date         | payment            |
| rental_date          | rental             |
+----------------------+--------------------+
6 rows in set (0.02 sec)
```

The six triggers affect four different tables, so there are only four .TRG files — one .TRG file for each table that is affected. When a table is renamed, the trigger files are renamed too, thus no triggers are lost during a table rename.

```
mysql> USE sakila;
Database changed
mysql> ALTER TABLE film RENAME foo;
Query OK, 0 rows affected (0.42 sec)

mysql> SELECT TRIGGER_NAME, EVENT_OBJECT_TABLE
    -> FROM INFORMATION_SCHEMA.TRIGGERS;
+----------------------+--------------------+
| TRIGGER_NAME         | EVENT_OBJECT_TABLE |
+----------------------+--------------------+
| customer_create_date | customer           |
| ins_film             | foo                |
| upd_film             | foo                |
| del_film             | foo                |
| payment_date         | payment            |
| rental_date          | rental             |
+----------------------+--------------------+
6 rows in set (0.02 sec)
```

And the corresponding directory now has:

- customer.TRG
- foo.TRG
- payment.TRG
- rental.TRG

253

Now reset the table back to the original sakila sample database:

```
mysql> ALTER TABLE foo RENAME staff;
Query OK, 0 rows affected (0.03 sec)

mysql> SELECT TRIGGER_NAME, EVENT_OBJECT_TABLE
    -> FROM INFORMATION_SCHEMA.TRIGGERS;
+----------------------+--------------------+
| TRIGGER_NAME         | EVENT_OBJECT_TABLE |
+----------------------+--------------------+
| customer_create_date | customer           |
| ins_film             | film               |
| upd_film             | film               |
| del_film             | film               |
| payment_date         | payment            |
| rental_date          | rental             |
+----------------------+--------------------+
6 rows in set (0.02 sec)
```

The corresponding .TRN files are:

- customer_create_date.TRN

- del_film.TRN

- ins_film.TRN

- payment_date.TRN

- rental_date.TRN

- upd_film.TRN

Triggers can be backed up using mysqldump and during cold and hot backups by copying the .TRG and .TRN files. For more information on backing up triggers, see Chapter 13.

Triggers and replication

CREATE TRIGGER and DROP TRIGGER statements are not replicated. Trigger actions are not saved to the binary log in statement-based replication. Therefore, to have an action triggered on both a master and slave when using statement-based replication, the trigger must be defined on each database instance. Row-based replication saves data changes to the binary log, making triggers easier to manage on such systems. When replication is in mixed mode, the effect of triggers is the same as in row-based replication.

Trigger limitations

Triggers cannot:

- Modify a table already being used by the statement that invoked the trigger without using the NEW and OLD aliases

- Be defined on a table in the mysql database

- Use SELECT without saving the results INTO variable_name

- Use SHOW commands
- Use LOAD DATA
- Use LOAD TABLE
- Use BACKUP DATABASE
- Use RESTORE
- Use dynamic SQL
- Use prepared statement commands (PREPARE, EXECUTE, DEALLOCATE PREPARE)
- Use statements that do a COMMIT or ROLLBACK:
  - COMMIT
  - ROLLBACK
  - START TRANSACTION
  - LOCK TABLES and UNLOCK TABLES when there were locked tables
  - SET AUTOCOMMIT=1 when it was not already set to 1
  - TRUNCATE TABLE
  - Most ALTER, CREATE, DROP and RENAME commands cause an implicit COMMIT (see Chapter 4)
  - Most CREATE commands cause an implicit COMMIT (see Chapter 4)
- Use FLUSH statements
- Invoke a user-defined function (UDF) to call an external application.
- Use ALTER VIEW
- Use RETURN

Using Stored Routines

A stored routine (either a stored procedure or a stored function) allows MySQL users to define a set of statements that they can later call in a query. Stored routines make repetitive tasks involving many queries much easier. Stored routines have been a part of many other databases for a long time; MySQL introduced stored routines as generally available (GA) in version 5.0.1, released in October 2005. Although MySQL stored routines are not as advanced as other databases, plenty of features make it easier to use the database. The most common reasons to use stored routines are:

- **Code reuse** — Different applications running against the same database can call a stored routine instead of having to write repetitive code.

- **Black box queries** — A developer can call a stored routine without having to know the exact queries or tables used. Stored routines make a database much more user-friendly; a developer can call save_profile_info(12345, "name", "Eli") instead of having to know about the underlying table structure and write a query such as UPDATE `user_profile SET name="Eli" WHERE user_id=12345`. This makes it easier for a database administrator to change the underlying schema without creating work for developers.

■ **Security via API** — Not only does a developer not need to know the underlying schema with a stored routine, a set of stored routines can act as an API into a database. If users only have permissions to use the stored routines created, they will be limited to exactly the actions allowed by the routines. This also means that functionality such as auditing and logging can be placed within a stored routine, to ensure that a database action is performed according to the policies of an organization.

■ **Security via ACL constraints** — Using GRANT statements, a database administrator can bestow privileges to see and change information on the global, database, table, and column levels. Instead, a database administrator could give privileges to execute stored routines, and thereby control access much more tightly. There is no way in MySQL to constrain a privilege — for instance, "user@host can update information in table, but no more than five rows at a time." However, with a stored routine, it is possible to enforce this type of privilege constraint.

Performance implications of stored routines

Stored routines are compiled by mysqld the first time they are invoked in a connection. Subsequent stored routine calls in the same connection are cached. This may seem advantageous; however, there is only an advantage if your application maintains the same connection (thread_id) throughout multiple stored routine calls. Many applications are designed to connect to the database, run one query or a few queries, and then disconnect. Those types of applications suffer when stored routines are used, because they have the penalty of compiling the code but very little benefit from the per-thread compile cache.

This is a particularly troublesome problem for database administrators who are experienced in other database systems. Many other database systems compile stored routines into native code when they are created. Database administrators accustomed to the database compiling stored routines at creation time are very surprised when their applications are running extremely slowly due to mysqld behaving differently than expected.

Stored procedures vs. stored functions

Both stored procedures and stored functions take zero or more arguments. A stored procedure can pass back values through output variables and result sets. A stored function can only output a scalar value, and is required to do so. MySQL follows the ISO:2003 SQL standard syntax for stored routines.

Creating a stored routine

Because of the similarities between stored procedures and stored functions, we will go through how to define a stored procedure, and then highlight where creating a stored function is different. While defining a stored procedure, we will use stored routine to mean either a stored procedure or a stored function, and specify stored procedure when we mean a stored procedure.

Ziesel wants to make a stored procedure that takes a store ID as input and outputs the number of films offered by the store. These offerings may or may not be in stock. The stored procedure she creates is very simple:

```
DELIMITER |
CREATE PROCEDURE store_offerings ( IN p_store_id TINYINT UNSIGNED,
    OUT p_count INT UNSIGNED)
        SELECT COUNT(*) INTO p_count
        FROM inventory WHERE store_id = p_store_id;
|
DELIMITER ;
```

Note that because the stored procedure has statements that end in the default delimiter (;), Ziesel must change the delimiter on her client to actually create the stored procedure. She changes the delimiter back when she is done creating the stored procedure.

The name of the procedure is store_offerings, and Ziesel declares one input parameter and one output variable. There can be zero or more input parameters and zero or more output variables in a stored procedure. The requirements for arguments are that each input parameter and output variable is specified as IN or OUT, named, and the type defined. Data types are discussed in depth in Chapter 5.

In the example store_offerings, the body of the stored procedure gets a count of the store offerings for the specified store_id, and puts that into the output variable.

If there are neither input parameters nor output variables, the parameter list must be specified as an empty list, using ( ):

```
DELIMITER |
CREATE PROCEDURE update_all_staff_time ()
        UPDATE staff SET last_update=NOW() WHERE 1=1;
|
DELIMITER ;
```

WHERE 1=1 is in the query to indicate the deliberate intention to update all the rows in the staff table. Otherwise, someone looking at this stored procedure might wonder if the WHERE clause was forgotten.

Warning: Data truncated for column ·sql_mode· at row 0

When trying to create a stored routine, you may get a warning such as Warning: Data truncated for column 'sql_mode'. This is a known issue (see MySQL bug 32633 — http://bugs.mysql.com/bug.php?id=32633), and was fixed in MySQL versions 6.0.5 and 5.1.24. The problem occurs when the sql_mode contains NO_ENGINE_SUBSTITUTION. If you receive this error, we strongly recommend upgrading. If you cannot upgrade, you can work

continued

continued

around the problem by removing NO_ENGINE_SUBSTITUTION from `sql_mode`, but that is not desirable.

Here is an example of receiving the error and fixing `sql_mode` in 6.0.4:

```
Welcome to the MySQL monitor.  Commands end with ; or \g.
Your MySQL connection id is 2625
Server version: 6.0.4-alpha-community MySQL Community Server (GPL)
Type 'help;' or '\h' for help. Type '\c' to clear the buffer.
mysql> DELIMITER |
mysql> CREATE PROCEDURE store_offerings ( IN p_store_id INT, OUT p_count INT )
    ->        SELECT COUNT(*) INTO p_count
    ->        FROM inventory WHERE store_id = p_store_id;
    -> |
ERROR 1655 (HY000): Cannot create stored routine `store_offerings`.
   Check warnings
mysql> DELIMITER ;
mysql> SHOW WARNINGS\G
*************************** 1. row ***************************
   Level: Warning
    Code: 1265
Message: Data truncated for column 'sql_mode' at row 0
*************************** 2. row ***************************
   Level: Error
    Code: 1655
Message: Cannot create stored routine `store_offerings`. Check warnings
2 rows in set (0.00 sec)
mysql> SELECT @@sql_mode;
+------------------------------------------------------------------+
| @@sql_mode                                                       |
+------------------------------------------------------------------+
| STRICT_TRANS_TABLES,NO_AUTO_CREATE_USER,NO_ENGINE_SUBSTITUTION   |
+------------------------------------------------------------------+
1 row in set (0.00 sec)
mysql> SET @@sql_mode="STRICT_TRANS_TABLES,NO_AUTO_CREATE_USER";
Query OK, 0 rows affected (0.02 sec)
mysql> SELECT @@sql_mode;
+------------------------------------------+
| @@sql_mode                               |
+------------------------------------------+
| STRICT_TRANS_TABLES,NO_AUTO_CREATE_USER  |
+------------------------------------------+
1 row in set (0.00 sec)
mysql> DELIMITER |
```

continued

```
continued
mysql> CREATE PROCEDURE store_offerings ( IN p_store_id INT, OUT p_count INT )
    ->        SELECT COUNT(*) INTO p_count
    ->          FROM inventory WHERE store_id = p_store_id;
    -> |
Query OK, 0 rows affected (0.00 sec)
mysql> DELIMITER ;
```

Invoking a stored procedure

To invoke a stored procedure, use the CALL statement. Make sure to specify all of the IN and OUT parameters. Note that you need the EXECUTE privilege in order to CALL the procedure; the creator of the stored procedure is given this privilege automatically. See Chapter 14 for more information about managing privileges.

NOTE The automatic_sp_privileges system variable can be set to 0 to change the default behavior of a stored procedure's creator getting automatic EXECUTE privilege.

In the following example, Ziesel invokes the store_offerings stored procedure, giving an input of 1 for the store_id and setting the output variable to @store_1_offerings:

```
mysql> CALL store_offerings(1,@store_1_offerings);
Query OK, 0 rows affected (0.00 sec)

mysql> SELECT @store_1_offerings;
+--------------------+
| @store_1_offerings |
+--------------------+
|               2270 |
+--------------------+
1 row in set (0.00 sec)
```

If you need to confirm the stored procedure did the right thing, you can double-check the result:

```
mysql> SELECT COUNT(*) FROM inventory WHERE store_id=1;
+----------+
| COUNT(*) |
+----------+
|     2270 |
+----------+
1 row in set (0.00 sec)
```

A stored procedure throws an error if the correct number of arguments is not given:

```
mysql> CALL store_offerings(1);
ERROR 1318 (42000): Incorrect number of arguments for PROCEDURE sak-
ila.store_offerings; expected 2, got 1
```

Errors are also thrown if the input variables are not of the right type, and if the output argument is not a proper variable:

```
mysql> CALL store_offerings("a",@store_1_offerings);
ERROR 1366 (HY000): Incorrect integer value: 'a' for column
   'p_store_id' at row 1
mysql> CALL store_offerings(1,1);
ERROR 1414 (42000): OUT or INOUT argument 2 for routine
   sakila.store_offerings is not a variable or NEW pseudo-variable
   in BEFORE trigger
```

If a stored procedure has neither input parameters nor output variables, the CALL statement can be specified with the empty parameter list ( ) or just invoked by itself. Recall the update_all_staff_time stored procedure, which has no arguments:

```
mysql> SELECT DISTINCT last_update FROM staff;
+---------------------+
| last_update         |
+---------------------+
| 2006-02-15 04:57:16 |
+---------------------+
1 row in set (0.00 sec)

mysql> CALL update_all_staff_time();
Query OK, 2 rows affected (0.19 sec)

mysql> SELECT DISTINCT last_update FROM staff;
+---------------------+
| last_update         |
+---------------------+
| 2008-08-27 08:16:26 |
+---------------------+
1 row in set (0.00 sec)

mysql> -- our stored procedure worked with CALL proc_name()
mysql> CALL update_all_staff_time;
Query OK, 2 rows affected (0.08 sec)

mysql> SELECT DISTINCT last_update FROM staff;
+---------------------+
| last_update         |
+---------------------+
| 2008-08-27 08:18:56 |
+---------------------+
1 row in set (0.00 sec)

mysql> -- our stored procedure worked with CALL proc_name
```

Dropping a stored routine

To drop a stored procedure, use the DROP PROCEDURE statement. To drop a stored function, use the DROP FUNCTION statement. If the routine does not exist, an error is returned from the DROP statement. This can be changed to a warning by using the IF EXISTS phrase in either DROP PROCEDURE or DROP FUNCTION:

```
mysql> DROP PROCEDURE store_offerings;
Query OK, 0 rows affected (0.01 sec)

mysql> DROP PROCEDURE store_offerings;
ERROR 1305 (42000): PROCEDURE sakila.store_offerings does not exist
mysql> DROP PROCEDURE IF EXISTS store_offerings;
Query OK, 0 rows affected, 1 warning (0.00 sec)

mysql> SHOW WARNINGS;
+--------+------+----------------------------------------------------+
| Level  | Code | Message                                            |
+--------+------+----------------------------------------------------+
| Note   | 1305 | PROCEDURE sakila.store_offerings does not exist    |
+--------+------+----------------------------------------------------+
1 row in set (0.00 sec)
```

Multiple SQL statements in stored routines

So far, you have created simple stored routines consisting of one SQL statement. You can create stored routines with multiple SQL statements by enveloping the SQL statements with BEGIN and END. See the subsection "Multiple SQL Statements in Triggers" for more information.

TIP Because there is no downside to surrounding a single SQL statement with BEGIN and END, it is good practice to always surround the body of a stored routine with BEGIN and END. From here forward, examples will follow this practice.

INOUT arguments to a stored procedure

Arguments to a stored procedure can be IN, OUT, or INOUT. The INOUT argument type is a variable, just as the OUT argument type is. The difference is that an INOUT argument can be used as both an input parameter and an output variable. Here is an example of a simple stored procedure that increases an INOUT argument by 1:

```
mysql> DELIMITER |
mysql> CREATE PROCEDURE increment_counter (
    -> INOUT p_count INT UNSIGNED)
    ->  BEGIN
    ->  SET p_count:=p_count+1;
    ->  END
    -> |
Query OK, 0 rows affected (0.00 sec)
```

```
mysql> DELIMITER ;
mysql> SELECT @count:=123;
+-------------+
| @count:=123 |
+-------------+
|         123 |
+-------------+
1 row in set (0.00 sec)

mysql> CALL increment_counter(@count);
Query OK, 0 rows affected (0.00 sec)

mysql> SELECT @count;
+--------+
| @count |
+--------+
|    124 |
+--------+
1 row in set (0.00 sec)

mysql> CALL increment_counter(@count);
Query OK, 0 rows affected (0.00 sec)

mysql> SELECT @count;
+--------+
| @count |
+--------+
|    125 |
+--------+
1 row in set (0.00 sec)
```

To summarize thus far, a simple CREATE PROCEDURE statement has the syntax:

```
CREATE
PROCEDURE p_name ([parameter[, ... ]])
{statement}

parameter is:
[IN|OUT|INOUT] name data_type
```

Local variables

In some cases, you may want to use a local variable in a stored routine. The scope of local variables is within an instantiation of a stored routine. This means that a local variable in a stored routine cannot be accessed from outside the stored routine. Also, different threads invoking the same stored routine cannot access each others' local variables (even if they are run at the same time).

To set a local variable within a stored routine, use the DECLARE syntax:

```
DECLARE var_name data_type
```

You can find more information about MySQL data types in Chapter 5.

The pct_increase stored procedure increases a number by a given amount, calculating the percentage increase. The INOUT variable p_int stores the input number and the number returned after the increase is performed. The IN parameter p_incr indicates the amount to increase p_int by, and the OUT variable p_pct_incr stores the percentage increase:

```
mysql> DELIMITER |
mysql> CREATE PROCEDURE pct_increase (INOUT p_int
    INT, IN p_incr INT, OUT p_pct_incr DECIMAL (5,2))
    -> BEGIN
    -> DECLARE p_int_new INT;
    -> SET p_int_new:=p_int+p_incr;
    -> SET p_pct_incr:=(p_int_new-p_int)/p_int*100;
    -> SET p_int:=p_int_new;
    -> END
    -> |
Query OK, 0 rows affected (0.00 sec)

mysql> DELIMITER ;
```

> **NOTE** DECLARE var_name data_type can be called only at the beginning of the body of the stored routine.

The following example increases the number 100, stored in the user variable @num, by 10 percent:

```
mysql> SET @num:=100;
Query OK, 0 rows affected (0.00 sec)

mysql> CALL pct_increase (@num, 10, @pct);
Query OK, 0 rows affected (0.00 sec)

mysql> SELECT @num, @pct;
+------+-------+
| @num | @pct  |
+------+-------+
|  110 | 10.00 |
+------+-------+
1 row in set (0.00 sec)
```

The stored procedure can also take negative numbers for p_incr. This will decrease p_int, and p_pct_incr will be negative:

```
mysql> SET @num:=100;
Query OK, 0 rows affected (0.00 sec)
```

```
mysql> CALL pct_increase (@num, -10, @pct);
Query OK, 0 rows affected (0.00 sec)

mysql> SELECT @num, @pct;
+------+--------+
| @num | @pct   |
+------+--------+
|   90 | -10.00 |
+------+--------+
1 row in set (0.00 sec)
```

Stored routine runtime behavior

Stored routines (like triggers) are defined by one user in one environment, and may be invoked from another user in another environment. This can lead to questions as to how the stored routine behaves with respect to sql_mode, collation, and whom the stored routine is run as.

sql_mode

By default, a stored routine is saved with the current sql_mode. This may lead to problems if the execution environment has a very different sql_mode than the definition environment. In fact, we saw earlier that the sql_mode may affect your ability to create a stored routine! If a stored routine is not acting as expected, you may want to check the sql_mode of the stored routine. For more information on sql_mode, see Chapter 5.

The sql_mode cannot be set as part of a CREATE PROCEDURE or CREATE FUNCTION statement. However, you can change the sql_mode for the current session, and any stored routines created after that change will then have the new sql_mode. You can change the sql_mode of an existing stored routine with the ALTER PROCEDURE and ALTER FUNCTION statements.

Character set and collation

The character set and collation are set as sql_mode is — by using the current environment variables when the stored routine is created. To set a stored routine with a different character set and collation, run SET CHARACTER SET charset and SET COLLATION_CONNECTION=collation commands before running the CREATE command. Changing the character set and collation cannot be done with the ALTER PROCEDURE and ALTER FUNCTION statements. For a further discussion of character sets and collations, see Chapter 4.

How the stored routine runs

By default, the stored routine is invoked as the user who defined the stored routine. However, the stored routine definer can be changed by using a DEFINER clause in the CREATE PROCEDURE statement:

```
CREATE
[DEFINER = { user | CURRENT_USER }]
```

```
PROCEDURE p_name ([parameter[, ... ]])
{statement}
```

and for a CREATE FUNCTION:

```
CREATE
[DEFINER = { user | CURRENT_USER }]
FUNCTION f_name ([parameter[, ... ]])
RETURNS type
{statement}
```

See the discussion in the subsection "Changing Whom a Trigger is Invoked As" for details on what the DEFINER clause allows.

Another way to change whom the stored routine runs as is to set the SQL SECURITY clause. The SQL SECURITY clause can be set to DEFINER or INVOKER, and the default is DEFINER. Thus, you can specify that a stored routine should run as a chosen user by specifying SQL SECURITY DEFINER; or you can specify that a stored routine should run as the user who invokes the stored routine by specifying SQL SECURITY INVOKER. Here is the CREATE PROCEDURE syntax with this information added:

```
CREATE
[DEFINER = { user | CURRENT_USER }]
PROCEDURE p_name ([parameter[, ... ]])
[SQL SECURITY {DEFINER | INVOKER}]
{statement}
```

and the CREATE FUNCTION syntax:

```
CREATE
[DEFINER = { user | CURRENT_USER }]
FUNCTION f_name ([parameter[, ... ]])
RETURNS type
[SQL SECURITY {DEFINER | INVOKER}]
{statement}
```

You can change the DEFINER and SQL SECURITY clauses of a stored routine with the ALTER PROCEDURE and ALTER FUNCTION statements.

Options when creating routines

SQL SECURITY is one of several options that are allowed in CREATE PROCEDURE and CREATE FUNCTION statements. Options are separated by spaces, and zero or more options can be specified.

Comments

A comment can be applied to a stored routine by specifying a COMMENT option with a string to the CREATE statement:

```
COMMENT 'comment string '
```

Language

Currently the only language supported for stored routines is SQL. The LANGUAGE option is a placeholder for the day when different languages may be supported. It can only be specified as LANGUAGE SQL, which is the default value. This parameter is somewhat meaningless currently, and its explanation is provided here for completeness.

Determinism

A stored procedure takes in zero or more inputs, runs specified SQL, and can change zero or more output variables. A stored function takes in zero or more inputs, runs specified SQL, and returns exactly one scalar value. If the same inputs always produce the same results — both the actions in SQL and the values of any output variables — a stored routine is said to be *deterministic*. A stored routine is said to be *non-deterministic* or *not deterministic* if the same inputs may not always produce the same results.

An example of a deterministic stored procedure is the increment_counter stored procedure we created earlier. An input value of 123 will *always* result in an output of 124. The following stored procedure is not deterministic:

```
CREATE PROCEDURE curr_time (OUT p_time DATETIME)
BEGIN
SET p_time:=CURRENT_DATE();
END
```

Because the stored procedure depends on CURRENT_DATE(), the output will be not *always* be the same. See the sidebar "Deterministic vs. Not Deterministic Routines in MySQL" for more information.

Deterministic vs. Not Deterministic Routines in MySQL

In computer science, a deterministic algorithm is one whose path and output do not change when given the same input. For example, regardless of why I need to get inside my office, I have to go to the office door, open the door, and step inside my office. A non-deterministic algorithm may change its path or its output given the same input. When driving to work, I may drive on the highway during light traffic, and take the back roads during heavy traffic. I start with the same input (starting from home) and end with the same output (arriving at work) but because of the traffic conditions, the path I take may change.

continued

continued

Whether or not a stored routine is deterministic is important due to binary logging. A deterministic stored routine will replicate without a problem; however, a stored routine that is not deterministic may have problems replicating. If binary logging is set as statement-based (see Chapter 16), the binary log contains the statements that change data, so they can be replayed during an incremental restore or during replication. A stored routine that is not deterministic may have a different output given the same input, which means that an incremental restore or slave will not have data that matches the original data.

Be very careful when using a stored routine that is not deterministic, because statement-based binary logging may not be adequate to store the data changes. If data integrity is a concern, use row-based binary logging or a deterministic stored routine instead.

Unfortunately, at the time of this writing, the DETERMINISTIC and NOT DETERMINISTIC options serve only as comments, and are not verified by mysqld. There are no warnings or errors if a non-deterministic routine is set as DETERMINISTIC.

MySQL will throw an error and refuse to create a stored function if binary logging of that function may be unsafe:

```
ERROR 1418 (HY000): This function has none of DETERMINISTIC, NO SQL, or
READS SQL DATA in its declaration and binary logging is enabled
(you *might* want to use the less safe log_bin_trust_function_
creators variable)
```

The best way to fix this problem is to declare the function to be DETERMINISTIC, NO SQL, or READS DATA. The next best way is to have a user with the SUPER privilege define the function. Turning binary logging off is another way to fix this issue, though it may not be possible. Setting log_bin_trust_function_creators to 1 will also fix this issue, though it is less safe because you may end up attempting to replicate a function that is not safe for replication.

SQL usage

The remaining option is what SQL statements the stored routine uses. These values are for informational purposes only, and do not affect the way mysqld handles the stored routine. The possible values are:

- MODIFIES SQL DATA — The stored routine may update data (with a DELETE, INSERT, or UPDATE command, for instance).

- READS SQL DATA — The stored routine does not contain SQL to write data (as in MODI-FIES SQL DATA) but does contain SQL that reads data (that is, SELECT statements). The store_offerings stored procedure is an example of a stored routine that qualifies as READS SQL DATA.

- CONTAINS SQL — The stored routine does not read or write data in the database. The curr_time and increment_counter stored procedures are examples of stored routines that qualify as CONTAINS SQL.

- NO SQL — The stored routine has no SQL statements in it.

The default is CONTAINS SQL. Any changes to the default are done manually by the user; MySQL does not check whether or not the option is correct. For example, the store_offerings stored procedure is created with the default of CONTAINS SQL even though READS SQL DATA is the correct option. Because this is for informational purposes only, there is no harm in having this option be incorrect. However, if you intend to use the information to guide decisions, make sure you set the appropriate option.

Full CREATE PROCEDURE syntax

The full CREATE PROCEDURE syntax is:

```
CREATE
[DEFINER = { user | CURRENT_USER }]
PROCEDURE p_name ([parameter[, ... ]])
[SQL SECURITY {DEFINER | INVOKER}]
[option ... ]
{statement}

option is one or more of:
SQL SECURITY {DEFINER | INVOKER}
COMMENT 'comment string'
LANGUAGE SQL
[NOT] DETERMINISTIC
{CONTAINS SQL | NO SQL | READS SQL DATA | MODIFIES SQL DATA}

parameter is:
[IN|OUT|INOUT] name data_type
```

Note that the CREATE ROUTINE privilege is needed in order to create a stored procedure. See Chapter 14 for more information about managing privileges.

Creating a basic stored function

A stored function outputs only one scalar value, so there is no such thing as an OUT parameter in a stored function. Therefore, the requirements for arguments to a stored function are that each input variable is named and the type defined. You must also specify the type of the return value, and most of the time, create a local variable to store the value to be returned. The differences between CREATE PROCEDURE and CREATE FUNCTION are:

- All arguments to a function are input parameters; arguments to a procedure may be input parameters, output variables, or INOUT variables.

- A function must use the RETURNS keyword after the input parameters to specify the type of the scalar value to be returned.

- A function must use the RETURN keyword in its body to specify the value to be returned.

The following defines a basic stored function to get the store_id of a staff member from the staff table given a staff_id:

```
mysql> DELIMITER |
mysql> CREATE FUNCTION get_store_id (f_staff_id TINYINT UNSIGNED)
    RETURNS TINYINT UNSIGNED
    -> READS SQL DATA
    -> BEGIN
    -> DECLARE f_store_id TINYINT UNSIGNED;
    -> SELECT store_id INTO f_store_id FROM staff WHERE
       staff_id=f_staff_id;
    -> RETURN f_store_id;
    -> END
    -> |
Query OK, 0 rows affected (0.03 sec)

mysql> DELIMITER ;
```

Full CREATE FUNCTION syntax

The full syntax for CREATE FUNCTION is:

```
CREATE
[DEFINER = { user | CURRENT_USER }]
FUNCTION f_name ([parameter[, ... ]])
RETURNS type
 [option ... ]
{statement}

option is one or more of:
SQL SECURITY {DEFINER | INVOKER}
COMMENT 'comment string'
LANGUAGE SQL
[NOT] DETERMINISTIC
{CONTAINS SQL | NO SQL | READS SQL DATA | MODIFIES SQL DATA}

parameter is:
name data_type
```

Note that both the CREATE ROUTINE and SUPER privileges are needed in order to create a stored function. See Chapter 14 for more information about managing privileges.

Invoking a stored function

A stored function is invoked just as a standard MySQL function is invoked — by using the function name and passing input parameters:

```
mysql> SELECT get_store_id(1);
```

```
+-----------------+
| get_store_id(1) |
+-----------------+
|               1 |
+-----------------+
1 row in set (0.20 sec)
```

Note that you need the EXECUTE privilege in order to invoke the function; the creator of the stored function is given this privilege automatically.

Changing a stored routine

MySQL supports the ALTER PROCEDURE and ALTER FUNCTION statements, by which you can change the SQL usage, SQL SECURITY option, and COMMENT of a stored routine. To change more than one of these in one ALTER command, separate the options by a space:

```
mysql> ALTER PROCEDURE increment_counter COMMENT "increments the
    INOUT variable by 1" CONTAINS SQL;
Query OK, 0 rows affected (0.00 sec)
```

Note that you need the ALTER ROUTINE privilege in order to change the stored routine; the creator of the stored routine is given this privilege automatically.

NOTE   The automatic_sp_privileges system variable can be set to 0 to change the default behavior of a stored routine's creator getting automatic ALTER ROUTINE privilege.

To change any other part of a stored routine (the DEFINER or the code body, for example), you must drop and re-create the stored routine.

To see details of a stored procedure, use the SHOW CREATE PROCEDURE command:

```
mysql> SHOW CREATE PROCEDURE increment_counter\G
*************************** 1. row ***************************
           Procedure: increment_counter
            sql_mode: STRICT_TRANS_TABLES,NO_AUTO_CREATE_USER,
              NO_ENGINE_SUBSTITUTION
    Create Procedure: CREATE DEFINER=`root`@`localhost` PROCE-
DURE `increment_counter`(INOUT p_count INT UNSIGNED)
    COMMENT 'increments the INOUT variable by 1'
SET p_count:=p_count+1
character_set_client: latin1
collation_connection: latin1_swedish_ci
   Database Collation: latin1_swedish_ci
1 row in set (0.03 sec)
```

To see details of a stored function, use the SHOW CREATE FUNCTION command:

```
mysql> SHOW CREATE FUNCTION get_store_id\G
```

```
*************************** 1. row ***************************
              Function: get_store_id
              sql_mode: STRICT_TRANS_TABLES,NO_AUTO_CREATE_USER,
                 NO_ENGINE_SUBSTITUTION
       Create Function: CREATE DEFINER=`root`@`localhost` FUNCTION
          `get_store_id`(f_staff_id TINYINT UNSIGNED)
              RETURNS tinyint(3) unsigned
    READS SQL DATA
BEGIN
DECLARE f_store_id TINYINT UNSIGNED;
SELECT store_id INTO f_store_id FROM staff WHERE staff_id=f_staff_id;
RETURN f_store_id;
END
character_set_client: latin1
collation_connection: latin1_swedish_ci
    Database Collation: latin1_swedish_ci
1 row in set (0.00 sec)
```

There is no shortcut to find all the stored routines associated with a database. To use SQL to find what stored routines are in the system, query the ROUTINES table in the INFORMATION_SCHEMA database:

```
mysql> SELECT ROUTINE_NAME, ROUTINE_TYPE FROM
    INFORMATION_SCHEMA.ROUTINES WHERE
ROUTINE_SCHEMA='sakila';
+-----------------------------+--------------+
| ROUTINE_NAME                | ROUTINE_TYPE |
+-----------------------------+--------------+
| film_in_stock               | PROCEDURE    |
| film_not_in_stock           | PROCEDURE    |
| get_customer_balance        | FUNCTION     |
| inventory_held_by_customer  | FUNCTION     |
| inventory_in_stock          | FUNCTION     |
| rewards_report              | PROCEDURE    |
+-----------------------------+--------------+
6 rows in set (0.09 sec)
```

For more about the INFORMATION_SCHEMA database, see Chapter 21.

Naming: stored routines

Stored routines can be named using reserved words. This is an extremely bad idea to do on purpose. Because it is possible you may accidentally give your stored routine a name that is a reserved word, we will explain how to name a stored routine using a reserved word.

To name a stored routine with a reserved word, there must be whitespace between the routine name (reserved word) and the opening parenthesis used for the parameters:

```
mysql> DELIMITER |
mysql> CREATE PROCEDURE count(INOUT p_count INT UNSIGNED)
```

```
            -> COMMENT 'this fails because count is a reserved word and no
               space exists between count and ('
            -> BEGIN
            -> SET p_count:=p_count+1;
            -> END
            -> |
    ERROR 1064 (42000): You have an error in your SQL syntax; check the
        manual that corresponds to your MySQL server version for the right
        syntax to use near 'count (INOUT p_count INT UNSIGNED) COMMENT
        'this will fail because count is a res' at line 1
    mysql> CREATE PROCEDURE count (INOUT p_count INT UNSIGNED)
            -> COMMENT 'this succeeds because of the space between count
               and (, but is a bad idea'
            -> BEGIN
            -> SET p_count:=p_count+1;
            -> END
            -> |
    Query OK, 0 rows affected (0.25 sec)
    mysql> DELIMITER ;
```

The same holds true for using a stored routine named with a reserved word: there must be a space between the routine name and the opening parenthesis used for the parameters:

```
    mysql> set @count:=123;
    Query OK, 0 rows affected (0.00 sec)

    mysql> CALL count(@count);
    ERROR 1064 (42000): You have an error in your SQL syntax; check the
        manual that corresponds to your MySQL server version for the right
        syntax to use near 'count (@count)' at line 1
    mysql> CALL count (@count);
    Query OK, 0 rows affected (0.11 sec)

    mysql> select @count;
    +--------+
    | @count |
    +--------+
    |    124 |
    +--------+
    1 row in set (0.00 sec)

    mysql> -- dropping the procedure right away for sanity's sake
    mysql> DROP PROCEDURE IF EXISTS count;
    Query OK, 0 rows affected (0.03 sec)
```

Note that the sql_mode named IGNORE_SPACE has no bearing on this rule — IGNORE_SPACE does not apply to stored routines.

If you get an SQL syntax error when attempting to execute a stored routine, check the name of the stored routine — you may have accidentally given your stored routine a name that is a reserved word!

Stored procedure result sets

A stored procedure can return information by way of OUT and INOUT variables; however, a stored procedure can also return information with SQL statements inside the stored procedure. For example, a SELECT statement inside a stored procedure will execute as it would on a command line, and when invoking the stored procedure you would see that result set.

Ziesel created the store_offerings stored procedure because she wanted to get the count of movies offered by a given store_id, whether or not that movie was in stock. To return the count, she took advantage of an OUT variable:

```
DELIMITER |
CREATE PROCEDURE store_offerings ( IN p_store_id INT,
    OUT p_count INT )
      SELECT COUNT(*) INTO p_count
      FROM inventory
      WHERE store_id = p_store_id;
|
DELIMITER ;
```

However, Ziesel could have also returned the count by issuing a simple SELECT statement, sending the result set back — the same way a result set is sent back when a user directly issues a SELECT statement:

```
mysql> DROP PROCEDURE IF EXISTS store_offerings;
Query OK, 0 rows affected (0.02 sec)

mysql> DELIMITER |
mysql> CREATE PROCEDURE store_offerings ( IN p_store_id INT )
    ->        SELECT COUNT(*)
    ->        FROM inventory
    ->        WHERE store_id = p_store_id;
    -> |
Query OK, 0 rows affected (0.05 sec)

mysql> DELIMITER ;
mysql> CALL store_offerings (1);
+----------+
| COUNT(*) |
+----------+
|     2270 |
+----------+
1 row in set (0.25 sec)

Query OK, 0 rows affected (0.25 sec)
```

Ziesel modified the stored procedure, changing the SELECT COUNT(*) INTO query to a SELECT COUNT(*) query, eliminating the need for an OUT variable to store the result in. The result is sent back to the client program that invoked the stored procedure (in this case, the mysql command-line client).

Sending Back Result Sets

Stored procedures can send information back in two ways: by updating a variable and by running queries that send back result sets. There is no need to choose only one method — a single stored procedure can update variables and run queries that send back results. There may be times when you want to minimize using user-defined variables; in these cases you may prefer to send back a result set. In other cases, perhaps when you do not want the overhead of processing a returned result set, user-defined variables are preferable.

The programs that call the stored procedure need to be able to handle all of the returned information, whether or not it is returned via a variable. OUT variables must be specified when the procedure is invoked, otherwise the command will fail. However, there is no error or warning from MySQL if information is returned via a result set and your application does not process that result set, or processes it incorrectly (perhaps by assuming the result set has exactly one row).

In the store_offerings example, only one SELECT query is part of the body. However, a stored procedure can issue many queries, including issuing many queries that return result sets to the client. Make sure your application can handle all possible output, including multiple result sets, errors, warnings, and unexpected result sets (empty result sets, or result sets with more rows than expected).

Stored routine errors and warnings

If you did not want to allow pct_increase to accept negative values for p_incr, you would have defined the input parameter as IN p_incr INT UNSIGNED:

```
mysql> DROP PROCEDURE IF EXISTS pct_increase;
Query OK, 0 rows affected (0.00 sec)

mysql> DELIMITER |
mysql> CREATE PROCEDURE pct_increase (INOUT p_int INT, IN p_incr
    INT UNSIGNED, OUT p_pct_incr DECIMAL (5,2))
  -> BEGIN
  -> DECLARE p_int_new INT;
  -> SET p_int_new:=p_int+p_incr;
  -> SET p_pct_incr:=(p_int_new-p_int)/p_int*100;
  -> SET p_int:=p_int_new;
  -> END
  -> |
Query OK, 0 rows affected (0.00 sec)
```

```
mysql> DELIMITER ;
mysql> SET @num:=100;
Query OK, 0 rows affected (0.00 sec)

mysql> CALL pct_increase (@num, -10, @pct);
ERROR 1264 (22003): Out of range value for column 'p_incr' at row 1
```

mysqld handles stored routine errors and warnings as if the client ran the commands interactively. A user invoking pct_increase with a negative number for the second argument receives the error Out of range value as seen in the preceding code. The error message is accurate, but it is confusing. There is no indication that p_incr refers to the second argument (-10). The error message specifies column 'p_incr', which is confusing because there are no columns being referenced, only variables and scalar values.

The user will have to examine the stored routine to figure out the problem. There is no debugger for stored routines, so logical errors can be difficult to detect and fix. One way to debug a stored procedure is to use a SELECT statement to print variables at certain positions. A SELECT statement before each line mimics stepping through the stored procedure and checking variable values at each step.

By the way, data type incompatibilities and overflows in a stored routine are treated the same as on the command line. Warnings or errors are generated, depending on the sql_mode. This holds true for arguments as well as local variables.

Conditions and handlers

Though the error handling in stored routines is not very advanced, MySQL allows you to specify handlers that can trap conditions. This allows you to handle known exceptions. Using the DECLARE syntax, you can create a handler to specify what to do when a condition is met. You can also create a condition using the DECLARE syntax for use in a handler.

You can find a full list of MySQL error codes, SQL states, and messages in the manual at http://dev.mysql.com/doc/refman/6.0/en/error-messages-server.html.

Handlers

The stored procedure pct_increase defined an OUT variable as a signed decimal with two decimal places. What happens if the OUT variable requires more precision?

```
mysql> SHOW CREATE PROCEDURE pct_increase\G
*************************** 1. row ***************************
            Procedure: pct_increase
             sql_mode: STRICT_TRANS_TABLES,NO_AUTO_CREATE_USER,
                NO_ENGINE_SUBSTITUTION
     Create Procedure: CREATE DEFINER=`root`@`localhost` PROCE-
DURE `pct_increase`
(INOUT p_int INT, IN p_incr INT UNSIGNED, OUT p_pct_incr DECI-
MAL (5,2))
```

```
BEGIN
DECLARE p_int_new INT;
SET p_int_new:=p_int+p_incr;
SET p_pct_incr:=(p_int_new-p_int)/p_int*100;
SET p_int:=p_int_new;
END
character_set_client: latin1
collation_connection: latin1_swedish_ci
  Database Collation: latin1_swedish_ci
1 row in set (0.00 sec)

mysql> SET @num:=100;
Query OK, 0 rows affected (0.00 sec)

mysql> CALL pct_increase (@num, 10, @pct);
Query OK, 0 rows affected (0.00 sec)

mysql> SELECT @num, @pct;
+------+-------+
| @num | @pct  |
+------+-------+
|  110 | 10.00 |
+------+-------+
1 row in set (0.00 sec)

mysql> CALL pct_increase (@num, 10, @pct);
Query OK, 0 rows affected, 1 warning (0.00 sec)

mysql> SHOW WARNINGS;
+--------+------+----------------------------------------------------------+
| Level  | Code | Message                                                  |
+--------+------+----------------------------------------------------------+
| Note   | 1265 | Data truncated for column 'p_pct_incr' at row 1          |
+--------+------+----------------------------------------------------------+
1 row in set (0.00 sec)

mysql> SELECT @num, @pct;
+------+------+
| @num | @pct |
+------+------+
|  120 | 9.09 |
+------+------+
1 row in set (0.00 sec)
```

There was data truncated for a variable, and a warning was generated. If the stored procedure had an sql_mode that was set to TRADITIONAL, there would have been an error generated. Note that the warning included at row 1, so there is no way of knowing which line in the stored procedure the truncation occurred at. Looking at the stored procedure definition, there is only one line that could have thrown this warning:

```
SET p_pct_incr:=(p_int_new-p_int)/p_int*100;
```

When the stored procedure was invoked, p_int was given a value of @num, which had a value of 110. p_int_new was set to p_int+p_incr, and had been given 10 as a value of p_incr. So p_int_new had a value of 120. What did the calculation actually produce?

```
mysql> SELECT (120-110)/110*100;
+-------------------+
| (120-110)/110*100 |
+-------------------+
|            9.0909 |
+-------------------+
1 row in set (0.00 sec)
```

p_pct_incr was defined as a DECIMAL(5,2), and the stored procedure tried to put 9.0909 into p_pct_incr. The warning is justified, as data was truncated. However, you might not care about data truncation in this calculation.

To not be notified, create a HANDLER for the warning. A handler is specified with the syntax:

```
DECLARE { CONTINUE | EXIT | UNDO } HANDLER FOR condition statement
```
condition is one of the following values:

- ■ SQLWARNING — The SQL state of all warnings.
- ■ NOT FOUND — The SQL state that occurs when a cursor has reached the end of a data set. For more information on cursors, see the "Using Cursors" section later in this chapter.
- ■ SQLEXCEPTION — Any SQL state other than OK, SQLWARNING, and NOT FOUND.
- ■ mysql_error_code — Replace mysql_error_code with the error number (that is, 1265) to handle.
- ■ condition_name — A user-defined condition name. See the "Conditions" subsection for more information.
- ■ SQLSTATE [VALUE] sqlstate — Replace sqlstate with the SQL state to handle (that is, SQLSTATE VALUE 01000).

statement is the SQL statement to run when the condition is met.

In the example, if data truncation happens, the stored procedure should continue. There is no need to exit or undo anything done previously in the stored procedure. Thus, specify CONTINUE. There are two different ways to specify the condition to handle — either SQLWARNING or 1265, the error code for data truncation. Because the SQLWARNING condition covers all warnings, not just data truncation, it is a good idea to limit the handler only to the condition where data is truncated. Note that the handler for error code 1265 will be invoked when any data is truncated, not just for the p_pct_incr variable.

The following example increments a user variable when the data truncation handler is invoked. The scope of the user variable is outside of the stored routine, so the stored procedure will display how many times the warning was issued.

```
mysql> DROP PROCEDURE IF EXISTS pct_increase;
Query OK, 0 rows affected (0.00 sec)

mysql> DELIMITER |
mysql> CREATE PROCEDURE pct_increase (INOUT p_int INT,
    IN p_incr INT, OUT p_pct_
incr DECIMAL (5,2))
    -> BEGIN
    -> DECLARE p_int_new INT UNSIGNED;
    -> DECLARE CONTINUE HANDLER FOR 1265
       SET @warn_count:=@warn_count+1;
    -> SET p_int_new:=p_int+p_incr;
    -> SET p_pct_incr:=(p_int_new-p_int)/p_int*100;
    -> SET p_int:=p_int_new;
    -> SELECT p_int, p_pct_incr, @warn_count;
    -> END
    -> |
Query OK, 0 rows affected (0.00 sec)

mysql> DELIMITER ;
```

Note the last SELECT query to show the variable values. This is for teaching purposes only. There is no need to see the values of the variables by calling SELECT @num, @pct, @warn_count.

> **TIP** When debugging a stored routine, use SELECT statements to print out information to help find the problem.

Here is an example of using the stored procedure with the handler for data truncation:

```
mysql> SET @warn_count:=0;
Query OK, 0 rows affected (0.00 sec)

mysql> SET @num:=100;
Query OK, 0 rows affected (0.00 sec)

mysql> CALL pct_increase (@num, 10, @pct);
+-------+-------------+-------------+
| p_int | p_pct_incr  | @warn_count |
+-------+-------------+-------------+
|   110 |       10.00 |           0 |
+-------+-------------+-------------+
1 row in set (0.00 sec)

Query OK, 0 rows affected (0.00 sec)
```

```
mysql> CALL pct_increase (@num, 10, @pct);
+-------+------------+-------------+
| p_int | p_pct_incr | @warn_count |
+-------+------------+-------------+
|   120 |       9.09 |           1 |
+-------+------------+-------------+
1 row in set (0.00 sec)

Query OK, 0 rows affected (0.00 sec)

mysql> CALL pct_increase (@num, 10, @pct);
+-------+------------+-------------+
| p_int | p_pct_incr | @warn_count |
+-------+------------+-------------+
|   130 |       8.33 |           2 |
+-------+------------+-------------+
1 row in set (0.00 sec)

Query OK, 0 rows affected (0.00 sec)
```

No warnings are showing up, and the @warn_count global user variable is being incremented each time the stored procedure is called. Is @warn_count being incremented *only* when a warning would happen?

```
mysql> SET @num:=0;
Query OK, 0 rows affected (0.00 sec)

mysql> CALL pct_increase (@num, 10, @pct);
+-------+------------+-------------+
| p_int | p_pct_incr | @warn_count |
+-------+------------+-------------+
|    10 |       NULL |           2 |
+-------+------------+-------------+
1 row in set (0.00 sec)

Query OK, 0 rows affected (0.00 sec)

mysql> CALL pct_increase (@num, 10, @pct);
+-------+------------+-------------+
| p_int | p_pct_incr | @warn_count |
+-------+------------+-------------+
|    20 |     100.00 |           2 |
+-------+------------+-------------+
1 row in set (0.00 sec)

Query OK, 0 rows affected (0.00 sec)

mysql> CALL pct_increase (@num, 10, @pct);
```

279

```
+-------+-----------+-------------+
| p_int | p_pct_incr | @warn_count |
+-------+-----------+-------------+
|    30 |     50.00 |           2 |
+-------+-----------+-------------+
1 row in set (0.00 sec)

Query OK, 0 rows affected (0.00 sec)

mysql> CALL pct_increase (@num, 10, @pct);
+-------+-----------+-------------+
| p_int | p_pct_incr | @warn_count |
+-------+-----------+-------------+
|    40 |     33.33 |           3 |
+-------+-----------+-------------+
1 row in set (0.00 sec)

Query OK, 0 rows affected (0.00 sec)
```

This is the first time @warn_count has incremented since @num was set to 0. And it is the first time that the percentage @num increased by a precision greater than two decimal places.

```
mysql> CALL pct_increase (@num, 10, @pct);
+-------+-----------+-------------+
| p_int | p_pct_incr | @warn_count |
+-------+-----------+-------------+
|    50 |     25.00 |           3 |
+-------+-----------+-------------+
1 row in set (0.00 sec)

Query OK, 0 rows affected (0.00 sec)

mysql> CALL pct_increase (@num, 10, @pct);
+-------+-----------+-------------+
| p_int | p_pct_incr | @warn_count |
+-------+-----------+-------------+
|    60 |     20.00 |           3 |
+-------+-----------+-------------+
1 row in set (0.00 sec)

Query OK, 0 rows affected (0.00 sec)

mysql> CALL pct_increase (@num, 10, @pct);
+-------+-----------+-------------+
| p_int | p_pct_incr | @warn_count |
+-------+-----------+-------------+
|    70 |     16.67 |           4 |
+-------+-----------+-------------+
1 row in set (0.00 sec)

Query OK, 0 rows affected (0.00 sec)
```

Indeed, the handler is handling the condition of data truncation (MySQL error code 1265) appropriately. To truly ignore the condition and not do any action, you could have specified an empty statement:

```
DECLARE CONTINUE HANDLER FOR 1265 BEGIN END;
```

Conditions

In the previous example, the "data truncated" error code (1265) was handled with this DECLARE statement:

```
DECLARE CONTINUE HANDLER FOR 1265 SET @warn_count=@warn_count+1;
```

The DECLARE syntax can be used to create and name a custom condition for use in a handler. The syntax is:

```
DECLARE condition_name CONDITION FOR { mysql_error_code |
SQLSTATE [VALUE] sqlstate }
```

To name error code 1265 instead of creating a handler that specifies the error code directly, use the following syntax:

```
DECLARE data_truncation CONDITION FOR 1265;
```

And the handler declaration changes to:

```
DECLARE CONTINUE HANDLER FOR data_truncation
    SET @warn_count=@warn_count+1;
```

This may seem like extra work; however, appropriate naming of conditions can make error handling much easier. Consider the difference between HANDLER FOR data_truncation and HANDLER FOR 1265 — which is more readable? If a stored routine has 100 error handlers, should they be declared by number? Named conditions are extremely useful when conditions are named appropriately. Conditions named error_handler and ignore_me are not useful.

> **TIP** Consider a database policy of always naming conditions explicitly and appropriately.

Order of DECLARE Statements

All DECLARE conditions must occur before any DECLARE handler. That makes sense; if a handler uses a condition, the condition must be defined before the handler is. MySQL takes this one step further and requires all conditions be defined before any handlers are defined. If a handler or condition uses a local variable, the local variable must be defined first. MySQL requires that all DECLARE variable statements must occur before any DECLARE condition statement.

In short, the required order of DECLARE statements is: variables, conditions, handlers. If a stored routine definition violates these requirements, mysqld raises an error and rejects the stored routine definition with the following error:

```
ERROR 1337 (42000): Variable or condition declaration after cursor or han-
dler declaration
```

Stored routine flow control

Many common flow control statements are supported in stored routines. These statements may be nested to create blocks of code and code loops. The flow control syntax is documented here, though advanced usage of flow control is out of the scope of this book. For more information about using flow control in stored routines, refer to Guy Harrison's book *MySQL Stored Procedure Programming* (O'Reilly, ISBN 0-596-10089-2).

Many commands discussed in this chapter require a BEGIN ... END block to allow multiple statements. However, most flow control statements allow multiple statements without using a BEGIN ... END block. When more than one statement can be defined in this manner, statement_list will denote that more than one statement can be used. For flow control statements that allow a statement list without a BEGIN ... END block, the end of the statement list is implied — for example, in an IF statement, the end of the statement list is implied by the next ELSEIF, ELSE, or END IF.

IF

The syntax for the IF statement is:

```
IF condition THEN statement_list
[ELSEIF condition THEN statement_list] ...
[ELSE statement_list]
END IF
```

> **NOTE** The IF flow control *statement* is different from the IF flow control *function*. The IF flow control statement described here is a procedural device. The IF flow control function has the syntax IF(test_expr, expr_if_true, expr_if_false).

CASE

As with other procedural code, it is often desirable to replace a nested IF statement with a CASE statement. The CASE statement has two acceptable syntaxes:

```
CASE expr
WHEN condition THEN statement_list [ ... ]
[ELSE statement_list]
END CASE
```

This first syntax takes an expression that evaluates to a value, compares it using one or more conditions, evaluating the appropriate statements if a condition matches, and ending with the optional catch-all ELSE.

The second syntax is similar, except that the condition includes the value:

```
CASE
WHEN condition THEN statement_list [ ... ]
[ELSE statement_list]
END CASE
```

NOTE The CASE flow control *statement* and the CASE flow control *function* have the same syntax.

To clarify, using the first syntax to see whether the flag is set:

```
CASE @flag
WHEN 0 THEN SELECT "flag is 0"
WHEN 1 THEN SELECT "flag is 1"
ELSE SELECT "flag is not 0 or 1, it is ", @flag;
END CASE;
```

And using the second syntax:

```
CASE
WHEN @flag=0 THEN SELECT "flag is 0"
WHEN @flag=1 THEN SELECT "flag is 1"
ELSE SELECT "flag is not 0 or 1, it is ", @flag;
END CASE;
```

In this case, either syntax can be used. There are times when only one of the syntaxes can express the conditional statement you want — when comparing different values, for example, the second syntax is required.

CASE statements must match on a condition; ELSE is the catch-all condition to use if you believe there might be a condition that does not match. If a condition is not matched — which means that none of the WHEN blocks matched and there is no ELSE block — an error is generated:

```
ERROR 1339 (20000): Case not found for CASE statement
```

WHILE

The most familiar way to create a loop in MySQL is with the WHILE statement. The syntax for WHILE is:

```
[label:] WHILE condition
statement_list
END WHILE [label]
```

REPEAT

REPEAT is similar to what many language call "until." In fact, the syntax contains the keyword UNTIL:

```
[label:] REPEAT statement_list
UNTIL condition
END REPEAT [label]
```

Similar to other procedural languages, the biggest difference between WHILE and REPEAT ("until") is that with REPEAT the code executes at least once, because the test condition is after the code.

The REPEAT block does not have to be labeled. However, the labels at the beginning and end of the loop must match, and if the label at the end is defined, the label at the beginning must also be defined.

LOOP

A loop allows for manual creation of loops, without using the WHILE or REPEAT statements. It is defined very simply:

```
[label:] LOOP
    statement_list
END LOOP [label]
```

The loop does not have to be labeled — labels are required for use with the LEAVE or ITER-ATE statements. However, the labels at the beginning and end of the loop must match, and if the label at the end of the loop is defined, the label at the beginning of the loop must also be defined.

Note that the name is somewhat misleading — a LOOP is simply a code block. To actually form a loop, other statements must be used to go back to the beginning of a LOOP and exit a LOOP without reaching END LOOP. In essence, LOOP ... END LOOP is just a label. To make a loop actually loop, use the ITERATE and LEAVE commands.

ITERATE

The ITERATE command is used to go to the beginning of a labeled block of code:

```
ITERATE label
```

LEAVE

To exit any labeled flow control construct, use the LEAVE statement. The syntax is:

```
LEAVE label
```

LEAVE can be used to exit LOOP, REPEAT, and WHILE statements.

Recursion

MySQL allows recursive stored procedures, but not recursive stored functions. The parameter max_sp_recursion_depth limits the number of times a procedure can be called recursively. This parameter is set to 0 by default, which disables the use of recursive stored procedures. If the value of max_sp_recursion_depth is not changed, a recursive stored procedure may be created, but when attempting to execute the stored procedure an error will occur:

```
ERROR 1456 (HY000): Recursive limit 0 (as set by the
    max_sp_recursion_depth variable) was exceeded for
    routine your_routine_name
```

The maximum value for `max_sp_recursion_depth` is 255. Note that this uses space in the thread stack, so increasing this value may require an increase of the `thread_stack` variable as well. See Chapter 10 for more information about the `thread_stack` system variable.

Stored routines and replication

The row-based and mixed replication modes write data changes to the binary logs, and are the safest way to obtain a copy of your data. In statement-based replication mode, statements that may change data are written to the binary logs, and the statements are applied to the data on the slave server. A small discrepancy in the data on a slave and master can have disastrous results in statement-based replication.

There are several important properties of stored routines combined with replication. If a stored routine is not replicating as you think it should, consider the following points:

- The `CREATE`, `ALTER`, and `DROP` statements for stored procedures and functions are written to the binary logs.
- Be careful when using statement-based replication — deterministic stored routines may not replicate properly. `mysqld` tries to prevent the creation of non-deterministic routines when binary logging is disabled, but is not always successful.
- Stored procedures and functions that call other stored procedures and functions may not replicate how you think they should using statement-based replication.
- A stored procedure is not invoked on a slave with a `CALL` statement; it replicates the actual SQL used by the stored procedure. The exception is when a stored procedure is called by a stored function (see previous point). If that happens, the stored procedure `CALL` is indeed replicated.
- If a function is defined differently on the master and on the slave, and statement-based replication is being used, there may be different results on the master and on the slave.
- Though a user invokes a stored function on a master, a slave using statement-based replication will invoke the stored function with full privileges.

Stored function limitations

Unlike stored procedures, stored functions cannot:

- Return a result set
- Be recursive
- Call statements that do a `COMMIT` or `ROLLBACK`
  - `COMMIT`
  - `ROLLBACK`
  - `START TRANSACTION`

- LOCK TABLES and UNLOCK TABLES when there were locked tables
- SET AUTOCOMMIT=1 when it was not already set to 1
- TRUNCATE TABLE
- Most ALTER, CREATE, DROP, and RENAME commands cause an implicit COMMIT (see Chapter 4)
- Most CREATE commands cause an implicit COMMIT (see Chapter 4)

Stored routine backup and storage

Stored routines are stored in the proc table of the mysql database. Manual manipulation of the proc table is not advised. Stored routine backup can be done by using mysqldump, and during hot and cold backups. For more information on backing up stored routines, see Chapter 13.

It is possible, but not recommended, to see a list of stored routines by querying the proc table:

```
mysql> SELECT db,name,type FROM mysql.proc;
+--------+---------------------------+-----------+
| db     | name                      | type      |
+--------+---------------------------+-----------+
| sakila | check_actors              | PROCEDURE |
| sakila | film_in_stock             | PROCEDURE |
| sakila | film_not_in_stock         | PROCEDURE |
| sakila | get_customer_balance      | FUNCTION  |
| sakila | increment_counter         | PROCEDURE |
| sakila | inventory_held_by_customer | FUNCTION  |
| sakila | inventory_in_stock        | FUNCTION  |
| sakila | rewards_report            | PROCEDURE |
| sakila | store_offerings           | PROCEDURE |
+--------+---------------------------+-----------+
9 rows in set (0.00 sec)
```

We recommend using the ROUTINES table of the INFORMATION_SCHEMA database to get this information, because using the proc table of the mysql database sets a bad example.

```
mysql> SELECT ROUTINE_SCHEMA, ROUTINE_NAME, ROUTINE_TYPE
    -> FROM INFORMATION_SCHEMA.ROUTINES;
+----------------+----------------------------+--------------+
| ROUTINE_SCHEMA | ROUTINE_NAME               | ROUTINE_TYPE |
+----------------+----------------------------+--------------+
| sakila         | check_actors               | PROCEDURE    |
| sakila         | film_in_stock              | PROCEDURE    |
| sakila         | film_not_in_stock          | PROCEDURE    |
| sakila         | get_customer_balance       | FUNCTION     |
| sakila         | increment_counter          | PROCEDURE    |
| sakila         | inventory_held_by_customer | FUNCTION     |
| sakila         | inventory_in_stock         | FUNCTION     |
| sakila         | rewards_report             | PROCEDURE    |
| sakila         | store_offerings            | PROCEDURE    |
+----------------+----------------------------+--------------+
6 rows in set (0.01 sec)
```

For more information on the INFORMATION_SCHEMA, see Chapter 21.

Using Cursors

As a declarative language, SQL can be difficult for developers used to procedural code to understand. For folks who are experts at algorithms, it can be unnerving to have to specify what data they would like to see, but not be able to specify *how* the database should get that data. One of the most common limitations that procedural programmers feel is not being able to go through all the data in a set, one by one, and apply a function to it. A cursor can be thought of as a position in a list; you can use a cursor to iterate through each entry in a result set. Cursors can be used in triggers, stored procedures, and stored functions.

As an example, Ziesel asks two employees to come up with a way to ensure that all of the actors in the actor table have at least one corresponding film to their credit. Samuel Benjamin, the SQL expert, comes up with:

```
mysql> SELECT actor.*
    -> FROM actor LEFT JOIN film_actor USING (actor_id)
    -> WHERE film_actor.actor_id IS NULL;
Empty set (0.00 sec)
```

However, Eli Solnik, the procedural expert, wants to specify an algorithm: go through every entry in the actor table and see if there is at least one entry in the film_actor table. This can be accomplished entirely in SQL by using a cursor in a stored procedure. There are a few steps to using cursors:

- Define the cursor
- Open the cursor
- Retrieve value(s) from the cursor
- Close the cursor

A cursor is defined using a DECLARE statement:

```
DECLARE cursor_name CURSOR FOR select_statement
```

In the example, Eli's cursor definition is:

```
DECLARE c_all_actors CURSOR FOR SELECT actor_id FROM actor;
```

Cursor declaration must occur after declaring variables and conditions, but before declaring handlers.

Opening a cursor is done with OPEN cursor_name. Eli opens his cursor with:

```
OPEN c_all_actors;
```

When he is finished with the cursor, he closes it similarly with CLOSE cursor_name:

```
CLOSE c_all_actors;
```

To retrieve values from the cursor, Eli has to use the FETCH ... INTO syntax:

```
FETCH cursor_name INTO variable_name [, variable_name ... ]
```

In this case, Eli's cursor only selected one field, actor_id, so he only needs one variable. He will create a variable cur_actor to be the target for the cursor's current value of actor_id.

The full stored procedure definition is:

```
mysql> DELIMITER |
mysql> CREATE PROCEDURE check_actors()
    -> BEGIN
    -> DECLARE cur_actor SMALLINT UNSIGNED;
    -> DECLARE film_count INT UNSIGNED;
    -> DECLARE done,actor_count INT UNSIGNED DEFAULT 0;
    -> DECLARE c_all_actors CURSOR FOR SELECT actor_id FROM actor;
    -> DECLARE CONTINUE HANDLER FOR NOT FOUND SET done=1;
    -> OPEN c_all_actors;
    -> WHILE done=0 DO
    -> FETCH c_all_actors into cur_actor;
    -> SET actor_count=actor_count+1;
    -> SELECT COUNT(*) INTO film_count FROM film_actor WHERE
       actor_id=cur_actor;
    -> IF film_count=0 THEN
    -> SELECT * FROM actor WHERE actor_id=cur_actor;
    -> END IF;
    -> END WHILE;
    -> CLOSE c_all_actors;
    -> SELECT actor_count;
    -> END
    -> |
Query OK, 0 rows affected (0.00 sec)
```

Eli has put a sanity check in to make sure all the actors are in fact being checked — the variable actor_count is incremented with each new actor_id. This stored procedure continues to FETCH the actor_id of the cursor until it gets an error of NOT FOUND SET, indicating that there are no more values in the set.

```
mysql> DELIMITER ;
mysql> CALL check_actors;
+--------------+
| actor_count |
+--------------+
|          201 |
+--------------+
1 row in set (0.02 sec)

Query OK, 0 rows affected (0.02 sec)
```

The `actor_count` is 201, even though the number of actors is 200. This occurs because the `FETCH` command that triggers the handler to change the `done` flag happens after the condition check in the `WHILE` loop. The condition to exit the `WHILE` loop is not triggered until the next time the condition is checked, at the beginning of the `WHILE` loop.

Cursors are very powerful tools. They can be indispensable when used properly. However, using stored procedures instead of learning proper SQL is not recommended. The cursor example we provided can be done more efficiently using a `LEFT JOIN`.

Using Events

An event is a set of SQL commands that can be scheduled to run once or at regular intervals, similar to the Unix cron daemon. On Windows systems the Task Scheduler provides similar functionality. The event scheduler in `mysqld` is platform-independent — it works exactly the same on these two platforms. The tight integration with the server allows you store almost all of your database maintenance tasks in the database, which means the data and maintenance tasks can be backed up at the same time with the same command. Using the event scheduler gets rid of the need to run a script that has login credentials saved to it. Not having to store a username and password in a file is very good for security purposes.

Events provide a powerful way to perform scheduled database administrator tasks such as performing backups or logging events. Events can be executed once, at a specific date/time, or they can occur at a defined interval. You have flexibility of setting a start date and end date too.

Turning on the event scheduler

Before an event will run, the event scheduler must be turned on. The event scheduler is the process thread that determines when it is time to run this event. Because each event has its own thread, parallel execution of events is allowed. You can schedule any number of events to occur simultaneously without any problem. Be warned that there is no guarantee that the event will happen exactly when scheduled. The server will attempt to run the event as close to the time scheduled as possible. Typically it will be the same time but this cannot be assumed.

Executing `SET GLOBAL event_scheduler = ON` starts the event scheduler. Setting `event_scheduler = OFF` will disable the event scheduler. While stopped, no new events will be run until the scheduler is turned back on. However, if any events are running when the scheduler is stopped, the currently running events will finish.

```
mysql> SHOW GLOBAL VARIABLES LIKE 'event_scheduler';
+-----------------+-------+
| Variable_name   | Value |
+-----------------+-------+
| event_scheduler | OFF   |
+-----------------+-------+
1 row in set (0.00 sec)
```

```
mysql> SET GLOBAL event_scheduler='ON';
Query OK, 0 rows affected (0.00 sec)

mysql> SHOW GLOBAL VARIABLES LIKE 'event_scheduler';
+-----------------+-------+
| Variable_name   | Value |
+-----------------+-------+
| event_scheduler | ON    |
+-----------------+-------+
1 row in set (0.00 sec)
```

WARNING As with all SET GLOBAL statements you will need SUPER privileges to run this command.

You can see if the event scheduler is working properly by checking the processlist:

```
mysql> SELECT ID, USER, HOST, DB, COMMAND, TIME, STATE, INFO
    -> FROM INFORMATION_SCHEMA.PROCESSLIST
    -> WHERE USER='event_scheduler'\G
*************************** 1. row ***************************
     ID: 10
   USER: event_scheduler
   HOST: localhost
     DB: NULL
COMMAND: Daemon
   TIME: 48
  STATE: Waiting for next activation
   INFO: NULL
1 row in set (0.00 sec)
```

In addition to ON and OFF, the event_scheduler system variable can have a value of DISABLED. This system variable is not dynamic; it can only be set from an option file or as an argument directly to mysqld, as in the following:

```
shell> mysqld --event_scheduler=DISABLED.
```

If the event scheduler is disabled, it cannot be modified from the command-line client. If you try to change the value of event_scheduler when it is set to DISABLED, you will see the following error:

```
mysql> SET GLOBAL event_scheduler='ON';
ERROR 1290 (HY000): The MySQL server is running with
    the --event-scheduler=DISABLED or --skip-grant-tables
    option so it cannot execute this statement
```

Events can be created, dropped, and modified when the event_scheduler is disabled.

Creating an event

Creating an event requires the EVENT privilege. See Chapter 14 for more information about managing privileges.

The simplest CREATE EVENT statement has the following syntax:

```
CREATE EVENT event_name
ON SCHEDULE schedule
DO statement;
```

where schedule defines either a one-time event using AT datetime_expr or a periodic event using EVERY n interval. The valid values for interval are all the interval data types in MySQL except those involving microseconds. See Chapter 5 for more detail on the available interval data types.

In this example, Ziesel wants to know when the event scheduler is working. So she creates a table:

```
mysql> USE test;
Database changed
mysql> CREATE TABLE event_scheduler_log (
    -> event_time DATETIME NOT NULL
    -> );
Query OK, 0 rows affected (0.39 sec)
```

And then she creates the event itself:

```
mysql> CREATE EVENT event_scheduler_test
    -> ON SCHEDULE EVERY 1 MINUTE
    -> DO INSERT INTO event_scheduler_log (event_time)
    -> VALUES (NOW());
Query OK, 0 rows affected (0.00 sec)
```

When the event scheduler is on, every minute the current timestamp is inserted into event_scheduler_log. If the event scheduler is on when the event is created, by default the first row is inserted immediately after the event is created, and the second row is inserted one minute later:

```
mysql> SELECT SLEEP(60); SELECT event_time from event_scheduler_log;
+-----------+
| SLEEP(60) |
+-----------+
|         0 |
+-----------+
1 row in set (1min 0.00 sec)

+---------------------+
| event_time          |
```

```
+---------------------+
| 2009-01-09 10:41:28 |
| 2009-01-09 10:42:28 |
+---------------------+
2 rows in set (0.00 sec)
```

If there is already an event with the same name, an error is raised:

```
mysql> CREATE EVENT event_scheduler_test
    -> ON SCHEDULE EVERY 5 DAY
    -> DO INSERT INTO event_scheduler_log (event_time)
       VALUES (NOW());
ERROR 1537 (HY000): Event 'event_scheduler_test' already exists
```

To raise a warning instead of an error, use the IF NOT EXISTS option:

```
mysql> CREATE EVENT IF NOT EXISTS event_scheduler_test
    -> ON SCHEDULE EVERY 5 DAY
    -> DO INSERT INTO event_scheduler_log (event_time)
       VALUES (NOW());
Query OK, 0 rows affected, 1 warning (0.00 sec)

mysql> SHOW WARNINGS;
+-------+------+---------------------------------------------+
| Level | Code | Message                                     |
+-------+------+---------------------------------------------+
| Note  | 1537 | Event 'event_scheduler_test' already exists |
+-------+------+---------------------------------------------+
1 row in set (0.00 sec)
```

Dropping an event

To drop an event, use the DROP EVENT statement. An error is thrown if the event does not exist, but this can be changed to a warning by using the IF EXISTS phrase:

```
mysql> DROP EVENT event_scheduler_test;
Query OK, 0 rows affected (0.00 sec)

mysql> DROP EVENT event_scheduler_test;
ERROR 1539 (HY000): Unknown event 'event_scheduler_test'
mysql> DROP EVENT IF EXISTS event_scheduler_test;
Query OK, 0 rows affected, 1 warning (0.00 sec)

mysql> SHOW WARNINGS;
+-------+------+-------------------------------------------+
| Level | Code | Message                                   |
+-------+------+-------------------------------------------+
| Note  | 1305 | Event event_scheduler_test does not exist |
+-------+------+-------------------------------------------+
1 row in set (0.00 sec)
```

Multiple SQL statements in events

So far, you have created and dropped a simple event consisting of one SQL statement. You can create stored routines with multiple SQL statements by enveloping the SQL statements with BEGIN and END. See the subsection "Multiple SQL Statements in Triggers" for more information.

Start and end times for periodic events

Periodic events can be set to start at a time in the future by using the optional clause STARTS timestamp_expr:

```
mysql> TRUNCATE event_scheduler_log;
Query OK, 0 rows affected (0.00 sec)

mysql> CREATE EVENT event_scheduler_test
    -> ON SCHEDULE EVERY 1 MINUTE
    -> STARTS NOW() + INTERVAL 10 MINUTE
    -> DO INSERT INTO event_scheduler_log (event_time)
       VALUES (NOW());
Query OK, 0 rows affected (0.00 sec)
mysql> SELECT * FROM event_scheduler_log;
Empty set (0.00 sec)
```

Instead of starting immediately, the event will start ten minutes from the time the event was created. The optional clause ENDS timestamp_expr can be used in the same way to set a time for the event to stop running periodically:

```
mysql> DROP EVENT event_scheduler_test;
Query OK, 0 rows affected (0.00 sec)

mysql> TRUNCATE event_scheduler_log;
Query OK, 0 rows affected (0.00 sec)

mysql> CREATE EVENT event_scheduler_test
    -> ON SCHEDULE EVERY 1 SECOND
    -> ENDS NOW() + INTERVAL 10 SECOND
    -> DO INSERT INTO event_scheduler_log (event_time)
       VALUES (NOW());
Query OK, 0 rows affected (0.00 sec)

mysql> SELECT event_time FROM event_scheduler_log;
+---------------------+
| event_time          |
+---------------------+
| 2009-01-09 11:19:54 |
| 2009-01-09 11:19:55 |
| 2009-01-09 11:19:56 |
| 2009-01-09 11:19:57 |
| 2009-01-09 11:19:58 |
```

```
| 2009-01-09 11:19:59 |
| 2009-01-09 11:20:00 |
| 2009-01-09 11:20:01 |
| 2009-01-09 11:20:02 |
| 2009-01-09 11:20:03 |
| 2009-01-09 11:20:04 |
+---------------------+
11 rows in set (0.00 sec)
```

If the STARTS clause is not specified, the event starts immediately by default. If the ENDS clause is not specified, the event does not end automatically. Using both the STARTS and ENDS clauses in the same event is supported.

Event status

Events are enabled by default at create time. To prevent an event from being enabled by default, use the DISABLE keyword in the CREATE EVENT statement:

```
mysql> DROP EVENT IF EXISTS event_scheduler_test;Query OK,
    0 rows affected (0.00 sec)

mysql> TRUNCATE event_scheduler_log;Query OK, 0 rows
    affected (0.00 sec)

mysql> CREATE EVENT event_scheduler_test
    -> ON SCHEDULE EVERY 1 SECOND
    -> ENDS '2028-09-17 22:30:00'
    -> DISABLE
    -> COMMENT 'This event should not start immediately'
    -> DO INSERT INTO event_scheduler_log (event_time)
       VALUES (NOW());
Query OK, 0 rows affected (0.00 sec)

mysql> SHOW EVENTS\G
*************************** 1. row ***************************
                   Db: test
                 Name: event_scheduler_test
              Definer: root@localhost
            Time zone: SYSTEM
                 Type: RECURRING
           Execute at: NULL
       Interval value: 1
       Interval field: SECOND
               Starts: 2009-01-09 12:33:19
                 Ends: 2028-09-17 22:30:00
               Status: DISABLED
           Originator: 0
 character_set_client: latin1
collation_connection: latin1_swedish_ci
```

```
         Database Collation: latin1_swedish_ci
1 row in set (0.00 sec)

mysql> SELECT event_time FROM event_scheduler_log;
Empty set (0.00 sec)
```

You can specify the ENABLED keyword, though it is unnecessary to do so because it is the default status value.

Another useful status is DISABLE ON SLAVE, which is used to indicate that the event should be enabled on the master but disabled on the slave. The server-id of the master is set as the Originator in the event metadata, so that a server can tell if it is the master server or a slave server.

 A comment can be applied to an event by specifying a COMMENT option with a string to the CREATE EVENT statement:

```
COMMENT 'comment string'
```

Finding all events

To view all the events in a database, use the SHOW EVENTS command:

```
mysql> SHOW EVENTS\G
Empty set (0.00 sec)
```

There are currently no events because the event scheduler drops events after their last execution time, if the ENDS clause was specified. You can also query the INFORMATION_SCHEMA.EVENTS table to find out information about events. For more about the INFORMATION_SCHEMA database, see Chapter 21.

Changing an event

To modify an event, use the ALTER EVENT command. The syntax is as follows:

```
ALTER
[DEFINER = { user | CURRENT_USER }]
    EVENT event_name
    [ON SCHEDULE schedule]
    [ON COMPLETION [NOT] PRESERVE]
    [RENAME TO new_event_name]
    [ENABLE | DISABLE | DISABLE ON SLAVE]
    [COMMENT 'comment']
    [DO statement]
```

The ALTER EVENT has the same clauses and syntax as CREATE EVENT and adds a RENAME clause:

```
mysql> SELECT EVENT_SCHEMA, EVENT_NAME
    -> FROM INFORMATION_SCHEMA.EVENTS;
```

```
+---------------+----------------------+
| EVENT_SCHEMA  | EVENT_NAME           |
+---------------+----------------------+
| test          | event_scheduler_test |
+---------------+----------------------+
1 row in set (0.00 sec)

mysql> ALTER EVENT event_scheduler_test RENAME TO
    event_scheduler_disabled;
Query OK, 0 rows affected (0.00 sec)

mysql> SELECT EVENT_SCHEMA, EVENT_NAME
    -> FROM INFORMATION_SCHEMA.EVENTS;
+---------------+--------------------------+
| EVENT_SCHEMA  | EVENT_NAME               |
+---------------+--------------------------+
| test          | event_scheduler_disabled |
+---------------+--------------------------+
1 row in set (0.00 sec)
```

As with the ALTER TABLE statement, the ALTER EVENT statement supports changing one or more attributes at the same time. However, the attributes are separated by spaces, not commas. For example:

```
mysql> ALTER EVENT event_scheduler_disabled
    -> ON SCHEDULE AT NOW()ON COMPLETION PRESERVE ENABLE;
Query OK, 0 rows affected (0.00 sec)
```

After the last execution of an event

By default, events are dropped from the database after their last execution. For one-time events scheduled with AT, the first execution is also their last execution. This behavior can be changed using the optional ON COMPLETION clause, which is set after the optional STARTS and ENDS clauses. Use the ON COMPLETION PRESERVE clause to preserve the event so it is not dropped automatically after its last execution. The default behavior is ON COMPLETION NOT PRESERVE.

```
mysql> DROP EVENT IF EXISTS event_scheduler_test;
Query OK, 0 rows affected (0.00 sec)

mysql> TRUNCATE event_scheduler_log;
Query OK, 0 rows affected (0.00 sec)

mysql> CREATE EVENT event_scheduler_test
    -> ON SCHEDULE EVERY 1 SECOND
    -> ENDS NOW() + INTERVAL 10 SECOND
    -> ON COMPLETION PRESERVE
    -> DO INSERT INTO event_scheduler_log (event_time)
```

```
             VALUES (NOW());
Query OK, 0 rows affected (0.00 sec)

mysql> SELECT SLEEP(15);
+-----------+
| SLEEP(15) |
+-----------+
|         0 |
+-----------+
1 row in set (15.00 sec)

mysql> SHOW EVENTS\G
*************************** 1. row ***************************
                  Db: test
                Name: event_scheduler_test
             Definer: root@localhost
           Time zone: SYSTEM
                Type: RECURRING
          Execute at: NULL
      Interval value: 1
      Interval field: SECOND
              Starts: 2009-01-09 12:19:32
                Ends: 2009-01-09 12:19:42
              Status: DISABLED
          Originator: 0
character_set_client: latin1
collation_connection: latin1_swedish_ci
  Database Collation: latin1_swedish_ci
1 row in set (0.00 sec)
```

Note that the Status of a past event is DISABLED.

Event logging

The event scheduler writes logging information to the mysqld error log:

```
090109 11:19:54 [Note] Event Scheduler: [root@localhost].
   [test.event_scheduler_test] started in thread 2082.
090109 11:19:54 [Note] Event Scheduler: [root@localhost].
   [test.event_scheduler_test] executed successfully in thread 2082.
090109 11:19:55 [Note] Event Scheduler: [root@localhost].
   [test.event_scheduler_test] started in thread 2083.
090109 11:19:55 [Note] Event Scheduler: [root@localhost].
   [test.event_scheduler_test] executed successfully in thread 2083.
...  [extra entries deleted, as it is more of the same
   starting and executing]
090109 11:20:03 [Note] Event Scheduler: [root@localhost].
   [test.event_scheduler_test] started in thread 2095.
090109 11:20:03 [Note] Event Scheduler: [root@localhost].
```

```
         [test.event_scheduler_test] executed successfully in thread 2095.
090109 11:20:04 [Note] Event Scheduler: Last execution of
         test.event_scheduler_test. Dropping.
090109 11:20:04 [Note] Event Scheduler: [root@localhost].
         [test.event_scheduler_test] started in thread 2097.
090109 11:20:04 [Note] Event Scheduler: Dropping
         test.event_scheduler_test
090109 11:20:04 [Note] Event Scheduler: [root@localhost].
         [test.event_scheduler_test] executed successfully in thread 2097.
```

Any errors generated are also logged to the error log. For example, the following event tries to INSERT into a nonexistent table:

```
mysql> CREATE EVENT event_scheduler_test
    -> ON SCHEDULE EVERY 1 SECOND
    -> ENDS NOW() + INTERVAL 1 SECOND
    -> DO INSERT INTO bad_table_name (event_time) VALUES (NOW());
Query OK, 0 rows affected (0.00 sec)
```

The error log stores the error message and the fact that the event failed:

```
mysql> 090109 11:35:44 [Note] Event Scheduler: [root@localhost].
         [test.event_scheduler_test] started in thread 2375.
090109 11:35:44 [ERROR] Event Scheduler: [root@localhost]
         [test.event_scheduler_test] Table 'test.bad_table_name'
         doesn't exist
090109 11:35:44 [Note] Event Scheduler: [root@localhost].
         [test.event_scheduler_test] event execution failed.
```

Event runtime behavior

Events are defined by a user in one environment, and may be invoked in another environment. This can lead to questions as to how the stored routine behaves with respect to sql_mode, collation, and whom the event is run as.

sql_mode

An event is saved with the current sql_mode. This may lead to problems if the execution environment has a very different sql_mode than the definition environment. If an event is not acting as expected, check the sql_mode of the event.

The SHOW CREATE EVENT and the EVENTS table in the INFORMATION_SCHEMA database contain the sql_mode associated with an event. There is no way to set the sql_mode as different from the defining environment. To change the sql_mode of an event:

- Drop the event
- Set the desired sql_mode with SET @@sql_mode={string}

- Re-create the event
- Reset the sql_mode back to what the client was originally running

For more information on sql_mode, see Chapter 5.

Character set and collation

The character set and collation are set the same way sql_mode is — by using the current environment variables when the event is created. To set an event with a different character set and collation, run SET CHARACTER SET charset and SET COLLATION_CONNECTION=collation commands before running the CREATE EVENT command. Changing the character set and collation cannot be done with the ALTER EVENT statement. For a further discussion of character sets and collations, see Chapter 4.

Changing whom an event is invoked as

By default, the event is invoked as the same user who defined it. However, the event definer can be changed by using a DEFINER clause in the CREATE EVENT statement:

```
CREATE
    [DEFINER = { user | CURRENT_USER }]
    EVENT
    [IF NOT EXISTS]
    event_name
    ON SCHEDULE schedule
DO statement;
```

See the discussion in the subsection "Changing Whom a Trigger is Invoked As" for details on what the DEFINER clause allows.

Event limitations

Nearly any SQL statement that can be used in a stored routine can also be used use in the DO clause of an event. The following SQL statements are not allowed in a CREATE EVENT statement:

- ALTER VIEW
- LOCK TABLES
- UNLOCK TABLES
- LOAD DATA
- LOAD TABLE
- BACKUP DATABASE
- RESTORE
- INSERT DELAYED (the server will allow the statement but INSERTs are not actually delayed)

Event backup and storage

Events are stored in the `event` table of the `mysql` database. Manual manipulation of the `event` table is not advised. Event backup can be done by using `mysqldump`, and during hot and cold backups. For more information on backing up events, see Chapter 13.

It is possible, but not recommended, to see a list of events by querying the `event` table:

```
mysql> SELECT db, name, status FROM mysql.event;
+------+----------------------------+----------+
| db   | name                       | status   |
+------+----------------------------+----------+
| test | event_scheduler_disabled   | DISABLED |
+------+----------------------------+----------+
1 row in set (0.00 sec)
```

We recommend using the `EVENTS` table of the `INFORMATION_SCHEMA` database to get this information, because using the `event` table of the `mysql` database sets a bad example.

```
mysql> SELECT EVENT_SCHEMA, EVENT_NAME, STATUS    -> FROM
    INFORMATION_SCHEMA.EVENTS;
+--------------+--------------------------+----------+
| EVENT_SCHEMA | EVENT_NAME               | STATUS   |
+--------------+--------------------------+----------+
| test         | event_scheduler_disabled | DISABLED |
+--------------+--------------------------+----------+
1 row in set (0.00 sec)
```

For more information on the `INFORMATION_SCHEMA`, see Chapter 21.

Summary

This chapter covered triggers, stored routines, and events, including:

- Creating, dropping, finding, backing up, and how MySQL stores triggers, stored routines, and events

- Using multiple SQL statements with triggers, stored routines, and events

- Changing stored routines and events

- Invoking stored routines

- Runtime behavior of triggers, stored routines, and events

- Flow control, error handling, and custom error handlers in stored routines

- How replication interacts with triggers, stored routines, and events

- The differences between stored procedures and stored functions

Although triggers, stored routines, and events are relatively new to MySQL, there are many features and details to master, particularly for database administrators who are accustomed to the way other database systems work.

Chapter 8

MySQL Views

A normalized schema is the best starting point for any application. OLTP (on-line transaction processing) and OLAP (on-line analytics processing) have often used separate schemas. Batch imports and the Extract-Transform-Load (ETL) process are commonly used to migrate data from a transactional schema to an analytical one. However, this takes time and effort, and introduces a delay in data getting to a reporting server.

The need for more real-time analysis is growing stronger. In addition, replication in MySQL is widespread and easy. Views are tools that assist in denormalizing data, such as for analysis, without changing the underlying system for transaction processing.

Views also allow for simplicity, abstraction, added security, and easier schema migration. Views do not necessarily improve performance, however.

Views allow for small schema changes that can have big effects without having to change a table with ALTER TABLE. Views can be used to:

- Restrict access to a subset of rows
- Simplify queries
- Simulate check constraints

IN THIS CHAPTER

Defining views

Changing a view definition

Replication and views

Defining Views

A view is a way to define a dynamic virtual table based on an SQL statement. It can be queried like a regular table can, and views appear in the TABLES table of the INFORMATION_SCHEMA database (see Chapter 22). A view is an object associated with a database, similar to a regular table. In fact, the SHOW TABLES and SHOW TABLE STATUS commands return tables and views:

```
mysql> SHOW TABLES LIKE 'staff%';
+---------------------------+
| Tables_in_sakila (staff%) |
+---------------------------+
| staff                     |
| staff_list                |
+---------------------------+
2 rows in set (0.02 sec)
```

SHOW TABLE STATUS can help you determine if an object is a table or a view. In the sakila sample database, staff is a table and staff_list is a view:

```
mysql> USE sakila;
Database changed
mysql> SHOW FULL TABLES LIKE 'staff%';
+---------------------------+------------+
| Tables_in_sakila (staff%) | Table_type |
+---------------------------+------------+
| staff                     | BASE TABLE |
| staff_list                | VIEW       |
+---------------------------+------------+
2 rows in set (0.00 sec)
```

The simplest CREATE VIEW statement has the following syntax:

```
CREATE [OR REPLACE] VIEW viewname AS {SELECT statement}
```

CREATE VIEW will attempt to create a VIEW. If the VIEW exists, an error will be thrown:

```
mysql> create view staff_list as select 1;
ERROR 1050 (42S01): Table 'staff_list' already exists
```

CREATE OR REPLACE VIEW will change the VIEW if it exists:

```
mysql> use test;
Database changed
mysql> CREATE VIEW staff_name AS
    -> SELECT first_name, last_name FROM sakila.staff;

Query OK, 0 rows affected (0.05 sec)
```

```
mysql> SELECT first_name, last_name FROM staff_name;
+------------+-----------+
| first_name | last_name |
+------------+-----------+
| Mike       | Hillyer   |
| Jon        | Stephens  |
+------------+-----------+
2 rows in set (0.03 sec)

mysql> CREATE OR REPLACE VIEW staff_name AS
    -> SELECT CONCAT(first_name, ' ', last_name) AS full_name
    -> FROM sakila.staff;
Query OK, 0 rows affected (0.00 sec)

mysql> SELECT full_name FROM staff_name;
+--------------+
| full_name    |
+--------------+
| Mike Hillyer |
| Jon Stephens |
+--------------+
2 rows in set (0.00 sec)
```

The SELECT statement in the view definition can be almost any SELECT query, including unions and multi-table joins. The DROP VIEW statement works like other DROP statements. The DROP VIEW IF EXISTS statement will DROP the view if it exists, and if it does not exist will issue a warning:

```
mysql> use test;
Database changed
mysql> DROP VIEW staff_name;
Query OK, 0 rows affected (0.00 sec)

mysql> DROP VIEW staff_name;
ERROR 1051 (42S02): Unknown table 'staff_name'
mysql> DROP VIEW IF EXISTS staff_name;
Query OK, 0 rows affected, 1 warning (0.00 sec)

mysql> SHOW WARNINGS;
+-------+------+--------------------------------+
| Level | Code | Message                        |
+-------+------+--------------------------------+
| Note  | 1051 | Unknown table 'test.staff_name' |
+-------+------+--------------------------------+
1 row in set (0.00 sec)
```

For a view, SHOW CREATE TABLE is an alias for SHOW CREATE VIEW.

View definition limitations and unexpected behavior

Not all SELECT statements are valid within a view definition. The SELECT statement in a view definition is not allowed to:

- Have a derived table (subquery in the FROM clause).
- Access user variables, system variables, local variables, stored routine variables, or prepared statement parameters.
- Refer to a TEMPORARY table.
- Refer to a table that does not exist. However, this is only checked at view creation time and any time a view is used. It is possible to drop an underlying base table or view that a view refers to without the DROP statement generating an error. Any attempt to use the view after an underlying base table or view is dropped will result in an error. The CHECK TABLE statement applied to a view will reveal if a referenced table or view no longer exists:

```
mysql> CREATE TABLE drop_test (foo int);
Query OK, 0 rows affected (0.36 sec)

mysql> CREATE VIEW v_drop_test AS SELECT foo FROM drop_test;
Query OK, 0 rows affected (0.00 sec)

mysql> CHECK TABLE v_drop_test\G
*************************** 1. row ***************************
   Table: test.v_drop_test
      Op: check
Msg_type: status
Msg_text: OK
1 row in set (0.00 sec)

mysql> DROP TABLE drop_test;
Query OK, 0 rows affected (0.00 sec)

mysql> CHECK TABLE v_drop_test\G
*************************** 1. row ***************************
   Table: test.v_drop_test
      Op: check
Msg_type: Error
Msg_text: Table 'test.drop_test' doesn't exist
*************************** 2. row ***************************
   Table: test.v_drop_test
      Op: check
Msg_type: Error
Msg_text: View 'test.v_drop_test' references invalid table(s) or
    column(s) or function(s) or definer/invoker of view lack rights to
    use them
```

```
*************************** 3. row ***************************
    Table: test.v_drop_test
       Op: check
 Msg_type: error
 Msg_text: Corrupt
3 rows in set (0.00 sec)
```

Several clauses and options within a SELECT statement may produce unexpected behavior when used as part of a view definition:

■ An ORDER BY in a view definition is not used if a query on the view has its own ORDER BY. That is, the query's ORDER BY statement overrides the view definition's ORDER BY statement.

■ Unlike with an ORDER BY clause, there are no guidelines on how a query with a certain option is processed when the query refers to a view defined with that same option. The options this applies to are:

  ▨ DISTINCT

  ▨ INTO

  ▨ FOR UPDATE

  ▨ ALL

  ▨ PROCEDURE

  ▨ SQL_SMALL_RESULT

  ▨ LOCK IN SHARE MODE

Security and privacy

Views in other database systems can act as security measures, by putting limitations and constraints in the view definition.

Views in other database systems use limitations and constraints as their only security measures. MySQL has added an SQL SECURITY extension to the view definition in standard SQL. With the SQL SECURITY parameter, MySQL gives views the ability to be a window into data that a user may not have permission to see. Thus, MySQL allows views to have extended means of security.

To define a MySQL view that acts like regular SQL, where the permissions are based on the user querying the view, use SQL SECURITY INVOKER. If the user does not have permission to run the SELECT query in the view definition, the user is not allowed to query the view.

It is very useful to give a user permission to see parts of a table. This can be done with column-level privileges (see Chapter 15), but there is a better way using views. With SQL SECURITY DEFINER specified, the access settings of the user who created the view are applied. SQL SECURITY DEFINER is the default value, and is useful when you want to give someone a partial window into the data without giving them full access to a table.

As an example, Ziesel has a new employee, Benjamin, to whom she delegates sending out New Year cards to the staff at their homes. Because Ziesel is very concerned with privacy, she would like to allow Benjamin access to the database to see staff members' phone numbers and mailing addresses, but not their e-mail addresses (or, for that matter, password hashes).

So Ziesel creates a view she calls `staff_list`. She starts with the `staff` table, taking the `staff_id` and `store_id` fields, and creating a `name` field that is a concatenation of the first and last names. The `staff` table contains a numeric reference to the `address` table, which in turn has numeric references to `city` and `country` tables, so she has to join to the `address`, `city`, and `country` to get a usable mailing address:

```
CREATE
SQL SECURITY DEFINER
VIEW staff_list
AS select s.staff_id AS ID,
    concat(s.first_name,_utf8' ',s.last_name) AS name,
    a.address AS address, a.postal_code AS `zip code`,
    a.phone AS phone, city.city AS city,
    country.country AS country, s.store_id AS SID
from staff s
        inner join address a on (s.address_id = a.address_id)
        inner join city on (a.city_id = city.city_id)
        inner join country on (city.country_id = country.country_id);
```

Even though Benjamin's MySQL user does not have permission to the `staff` table, he can get the information he needs because he has the permission to SELECT from the `staff_list` view, and the view was created with `SQL SECURITY DEFINER`.

Depending on your organization's policies, you may opt to put views in a separate database on the same MySQL server. This allows you to control view access using database-level granularities instead of table-level granularities.

Views can also let a user see a subset of rows in one or more base tables they do not have access to, which cannot be done with the privilege system in MySQL. This is accomplished by creating a view using `SQL SECURITY DEFINER` with a definition that filters some rows.

Specify a view's definer

A user with a lot of permissions uses the `SQL SECURITY DEFINER` property of views in order to easily give another user a look at some of the data. In our example, Ziesel wanted Benjamin to be able to see address information of the staff, but not e-mail or password information. Because `SQL SECURITY DEFINER` was specified, when Benjamin queries the view, he queries it as if he has Ziesel's permissions. What if Ziesel wants Benjamin to run the view as if he had someone else's permissions, though?

MySQL has another extension to standard SQL — the ability to change the view's definer; by default, `DEFINER = CURRENT_USER`. However, users with the SUPER privilege may specify a definer other than themselves. If a view specifies SQL SECURITY DEFINER and changes the value of DEFINER, then when the view is run it is as if the user invoking the view has the same permissions as the DEFINER.

Going back to our example, Ziesel can specify that anyone who queries the staff_list view should query it as if they were logged in as Rachel, Ziesel's administrative assistant. Rachel has the user rachel@localhost:

```
CREATE
DEFINER=rachel@localhost
SQL SECURITY DEFINER
VIEW staff_list
AS select s.staff_id AS ID,
    concat(s.first_name,_utf8' ',s.last_name) AS name,
    a.address AS address, a.postal_code AS `zip code`,
    a.phone AS phone, city.city AS city,
    country.country AS country, s.store_id AS SID
from staff s
     inner join address a on (s.address_id = a.address_id)
     inner join city on (a.city_id = city.city_id)
     inner join country on (city.country_id = country.country_id);
```

Now when Benjamin runs SELECT * FROM staff_list, it is run as if he were logged in as rachel@localhost. If the user rachel@localhost did not exist, the view would have been created and a warning would have been generated:

```
Query OK, 0 rows affected, 1 warning (0.00 sec)

mysql> show warnings;
+-------+------+-------------------------------------------------+
| Level | Code | Message                                         |
+-------+------+-------------------------------------------------+
| Note  | 1449 | There is no 'rachel'@'localhost' registered     |
+-------+------+-------------------------------------------------+
1 row in set (0.00 sec)
```

Only a user with the SUPER privileges can set the DEFINER to be anything other than CURRENT_USER. Specifying a different definer has no effect on views that specify SQL SECURITY INVOKER.

Abstraction and simplification

In the previous example, Ziesel created a view for Benjamin to access relevant staff data. Another effect that a view can have is simplifying end-user queries. Instead of having to write a query joining four tables, Benjamin can write a very simple SELECT * FROM staff_list query. Views are a way to simplify queries for programmers more familiar and comfortable with procedural languages than they are with SQL.

Many database administrators take advantage of the abstraction that views can provide and make schemas with views of views — meaning that a view is defined with a query that uses another view. This is perfectly valid, and can ease the tension that arises between developers and schema designers when developers want to write simple queries, and schema designers want to have efficient schemas.

The downside to making queries more simple is that someone using the query may assume that a simple SELECT * FROM staff_list query does a full table scan of one table. In reality, four tables are being joined in the query and the performance cost is a lot more than the simple query implies.

Performance

Views in MySQL are always dynamic. Whenever Benjamin runs SELECT * FROM staff_list the query performs as if he is running that four table join query. The results are not cached or materialized into a permanent structure. The exception to this is if the query_cache is turned on the results may be cached, following standard query_cache rules.

The dynamic nature of views makes them perform poorly for many uses, including aggregations. When reporting rentals per day, Ziesel decided a view would make reporting easier:

```
CREATE VIEW test.rentals_per_day AS
SELECT COUNT(*), DATE(rental_date) AS business_day
FROM sakila.rental
GROUP BY business_day;
```

Ziesel realized that there were redundant calculations going on. Once a day is over, the number of movies rented that day will not change. However, the query cache was invalidated whenever the rental table was updated — every time a new rental was made or a rental was returned. When she ran

```
SELECT * FROM rentals_per_day WHERE business_day='2005-08-01'
```

the query took a long time to complete. So Ziesel ran an EXPLAIN query:

```
mysql> EXPLAIN SELECT * FROM rentals_per_day WHERE
    business_day='2005-08-01'\G
*************************** 1. row ***************************
           id: 1
  select_type: PRIMARY
        table: <derived2>
         type: ALL
possible_keys: NULL
          key: NULL
      key_len: NULL
          ref: NULL
         rows: 41
        Extra: Using where
```

```
*************************** 2. row ***************************
           id: 2
  select_type: DERIVED
        table: rental
         type: index
possible_keys: NULL
          key: PRIMARY
      key_len: 4
          ref: NULL
         rows: 15596
        Extra: Using temporary; Using filesort
2 rows in set (0.05 sec)
```

She realized that MySQL was first calculating DATE(rental_date) for every single row in the base table rental, then grouping similar dates together, and only afterwards checking for matching rows. Her simple SELECT query was actually parsed into:

```
SELECT * FROM
  (SELECT COUNT(*), DATE(rental_date) AS business_day
   FROM sakila.rental
   GROUP BY business_day) AS view_defn
WHERE business_day='2005-08-01'
```

Ziesel quickly understood that simplifying her query with a view did not have acceptable performance. A more optimized query to get the data she wanted would be:

```
SELECT COUNT(*)
FROM rental
WHERE rental_date between '2005-08-01 00:00:00'
AND '2005-08-01 23:59:59';
```

But there is no way to define a view that groups by dates to obtain that optimization. It can only be done without a view.

View algorithm

MySQL has an extension to the standard SQL to help with view performance. The ALGORITHM clause specifies which algorithm MySQL will use to process the view. The MERGE algorithm processes a query on a view by *merging* the query with the view definition. This is what Ziesel saw in the previous example — the query

```
SELECT *
FROM rentals_per_day
WHERE business_day='2005-08-01'
```

on the rentals_per_day view defined by the SQL query

```
CREATE VIEW test.rentals_per_day
AS
SELECT COUNT(*), DATE(rental_date) AS business_day
```

```
     FROM sakila.rental
     GROUP BY business_day
```

was processed as:

```
SELECT *
 FROM
   (SELECT COUNT(*), DATE(rental_date) AS business_day
    FROM sakila.rental
    GROUP BY business_day) AS view_defn
 WHERE business_day='2005-08-01'
```

MySQL offers another way to process a view. If the ALGORITHM is defined as TEMPTABLE, the VIEW is processed and the output is stored in a temporary table. Then the temporary table is used in the query.

The default setting is ALGORITHM=UNDEFINED, which means MySQL will choose which is more efficient. The MERGE algorithm is preferred over the TEMPTABLE algorithm in most cases because it is faster overall. However, locks on the base tables are released when the temporary table is generated, so TEMPTABLE can lead to better server performance overall because there is less time spent waiting for locks to be released.

If ALGORITHM=MERGE is set for a view that can only use TEMPTABLE, MySQL issues a warning and saves the view as ALGORITHM=UNDEFINED.

Materialized views and view indexes

Some popular database systems offer materialized views, also called snapshots. Unlike a regular view, a materialized view contains data, and can be indexed. The dynamic nature of a view in MySQL does not allow a view to have an index — though MySQL can and does use indexes on base tables.

Simulating check constraints

A check constraint is a predicate that limits the data that can be stored inside a table. MySQL does not offer check constraints, though data can be limited through data types, primary keys, unique keys, and foreign keys.

Check constraints can be simulated with the WITH CHECK OPTION in a view definition. WITH CHECK OPTION means that data updates made to the view will not occur in the base table unless the WHERE clause of the view definition is satisfied.

As an example, Ziesel wants only corporate e-mail addresses to be stored for staff members. First, she examines the case where no WITH CHECK OPTION clause is defined in the view, and sees that an UPDATE violating the WHERE clause of the view definition is allowed:

```
mysql> CREATE OR REPLACE ALGORITHM=UNDEFINED
    -> DEFINER=root@localhost SQL SECURITY DEFINER
    -> VIEW staff_email AS
    -> SELECT first_name, last_name, email
    -> FROM staff WHERE email like '%@sakila%.com';
Query OK, 0 rows affected (0.00 sec)
```

```
mysql> SELECT first_name, last_name, email FROM staff_email;
+------------+-----------+----------------------------+
| first_name | last_name | email                      |
+------------+-----------+----------------------------+
| Mike       | Hillyer   | Mike.Hillyer@sakilastaff.com |
| Jon        | Stephens  | Jon.Stephens@sakilastaff.com |
+------------+-----------+----------------------------+
2 rows in set (0.00 sec)

mysql> UPDATE staff_email SET email="Mike.Hillyer" WHERE
    first_name='Mike' and last_name='Hillyer';
Query OK, 1 row affected (0.53 sec)
Rows matched: 1  Changed: 1  Warnings: 0
```

This UPDATE statement violated the view definition of WHERE email LIKE '%@sakila%.com', but one row was changed in the base table anyway. The view no longer shows Mike Hillyer, because he is filtered out. The base table should have an updated e-mail for Mike Hillyer:

```
mysql> SELECT first_name, last_name, email FROM staff_email;
+------------+-----------+----------------------------+
| first_name | last_name | email                      |
+------------+-----------+----------------------------+
| Jon        | Stephens  | Jon.Stephens@sakilastaff.com |
+------------+-----------+----------------------------+
1 row in set (0.00 sec)

mysql> SELECT first_name, last_name, email FROM staff;
+------------+-----------+----------------------------+
| first_name | last_name | email                      |
+------------+-----------+----------------------------+
| Mike       | Hillyer   | Mike.Hillyer               |
| Jon        | Stephens  | Jon.Stephens@sakilastaff.com |
+------------+-----------+----------------------------+
2 rows in set (0.02 sec)
```

Now, Ziesel resets the data and changes the view to have a WITH CHECK OPTION clause:

```
mysql> UPDATE staff SET email="Mike.Hillyer@sakilstaff.com"
    -> WHERE first_name='Mike' and last_name='Hillyer';
Query OK, 1 row affected (0.42 sec)
Rows matched: 1  Changed: 1  Warnings: 0
mysql> CREATE OR REPLACE ALGORITHM=UNDEFINED
    -> DEFINER=root@localhost SQL SECURITY DEFINER
    -> VIEW staff_email AS
    -> SELECT first_name, last_name, email
    -> FROM staff WHERE email like '%@sakila%.com'
    -> WITH CHECK OPTION;
Query OK, 0 rows affected (0.00 sec)
```

```
mysql> SELECT first_name, last_name, email FROM staff_email;
+------------+-----------+-----------------------------+
| first_name | last_name | email                       |
+------------+-----------+-----------------------------+
| Mike       | Hillyer   | Mike.Hillyer@sakilastaff.com |
| Jon        | Stephens  | Jon.Stephens@sakilastaff.com |
+------------+-----------+-----------------------------+
2 rows in set (0.00 sec)
```

The WITH CHECK OPTION clause means that updates that violate the view's definition will not be allowed:

```
mysql> UPDATE staff_email SET email="Mike.Hillyer"
    -> WHERE first_name='Mike' AND last_name='Hillyer';
ERROR 1369 (HY000): CHECK OPTION failed 'sakila.staff_email'
```

And indeed, no modification was made:

```
mysql> SELECT first_name, last_name, email FROM staff_email;
+------------+-----------+-----------------------------+
| first_name | last_name | email                       |
+------------+-----------+-----------------------------+
| Mike       | Hillyer   | Mike.Hillyer@sakilastaff.com |
| Jon        | Stephens  | Jon.Stephens@sakilastaff.com |
+------------+-----------+-----------------------------+
2 rows in set (0.00 sec)

mysql> select first_name,last_name,email from staff;
+------------+-----------+-----------------------------+
| first_name | last_name | email                       |
+------------+-----------+-----------------------------+
| Mike       | Hillyer   | Mike.Hillyer@sakilastaff.com |
| Jon        | Stephens  | Jon.Stephens@sakilastaff.com |
+------------+-----------+-----------------------------+
2 rows in set (0.00 sec)
```

Ziesel successfully used the WITH CHECK OPTION of a view to simulate a check constraint. In the latter example, she was able to make sure that staff members' e-mail addresses were limited to a domain of sakila[something].com.

WITH CHECK OPTION on views that reference other views

By default, WITH CHECK OPTION will check all filters against all underlying views. In other words, if a view definition references another view, WITH CHECK OPTION will cascade and check all the WHERE clauses of all the underlying views.

You can specify that a view checks only its own definition and not that of any underlying views by specifying WITH LOCAL CHECK OPTION. If the LOCAL keyword is not specified, the view definition is stored containing WITH CASCADED CHECK OPTION:

```
mysql> SHOW CREATE VIEW staff_email\G
*************************** 1. row ***************************
```

```
               View: staff_email
         Create View: CREATE ALGORITHM=UNDEFINED
               DEFINER=`root`@`localhost` SQL
 SECURITY DEFINER VIEW `staff_email` AS select `staff`.`first_name` AS
     `first_name`,`staff`.`last_name` AS `last_name`,`staff`.`email` AS
     `email` from `staff` where (`staff`.`email` like _utf8'%@sakila%
     .com') WITH CASCADED CHECK OPTION
 character_set_client: latin1
 collation_connection: latin1_swedish_ci
 1 row in set (0.00 sec)
```

Updatable views

As shown earlier, views are not queried using only SELECT; it is possible to use DML on a view as well. As another example, if Benjamin needs to update a staff member's address, he can run the following query:

```
mysql> UPDATE staff_list SET address="20 Workhaven Lane"
    -> WHERE ID=1;
Query OK, 1 row affected (0.05 sec)
Rows matched: 1  Changed: 1  Warnings: 0

mysql> SELECT ID, name, address, zip code, phone, city, country, SID
    -> FROM staff_list\G
*************************** 1. row ***************************
      ID: 1
    name: Mike Hillyer
 address: 20 Workhaven Lane
zip code:
   phone: 14033335568
    city: Lethbridge
 country: Canada
     SID: 1
*************************** 2. row ***************************
      ID: 2
    name: Jon Stephens
 address: 1411 Lillydale Drive
zip code:
   phone: 6172235589
    city: Woodridge
 country: Australia
     SID: 2
2 rows in set (0.00 sec)
```

INSERT and DELETE statements work the same way. Benjamin is allowed to update the VIEW because the VIEW was defined with SQL SECURITY DEFINER and DEFINER=root@localhost. If Benjamin was not allowed to update the base tables and SQL SECURITY INVOKER was defined, he would not be allowed to use UPDATE, INSERT, or DELETE statements on the view.

The INFORMATION_SCHEMA shows whether a view is marked updatable:

```
mysql> USE INFORMATION_SCHEMA
Database changed
mysql> SELECT table_schema, table_name, is_updatable FROM views
    -> WHERE table_name IN ('staff_email','staff_list');
+--------------+-------------+--------------+
| table_schema | table_name  | is_updatable |
+--------------+-------------+--------------+
| sakila       | staff_email | YES          |
| sakila       | staff_list  | YES          |
+--------------+-------------+--------------+
2 rows in set (0.00 sec)
```

Updatable view limitations

To use INSERT, UPDATE, and DELETE on a view, base tables must have a one-to-one relationship with their analogous rows in the view. The staff_email view adhered to this rule. This means that a view is not updatable if the definition contains:

- Aggregations such as COUNT, SUM, MIN, MAX
- GROUP BY or GROUP BY...HAVING
- SELECT DISTINCT
- UNION ALL or UNION
- Joins that do not have a one-to-one relationship

Additionally, there are other limitations that render a view non-updatable:

- There are no base tables in the definition or the FROM clause is FROM DUAL
  - If only literal and constant values are used, because there is nothing to update.
- The FROM clause references a non-updatable view
  - If an underlying view is non-updatable, so is any view referencing it, because updates actually happen on base tables, not views.
- The SELECT clause contains a subquery
  - MySQL does not allow a table to be both changed and selected from in a subquery.
- ALGORITHM=TEMPTABLE
  - If an intermediate temporary table is used instead of going directly to the underlying base table, the underlying base table cannot be updated.

Finally, there are limitations that affect whether an INSERT statement is allowed on a view:

- View field names must be unique.
  - If field names are not unique, an INSERT cannot determine which field to put the corresponding value with.
- The view must be defined with all fields in the base table(s) that have no default values.

- There is no way to specify values for base tables when inserting into a view, so there must be default values for all fields in base tables that are not in the view.
- Views with calculated fields.
  - There is no way to reverse the calculation to obtain the right value to insert into a base table.

Updatable view problems

Because a view abstracts the data, updating information may not result in the desired behavior. Benjamin submitted what looked like a simple update to Mike Hillyer's address using the staff_list view. In reality, though, Benjamin changed a row in the base table address:

```
mysql> select address_id from staff where staff_ID=1;
+------------+
| address_id |
+------------+
|          3 |
+------------+
1 row in set (0.02 sec)

mysql> select * from address where address_id=3\G
*************************** 1. row ***************************
 address_id: 3
    address: 20 Workhaven Lane
   address2: NULL
   district: Alberta
    city_id: 300
postal_code:
      phone: 14033335568
last_update: 2008-06-15 22:07:31
1 row in set (0.00 sec)
```

Earlier, we showed that Benjamin successfully changed Mike Hillyer's address using the staff_list view. However, the address table is separate from the staff table. Benjamin's UPDATE statement actually changed the address associated with address_id=3, which may or may not be associated with other staff members — or customers, because the customer table also has an address_id reference.

What if Mike Hillyer was moving from one apartment shared with a customer, to another apartment shared with a staff member? Table 8-1 shows a sample list of addresses and staff members before any update.

If Mike Hillyer moves to into Ashton Kramer's apartment, the desired change is that Mike Hillyer's row in the staff table contains an address_id of 5. If the UPDATE was done as in the preceding example, Mike Hillyer would still have an address_id of 3, and there would be a side effect of Rachel Cosloy's address being changed even though she did not move. This discrepancy is shown in Table 8-2.

TABLE 8-1

Addresses Before Any Update

address_id	Address	Resident
3	23 Workhaven Lane	Mike Hillyer
3	23 Workhaven Lane	Rachel Cosloy
4	1411 Lillydale Drive	Jon Stephens
5	1913 Hanoi Way	Ashton Kramer

TABLE 8-2

INCORRECT: Addresses After Updating the View

address_id	Address	Resident
3	1913 Hanoi Way	Mike Hillyer
3	1913 Hanoi Way	Rachel Cosloy
4	1411 Lillydale Drive	Jon Stephens
5	1913 Hanoi Way	Ashton Kramer

Benjamin does not have underlying permissions to the base tables, and can only run an UPDATE statement on the view, not the base tables. The appropriate update is to the staff table, changing Mike Hillyer's address_id to 5, as shown in Table 8-3.

TABLE 8-3

CORRECT: Addresses After Updating the Base Table

address_id	Address	Resident
5	1913 Hanoi Way	Mike Hillyer
3	23 Workhaven Lane	Rachel Cosloy
4	1411 Lillydale Drive	Jon Stephens
5	1913 Hanoi Way	Ashton Kramer

Note that updating the view presents a logical error. Even if Benjamin had privileges to the base tables, updating the view would generate no warning or error, but produces incorrect results.

Changing a View Definition

There are two ways to change a view. One method has already been discussed — using the CREATE OR REPLACE when defining a view. In addition, MySQL has an ALTER VIEW command.

ALTER VIEW works much like ALTER TABLE. The SELECT statement that defines the view must always be included in the ALTER VIEW statement, even if that part of the view definition is not being modified.

You may have noticed that in the CREATE VIEW statement, four different clauses may come between the words CREATE and VIEW:

```
CREATE
[OR REPLACE]
[ALGORITHM = {UNDEFINED | MERGE | TEMPTABLE}]
[DEFINER = { user | CURRENT_USER} ]
[SQL SECURITY { DEFINER | INVOKER }]
VIEW view_name [(column_list)]
AS select_statement
[WITH [CASCADED | LOCAL] CHECK OPTION]
```

Similarly, the syntax of the ALTER VIEW statement is:

```
ALTER
[ALGORITHM = {UNDEFINED | MERGE | TEMPTABLE}]
[DEFINER = { user | CURRENT_USER} ]
[SQL SECURITY { DEFINER | INVOKER }]
VIEW view_name [(column_list)]
AS select_statement
[WITH [CASCADED | LOCAL] CHECK OPTION]
```

Only the view's definer or a user with the SUPER privilege can ALTER a view.

Replication and Views

In both row- and statement-based replication, MySQL treats a view the same way it treats a base table. In statement-based replication, CREATE VIEW, ALTER VIEW, and DROP VIEW statements are written to the binary log, and thus replicated. In row-based replication, the underlying data is replicated.

The replicate-do-table and replicate-ignore-table replication options are applied to views and tables in both statement- and row-based replication, with the following outcomes:

- A view that matches a `replicate-do-table` pattern will be written to the binary log, and thus replicated.

- A view that matches a `replicate-ignore-table` pattern will not be written to the binary log, and thus not be replicated.

- `replicate-do-table` and `replicate-ignore-table` patterns match the object name only. Therefore, those options will only be applied to views matching the pattern — even if the view references a matching table name.

Summary

In this chapter, we have described:

- How to create, change, and drop views
  - Invalid `SELECT` statements in view definitions
- Using views to limit field and row data for security purposes
- How views can simplify and abstract queries
- Performance implications of views
- Using views as check constraints
- How to update underlying base tables using an updatable view
  - Reasons a view may not be updatable
  - Logical errors that may occur when updating data using an updatable view
- How replication handles views

Chapter 9

Transactions in MySQL

When reading about relational database management systems (RDBMSs), you will see the terms *transaction* and *ACID compliance*. A *transaction* is a set of SQL statements that are executed as if they were one statement. For a transaction to be finished and save data changes permanently, all the statements in the transaction have to be completed. If a transaction is not completed for any reason, the changes to the dataset that the transaction already made are removed, placing the database in its original state before the transaction began.

A transaction is a transaction only if it is *ACID-compliant*. ACID is an acronym that stands for atomicity, consistency, isolation, and durability. A proper implementation of these properties guarantees reliable processing of database transactions. The properties of ACID are explained in detail in the next section.

To begin understanding what transactions are and why they are important, it will be helpful to walk through an example of how transactions are used. The classic transaction example is the database system used by a bank. Consider the following situation: Ziesel wants to move $1,000 from her checking account to the checking account of her neighbor Hudson, who is selling Ziesel his car.

If Ziesel has an account id of 145356 and Hudson has an account id of 118254, the following two SQL statements might be used to accomplish this bank transaction:

```
UPDATE checking SET balance = balance - 1000 WHERE id = 145356;
UPDATE checking SET balance = balance + 1000 WHERE id = 118254;
```

The inherent problem with this is that it takes two statements to accomplish the goal of moving the money from one account to another. What happens if the server experiences a system failure between execution of the first and second statement? The $1000 is lost somewhere — poor Ziesel is left with $1000 less in her checking account and Hudson has the same amount of money as when things started.

To keep this situation from happening, a *transactional wrapper* is used. This tells the database server that unless all the statements are completed the results of the statements should not be saved to the database. To do this:

```
START TRANSACTION;
UPDATE checking SET balance = balance - 1000 WHERE id = 145356;
UPDATE savings SET balance = balance + 1000 WHERE id = 118254;
COMMIT;
```

The START TRANSACTION and COMMIT statements are wrapped around the statements to denote the beginning and end of a transaction. In MySQL, transactions can start with START TRANSAC-TION, and transactions are ended with COMMIT (successful transaction) or ROLLBACK (indicating the data should be reset back to the original). See the next section, "Using Transactional Statements," for more information.

Revisiting the scenario of the server experiencing a system failure while executing the second UPDATE statement, this time after the server starts up it will realize the transaction was not finished and issue a ROLLBACK, which resets any changes left unfinished that were made before system failure. Wrapping both statements in a transaction means that either both statements happen, or neither statement happens. If there is a failure, Ziesel gets her money back and the transaction can be executed again.

NOTE mysqld supports multiple storage engines. Storage engines are the server components that are used to create and support database tables. These storage engines have different characteristics. Some of them do not support transactions, including the MyISAM storage engine. However, there are storage engines that do support transactions, including the InnoDB and Falcon storage engines. There is more information about storage engines in Chapter 11, "Storage Engines."

Understanding ACID Compliance

As previously mentioned, ACID compliance is an acronym for the characteristics of a transactionally safe database. Enforcing atomicity, consistency, isolation, and durability is what ensures that a series of statements is indeed a transaction. That is, it ensures that a series of statements either completes with the resulting changes reliably stored, or, if interrupted, the set of statements is *rolled back* to where it began so the database is not changed.

Atomicity

Atomicity refers to concept that either all of the statements inside a transaction are completed, or none of them are performed. As with the previous example, in a banking system, the transfer of funds can be completed or it could fail. However, the transfer of funds is not allowed to fail leaving the work half-done.

The atomicity property guarantees that one account will not be debited unless the other account is credited. Each transaction is said to be *atomic* (indivisible) — even though there are actually two statements, they act as if they are one statement. If any part of the transaction fails, the entire transaction must fail.

Consistency

The *consistency* property ensures that the database moves from one consistent state to another. If the server were to fail while executing the transfer of money from Ziesel's account to Hudson's account, the database would be left in an inconsistent state. The only way to resolve this inconsistency is to undo changes already made. Before a transaction begins the database should be in a consistent state. Once the transaction either completes successfully or is rolled back the database should still be in a consistent state.

In a transactional system (ACID-compliant by definition), if one or more statements in the transaction do not succeed, the entire transaction must be rolled back to a consistent state. If a transaction is successful, the database moves from one consistent state to another.

Isolation

The *isolation* property specifies that data being modified for one transaction cannot be viewed or modified by a second transaction until the completion of the first transaction. This is important to support concurrent execution of queries, which is critical in any modern database system. With isolation, separate transactions can run at the same time without compromising the consistency of the data. In MySQL, the level of isolation that transactions have can be configured. The meanings of different isolation levels and how to set the isolation level are discussed in more detail in the section "Using Isolation Levels" later in this chapter.

Durability

Durability describes the principle that once a transaction has been successfully completed, the results are recorded by the database server permanently. After this point the transaction is complete, and the data changes must survive even if the database or operating system fails. This is important, because modern-day operating systems do not always perform operations immediately. If there is an operating system failure between the time that a transaction successfully completes and the time the data is actually written to the disk permanently, the database has marked the transaction as complete but the data has not been changed appropriately.

Many databases implement durability by writing complete transactions into a log that can be *played back* to re-create the database state right before a failure. A transaction is considered successfully committed only after it has been written to this log, called a *redo* log.

Using Transactional Statements

Now that you have some theory under your belt it is time to see how you actually work with transactions in MySQL. It has been touched on previously, but it is important to understand that with MySQL you have a choice of the type of storage engine to use for each table. To utilize transactions the storage engine used for each table involved in the transaction must support transactions. Failure to do so will lead to inconsistent results. Five SQL commands are used to work with transactions. We cover each of these in the following subsections.

BEGIN, BEGIN WORK, and START TRANSACTION

BEGIN, BEGIN WORK, and START TRANSACTION all can be used to start a transaction. Technically, both BEGIN and BEGIN WORK are aliases of the START TRANSACTION command.

If you execute any of these statements, it causes an implicit COMMIT of any previous pending transactions that are open by the client thread. In addition, if you had previously executed a LOCK TABLES statement the tables will be unlocked just as though you had issued an UNLOCK TABLES statement.

COMMIT

The COMMIT statement is used to signify the end of a transaction. At this point all changes to the tables are considered to be durable and will survive server failure.

ROLLBACK

ROLLBACK is used to roll back a transaction to either the state it was in before execution of the transaction or to a certain point prior to where execution is currently occurring. This point is called the SAVEPOINT.

> **WARNING** Some statements cannot be rolled back, because they perform an implicit COMMIT when they complete. These include DDL (Data Definition Language) statements like CREATE DATABASE, CREATE TABLE, DROP DATABASE, DROP TABLE, and ALTER TABLE. If you have issued a DDL statement early in a transaction and another statement fails, you cannot roll back the transaction by issuing the ROLLBACK statement. Many of these statements also perform an implicit COMMIT when they begin, too. For the full, up-to-date list of statements that perform an implicit COMMIT, see http://dev.mysql.com/doc/refman/6.0/en/implicit-commit.html.

Savepoints

A *savepoint* is a defined point in a transaction. The SAVEPOINT statement is used to set a save-point with a name. The ROLLBACK TO SAVEPOINT statement is used to roll back the transaction to the named savepoint specified. Instead of rolling back all the changes in the transaction, ROLLBACK TO SAVEPOINT savepointname rolls back modifications to rows made in the current transaction after the savepoint at savepointname. The data is in the same state it was in at the time the savepoint was reached by the transaction. To remove the named savepoint from the set of defined savepoints in the current transaction, use the RELEASE SAVEPOINT command.

Here is an example showing the use of SAVEPOINT and RELEASE SAVEPOINT:

```
mysql> use test;
Database changed
mysql> DROP TABLE IF EXISTS trans_test;
Query OK, 0 rows affected, 1 warning (0.00 sec)

mysql> CREATE TABLE trans_test (id INT PRIMARY KEY AUTO_INCREMENT,
    -> name VARCHAR(8)) ENGINE=InnoDB;
Query OK, 0 rows affected (0.12 sec)

mysql> INSERT INTO trans_test (name) VALUES ('a'), ('b');
Query OK, 2 rows affected (0.00 sec)
Records: 2  Duplicates: 0  Warnings: 0

mysql> SELECT id,name FROM trans_test;
+----+------+
| id | name |
+----+------+
|  1 | a    |
|  2 | b    |
+----+------+
2 rows in set (0.00 sec)

mysql> START TRANSACTION;
Query OK, 0 rows affected (0.00 sec)

mysql> UPDATE trans_test SET name='z' WHERE id = 1;
Query OK, 1 row affected (0.00 sec)
Rows matched: 1  Changed: 1  Warnings: 0

mysql> SAVEPOINT savepoint_one;
Query OK, 0 rows affected (0.00 sec)

mysql> UPDATE trans_test SET name='y' WHERE id = 2;
Query OK, 1 row affected (0.00 sec)
Rows matched: 1  Changed: 1  Warnings: 0
```

```
mysql> SELECT id,name FROM trans_test;
+----+------+
| id | name |
+----+------+
|  1 | z    |
|  2 | y    |
+----+------+
2 rows in set (0.00 sec)

mysql> ROLLBACK TO SAVEPOINT savepoint_one;
Query OK, 0 rows affected (0.00 sec)

mysql> SELECT id,name FROM trans_test;
+----+------+
| id | name |
+----+------+
|  1 | z    |
|  2 | b    |
+----+------+
2 rows in set (0.00 sec)

mysql> COMMIT;
Query OK, 0 rows affected (0.03 sec)
```

Notice that the first row still has a NAME field value of z, whereas the last row, whose NAME field value was changed to y, has reverted to 1.

AUTOCOMMIT

The use of the AUTOCOMMIT statement is another way to work with transactions rather than the more traditional START TRANSACTION or BEGIN. To a transactional storage engine such as InnoDB or Falcon every statement is considered a transactional statement in itself if AUTOCOMMIT is enabled (AUTOCOMMIT = 1). The result of this is that if AUTOCOMMIT is enabled, which it is by default, mysqld wraps every statement with START TRANSACTION and COMMIT statements. However, if you explicitly start a transaction with START TRANSACTION, a new transaction is started and AUTOCOMMIT is off for the new transaction.

WARNING After execution of a transaction using the START TRANSACTION and COMMIT commands mysqld reverts to the autocommit mode it was in before the transaction began. This can cause unpredictable and undesirable results.

From our previous example of Ziesel and Hudson at the bank, here are the SQL statements we initially used to update the two accounts:

```
UPDATE checking SET balance = balance - 1000 WHERE id = 145356;
UPDATE checking SET balance = balance + 1000 WHERE id = 118254;
```

If you have AUTOCOMMIT enabled (which it is by default), here is what mysqld actually executes:

```
START TRANSACTION;
UPDATE checking SET balance = balance - 1000 WHERE id = 145356;
COMMIT;
START TRANSACTION;
UPDATE checking SET balance = balance + 1000 WHERE id = 118254;
COMMIT;
```

This ensures that each modification is actually committed to the database, performing everything that happens on COMMIT, including issuing a disk flush if the storage engine is configured to do so.

Disabling AUTOCOMMIT (using SET AUTOCOMMIT=0) is equivalent to executing a START TRANSACTION statement for every statement in the session. You now have a transaction open that will not be closed until a COMMIT or ROLLBACK is issued.

```
mysql> SELECT id,name FROM trans_test;
+----+------+
| id | name |
+----+------+
|  1 | z    |
|  2 | b    |
+----+------+
2 rows in set (0.00 sec)

mysql> SET AUTOCOMMIT=0;
Query OK, 0 rows affected (0.00 sec)

mysql> UPDATE trans_test SET name='a' WHERE id='1';
Query OK, 1 row affected (0.00 sec)
Rows matched: 1  Changed: 1  Warnings: 0

mysql> COMMIT;
Query OK, 0 rows affected (0.06 sec)
```

As you can see the SET AUTOCOMMIT=0 statement works just as a BEGIN or START TRANSACTION statement. After the COMMIT, a new transaction is started without needing to use START TRANSACTION, BEGIN, or BEGIN WORK.

Using Isolation Levels

Isolation levels determine how data is isolated among different transactions. If you begin a transaction, read a row from a table, change the row, read the same row from the table, and then commit, what do you see at each step? What does another transaction reading the same row see at each step? The exact nature of what is isolated and under what conditions is determined by the isolation level.

In MySQL, the server can be set to a particular isolation level, and connections can also set their isolation level, overriding the global isolation level. For the purpose of defining isolation levels, we will describe the behavior when all connections have the same isolation level as the server. After describing each level, we go into detailed examples of each isolation level.

MySQL supports the four standard isolation levels:

- READ UNCOMMITTED — This setting allows all transactions to see all uncommitted changes, whether within their own transaction or in another transaction. These are called *dirty reads* — the data is said to be *dirty* because the change is not permanent yet. Queries inside one transaction are affected by uncommitted changes in another transaction. This is not desirable, and in fact violates ACID compliance. Setting the isolation level to READ UNCOMMITTED gets rid of transaction support — though you can still wrap transactions with START TRANSACTION, ROLLBACK, and COMMIT, there is no isolation and thus your system is no longer transactional.

- READ COMMITTED — Only data changed by committed transactions are visible to other transactions. However, within a transaction, dirty data can still be read. This means identical queries within a transaction can return differing results. For example, if a transaction reads a row, changes the row, and reads the row again, both reads will produce different data, because the data was changed inside the transaction. Other connections will see only the unchanged data, until the transaction is committed.

   READ COMMITTED is the default isolation level for SQL Server and Oracle.

- REPEATABLE READ — The default isolation level for MySQL is REPEATABLE READ. At the time of this writing, only the Falcon and InnoDB storage engines are transactional, so changing isolation levels only applies to transactions that query tables that use Falcon or InnoDB.

   Using the REPEATABLE READ isolation level, all reads within a transaction show the same data values, even if a second transaction has committed a data change while the first transaction was still running. If a transaction starts, reads a row, waits 60 seconds, and reads the same row again, both data reads will be the same — even if in those 60 seconds another transaction has changed and committed data. The first transaction has the same data when it repeats the read. Any transactions started after the data commit will see the new data.

   REPEATABLE READ may not seem like a good idea — after all, if the data changes, shouldn't a transaction be aware of that? The problem is that a transaction may take different actions based on the values of the data. Data values changing in the middle of a transaction may lead to unexpected consequences. Consider what would happen if the schema changed in the middle of a transaction, and the desired fields or tables cease to exist!

- SERIALIZABLE — In the SERIALIZABLE isolation level of MySQL, data reads are implicitly run with a read lock (the LOCK IN SHARE MODE clause; see the example in the

"Row-Level Locks" section later in this chapter). Other transactions can read the data, but no transactions can update this data until all the read locks are released.

READ UNCOMMITTED is the easiest isolation level to implement and provides the fastest performance. The problem with READ UNCOMMITTED is that it provides no isolation between transactions. READ COMMITTED provides some isolation and slightly slower performance, because only committed data changes are seen by other transactions. However, READ COMMITTED does not address the issue of data changing in the middle of a transaction. REPEATABLE READ provides more isolation from a transaction, ensuring that data reads are the same throughout the transaction even if the data has been changed and committed by a different transaction. The SERIALIZABLE isolation level provides the slowest performance but also the most isolation between transactions.

The mysqld isolation level is set by the tx_isolation system variable. All connections to the database default to using the isolation level set by the system variable. If the system variable is changed, new connections will use the new isolation level but existing connections continue to use the previous isolation level.

In addition, isolation levels can be set per connection. Though the flexibility of this system is nice, it does bring complexity in that you may have a server level setting of READ COMMITTED and a connection with a session setting of READ UNCOMMITTED. The connection with the READ UNCOMMITTED isolation setting will see uncommitted changes, even from connections with uncommitted transactions that changed data using the READ COMMITTED isolation level. In simpler terms, the isolation setting of the connection is the isolation setting used for any transactions within that connection.

To determine the isolation level of your connection:

```
mysql> SHOW SESSION VARIABLES LIKE 'tx_isolation';
+---------------+------------------+
| Variable_name | Value            |
+---------------+------------------+
| tx_isolation  | READ-UNCOMMITTED |
+---------------+------------------+
1 row in set (0.00 sec)

mysql> SELECT @@session.tx_isolation;
+------------------------+
| @@session.tx_isolation |
+------------------------+
| READ-UNCOMMITTED       |
+------------------------+
1 row in set (0.00 sec)

mysql> SELECT VARIABLE_NAME, VARIABLE_VALUE
    -> FROM INFORMATION_SCHEMA.SESSION_VARIABLES
    -> WHERE VARIABLE_NAME='tx_isolation';
```

```
+-----------------+---------------------+
| VARIABLE_NAME   | VARIABLE_VALUE      |
+-----------------+---------------------+
| TX_ISOLATION    | READ-UNCOMMITTED    |
+-----------------+---------------------+
1 row in set (0.07 sec)
```

To see the isolation level for the server:

```
mysql> SELECT @@global.tx_isolation;
+-----------------------+
| @@global.tx_isolation |
+-----------------------+
| REPEATABLE-READ       |
+-----------------------+
1 row in set (0.00 sec)

mysql> SHOW SESSION GLOBAL VARIABLES LIKE 'tx%';
+----------------+------------------+
| Variable_name  | Value            |
+----------------+------------------+
| tx_isolation   | REPEATABLE-READ  |
+----------------+------------------+
1 row in set (0.00 sec)

mysql> SELECT VARIABLE_NAME, VARIABLE_VALUE
    -> FROM INFORMATION_SCHEMA.GLOBAL_VARIABLES
    -> WHERE VARIABLE_NAME='tx_isolation';
+----------------+------------------+
| VARIABLE_NAME  | VARIABLE_VALUE   |
+----------------+------------------+
| TX_ISOLATION   | REPEATABLE-READ  |
+----------------+------------------+
1 row in set (0.07 sec)
```

To change the server (global) or connection (session) isolation level you can execute either of the following SET commands:

```
SET @@{global|session}.tx_isolation= {read-uncommitted|
 read-committed|repeatable-read|serializable}
SET {GLOBAL | SESSION} TRANSACTION ISOLATION LEVEL {READ
 UNCOMMITTED | READ COMMITTED | REPEATABLE READ | SERIALIZABLE}
```

The transaction_isolation variable can be set in an option file to change the default tx_isolation level.

READ UNCOMMITED

Recall that the READ UNCOMMITTED isolation level provides no isolation, allowing dirty reads. To see how READ UNCOMMITTED behaves, open a connection, set the isolation level, and check to make sure it is set appropriately:

```
mysql> SET @@session.tx_isolation='READ-UNCOMMITTED';
Query OK, 0 rows affected (0.00 sec)

mysql> SHOW VARIABLES LIKE 'tx_isolation';
+---------------+------------------+
| Variable_name | Value            |
+---------------+------------------+
| tx_isolation  | READ-UNCOMMITTED |
+---------------+------------------+
1 row in set (0.00 sec)
```

> **TIP** To make it easier to keep track of connections, change the prompt of this connection to 'my1> ' — make sure there is one space after >:

```
mysql> prompt my1>
PROMPT set to 'my1> '
my1>
```

Open a second connection without closing the first connection, and set the prompt and isolation level to READ UNCOMMITTED. Return to your first connection and perform the following:

```
my1> use test;
Database changed
my1> CREATE TABLE isolation_test (id INT PRIMARY KEY AUTO_INCREMENT,
    -> name VARCHAR(8)) ENGINE=InnoDB;
Query OK, 0 rows affected (0.35 sec)
my1> INSERT INTO isolation_test (name)
    -> VALUES ('a'),('b');
Query OK, 2 rows affected (0.00 sec)
Records: 2  Duplicates: 0  Warnings: 0

my1> SELECT id,name FROM isolation_test;
+----+------+
| id | name |
+----+------+
|  1 | a    |
|  2 | b    |
+----+------+
2 rows in set (0.00 sec)
```

Next execute the following commands in your second connection:

```
my2> use test;
Database changed
my2> BEGIN;
Query OK, 0 rows affected (0.00 sec)

my2> INSERT INTO isolation_test (name) VALUES ('c'),('d');
Query OK, 2 rows affected (0.00 sec)
Records: 2  Duplicates: 0  Warnings: 0
```

Returning to your first connection:

```
my1> SELECT id,name FROM isolation_test;
+----+------+
| id | name |
+----+------+
|  1 | a    |
|  2 | b    |
|  3 | c    |
|  4 | d    |
+----+------+
4 rows in set (0.00 sec)
```

Notice that the first connection can read the uncommitted c and d values of connection two. This is the essence of the READ UNCOMMITTED isolation level.

Returning to the second connection:

```
my2> ROLLBACK;
Query OK, 0 rows affected (0.01 sec)
```

Now that you have rolled the transaction back in the second connection, return to the first:

```
my1> SELECT id,name FROM isolation_test;
+----+------+
| id | name |
+----+------+
|  1 | a    |
|  2 | b    |
+----+------+
2 rows in set (0.00 sec)
```

The first connection sees the data rolled back. READ UNCOMMITTED can provide for unpredictable results!

READ COMMITTED

As stated before, an isolation level of READ COMMITTED eliminates dirty reads. To see an example you once again use two connections, setting the isolation level in both to READ COMMITTED. Once they are set and double-checked, do the following in the first connection:

```
my1> START TRANSACTION;
my1> SELECT id,name FROM isolation_test;
+----+------+
| id | name |
+----+------+
|  1 | a    |
|  2 | b    |
+----+------+
2 rows in set (0.00 sec)
```

In the second connection:

```
my2> BEGIN;
Query OK, 0 rows affected (0.00 sec)

my2> INSERT INTO isolation_test (name) VALUES ('c'),('d');
Query OK, 2 rows affected (0.00 sec)
Records: 2  Duplicates: 0  Warnings: 0
```

Returning to your first connection:

```
my1> SELECT id,name FROM isolation_test;
+----+------+
| id | name |
+----+------+
|  1 | a    |
|  2 | b    |
+----+------+
2 rows in set (0.00 sec)
```

Notice that this connection does not see the data changes the second connection made — there are no dirty reads.

Unfortunately, a second situation called an *inconsistent read* is possible. An inconsistent read is when a transaction reads data that has changed during transaction execution. Though the changed data was committed by another transaction, a transaction already in progress depends on the data not being changed by another transaction.

331

To show this, commit the changes made in the second connection:

```
my2> COMMIT;
Query OK, 0 rows affected (0.05 sec)
```

Returning to the first connection, check the isolation_test table and you will see the new data:

```
my1> SELECT id,name FROM isolation_test;
+----+------+
| id | name |
+----+------+
|  1 | a    |
|  2 | b    |
|  3 | c    |
|  4 | d    |
+----+------+
4 rows in set (0.00 sec)
```

Once the transaction in the second connection was committed the results became visible to the first connection, even though the first connection was already open and had already read the data once, with the original values.

REPEATABLE READ

With a REPEATABLE READ isolation level there is no possibility of either dirty or inconsistent reads. To prove this to yourself, repeat the previous example with the tx_isolation level set to REPEATABLE READ for both connections.

The REPEATABLE READ isolation level allows a transaction to see the same data for values it has already read regardless of whether or not the data has been changed. Unfortunately, this leads to a problem called a *phantom read*, because it reads data that no longer exists.

As an example, a company generates reports based on customer invoice data. Set your connections to the REPEATABLE READ isolation level, and in the first connection populate a table and start a transaction:

```
my1> CREATE TABLE invoice (customer_id INT NOT NULL,
    -> invoice_date DATE NOT NULL) ENGINE=InnoDB;
Query OK, 0 rows affected (0.38 sec)

my1> INSERT INTO invoice (customer_id,invoice_date)
    -> VALUES (1,'2008-10-07'), (1,'2008-11-15'), (2,'2009-01-01');
Query OK, 3 rows affected (0.00 sec)
Records: 3  Duplicates: 0  Warnings: 0

my1> START TRANSACTION;
Query OK, 0 rows affected (0.00 sec)
```

```
my1> SELECT customer_id, invoice_date
    -> FROM invoice WHERE invoice_date > '2008-10-01';
+-------------+--------------+
| customer_id | invoice_date |
+-------------+--------------+
|           1 | 2008-10-07   |
|           1 | 2008-11-15   |
|           2 | 2009-01-01   |
+-------------+--------------+
3 rows in set (0.00 sec)
```

The first connection represents a data processor — imagine that it processes the data for reporting. While this is going on, the following happens in a second connection:

```
my2> BEGIN;
Query OK, 0 rows affected (0.00 sec)

my2> DELETE FROM invoice WHERE invoice_date < '2009-01-01';
Query OK, 2 rows affected (0.01 sec)

my2> COMMIT;
Query OK, 0 rows affected (0.00 sec)

my2> SELECT customer_id, invoice_date FROM invoice;
+-------------+--------------+
| customer_id | invoice_date |
+-------------+--------------+
|           2 | 2009-01-01   |
+-------------+--------------+
1 row in set (0.00 sec)
```

In the first connection, however, three rows of data appear:

```
my1> SELECT customer_id, invoice_date FROM invoice;
+-------------+--------------+
| customer_id | invoice_date |
+-------------+--------------+
|           1 | 2008-10-07   |
|           1 | 2008-11-15   |
|           2 | 2009-01-01   |
+-------------+--------------+
3 rows in set (0.00 sec)
```

The first transaction is still seeing the first two records, which have already been deleted. It is doing a phantom read of those two records.

The phantom read was introduced by trying to fix the inconsistent read problem in READ UNCOMMITTED. However, READ UNCOMMITTED still allows other transactions to change the data. The ideal scenario is one where data read by one transaction cannot be modified by another at all. This is the SERIALIZABLE isolation level.

333

SERIALIZABLE

With the SERIALIZABLE isolation level, updates are not permitted by a transaction if another transaction has already read the data. Set both connections to use the SERIALIZABLE isolation level, and in the first connection:

```
my1> START TRANSACTION;
Query OK, 0 rows affected (0.00 sec)

my1> SELECT id,name FROM isolation_test;
+----+------+
| id | name |
+----+------+
|  1 | a    |
|  2 | b    |
|  3 | c    |
|  4 | d    |
+----+------+
4 rows in set (0.00 sec)
```

In the second connection begin a transaction:

```
my2> START TRANSACTION;
Query OK, 0 rows affected (0.00 sec)

my2> UPDATE isolation_test SET name='z' WHERE id=1;
```

The query in your second connection hangs — it is waiting for the first connection to release the implicit read lock it has on the data. If the second connection exceeds the lock wait timeout value, you will see:

```
ERROR 1205 (HY000): Lock wait timeout exceeded; try restarting
  transaction
```

If your second connection has timed out, run the UPDATE again, and COMMIT the transaction in connection one:

```
my1> COMMIT;
Query OK, 0 rows affected (0.00 sec)
```

Your second connection should show that the update completed. Note the amount of time required to complete the update in connection two because of this locking:

```
Query OK, 1 row affected (14.09 sec)
Rows matched: 1  Changed: 1  Warnings: 0
```

At this point both connections should see the update to the table — the first connection has committed, and any new transactions will see the new data. Do not forget to commit your transaction in connection two:

```
my2> COMMIT;
Query OK, 0 rows affected (0.09 sec)
```

Although the SERIALIZABLE isolation level provides the most isolation available, it is often both excessive and not efficient. With both the InnoDB and Falcon storage engines techniques are implemented such as next-key locking and multi-version concurrency control (see the next section) that effectively eliminate problems caused by phantom rows. The REPEATABLE READ isolation will provide for better concurrency, so unless there is some special reason, this should be the preferred isolation level. Changing the isolation level is very rare and should only be done very carefully.

> **TIP** You can find a good article written by one of the book's authors showing more examples of each isolation level at http://sheeri.com/node/144.

Multi-version concurrency control

The REPEATABLE READ isolation level can only occur if each transaction has its own virtual view of the data it reads and writes. This is accomplished in InnoDB and Falcon by using *multi-version concurrency control* (MVCC).

MVCC is a versioning system for data, just like there are version control systems for code (cvs, Subversion, Mercurial, and so on). When a transaction starts, you can think of it as checking out a copy of the data as it is at the start of the transaction. Note that the mechanics are not the same, but the concept is — in version control systems, an actual local copy of code is made, which would be impossibly unwieldy on a system with many transactions and a large amount of data. Needless to say, MVCC has a very complex job when managing hundreds of concurrent transactions.

If a second transaction starts, it "checks out" its own copy of the data. If the first transaction makes changes and commits, the second transaction will not see the data. The second transaction can only work with the data it has. There is no way to update the data that the second transaction sees, though the second transaction could issue a ROLLBACK and start the transaction again to see the new data.

The drawback of MVCC is the cost of storing multiple versions of objects in the database. The benefit is that queries are not blocked as they are in the SERIALIZABLE isolation level. MVCC greatly increases the concurrency ability for transactional storage engines.

Explaining Locking and Deadlocks

Locks are used by a thread to keep other threads from modifying data in the area of the database that is locked. Locks are one way to enforce isolation — if a transaction cannot read or write data, it is isolated from other transactions. There are two types of locks — read locks and write locks:

- **Read Lock** — The locked data is reserved for reading by the current thread. Other threads can read the locked data, but they cannot change the locked data. A read lock is also called a shared lock, because more than one thread can have a read lock on data.

- **Write Lock** — The locked data is reserved for writing by the current thread. Other threads can neither read nor write the locked data. A write lock is also called an exclusive lock, because only one thread at a time can have a write lock on data.

There are three levels of locking:

- **Table Lock** — The entire table is locked.

- **Page Lock** — The lock is set at the memory page level. A page is a group of rows. The exact row count can vary depending on a number of factors but it will typically be a subset of one entire table.

- **Row Lock** — The lock is set at the row level. Each row being read or written to is locked.

Different storage engines use different levels of locking. We cover each of these locking levels in the next three sections.

A *deadlock* is when two transactions are simultaneously trying to access the same data in the database, and each transaction has locked data that the other transaction needs to continue. Without being able to continue, the transactions will not release their existing lock on the data. More specifically, one transaction holds a lock on one set of rows and is requesting a lock on another set of rows; those rows are locked by a second transaction that is simultaneously requesting a lock on the rows locked by the first transaction.

For example, consider the following timeline:

1. Transaction one (T1) requests a write lock on Table B, rows 23 and 78.
2. T1 receives a write lock on Table B, rows 23 and 78. No other transaction can read or write these rows.
3. Transaction two (T2) requests a write lock on Table A, rows 10 and 15.
4. T2 receives a write lock on Table A, rows 10 and 15. No other transaction can read or write these rows.
5. T1 requests a write lock on Table A, rows 10 and 15.
6. T1 waits for the write lock to be granted, which cannot happen until T2 releases its lock.

7. T2 requests a write lock on Table B, rows 23 and 78.

8. T2 waits for the write lock to be granted, which cannot happen until T1 releases its lock.

T1 and T2 are waiting for each other to release the lock, but neither will release its own lock because they are not done using it yet. Figure 9-1 shows the stalemate happening.

FIGURE 9-1

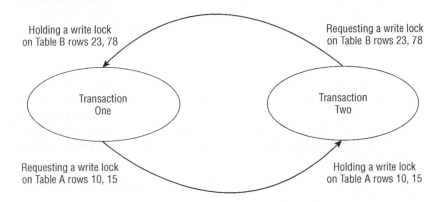

Holding a write lock on Table B rows 23, 78

Requesting a write lock on Table B rows 23, 78

Transaction One

Transaction Two

Requesting a write lock on Table A rows 10, 15

Holding a write lock on Table A rows 10, 15

Unless there is some intervention by the client or the database server, these two transactions would wait forever for the other to release the lock. The database server can manage the deadlock by having what is called a lock wait time value. What this means is that if the time that the locks that are held by the transactions exceed the lock wait time value waiting to be released, one of the transactions is rolled back so the other transaction can complete. The InnoDB storage engine will often recognize that a deadlock has occurred and kill one of the transactions before this limit is actually reached.

NOTE   There are three different lock wait timeout variables:

```
mysql> SHOW GLOBAL VARIABLES LIKE '%lock_wait_timeout';
+-----------------------------+-------+
| Variable_name               | Value |
+-----------------------------+-------+
| falcon_lock_wait_timeout    | 50    |
| innodb_lock_wait_timeout    | 50    |
| table_lock_wait_timeout     | 50    |
+-----------------------------+-------+
3 rows in set (0.00 sec)
```

These system variables can be set dynamically, and can be set on a GLOBAL or SESSION level. The default values are, as shown, 50 seconds for table-level locks and row-level locks in Falcon and InnoDB.

Table-level locks

Using only table-level locking, if a query accesses the table it will lock the entire table. It is possible to request many table-level locks at one time; however, a table-level lock request releases all currently held table-level locks. One benefit of this type of locking is that it entirely eliminates deadlocking issues, because all locks are requested at the same time. There is no way to request a table-level lock, wait, and request another table-level lock without releasing the first table-level lock. Another benefit is that only one lock is needed to change all the rows in a table — larger tables require more overhead with more granular locking levels. For example, a thread updating a table with a million rows using row-level locking must acquire and release a million locks, whereas updating the same table with table-level locking requires only one lock to be acquired and released.

The biggest disadvantage of table-level locking is that when a thread has locked a table with a write lock, no other queries have access to the table. If you have a table with a million rows and need to modify one row, the entire table is inaccessible by other threads for the time it takes to modify that one row. The LOCK TABLES and UNLOCK TABLES commands are used by mysqld to acquire and release table-level locks on any table, regardless of storage engine. The MyISAM and MEMORY storage engines use table-level locking by default because it is the only level of locking available to those storage engines.

The LOCK TABLES statement tries to acquire table-level locks on one or more tables. It implicitly releases all previously held locks by the thread:

```
LOCK TABLES tbl_name {READ | WRITE}[, tbl_name {READ | WRITE}, ...];
```

The UNLOCK TABLES statement can be used to explicitly unlock all previously held locks by the thread:

```
UNLOCK TABLES;
```

The following example code shows how a read-locked table in one session will affect the same table's usage in a second session.

To begin, set a prompt for the first connection and create a new table:

```
mysql> prompt my1>
PROMPT set to 'my1> '
my1> use test;
Database changed
my1> DROP TABLE IF EXISTS lock_test;
Query OK, 0 rows affected, 1 warning (0.00 sec)

my1> CREATE TABLE lock_test (id INT PRIMARY KEY AUTO_INCREMENT,
    -> name VARCHAR(8)) ENGINE=MyISAM;
Query OK, 0 rows affected (0.37 sec)

my1> INSERT INTO lock_test (name) VALUES ('a');
Query OK, 1 row affected (0.00 sec)
```

```
my1> LOCK TABLES lock_test READ;
Query OK, 0 rows affected (0.00 sec)
Open a second connection and execute the following:mysql> prompt my2>
PROMPT set to 'my2> '
my2> use test;
Database changed
my2> SELECT id,name FROM lock_test;
+----+------+
| id | name |
+----+------+
|  1 | a    |
+----+------+
1 row in set (0.00 sec)

my2> INSERT INTO lock_test (name) VALUES ('b');
```

When you enter the INSERT statement it will not return a prompt. This connection is now blocked waiting for the first connect to release the read lock that it is holding on the table lock_test.

If you return to the first connection and issue the following command:

```
my1>UNLOCK TABLES;
Query OK, 0 rows affected (0.00 sec)
the connection will release the lock on the table. At this point
the INSERT command in the second connection will finish and return
the results followed by the mysql prompt. You should see
something like this in connection two at this point:my2> INSERT
INTO lock_test (name) VALUES ('b');
Query OK, 1 row affected (3 min 2.26 sec)
```

Notice that it took over three minutes to complete this INSERT command, because it waited for the lock to be released. After connection two finishes the INSERT statement, look at the table:

```
mysql> SELECT id,name FROM lock_test;
+----+------+
| id | name |
+----+------+
|  1 | a    |
|  2 | b    |
+----+------+
2 rows in set (0.00 sec)
```

The next part of the example shows the use of a write lock. To begin, lock the table from your first connection:

```
my1> LOCK TABLES lock_test WRITE;
Query OK, 0 rows affected (0.00 sec)
```

Once this is done, attempt to read data from the lock_test table from your second connection:

```
my2> SELECT id,name FROM lock_test;
```

When you attempt to do this your SELECT statement will be blocked waiting for the release of the write lock acquired by your first connection. Go back to your first connection and release the write lock:

```
my1> UNLOCK TABLES;
Query OK, 0 rows affected (0.00 sec)
```

Once the write lock is released the SELECT statement in your second connection finishes:

```
+----+------+
| id | name |
+----+------+
|  1 | a    |
|  2 | b    |
+----+------+
2 rows in set (22.34 sec)
```

Notice that the SELECT statement could not be fulfilled until the write lock was released. In this case it took 22.34 seconds to wait for the write lock to be released and perform the SELECT.

In the first part of the example the second connection could see the data in the table the first connection had locked. In the second part of the example the second connection could not even see the data that was locked. This is the fundamental difference between a read and write lock.

Managing multiple table-level lock requests is a bit complicated. If a thread requests either type of table-level lock and no thread currently holds any locks on the table, the lock is immediately acquired by the thread. If a lock cannot be acquired immediately, it is placed in a queue. There is one queue for table-level read locks, and another for table-level write locks.

If a thread already has a write lock on a table, no locks can be acquired immediately. If a thread already has a read lock on a table, only another read lock can be acquired immediately. Table-level write locks have higher precedence than table-level read locks by default in MySQL. When a thread releases the final lock on a table, a lock on that table from the write lock queue is acquired next. Table-level locks in the read lock queue are acquired only after all the write locks for that table are acquired and released.

If your database server has a large number of INSERT, DELETE, or UPDATE statements being processed on a table that is using table-level locking, there is a real possibility that SELECT statements on that table will be waiting for a long period of time. The write lock precedence behavior can be changed in many ways. Write locks can be set as lower priority than read locks globally by starting mysqld with the low-priority-updates option, or by issuing:

```
mysql> SET GLOBAL low_priority_updates=1;
```

Though this is a dynamic system variable, only new connections will use the new value. To set all writes in a session as lower priorities than reads, use the following command:

```
mysql> SET SESSION low_priority_updates=1;
```

To set individual writes as lower priorities, use the LOW PRIORITY clause in INSERT, UPDATE, and DELETE statements. To set individual reads as higher priorities, use the HIGH PRIORITY clause in a SELECT statement. See Chapter 4 for more details.

> **TIP** Lock acquisition behavior can also be controlled with the max_write_lock_count and concurrent_insert system variables. The MySQL manual has this tip and many ideas on how to work around table locking issues at http://dev.mysql.com/doc/refman/6.0/en/table-locking.html.

Page-level locks

Page-level locking is when a memory page is locked. This will lock a group of rows instead of the entire table. The number of rows locked will vary based on a number of factors, including the amount of memory allocated to a page, the size of the rows, and amount of fragmentation. Going back to our previous example of a table with a million rows, assume a page-level lock is used. If a page consists of 1,000 rows, a lock would be placed on 1,000 rows at a time. Any of the other 999,000 rows (stored in 999 memory pages) could be used by other queries without waiting, because there is no lock for that data. Unlike table-level locking, page-level locking allows deadlocking to occur. The BDB storage engine is the only storage engine using page-level locking and it was removed from mysqld by version 5.1.

Row-level locks

Row-level locking allows locks to be acquired on the row-by-row basis. This will both block the minimal amount of table content and allow for the most concurrency on a table. InnoDB and Falcon implement row-level locking. Deadlocking can occur with row-level locking. Following is an example using the InnoDB storage engine.

To demonstrate row-level locking, use the LOCK IN SHARE MODE clause of the SELECT statement to place a row-level lock on data. To begin, open your first connection to the database server and do the following:

```
mysql> prompt my1>
PROMPT set to 'my1> '
my1> DROP TABLE IF EXISTS lock_test;
Query OK, 0 rows affected (0.00 sec)

my1> CREATE TABLE lock_test (id INT PRIMARY KEY AUTO_INCREMENT,
    -> name VARCHAR(8)) ENGINE=InnoDB;
Query OK, 0 rows affected (0.38 sec)
```

```
my1> INSERT INTO lock_test (name) VALUES ('a');
Query OK, 1 row affected (0.01 sec)

my1> START TRANSACTION;
Query OK, 0 rows affected (0.00 sec)

my1> SELECT id,name FROM lock_test WHERE id=1 LOCK IN SHARE MODE;
+----+------+
| id | name |
+----+------+
|  1 | a    |
+----+------+
1 row in set (0.00 sec)
```

Now open a second connection and do the following:

```
mysql> prompt my2>
PROMPT set to 'my2> '
my2> INSERT INTO lock_test (name) VALUES ('b');
Query OK, 1 row affected (0.00 sec)

my2> SELECT id,name FROM lock_test;
+----+------+
| id | Name |
+----+------+
|  1 | a    |
|  2 | b    |
+----+------+
2 rows in set (0.02 sec)


my2> UPDATE lock_test SET name='d' WHERE id=2;
Query OK, 1 row affected (0.00 sec)
Rows matched: 1  Changed: 1  Warnings: 0

my2> UPDATE lock_test SET name='c' WHERE ID='1';
```

Your second connection will now be waiting because of a write lock held by your first connection on the row where id=1. The first UPDATE had no problem updating the row where id=2 because there was no lock on that row. Returning to your first connection run the following:

```
mysql> COMMIT;
Query OK, 0 rows affected (0.00 sec)
```

At this point your second connection now completes the update.

Storage Engines and Locking

Locking is implemented by both `mysqld` and particular storage engines. Falcon and InnoDB implement row-level locking, and `mysqld` implements table-level locking. The result is that any storage engine can be locked with a table-level lock, because table-level locking is implemented in the server. There are storage engines we have not mentioned with regards to locking, such as ARCHIVE and BLACKHOLE. Unless the storage engine specifically implements locking, only table-level locking is available. At the time of this writing, Falcon and InnoDB have working implementations of row-level locking. The status of locking in Maria is unknown. Note that storage engines that implement their own locking can also use the default `mysqld` implementation of table-level locking.

Storage engines other than Falcon, InnoDB, and Maria can only use the `mysqld` implementation of table-level locking.

Recovering MySQL Transactions

To be ACID-compliant, a database system must resolve situations where a transaction is interrupted and where data from a completed transaction has not been written to disk. Perhaps the power goes out, the hard drive crashes, or the database tries to use too much memory and crashes.

If such an interruption occurs, when `mysqld` starts again there is potentially inconsistent data. Inconsistent data is resolved through a recovery process involving log files that are called transactional logs. There are two types of transactional logs — the *redo logs* and *undo logs*.

Redo logs are used to apply changes that were made in memory but not flushed to the permanent table records. Before a `COMMIT` statement is successful, the redo log is written to. Logging is done in this manner because it provides for faster database operation. This might be seen as counter-intuitive at first look. Instead of writing to only the data file(s), `mysqld` additionally writes the redo log. Writes to the redo logs are always sequential, whereas often data files are not written to sequentially. Sequential writes are faster than non-sequential writes. Therefore, the much faster redo log writes occur when a statement is committed, and the slower writes to the data files can be batched periodically. Thus, the database actually operates faster writing to both files rather than just one file.

The redo logs are stored in different places for different transactional storage engines — the storage engine defines the exact redo log implementation. When `mysqld` starts up after a crash, it checks and applies all redo logs. This application of the redo logs provides the durability part of ACID compliance in transactional storage engines within MySQL.

Undo logs are used to roll back uncommitted transactions. When a transaction is started and commands are executed, the storage engine does not know if the transaction will end with a COMMIT, ROLLBACK, or with an interruption from a crash. Ending with a COMMIT means all the changes made in the course of the transaction will be preserved (fulfilling the consistency requirement of ACID compliance). This is true whether the COMMIT was explicitly issued to end the transaction, or an implicit COMMIT occurred — see the section "Using Transactional Statements" earlier in this chapter for more information on statements that perform an implicit COMMIT.

If the transaction ends with a ROLLBACK command, all changes made by the transaction need to be undone. Changes also need to be undone if the transaction gets interrupted for some reason, such as mysqld crashing or the client disconnecting before ending the transaction. The undo logs store the changes that need to be done. The undo logs also store the savepoints, and are used when a ROLLBACK TO SAVEPOINT statement is issued.

In the crash recovery process, after the redo log files are applied mysqld will need to roll back the transactions that were not committed but had already made changes to the database. Undo logs are used to roll back these transactional changes.

As an example, imagine running a transaction adding 1,000,000 rows, and the operating system crashes after 800,000 inserts are performed. When mysqld restarts after the operating system is back up, first the redo logs are applied to get the database server into a consistent state — with the 800,000 inserts done. Then mysqld will perform a rollback of the 800,000 inserts using the undo logs.

In InnoDB, undo logs are stored in the data files, and redo logs are stored in the innodb log files. For Falcon the undo and redo logs are stored in the serial log file. The binary logs (bin-log) are not used in crash recovery and do not contain undo or redo information.

> **TIP** One of the book's authors has an article explaining how InnoDB stores and uses redo logs at http://www.pythian.com/blogs/1242/innodb-logfiles. The article explains the system variables that pertain to the InnoDB redo logs and crash recovery and how they interact.

Summary

This chapter covered how transactions work in MySQL. Specifically, it covered:

- The four parts of ACID compliance
- How to use transactions in MySQL and interactions with AUTOCOMMIT
- Isolation levels — Read Uncommitted, Read Committed, Repeatable Read, Serializable
- MVCC

■ Types of levels of locking

■ Deadlocks

■ Redo and undo logs

Although transactions can be complicated, they are a fundamental part of a modern database system and a DBA should understand how they work — in theory and in actual implementation.

Part III

Core MySQL Administration

Chapter 10

MySQL Server Tuning

There are four main areas of a server running `mysqld` that the database administrator can analyze and optimize for best performance. These areas are SQL tuning, schema and index tuning, `mysqld` tuning, and operating system tuning. SQL tuning and index optimizations are covered in Chapter 18. This chapter covers tuning `mysqld` for top performance. In addition to tuning `mysqld`, the operating system and hardware that the server runs on requires tuning for best performance. While these are not necessarily under the direct control of a database administrator, recommendations can be made to the system administrators for the best hardware and operating system to run `mysqld` on.

Choosing Optimal Hardware

Computer hardware changes very quickly. Because of this, specific hardware recommendations will not be made. However, there are some characteristics that you can look for when purchasing server hardware.

The first consideration is that you should always buy 64-bit hardware, because `mysqld` can take advantage of the larger amounts of per-process memory supported by 64-bit operating systems. On a 32-bit operating system, each process can only use about 2.4 Gb of RAM per process, and `mysqld` is currently single-threaded. Make sure that the motherboard can support a sufficient amount of RAM. If the server is going to be used in a high-load environment, we recommend that the motherboard be able to support 16 Gb of RAM, if not 32 Gb. While you might not need it now, do not put yourself in the position of realizing you need to add more RAM to your server but the motherboard will not support any more.

When it comes to RAM, the amount needed is going to vary greatly depending on your application. If the entire database is 1 Gb in size and will not increase over time, the server does not need 8 Gb of RAM. However, many applications have databases that are much larger than the amount of memory available. What is most important is the size of the *working set* of the database. The working set of the database is the amount of data that is being worked on at a time. If the database is 100 Gb in size, but has a working set of 10 Gb (only 10 percent needs to be in RAM at any time) then 16 Gb of RAM on a properly configured mysqld instance will be fine. The amount of data in the working set is varies on how the data is used.

Your I/O subsystem is often one of the most difficult parts of the server to accurately forecast requirements for. Current options for hard drives include traditional SCSI drives, SATA (Serial ATA) drives, SAS (Serial Attached SCSI) drives and the new solid state drives. At this point, very few systems are being bought with traditional SCSI drives. SATA drives are not as reliable as the SAS drives. Unless the server is very low end, it should use SAS drives. Currently both SAS and SATA are limited to 3 gigabits per second, but the SAS protocol will be upgraded to 6 Gb per second in 2009. SATA drives will most likely reach that speed even sooner.

In larger production system, there will often be a hardware RAID controller or RAID configured through software at the operating system level. *RAID* stands for redundant array of independent disks. As its name implies, RAID brings together disks to be used as a unit with some data mirroring. There are various levels of RAID. Table 10-1 lists the most common levels used for databases servers.

TABLE 10-1

RAID Levels

RAID Level	Description
RAID 0	Only one copy of the data, but the data is spread out (*striped*) across multiple disks. If one disk fails, all of the data is lost — from all disks.
RAID 1	Two disks of equal size combine to form one redundant array. Each disk is a copy (*mirror*) of the other. If one disk fails, all the data is intact on the other.
RAID 5	Combines three or more disks in a way that protects data against loss of any one disk; the storage capacity of the array is reduced by one disk.
RAID 10	A combination of RAID 1 (mirroring) and RAID 0 (striping). The storage capacity of the array is 50 percent of total capacity of the hard drives, but each drive is mirrored.

For a very visual example of RAID levels, see www.flickr.com/photos/tirrell/128638167.

RAID 10 offers the best write performance. However, it does require a lot of overhead in the form of lost storage space. If you use an array of ten 160-GB drives your total capacity is only 800 GB, so you are effectively losing 50 percent of your storage capacity. However, where top performance in terms of write throughput is needed, this is the best option. If you find yourself needing better read performance, consider using the scaling techniques discussed in Chapter 22, the caching suggestions in Chapter 12, or the query optimizations techniques in Chapter 18.

> **NOTE** Some organizations choose to use the faster RAID 1 or RAID 0 levels because they have very large numbers of slaves, and it is easier for them to maintain 500 slaves using RAID 1 or RAID 0 than to have more redundancy at the RAID level. In effect, they have a different kind of RAID — a redundant array of independent databases! This solution is appropriate for larger infrastructures that can easily rebuild a server (usually in a mostly automated fashion), have extra server capacity, and are very wary of RAID controller failures.
>
> Organizations that have used this method have found that the extra server capacity comes in handy when needing to perform unscheduled maintenance, and enables most maintenance (scheduled or not) to not cause an application-level downtime. In addition, if a machine needs to be repurposed, they can remove a machine from production and repurpose it immediately. They place an order for hardware to replace the machine they repurposed, but they can wait if the vendor takes 6–8 weeks to deliver.

When looking for a RAID controller, you should choose one that supports the needed RAID level. In addition, most hardware RAID controllers have a RAM cache. This is used as a buffer for reads from the array and writes to the array. When looking at the specifications of the controller, look for what is called *battery-backed write cache*. This means that the cache on the controller utilizes a battery so that, if power is lost, the contents of the cache are retained for a period of time. This enables you to safely utilize the writeback feature, which means that, when the RAID controller receives a write request from the server it can immediately return a signal to the operating system that the write is complete. This can provide a good performance boost, as the operating system does not have to wait for the hard drive to actually write the data to the platter and signal that it is complete. As with system RAM, the more RAM cache on the RAID controller the better.

> **WARNING** RAID is not always the best solution. Besides the tradeoffs already discussed, the RAID controller is a single point of failure. Even if you have mirrored disk drives, if the RAID controller fails, you will not be able to access any of the drives.

Recently *solid-state* hard drives have gained a lot of attention. Solid-state hard drives do not have spinning heads like traditional disks do. These devices either have nonvolatile flash memory or are DRAM-based. The main advantage includes fast random access reading, as there is no head to move for reads and writes. DRAM-based drives also have an extremely fast write. At this time the cost for sold-state drives is extremely high compared to typical hard drives. However, for some applications, these might be necessary. In addition, prices are dropping, and both capacity and performance are improving. There will be a time in the not too distant future when it makes sense to utilize solid-state disk hardware for a high-performance server. You might not use solid-state drives for all storage needs, but if you get a 30 percent I/O boost by moving your data files to solid-state disks this begins to be attractive if the price increase is not substantial.

Of course, there are large drawbacks other than the price. Currently non-DRAM–based solid-state disk drives have a higher rate of data corruption than traditional spinning disks, and there is a limited number of writes that can be done to each block. At the time this book was written, there had not been enough long-term studies to compare how the life of a solid-state disk drive compares to the life of a traditional disk drive.

Tuning the Operating System

The three most popular operating system platforms that `mysqld` runs on are Linux, Windows, and Solaris. While the methods of tuning the various operating systems are different, the principles are the same. We will spend time discussing the principles involved and then implementation details for various operating systems. Specific differences in implementation due to operating system will be noted.

Operating system architecture

With all modern operating systems, there are both 32- and 64-bit architectures. No matter what operating system you choose, your operating system should be a 64-bit architecture in order to run a production-quality database server. A 32-bit architecture has a theoretical per-process limit of 4 Gb of RAM. In reality, a single process can use a maximum amount of 2.4–2.7 Gb of RAM on a 32-bit server. As `mysqld` is single-threaded, a 64-bit architecture is necessary to be able to have your entire database use more than 2.4–2.7 Gb of memory.

> **NOTE** In order to use a 64-bit operating system, the hardware must be able to support it. However, almost all hardware being sold in recent times can support 64-bit operating systems.

If you are using the Windows operating system for production use of `mysqld.exe` we would recommend that you use Windows Server 2003 or later. The reasons for this include:

- Up to 32 CPUs and 64 Gb of RAM are now supported using Intel x86 64-bit chips. While MySQL cannot currently support that amount of RAM or a CPU count that high, it may do so in the future, and the operating systems should support it. When the time comes to, say, install more RAM, you want to be sure that your operating system can use it. Being required to upgrade the operating system when all you wanted to do was upgrade the RAM turns a short process into a long and frustrating one.

- I/O performance has been substantially improved from previous versions. Additionally, the CPU resources required to service I/O have been reduced. Together, these will greatly speed up database performance.

- The TCP/IP protocol is up to 25 percent faster than the TCP/IP implementation in Windows 2000.

With the recent introduction of Windows Server 2008, Microsoft has given the administrator the ability to install what is called a *Server Core*. This is a very stripped-down version of Windows Server that does not include the Windows Explorer (no graphical login, similar to having a non-Windows system where X Server is not installed). This will provide for a more secure environment and a faster server.

With Linux the changes tend to happen much faster than the Windows or Solaris platform. However, there is wisdom in not being on the forefront of innovation — at least not in production. Along with all the benefits of having the latest features comes the problem of having the latest features crash (and perhaps corrupt your data) for no apparent reason. Two widely used Linux distributions in the enterprise are Red Hat Enterprise and the stable branch of the Debian distribution. Neither of these distributions is necessarily the most innovative, but they tend to be very stable.

TIP Debian is a very stable version of GNU/Linux, and `mysqld` runs very smoothly on it. Even so, it should be noted that MySQL Enterprise does not officially support 64-bit Intel versions of `mysqld` on Debian. See the supported platforms part of the MySQL Enterprise website at `http://mysql.com/support/supportedplatforms/enterprise.html`.

The Solaris operating system has always been targeted at the enterprise market. Because of this, it tends to be very conservative and very stable. Solaris has a reputation as a solid platform but also has some very innovative features such as `dtrace` and the ZFS file system.

File systems and partitions

All operating systems use *file system partitions*. File system partitions are the divisions of the hard drive(s). A hard drive can be divided into one or more *partitions*, which are logical divisions. On Solaris, partitions are called *slices*.

The file system that the operating system utilizes, along with the partitioning scheme of the file system, lays the foundation for operating system performance characteristics. A machine running Linux might have a disk partition that looks like Figure 10-1.

FIGURE 10-1

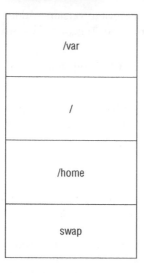

Of course, the exact layout will vary depending on the needs of the users.

When considering how to lay out your partitions you should keep the following points in mind:

- Directories that can expand in size rapidly, such as the Unix-system /tmp and /var should be in dedicated partitions. That way there is less chance of interfering with overall server operation if they start growing rapidly.

- Data transfer within a partition is much faster than data transfer from one partition to another. In particular, moving files within a partition is almost instant — the operating system just changes the pointers to where the files are located. However, moving files from one partition to another takes time to copy the file from one partition to another and then delete the original file.

- There are security considerations for giving a directory its own partition. Typically the /home (home directory files) on a Unix-based system has its own partition for this reason.

- Having major directories in their own partition will help with recovery if there are issues with file system corruption and another partition becomes unusable.

- On Unix-based systems, swap space will need its own partition.

- The operating system is more likely to run into (file system) fragmentation problems if you have a series of slowly growing data files on the same partition with other operating system files that are growing.

All of the preceding points are applicable to a system that is running off a single hard drive. In order to improve performance, you can use multiple drives either configured with partitions or using a RAID setup to manage a number of drives and make them appear to be a single drive to the server. With `mysqld`, you will have better performance with dedicated partitions on separate disks for your data and log files directories. If you are using a RAID array for optimal performance, you might want to have your data files on the RAID array and the log files on a separate individual hard drive. The principle is that you are separating random I/O (the data files) from sequential I/O (writing log files).

Unfortunately, there is a downside to having multiple partitions configured. Under Linux, a very popular tool for performing backups is the LVM (Logical Volume Manager) tool. We cover this tool in Chapter 13, "Backups and Recovery," but it should be pointed out that LVM can not guarantee consistency of snapshots across multiple partitions.

Once you have a partitioning scheme, the next choice is what file system to use for the server. With the Windows Server family (2000/2003/2008), there is really only one choice — NTFS. With Linux there are a few more choices:

- ext2 has been around for a long time. It is not a journaling file system but does provide for very good performance. Because of its lack of journaling capabilities, after a crash recovery is much slower. We do not recommend ext2 for database log and data/index files.

- ext3 is the default operating system of many GNU/Linux operating systems. As the successor to ext2, it is a journaling operating system that has pretty good performance with low overhead on the system.

- JFS is IBM's journaling file system. It has a history of being used in enterprise environments and is a reliable choice. It has fast recovery after a file system failure. The GNU/Linux version is not as well supported as other choices.

- XFS has very good performance and the ability to do snapshots of partitions without seriously impacting server performance. It does tend to utilize the CPU more than ext3, but with `mysqld` CPU usage typically is not a bottleneck.

- ReiserFS has really good performance and the ability to grow partitions without any server downtime. Unfortunately, the future of the file system is in doubt, as the creator and main driving force behind ReiserFS is in jail.

On Solaris there are two main file system options. The default file system is UFS with a new option of ZFS available in Solaris 10 and later. In Solaris 7 and later, UFS has journaling capabilities. It is a mature, high-performing operating system that works very well with database servers. The much newer ZFS is really a hybrid file system and volume manager. The ability of ZFS to work with volumes is very attractive and provides for a great deal of flexibility.

When comparing files systems, people often want to know which one is the fastest. Comparisons of the different file systems typically consist of claims like "file system A will be faster than file system B at random file reads, but B will be faster than A at sequential reads." Really the difference is so marginal that the bottom line is that it does not matter. There are many file system speed comparison tests available on the Internet. Feel free to read them or even perform your own. While many database administrators have their preferred file system, in the end the difference in a typical production setup is very minimal. It is more important, in almost every case, to be concerned with the features supported by the operating system. A well-tuned file system will perform better than a poorly tuned file system.

A journaling file system is a fault-resilient file system, which writes a journal that keeps track of where data has been written or removed. The journal keeps track of where the file system puts each extent. Then, if your system crashes, you can be back up and operational much more quickly with a journaling file system. It also recovers unsaved data and stores it in the location where it would have gone if the computer had not crashed, making it an important feature for mission-critical applications.

The journaling file system can ensure file system consistency and fast recovery in the unlikely event of a system crash or other abnormal failure. With the journaling file system, NAStorage can recover from an abnormal shutdown in a few minutes.

It is very important that the file system support *journaling*. A journaling file system is a fault-resistant file system in which data integrity is strengthened because file system updates are constantly written to a serial log before the file system is updated. In the event of a system failure, a journaling file system has a better chance of restoring changes on the disk to a pre-crash configuration. The end result for a database administrator is that after a server crash the recovery time for a file system with journaling is much quicker than for a non-journaling file system — and, perhaps more importantly, less information is lost and less corruption occurs. Of the file systems listed previously all support journaling, except ext2. Because of this limitation, I would recommend that you not use ext2 in production.

Two other characteristics of file systems that are important to database administrators is the ability to work with large file sizes and to provide support for a large number of directories and files. Except for ext2, all the preceding file systems provide journaling capabilities plus support for larger files and more files per directory.

Two other characteristics of file systems that are important to database administrators is the ability to support large file sizes and large numbers of files and directories.

Buffers

Buffers are areas of system memory that are allocated for use to speed up program and system processes. File system buffers are an example of this, where the server buffers information read from the hard drives because it is significantly faster to read information from system memory than from hard drives. If the data is stored in the file system buffer, then the next time it is needed it is retrieved from the buffer.

While the operating system can have buffering, so can individual applications. For example, mysqld has multiple buffers and can be configured to create a buffer for data and indexes from InnoDB tables (the Innodb buffer pool). MyISAM can buffer indexed fields in the MyISAM key buffer.

As previously stated, the goal of buffering is to increase the performance of programs and the overall system. However, there are situations where performance is actually decreased. This happens when a situation called *double-buffering* occurs. For example, if you are running mysqld on a Linux server, you have no control over the file system buffer (Linux manages it completely independently of the user). If you are using primarily InnoDB tables, you can configure a large InnoDB buffer. However, before the data gets into the Innodb buffer it may be stored in the file system buffer. Hence you have the same data stored in two buffers, and this is going to cause performance degradation.

With Linux the only way to resolve this is to use what is called direct I/O. Direct I/O bypasses the file system buffer and relies on the daemon to provide any needed buffering. As the database administrator you can control the InnoDB buffer. Better performance and more efficient use of resources is typically achieved this way.

Kernel parameters

The *kernel* of the operating system provides the fundamental components needed for the server to function. With Unix-based systems there are sometimes optimizations to be made by changing various parameter values for optimizations for your specific configuration.

Linux

There are several areas of possible optimizations with the kernels running the various Linux distributions.

Open files limit

When running mysqld on busy Linux-based operating systems it is often necessary to raise the number of allowable open files. This is a *per-process* limit, meaning that this value is how many files are allowed to be open by a single process, not all processes. However, recall that mysqld runs in a single process. In addition, reading table structures, data and indexes all require opening files.

With Red Hat-based systems the value of the open files limit is set in the file /etc/security/ limits.conf, which looks similar to this:

```
# /etc/security/limits.conf
#
#Each line describes a limit for a user in the form:
#
#<domain>        <type>   <item>        <value>
#

#*              soft     core          0
#*              hard     rss           10000
#@student       hard     nproc         20
#@faculty       soft     nproc         20
```

```
#@faculty        hard     nproc        50
#ftp             hard     nproc        0
#@student        -        maxlogins    4
```

```
# End of file
```

To set a maximum of 4096 open files for the `mysql` user add this line:

```
Mysql      hard     nofile      4096
```

This assumes that `mysqld` runs under the `mysql` user. While 4096 open files might seem like a lot, consider that every connection is going to have several open files.

As an alternative, you can use the `open_files_limit=num` in the `[mysqld_safe]` directive of the configuration file (for this example, `num` would be 4096). If this option is present, then `mysqld_safe` executes the `ulimit` command during startup, which accomplishes the same thing as the previous example. The `open_files_limit` should be used in Linux only.

I/O schedulers

One area of possible optimization is the I/O scheduler. As the name implies the I/O scheduler is what determines how the server manages I/O. In older versions of Linux (kernel version 2.4), there was only one I/O scheduler, the Linux Elevator. Whimsical name aside, it was a fairly simple I/O scheduler that could easily *starve* a process waiting for an I/O resource. The new 2.6 kernel has introduced four schedulers:

- Deadline I/O scheduler
- Anticipatory I/O scheduler
- CFQ (Completely Fair Queuing) scheduler (default scheduler after kernel version 2.6.18)
- Noop scheduler

There is no strong evidence that supports that you should definitely use one scheduler over another. If you have time, benchmark your application with the different schedulers and determine which one is best for your needs. If you have a good quality RAID controller, it very likely might be best to use the noop scheduler. As always, test this in your environment.

If you want to change your scheduler, it is fairly easy. It can be configured differently for each drive (or RAID arrays of drives that appear as a single drive). Assuming that your disk name is `/dev/sda`:

```
shell> cat /sys/block/sda/queue/scheduler
```

Your output should look like this:

```
noop anticipatory deadline [cfq]
```

To set new scheduler temporarily, type the command as follows:

```
shell> echo noop > /sys/block/had/queue/scheduler
```

This would set noop as the scheduler for the /dev/sda drive. If you decide to use a different scheduler all the time, you could add the appropriate echo statement to the /etc/rc.d/rc.local file.

Swap memory

The kernel uses heuristics to determine which pages of memory are most likely to be needed in the near future. The kernel then tries to keep those pages in memory, regardless of whether they belong to processes or kernel caches. It is normal for the kernel to swap out process memory even when there is plenty of cache memory that could be easily freed.

For most applications, this approach makes sense. Parts of a memory-hungry process are better off being pushed out to disk, leaving more memory to be used for file system caches.

However, for a database application like mysqld, this favoring of file system caches can be bad. When mysqld loads the contents of a file on disk into a buffer, it is making the assumption that this will be in memory. If the buffer is swapped out by the operating system, it makes more sense for mysqld to use smaller buffers in the first place. These heuristics can be tuned by changing the vm.swappiness parameter of the sysctl command, which is used to modify kernel parameters. The default value of 60 is reasonable for most workloads. When you increase this value it will make the system more inclined to swap which is not a good practice for database severs.

Decreasing this value will make the system less inclined to swap, and may improve server responsiveness. Often mysqld benefits from smaller values.

Configuring the parameter is very easy. To set the vm.swappiness parameter to 50:

```
shell> echo '50'> /proc/sys/vm/swappiness
```

This sets it to 50. To make this setting change permanent, you need to add a line to the /etc/sysctl.conf file:

```
vm.swappiness = 50
```

Tuning vm.swappiness may hurt performance. Different workloads might behave differently. Changes to this parameter should only be made in small increments and it should be bench-marked under the same conditions that the system normally operates. Do not be afraid to experiment. Some places even set this parameter to 0. This doesn't actually disable swapping, just the conditions under which swapping occurs.

Other daemons

If performance and stability of mysqld is very important, you should not run other daemons on the same server. With small setups, it is quite common to see the Apache web server (httpd) and mysqld running on the same host server. If this is the case, then both daemons are going to be competing for CPU, I/O, memory and disk scheduling resources. Both daemons will suffer. In addition to performance problems, if a daemon crashes, it can often cause problems with other daemons running on the server. Finally, more daemons mean more potential security holes.

If you must run multiple daemons, very careful monitoring is needed. Chapter 19 discusses the system-monitoring options commonly available and in use.

Often with a server installation there will be many small programs that are running continuously but often are not necessary. Just as with the larger programs such as Apache, these programs are going to be competing for the same server resources as mysqld. If it is not needed and can be turned off, then it should be! Unfortunately, these programs are going to vary from operating system to operating system and even version to version so much that there is no way to provide a definitive list of programs you should shut down. As a brief example, the X Windows program provides for the foundation of graphical interfaces on Unix-based systems. It is not required for a mysqld installation and yet is still installed on servers quite often. If it is not needed and can be removed — remove it (very carefully).

Tuning MySQL Server

Having a properly configured operating system is important to optimal performance. However, it is only half of the performance equation. The other half is mysqld itself. Tuning mysqld requires an understanding of how to use the mysqld status variables to determine values for system variables, which are set in the configuration file. In this section, we will spend a great deal of time covering the variables that affect performance.

Status variables

You can use the SHOW STATUS command to see the values of over 250+ status variables. Because of the number of status variables, it is useful to use the LIKE clause to show a subset of the entire list. With the SHOW STATUS command, you can specify either GLOBAL or SESSION modifiers.

> **TIP**   By default, SHOW STATUS will show SESSION variables. This may or may not be your intention, so to avoid confusion, always specify GLOBAL or SESSION as a keyword.

With the GLOBAL modifier SHOW STATUS shows the status for all connections to the server. With the SESSION modifier it shows the status for the current connection. If neither is specified it show the session status. As an example, here are the statistics of the temporary table creation on a busy server:

```
mysql> SHOW GLOBAL STATUS LIKE '%tmp%';
+------------------------+---------+
| Variable_name          | Value   |
+------------------------+---------+
| Created_tmp_disk_tables | 2744623 |
| Created_tmp_files      | 147344  |
| Created_tmp_tables     | 5003238 |
+------------------------+---------+
3 rows in set (0.03 sec)
```

These values show that a total of 5,003,238 temporary tables were created. Of those created, 2,744,623 were written to disk. This is a 54 percent conversion ratio of in memory tables to disk-based tables which is not good. Increasing the amount of memory that can be allocated for in-memory temporary tables should help lower this ratio. We will cover how this is done later in the chapter.

System variables

The SHOW VARIABLES can be used to determine the values of system variables. This is a very useful command when tuning a server. As with the SHOW STATUS command, it can use the LIKE modifier, and you should always specify GLOBAL or SESSION to avoid possible confusion. If you wanted to see the global settings for temporary tables:

```
mysql> SHOW GLOBAL VARIABLES LIKE '%tmp\_%';
+--------------------+----------+
| Variable_name      | Value    |
+--------------------+----------+
| max_tmp_tables     | 32       |
| tmp_table_size     | 33554432 |
+--------------------+----------+
2 rows in set (0.00 sec)
```

In this case, the temporary table size (the lower of tmp_table_size and max_tmp_tables) is set to 32 Mb — unfortunately, tmp_table_size is specified in bytes and max_tmp_tables is specified in megabytes, so it is difficult to compare them at a glance. Temporary tables can be created by mysqld during query execution to store intermediate results. These tables are created in memory. However, if the temporary table exceeds the size of the smaller of tmp_table_size and max_heap_table_size then the table is converted to a disk based table. Disk-based tables are also created under other circumstances, such as when a temporary table field is a BLOB or TEXT type, and when row length of greater than 8 Kb. Disk-based tables are much slower than in-memory tables.

Option file

The option file (also known as the configuration file, my.cnf, and on Windows, my.ini) is used manage the configuration of mysqld. Though static server variables can be set when starting mysqld from the operating system command line (mysqld --variable=value), and dynamic server variables can be set using a database command (SET GLOBAL VARIABLE=value), being able to save options to a file is much easier.

The server variable settings (options) in the configuration file can play a crucial role in the performance of your server. The proper setting here in tandem with the proper hardware choices will make a difference in what your server is capable of doing.

The configuration file supports options for multiple programs. Each program has its own *directive*, which is a keyword in square brackets, such as [mysqld] or [client]. Here is a sample configuration file from a production system:

```
# The following options will be passed to all MySQL clients
[client]
port            = 3306
socket          = /var/lib/mysql/mysql.sock


[mysqld]
#this will prevent mysql from starting
port            = 3306
socket          = /var/lib/mysql/mysql.sock
datadir         =/var/lib/mysql
log_slow_queries = /var/log/mysql/mysqld_slow-queries.log
long_query_time = 4

max_connections=200
max_connect_errors = 400
wait_timeout=7200
connect_timeout=10
key_buffer = 512M
tmp_table_size = 32M
max_heap_table_size = 32M
max_allowed_packet = 32M
table_cache = 1800
join_buffer_size = 8M
sort_buffer_size = 16M
read_buffer_size = 8M
read_rnd_buffer_size = 524288
myisam_sort_buffer_size = 256M
thread_cache_size = 384
bulk_insert_buffer_size = 8M
query_cache_limit = 4M
query_cache_size = 128M
query_cache_type = 1
```

```
query_prealloc_size = 65536
query_alloc_block_size = 131072
# Try number of CPU's*2 for thread_concurrency
thread_concurrency = 4

#innodb configuration

innodb_data_home_dir    = /mysql/data
innodb_data_file_path=ibdata1:200M:autoextend
innodb_log_group_home_dir = /mysql/data/data
innodb_log_arch_dir     = /mysql/data/data
innodb_buffer_pool_size = 24576M
innodb_additional_mem_pool_size = 32M
innodb_log_file_size    = 1024M
innodb_log_files_in_group = 2
innodb_log_buffer_size  = 16M
innodb_flush_log_at_trx_commit = 1
innodb_lock_wait_timeout = 120
sync-binlog             = 1
innodb_support_xa       = 0
innodb_thread_concurrency = 128
innodb_file_per_table


# binary logging is required for replication
log-bin=mysql-bin
max_binlog_size = 1024M
server-id       = 4
slave-skip-errors = 1062
expire-logs-days = 7

[mysqldump]
quick
max_allowed_packet = 16M

[mysql.server]
user=mysql
group=mysql
basedir=/var/lib

[mysqld_safe]
nice = -5
open_files_limit = 8192
log-error=/var/log/mysql/mysqld.log
pid-file=/var/run/mysqld/mysqld.pid
```

With so many settings in several directives, it is necessary to store the configuration in a file instead of typing the options in all the time. We cover the more important options related to performance in the following sections. If you need to look up other variables the MySQL manual page, located at `http://dev.mysql.com/doc/refman/6.0/en/server-system-variables.html`, is a great place to start.

There are a number of configuration values in your option file that you can change and potentially affect the performance of `mysqld`. In each of the following sections, we will cover a related group of variables.

Overall mysqld options

There are several options that relate to the overall MySQL Server, not just a particular storage engine or feature. Table 10-2 lists the configuration options that relate to `mysqld` itself.

TABLE 10-2

Overall MySQL Server Options

Option Name	Global or Session	Purpose
memlock	Global	Locks the `mysqld` daemon into server memory. While this can improve performance if the server runs out of RAM, the `mysqld` daemon will crash.
sort_buffer_size = buffer_size	Session	Determines the amount of system memory allocated for SQL sorts. If this size is exceeded, the server will use hard drive space for sorting data.
thread_cache_size = num_of_threads	Global	`mysqld` creates a cache of unused connection threads rather than destroying threads and creating new ones as need.
thread_concurrency = N	Global	Only use on Solaris systems. This should typically be set to twice the number of CPUs. It should be tested carefully before using in production.
tmp_table_size	Global	Both this and the `max_heap_table_size` setting are used to determine the maximum size allowed of an in-memory temporary table before it is converted to a MyISAM table. The smallest value for these two settings is the one utilized.

The `memlock` option can provide a performance boost, but potentially creates instability. Because of this the database administrator needs to be very careful with `memlock`. The `memlock` option locks `mysqld` into system memory. If this option is used, `mysqld` cannot be stored into swap space. This is where the performance benefits come from. However, if for some reason the server were to run out of memory and `mysqld` did not have enough memory to operate, it would crash and potentially corrupt data.

MyISAM storage engine options

The MyISAM engine is one of the oldest storage engines, introduced in version 3.2. Even so, it is still in use by many production servers. Table 10-3 lists the configuration options for MyISAM.

TABLE 10-3

MyISAM Configuration Options

Option Name	Purpose
`concurrent_inserts = {0	1	2}`	Allows for inserts into MyISAM tables without blocking reads.
`delayed_key_write = {OFF	ON	ALL}`	Delays flushing to disk for index changes to batch the changes for greater performance.
`key_buffer = buffer_size`	This configures the size of the MyISAM index buffer.

These three server variables are `GLOBAL` in scope.

The `concurrent_inserts` server variable defaults to a setting of 1. With this setting, if there are any deleted rows in the data file that space is filled. Only if there are no deleted rows are inserts allowed to be added while reads occur at the same time. With a setting of 2, MyISAM operates slightly differently. If no selects are occurring the empty space in the data file is filled. If there are any reads, then the inserts are written to the end of the data file at the same time. The `key_buffer` variable sets up a buffer for the MyISAM table indexes. MyISAM does not have a buffer for the data, so the only caching for data is done by the operating system buffers.

When trying to determine how much memory to allocate to the `key_buffer`, you should consider the server usage patterns. Are you using MyISAM for most tables? Do a lot of your queries use indexes? Allocate some amount of memory — say, between 10 and 20 percent of the memory available to `mysqld` — and after some actual usage, see if you need to increase or decrease the `key_buffer`.

You can monitor `key_buffer` usage by checking the *cache hit ratio* (see Chapter 12 for more information on caching). The cache hit ratio is the number of times a value in the buffer was read as a percentage of the total number of times a value in the buffer was looked for. To determine the cache hit ratio, run:

```
SHOW GLOBAL STATUS LIKE 'key_read%'
```

And use the `key_reads` and `key_read_requests` status variables in the following formula (a higher hit ratio is better):

```
hit_ratio=(key_reads/key_read_requests)*100
```

To increase the hit ratio, use the `key_buffer` option to set the `key_buffer_size` larger.

For overall MyISAM index buffer usage, you will need to determine the value of the status variable `key_blocks_unused` and the values of the system variables `key_cache_block_size` and `key_buffer size` by running:

```
SHOW GLOBAL STATUS like `key_blocks_unused`;
SHOW GLOBAL VARIABLES LIKE 'key%'
```

The algorithm for finding the overall MyISAM index buffer usage is:

- Find the size of the unused part of the index buffer (`key_blocks_unused*key_cache_block_size`).
- Divide the unused size by the total size of the index buffer (`key_buffer_size`). This is the ratio of the unused part of the index buffer as a part of a whole.
- Subtract the unused ratio from 1 to get the ratio of the used part of the index buffer.
- Multiply the used ratio by 100 to get the percentage of the index buffer that is in use.

The formula for finding the percentage of the index buffer that is in use is:

```
100* (1 - (key_blocks_unused * key_cache_block_size) / key_buffer_size)
```

From the value calculated for index buffer usage, look for at least 80 percent usage or you probably have too much memory allocated to the key buffer.

If the `delay_key_write` system variable is enabled the server will not immediately flush to disk changes to the MyISAM index buffer. Delaying the flushing operation allows for greater performance. The tradeoff is that if you enable this setting, a server crash could cause corrupted indexes on disk. The data will probably be fine, it's just the indexes that are affected. However, this index corruption may not be detectable automatically, so you need to make sure to rebuild the indexes using `myisamcheck` during server startup. The default value is `ON`, which enables delayed writing for all MyISAM tables created with the `DELAYED_KEY_WRITE` option of `CREATE TABLE`. Using the `ALL` option enables delayed writes for all MyISAM tables, and the `OFF` option disables delayed key writing.

Rebuilding indexes for MyISAM tables takes time. With very large tables it is going to take a significant amount. With the `delayed_key_write` setting, you are trading off performance for speed of recoverability and is something you should think about very carefully.

InnoDB storage engine options

InnoDB is a very widely used storage engine in production systems. There are a number of configuration options for the InnoDB engine, and Table 10-4 covers these options.

TABLE 10-4

InnoDB Configuration Options

Option Name	Purpose
innodb_buffer_pool_size = buffer_size	A static variable that specifies the size of the cache for InnoDB data and indexes.
innodb_flush_log_at_trx_ commit = number	There are three possible options {0|1|2}. This dynamic system variable manages how often the InnoDB log buffer is written (flushed) to the log file.
innodb_flush_method = IO_access_method	This static variable determines how the InnoDB storage engine interacts with the operating system with respect to I/O operations.
innodb_log_buffer_size = buffer_size	Buffer used for writes to the InnoDB logs. Unless you use very large BLOBs this static variable should not be over 8 MB, and can be set to 2 Mb.
innodb_log_file_size = log_file_size	A static variable that determines the size of each Innodb log file (ib_logfile).
innodb_log_files_in_group = number_log_files	A static variable that determines the total number of Innodb log files.
innodb_max_dirty_pages_pct= N	This dynamic variable specifies the maximum percentage of pages in the in Innodb buffer pool that can be *dirty* — that is, changed in the buffer pool in memory without being saved to disk. Defaults to 90 (%).
innodb_thread_concurrency = N	This dynamic variable determines the maximum number of system threads inside InnoDB. A good number to start is twice the number of CPUs.

All of the InnoDB server variables are GLOBAL in nature.

The single most important InnoDB configuration variable is the innodb_buffer_pool_size. Assuming the server is only running mysqld and most of your tables are InnoDB tables, the majority of your memory should be dedicated to the InnoDB buffer pool. It is safe to begin at

50–70 percent of your system memory allocated the InnoDB buffer, and adjust up or down as you need to.

If you have a large amount of RAM (16 Gb or more) on a dedicated MySQL server, then the buffer pool can be an even larger percentage of overall memory. When configuring a server, choose a starting value for the InnoDB buffer pool, set the other configuration values, then determine how much memory is still available. On Unix, the vmstat, top, and free commands show memory information. In Windows, the Task Manager can show you memory usage.

To determine if the InnoDB buffer pool is appropriately sized, run:

```
SHOW GLOBAL STATUS LIKE 'innodb_buffer_pool_pages%';
```

- Innodb_buffer_pool_pages_data is the total number of used data pages (clean and dirty).
- Innodb_buffer_pool_pages_dirty is the number of dirty data pages. The number of clean data pages can be calculated from these first two status variables.
- Innodb_buffer_pool_pages_flushed is the number of data pages that have been flushed to disk.
- Innodb_buffer_pool_pages_free is the number of unused data pages.
- Innodb_buffer_pool_pages_misc is the number of data pages used for InnoDB overhead.
- Innodb_buffer_pool_pages_total is the total number of pages.

Calculate the ratio of unused data pages to the total number of pages:

```
Innodb_buffer_pool_pages_free / Innodb_buffer_pool_pages_total
```

If the ratio is high (close to 1), then the InnoDB buffer pool is probably set too high. A less likely cause is that the innodb_max_dirty_pages_pct system variable is set too low, and dirty pages are being flushed very often, freeing up pages long before they are needed.

Conversely, if the ratio is low, the size of the InnoDB buffer pool may need to be set higher. Using the information you have about the free memory on your system, increase the InnoDB buffer pool size, restart mysqld, and continue to monitor the status variables after the newly sized InnoDB buffer pool has been used for a while. Continue the adjust-monitor-adjust cycle, and once your system is at the right level, continue to monitor levels, making sure to check performance once every month or two.

Make sure to always leave a buffer of a half-gigabyte or so of memory because mysqld performs very poorly when it is forced to use swap space. Keep in mind that under high load, mysqld will use more memory.

The `innodb_flush_log_at_trx_commit` system variable is used to manage how often the InnoDB log buffer sends writes to the InnoDB log. When this parameter is set to 0, the log buffer is written every second and the logs file flushes to disk. When this value is 1 (the default), every commit will make the log buffer write to the log file. The log file is flushed to disk on each commit as well. This is required for ACID compliance. For more information on ACID compliance and transactions, see Chapter 9.

When set to 2, every commit makes the log buffer write to the file, just as when the value is 1. However, the log file flushes to disk every second, just as when the value is 0. Setting this variable to 0 or 2 changes the database to no longer be ACID–compliant — it does not meet the requirements for durability. Because of the log file flushing being different from the transaction commit, it is possible that a crash could lose a second of transactions (actually, slightly more than a second, because of process-scheduling issues). When the variable is set to 0, a crash of `mysqld` or the operating system may cause this lack of durability; when this variable is set to 2, only an operating system crash may cause this lack of durability.

Note that many operating systems and some disk hardware tell `mysqld` that the flush has taken place even though a flush has not happened. In these cases, the durability requirement of ACID compliance not met, regardless of the value of `innodb_flush_log_at_trx_commit`. A crash (for example, due to a power outage) can even corrupt the InnoDB database. Using a battery-backed disk cache in the disk or disk controller will protect against this scenario, and regular file flushes will be faster, too.

The `innodb_flush_method` variable has three possible values:

- `fsync` is the default option and uses the `fsync()` system call to flush both data and log files.
- `O_DIRECT` will bypass the operating system cache for both reads and writes of data and log files.
- `O_SYNC` uses the `fsync()` system call for data files but for log files uses `O_SYNC`.

There are many times when using `O_DIRECT` will significantly improve performance of `mysqld`. This is because it removes the buffering of the operating system. Do not use `O_DIRECT` without using a RAID controller that has a battery backed write cache. This can overcome problems because of operating system crashes that otherwise do not complete a write to the hard drives. In addition, you should enable what is called writeback on the cache. When the server sends data to be flushed to the RAID controller, the controller immediately tells the server the flush is complete. The server considers it committed and is free to do other task. The RAID controller then flushes the writes stored in the cache periodically. This batches the writes and makes them more efficient.

If you are considering using `O_DIRECT`, carefully test your setup to make sure you are getting the best performance possible. With some configurations using `O_DIRECT` can actually impede performance so be careful!

Using O_SYNC is usually a slower alternative than using O_DIRECT, but there are some edge cases where it can prove to be faster. As with O_DIRECT, it is important that you test your setup to see if server performance benefits.

On very write-intensive systems a performance boost can be found by creating larger InnoDB log files. The reason why is that the larger the size of the log file, the less checkpoint flush activity, which saves disk I/O. However, the larger your log files are the longer the recovery time will be after a crash. The default size for the InnoDB log files is only 5 MB. Even with 64-MB log files you should have recovery times under a minute. The maximum size is 4 GB for all the InnoDB log files. It is very common to set these to between 128 and 256 MB. See tip for how to change the InnoDB log file size.

To change the size of your InnoDB log files:

- Shut down mysqld.
- Edit the configuration file, setting a new log file size with the innodb_log_file_size option.
- Move the existing InnoDB log files to a backup location.
- Start mysqld.
- Verify that the new log files are the correct size.
- The previous InnoDB log files can be deleted.

The innodb_max_dirty_pages_pct server variable sets the percentage of pages allowed to be changed ("marked dirty") before a flush to disk is performed. A page in this context is a fixed amount of system memory. With the InnoDB storage engine a page is 16k in size. Allowing a higher percentage of dirty pages before a disk flush could increase performance. The default is 90 percent.

Falcon storage engine options

The new Falcon storage engine is designed to utilize large amount of memory to increase performance. Table 10-5 shows the configuration option that will affect performance on your server.

TABLE 10-5

Falcon Configuration Options

Option Name	Purpose
falcon_record_memory_max=buffer_size	Sets the maximum size of the data cache

The falcon_record_memory_max variable is used to determine the size of the buffer used for the Falcon storage engine. If your server is only using Falcon tables then this should be set to use most of the available memory (much like the previous suggestions for the InnoDB buffer pool).

Maria storage engine options

The Maria storage engine is designed to be a replacement for MyISAM. It has many similar characteristics to MyISAM but includes transactional support and automatic crash recovery. Table 10-6 shows the configuration option that affects performance for the Maria storage engine.

TABLE 10-6

Maria Configuration Options

Option Name	Purpose
maria_pagecache_buffer_size	Configures the cache size for data and index pages. This is similar to the InnoDB buffer pool.

If you are using a large number of Maria tables you should increase the buffer size. By default it is only 8 MB.

Query cache options

Effectively utilizing the query cache can significantly improve the performance of mysqld. The query cache is covered in great detail in Chapter 12, including explanations of the options and how to tune the query cache.

Dynamic variables

So far, we have been discussing how to change your system variables by modifying the configuration file. While changing the option file is necessary for a change that will persist across mysqld restarts, there are times when you do not want to restart mysqld to change a system variable — perhaps you are testing and only want to set a variable temporarily.

However, it is possible to dynamically change many of the server variables. For example, the variables relating to query cache setup and management can be changed without a server restart. However, the innodb_buffer_pool_size variable cannot be changed dynamically and requires a server restart with the option specified. Session variables, by their nature, are always dynamic, as they are set per session.

WARNING If you make a change to a dynamic variable while it is running, do not forget to change your configuration file or the next time you restart the server you may have an unexplained performance drop, or other behavior revert to an unpleasant state.

The MySQL manual maintains a list of `mysqld` system variables, their scope (`GLOBAL` or `SESSION`), and if they are dynamic or static. The web page for version 6.0 is:

```
http://dev.mysql.com/doc/refman/6.0/en/server-system-variables.html
```

Similarly, the MySQL manual page for status variables, which can be used for monitoring performance, is located at:

```
http://dev.mysql.com/doc/refman/6.0/en/server-status-variables.html
```

To access information for other release series (5.1, for example), just replace the 6.0 in the above address with the release series. If a system variable can be changed dynamically it is modified using the `SET GLOBAL`, `SET SESSION`, `SELECT @@global` or `SELECT @@session` command. Recall our previous example of the `SHOW GLOBAL STATUS` command and the temporary tables for the server with a 54 percent conversion ratio of in-memory temporary tables to on-disk temporary tables. To see the current maximum temporary table size, use the following `SHOW VARIABLES` command:

```
mysql> SHOW GLOBAL VARIABLES LIKE '%tmp%';
+-------------------+----------+
| Variable_name     | Value    |
+-------------------+----------+
| max_tmp_tables    | 32       |
| slave_load_tmpdir | /tmp/    |
| tmp_table_size    | 33554432 |
| tmpdir            | /tmp     |
+-------------------+----------+
4 rows in set (0.00 sec)
```

This shows a current setting of 32 MB. To increase this to 48 MB, we issue either of the following commands:

```
mysql> SET GLOBAL max_tmp_tables=48;
Query OK, 0 rows affected (0.00 sec)

mysql> SET @@global.max_tmp_tables=48;
Query OK, 0 rows affected (0.00 sec)
```

After some time, recalculate the conversion ratio to see if the change is helping. Of course, once a final decision is made on the size allowed for temporary tables, edit the configuration file and set the new value to persist when `mysqld` restarts.

SUMMARY

This chapter covers a great deal of information. While there is not enough space to cover every part of server tuning you should understand the basics of tuning the hardware, operating system, and `mysqld`.

Topics covered included:

- Choosing the best hardware
    - CPU choice
    - Memory
    - Disk storage
- Operating system tuning
    - Choosing an operating system
    - File system tuning
- Tuning `mysqld`
    - The configuration file
    - Storage engine configuration
    - Dynamic variables

## Chapter 11

Storage Engines

The storage engines of MySQL are one of the most unique features of the server. Approximately twenty major storage engines are currently available, and though they allow for the ultimate flexibility when working with your data, this diversity can be intimidating to the beginning or even intermediate level database administrator. Most database administrators regularly work with two storage engines, MyISAM and InnoDB, and may use others in a handful of projects.

Understanding Storage Engines

A *storage engine* is a subsystem that manages tables. Most database management systems have one subsystem to manage tables; MySQL Server can use different subsystems. Because a storage engine is applied at the table level, it is sometimes called *table type*. CREATE TABLE and ALTER TABLE statements can use the ENGINE option to set (or change) the storage engine that is associated with the table.

The MySQL *pluggable storage engine* is an architectural design that separates the code that manages the tables from the database server core code. This core code manages the components such as the query cache, the optimizer, and the connection handler. The storage engine code handles the actual I/O of the table. This separation of code allows for multiple storage engines to be used by the same core server. Once you have the ability to have multiple storage engines at the same time, the database administrator can choose a storage engine based on its ability to meet the requirements of an application. This is vastly different from most other database management systems, where there is no choice.

Though each storage engine handles its own I/O, `mysqld` requires a table format file for each file. These files have an `.frm` extension.

Having different storage engines allows MySQL to have many different features, and many storage engines are produced by third-party companies. InnoDB, the most frequently used transactional storage engine, is actually produced by a different company. This means that people can develop storage engines that meet their own needs, without having to wait for a feature to be released.

Storage engines as plugins

Even though the name implies that storage engines are easily added and removed from MySQL, it was only starting in MySQL Server version 5.1 that storage engines have been able to be plugins. The *pluggable* part of pluggable storage engines reflects the separation of code, not the nature of how to add a storage engine (compiled-in vs. plugin).

Innobase Oy, the company that created the InnoDB storage engine (`www.innodb.com`), has a plugin version of its storage engine. This plugin includes several features not available in the compiled-in InnoDB that ships with MySQL, including:

- Ability to `ADD` or `DROP` indexes (except primary keys) without requiring a table copy
- On-the-fly compression and decompression of table data
- New tables in the `information_schema` database

Another storage engine that uses the same plugin methodology is the PBXT engine developed by PrimeBase Technologies (`www.primebase.org`). The benefit to this architecture is immediately obvious; the release cycle of the storage engine plugin can be completely independent from the server. Neither Innobase nor Primebase Technologies have to wait for Sun Microsystems to release a new version of MySQL Server for a bug fix or a feature addition to either storage engine. A new version of the storage engine plugin can be released at any time and an administrator can upgrade just that one component.

One example of how this is beneficial is that beginning with version 5.1, MySQL Server allows a storage engine to be able to create or drop indexes without copying the contents of the entire table. However, a storage engine has to write the code to implement this functionality. The InnoDB storage engine integrated into MySQL Server version 5.1 does not take advantage of this capability. With the InnoDB plugin, however, users can add and drop non-primary indexes much more efficiently than with prior releases. Using the plugin, a database administrator can upgrade the plugin instead of the entire MySQL Server, and have this functionality.

Storage engine comparison

You can easily use multiple storage engines in a single application. This ability to use multiple storage engines can lead to optimal results for the application. This is because different parts of the application will have different requirements. One storage engine cannot be a perfect fit for every situation. Using multiple storage engines allows you to fit the storage engine to the requirements of any particular area of the application.

What are some of these features and abilities that make one storage engine different from another?

- **Transaction support** — Support of transactions requires more overhead in terms of memory, storage space, and CPU usage. Every application does not require transactions and using a non-transactional storage engine can be faster in some cases.

- **Table-level features** — MySQL provides a handler for tables to have a `CHECKSUM` attribute, which can be seen in the `TABLES` system view in the `INFORMATION_SCHEMA` database. Whether or not the table has a value for `CHECKSUM` depends on the storage engine — only MyISAM currently handles the `CHECKSUM` attribute.

- **Locking** — MySQL Server supports the ability to lock an entire table. However, storage engines can implement their own locking methods, to be able to lock at more granular levels, such as locking a set of rows. Further locking granularity implemented by the designers of the storage engine helps determine the amount of overhead, the overall speed, the possibility for lock contention, and the ability to support higher concurrency workloads.

- **Index implementation** — Different applications can benefit from different index implementation strategies. Several common methods of implementing indexing exist and the designers of each storage engine choose the one they think will perform best in their targeted situation.

- **Foreign keys** — Using foreign keys to enforce relational integrity among tables is quite common. However, not every application needs foreign keys and many storage engines do not support them.

- **Buffering** — Data, index, and log buffers are handled by storage engines. Some choose not to implement buffering in some areas at all, and others can allow multiple buffers. For example, MyISAM does not have a buffer for data, but supports multiple buffers for indexes.

- **File storage** — Some storage engines store their data and indexes in self-contained files, meaning that a table can be copied by copying the files. Other storage engines use centralized metadata, and thus a table cannot be copied simply by copying the data and index files.

- **Backup** — Some storage engines have tools to allow consistent, non-blocking backups to be taken, whereas others will cause application disruption if a backup is run while the table is in use by the application.

Table 11-1 provides a summary table of some of the more common storage engines with their higher-level features.

Because you have such flexibility and choice with MySQL Server, you should carefully weigh your application's requirements before selecting a particular storage engine for use. Though it is easy to change the storage engine that handles a table, the entire table must be rebuilt, which can take a long time for large tables.

TABLE 11-1

MySQL Server Storage Engine Overview

Storage Engine	Transactional Support	Locking Level	Online Non-blocking Backup	Server Version(s) Available
MyISAM / Merge	No	Table	No	5.1, 6.0
InnoDB	Yes	Row	Yes	5.1, 6.0
MEMORY	No	Table	No	5.1, 6.0
Maria	Yes	Row	No	5.1, 6.0
Falcon	Yes	Row	Yes	6.0
PBXT	Yes	Row	Yes	5.1, 6.0
FEDERATED	No	Not applicable	Not applicable	5.1, 6.0
NDB	Yes	Row	Yes	5.1 up to 5.1.24; After that, available in MySQL Cluster
Archive	No	Row	No	5.1, 6.0
Blackhole	No	Not applicable	Not applicable	5.1, 6.0
CSV	No	Table	No	5.1, 6.0

Using Different Storage Engines

Now that we have covered the basics of the storage engines, it is time to cover in some depth the most used storage engines available. This will give you a good idea of which storage engine might be best for your application and how to best utilize the storage engine you choose.

 The default storage engine for mysqld is MyISAM. To change this, set the default_storage_engine option in the configuration file. For example:

```
default_storage_engine=InnoDB
```

MyISAM storage engine

MyISAM is the default storage engine in mysqld, and is the storage engine used by the system tables. It has been a reliable storage engine for MySQL Server since MySQL Server version 3.2, replacing the original ISAM engine. It is non-transactional and does not implement additional locking mechanisms. MyISAM depends on the global table-level locking in MySQL, but because it has very little overhead can be quite fast for reads. However, a large number of concurrent writes to a MyISAM table can be problematic. If your application has a lot of write activity, the writes will end up blocking the reads and your database server might exhibit a high number of connections to the server as SELECT statements are blocked waiting for any write threads to complete. If your application has this problem you should consider using a storage engine such as InnoDB or Falcon that locks at the row level instead of the table level.

One method of reducing the contention between reads and writes to a MyISAM table is allowing what are called *concurrent inserts*. Concurrent inserts allow more than one insert at a time to be added at the end of a table. The concurrent_insert option to mysqld defaults to 1, meaning that inserts are allowed at the same time as reads if there are no data gaps caused by UPDATE or DELETE statements. A value of 2 indicates that inserts are allowed regardless of data gaps, and a value of 0 means concurrent inserts are not allowed.

There are three files on disk that represent a MyISAM table. Those three files have the table name and an extension, where the extension is either frm for the table format file, MYD for the data file, or MYI for the index file. A nice feature of MyISAM tables is that the three files compromising a table are the entire table. This means they can be copied without any problem from the server to a backup location for a raw backup or even directly to another server for use on a new server. There are two stipulations. The first problem is that the tables should not be written to when the files are copied off or there is a possibility of corruption. This can be accomplished with a read lock or by shutting down mysqld.

The second problem is that the target server must be of the same *endian* format as the source server. This simply means that the servers use the same byte order. There are two endian formats — little endian and big endian. As an example, you cannot copy MyISAM tables from an x86 or x86_64 server to a SPARC server, because they do not have the same endian format. However, you could copy from an x86-based Linux server to a Windows-based server, because they use the same endian format.

Feature summary:

- Non-transactional
- No foreign key support
- FULLTEXT indexes for text matching
- No data cache
- Index caches — can be specified by name
- Implements both HASH and BTREE indexes (BTREE by default; see Chapter 6 for more information about indexes)
- Table-level locking
- Very fast read activity, suitable for data warehouses
- Compressed data (with myisampack)
- Online backup with mysqlhotcopy (see Chapter 13)
- Maximum of 64 indexes per table

MyISAM configuration options

A number of my.cnf configuration options are used for MyISAM tables. Table 11-2 lists the common configuration options for MyISAM tables.

TABLE 11-2

MyISAM Configuration Options

Configuration Option	Description
key_buffer_size	Determines the size of the memory cache used for storing MyISAM indexes. MyISAM depends on the operating system to cache MyISAM data. The default is 8 Mb, and the maximum is 4 Gb.
concurrent_insert	Determines the behavior of concurrent inserts. Concurrent inserts in tables with no data gaps are enabled (set to 1) by default. A setting of 0 disables concurrent inserts and a setting of 2 allows concurrent inserts for tables with data gaps.
delay_key_write	Delays updating indexes for MyISAM tables until tables are closed. This will provide a boost in performance but tables will be corrupted if mysqld crashes. The default is ON, which means that MyISAM tables that have the DELAY_KEY_WRITE option defined (in a CREATE TABLE or ALTER TABLE statement) will delay index updates. Other values are OFF, disabling delayed index writes entirely, and ALL, which will make all MyISAM tables delay index writes.
max_write_lock_count	Determines how many writes to a table take precedence over reads. This could resolve issues with read starvation if there are constant writes to a table. This works with storage engines that use table-level locking so it applies to both MyISAM and MEMORY tables. The default is 4294967295 (which is the maximum), to give high precedence to writes. See Chapter 4 for more information on the HIGH_PRIORITY and LOW_PRIORITY options to queries, and Chapter 9 for an explanation of locking precedence.
preload_buffer_size	Determines the size of the buffer used for index preloading of the key cache. The default size is 32 Kb.

MyISAM utilities

Three utility programs are designed for working with MyISAM tables:

- myisamchk — Used to analyze, optimize, and repair MyISAM tables.
- myisampack — Used to create compressed, read-only MyISAM tables.
- myisam_ftdump — Used to display information about fulltext fields in MyISAM tables.

Each of these programs provides for specific uses. Each program must be run locally on the server where the MyISAM tables are located.

myisamchk

The myisamchk program has four different modes of operation. It can be used to analyze, optimize, check, and repair MyISAM tables. The default mode of operation is the check mode where it checks for possible corruption. Though you can specify a specify table, the myisamchk program also works with wildcard conditions. This makes it easy to have it check all tables in a database. The following command will check all the MyISAM tables in the mysql database:

```
$ myisamchk /var/lib/mysql/mysql*.MYI
Checking MyISAM file: columns_priv.MYI
Data records:         0   Deleted blocks:        0
- check file-size
- check record delete-chain
- check key delete-chain
- check index reference
- check data record references index: 1

---------

Checking MyISAM file: db.MYI
Data records:         0   Deleted blocks:        2
- check file-size
- check record delete-chain
- check key delete-chain
- check index reference
- check data record references index: 1
- check data record references index: 2
```

The output is too long to include all of it here, but you can see what is happening. The utility actually checks the index files of the MyISAM tables. If it had returned that one of the tables needed repair you could just run:

```
$ myisamchk -r /var/lib/mysql/mysql/table_name.MYI
```

WARNING When running myisamchk you must manually block all access to the tables being checked. Otherwise, corruption could occur. The easiest and best way to accomplish this is simply to shut down mysqld. If you need to check tables while mysqld is running, consider using the CHECK TABLE command as described in Chapter 4.

myisampack

Using myisampack to create compressed read-only versions of tables can provide for a good performance increase for data that is no longer being updated but still needs to be accessed. As with myisamchk, it is best to stop the database server before running, although ensuring the tables are not written to (for example, doing a FLUSH TABLES WITH READ LOCK) is another way to avoid corruption.

Though the Archive storage engine has better compression than read-only MyISAM tables, the Archive storage engine can support only one index. A compressed MyISAM table is read-only, and cannot have new rows inserted like an Archive table can.

The basic running of myisampack is very simple. In the data directory of the database the table is in, run:

```
shell> myisampack table_name.MYI
```

Remember to specify the MyISAM index file (.MYI) of the table you are compressing.

Once the compression is done you have to run the myisamchk program to rebuild indexes. For optimal performance you can also sort the index block and analyze the table to help the optimizer work better:

```
shell> myisamchk --rq --sort-index -analyze
    table_name_MYI
```

If the compression process was done while the server is online, release any read locks on the table and issue a FLUSH TABLES command to force mysqld to recognize and begin using the new table. If mysqld was shut down, restart it.

Additional information is available on the various options in the MySQL Manual at http:// dev.mysql.com/refman/6.0/en/myisampack.html.

myisam_ftdump

The myisam_ftdump program will provide information about the FULLTEXT indexes in MyISAM tables.

When running myisam_ftdump you must specify which index you want the program to analyze. You can determine this by looking at the output of the SHOW CREATE TABLE command:

```
mysql> SHOW CREATE TABLE film_text\G
*************************** 1. row ***************************
       Table: film_text
Create Table: CREATE TABLE `film_text` (
  `film_id` smallint(6) NOT NULL,
  `title` varchar(255) NOT NULL,
  `description` text,
  PRIMARY KEY (`film_id`),
  FULLTEXT KEY `idx_title_description` (`title`,`description`)
) ENGINE=MyISAM DEFAULT CHARSET=utf8
1 row in set (0.00 sec)
```

Notice that FULLTEXT KEY is listed second, after the PRIMARY KEY. To specify the appropriate index you provide a number. The numbering begins at 0 so this text index is number 1. Now to run myisam_ftdump, change to the directory where the table files are (for example, /var/lib/mysql/sakila) and run:

```
shell> myisam_ftdump film_text 1
Total rows: 1000
Total words: 9602
Unique words: 1080
Longest word: 13 chars (administrator)
Median length: 7
Average global weight: 5.904181
Most common word: 158 times, weight: 1.673185 (boat)
```

 If you do not run myisam_ftdump **in the directory where the table files are, you will receive an error such as:**

```
got error 2
```

Additional information about myisam_ftdump is available from the MySQL Reference Manual at http://dev.mysql.com/doc/refman/6.0/en/myisam-ftdump.html.

Merge storage engine

The Merge storage engine is actually a sort of *wrapper* table that wraps around MyISAM tables with the same schemas. All the underlying tables can be queried at once by querying the Merge table. This is one way to implement partitioning; see Chapter 15 for more information on partitioning and Merge tables. Using Merge tables is one solution for typical reporting needs where you have massive tables of data.

Merge tables will use the same buffers and configuration options as for the underlying MyISAM tables so configuration options will not be covered here. Please refer to section "MyISAM Configuration Options" in this chapter for the various options available. See Chapter 15 for actual examples of CREATE TABLE statements to create Merge tables.

When you create a Merge table, two files are always created in the file system. There is one file containing the table format that has a filename of the table followed by a suffix of .frm. The second file also has a filename of the table but ends with a suffix of .MRG. This file contains the names of the underlying MyISAM tables.

After creating the Merge table, you can query the underlying individual tables or the Merge table. When a SELECT is executed against the Merge table it begins with the first table specified in the Merge table definition. Where INSERT statements occur depends on setting of the INSERT_METHOD clause, as discussed in Chapter 15.

WARNING The REPLACE statement does not work when executed against a Merge table.

The benefits of using Merge tables are better manageability of tables and better performance. When your table sizes become large your maintenance and repair operations will take a long time. Using a Merge table with smaller underlying tables not only speeds up these operations because of the smaller table size, but it will also allow you to rotate out the table from use by modifying the Merge table definition to exclude it while maintenance is occurring.

The performance benefits actually come in several ways. With Merge tables it is perfectly feasible to use compressed MyISAM tables, which leads to less use of disk space and faster searches of the tables. You can also put the individual MyISAM tables on different hard drives to help increase performance. Also, you can query individual MyISAM tables as well as the Merge table. This can sometimes provide a tremendous performance boost.

InnoDB storage engine

The most widely used transactional storage engine is the InnoDB storage engine. InnoDB brought support for foreign keys to `mysqld`.

Feature summary:

- Transactional support provided by MVCC (Multi Version Concurrency Control)
- Row-level locking
- Foreign key support
- Indexing using clustered B-tree indexes
- Configurable buffer caching of both indexes and data
- Online non-blocking backup through separate commercial backup program

InnoDB provides some scalability on up to eight CPU cores and 64 gigabytes of RAM. It supports a high level of concurrent writes and is heavily used in typical online transactional environments.

Tablespace configuration variables

With the InnoDB storage engine you have control over the format and the location of the *tablespace*. A tablespace is a logical group of one or more data files in a database. Table 11-3 lists the variables used to configure the tablespace.

The full path to each shared tablespace is formed by adding `innodb_data_home_dir` to each path specified in the `innodb_data_file_path`. The file sizes are specified in kilobytes, megabytes, or gigabytes by appending K or M or G to the size value, otherwise numbers are assumed to be in bytes. The centralized data files must add up to 10 Mb or more. A raw disk partition can be used as a shared tablespace.

By default if `innodb_data_file_path` is not defined, a 10 Mb `ibdata1` file is created in the data directory (`datadir`). The maximum size of an InnoDB shared tablespace depends on the operating system.

TABLE 11-3

Tablespace Configuration Variables

Tablespace Configuration Variable	Description
Innodb_data_file_path	Determines both the path to individual centralized data files (shared tablespace) and the size of the files.
Innodb_data_home_dir	The common part of the directory path for all InnoDB data files. If you do not explicitly set this value it will default to the MySQL data directory. You can specify the value as an empty string, in which case you must use absolute file paths in the innodb_data_file_path variable.
Innodb_file_per_table	If innodb_file_per_table is enabled, then new InnoDB tables will be using their own .ibd file for both data and indexes rather than in the shared tablespace. There is still a common tablespace used for metadata. The default is to store data and indexes in the shared tablespace.

WARNING You cannot move InnoDB table files around as you can MyISAM tables. When the innodb_file_per_table option is set, the .ibd file contains the data and indexes for an InnoDB table; however, the shared tablespace still contains metadata. Copying the .ibd file to another server will not result in actually copying the table.

Performance configuration variables

Several variables directly affect the performance of your InnoDB tables. Table 11-4 lists these variables.

A larger buffer configured by innodb_buffer_pool_size means there is less I/O needed to access data in tables. This is because the InnoDB storage engine stores your frequently used data in memory. On a dedicated database server primarily using InnoDB tables, this should be a significant percentage of the total memory available to mysqld. Be very careful with this setting because if it is configured to use too much memory it will cause swapping by the operating system, which is very bad for mysqld performance. In the worst-case scenario, using too much memory will cause mysqld to crash. See Chapter 10 for more details on tuning this parameter.

SHOW ENGINE InnoDB STATUS

The SHOW ENGINE InnoDB STATUS command can be used to provide detailed information about the workings of the InnoDB storage engine.

TABLE 11-4

InnoDB Performance Configuration Variables

Performance Configuration Variable	Description
innodb_buffer_pool_size	Determines the size of the buffer that the InnoDB storage engine uses to cache both data and indexes.
innodb_flush_log_at_trx_commit	Configures how frequently the log buffer is flushed to disk. The three valid values are 0, 1, and 2. The default value of this variable is 1. This default setting is required for ACID-compliance. See Chapter 10 for more details on this parameter.
innodb_log_file_size	Determines the size, in bytes, of each of the InnoDB log files. The default size is 5 megabytes. A larger log file means there is less disk I/O. Unfortunately, larger log files also mean that recovery is slower in the case of a server crash. In our experience, reasonable values for this range between 128 megabytes and 256 megabytes.

The following is sample output from a production server. The output has been modified to take up less space but will give you a good idea of the information available:

```
mysql> SHOW ENGINE INNODB STATUS\G
*************************** 1. row ***************************
Status:
=====================================
081124 14:47:30 INNODB MONITOR OUTPUT
=====================================
Per second averages calculated from the last 59 seconds
----------
SEMAPHORES
----------
OS WAIT ARRAY INFO: reservation count 56930532, signal count 48711739
Mutex spin waits 0, rounds 2643139276, OS waits 43490665
RW-shared spins 22064383, OS waits 6936948; RW-excl spins 21037008,
   OS waits 1461843
------------------------
LATEST FOREIGN KEY ERROR
------------------------
081124 12:08:15 Transaction:
TRANSACTION 1 2114794386, ACTIVE 0 sec, process no 30716, OS thread
   id 1349732704 inserting, thread declared inside InnoDB 500
mysql tables in use 1, locked 1
4 lock struct(s), heap size 368, undo log entries 1
```

```
MySQL thread id 335227181, query id 1962772590 172.17.0.66 db1user
    update
insert into mm.cc_transaction (
member_id,
product_id,
wallet_id

{cut for brevity}


------------
TRANSACTIONS
------------
Trx id counter 1 2117126607
Purge done for trx's n:o < 1 2117125779 undo n:o < 0 0
History list length 40
Total number of lock structs in row lock hash table 0
LIST OF TRANSACTIONS FOR EACH SESSION:
---TRANSACTION 1 2117126606, not started, process no 30716, OS thread
    id 1195391328
MySQL thread id 336895572, query id 1972768750 172.17.0.67 db1user
---TRANSACTION 1 2117126605, not started, process no 30716, OS thread
    id 1175120224
MySQL thread id 336895571, query id 1972768749 172.17.0.66 db1user
---TRANSACTION 1 2117126604, not started, process no 30716, OS thread
    id 1179134304
MySQL thread id 336895567, query id 1972768746 172.17.1.71 db1user
---TRANSACTION 1 2117126602, not started, process no 30716, OS thread
    id 1168898400
MySQL thread id 336895564, query id 1972768743 172.17.0.66 db1user
    Sending data
SELECT * FROM blocklist WHERE userid = '572692'
---TRANSACTION 1 2117126598, not started, process no 30716, OS thread
    id 1370806624
MySQL thread id 336895563, query id 1972768711 172.17.0.67 db1user
---TRANSACTION 1 2117126371, not started, process no 30716, OS thread
    id 1375623520
MySQL thread id 336895338, query id 1972767576 172.17.1.71 db1user

{cut for brevity}


--------
FILE I/O
--------
I/O thread 0 state: waiting for i/o request (insert buffer thread)
I/O thread 1 state: waiting for i/o request (log thread)
I/O thread 2 state: waiting for i/o request (read thread)
I/O thread 3 state: waiting for i/o request (write thread)
Pending normal aio reads: 0, aio writes: 0,
 ibuf aio reads: 0, log i/o's: 0, sync i/o's: 0
```

```
Pending flushes (fsync) log: 0; buffer pool: 0
230203666 OS file reads, 44385900 OS file writes, 4666794 OS fsyncs
94.54 reads/s, 20167 avg bytes/read, 17.81 writes/s, 1.97 fsyncs/s
--------------------------------------
INSERT BUFFER AND ADAPTIVE HASH INDEX
--------------------------------------
Ibuf: size 37, free list len 5038, seg size 5076,
3338036 inserts, 3329377 merged recs, 2005268 merges
Hash table size 3735439, used cells 2697846, node heap has 7063
    buffer(s)
16232.45 hash searches/s, 1891.78 non-hash searches/s
---
LOG
---
Log sequence number 78 406104101
Log flushed up to   78 406102209
Last checkpoint at  78 382788515
0 pending log writes, 0 pending chkp writes
24794495 log i/o's done, 10.44 log i/o's/second
----------------------
BUFFER POOL AND MEMORY
----------------------
Total memory allocated 2159124168; in additional pool allocated
    8388608
Buffer pool size    115200
Free buffers        0
Database pages      108137
Modified db pages   8259
Pending reads 0
Pending writes: LRU 0, flush list 0, single page 0
Pages read 276041718, created 232171, written 21610976
116.37 reads/s, 0.07 creates/s, 8.15 writes/s
Buffer pool hit rate 998 / 1000
---------------
ROW OPERATIONS
---------------
0 queries inside InnoDB, 0 queries in queue
1 read views open inside InnoDB
Main thread process no. 30716, id 1157658976, state: sleeping
Number of rows inserted 4518386, updated 16346615, deleted 1410250,
    read 129367646239
2.78 inserts/s, 5.98 updates/s, 1.00 deletes/s, 35214.79 reads/s
----------------------------------
END OF INNODB MONITOR OUTPUT
================================

1 row in set (0.02 sec)

mysql>
```

The output from a SHOW ENGINE InnoDB STATUS command breaks down into nine sections. These sections provide a snapshot of activity occurring inside the InnoDB storage engine. Table 11-5 lists these sections.

TABLE 11-5

InnoDB Status Sections

Section Name	Description
Semaphores	Reports threads waiting for a semaphore and statistics on how many times threads have been forced to wait for an OS call, waiting on a spin wait, or a mutex or rw-lock semaphore. A large number of threads waiting for semaphores indicate either disk I/O or contention problems inside InnoDB. Contention can be due to heavy parallelism of queries or problems in operating system thread scheduling.
Foreign key errors	Displays information about foreign key problems.
Deadlocks	Displays information about the last deadlock that occurred.
Transactions	Reports lock waits, which could indicate your application may have lock contention. The output can also help to trace the reasons for transaction deadlocks.
File I/O	Shows information about the threads used by InnoDB for I/O activity.
Insert buffer and adaptive hash index	Displays information about the insert buffer including size and amount of free space. Also contains information about the adaptive hash index.
Log	Shows information on InnoDB log files.
Buffer pool and memory	Shows buffer pool activity (including hit rate).
Row operations	Shows the activity of the main thread.

There is a lot of information contained the SHOW ENGINE INNODB STATUS command output. It can be very useful when debugging problems relating to the InnoDB engine. All statistics are calculated using data from either the time of the last run of SHOW ENGINE INNODB STATUS or the last system reset. The length of time used for calculations is displayed in the header information.

It is possible to have InnoDB configured to write the same information shown by SHOW ENGINE InnoDB STATUS to the standard output of mysqld. Standard output would typically be your error log. This done by creating a table called innodb_monitor:

```
mysql> CREATE TABLE innodb_monitor (a INT) ENGINE=INNODB;
Query OK, 0 rows affected (0.03 sec)
```

Now until you drop the table it will log similar information as was shown previously to your standard output every fifteen seconds. When you are done troubleshooting the issue, just drop the table:

```
mysql> DROP TABLE innodb_monitor;
```

Using this method of logging your InnoDB storage engine status is much easier than manually running a SHOW ENGINE InnoDB STATUS command by hand.

InnoDB tablespace management

By default InnoDB uses a shared tablespace for all tables that consists of one or more files. These files are used to store metadata for all the InnoDB tables across all databases on the server, and are usually referred to as ibdata files, because the default name for the first file is ibdata1. These ibdata files are, by default, stored in the datadir directory.

By default, ibdata files also contain all the data and indexes for all the InnoDB tables. When an InnoDB table is defragmented in a shared tablespace configuration, the ibdata files will not shrink, even though the data and indexes are successfully defragmented. The good news is that the space is not lost — InnoDB will add that space to its pool of free space and put new rows in it. The amount of InnoDB free space that is reported in the TABLE_COMMENT field of the INFORMATION_SCHEMA.TABLES system view and the Comment field of SHOW TABLE STATUS for a defragmented InnoDB table will increase. The bad news is that the operating system cannot reclaim that disk space and use it for other purposes if needed. The space is used by the tablespace files.

A second option is to configure a per-table tablespace using the innodb_file_per_table option which, as the name suggests, stores the indexes and data for each table in a separate file, named with the table name and an extension of ibd. There is still some metadata stored in the ibdata files but the end result of using innodb_file_per_table is that the overall system can be more manageable. When an InnoDB table is defragmented (using OPTIMIZE TABLE, for example), the associated .ibd file will shrink and disk space will automatically be reclaimed.

Defragmenting of InnoDB tablespace, regardless of configuration, is typically done through the previously mentioned OPTIMIZE TABLE command. This command is discussed in the "Table Maintenance Commands" section of Chapter 4. An ALTER TABLE that rebuilds the entire table will also defragment the table.

Working with ibdata files

By default ibdata files are located in datadir. Any options for the InnoDB storage engine should be listed in the [mysqld] directive of the configuration file. The following example shows two ibdata files in the default data directory. One file is a gigabyte in size, and the second is configured to begin at a gigabyte in size but grow larger as needed:

```
innodb_data_file_path=ibdata1:1024M;ibdata2:1024M:autoextend
```

The innodb_data_home_dir option is used to specify the location of the ibdata files explicitly, to store them somewhere other than datadir. In the following example two ibdata files are in the /data directory:

```
innodb_data_home_dir = /data
innodb_data_file_path=ibdata1:1024M;ibdata2:1024M:autoextend
```

A third option would be to have the ibdata files located in different directories from each other. Using this method the files can be placed on separate hard drives for performance gains or because of low storage space. Here is how it is done:

```
innodb_data_home_dir =
innodb_data_file_path=/d1/ibdata1:1024M;/d2/ibdata2:1024M:autoextend
```

Adding an additional ibdata file to a shared tablespace

A single ibdata file can grow very large (over 300 gigabytes). In these cases, it may be desirable to add a new tablespace. Maybe the partition where the ibdata file is located is running out of space. The procedure to add an additional ibdata file is straightforward:

- Configure the innodb_data_home_dir (if necessary) and the innodb_data_file_path variable. If the current configuration is the following:

```
innodb_data_file_path=ibdata1:1024M:autoextend
```

- Determine the actual size of ibdata1. This must be done to the nearest megabyte. On Unix-based systems a simple ls -lh command executed in the data directory will return the current size in megabytes.

- Once this is known the new innodb_data_file_path can be written. If the size of the ibdata1 file is 1824 megabytes and the second ibdata is to begin at 2 gigabytes in size, the new line would look this:

```
innodb_data_file_path=ibdata1:1824M;ibdata2:2G:autoextend
```

- The autoextend option on the innodb_data_file path allows a file to grow as needed.

- Once this change to innodb_data_file_path is completed a restart of mysqld is necessary. It will take some time to initialize the ibdata2 file, but after a minute or two the file should be present in the data directory.

Adding this file is not very complicated. The previous section shows how you can configure your innodb_data_file_path and innodb_data_home_dir options for placing these data files in other directories.

> **TIP**   Do not think that just because an additional `ibdata` file is added that data will be balanced across the files. If there were only 400 megabytes of data in `ibdata1` (out of a configured 1 gigabyte of space) when `ibdata2` was added no table data will be written to `ibdata2` until `ibdata1` is completely full. Similarly, when `ibdata1` is full, new data is written to `ibdata2`, and tables can be thus split across data files.

Removing or reorganizing shared tablespace files

If you overestimated the size of the shared tablespace or it has grown much larger than your data (for example, if you have dropped some larger tables or your data is heavily fragmented), you may wish to remove an `ibdata` file from a shared tablespace. You may also wish to reorganize the current `ibdata` files — for example, if one `ibdata` file is 100 Mb and another is 500 Mb, you may wish to have each `ibdata` file be 300 Mb. Unfortunately, this is not as easy as adding an `ibdata` file. To remove or reorganize shared tablespace files:

- Perform a logical export (using a logical export tool such as `mysqldump`) of all the InnoDB tables.
- Shut down `mysqld`.
- Change the configuration options as desired to remove or reorganize a tablespace.
- Move the existing `ibdata` files, `ib_logfile` log files, and `.frm` table definition files to a backup location.
- Restart `mysqld`. The new `ibdata` file(s) will take some time to initialize.
- Import the InnoDB tables.
- After a successful import, you can delete the backup `ibdata`, `ib_logfile`, and `.frm` files. Should you need to roll back to the previous `ibdata` files, shut down `mysqld`, change the configuration options back to the previous values, and move the `ibdata`, `ib_logfile`, and `.frm` files back.

You can find more information on logical backup and restore techniques in Chapter 13.

Moving from a shared tablespace file to per-table tablespace

If you decide to move from a shared tablespace to using per-table tablespaces the process is somewhat involved. Moving to a per-table tablespace allows you to easily see on-disk how large the data and indexes for the tables are. If a tablespace is significantly larger than the metadata from `SHOW TABLE STATUS` and the `TABLES` system view of the `INFORMATION_SCHEMA` database, it is very likely the table is fragmented. As previously stated, with per-table tablespaces, defragmentation reclaims disk space; storing all the data and indexes in the shared tablespace does not.

Converting your database to use per-table data and index files is very similar to reorganizing or removing shared tablespace files:

- Perform a logical export (using a logical export tool such as `mysqldump`) of all the InnoDB tables.

- Shut down mysqld.

- Edit the configuration file and add innodb_file_per_table in the [mysqld] directive. Though it is still necessary to retain an ibdata1 file it will remain relatively small compared to the overall amount of data in InnoDB tables. This is because it will only contain metadata about the tables. Because of this you will almost certainly want to edit your innodb_data_file_path. Something like this will probably be more appropriate:

  innodb_data_file_path=ibdata1:256M:autoextend

- Move the current InnoDB table format files (.frm files), ibdata file(s), and the InnoDB log files (ib_logfile) to a backup location until you are assured everything works properly.

- Restart mysqld. At this point a new central tablespace and InnoDB log files will be initialized.

- Verify that you can create an InnoDB table and that an individual .ibd data file is created in the database directory.

- Restore your files from the backup. Once this is done the InnoDB tables are all stored in per-table tablespace.

- After a successful import, you can delete the backup ibdata and .frm files. Should you need to roll back to the previous ibdata files, shut down mysqld, change the configuration options back to the previous values, and move the ibdata and .frm files back.

You can find more information on logical backup and restore techniques in Chapter 13.

InnoDB log files and crash recovery

The unsung heroes of InnoDB are the log files. They are what makes InnoDB automatic crash recovery possible.

Database administrators of other DBMSs may be familiar with the concept of a "redo" log. When data is changed, affected data pages are changed in the innodb_buffer_pool. Then, the change is written to the redo log, which in mysqld is stored in the InnoDB log files (ib_logfile0 and ib_logfile1). The pages are marked as *dirty*, because they have been changed, and eventually get flushed and written to disk.

If mysqld crashes, there may be data that is changed that has not been written to disk. Those data pages were marked as dirty in the innodb_buffer_pool, but the innodb_buffer_pool is an in-memory cache, so after a crash the information inside the buffer pool no longer exists. However, all changes were written to the redo log. On crash recovery, mysqld can read the redo log (InnoDB log files) and apply any changes that were not written to disk.

Some of the different parameters for the InnoDB log files and their ramifications are:

- innodb_log_files_in_group is set with a default of 2. The log files are written in a circular manner — ib_logfile0 is written first, and when it is full of changed data, ib_logfile1 will be written to. The log files are initialized to their full size when mysqld starts up, if they are not already initialized.

- `innodb_log_file_size` is the size of each log file in the log group. The total, combined size of all the log files has to be less than 4 Gb (according to the MySQL Manual — this has nothing to do with the size of files an operating system can handle). Because the log files contain changes in the buffer pool that have not been written to disk, the total, combined size of all the log files should not be more than the `innodb_buffer_pool_size`. If so, the log files are wasting space that will never be used.

- If all the log files in the group are full of changes that have not been written to disk, `mysqld` will start to flush dirty pages from the InnoDB buffer pool, writing the changes to disk. If the log files are small, changes will be written to disk more often, which can cause more disk I/O. When InnoDB does a crash recovery, it reads the log files. If the log files are large, it will take longer to recover from a crash.

- If `innodb_fast_shutdown` is set to 0, the log files are purged when `mysqld` shuts down — larger files mean a longer shutdown time. The default for `innodb_fast_shutdown` is 1, which means that the log files are not purged before a shutdown. A value is 2 simulates a crash, and at the next startup InnoDB will do a crash recovery. This can be useful when testing to see approximately how long InnoDB takes to recover from a crash, to determine if the size of your log files is too large.

- `innodb_flush_log_at_trx_commit` controls how often the log files are written to. A value of 0 causes the log files to be written and flushed to disk once per second. The default is 1, which causes the log buffer to be written and flushed to disk after every transaction commit. The value can also be set to 2, which causes the log buffer to be written after every transaction commit and flushes the log files to disk once per second. A value of 2 means that MySQL might think that some changes are written to the log file, but do not persist in the log file after an operating system crash, because the log file was not flushed to disk before a crash.

- Note that some file systems are not honest about flushing to disk, so even though you may have the default value of 1, your system may be acting as if it has a value of 2. Setting this parameter to 2 means that there will be less I/O, at the cost of not being able to recover data from a crash.

- `innodb_flush_method` changes how InnoDB opens and flushes data and log files. See Chapter 10 for more information; the end result is a tradeoff in I/O performance versus whether or not an operating system crash would leave the InnoDB log files in an inconsistent state.

- `innodb_log_buffer_size` is the write buffer for InnoDB log files. The larger the buffer is, the less often the log files are written to. This can save I/O.

MEMORY storage engine

The MEMORY storage engine creates tables stored in memory only. Because the MEMORY storage engine stores all data in RAM it provides for extremely fast access with the downside that no data is stored on disk. Data does not persist across restarts — a MEMORY table will have no data in it when a server starts. In addition, if a MEMORY table is replicated and the master restarts, the slave will have its MEMORY table truncated as well — even though the slave did not restart. Though you can use an initialization file to repopulate the table, it is not really practical to use a MEMORY table for data that needs to be saved across restarts. Ideal candidates for MEMORY tables are data that do not need to persist across restarts — for example, session data.

There are no extra files for MEMORY tables; they are only associated with their table format file (.frm extension).

> **TIP** When you delete rows from a MEMORY table it does not reduce the amount of memory the table actually uses — just as deleting rows from any other table does not reduce the amount of disk space used. Running an ALTER TABLE or OPTIMIZE TABLE command on the MEMORY table would defragment the table and reduce the amount of memory used.

Feature summary:

- All data is stored in memory
- Non-transactional
- No foreign key support
- Very fast read and write activity due to being entirely in-memory
- Table-level locking
- A MEMORY table can include up to thirty-two indexes per table
- Implements both HASH and BTREE indexes (HASH is used by default; see Chapter 6 for more information on indexes)
- MEMORY tables use a fixed-length row storage format, and thus cannot be defined with data types of BLOB or TEXT (see Chapter 5 for more information on data types)

MEMORY configuration options

The MEMORY storage engine has only a few configuration options. Table 11-6 lists the options for the MEMORY storage engine.

TABLE 11-6

MEMORY Storage Engine Configuration

MEMORY Storage Engine Parameter	Description
max_heap_table_size	The maximum size of MEMORY tables is limited by the system variable. It has a default value of 16 megabytes.
init_file	This can be used to specify a file to use to populate a MEMORY table when mysqld starts. For example, the file may contain a LOAD DATA INFILE command.

> **NOTE** The init_file option is used by mysqld to run a set of commands in a file on
> startup. These commands need not populate a MEMORY table; they can also be used
> to set parameters or run any other statements you wish upon startup.

Maria storage engine

The Maria storage engine is a crash-safe version of MyISAM. The Maria storage engine supports
all of the main functionality of the MyISAM engine, but includes recovery support (in the event
of a system crash), full logging (including CREATE, DROP, RENAME, and TRUNCATE operations),
all MyISAM row formats, and a new Maria-specific row format.

At the time of this writing, the Maria storage engine is not production-ready. Overall the Maria
storage engine is very similar to MyISAM with the additional functionality in that it is crash-safe
and will include full transactional support in the future. As with MyISAM, the Maria storage
engine uses three files per table in your databases. These files include the table definition file
(suffix of .frm), the data file (suffix of .mad), and the index file with a suffix of .mai.

In addition to the files used to define and store the Maria table data, there are two additional file
types in the data directory. These are the log files and the control file. The log files use a naming format of maria_log.num (where num is an integer). Just like the binary logs these files are
numbered sequentially. There is also a control file called maria_log_control that is used to
store information about the state of the Maria engine.

> **WARNING** You should not delete the maria_log_control file from a running mysqld cur-
> rently using Maria tables because it records information about the current state of the
> Maria engine, including log file details and the default page block size used for the log and data
> files.

Feature summary:

- Crash-safe non-transactional support
- Transactional support planned
- Page cache for caching indexes and data
- Row-level locking
- Replacement for system tables (currently MyISAM) in the future

Maria configuration options

Maria supports a number of configuration options to control the operation and performance
of the storage engine. Many of the options are similar to options that are already available within
the MyISAM configuration options.

The maria_block_size server variable sets the block size to be used by Maria for both index
and data pages for the PAGE row format.

> **TIP** To change the block size of existing tables, you should use `mysqldump` to create a backup of the table data, stop `mysqld`, remove the `maria_log_control` file, and change the `maria_block_size` parameter before starting up `mysqld` again.

The configuration settings are stored in the `maria_log_control` file when `mysqld` is started with the Maria engine enabled. The default block size is 8192 bytes (8kb).

Log configuration parameters

Maria, unlike MyISAM, uses log files. These are used to store transactional information for recovery after a crash. Table 11-7 lists the log configuration variables for Maria tables.

TABLE 11-7

Maria Log File Configuration Variables

Maria Log File Configuration Variable	Description
`maria_log_dir_path`	This configuration value specifies where the transactional log files are located. The default value is `datadir`. You might want to change the path to another partition, hard drive, or storage unit for disk management or performance improvements.
`maria_log_file_size`	This configuration value specifies the maximum size of a Maria log file. When a log file reaches this limit two actions occur. A new log file is created and the `maria_log_control` file is updated. The default size is 1 gigabyte. The minimum log file size is 8 megabytes and the maximum log file size is 4 gigabytes.
`maria_log_purge_type`	This configuration value specifies the method used for removal of transactional logs. There are three options, `at_flush`, `immediate`, and `external`. The default value is `immediate`.
`maria_sync_log_dir`	This parameter controls the synchronization of the directory after the log file has been extended or a new log file has been created. Supported values are `never`, `newfile` (only when a new log file is created), and `always`. The default setting is `newfile`.

The `maria_log_purge_type` variable has three possible options. If it is configured to be `at_flush`, the log files are removed when all transactions in the log have completed and a `FLUSH LOGS` statement has been run. If configured to be `immediate`, the log files are removed as soon as all transactions in the log file are complete. If configured to a value of `external`, log files are never removed by the storage engine and must be done with an external utility program.

Page cache configuration

The Maria storage engine has several configuration parameters relating to the *page cache*. The page cache is the area of memory allocated to storing table information for faster access. Unlike MyISAM this information includes both data and indexes. Table 11-8 describes the page cache configuration parameters.

TABLE 11-8

Maria Page Cache Configuration Variables

Page Cache Configuration Variable	Description
`maria_pagecache_age_threshold`	Determines the number of times the page cache receives a hit without touching a hot block until the block is downgraded to a warm block. The default value is 300.
`maria_pagecache_buffer_size`	Sets the size of the buffer used for both data and index pages of Maria tables. Increasing this value (with the appropriate amount of system memory) will improve performance on data and index reads and writes. The default value is 8 megabytes.
`maria_pagecache_division_limit`	Specifies the minimum percentage of warm blocks that can be in the page cache. The default value of 100 means that before data is stored in the cache it has to have been in use.

Maria table options

A number of options are available when you create a new Maria table. These options control the behavior of these Maria tables. Table 11-9 lists the parameters.

When you are using Maria tables that are less than version 2.0, TRANSACTIONAL does not mean the tables support transactional statements. It means the tables are crash-safe. With a Maria table of version 2.0 or greater there is full transactional support available.

It should be pointed out that the `maria_page_checksum` variable is a server-level variable you would configure in your `my.cnf` file. The PAGE_CHECKSUM, TABLE_CHECKSUM, and TRANSAC-TIONAL options are used during creation of Maria tables. Here is an example of the creation of a Maria table. This shows the default settings:

```
mysql> create table maria_trans (
id int NOT NULL AUTO_INCREMENT,
title char(20),
age int
) engine=Maria;
Query OK, 0 rows affected (0.05 sec)
```

```
mysql> SHOW CREATE TABLE maria_trans;
+-------------+------------------------------------------+
| Table       | Create Table                             |
+-------------+------------------------------------------+
| maria_trans | CREATE TABLE `maria_trans` (
    `id` int(11) DEFAULT NOT NULL auto_increment,
    `title` char(20) DEFAULT NULL,
    `age` int(11) DEFAULT NULL
) ENGINE=MARIA DEFAULT CHARSET=latin1 PAGE_CHECKSUM=1 |
+-------------+------------------------------------------+
1 row in set (0.00 sec)
```

TABLE 11-9

Maria Table Creation Options

Table Option	Description
maria_page_checksum	This variable is used to enable or disable page checksums. When a Maria table has page checksum enabled the storage engine will use the checksums to ensure the page information has not been corrupted. This setting can be configured on a table-level basis by using the PAGE_CHECKSUM or CHECKSUM option during execution of the CREATE TABLE statement. The default setting is for maria_page_checksum to be enabled.
PAGE_CHECKSUM	This option specifies if page checksums for the table are turned on or off. Setting PAGE_CHECKSUM to 1 turns page checksums on, and setting it to 0 turns page checksums off. The default value is determined by the maria_page_checksum variable.
TRANSACTIONAL	Maria tables, unlike any other storage engines, can be created either transactional or non-transactional.
TABLE_CHECKSUM	When this is enabled a rolling checksum is kept on the Maria table. It is used to identify corrupted tables. This is identical in operation to checksums on MyISAM tables.

Transactional support and page checksums are the default in creation of a Maria table as you can see from the SHOW CREATE TABLE output. Changes to any version of a Maria transactional table are recorded in the Maria log file. The default setting is that all Maria tables are transactional (that is, TRANSACTIONAL=1 is implied within the CREATE TABLE definition). Because of this, unless you specify a TRANSACTIONAL=0 clause in the CREATE TABLE statement the transactional status of the table is not written in the output of the SHOW CREATE TABLE output. This is the case with the CREATE TABLE statement just shown.

Along with transactional support, either crash-proof or actual transactional support, Maria offers three different row formats. The FIXED row format is the same as the FIXED row format used for MyISAM tables. The DYNAMIC row format is the same as the DYNAMIC row format used for MyISAM tables.

Both FIXED and DYNAMIC row format can only be used with non-transactional tables.

In addition, Maria has a new format called PAGE where both data and index information is written to pages. Using a PAGE format for Maria tables allows for the use of the page cache to increase performance. This format can be used with either transactional or non-transactional tables.

Miscellaneous configuration

You have several miscellaneous options for working with Maria tables. Table 11-10 lists these options.

TABLE 11-10

Maria Miscellaneous Options

Option	Description
maria_repair_threads	Specifies the number of threads used executing a REPAIR TABLE command to repair a Maria table. The default value of 1 disables parallel repair.
maria_sort_buffer_size	Configures the size of the buffer used for sorting indexes while a REPAIR TABLE, CREATE INDEX, or ALTER TABLE command is running. Increasing this buffer size should improve the speed of the index creation process. The default value is 8 megabytes.
maria_max_sort_file_size	Forces Maria not to use the fast sort index method to create an index if the temporary file would get bigger than this size. Default is the maximum file size.
maria_stats_method	Determines how the calculation of index statistics manages NULL. The available values include nulls_unequal, nulls_equal, and nulls_ignored. The default setting is nulls_unequal.
maria_checkpoint_interval	Specifies the amount of time between the automatic checkpointing of data from memory to disk. Checkpoints are a method used to speed up the recovery process because the process is able to begin at the last stable checkpoint in the log. The default checkpoint interval is thirty seconds. You can disable checkpoints by setting the value to 0, but disabling checkpoints will increase the time taken to recover in the event of a failure. You should only set the value to 0 during testing.

Maria command-line tools

Maria supports a number of command-line tools that operate in a similar fashion to the corresponding MyISAM tools. Table 11-11 lists these tools.

TABLE 11-11

Maria Command-Line Tools

Command-line Tool	Description
maria_chk	Analyzes Maria tables for corruption. Similar to the myisamchk command.
maria_dump_log	Used for debugging of transactional log internals.
maria_ftdump	Displays information about the fulltext indexes of Maria tables. Similar to the myisam_ftdump command.
maria_pack	Compresses a Maria table. Similar to the myisampack command.
maria_read_log	Used to view a Maria log file.

The Maria storage engine has great promise as a replacement for aging MyISAM tables. The ability to recover from crashes without intervention is a great benefit for database administrators.

Falcon storage engine

Falcon has been specially developed for systems that are able to support large memory architectures and multi-threaded or multi-core CPU environments. Though it performs optimally on 64-bit architectures Falcon can be deployed on 32-bit platforms. A CPU count of up to eight cores and eight gigabytes is the current sweet spot.

Feature summary:

- Multi Version Concurrency Control (MVCC).
- Flexible locking, including flexible locking levels and smart deadlock detection keep data protected and transactions and operations flowing at full speed.
- Serial log files are used to improve both performance and recovery times.
- Utilizes B-Tree indexes for data retrieval.
- Data compression techniques are used to store data on disk using a compressed format. The compression and decompression of data is done on the fly by Falcon.
- Space created by deletion of data in both log and data files is automatically reclaimed by Falcon.

■ Data and index caching for performance boost.

■ Metadata stored in the INFORMATION_SCHEMA database.

Architectural overview

The Falcon storage engine is a marked departure from previous storage engines. It is part of a new generation of storage engines designed from the ground up to take advantage of the modern operating system configurations with optimal usage of large amounts of RAM and higher numbers of CPUs.

Figure 11-1 gives an overview of the Falcon storage engine architecture.

FIGURE 11-1

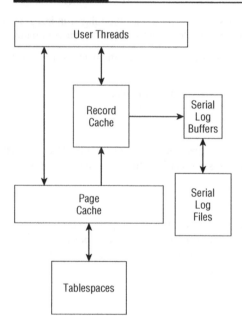

From the architecture diagram you can see the flow of data through the storage engine. All user thread activity begins with the record and page caches. The record cache is a memory cache used to maintain copies of both active and uncommitted records. The page cache is a memory cache used to hold database pages that are either being written to the database or being read from currently.

The tablespace is a logical group of one or more data files in a database. This is the same as with other storage engines. With the Falcon storage engine, by default, all data for a database is stored in a single file. This file has a filename of the database with an extension of .fts.

Three additional tablespaces are created automatically. They are used to hold systems tables, user-defined tables, and temporary tables.

Falcon tablespaces do not need to be manually extended and the Falcon storage engine automatically reclaims unused space.

The *serial log* is a log file that contains recently committed data and index changes along with transactional information. This information is used during crash recovery. *Gopher threads* are processes used to commit changes from the serial logs to the Falcon tablespace.

Falcon configuration options

The Falcon storage engine has several miscellaneous parameters. Table 11-12 lists these parameters.

TABLE 11-12

Miscellaneous Falcon Parameters

Parameter	Description
falcon_checkpoint_schedule	Determines how often the fsync() system call is made to synchronize the data in memory to the Falcon tablespace. The schedule is specified in a crontab-style format.
falcon_debug_mask	Determines the log information that is sent to the standard output of mysqld when an error occurs. The value that you specify is a bit mask and it allows you to combine values for different combinations of error messaging.
falcon_debug_server	Determines if the debug server should be enabled. The default value is OFF.

The falcon_checkpoint_schedule parameter uses a schedule in the form of a crontab-style series of values, each separated by spaces. Each schedule has six fields with the field using a similar format to the Unix crontab utility. Within the schedule these fields are:

- Seconds (0–59)
- Minutes (0–59)
- Hours (0–23)
- Day of month (1–31)
- Month (1–12)
- Day of week (0–7 — both 0 and 7 are Sunday)

The values for each field specified can be one of three things: an absolute value, a range of values, or a comma-separated list of matching values. The default setting is once a minute, running at seven seconds past the minute.

The `falcon_debug_mask` parameter has ten possible values. Table 11-13 lists these values along with their descriptions.

TABLE 11-13

falcon_debug_mask Values

Value	Name	Description
1	LogLog	This will log an error of any kind.
2	LogDebug	This will log both status and progress information.
4	LogInfo	This will log both general information and status messages
8	Unused	not used
16	Unused	not used
32	LogGG	
64	LogPanic	
128	LogScrub	
256	LogException	This will log exceptions and SQL errors.
512	LogScavenge	This will log the statistics of the record scavenger.

Performance optimization configuration

Some specific configuration parameters are used to optimize the performance of Falcon-based tables. Table 11-14 lists these parameters.

With `falcon_page_size`, the specified page size also affects the maximum index key lengths supported. Table 11-15 shows the relationship between the page size and the maximum index key length.

Transactional support configuration

A number of parameters are used to manage transactional behavior with Falcon tables. Table 11-16 shows these parameters.

Record cache configuration

The record cache is used to store copies of both active and uncommitted records. It is one of the primary methods of increasing the performance of Falcon tables. Table 11-17 lists the record cache configuration parameters.

TABLE 11-14

Performance Optimization Parameters

Parameter	Description
falcon_disable_fsync	Setting this to true means that the periodic fsync operation to synchronize data in memory to disk is disabled. Setting this value to true could potentially increase performance but could potentially lead to data loss.The default value is false (fsync is enabled).
falcon_io_threads	Determines the number of asynchronous threads used for executing writes to disk. The default value is two threads.
falcon_large_blob_ threshold	When BLOB data is smaller than the value specified, the data is stored in data pages instead of BLOB pages. Performance can improve for smaller blobs because if all blobs in a transaction are smaller than this value only the serial log will need to be flushed at the end of the transaction.
falcon_page_cache_size	This determines the size of the cache used for caching pages from the tablespace file. The default value is 4 megabytes.
falcon_page_size	This determines the page size used to store data in the Falcon tablespace. Valid sizes are 1, 2, 4, 8, 16, and 32 KB. The default setting is 4 KB.

TABLE 11-15

Falcon Page Size and Index Length

Page Size	Maximum Index Key Length
1K	255
2K	540
4K	1100
8K	2200
16K	4500
32K	9000

TABLE 11-16

Transactional Support Parameters

Variable	Description
falcon_consistent_read	This parameter configures the transaction isolation level. When set to On, repeatable read transactions are truly consistent-read. Changes made by newer transactions will not be exposed and newer records cannot be read or written within a repeatable read transaction. Set to Off, Falcon works in read-committed transaction isolation level. The default is On.
falcon_index_ chill_threshold	The number of bytes of pending index data that should be stored during transaction processing before the index changes are flushed to the serial log. If the index is unique, or the transaction is frequently re-reading the index data, the index data is stored in memory. The flushing of the index data to the serial log is called *chilling*. The chilling of pending indexes allows Falcon to load large data sets in a single transaction without running out of memory. The minimum value is 1048576, the maximum is 1073741824, and the default value is 4194304.
falcon_lock_ wait_timeout	This determines the deadlock timeout value for Falcon. It is the amount of time in seconds that a transaction will wait for another transaction to complete when both transactions need access to a locked table. A value 0 indicates that Falcon will wait indefinitely for another transaction to complete. The default value is 50.
falcon_record_ chill_threshold	The number of bytes of pending record data that Falcon stores in memory during a transaction before these records are flushed to the serial log. The flushing of records to serial logs is called chilling. Accessing chilled records during a transaction will immediately restore them from the serial log. This process is called *thawing*. The chilling process allows Falcon to manage large transactions without running out of available memory. The minimum accepted value is 1048576, the maximum is 1073741824, and the default value is 5242880.

TABLE 11-17

Falcon Record Cache Configuration Parameters

Parameter	Description
falcon_record_memory_max	Determines the maximum amount of memory set aside for the caching of record data. The default size is 20 megabytes.
falcon_record_scavenge_threshold	Determines the percentage filled of the record cache that will trigger the scavenger thread to remove old records from the cache. The default value is 67. The minimum accepted value is 10 and the maximum is 100.
falcon_record_scavenge_floor	Determines the percentage of records that will be retained in the record cache after the scavenger thread has completed execution. The default is 50. The minimum value is 10 and the maximum is 90.
falcon_scavenge_schedule	Determines the record scavenging schedule. This is specified in a crontab-style schedule.

As with the falcon_checkpoint_schedule, the falcon_scavenge_schedule is specified in a crontab-style schedule. This schedule is a list of values that are separated by spaces. The fields in this schedule specify the following, going from left to right:

- seconds (0–59)
- minutes (0–59)
- hours (0–23)
- day of month (1–31)
- month (1–12)
- day of week (0–7 with both 0 and 7 being Sunday)

The default value is 15, 45 * * * * *, which means the record scavenger runs twice a minute at the 15-second and 45-second mark.

Serial log configuration

Only three parameters relate to the serial log. Table 11-18 lists these parameters and what they control.

TABLE 11-18	

Falcon Serial Log Parameters

Serial Log Parameter	Description
falcon_serial_log_buffers	Determines the number of memory windows that Falcon sets aside for the Falcon serial log. Each memory window is 1 megabyte in size. The minimum accepted value is 10, the maximum is 32768, and the default value is 10.
falcon_serial_log_dir	Specifies the directory used for storing the serial log. The filenames used by the serial log are determined by the name of the tablespace. The default location is in the same directory as the tablespace file.
falcon_gopher_threads	Specifies the number of threads used that write committed changes in the serial log to the database. The default is five gopher threads.

Falcon tablespace management

Falcon has several compelling features for tablespace management. One of the most innovative features is the ability to change the page size of tablespace. The page size can range from 2–32K in size. This can be changed at any time but will only take effect for any new tablespaces created. To change the page size of previously created tablespaces you must:

- Back up any Falcon tables
- Drop the Falcon tablespaces and log files
- Restart the MySQL Server with the new Falcon page size
- Restore all Falcon tables

The management by the Falcon storage engine of tablespaces to eliminate fragmentation is another great feature for database administrators. This is all done in background with no need for manual intervention by the administrator.

Three initial tablespaces are created:

- falcon_master.fts — System tablespace
- falcon_temporary.fts — Temporary table workspace
- falcon_user.fts — Default tablespace for user tables, indexes, and BLOB data

By default these tablespaces are created in the MySQL data directory.

With Falcon tablespaces, there are no separate tablespaces for data and index information. This is a departure from the common strategy of database servers to have separate tablespaces for indexes and data.

Creating a new tablespace

Creating a new tablespace is very easy. You use the CREATE TABLESPACE command:

```
mysql> CREATE TABLESPACE FALCON_DATA
    -> ADD DATAFILE '/data/falcon_data.fts'
    -> ENGINE=FALCON;
Query OK, 0 rows affected (0.03 sec)
```

Your tablespace name must be different than any other tablespaces and use a single data file name. The ENGINE=FALCON clause must always be used because the NDB storage engine also uses the CREATE TABLESPACE command to manage its tablespace.

> **TIP** Falcon initially creates a data file the size equal to four times the Falcon page size, which defaults to 4k.

Falcon tablespaces can be created and dropped as needed without impacting the database server. Tablespaces will also grow as needed automatically.

Creating tables and indexes

Creating tables and indexes in Falcon tablespaces is done with the CREATE TABLE syntax:

```
mysql> CREATE TABLE x (a int) ENGINE=falcon TABLESPACE FALCON_DATA;
Query OK, 0 rows affected (0.07 sec)
```

This would create the table in the FALCON_DATA tablespace created previously. If no tablespace is specified the table is placed in the default FALCON_USER tablespace. Once the table is created you work with it no differently than other storage engines.

> **TIP** Falcon tablespace names are case-sensitive. If you try to use falcon_user instead of FALCON_USER it will not be using the default tablespace.

It is possible (and very easy) to move a Falcon table from one tablespace to another. What if you decide to move the previous table to the newly created FALCON_DATA tablespace? You use the ALTER TABLE command and specify the new tablespace:

```
mysql> ALTER TABLE x TABLESPACE falcon_data;
Query OK, 0 rows affected (0.09 sec)
```

If a tablespace is storing any data that tablespace cannot be dropped. When empty, the tablespace can be dropped with the DROP TABLESPACE tablespace name ENGINE=FALCON command. This removes the Falcon data files from the server:

```
mysql> DROP TABLESPACE falcon_data;
Query OK, 0 rows affected (0.09 sec)
```

PBXT storage engine

PBXT is an ACID-compliant transactional storage engine. The PBXT engine is efficient at processing I/O operations. It takes a different approach than any other storage engine by performing any needed writes in a sequential manner and only a single time. This is in contrast to the more traditional approach where a transactional log file is written first and the database is updated with information from the transactional log. The immediate writing of log data actually accomplishes two things: the record cache is never dirty and creates extremely fast rollbacks.

ON the WEBSITE On recovery PBXT creates a filed called `recovery-progress` in the PBXT database. The recovery percentage complete is written to this file as recovery progresses. This file will not be created if PBXT estimates that it will read less than 10 megabytes to perform a recovery.

Feature summary:

- Transactional support
- Row-level locking
- Data and index caching (in separate caches)
- Sequential, write-once I/O
- Instantaneous deadlock detection, commits and rollbacks of transactions
- Foreign key support
- B-tree indexing
- `BLOB` streaming (in combination with the `BLOB` streaming engine)

Architectural overview

Because the PBXT storage engine operates quite differently than other storage engines, an overview of the architecture will be helpful. Figure 11-2 shows the major parts of the PBXT engine and how they interact with each other.

PBXT uses two caches for table contents. The record cache stores table data. One feature of the record cache is that full table scan results are never stored in the record cache. The only data stored in the record cache is the data that is returned from some type of index lookup. The complement of the record cache is the index cache, which is used to store index data.

Data files are used to store the table data that is fixed-length. These data files are able to grow in size as needed and their filenames have a suffix of `.xtd`. The complement to the data files is the data logs that contain the variable length (`VARCHAR` and `BLOB`) portion of a PBXT table's data. As with PBXT data files, these will grow in size as needed. All data log files have a suffix of `.xtl`.

Index files contain index data and have an `.xti` file suffix. B-tree indexing is used for lookups.

Transaction log files are used in the management of transactions. Unlike a traditional transactional log, the PBXT transactional log only has references to new data in the data files. All transaction log files end with an `.xt` file suffix.

FIGURE 11-2

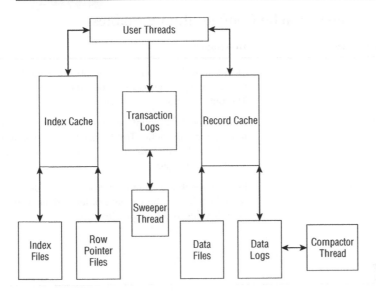

The PBXT storage engine uses two types of threads to manage the processes that run in the background. The *sweeper thread* is the thread used to read the transaction log files after transactions have been completed. As it reads through the transaction log it removes data that is no longer needed. This includes transactions that have been rolled back and committed and also old record versions. These will delete a transaction log after the thread finishes scanning the log file. In addition to the management of the transaction logs, the sweeper thread is also used during crash recovery. There is a separate sweeper thread for each database containing PBXT tables.

The *compactor thread* is the thread that is used to reduce the size of the data logs. It does this waiting until the data marked as garbage in the data log reaches a threshold that is configurable by the pbxt_garbage_threshold setting. It accomplishes this by copying all valid data into a new data log and then deleting the old data log. As with sweeper threads, compactor threads are assigned one to each database that uses PBXT tables.

PBXT configuration options

PBXT has three caches: index, record, and log caches. The current memory usage in these areas can be determined using SHOW ENGINE PBXT STATUS. Table 11-19 lists the configuration variables for the PBXT caches.

Transaction configuration

Three configuration values are used to manage how transactions are performed. Table 11-20 lists the configuration variables that relate to the transaction logs.

TABLE 11-19

PBXT Cache Configuration Variables

Cache Configuration Variables	Description
pbxt_index_cache_size	Determines the amount of memory set aside for the index cache, which is used for caching index pages. The default value is 32 megabytes.
pbxt_log_cache_size	Determines the amount of memory set aside for the transaction log cache. The transaction log cache is used to cache the transaction log data. The default value is 16 megabytes.
pbxt_record_cache_size	Determines the amount of memory set aside for the record cache for the caching of table data. The default value is 32 megabytes.

TABLE 11-20

Transaction Log Variables

Transaction Log Configuration Variables	Description
pbxt_log_file_threshold	Determines the size of a transaction log before it is closed and a new log file is created. The default size is 32 megabytes.
pbxt_transaction_buffer_size	Determines the size of the global transaction log buffers. The default size is 1 megabyte. The storage engine creates two buffers of the specified size.
pbxt_checkpoint_frequency	Determines the amount of data written to the transaction log before a checkpoint is written to the log. The default value is 24 megabytes. The amount written between checkpoints affects the rate of recovery with more data written between checkpoints meaning a longer recovery time.

Data log configuration

PBXT stores variable-length data in the data logs. This should be mostly data from rows containing VARCHAR or BLOB data. These data logs are managed by the *compactor* thread. Table 11-21 lists the configuration variables relating to the data logs.

TABLE 11-21

Data Log Variables

Data Log Configuration Variables	Description
pbxt_auto_increment_mode	Determines the behavior of the AUTO INCREMENT clause in a CREATE TABLE statement for PBXT tables.
pbxt_data_log_threshold	Determines the maximum size of a data log file. The default value is 64 megabytes. The maximum number of data logs the PBXT storage engine can create is 32,000 data logs. This means the maximum size of the PBXT tablespace is 2,048,000 megabytes or 2 terabytes of data with a pbxt_data_log_threshold = 64 MB.
pbxt_garbage_threshold	The percentage of garbage (deleted rows) in a data log file before compaction occurs. This can be an integer between 1 and 99. The default value is 50.
pbxt_log_buffer_size	Determines the size of the buffer used for writing a data log. One buffer per thread is allocated by the engine when the thread needs to write a data log. The default size is 256 megabytes.
pbxt_sweeper_priority	The sweeper cleans up deleted records occurring from DELETE or UPDATE commands. These deleted records can slow searches if they are allowed to build up too much. Higher priority for the sweeper is recommended on systems with four or more cores. Allowable settings are 0 (default / low priority), 1 (normal priority), and 2 (high priority).

The pbxt_auto_increment_mode variable requires some additional explanation. The default behavior of mysqld is that auto-increment values will be re-issued if you delete the row containing the current maximum auto-increment value and immediately restart the server. To prevent this you can use the command:

```
ALTER TABLE table AUTO_INCREMENT = <curr-max-auto-increment> + 1
```

Once this is done you can delete the current maximum auto-increment value and restart the server.

When the pbxt_auto_increment_mode variable is set to 0 (the default) auto-increment values will work as described in the previous paragraph. When set to 1, the AUTO_INCREMENT value of the table is set automatically to prevent previously issued auto-increment values from being reused. However, this can cause performance degradation because it requires a disk flush of the table file.

The index statistics are recalculated three ways: when the table row count initially exceeds 200, when a FLUSH TABLES command is executed, and when the server is restarted.

The PBXT storage engine creates a database called pbxt that is used to store metadata for the PBXT tables used in the server. It is automatically created when the first PBXT table is created and should only be dropped if there are no remaining PBXT tables in any databases. Dropping the pbxt database will additionally cause all PBXT transaction and data logs to be deleted.

File growth variables

Both the handle data and row pointers files are grown in chunks as needed. Table 11-22 lists the configuration variables used to manage these files.

TABLE 11-22

File Growth Variables

File Growth Configuration Variable	Description
pbxt_data_file_grow_size	The amount the handle data (.xtd) files grow when they become full.
pbxt_row_file_grow_size	The amount the row pointer (.xtr) files grow when they become full.

SHOW ENGINE PBXT STATUS

As with the InnoDB storage engine, the PBXT engine can display statistics about the storage engine using the SHOW ENGINE PBXT STATUS command. As you can see from the following example, it shows the record (data) cache size and usage, the index cache size and usage, the log cache size and usage, and information about the data log files. The g% status for each of the data logs shows what percentage of the log file is garbage (deleted rows).

```
mysql> SHOW ENGINE PBXT STATUS\G
*************************** 1. row ***************************
  Type: PBXT
  Name:
Status:
081118 11:21:02 PBXT 1.0.07 Beta STATUS OUTPUT
Record cache usage: 3123403
Record cache size: 33554432
Record cache high: 3123403
Index cache usage: 557056
Index cache size: 33554432
Log cache usage: 16137600
Log cache size: 16760800
Data log files:
d-log: 5 status=x-locked eof=28543757 garbage=12998183 g%=45 open=1
```

```
d-log: 6 status=to-compact eof=67114253 garbage=47625774 g%=70 open=1
d-log: 7 status=to-compact eof=67119082 garbage=66498898 g%=99 open=2
d-log: 8 status=read-only eof=67113923 garbage=16114330 g%=24 open=1
d-log: 9 status=x-locked eof=45015359 garbage=0 g%=0 open=0
d-log: 10 status=x-locked eof=43300442 garbage=11279103 g%=26 open=1
```

The SHOW ENGINE PBXT STATUS command gives a concise view of the state of your PBXT tables. It can be used for both monitoring purposes and troubleshooting of PBXT databases.

Installing the PBXT binary plugin

To use the PBXT storage engine you will need to install it first. The easiest method is to use a binary plugin distributed by Primebase Technologies. The website for downloading a binary plugin is www.primebase.org/download.

Once you have downloaded the plugin, you will need to know the plugin directory used on your MySQL Server. Log in to mysqld and run the following:

```
mysql> SHOW GLOBAL VARIABLES LIKE 'plugin%';
+---------------+----------------------+
| Variable_name | Value                |
+---------------+----------------------+
| plugin_dir    | /usr/lib/mysql/plugin |
+---------------+----------------------+
1 row in set (0.00 sec)
```

After determining this, you copy the plugin file to this directory.

Once this is done you will need to tell mysqld that the plugin is present:

```
mysql> INSTALL PLUGIN PBXT SONAME 'libpbxt.so';
```

When you complete this step the storage engine should be available. To verify you can use the SHOW ENGINES command.

If you need to compile from source, refer to the Primebase website (www.primebase.org).

FEDERATED storage engine

The FEDERATED storage engine is not a storage engine in the traditional sense in that, strictly speaking, FEDERATED tables are only an interface to other remote tables. When an SQL query is issued against a FEDERATED table, the query is sent to the remote server where it is executed, and the result set is returned to the local server where it is relayed to the client. It sounds complicated but is actually very easy to configure and utilize.

Feature summary:

- Non-transactional
- No data or index caches

415

- No foreign key support
- Allows access to data on remote servers

Though many database administrators do not use the FEDERATED engine in day-to-day usage, there are definite scenarios where it makes sense. When working with data there are going to be situations where a query needs to access table data that is located on another physical server for whatever reason. Both Oracle and SQL Server implement methods to create these connections. With Oracle they are referred to as *database links*, and on SQL Server the concept is called *linked servers*. A common scenario is where historical/archival data is stored on a secondary that might not be as powerful as the main database server but is used to hold this older data that is not accessed very frequently.

TIP The FEDERATED engine has to be enabled before use. To enable the FEDERATED storage engine add the line `federated` to the [mysqld] directive of your configuration file.

To access this data you create a FEDERATED table on the primary server that is identical in structure to the table being referenced on the secondary other than the storage engine type being set to FEDERATED. For example, if there were archival tables of invoices from previous years stored on the secondary server with the following table structure:

```
CREATE TABLE `invoice_0108` (
  `invoice_id` int(11) NOT NULL AUTO_INCREMENT,
  `sales_date` datetime NOT NULL,
  `customer_id` mediumint(8) unsigned NOT NULL,
  `staff_id` tinyint(3) unsigned NOT NULL,
  PRIMARY KEY (`invoice_id`)
) ENGINE=InnoDB DEFAULT CHARSET=utf8
```

you would create the following table on the primary server:

```
CREATE TABLE `invoice_0108` (
  `invoice_id` int(11) NOT NULL AUTO_INCREMENT,
  `sales_date` datetime NOT NULL,
  `customer_id` mediumint(8) unsigned NOT NULL,
  `staff_id` tinyint(3) unsigned NOT NULL,
  PRIMARY KEY (`invoice_id`)
) ENGINE=FEDERATED DEFAULT CHARSET=utf8 CONNECTION=
  'mysql://user:pword@192.168.2.11:3306/test/invoice_0108'
```

As you can see there is no difference until you get to the very last line. This `Connection` clause is the information needed by the FEDERATED table in order to establish the connection to the remote table. You will need to replace `user` with the username used to establish the connection and `pword` with the password of the user account. The IP address must be specified, whereas the port number is optional. If no port number is specified it defaults to port 3306. The character string after the first "/" is the name of the database where the remote table is located and the character string after the second "/" is the name of the remote table.

Once this is done you can SELECT from the FEDERATED table and see the rows in the remote table.

Limitations of FEDERATED tables

Although FEDERATED tables can be extremely useful they do have some limitations. FEDERATED tables are non-transactional in nature regardless of the support that the remote table might have for transactions. In addition, indexes are not always handled the same for the FEDERATED table as they are for the remote table. FEDERATED tables do not support index prefixes on CHAR, VARCHAR, TEXT, or BLOB columns. There are instances where indexes are not used as expected.

Though it is a fairly minor issue, FEDERATED tables do not support the use of ALTER TABLE. To change the table definition of a FEDERATED table you must drop the table and re-create it.

Even with these limitations the FEDERATED engine can be very useful when remote data access is needed.

NDB storage engine

The NDB storage engine is used to build a MySQL Cluster. MySQL Cluster is a shared-nothing, highly available system. MySQL Cluster is designed to avoid a single point of failure. A cluster will contain one or more SQL nodes (traditional MySQL Servers), one or more data nodes, and one or more management servers. For more information about MySQL Cluster, see Chapter 22.

Feature summary:

- Built to provide high availability with redundant sets of data for node failure scenarios.
- Transactional support.
- No foreign key support.
- Row-level locking.
- Operates either entirely in memory or supports on-disk storage of data columns. Indexes must always be stored in memory.

Beginning with MySQL Server version 5.1.24 the standard binaries built by Sun Microsystems will not include the NDB storage engine. Though it is still available with the source code (for now), the code for the NDB storage engine will not be updated to keep pace with changes in the NDB storage engine. If you need to use the NDB storage engine, use the MySQL Cluster server instead of MySQL Server.

Archive storage engine

The Archive storage engine is a good option for those needing to store data long term or perform data auditing on application operations. For quite some time MySQL has offered an option of using compressed MyISAM tables. There are performance benefits to using compressed

MyISAM tables for read operations, but there are several problems with MyISAM compressed tables:

- Compressing (or *packing*) a MyISAM table requires that the database be taken offline while the table is compressed. This is done through the use of the of the myisampack utility from the shell prompt.

- Compressed MyISAM tables are read-only. You cannot INSERT, DELETE, or UPDATE on a compressed table.

Archive tables are, in several ways, an improvement over these older MyISAM packed tables. The designers of the Archive storage engine were definitely looking at what was good about compressed MyISAM tables and improving on the areas of weaknesses of compressed MyISAM tables.

Feature summary:

- Non-transactional.

- Archive tables allow INSERT operations on the table. However, Archive tables do not allow UPDATE or DELETE operations. For data auditing purposes this is ideal because auditing requirements specify that once data has been created it cannot be changed in any manner.

- Very good data compression factor. The compression factor on an Archive table is higher than a packed MyISAM table.

- For reading data, much like the InnoDB engine, the Archive engine uses a snapshot read. This ensures that read operations do not block write operations.

- The Archive engine uses row-level locking.

- The Archive storage engine supports only one index. However, in tests, the Archive storage engine performs better with read queries than MyISAM packed tables, even when the packed tables have indexes the Archive tables do not.

Archive tables use up to four files during operation. All files begin with a filename of the table name. The table definition file has a suffix of .frm. The data file has a suffix of .ARZ. The file with metadata information for the table (if present) has a suffix of .ARM. During table optimization operations it is also possible that there is a file with a suffix of .ARN. These files will all be located in the directory of the database in which the tables are located.

The following shows a modified version of the rental table from the sakila database. Changes were made because Archive tables do not support foreign keys and the rental table had more than one index:

```
mysql>  CREATE TABLE `rental_archive` (
    ->    `rental_id` int(11) NOT NULL AUTO_INCREMENT,
    ->    `rental_date` datetime NOT NULL,
    ->    `inventory_id` mediumint(8) unsigned NOT NULL,
    ->    `customer_id` smallint(5) unsigned NOT NULL,
```

```
        -> `return_date` datetime DEFAULT NULL,
        -> `staff_id` tinyint(3) unsigned NOT NULL,
        -> `last_update` timestamp NOT NULL DEFAULT CURRENT_TIMESTAMP,
        -> PRIMARY KEY (`rental_id`)
        -> ) ENGINE=Archive DEFAULT CHARSET=utf8;
Query OK, 0 rows affected (0.01 sec)
```

This creates an archival version of the table. Now to demonstrate the ability to perform INSERT statements but not UPDATE or DELETE statements on an Archive table:

```
mysql> INSERT INTO rental_archive
    -> (rental_date, inventory_id, customer_id,
    -> return_date, staff_id) values (NOW(),'1','23',NOW(),'1');
Query OK, 1 row affected (0.00 sec)

mysql> SELECT rental_id, rental_date, inventory_id, customer_id
    -> return_date, staff_id, last_update
    -> FROM rental_archive\G
*************************** 1. row ***************************
    rental_id: 1
  rental_date: 2009-01-16 16:44:41
 inventory_id: 1
  customer_id: 23
  return_date: 2009-01-16 16:44:41
     staff_id: 1
  last_update: 2009-01-16 16:44:41
1 row in set (0.00 sec)

mysql> UPDATE rental SET rental_date=NOW() WHERE rental_id='1';
ERROR 1031 (HY000): Table storage engine for 'rental_archive' doesn't
    have this option
mysql> DELETE FROM rental_archive WHERE rental_id='1';
ERROR 1031 (HY000): Table storage engine for 'rental_archive' doesn't
    have this option
```

In a nutshell, what is demonstrated here, along with the data compression capabilities, are the two primary reasons for using Archive tables.

Blackhole storage engine

The Blackhole storage engine does not actually store data in tables as with other storage engines. This might seem to be very counter-intuitive. It is a storage engine that does not store data. But there are uses for this setup.

A master server may have an extremely high-write table whose data is only ever used on a slave. For example, session information including where a user clicked may be used in reporting queries, but are never queried on the master server. In this case, the table on the master can be created with ENGINE=BLACKHOLE and the table on the slave can be modified to use any storage engine. In this way, data updates on the master happen instantaneously, because INSERT, UPDATE, and DELETE statements return immediately as successful (so long as they are valid DML statements according to the table schema). This is a frequently used method of having a high-write table cause almost no extra I/O on the master (the binary logs are still written to).

Something quite common with large setups is the use of multiple slaves from a master server. If you have too many slaves this can cause load issues on the master server. You can implement a relay slave that acts as an intermediary to reduce this load. We discuss this in detail in Chapter 16. This relay slave can be configured using the Blackhole storage engine for all tables being replicated. Even though the Blackhole tables do not store any data changes, the binary logs are still written if logging is enabled. The relay slave operates much more efficiently because of the minimization of I/O activity.

CSV storage engine

The CSV (Comma Separated Value) storage engine is an engine of a decidedly different nature. A CSV data file is simply a text file that can be manipulated with a simple text editor or command-line text tools if needed. One of the primary uses for CSV is for data exchange and fast importing.

Feature summary:

- Plain text data file in CSV format
- Can have an instantaneous import time
- Easily imported into programs such as Microsoft Excel
- Table-level locking
- No foreign key support
- Non-transactional
- Trivial backups and restores (copy the files)
- Does not support indexing or partitions

Three files are created with any CSV table: an .frm file, which contains the table format; a .CSM file, which contains metadata; and the .CSV file, which contains the data. Each of these files has a prefix that consists of the table name.

Here is a brief example from a snippet of a data file of a three-field CSV table:

```
"1","Overstreet","Joe"
"2","Beal", "Sally"
"3","Murphy","Ashton"
"4","McGhee", "Sam"
```

> **TIP**   Want an instantaneous import time? Just have the data that you want to be imported stored in the CSV format in an export file. Create a new CSV table with the desired fields and then just copy the export file to the directory of the database. Then move the file to `table_name.CSV`. Issue a `FLUSH TABLES` command and the data is instantly available.

Working with Storage Engines

A number of commands are used specifically to work with any storage engine. These commands are extremely useful in the day-to-day work of a system administrator.

CREATE TABLE

The `CREATE TABLE` statement is used to create a database table. You can specify the storage engine that you want to use for the table by using the `ENGINE` clause or the server will use the default storage engine.

For example, to create an InnoDB table:

```
CREATE TABLE innodb_example (
id INTEGER UNSIGNED NOT NULL PRIMARY KEY AUTO_INCREMENT,
name VARCHAR(20) NOT NULL
) ENGINE = InnoDB;
```

ALTER TABLE

The `ALTER TABLE` command is used to modify previously created tables. The full syntax for the command is covered in Chapter 4. If you need to change a table type from one storage engine to another the `ALTER TABLE` command makes this simple. If you executed the previous `CREATE TABLE` without specifying an `ENGINE` clause it would create a MyISAM table by default:

```
CREATE TABLE innodb_example (
id INTEGER UNSIGNED NOT NULL PRIMARY KEY AUTO_INCREMENT,
name VARCHAR(20) NOT NULL
);
```

After you create the table you realize it needed to be an InnoDB table. To change this you simply run the `ALTER TABLE` command:

```
mysql> ALTER TABLE innodb_example ENGINE=InnoDB;
```

That is all there is to it!

DROP TABLE

The DROP TABLE command is used to drop a table and all its contents. Be careful, because this action cannot be undone. If it is executed inside a transaction the DROP TABLE command will implicitly commit the transaction before performing the actual DROP TABLE command.

```
mysql> DROP TABLE innodb_example;
```

Summary

The amazing variety of storage engines available for MySQL Server can be a great benefit to the database administrator. It allows you to choose the storage engine that best fits the needs of your application. You even have the choice of having more than one storage engine at the same time in your database, and having a table on a slave server have a different storage engine than the same table on the master server. This range of options brings complexity. There are typically many options to configure each storage engine. A beginning administrator should concentrate on understanding the MyISAM and InnoDB storage engines because these are going to be the ones you work with most often in a typical MySQL Server environment.

Some of the topics that were taught in this chapter include:

- Pluggable storage engine architecture
- Storage engine plugins
- Available storage engines:
  - MyISAM / Merge
  - InnoDB
  - MEMORY
  - Maria
  - Falcon
  - PBXT
  - FEDERATED
  - NDB
  - Archive
  - Blackhole
  - CSV
- Commands used to work with storage engines

Chapter 12

Caching with MySQL

IN THIS CHAPTER

Implementing Cache Tables

Working with the Query Cache

Utilizing Memcached

One of the ways of making queries respond faster is to implement caching. A cache stores frequently used information in a place where it can be accessed faster. For example, a web browser like Firefox uses a cache to store the text, images, and other objects from recently visited websites on your hard drive. When you visit a page you have recently been to, the text and images do not have to be downloaded a second time. Another way objects on web pages are cached is through a caching proxy server such as Squid (www.squid-cache.org). A caching proxy server is a proxy between the Internet and a set of machines. It eliminates the redundancy of each machine having a private cache. Furthermore, a cache of web objects from sites that all the machines have recently visited are stored, so a machine can benefit from a proxy cache even if it has never visited a particular web page before. Figure 12-1 shows a simplified diagram of a network of desktops that utilize a caching proxy server for web pages.

When users visit a web page their computer will first check the web page cache in their browser as described previously. If the page is not stored locally, the next step is to check the Squid cache. If the web page is not stored in the Squid cache, the web page is downloaded from the actual website — storing objects in the Squid and local browser cache along the way.

This may sound complicated, but there is very little overhead from checking these caches. When a cache can be used it is much faster than downloading content over the Internet. If you have a hundred people behind a caching proxy, there are going to be many cached web objects that can be accessed by someone else. Everyone behind the web caching proxy benefits from the entire cache. Not only is the user experience faster, but because there is less need to go to the Internet to download a web page, less bandwidth is used. The drawback is sometimes a web page has been updated and a cache has older information.

FIGURE 12-1

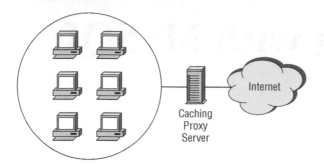

Like caching in any other application, caching with MySQL is designed to return data from a query quickly. There are three common ways to cache data with MySQL: creating manual cache tables, using internal caching in `mysqld`, and using the memcached distributed caching system.

Implementing Cache Tables

Developers and database administrators spend lots of time optimizing queries. However, one aspect of query optimization that is often overlooked is that a simple data access is much faster than a query with calculations, sorting, and aggregations. A *cache table* is a regular table in a database that stores the results of one or more queries for faster retrieval. Common query results that could be cached in a table are counts, ratings, and summaries.

For example, instead of calculating the number of total site visitors every time someone visits a particular web page, you can set an event in the Event Scheduler to calculate the total number of visitors every 30 minutes and store that information in a visitor count table. Then the slower query to calculate count is run once every 30 minutes, and every single time the web page is visited it does a simple query of the visitor count table. For more information on the Event Scheduler and how to create events, see Chapter 7.

As an example, assume it takes 4 seconds to calculate the total visitor count and a quarter of a second to return the results from the visitor count cache table. If there are 100 visitors to a site in 30 minutes, it would take 4 seconds per visitor * 100 visitors = 400 seconds of query processing time to run the query for every visitor. However, if you ran the query once every 30 minutes, it would take 4 seconds for the query to run once + 1/4 second to retrieve data from the cache table * 100 visitors to the site = 29 seconds of query processing time. The benefit is obvious.

The tradeoff is that the total count may not be 100% accurate. However, it is likely good enough — visitor count is usually used to show how many people have visited the site, and the count still adds value even if it is off by a few percentage points. The decision of whether or not the number is good enough has to be made through a joint effort between the database administrator and the business to determine if this is a reasonable tradeoff.

There is one other tradeoff of using the Event Scheduler — the query is run every 30 minutes, regardless of whether or not the information is used. For example, if nobody visits the website for an hour, there is no reason to recalculate the visitor count. If this is an issue you need to overcome, you will have to coordinate with application developers as well to create querying code that uses the following logic:

- Check the age of the data in the cache table
- If the data age is 30 minutes or less, use the data in the cache table
- If the data age is greater than 30 minutes, re-run the query, storing the results and new time in the cache table

It is preferable to schedule an event in the Event Scheduler, but for resource-heavy queries that are run on data that does not change very often, it may be necessary to create custom application code instead.

Going back to our example using the Event Scheduler — after the decision to store total visitor count every 30 minutes is made, there is a problem. The business has changed its requirements, and tells you that the count needs to be 100% accurate; it is unacceptable to have the query take 4 seconds, and there is no money in the budget for faster hardware.

This issue can be solved by storing the total visitor count for a time period in the past and then adding the count of visitors since the last calculation. For example, at midnight daily, calculate the total visitor count for the previous day. This count will never change once the day is over, so the count for an entire day never needs to be recalculated. The running total of visitors can be calculated as well, and then a 100% accurate count can be done at any time by calculating the total visitor count so far today and adding it to the running total calculated once per day. Computing the count for one day is much less resource-intensive than running full count every time someone visits a page.

Not only will this allow for accurate counts of total visitors, but it will allow for easy computation of number of visitors in a given data range — in our example, the number of visitors in a week can be calculated by adding the seven daily totals of visitors. The previous method did not easily allow for this type of data manipulation.

Here is an example of how to create such a system:

```
CREATE TABLE visitors_today (
today INT UNSIGNED NOT NULL DEFAULT 0,
vcount BIGINT UNSIGNED NOT NULL DEFAULT 0
) ENGINE=InnoDB;
```

```
CREATE TABLE visitors_stored (
vcount BIGINT UNSIGNED NOT NULL DEFAULT 0,
vcount_date DATE NOT NULL PRIMARY KEY
) ENGINE=MyISAM;
```

The visitors_stored table holds a historic record of the count of visitors per day. There can only be one entry per day. The visitors_today table holds the current count of visitors so far today (in the today field) and the total count of visitors up to today (in the vcount field).

With each new visitor, update the visitors_today.count field:

```
UPDATE visitors_today SET today = today + 1;
```

To retrieve the current total visitor count:

```
SELECT today + vcount FROM visitors_today;
```

Every day at midnight, schedule an event that:

- Inserts a new row with yesterday's date and count in the visitors_stored table
- Calculates and stores the total running count in visitors_today.vcount
- Resets the vistors_today.today field to zero

Here is a sample event that updates the current and historic visitor count tables:

```
CREATE EVENT update_vcount
ON SCHEDULE EVERY 1 DAY
STARTS '2009-01-01 00:00:00'
DO BEGIN
INSERT INTO visitors_stored (vcount, vcount_date)
SELECT today, CURRENT_DATE() - INTERVAL 1 DAY FROM visitors_today;
UPDATE visitors_today set today=0, vcount=(
  SELECT SUM(vcount) as vcount FROM visitors_stored);
END
```

Do not forget to enable the Event Scheduler with SET GLOBAL event_scheduler='ON', and recall from Chapter 7 that you will need to change the DELIMITER to define an event with multiple statement events. Also, for the system to function it must be initialized; at minimum you must populate the visitors_today table. If today already had 37 visitors and the total number of visitors at the start of the day was 1,638,492, the following would populate the table properly:

```
INSERT INTO visitors_today (today, vcount) VALUES (37,1638492);
```

For a new system, simply use INSERT INTO visitors_today (today, vcount) VALUES (0,0);.

These two tables achieve the business goals of allowing for accurate counts and faster counting without buying new hardware. For more ways to optimize this and other queries, see Chapter 18.

As a final example before moving on, another way to keep a counter accurate is through the use of a trigger. If you need to keep an accurate count of the number of rows in a table and it is resource-intensive to run the SELECT COUNT(*) query (as is the case on InnoDB tables), just have a trigger update a count statistic on every INSERT or DELETE from the table. Keep in mind that using triggers brings its own overhead and might not be ideal for your situation. As well, it is useful for simple calculations such as a running counter, but there is not an equivalent useful solution for more complex calculations such as ranking.

System-intensive queries, whose results can be slightly inaccurate, are often perfect candidates for cache tables. Some of these queries may be required to use a cache table because the calculations use so many resources!

Working with the Query Cache

Internally, mysqld can cache the result sets of SQL statements. Similar to the concept of a local cache of a web page, mysqld can compare a query to the queries stored in the query cache. If the query is stored in the query cache, the result set is retrieved without having to execute the query again. If the query is not stored in the query cache, the query is executed and the result set can be stored in the query cache so the next time the query is called the result set will be there.

By default, the query cache is not enabled. Using the query cache adds more overhead — memory is used to store the query cache, and it takes processing time to check the query cache. If the query cache is frequently checked and matches are rarely found, the additional processing time required may hurt performance instead of helping it. Make sure to thoroughly test the query cache before implementing it.

In some cases, turning the query cache on will produce amazing performance improvements. However, it is a common mistake for database administrators new to MySQL to believe that the query cache will solve most performance issues. In reality, only queries with certain characteristics will benefit from using the query cache. This section discusses how the query cache works, to better provide you with information to help you decide when the query cache is appropriate for you.

What gets stored in the query cache?

The MySQL query cache is simple in operation. It only caches SELECT statements and their corresponding result sets, and only for deterministic SELECT statements. Deterministic SELECT statements are statements that always produce the same results no matter what, given the same

427

data set. For example, `SELECT COUNT(*) FROM tbl` is always the same given the same data set, but `SELECT NOW()` is not always the same.

The query cache stores a rudimentary hash of the query along with its result set. This means that the query being compared must be byte-for-byte identical to the cached query — the queries themselves are not compared; their hashes are compared. This means that in order to match, the queries must match with regard to case sensitivity and whitespace. Consider the following two queries:

```
SELECT customer_id,name from sakila.customer;
SELECT customer_id,name FROM sakila.customer;
```

Both queries executed from the command line will return identical result sets. However, from the perspective of the query cache, both queries are not identical. With the first query `from` is not capitalized and with the second query `FROM` is capitalized. From the perspective of the query cache these are not the same query. As mentioned previously, different spacing in the queries will also result in no match being found.

In addition to spacing and capitalization, queries are viewed as different by the query cache if they use different databases, protocol versions, or character sets. Furthermore, not all `SELECT` statements will be cached. `SELECT` statements with the following properties are not cached:

- Use of non-deterministic functions
- Most subqueries
- Use of user-defined functions
- Use of temporary tables
- `SELECT` statements in stored functions, triggers, views, and events
- Using `LOCK IN SHARE MODE` or `FOR UPDATE`
- Result sets larger than `query_cache_limit` (1 Mb by default; see the section in this chapter on query cache configuration)
- Using `SQL_NO_CACHE`

Just because a query can be cached, however, does not mean it should be cached. If a query is being executed frequently and does not have a result set that exceeds the `query_cache_limit`, it may be a good candidate for caching. However, another factor to consider is how many times a cached query is used before it is removed from the query cache.

Query cache invalidation is when a query is removed from the query cache because its result set may have changed. When a table is modified by either DDL or DML (either schema changes or data changes), all of the queries in the query cache referencing that table are invalidated and removed. This query cache invalidation is not very granular — it invalidates query cache results based on tables, not rows. A query may be removed from the query cache even though its result set has not changed, because a table it references has changed.

Query cache pruning is when a query is removed from the query cache because the query cache cannot find a free block in which to store a new query. The query cache prunes older entries using a least recently used (LRU) algorithm.

The overhead of query removal must be considered when determining if a query is a good candidate for caching. Queries that reference tables that are frequently updated and queries that are pruned before being used several times are not good candidates for the query cache. In addition, if there are many queries that can be cached, enabling the query cache for all queries is not a good idea — we have seen many database administrators turn on the query cache, and query performance gets worse, because every single query is being cached, and there are so many queries being cached that the savings of using a cache are never recognized.

WARNING When using the query cache, each SELECT statement has overhead. First, a hash of the query is calculated, and the query cache is checked for a match. If the query does not match, the query proceeds as usual. If the query can be cached, the result set is stored in the query cache when the query is completed. All queries that do not have a match in the query cache will use more resources than if the query cache was turned off.

However, DML such as UPDATE, INSERT, and DELETE and DDL such as ALTER TABLE also have extra overhead even though these statements are never cached. When a table is changed, the cache is checked in order to remove any queries that are invalidated.

If you realize you do not want to store every query in the query cache, you can use the server variable query_cache_type. It has three possible options: OFF, ON, and DEMAND. Setting the query_cache_type to OFF turns off the query cache. If you do not want to cache every result set, you have two options:

■ Cache all queries, except for a few chosen queries. Setting the query_cache_type to ON and setting a query_cache_size larger than 0 enables the query cache for SELECT statements as specified by the rules above. This means the query cache will cache all possible queries, and you can choose certain queries not to cache by using SELECT SQL_NO_CACHE.

■ Do not cache any queries, except for a few chosen queries. Setting the query_cache_type to DEMAND and setting a query_cache_size larger than 0 enables the query cache only for SELECT statements with the SQL_CACHE clause. In other words, the query cache does not cache any queries except for the ones you choose, which will use SELECT SQL_CACHE.

Query cache memory usage and tuning

The query cache for the server is stored completely in memory, and does not persist across mysqld restarts. Aside from about 40k of memory used by the query cache, the entire pool of memory is initialized as a single contiguous chunk of memory. During query cache operation this chunk of memory is divided up into smaller blocks. These blocks are used to store the result sets of the cached queries. Each block must be at least the size specified by query_cache_min_res_unit, which defaults to 4 Kb. For result sets smaller than 4 Kb, it still uses 4 Kb of memory.

In addition to these blocks containing the result sets of the queries there are two hash tables. One hash table stores query hashes. The second hash table contains the list of database tables that each cached query references. When a table is modified, this second hash table is consulted to determine which queries should be removed due to query cache invalidation.

Seven system variables are used to control the configuration and memory usage of the query cache. The values of these can be seen by using SHOW GLOBAL VARIABLES statement or in the GLOBAL_VARIABLES system view in the INFORMATION_SCHEMA (see Chapter 21 for more information about INFORMATION_SCHEMA).

Table 12-1 lists these variables and a brief description of each one.

TABLE 12-1

Query Cache System Variables

Variable Name	Description
query_alloc_block_size	Specifies the size of memory blocks allocated by the query cache during query processing. The default is 8 Kb.
query_cache_limit	Result sets larger than this are not cached. The default is 1 Mb.
query_cache_min_res_unit	Specifies the minimum size for blocks in the query cache. The default value is 4 Kb.
query_cache_size	The total memory allocated by mysqld for the query cache. The default is 0, which disables the query cache. This can be changed dynamically — changes do not require a mysqld restart.
query_cache_type	Determines the mode of operation of the query cache. Options are OFF, ON, and DEMAND. The default is ON.
query_cache_wlock_invalidate	If set to TRUE, queries referencing MyISAM tables are invalidated when a write lock for that table is obtained, even if none of the data is changed when the write lock is released. The default is FALSE.
query_cache_prealloc_size	Specifies the size of the buffer used for query parsing by the cache. Defaults to 8 Kb.

There are eight status variables relating to the query cache. These variables are used for managing and tuning the query cache. The values of these can be seen by using the SHOW GLOBAL STATUS statement or in the GLOBAL_STATUS system view in the INFORMATION_SCHEMA (see Chapter 21 for more information about INFORMATION_SCHEMA).

Table 12-2 lists each query cache status variable with a brief description.

TABLE 12-2	

Query Cache Status Variables

Counter Name	Description
Qcache_free_blocks	Number of memory blocks free in the query cache
Qcache_free_memory	Total bytes of memory free in the query cache
Qcache_hits	Number of times a query matched the query cache
Qcache_inserts	Number of times a query and result set were inserted into the query cache
Qcache_lowmem_prunes	Number of times a query was removed due to query pruning
Qcache_not_cached	Number of queries that could not be cached
Qcache_queries_in_cache	Number of queries currently stored in the query cache
Qcache_total_blocks	Total number of memory blocks in cache

To see how useful your query cache is:

■ Determine the percentage of SELECT queries that are getting their result sets from the query cache. This rate, known as the query cache *hit ratio*, is calculated by taking the number of query cache *hits* (matches) and dividing it by the total number of hits plus the number of non-hits. Com_select is the status variable that holds the number of executed SELECT queries that go through the full execution plan. To calculate the query cache hit ratio:

Qcache_hits / (Qcache_hits + Com_select)

For example, if Qcache_hits is 15,593 and Com_select is 10,193:

15,593 / (15,593 + 10,193) = .60470 = 60.47%

Depending on your application, this can be a good hit ratio or not. If your application has many different SELECT statements, or if many statements cannot be cached or are not being cached on purpose (that is, using SELECT SQL_NO_CACHE), the hit ratio will never be high. To increase your hit ratio, consider caching more queries (see the sidebar on caching more queries).

- Calculate the percentage of SELECT queries that are placed in the query cache. This rate is known as the *insert ratio* and, like the hit ratio, is calculated using the Com_select status variable:

```
Qcache_inserts / Com_select * 100
```

If this percentage is high, it means that most of your SELECT queries are being put into the query cache. If Qcache_lowmem_prunes is also low, it means that even though most of your SELECT queries are being put into the query cache, they are not causing your query cache to fill up, thus pruning queries from the query cache. However, this may not necessarily indicate a well-tuned query cache, because there could be a lot of query cache invalidation happening. Unfortunately there is no parameter to see exactly how much query cache invalidation is happening. You may be able to estimate how many queries are being removed by watching how the Qcache_queries_in_cache variable changes over time.

- Calculate the percentage of free memory, in bytes and blocks, left in the query cache:

```
Qcache_free_memory / query_cache_size * 100
Qcache_free_blocks / Qcache_total_blocks * 100
```

If the percentage of free memory is high, either lower the query_cache_size so that you are not wasting memory by allocating it to the query cache, or cache more queries (see the sidebar on caching more queries).

If the percentage of free memory is low and Qcache_queries_in_cache is also low, it means that in addition not having a lot of memory for more queries, there are very few queries in the query cache. This may indicate that:

- The query_cache_size needs to bigger
- The query_cache_limit needs to be smaller
- The query cache is heavily fragmented. See the next section on query cache fragmentation for more information.

Caching More Queries

If you determine that your query cache is not being utilized enough, you may need to try caching more queries. To do this, you can:

1. Use fewer SELECT SQL_NO_CACHE statements if your query_cache_type is ON.
2. Use more SELECT SQL_CACHE statements if your query_cache_type is DEMAND.

continued

continued

3. `Qcache_not_cached` is the number of queries that could not be cached. If this is large, increasing the `query_cache_limit` parameter enables queries with larger result sets to be stored in the query cache.

4. `Qcache_lowmem_prunes` is the number of times a query has had to be pruned due to not enough memory. If `Qcache_free_blocks` and `Qcache_free_memory` are also high, you likely have fragmentation (see the next section on query cache fragmentation). If the free memory in the query cache is low, increasing the `query_cache_size` parameter will allow more queries to be cached in the query cache.

Query cache fragmentation

Fragmentation of the query cache is analogous to fragmentation of hard drives. With a typical desktop computer, after you utilize it for a while your hard drive gets fragmented with files *scattered* all over the hard drive. The fragmentation is caused by files being deleted that leave *holes* in the layout of files on your hard drive. Though the operating system will try and fill in these holes with other files, they will almost never be an exact fit. Over time you end up with hundreds or thousands of these holes and they consume extra hard drive space and slow down the system. To resolve the problem the hard drive must be defragmented. This involves moving the files around to remove the gaps and make everything as compact as possible.

With a query cache there are two causes of fragmentation. The first cause is that the result sets do not always fit exactly into a block of memory. The query cache program has to estimate the size of the result set it will be storing in the cache and allocate a block of memory for storage of the result set. The estimation is necessary because it receives the result set row by row instead of in one large chunk. Once the query cache is done storing the result set it will trim the allocated block of memory down in size so that there is just enough memory for the size of the result set. This leaves a gap between the blocks of memory.

The second cause of query cache fragmentation is the invalidation of queries stored in the cache. When a query is invalidated it is deleted from the cache. As with hard drive fragmentation, a hole is created when the deletion occurs.

Often both trimming of blocks and invalidation of queries leads to blocks of memory that are too small to store query results. The best way to handle query cache fragmentation is to minimize the amount of fragmentation. One way to minimize fragmentation is to set the block size of the query cache to the average result set size of your queries. To determine the average result size:

```
(query_cache_size-Qcache_free_memory)/Qcache_queries_in_cache
```

Unfortunately this will not help for every application. Situations where this might not be helpful include when the application has a combination of both large and small queries.

433

Another way to minimize fragmentation is to minimize the query cache invalidation and pruning. The more queries removed, the more fragmentation can occur. Often, it is not possible to change the frequency of UPDATE, INSERT, and DELETE statements on a table. However, query cache invalidation may be minimized by splitting large tables into smaller tables by using MERGE tables (see Chapter 11) or partitioning (see Chapter 15).

In situations where fragmentation is likely and difficult to minimize, it may be best to choose which queries to cache by setting the query_cache_type to DEMAND and using the SQL_CACHE hint to select the queries you want cached.

The previous section on query cache memory usage and tuning showed how to determine if the query cache is fragmented. Executing the FLUSH QUERY CACHE command will defragment the cache. FLUSH QUERY CACHE does not flush the cache; it compacts the cache by locking the query cache and re-ordering it so there are no gaps between blocks of memory. With larger caches the re-ordering can be a significant period of time. At the time of this writing, we recommend the maximum size of query_cache_size to be 256 Mb, so the defragmentation process is not too long. If, instead of compacting the query cache, it is necessary to empty the query cache use the RESET QUERY CACHE command.

WARNING   Be careful using the FLUSH QUERY CACHE command. DML and DDL use the query cache to invalidate queries after the table changes are made, so these queries will not complete until the lock on the query cache is released. In addition, any SELECT queries checking the query cache must also wait for the lock on the query cache to be released. If the query_cache_type is ON, this means that *all* SELECT queries except for those specifying SQL_NO_CACHE depend on the query cache. Performing a FLUSH QUERY CACHE may block many or all queries, so be careful when defragmenting!

Utilizing memcached

The memcached caching system is a distributed, in-memory cache system that speeds up web applications by minimizing the amount of database queries needed. It was originally developed by Danga Interactive for the LiveJournal website. The official website for memcached is at http://danga.com/memcached/.

The basic principle of memcached is that a number of memcached daemons work together to provide data caching. memcached is *distributed* because many daemons can work together to cache data — there is no need for one centralized cache. It is an *in-memory* cache, which means that when a daemon is restarted the cache data it held is lost. As with the query cache in mysqld, memcached stores a hash of a query along with its result set. The application code must be changed to first retrieve the result set corresponding to the hash of the query — if nothing is returned, there was no match in the memcached cache, and the application code should proceed to query the database as normal. The application code has the power to store the query and the new result set, if desired.

Installing memcached is not difficult for those with system administration experience. memcached runs on Unix-based platforms. A third-party Windows port of memcached is available at http://jehiah.cz/projects/memcached-win32. The only prerequisite memcached requires is the libevent library.

> **TIP** The Frequently Asked Questions page for memcached has a lot of good information for a memcached beginner, including where to download memcached and how to install it:
>
> http://code.google.com/p/memcached/wiki/FAQ

Configuration of memcached is not difficult. In fact, it has just a handful of command-line options. Table 12-3 lists the memcached options and what they do.

TABLE 12-3

memcached Command-Line Options

Option	Description
-d	Runs in daemon mode (in the background). Without this option, memcached runs in the foreground.
-l	Listens on specific IP address. By default, memcached listens on all IP addresses configured on the server.
-s	Listens via the specified Unix socket file only.
-m	Amount of memory to use (in megabytes).
-p	Listens on specified port (11211 by default).
-u	User who runs the daemon.

One consideration is the amount of memory you can allocate to each memcached daemon. If you are running memcached on a 32-bit machine, each process can only address approximately 2.4 Gb of memory. However, because memcached is designed to be distributed, it is very easy to run multiple instances on 32-bit machines. In fact, to maximize the cache memcached provides, run as many memcached daemons as possible — using dedicated memcached machines with one or more instances, and putting memcached instances on the same machines as their web servers. Both of these practices are recommended and encouraged.

Web servers are particularly well-suited to share resources with memcached processes. For typical dynamic content, web servers use much more CPU than memory, and memcached processes use much more memory than CPU.

> **WARNING** No authentication or security measures are built into memcached. Never expose memcached ports to the Internet.

Once memcached is configured and running, it is time to begin utilizing the cache. You do this via application code. In each place that your application queries the database, add in a check of the cache in memcached first. If memcached returns nothing, the application must then go to the database, get the result set, and store it in memcached.

A number of programming APIs are available that interface with memcached. Table 12-4 lists some of the more popular ones and their locations.

TABLE 12-4

memcached Programming API Libraries

API Language	API Name	Download Location
C	libmemcachedapr_memcache	http://tangent.org/552/libmemcached.html http://www.outoforder.cc/projects/libs/apr_memcache/
C#	memcacheddotnetEnyim Memcachedbeitmemcached	https://sourceforge.net/projects/memcacheddotnet/ http://www.codeplex.com/EnyimMemcached/ http://code.google.com/p/beitmemcached/
Java	spymemcached	http://code.google.com/p/spymemcached/
Lua	memcached.lua	http://luamemcached.luaforge.net/
Perl	Cache::Memcached Cache::Memcached::Fast	http://search.cpan.org/dist/Cache-Memcached/ http://search.cpan.org/dist/Cache-Memcached-Fast/
PHP	memcache	http://pecl.php.net/package/memcache
Python	python-memcached	ftp://ftp.tummy.com/pub/python-memcached/
MySQL UDFs	Memcached Functions for MySQL	http://tangent.org/586/Memcached_Functions_for_MySQL.html

Though we do not have the space to provide a complete programming guide, we will show a simple example to show you what it is like to work with memcached.

In order to be utilized, memcached will need to be integrated into your application. In this example, the application is using PHP and the memcache API for PHP.

The first thing to do is create a new Memcache object and establish a connection to our memcached server:

```php
<?php
$memcache = new Memcache;
$memcache->connect('localhost', 11211) or die ("Could not connect");
?>
```

For this example we are running memcached on the local machine with default settings. You would typically initiate this connection once, when you open a database connection. If you want to connect to more than one memcached server, call $memcache->connect() again and with the host and port additional server. For comparison purposes, before we show you how to integrate memcached with your code, here is the code for a database query that does not use memcached:

```php
<?php
$sql = "SELECT first_name, last_name FROM sakila.customer WHERE cus-
tomer_id = 1";
$query = mysql_query($sql) or die(mysql_error()." : $sql");
if(mysql_num_rows($query)> 0) {
  $result = mysql_fetch_object($query);
$content = $result->content;
  }
?>
```

Here is one way to integrate memcached:

```php
<?php
$sql = "SELECT first_name, last_name FROM sakila.customer WHERE cus-
tomer_id = 1";

//create a hash of the query
$key = md5('query'.$sql);

//lookup the hash
$result = $memcache->get($key);

//if we memcached does not return a result set
//query the database normally
if($result == null) {
  $query = mysql_query($sql) or die(mysql_error()." : $sql");
  if(mysql_num_rows($query)> 0) {
    $result = mysql_fetch_object($query);

//store the result in memcache
    $memcache->set($key,$result,0,1800);
$content = $result->content;
    }
  }
?>
```

The code first checks to see if it can find the result set in memcached. If no results are returned, the result set is fetched from the database, returned for use, and stored into memcached. In the code sample, the set() function takes four arguments: the query hash ($key), the result set ($result), whether or not the result set should be compressed (0, which means no), and an expiration time (1800 seconds, which is 30 minutes).

There are two ways to resolve the problem of stale data in the memcached cache. The easiest method is to use a low cache expiration time, applied to the result set when the data is stored using the set() function. Though this is simple to implement, there can still be a lag from the time you updated the database to when the updates will appear in the cache. For example, if we set the expiration time for the previous query to 60 seconds, the data may be up to 60 seconds out of date. Though this is better than up to 30 minutes out of date, the data is still changed.

The second method is to update the cache immediately when data is changed. This requires more work because you have to update each result set that has changed in the cache.

There is another way for memcached to interact with mysqld: the memcache_engine storage engine, developed by MySQL architect Brian Aker. The website for memcache_engine is:

```
http://tangent.org/index.pl?node_id=506
```

memcache_engine makes memcached look like a table in mysqld. Instead of API calls such as get() and set() in the preceding example, API calls are in the format of SELECT, INSERT, UPDATE, and DELETE queries on a table representing the memcached cache.

memcached can make a dramatic difference in the response time of your application and the load on your database servers. Although the speed of memcached is impressive, surpassing that of the query cache in mysqld, the ability to scale by adding additional servers and updating your application code is equally important. memcached can be a great way to scale a rapidly growing website.

Summary

Caching at any level with database servers is a win-win situation when the end user frequently gets faster responses from the application and the database server does not have to work as hard to return those results. Combining multiple layers of caching provides even better results. The following topics were covered in this chapter:

- What caching is
- Using cache tables to cache counts
- The mysqld query cache
- The memcached caching server

Chapter 13

Backups and Recovery

IN THIS CHAPTER

Backing up MySQL

Recovering from crashes

Planning for disasters

he most important responsibility a database administrator has is performing backups and recoveries. In almost every case, data is an organization's primary asset and keeping that asset safe is of utmost importance. Backups and recovery are necessary in case of disaster, but are also critical in setting up replication, upgrading, migrating, and troubleshooting unexpected data changes.

This chapter has two goals. The first goal is to give an overview of the various methods of backups available to a database administrator. The second goal is to help you to understand that there is more to backups and recovery than just being able to perform the actual operations of backup and recovery. Backup and recovery are parts of the big picture of planning for disasters and recovering from them, as well as setting up new slave servers and test/development environments.

Backing Up MySQL

A number of terms are associated with backup and recovery. Before covering the various methods of performing backups, it's important to define some terminology first:

- **Logical backup** — A *logical backup* is created by saving information that represents the logical database structures using SQL statements like CREATE DATABASE, CREATE TABLE, and INSERT. It is not correct to say that a logical backup is a text representation of the database server because there can be non-text binary data in logical backup. Other names for a logical backup are a *logical export* and an *export*.

439

The advantages of a logical backup are that it allows the database administrator to manipulate the backup data using tools such as dd and grep and programming languages such as awk and Perl. In addition, logical backups are more compatible between different versions of mysqld when you are upgrading your database server. Sun recommends a logical backup and restore of your database as a standard practice when upgrading between different release series (that is, when upgrading from version 5.1 to 6.0) of mysqld. The disadvantages compared to a physical backup are that a logical backup is slower to back up and restore and may take up more space (but compresses well).

■ **Physical backup** — A *physical backup* is a backup of the actual database files or disk partitions. This can be much faster to back up and restore than logical backups. Though physical backups do not compress much (the data is usually in a binary format and thus somewhat compressed already), physical backups are often smaller than uncompressed logical backups. Physical backups may also be called *raw backups*.

■ **Full backup** — A *full backup* is a standalone backup containing everything in the database. If necessary you could use the results of the full backup to re-create a server somewhere else. A full backup can be either a logical or physical backup.

■ **Incremental backup** — An *incremental backup* is a backup that only contains the data changed since the previous backup. The previous backup may have been full or incremental. The advantage of an incremental backup compared to a full backup is quicker backup times. Incremental backups are used to be able to back up data more frequently than a full backup may allow.

For example, a full backup of a large data set may take 3 hours, and a daily incremental backup may take 30 minutes. An organization may only be able to run a 3-hour full backup once a week on Sundays, but during the other six days of the week an organization can run an incremental backup. In this way, the data set can be restored to how it was on Sunday, Tuesday, or any other day of the week. To restore to Tuesday, first the Sunday full backup is restored. Then the Monday incremental backup is applied to the Sunday restore, restoring the data to how it was on Monday. Then the Tuesday incremental backup can be applied.

The biggest disadvantage of an incremental backup is that it is not a full data set, and cannot be used by itself to restore a full data set. This means that incremental backups have longer recovery times than full backups, because the latest full backup and all intermediate incremental backups need to be restored.

■ **Consistent backup** — A *consistent backup* is a backup at an exact moment in time. A backup process takes time to complete. Consider the following scenario:

    ▨ The customer table has a field that references a record in the address table.

    ▨ The address table is backed up at 1:00 am.

    ▨ The customer table is backed up at 1:05 am.

    ▨ Between 1:00 am and 1:05 am, a customer named Henry Inge signs up for a new account using an address not previously in the system.

The address table was backed up at 1:00 am, before Henry signed up for a new account. Therefore, the backup of address will not contain Henry's address. However, customer is backed up at 1:05 am, and by then Henry's address is in address, and there is a reference to that record in customer. Thus, a problem occurs: in the backup of customer, Henry's record references an address that does not exist in the backup of address!

An *inconsistent backup* is usually simpler and less resource-intensive to produce than a consistent backup. However, an inconsistent backup cannot be used as a standalone backup. An inconsistent backup may be used for partial data restores (such as restoring only Henry's e-mail address).

■ **Hot backup** — A *hot backup* is a backup of a database that is still running. During a hot backup, neither reads nor writes are blocked.

■ **Warm backup** — A *warm backup* is a backup of a database that is still running. During a warm backup, read queries are not blocked but writes are prohibited from making any modifications to the database for the duration of the backup.

■ **Cold backup** — A *cold backup* is a backup performed while the database is shut down. This makes it very easy to make a consistent copy of your data. The disadvantage is that the server is not accessible during the time the backup is performed.

■ **Point-in-time restore** — A *point-in-time restore* is a restoration of a database to a specified date and time. If this does not correspond to the time a full backup was performed, incremental backups and/or server logs must be used to finish the restoration process.

Uses for backups

There are many reasons to have data backups. This section outlines the main reasons; you may have additional backup uses specific to your environment.

Disaster recovery

Most people think of disaster recovery as the sole reason backups are performed. However, disaster recovery itself is a misnomer. You have many different types of disasters to plan for; an important part of a backup plan is determining both common and uncommon disasters and planning the appropriate responses to them.

For example, hard drive failure could be handled several ways. One plan is to use RAID arrays to handle a single drive failure, which will allow the file system to continue to be used (at a reduced speed) until the drive can be replaced. This disaster recovery plan must also include how to notice that a drive has failed, and how and when the replacement is done — is there a vendor or third-party that will replace the drive within a certain period of time? Whose responsibility in-house is it to make sure the correct parts are on hand (or ordered with rush delivery), and make sure the replacement happens?

Of course this plan does not take into account what happens if the RAID controller fails. You should try and think of as many possible failure scenarios and your response to them as possible. What happens if a motherboard malfunctions? Many databases are stored on in-house systems — what happens if the office building loses power? What if the office building has a fire and the machines are unsalvageable? If you have your data in a data center, what happens if a natural or man-made disaster occurs such as a hurricane or act of war? If you have a backup data center, is it near the first data center? A blizzard may hit Boston and New York City on the same day.

It may seem ridiculous to go through this scenario ("what happens if all of Europe is vaporized?"). However, it is extremely important for both the IT department and management to understand that *disaster* takes many forms, and that situations occur in which it is acceptable to have downtime, or perhaps lose data. Many times a directive will come down to have all systems running 24 hours a day, 7 days a week, 52 weeks a year, with 99.999% uptime. Is it possible to release a code update, upgrade your systems, and perform regularly scheduled maintenance with fewer than 5 minutes and 15 seconds of downtime per year?

For many actual natural and man-made disasters, customers will understand. If you had ordered a book from Amazon.com and were informed that before the backups that night, a major tornado destroyed the building, it is very likely you would not be upset having to re-order. Keep in mind that these sorts of disasters happen very infrequently, but must be considered.

In addition, it is important to stress the difference between *disaster recovery* and *high availability*. Often, being able to recover from a disaster is taken for granted, and people actually mean *high availability* when they use the words *disaster recovery*. However, disaster recovery means that information and status can be recovered, not that they can be recovered instantly. Good disaster recovery plans will include details and timing. How much spare equipment and parts are on hand? A large backup can take hours to copy to a new machine — is it acceptable to have that sort of downtime, or should another plan be in place, such as having a slave machine with similar specifications as the master? If it is a business requirement that your database servers are available a very high percentage of the time, you need to plan for server failover and using an option like replication to ensure that you have two servers at all times with the same data set. We cover this in Chapter 22.

Planning for disaster recovery takes time. A plan for hard drive issues might be researched and written in thirty minutes. Planning for a catastrophic natural disaster such as a major hurricane destroying your data center is another matter entirely. Creating a disaster recovery plan for loss of a data center may take several people many weeks to research, test, and document.

Data recovery

What do you do when a long-time customer (or the president of your company) deletes data and realizes a week later he needs it back? What about if some new code updates the wrong records? What if you are legally required to hand over historical data (for example, if you receive a subpoena)? Alternatively, maybe you decide to back up the `mysqld` users and their privileges separately.

 Physical backups are very useful for disaster recovery, but logical backups are much more useful when restoring partial amounts of data.

Easy test server creation

Development, testing, load test, QA, and content staging servers can be created. Some companies have a regular weekly restores so their non-production environments mimic the production environment. Using a backup to create a test server is a good reason to back up only part of the database.

Easy slave creation

If you have a properly configured backup it makes it easy to create a new slave. When your backup is taken, save the binary log position along with the backup. To create a slave of the backed-up server, restore the database and execute a CHANGE MASTER command to configure the slave, using the saved binary log position. Setting up a slave is covered in detail in Chapter 16.

WARNING A replicated slave can serve as a backup for disaster recovery, but not for data recovery. If you accidentally delete data on the master this will be replicated to the slave and you then have no method of recovering that data. However, slaves often make ideal platforms for backups because it is often easier to have a slave out of service for a time.

Backup frequency

When talking about backups an important part of the discussion is how often and what kind of backups should be done. The answer to how often and what kind of backup is a firm "it depends." Some companies are perfectly comfortable with a full backup once a month and no other backups are performed. Those companies must be prepared to lose up to a month's amount of data changes. Performing a full backup once a month and retaining incremental backups may not lose as much data, but the restore takes longer because the incremental backups must be applied.

On the other hand, some companies perform a full backup every night, perform incremental backups every 5 minutes and copy them to an off-site server, and have an extra data center configured and ready in case of the loss of the primary data center. This is an extremely expensive solution; however, if a company loses $10,000 a minute when data is unaccessible, it is appropriate.

Factors that affect how often backups are taken and what type of backups to take include:

- The amount of resources a backup can consume, and for what duration. Can a backup consume the entire database (as with a cold backup) for 5 hours? The answer may be "Yes, but only once per month."

- The definition of an *acceptable* resource use and duration for the restore of a full data set. Similarly, an acceptable resource use and duration for the restore of a partial data set. Resource use and duration will depend on the importance and age of the data: It can be acceptable to take a day or longer to locate correct financial data from 6 months ago, but finding the same data from last week should not take as long.

- The type of data being backed up. A database with mostly static data such as a list of countries can be backed up less frequently than an invoicing database. In-memory, transient, temporal, or interim data such as current session information may never be backed up.

- The amount of time to store a backup for. For example, if full backups are taken weekly, for how many weeks are full backups saved, and in what locations? How long are incremental backups saved?

Often, a *grandfather-father-son* backup rotation is implemented. This term refers back to when tape storage was used for backups and it was important to rotate tape stock. A company whose backup filled a backup tape might rotate 20 backup tapes in the following manner: keep the first backup of the month for 6 months, the first backup of the week for the past 7 weeks, and the last week's worth of daily backups. Even though many companies no longer use tape storage for backup, it still provides a great strategy for backups. With this strategy there are three defined sets of backups: daily (*son*), weekly (*father*), and monthly (*grandfather*).

Daily backups may be either full or incremental; monthly backups are full backups. Weekly backups are usually full, though occasionally companies will do weekly backups as incremental backups. A monthly backup can be used to compare historical data or to retrieve data from a particular point in time. A monthly backup will not likely be used to recover from a full data disaster; however, it can be quite useful to retrieve a snapshot of the data at a certain time.

To illustrate a grandfather-father-son backup rotation, a company with a grandfather-father-son backup rotation of 6-7-7 will have the following backups as of June 15, 2009 as shown in Table 13-1.

TABLE 13-1

Sample Grandfather-Father-Son Backups Available as of June 15, 2009

Monthly Backups	Weekly Backups	Daily Backups
Thursday, January 1, 2009	Sunday, May 3, 2009	Tuesday, June 9, 2009
Sunday, February 1, 2009	Sunday, May 10, 2009	Wednesday, June 10, 2009
Sunday, March 1, 2009	Sunday, May 17, 2009	Thursday, June 11, 2009
Wednesday, April 1, 2009	Sunday, May 24, 2009	Friday, June 12, 2009
Friday, May 1, 2009	Sunday, May 31, 2009	Saturday, June 13, 2009
Monday, June 1, 2009	Sunday, June 7, 2009	**Sunday, June 14, 2009**
	Sunday, June 14, 2009	Monday, Jun 15, 2009

Note that the Sunday, June 14, 2009 backup is stored twice.

What to back up

The question of what to back up seems simple on the surface. We have already described situations (non-production servers, `mysqld` user accounts, static data) in which you may decide not to back up all your data. However, there is more to consider than full vs. incremental data and complete vs. partial data. Some other information that might need to be backed up includes:

- Binary logs (for incremental backups, or to create a slave of the backed-up machine)
- InnoDB log files (for physical backups)
- `mysqld` option file (such as `/etc/my.cnf`)
- Slave position information (`master.info`) if backup occurs on a slave
- Relay logs on slave server if backup occurs on a slave

Backup locations

A production server that is in use and serving queries can be backed up using a hot backup method. Though a hot backup is non-blocking, it will impact the server and slow operations. Disk I/O, CPU, and RAM are all used by backups, which will make fewer resources available for `mysqld`. Often a slave server is implemented, and backups can be performed on the slave instead of the master.

Unfortunately one of the limitations of replication in `mysqld` is that a slave cannot have more than one master. This means that it becomes more difficult to have a centralized backup of all the database servers in an organization. Most organizations already have a slave to minimize downtime from maintenance and system failures — backups can be performed there with little impact. If backup centralization is desired, after backups are performed the results can then be copied to a central file server. Alternatively, a machine can run more than one instance of `mysqld`, so a centralized backup server can run many instances of `mysqld`, each instance having a different master.

A cold backup is the easiest way to get a consistent physical backup of a server. In a cold backup, `mysqld` is shut down, which flushes all buffers to disk and then the appropriate files can be copied to the backup location. Many companies utilize a slave server to perform backups, to get consistent backups with no downtime on the master.

Backup methods

You have multiple options for performing backups with MySQL. This provides a great deal of flexibility when planning backups. Table 13-2 provides an overview of the most common backup methods available at the time of this writing.

The next sections cover each of the major methods including examples.

TABLE 13-2

Backup Tools Overview

Backup Method	Storage Engines	Impact	Backup Speed	Recovery Speed	Recovery Granularity
mysqldump	ALL	WARM	MEDIUM	SLOWEST	MOST FLEXIBLE
mysqldump	INNODB	HOT	MEDIUM	SLOWEST	MOST FLEXIBLE
SELECT INTO OUTFILE	ALL	WARM	SLOW	SLOW	MOST FLEXIBLE
mk-parallel-backup	ALL	WARM	MEDIUM	MEDIUM	FLEXIBLE
ibbackup	INNODB	HOT	FAST	FAST	FLEXIBLE
ibbackup	ALL	WARM	FAST	FAST	FLEXIBLE
BACKUP command in mysqld	ALL	HOT	FAST	FAST	FLEXIBLE
Filesystem (copy files)	ALL	COLD	FASTEST	FASTEST	NOT FLEXIBLE
Snapshot (that is, with LVM, ZFS)	ALL	ALMOST HOT	FAST	FAST	LEAST FLEXIBLE
mysqlhotcopy	MyISAM	MOSTLY COLD	FAST	FAST	FLEXIBLE

mysqldump

The mysqldump program has been a backup tool for mysqld for a long time. It provides a logical backup of entire database servers, individual databases, individual tables, or even subsets of data using the --where option. The logical backup created using mysqldump is often called a data *dump*. The output is in ASCII format — easily readable and manipulated. As an example, here is a portion of the dump of the sakila database:

```
-- MySQL dump 10.13  Distrib 6.0.8-alpha, for apple-darwin9.4.0
   (i386)
--
-- Host: localhost    Database: sakila
-- ------------------------------------------------------
-- Server version     6.0.8-alpha

/*!40101 SET @OLD_CHARACTER_SET_CLIENT=@@CHARACTER_SET_CLIENT */;
/*!40101 SET @OLD_CHARACTER_SET_RESULTS=@@CHARACTER_SET_RESULTS */;
```

```
/*!40101 SET @OLD_COLLATION_CONNECTION=@@COLLATION_CONNECTION */;
/*!40101 SET NAMES utf8 */;
/*!40103 SET @OLD_TIME_ZONE=@@TIME_ZONE */;
/*!40103 SET TIME_ZONE='+00:00' */;
/*!40014 SET @OLD_UNIQUE_CHECKS=@@UNIQUE_CHECKS, UNIQUE_CHECKS=0 */;
/*!40014 SET @OLD_FOREIGN_KEY_CHECKS=@@FOREIGN_KEY_CHECKS, FOREIGN_
  KEY_CHECKS=0 */;
/*!40101 SET @OLD_SQL_MODE=@@SQL_MODE, SQL_MODE='NO_AUTO_VALUE_
  ON_ZERO' */;
/*!40111 SET @OLD_SQL_NOTES=@@SQL_NOTES, SQL_NOTES=0 */;


--
-- Table structure for table `actor`
--

DROP TABLE IF EXISTS `actor`;
SET @saved_cs_client     = @@character_set_client;
SET character_set_client = utf8;
CREATE TABLE `actor` (
  `actor_id` smallint(5) unsigned NOT NULL AUTO_INCREMENT,
  `first_name` varchar(45) NOT NULL,
  `last_name` varchar(45) NOT NULL,
  `last_update` timestamp NOT NULL DEFAULT CURRENT_TIMESTAMP ON
UPDATE CURRENT_TIMESTAMP,
  PRIMARY KEY (`actor_id`),
  KEY `idx_actor_last_name` (`last_name`)
) ENGINE=InnoDB AUTO_INCREMENT=201 DEFAULT CHARSET=utf8;
SET character_set_client = @saved_cs_client;


--
-- Dumping data for table `actor`
--

LOCK TABLES `actor` WRITE;
/*!40000 ALTER TABLE `actor` DISABLE KEYS */;
INSERT INTO `actor` VALUES (1,'PENELOPE','GUINESS','2006-02-15
10:34:33'),(2,'NICK','WAHLBERG','2006-02-15 10:34:33'),(3,'ED',
'CHASE','2006-02-15 10:34:33'),(4,'JENNIFER','DAVIS','2006-02-15
10:34:33'),(5,'JOHNNY','LOLLOBRIGIDA','2006-02-15 10:34:33'),
[ ... ]
(196,'BELA','WALKEN','2006-02-15 10:34:33'),(197,'REESE','WEST',
'2006-02-15 10:34:33'),(198,'MARY','KEITEL','2006-02-15 10:34:33'),
(199,'JULIA','FAWCETT','2006-02-15 10:34:33'),(200,'THORA','TEMPLE',
'2006-02-15 10:34:33');
/*!40000 ALTER TABLE `actor` ENABLE KEYS */;
UNLOCK TABLES;
```

An administrator can spot-check or review this for potential issues using text editor (for small dumps). Text file manipulation can be done with commands like tail, head, cut, and grep or a script in a programming language. The default behavior is to use an *extended* INSERT statement as seen in the preceding example. When restoring, the extended INSERT syntax is faster than performing a separate insert for each row. However, it may be more beneficial to use standard INSERT statements (one record per INSERT statement) in a logical dump used for partial data restore. For example, finding all article ID numbers belonging to a specific user can easily be done using a grep statement on a dump that has one record per INSERT statement.

Though mysqldump has a large number of options (which can be seen by running mysqldump -?), there is a smaller subset that is used quite frequently. Table 13-3 lists the most frequently used options for using mysqldump, other than the common options for command-line clients discussed in Chapter 3.

TABLE 13-3

Frequently Used Options for mysqldump

Option	Description
db_name [tbl1 [tbl2]]	The first argument that is not an option (options begin with - or --) is considered a database name to dump from. Any non-option arguments after the first are considered tables to back up. In this way, mysqldump can easily dump all the tables in a database (just specify db_name) or any number of tables in a database.
--all-databases	Performs a backup of all databases on the server.
--databases	Exports more than one database.
--events	Exports CREATE EVENT statements.
--extended-insert	The extended (multi-record) INSERT syntax is used. This is faster during restore than the default of having an INSERT statement for each row. This is enabled by default; use --skip-extended-insert to disable.
--flush-logs	Issues a FLUSH LOGS before the export of each database begins. If used with --master-data=n or --lock-all-tables, FLUSH LOGS is only issued at the beginning of the export, because the export is consistent.
--insert-ignore	Export statements use INSERT IGNORE instead of INSERT. See Chapter 4 for details on INSERT IGNORE.
--lock-all-tables	Locks all tables before backup begins, for a consistent backup.
--lock-tables	Places a lock on a table just before backup of the table begins. When a table has been backed up the lock is released. If the backup includes more than one table, this may not provide a consistent view of the data.

TABLE 13-3	(continued)
Option	**Description**
`--master-data=n`	Exports binary log file name and position. If n is set to 1, the information is saved as a CHANGE MASTER statement. If n is set to 2, the information is saved as a commented out CHANGE MASTER statement. If this option is specified mysqldump assumes you want a consistent backup, and will use `--lock-all-tables` unless `--single-transaction` is also given as an option. The `--lock-tables` option in conjunction with this option is ignored.
`--no-data`	Does not export data; only table and view creation statements.
`--opt`	Creates optimal output. It is the same as specifying `--add-drop-table, --add-locks, --create-options, --disable-keys, --extended-insert, --lock-tables, --quick,` and `--set-charset`. This option is enabled by default; use `--skip-opt` to disable all of the features or `--skip-option` to disable an individual option (for instance, `--opt --skip-extended-insert` will specify all the options except `--extended-insert`).
`--replace`	Export statements use REPLACE instead of INSERT. See Chapter 4 for details on REPLACE.
`--routines`	Exports CREATE PROCEDURE and CREATE FUNCTION statements.
`--single-transaction`	For transactional engines such as InnoDB this option provides a consistent view of the data without requiring a global read lock.
`--triggers`	Exports CREATE TRIGGER statements.
`--where "WHERE clause"`	Exports a subset of data. See the following example.

A simple example of using mysqldump is an export of the entire server using the `--all-database` option:

```
$ mysqldump --user=root --password --all-databases > dump.sql
```

This will create a single dump file of all the databases in the server into the file dump.sql in the current directory.

To export a single database, or a single table:

```
$ mysqldump --user=root --password sakila > sakila.sql
Enter password:
$ mysqldump --user=root --password sakila actor > actor.sql
Enter password:
$
```

To export the actor table schema and records in the actor table where the last_name field is WALKEN:

```
$ mysqldump --user=root --password sakila actor \
--where "last_name='WALKEN' ORDER BY first_name" > walken.sql
Enter password:
$
```

To export multiple databases:

```
$ mysqldump --user=root --password --databases sakila test > dbs.sql
```

mysqldump exports one table at a time. If you need to be able to export tables and databases in parallel, look into mk-parallel-dump and mk-parallel-restore from the maatkit toolkit, described later in this chapter.

> **TIP** In MySQL 6.0, mysqldump has a --dump-slave=n option that acts like the --master-data=n option, except it exports the binary log information for the server's master, not the binary log information for the server itself. In this way, a slave can be backed up to create another slave of the same master.

SELECT INTO OUTFILE

You can use the INTO OUTFILE clause of the SELECT statement to back up individual tables on a server. The command used to load the dump created is LOAD DATA INFILE.

Here is an example showing the creation of a dump of the accounts table:

```
mysql> SELECT * INTO OUTFILE '/tmp/accounts.txt' FROM accounts;
```

If you need to load the data from /tmp/accounts.txt you would do it like this:

```
mysql> LOAD DATA INFILE '/tmp/accounts.txt' INTO TABLE accounts;
```

Though you probably would not want to use SELECT INTO OUTFILE to perform backups of your entire database, it is very useful when you are working on a server and need a backup of one or two tables.

For more information on SELECT INTO OUTFILE including usage, see Chapter 4.

maatkit parallel dump/restore

The third-party maatkit toolkit (see http://www.maatkit.org/ for information and downloads) contains two useful scripts that are wrappers around the mysqldump program. These programs are mk-parallel-dump and mk-parallel-restore. Both backups and restores are performed in parallel. The way this works is that if your server has eight core processors and you are dumping a database with forty different tables the script will (by default) start up eight separate copies of mysqldump, which each dump a separate table. With the appropriate storage, such as a nice RAID array of SAS drive, this will be much faster than running a single mysqldump of the entire database. The restore functionality works in the same manner.

If you need a logical backup of a large database and you are not running mysqld 6.0 or higher (with the option of online logical backups) this is your best option.

The defaults for both mk-parallel-dump and mk-parallel-restore are very sensible, though you can use the help option to see all the available options. Typically a backup will look like:

```
$ mk-parallel-dump --basedir=/backups
```

The --basedir option specifies the directory to store the exports. If you do not specify a base directory the exports will be located in the current working directory.

The restore program is just as easy to use. To restore your previous dump just do this:

```
$ mk-parallel-restore /backups
```

The options for mk-parallel-dump and mk-parallel-restore are very similar to the options for mysqldump.

File system snapshot

Using snapshot functionality of file systems is one of the best ways to create a consistent, physical hot backup of your database files. A file system snapshot provides a point-in-time view (*snapshot*) of a disk partition.

Consider what would happen if you did not use a snapshot to create this point-in-time view. You can have a physical backup of your data directory performed while the server is running, but all the files are not going to be copied at the same time. It might be 30 minutes or more before a file is copied, whereas others are copied within a few seconds of the backup starting. Now when the restore is performed you potentially end up with some files having no changes since the time the backup began and some files with many changes. You have an inconsistent backup of your data. Most likely mysqld will refuse to start with the restored files.

Though the methods used to implement a snapshot vary, the end result is the same. After a snapshot is created you have a disk partition that you can mount and these files will remain consistent with each other even though the original partition continues to change. Some file systems support snapshots natively, such as ZFS, and you can also do file system snapshots through LVM (Logical Volume Manager) for the Linux kernel. See the appropriate documentation for how to use your snapshot implementation.

Using file system snapshots makes it easy to perform consistent, physical hot backups of a server. Although it is best if mysqld can be shut down before a physical backup is performed, it is not strictly necessary. You can use file system snapshots to create a snapshot of a running system and then copy the snapshot partition to your backup location. Restoration is just copying the backup files to the appropriate location on your host server and starting mysqld. If the snapshot was created while mysqld was shut down, the restore will produce a normal startup. If the snapshot was created while mysqld was running, mysqld may think it is recovering from a crash and perform the recovery process.

The basic procedure for performing a backup of a running MySQL server using file system snapshots is the same across all platforms that support snapshots. This can be scripted or performed manually:

1. Open a mysql client session to mysqld and issue a FLUSH TABLES WITH READ LOCK command. This will lock the tables, preventing modifications from happening during the backup, flush MyISAM buffers to disk, and close any open file descriptors. So that you know the position in the binary logs for a restore you should also issue a SHOW MASTER STAUS command and record the output from it.

> **WARNING**   On systems with long-running queries the FLUSH TABLES WITH READ LOCK command can take a long time to finish and return control to the command line. FLUSH TABLES has to wait until all queries are done executing so keep this in mind.

2. From a shell prompt on the host server the appropriate command to take a snapshot.

3. Issue an UNLOCK TABLES command in mysqld so that database activity can continue.

4. Mount the new snapshot partition and copy the data to your backup location.

5. Once the copy is complete, unmount and delete the snapshot partition.

While the database tables are locked with the FLUSH TABLES WITH READ LOCK no read or write activity takes place on the server. This occurs between steps 1 and 3.

If you have the luxury of being able to shut down mysqld it becomes even easier:

1. Shut down mysqld. There is no need to record binary log positions because it will rotate to a new binary log when the server starts up. Just use this log for your start position.

2. From a shell prompt on the host server issue the appropriate command to take a snapshot.

3. Restart mysqld.

4. Mount the new snapshot partition and copy of the data to your backup location.

5. Once the copy is complete, unmount and delete the snapshot partition.

One problem with this scenario is that mysqld may have files in several disk partitions. There may be data files in one partition, log files in a second partition, and the InnoDB tablespace in a third partition. For example, LVM does not have the ability to guarantee that snapshots across multiple partitions are in sync with each other, because LVM does not flush information from memory to disk exactly at the same time for all volumes. Unless you shut down mysqld and then create your snapshots of each partition, you will not be able to get a reliable physical backup with this configuration. The following sections cover ZFS snapshots and LVM snapshots in detail because these are the two most popular snapshot implementations.

ZFS

Sun Microsystems released the ZFS file system in 2004. It has been designed to remove many of the limits on current file system storage. The ZFS file system is a 128-bit file system with fast snapshots and optional compression. It currently runs on Solaris, Apple OS X, and FreeBSD 7.0.

When working with ZFS you will see the term *pool*. A pool is a set of at least one storage unit(s). You can add storage units to a pool on-the-fly. When adding a new device to the pool the space becomes available to any file system that needs it, which provides very flexible storage management.

To take a newly attached disk and use the whole disk for a new ZFS pool you would use the command:

```
# zpool create data c3t0d0
```

This will create a pool called data. It also creates a single file system mounted at /data. Later on, if you run out of space, just add another device to the pool, and the file system will grow:

```
# zpool add data c4t0d0
```

One nice feature is that when you add a second hard drive ZFS will automatically implement striping of data across the hard drives in the pool. This should improve performance because the data load is moved across multiple hard drive controllers.

Need another file system? You can mount one on the same pool:

```
# zfs create data/logs
# zfs set mountpoint=/logs data/logs
```

You can build a disk pool that uses both mirroring and striping (software RAID). This provides both redundancy (to lessen the chance of system failure) and increased I/O throughput. This configuration of software RAID is done with a simple one-line command. Going back to our original creation of the data pool:

```
# zpool create data mirror c3t0d0 c4t0d0
```

Now we have a mirrored pool. If one drive fails the pool will continue to be available, just as it is on a disk using RAID.

However, we created a mirrored pool when the pool was initially created. What about when adding a drive (c4t0d0) to an already existing pool of one drive (c3t0d0) to create a new mirror?

```
# zpool attach data c3t0d0 c4t0d0
```

This is all interesting technology, and if you are a system administrator this removes a big headache from your life. However, how does this directly benefit you as a database administrator? One example would be that often in a production system you have multiple InnoDB tablespace files on different partitions or disks. This is because either the original partition was close to full or the administrator is trying to increase system performance by spreading the InnoDB table across multiple drives.

The InnoDB tablespace information from a my.cnf file might look like this:

```
innodb_data_file_path =
/d1/dt/ibdata1:20G;/d2/dt/ibdata2:20G;/d3/dt/ibdata3:20G:autoextend
```

In this example, the InnoDB tablespace is spread out over three drives. In theory this should help spread I/O activity across the three drives. In actuality, this is more difficult than it might seem. InnoDB fills these tablespace files in the order listed — ibdata1 is the first to be filled, then ibdata2, then ibdata3. Until the 20 gigabytes of tablespace on the first drive is full the second and third tablespaces will not be utilized. In addition, expanding this tablespace, if you run out of drive space, is not easy. It requires a restart of the mysqld daemon.

Using ZFS for your file system management makes this much easier. Something similar to the following InnoDB tablespace definition would be all you need:

```
innodb_data_file_path = /data/ibdatafile:20G:autoextend
```

Without ever restarting the server you can extend a pool over as many drives as you need. ZFS will automatically balance the I/O load intelligently, striping data across multiple drives (if available) in a pool. You can perform software mirroring and even take a failed disk offline, all without restarting. This means the database administrator's job is a little easier.

Now that you have a ZFS file system created and mounted it is time to use it for creating your physical backups of your MySQL database server. Earlier we outlined the five basic steps of the process. Step two is the creation of the actual snapshot. With ZFS the command to create a snapshot will be similar to this:

```
# zfs snapshot data@0080913
```

Simply specify the pool or pool/file system name, the @ symbol, and then a name for the snapshot.

Once a snapshot is created it is very easy to work with. Snapshots are viewed with the zfs list command, the same as any other ZFS file system, and you can mount a snapshot in a directory using the zfs set mountpoint command. When you are finished with the snapshot it can be deleted with the zfs destroy command. This is the same method used to delete any other ZFS file system.

The ZFS file system is known to have extremely fast snapshots. If you take the time to develop a script for your environment you can have a very fast backup system.

LVM

The Logical Volume Manager program provides volume management and snapshot capabilities on Linux servers. It was initially implemented in 1997. LVM is agnostic about what file systems are used "underneath." Chapter 10 covered file system choices for Linux so this is not covered here.

LVM operates as an additional layer above the actual file system to provide this functionality. In addition to the snapshot implementation, it also has some very good volume management functionality. In contrast, ZFS is its own file system.

When working with LVM there is some terminology to understand. There are three basic terms: *physical volume*, *volume group*, and *logical volume*.

Physical volumes are any block device — usually standard hard drive partitions or software RAID volumes. The partition types for these volumes must set to LVM. A *volume group* is a collection of one or more physical volumes. Physical volumes can be added to or removed from the volume group while the files remain usable.

Volume groups do not have file systems mounted and do not have file systems created on them directly. This is done through what are called *logical volumes*. There can be one or more logical volumes in a volume group. These logical volumes are used to both create and mount file systems.

Figure 13-1 shows a diagram of the layout of a LVM-based MySQL server.

FIGURE 13-1

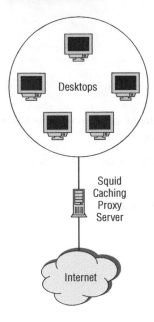

In this example, the operating system is mounted on /dev/sda so it is not displayed in the diagram. The other seven drives are used to create one volume group (vg0). The logical volumes created can span multiple physical volumes as do all three of these logical partitions. It is also helpful to leave some space unused so later it can be used to expand any of the logical volumes if needed. Some of the Linux-based file systems allow you to grow the file system on-the-fly so it does not even require unmounting the partition (and thus making the files unavailable) during expansion.

Using the layout from Figure 13-1, we will walk through the creation process for the volume group and logical volumes. First, the installation of the operating system is done on /dev/sda, with an fdisk command. The output of the fdisk command is too long for inclusion. After the operating system, each of the remaining drives is formatted with a single partition of type Linux LVM (type 8E in the fdisk formatting menu). Once this is done, create physical volumes:

```
# pvcreate /dev/sdb1 /dev/sdc1 /dev/sdd1 /dev/sde1 /dev/sdf1
  /dev/sdg1 /dev/sdh1
```

The pvdisplay command will show you the physical volumes created. The following is truncated for space considerations but pvdisplay will show you one group for each physical volume:

```
# pvdisplay
  --- NEW Physical volume ---
  PV Name                /dev/sdb1
  VG Name
  PV Size                150.79 GB
  Allocatable            NO
  PE Size (KByte)        0
  Total PE               0
  Free PE                0
  Allocated PE           0
  PV UUID                G8lu2L-Hijl-NVde-sOKc-OoVI-fadg-Jd1vyU
```

Now that the physical volumes are created it is time to create the next layer — the volume group. The vgcreate command is used to create the volume group:

```
# vgcreate vg0 /dev/sdb1 /dev/sdc1 /dev/sdd1 /dev/sde1 /dev/sdf1
  /dev/sdg1 /dev/sdh1
```

Once the volume group has been created you can see the characteristics with the vgdisplay command:

```
server1:~# vgdisplay
  --- Volume group ---
  VG Name                vg0
  System ID
```

```
Format                 lvm2
Metadata Areas         7
Metadata Sequence No   1
VG Access              read/write
VG Status              resizable
MAX LV                 0
Cur LV                 0
Open LV                0
Max PV                 0
Cur PV                 7
Act PV                 7
VG Size                1055.53 GB
PE Size                4.00 MB
Total PE               270216
Alloc PE / Size        0 / 0
Free  PE / Size        270216 / 1055.53 GB
VG UUID                3Z2XVF-BIAT-PmKs-Qnss-SXxI-WrNO-dTqhFP
```

After the volume group has been created, the final step of the LVM creation process is to create the logical volumes. Remember that these logical volumes are what are formatted and mounted as file systems.

This example will create three logical volumes. The logical volume data will be 300 GB in size. The logs partition will be 210 GB in size and backups will be 400 GB in size. This will leave approximately 145 GB of space. To create a logical volume you use the lvcreate command:

```
# lvcreate --name data --size 300G vg0
  Logical volume "data" created
# lvcreate --name logs --size 210G vg0
  Logical volume "logs" created
# lvcreate --name backups --size 400 G vg0
  Logical volume "backups" created
#
```

You can use the lvdisplay command to show you the statistics about each logical volume.

Now that you have created the logical volumes it is time to create the file systems and mount the logical volumes. This example uses the ReiserFS file system because it allows you to easily expand the size of a partition without unmounting the partition.

First, create the file system on /dev/vg0/logs:

```
# mkfs.reiserfs /dev/vg0/logs
```

You will need to repeat this command, changing the logical volume name, for the other two partitions.

Once the file systems are created they must be mounted on a directory. These directories will vary depending on your needs. For this example, mount them in /data, /var/logs/mysql, and /backups. The command to create the directories is:

```
# mkdir /data /var/logs/mysql /backups
```

After creating the directories you need to mount the partitions. This is done like this:

```
# mount /dev/vg0/data /data
# mount /dev/vg0/logs /var/logs/mysql
# mount /dev/vg0/backups /backups
```

Now your logical volumes are ready to use. You can modify the /etc/fstab file to have these partitions mounted automatically at boot time.

Finally, the lvextend command is used to expand logical volume. Because you have about 145 GB of free space there is room to grow as needed. If you decide to increase the logical volume backups by an additional 50 GB the command would be this:

```
# lvextend -L450G /dev/vg0/backups
    Extending logical volume backups to 450 GB.
    Logical volume backups successfully resized.
#
```

Now that the volume has been extended the file system has to be resized. With ReiserFS this would be:

```
# resize_reiserfs -s +50G /dev/vg0/backups
```

Though this introduction to LVM is by no means exhaustive it gives you the basic tools to work with logical volumes under Linux. For more information, an excellent how-to is available at www.tldp.org/HOWTO/LVM-HOWTO/index.html.

After all your logical volumes are created and mounted you can use the LVM snapshot functionality to create your backups. Remember from our previous discussion that the basic outline of the five basic steps for taking a file system snapshot is as follows:

1. Open a session in mysqld and issue a FLUSH TABLES WITH READ LOCK command. This will lock the tables and prevent any modifications from happening during the backup. So that you know the position in the binary logs for a restore you should also issue a SHOW MASTER STATUS command and record the output from it.

2. From a shell prompt on the server, issue whatever command it is to actually create the snapshot.

3. Issue an UNLOCK TABLES command in your MySQL server command so that database activity can continue.

4. Mount the new snapshot partition and copy of the data to your backup location.

5. Once the copy is complete, unmount and delete the snapshot partition.

With the previous LVM example /data was mounted on the /dev/vg0/data logical volume. This contains all the mysqld data files so it is the partition to copy for a backup. The command to create the snapshot would be:

```
# lvcreate -L16G -s -n data_snapshot /dev/vg0/data
```

This will create a new logical volume called data_snapshot that has 16 GB allocated to it. It is a snapshot of the logical volume data. What is written to the snapshot are changes that have occurred to the original logical volume since the time the snapshot was taken. If you have a very active system with a large partition to copy this might need to be larger. After you mount the snapshot partition, you can check the amount that the snapshot partition is full by running a df command.

TIP When performing any type of physical backup it is important that you copy the InnoDB log and tablespace files. If you do not copy them, any restore will be unsuccessful.

To mount the partition you need to have a directory on which to mount it. In this case you will create the /snapshot directory first and then mount the snapshot on this new directory:

```
# mkdir /snapshot
# mount /dev/vg0/data_snapshot /snapshot
```

Once this is done the directory /snapshot contains the files of the /data directory at the point in time the snapshot was taken. You can copy the files off to a remote server, an NFS mount on the local server, or even to a local directory.

When you are done with the copy, to remove the snapshot you just unmount the snapshot partition and delete it. For this example it would be:

```
# umount /dev/vg0/data_snapshot
# lvremove /dev/vg0/data_snapshot
```

As you can see, using LVM takes a little bit of learning to set up the physical volumes, logical volumes, and logical volume groups appropriately. Using LVM snapshots is easy once this initial setup is done.

WARNING Do not allow the snapshot partition to become 100% full!

Special mention should be made of the mylvmbackup script. The homepage for this script is http://lenz.homelinux.org/mylvmbackup. Lenz Grimmer, a MySQL developer working for Sun Microsystems, created and maintains the script. The script manages the entire process of creating an LVM snapshot and creating a compressed archive file.

If you are using LVM for volume management on your Linux servers, it is worthwhile to take the time to explore `mylvmbackup` as an alternative to manually performing file system snapshots or using a custom script.

SAN-based

Many SAN (Storage Area Network) storage units have snapshot capabilities. The commands to create snapshots vary from manufacturer to manufacturer but the functionality remains the same. You create a snapshot of the data directory while the tables are locked and then copy the snapshot partition off to a backup location.

Microsoft VSS

Microsoft offers a solution called Volume Shadow Copy Service (VSS) that can be used to perform file system snapshots. Both the Zmanda Recovery Manager (ZRM) and R1Soft commercial backup programs use this technology to provide hot backups of Microsoft servers.

Online backup

One of the most important new features of MySQL 6.0 Server is the online, logical hot backup feature called MySQL Backup. It provides for an integrated method of performing hot backups. In addition there is optional compression and encryption available when performing backups.

Here is a sample of a backup session and the corresponding restore session:

```
mysql> BACKUP DATABASE sakila TO 'sakila-backup.sql';
+-----------+
| backup_id |
+-----------+
| 271       |
+-----------+
1 row in set (0.37 sec)
```

The `sakila-backup.sql` file is stored in your data directory (the `datadir` server variable).

Once you have performed a backup it is equally simple to restore the backup. The `RESTORE FROM` command is used for restoration. It expects the backup file to be located in the data directory:

```
mysql> RESTORE FROM 'sakila-backup.sql';
+-----------+
| backup_id |
+-----------+
| 272       |
+-----------+
1 row in set (3.09 sec)
```

If successful, the RESTORE FROM command returns only the backup ID of the backup being restored.

MySQL Backup is significantly faster than an export using the traditional mysqldump. And there is the added benefit that it allows read and write access to your system (other than executing DDL statements) while backups are being performed if you are using native or consistent snapshot drivers (explained next).

There is additional information stored in the mysql database about that status of your backup and restore operations. Among other items, it shows the total size of the backup or restore, the start and stop time, the user who executed the command, and the filename used. To view this information you just SELECT from the backup_history and backup_progress tables in the mysql database. Here is an example showing data about the previous backup:

```
mysql> SELECT * FROM backup_history WHERE backup_id = 271\G
*************************** 1. row ***************************
           backup_id: 271
          process_id: 0
          binlog_pos: 0
         binlog_file:
        backup_state: complete
           operation: backup
           error_num: 0
         num_objects: 16
         total_bytes: 1964297
 validity_point_time: 2009-01-16 22:57:18
          start_time: 2009-01-16 22:57:18
           stop_time: 2009-01-16 22:57:18
  host_or_server_name: localhost
            username: root
         backup_file: sakila-backup.sql
    backup_file_path: /usr/local/mysql/data/
        user_comment:
             command: backup database sakila to 'sakila-backup.sql'
             drivers: Snapshot, MyISAM
1 row in set (0.00 sec)
```

Unfortunately, because MySQL Backup stores information in the mysql system database, MySQL Backup cannot be used to back up the mysql system database.

When using online backup, three types of drivers can be used to back up an engine:

- **Native driver** — The storage engine can use a *native driver* for creating backup images in the most efficient manner for the particular engine.

- **Consistent snapshot driver** — For engines that do not have a native driver but that support a consistent snapshot (such as InnoDB), there is a *consistent snapshot* algorithm used to perform backups of these engines.

■ **Default driver** — For engines that do not have a native driver and do not support consistent snapshot, there is a *default* algorithm that does a backup of the engine. If online backup has to use the default driver, the backup blocks other DML statements.

There are currently some limitations to online backup. The major limitations include:

■ No backup of the internal `mysql` database

■ No native driver for InnoDB tables

■ No native driver for Maria

■ No native drive for Falcon

■ No backup of partitions

■ No incremental backup

These might affect your usage of MySQL Backup. Remember that with both Falcon and InnoDB the lack of native driver support does not mean that backups will block server operation. The backups will not be as efficient as when using native drivers but will be a non-blocking operation.

All of these limitations are scheduled to be fixed in MySQL Server 6.1 or later.

mysqlhotcopy

The `mysqlhotcopy` program is a Perl script written to provide a consistent backup of MyISAM and ARCHIVE tables. Though it has limitations, a number of installations are still in use and it is important to understand the usage of the program. When run, `mysqlhotcopy` uses the `LOCK TABLES` command to create read locks on the tables being backed up. This allows a consistent backup across all the tables to be executed. The backup is done using either the `cp` or `scp` commands. The name of the script leads to the conclusion this performs a hot backup. Though the server does not have to be shut down, any writes to the tables being backed up are blocked. By definition this means it is not a hot backup, though it is a warm backup.

The `mysqlhotcopy` script must be run on the host server where the `datadir` is located, and the operating system user running the script must have permissions to read the data files in the data directory. There is no Windows version of `mysqlhotcopy`.

The following example will copy the database `sakila` to the directory /backup:

```
$ mysqlhotcopy sakila /backup
```

This creates a backup on the local server. To send the backup to another server use the `scp` command. In this example you will backup the `sakila` database to the `/backup` directory of `backup.company.com`:

```
$ mysqlhotcopy --method=scp sakila \ username@backup.company.
com:/backup
```

You can also back up multiple databases. To back up databases sakila, mysql, and test to the /backup directory use this command:

```
$ mysqlhotcopy sakila mysql test /backup
```

You can use regular expressions that perform pattern matching of both database and tables. To back up all tables in sakila that start with film to the directory /backup do this:

```
$ mysqlhotcopy sakila./^film/ /backup
```

The mysqlhotcopy program has a number of options, which can be seen by running mysql-hotcopy -?. Table 13-4 lists the most frequently used options for using mysqlhotcopy, other than the common options for command-line clients discussed in Chapter 3. In addition to command-line options mysqlhotcopy will read options from two of the mysqld configuration file directives: [client] and [mysqlhotcopy].

TABLE 13-4

Frequently Used mysqlhotcopy Options

Option	Description
--addtodest	Adds to the destination directory if it already exists. To rename the destination directory if it already exists instead of adding to it, use the --allow-old option instead.
--allowold	Renames the destination directory if it exists by adding a suffix of _old to the directory name. To add to the destination directory instead of renaming it, use the --add-to-dest option instead.
--checkpoint=db_name.table_name	Inserts checkpoint entries in the database and table specified.
--dryrun	Performs a dry run of the backup (only displaying what would happen but not actually performing the backup).
--flushlogs	Executes the FLUSH LOGS command after tables are locked. This rotates the binary log files.
--keepold	Does not delete previous destination when backup is done.
--method	Specifies the method used to copy files. This can be either cp or scp.
--regexp	Uses the regexp pattern to copy all databases or tables that match the pattern.
--resetmaster	Runs the RESET MASTER command after tables are locked. This resets the binary logs.
--resetslave	Runs the RESET SLAVE command after tables are locked.

Commercial options

There have been a number of companies that have provided alternative backup options for MySQL Server. Three of the most common commercial options are the InnoDB hot backup program, Zmanda's backup wrapper GUI, and R1soft's backup program.

InnoDB hot backup

The InnoDB hot backup program (ibbackup) has been available for quite some time. It can be used to perform non-blocking hot backups of InnoDB tables. The program is entirely command-line driven, which makes it very easy to integrate into scripts and execute from crontab.

The ibbackup program uses two files (explained in a moment) to determine how the backup is run. A basic backup run will look like this:

```
$ ibbackup my.cnf backup-my.cnf
```

It is possible to have ibbackup compress the backup while it is being performed. To do this use the compress option:

```
$ ibbackup --compress my.cnf backup-my.cnf
```

In addition you can control the *level* of compression. The compression level is an integer between 0 and 9. A 1 gives the fastest backup/worst compression level, and a 9 gives the slowest backup/best compression. A 0 means no compression is performed. A compression level of 1 is the default. For the best compression level use something like this:

```
$ ibbackup --compress=9 my.cnf backup-my.cnf
```

Note that higher levels of compression are going to create more load on the CPU of the host server performing the backup. Though 9 will give you the most compressed backup you might want to start at a lower level of 6 or 7 and monitor how this impacts your server's performance. The ibbackup program uses my.cnf to determine the location of both the ibdata and ib_logfiles. It then creates a backup of these files using the location specified in the backup-my.cnf file. Your my.cnf must contain the following options:

```
datadir
innodb_data_home_dir
innodb_data_file_path
innodb_log_group_home_dir
innodb_log_files_in_group
innodb_log_file_size
```

Anything else is ignored. There are a few prerequisites. The directory paths specified must be absolute paths (not relative paths). Both the number and the size of the innodb_data files must match in the two configuration files.

Here is a sample my.cnf file:

```
[mysqld]
datadir = /var/lib/mysql/data
innodb_data_home_dir = /var/lib/mysql/data
innodb_data_file_path = ibdata1:20G:autoextend
innodb_log_group_home_dir = /var/lib/mysql/data
set-variable = innodb_log_files_in_group=2
set-variable = innodb_log_file_size=256M
```

To store the backup in the directory /backup, the backup-my.cnf should be similar to:

```
datadir = /backup
innodb_data_home_dir = /backup
innodb_data_file_path = ibdata1:20G:autoextend
innodb_log_group_home_dir = /backup
set-variable = innodb_log_files_in_group=2
set-variable = innodb_log_file_size=256M
```

You must ensure that the backup directory is clear of old backups because ibbackup will error instead of writing over any files.

The ibbackup program has a number of options, which can be seen by running ibbackup -?. Table 13-5 lists the most frequently used options for using ibbackup, other than the common options for command-line clients discussed in Chapter 3.

TABLE 13-5

ibbackup Options

Option	Description
--apply-log	Used to create a consistent view of the database.
--compress	Creates a compressed backup. The compressed data files will have a suffix of .ibz.
--sleep=sleep_time	During backup the ibbackup program will sleep for sleep_time (in milliseconds) after each one megabyte of copied data. It is used to manage disk I/O.
--suspend-at-end	Creates a file called ibbackup_suspended in the backup directory when the backup is almost complete. Backup does not continue until ibbackup_suspended is deleted. Used for scripting the backup of MyISAM files.
--uncompress	This uncompresses backups created with the compress option. Used during apply-log operations.
--use-memory= amount_memory	Specifies the amount of memory in megabytes the ibbackup uses during recovery. Defaults to 100 MB.

The apply-log option is used to create a consistent view of the backed-up database. During backup different database pages are copied at different times. While backing up, the ibbackup program also copies the InnoDB log to a file called ibbackup_logfile. This file is what is applied to create a consistent view of the database.

Here is an example of how this is done:

```
$ ibbackup --apply-log /home/kmurphy/backup-my.cnf
```

If the backup had been created using the compress option, when applying log files you must tell ibbackup to uncompress:

```
$ ibbackup --apply-log --uncompress /home/kmurphy/backup-my.cnf
```

Overall the ibbackup program is very well done. It is currently one of the best methods for performing hot backups of InnoDB-based servers.

The homepage of InnoDB Hot Backup is www.innodb.com. The website contains a freely downloadable wrapper script called innobackup.pl that uses mysqlhotcopy to back up MyISAM tables and ibbackup to back up InnoDB tables.

Zmanda

Zmanda has multiple versions of its backup software. The Amanda Enterprise Edition provides for centralized backup of multiple desktops and servers. These backups can be sent to disk, tape, or even Amazon S3 storage. The Zmanda Enterprise Recovery Manager (ZRM) product is designed strictly for backups of mysqld. It can be used to perform all types of backups (full, incremental, physical, and logical) and can utilize file system snapshots for hot backups. With its web-based graphical interface it is easy to configure and manage backups. In addition, Zmanda supports both encryption and compression of backups.

It should be pointed out that Zmanda uses other existing backup technology to accomplish backups. For example, it can use the mysqldump program, the ibbackup program, and others to accomplish backups. Even so, it is a very smooth and integrated package that can be used effectively.

Zmanda also has an open source community project called ZRM Community. This is very similar to the Enterprise ZRM program — the major difference is that the Enterprise version includes the web-based Management Console.

The homepage of Zmanda is www.zmanda.com.

R1Soft

R1Soft provides a completely graphical environment for performing a MySQL server backup. Like Zmanda it offers backups with compressions and encryption. One of the major features of

R1Soft is that it provides what it calls near-Continuous Online Backups. It does this by performing backups very frequently (every 15 minutes or less). This provides for a very small window of time that data can be lost. In addition, the R1Soft software also provides for complete bare-metal restore for MySQL servers.

The homepage of R1Soft is: www.r1soft.com.

Copying Databases to Another Machine

You can copy the .frm, .MYI, and .MYD files for MyISAM tables and the .frm and data files (.ibd or ibdata) for InnoDB between different hardware architectures that support the same floating-point format (Endianness). This means that you can transfer InnoDB and MyISAM tables from Windows to Linux without doing a logical export and import. Simply shut down the database (or lock the tables involved) and use scp to copy the database. Or, restore a physical backup to a different machine.

In cases where you need to transfer databases between different architectures, you can use mysqldump to create a file containing SQL statements. You can then transfer the dump file to the second machine (the *destination* host) and feed it as input to the mysql client.

To move a database from one machine to another, run the following from the machine currently holding the database (the *target* host):

```
shell> mysqldump --databases sakila | mysql -h destination_host
sakila
```

For large tables, exporting a tab-delimited file and using mysqlimport is much faster than using mysqldump to export INSERT statements and restoring with source or the redirection operator (<). The --tab=/path/to/backup option to mysqldump creates a tab-delimited ASCII data file (.txt) and schema file (.sql) for each table, when mysqldump is run locally.

First, create the backup directory and dump the database:

```
shell> mkdir /path/to/backup
shell> mysqldump --tab=/path/to/backup --databases sakila
```

Then copy the files in /path/to/backup directory to the destination machine and load the files into mysqld there:

```
shell> cat /path/to/backup/*.sql | mysql sakila
shell> mysqlimport sakila /path/to/destination/copy/*.txt
```

WARNING The grant tables (user permissions) are stored in the mysql database. If you do not have a mysql database, mysqld may not start up on the new machine. Make sure to FLUSH PRIVILEGES or restart mysqld when the grant tables are imported.

Recovering from Crashes

Many administrators spend a significant amount of time on backups and then do not spend time on their recovery strategies. However, they make a serious mistake by not planning for how they will recover or ever testing backups and the recovery process by performing a recovery.

The recovery process is going to vary depending on your objectives. It will always begin with the restoration of a backup. With physical backups you just copy the files to the server where the recovery is taking place and restart the server. For a logical backup the techniques used for recovery are going to vary — recovery may consist of loading of files with the source command, redirecting files with the < operator, or using mysqlimport.

Often after the backup is restored you will need to restore the server to a point-in-time after the last backup. If this is the case you need to perform what is called a point-in-time recovery.

You can perform a point-in-time recovery with any backup process because you are using incremental backups (such as the binary log files) to bring the server up to a certain point-in-time after restoring a previous backup.

MySQL server uses a binary format for the log files to save space. This means you cannot view it directly. MySQL supplies a utility called mysqlbinlog to convert these logs to a text format that you can view. For more on binary logging, see Chapter 16.

The process for performing a point-in-time restore is as follows:

- Restore the database using the last backup
- Determine the first binary log and starting position needed
- Determine the last binary log needed
- Convert the binary log(s) to text format with the mysqlbinlog utility, using options to specify the start and stop time
- Import the converted binary log(s)

As with any recovery process, the first step is to restore the last backup performed. This restoration will vary depending on how the backup was performed. For this example assume a file system snapshot was performed at midnight of the 16th of September and the logs were flushed at the same time. This means you have a physical backup and the restoration should just be copying the files to the server and starting up mysqld again.

Once the basic restoration is complete it is time to restore the data changes since the backup was performed.

Here is a listing of the binary log directory:

```
$ ls -lh mysql-bin*
-rw-rw---- 1 mysql mysql 257M Sep 16 23:48 mysql-bin.010309
-rw-rw---- 1 mysql mysql 257M Sep 17 00:02 mysql-bin.010310
-rw-rw---- 1 mysql mysql 257M Sep 17 03:48 mysql-bin.010311
-rw-rw---- 1 mysql mysql 257M Sep 17 19:01 mysql-bin.010312
-rw-rw---- 1 mysql mysql 162M Sep 17 19:03 mysql-bin.010313
-rw-rw---- 1 mysql mysql 8.3K Sep 17 19:01 mysql-bin.index
```

This means that mysql-bin.010310 is the first binary log created after the backup was performed. This was determined by looking at the timestamp of the log files, which shows the last time the log file was modified. Knowing the backup was performed at midnight you can see that mysql-bin.010309 was the last log written before midnight. Therefore the next log file is the one with which you want to start your restoration.

For this example, you need to restore the server through the last log listed, which is mysql-bin.010313.

If you have a large number of binary logs (such as in this case) to convert it would probably be beneficial to script this process. The command to convert an entire binary file will look similar to this:

```
$ mysqlbinlog mysql-bin.010310 > mysql-bin.010310.sql
```

This would convert the mysql-bin.010310 log to text format and store it in the mysql-bin.010310.sql file. You will have to do this for each log file needed. The final part of the process is the import of the log files into the database server:

```
$ mysql --user=root --pasword < mysql-bin.010310.sql
```

This would need to be done for each converted binary log. Once again, scripting might be helpful.

To create text files from parts of binary logs using mysqlbinlog, specify a starting place with either --start-datetime='YYYY-MM-DD' or --start-position=# and ending place with either --stop-datetime='YYYY-MM-DD' or --stop-position=#. To determine the exact position to start or stop you have to examine the binary log contents. The problem is that this can be a large file. To start you have to convert the log to text format:

```
$ mysqlbinlog mysql-bin.010312 > mysql-bin.010312.sql
```

Once you convert the log file you can view the text-format log with a text editor. With a binary log of 162 MB in size this may be tricky. If you are looking to end at a specific time you can specify a stopping time:

```
$ mysqlbinlog --stop-datetime='2008-09-17 18:42:48' mysql-bin.010312
> mysql-bin.010312.sql
```

Once you have trimmed the file it becomes much easier to view with the `tail` command. Now you will still have to potentially look through a number of entries because a busy database server is going to be executing hundreds, if not thousands, of queries a second. Here are the last 25 lines after trimming:

```
$ tail -25 mysql-bin.010312.sql
use usersession/*!*/;
SET TIMESTAMP=1221702167/*!*/;
UPDATE XXXXX /*!*/;
# at 185118382
#080917 18:42:47 server id 16   end_log_pos 185118409      Xid =
9731310851
COMMIT/*!*/;
# at 185118409
#080917 18:42:47 server id 16   end_log_pos 185118473      Query
thread_id=1273437368     exec_time=1      error_code=0
SET TIMESTAMP=1221702167/*!*/;
BEGIN/*!*/;
# at 185118473
#080917 18:42:47 server id 16   end_log_pos 185118508      Rand
SET @@RAND_SEED1=700138339, @@RAND_SEED2=45664511/*!*/;
# at 185118508
#080917 18:42:47 server id 16   end_log_pos 185119173      Query
thread_id=1273437368     exec_time=1      error_code=0
use usersession/*!*/;
SET TIMESTAMP=1221702167/*!*/;
UPDATE XXXXX /*!*/;
# at 185119173
#080917 18:42:47 server id 16   end_log_pos 185119200      Xid =
9731310854
COMMIT/*!*/;
DELIMITER ;
# End of log file
ROLLBACK /* added by mysqlbinlog */;
/*!50003 SET COMPLETION_TYPE=@OLD_COMPLETION_TYPE*/;
$
```

In this case you want to execute the first COMMIT statement and then stop. The line after the COMMIT statement shows the log position. The log position is 185118473. Now you can create your final text format file with exactly the right information:

```
$ mysqlbinlog --stop-position=185118473 mysql-bin.010312 >
mysql-bin.010312.sql
```

This file (mysql-bin.010656.sql) is what you will want to import.

```
$ mysql --user=root --password <  mysql-bin.010656.sql
```

It would be wise to examine the resulting file to ensure it is correct before execution of the log file.

Table 13-6 lists common options for the mysqlbinlog program.

TABLE 13-6

mysqlbinlog Options

Option	Description
--start-datetime= "date_time"	Begins reading the binary log file at a timestamp equal to or greater than the datetime argument.
--stop-datetime= "date_time"	Ends reading the binary log file at a timestamp equal to or greater than the datetime argument.
--start-position= start_log_position	Begins reading the binary log file beginning at the first log position equal to or greater than start_log_position.
--stop-position=stop_ log_position	Ends reading the binary log file at the first event having a log position equal to or greater than stop_log_position.

Planning for Disasters

Database recovery is part of the disaster planning process. What to do, who does it, and how long the recovery process takes when things break requires thought, planning, and usually coordination with other people and departments. It is important that you rehearse plans and perform drills to make sure that the proper preparations are in place.

A backup plan and corresponding periodic restores of your backups should be part of the disaster preparation. An incomplete list of issues covered could include:

- Power
- Employee termination process
- Data center failover plan
- Data retention strategies

A disaster plan should be written down and approved by everyone involved, including management. It should include checklists and processes to carry out for various scenarios.

Summary

You have multiple methods of backing up your data, and depending on your situation, some options are going to be better than others. Do not underestimate the importance of performing backups and testing the recovery procedure. Ensure the backups and recovery processes are actually working and current by testing frequently, preferably at least once per quarter. Other periodic tasks may include a test of the backups and recovery processes, such as periodically refreshing a QA server by recovering a production backup to it.

The following topics were covered in this chapter:

- Backup and recovery terminology
- Why backups are necessary
- Backup methodology
- The recovery process
- Disaster planning

Chapter 14

User Management

Managing the users for a MySQL server is one of the most important tasks of a MySQL database administrator. Because of the flexibility of the permissions system, it is not necessarily a trivial task. There are many tips to help manage users.

IN THIS CHAPTER

Learning about MySQL users

Managing user accounts

Resetting the root password

Debugging user account problems

Learning about MySQL Users

A user in MySQL is a combination of a username and *host string*. A host string can be an IP address, hostname, fully qualified domain name, or netmask. This means that even though they share a username, admin@192.168.2.10 is different from admin@'192.168.2.%', and both users can have different passwords and permissions. In the following example, we set up two users with the same username and different passwords and permissions:

```
shell> mysql -u root -prootpass
Welcome to the MySQL monitor.  Commands end with ; or \g.
Your MySQL connection id is 8
Server version: 6.0.8-alpha-community MySQL Community Server (GPL)

Type 'help;' or '\h' for help. Type '\c' to clear the buffer.

mysql> GRANT USAGE ON *.* TO admin@'192.168.2.10'
    IDENTIFIED BY 'easytoguess';
Query OK, 0 rows affected (0.22 sec)

mysql> GRANT ALL ON sakila.* TO admin@'192.168.2.20'
    IDENTIFIED BY 'anotherpassword';
```

473

```
Query OK, 0 rows affected (0.41 sec)

mysql> select user,host,password from mysql.user where user='admin';
+--------+--------------+----------------------------------------------+
| user   | host         | password                                     |
+--------+--------------+----------------------------------------------+
| admin  | 192.168.2.10 | *2F9A309FBEA7337E61AA2953EB48179BF9300B7C     |
| admin  | 192.168.2.20 | *4CBC947A0D5CF017233C027F4597C92A92D02F92     |
+--------+--------------+----------------------------------------------+
2 rows in set (0.05 sec)

mysql> exit
Bye
```

This allows for a flexible control system but can also cause confusion. How the server determines who a user is and what permissions are allowed for that user will be discussed in the next section.

Access Control Lists

An ACL (Access Control List) is a list of permissions that is associated with an object. This list is the basis for MySQL server's security model and once you understand this it helps greatly when troubleshooting problems with users not being able to connect.

MySQL keeps the ACLs (also called grant tables) cached in memory. When a user tries to authenticate or run a command, MySQL checks the authentication information and permissions against the ACLs, in a predetermined order. If you had two users, admin@'192.168.2.%' and then admin@192.168.2.10, the user admin@'192.168.2.%' user comes before admin@192.168.2.10 in the Access Control List. When MySQL checks authentication, the admin@'192.168.2.%' user is the first user whose credentials match the credentials provided. Remember how users with the same username but different host strings can have different passwords? The following example shows what happens in this case; the computer used by the user has an IP address of 192.168.2.20:

```
shell> mysql -u admin -peasytoguess -h 192.168.1.5
ERROR 1045 (28000): Access denied for user 'admin @'192.168.2.20'
 (using password: YES)
```

What happened was the account attempted to connect using the account admin@192.168. 2.10, which was configured with the password of easytoguesss. When attempting to connect the server authenticated against the user account admin@192.168.2.20, which has a password of anotherpassword.

If they had same passwords the connection would be allowed — but the connection may be using an account with different privileges than expected. If you are not sure what user you are actually logged in as you can use the USER() and CURRENT_USER() functions to determine how you are connected.

The USER() function shows which username and host the MySQL server sees the connection as coming from. The CURRENT_USER() function shows which username and host the connection is actually authenticated. Note that the SHOW GRANTS statement with no arguments shows the privileges for the user the connection was authenticated — the privileges for the CURRENT_USER().

Wildcards

Wildcard characters (% and _) are allowed in host strings. This is another source of confusion as admin@192.168.2.10 is a completely different user than admin@'192.168.2.%'. As stated above, MySQL checks the access control list in order. However, we did not reveal how the MySQL server orders the access control list.

MySQL orders the access control list with the least specific hosts last. This means that hostnames and IPs without wildcards or netmasks are placed before hostnames and IPs with wildcards and netmasks. MySQL matches the most specific user and hostname.

In the following example, after deleting the users from the previous example, admin@192.168. 2.10 is given full read/write permissions to the sakila database, and admin@'19.168.2.%' is given read-only permissions to the sakila database:

```
mysql> DROP USER admin@192.168.2.20;
Query OK, 0 rows affected (0.01 sec)
mysql> DROP USER admin@192.168.2.10;
Query OK, 0 rows affected (0.01 sec)


mysql> SELECT USER, HOST, PASSWORD FROM MYSQL.USER WHERE
   USER='admin';
Empty set (0.01 sec)

mysql> GRANT SELECT ON sakila.* TO admin@'1921.68.2.%'
   identified by 'adminpass';
Query OK, 0 rows affected (0.39 sec)

mysql> GRANT ALL ON sakila.* TO admin@'192.168.2.10' identified by
   'adminpass';
Query OK, 0 rows affected (0.00 sec)

mysql> exit
Bye

shell> mysql -u admin
Welcome to the MySQL monitor.  Commands end with ; or \g.
Your MySQL connection id is 8
Server version: 6.0.8-alpha-community MySQL Community Server (GPL)

Type 'help;' or '\h' for help. Type '\c' to clear the buffer.
```

475

```
mysql> SHOW GRANTS\G
*************************** 1. row ***************************
Grants for admin@192.168.2.10: GRANT USAGE ON *.* TO 'admin'@'192.
168.2.10' IDENTIFIED BY PASSWORD '*2C6396ADEEF1AF865672D48735
C0E3EC8B1A9CEC'
*************************** 2. row ***************************
Grants for admin@192.168.2.10: GRANT ALL PRIVILEGES ON `sakila`.*
TO 'admin'@'192.168.2.10'
2 rows in set (0.00 sec)

mysql> exit
Bye
```

The connection was authenticated as the user admin@192.168.2.10 because it has a more specific host than the user admin@'192.168.2.%' and, therefore, appeared earlier in MySQL's access control list. This would only happen if the user connected from the IP address 192.168.2.10. If they connected from 192.168.2.20, it would use the more general host of '192.168.2.%'. If they attempted to connect from 192.168.3.10, they would not be authenticated.

System tables

All the user and permission information is stored in the mysql database in a set of tables known as the *grant tables*. If you execute 'SHOW DATABASES' on a typical default install of MySQL it will look like the following:

```
mysql> SHOW DATABASES;
+--------------------+
| Database           |
+--------------------+
| information_schema |
| mysql              |
| test               |
+--------------------+
3 rows in set (0.02 sec)
```

The information_schema database really is not a database but an interface to various system metadata (see Chapter 21 for more information about the information_schema database). The test database is an empty database used for testing purposes and as mentioned the mysql database stores the user information. In addition to the grant tables, the mysql database has tables containing other system information. For example, a table called event is used by the event scheduler (see Chapter 7 for more information about events). Because of new additions such as this, the tables in the mysql database vary from version to version. Here are the tables in a server running mysqld 6.0.8-alpha:

```
mysql> SHOW TABLES;
+---------------------------+
| Tables_in_mysql           |
+---------------------------+
| backup_history            |
| backup_progress           |
| columns_priv              |
| db                        |
| event                     |
| func                      |
| general_log               |
| help_category             |
| help_keyword              |
| help_relation             |
| help_topic                |
| host                      |
| ndb_binlog_index          |
| plugin                    |
| proc                      |
| procs_priv                |
| servers                   |
| slow_log                  |
| tables_priv               |
| time_zone                 |
| time_zone_leap_second     |
| time_zone_name            |
| time_zone_transition      |
| time_zone_transition_type |
| user                      |
+---------------------------+
25 rows in set (0.18 sec)
```

The tables that are of interest when it comes user management are columns_priv, db, host, procs_priv, tables_priv, and user. It is possible to directly manipulate these tables using SQL to add, delete, or update user information. In fact, that used to be the only way privileges were managed. These days, however, it is much easier and less error prone to use the GRANT, REVOKE, CREATE USER, DROP USER, and RENAME USER commands designed for user management. We will cover the commands used to manipulate users in the next section.

One of the more common problems of a database administrator is seeing what users are already exist and what privileges they have. If you are logged in to the server with appropriate privileges, the following will show all usernames, hosts, and password hashes on the system:

```
mysql> SELECT user,host,password FROM mysql.user;
+-------------+---------------+-----------------------------------+
| user        | host          | password                          |
+-------------+---------------+-----------------------------------+
| root        | %             | *ACC4836009D0D7911EFE143E154D3E7C |
|             |               | 32AB8EEB                          |
| root        | localhost     | *ACC4836009D0D7911EFE143E154D3E7C |
|             |               | 32AB8EEB                          |
| developer   | localhost     | *50C0E8BEE396F2367258EC80901409C4 |
|             |               | BE300238                          |
| production_ | slave.        | *891A44E50A5E8286F04BC1EFB0292BE3 |
| slave       | company.com   | AFE74D5E                          |
| production_ | 192.168.2.191 | *891A44E50A5E8286F04BC1EFB0292BE3 |
| slave       |               | AFE74D5E                          |
| ops         | localhost     | *99FFA08BDD2C5D80552F52F441AA632D |
|             |               | FA1DE9E3                          |
| cto         | 192.%         | *B81134DE91B9BE86259180DC8446A254 |
|             |               | 008A1D9E                          |
+-------------+---------------+-----------------------------------+
7 rows in set (0.00 sec)
```

> **NOTE** If a user has a blank password, the password field will be empty.

Managing User Accounts

MySQL server provides a number of commands used for managing users. To create a user, you can use the CREATE USER command. To drop a user, you should use the DROP USER command. In the following example, we create a user and give them privileges and finally drop the user.

```
mysql> CREATE USER 'ops'@'192.168.%' IDENTIFIED BY 'password';
Query OK, 0 rows affected (0.00 sec)

mysql> GRANT ALL PRIVILEGES ON test.* TO 'ops'@'192.168.%';
Query OK, 0 rows affected (0.00 sec)

mysql> DROP USER 'ops'@'192.168.%';
Query OK, 0 rows affected (0.00 sec)
```

```
mysql> select User,Host,Password from user;
+------+-----------+-------------------------------------------+
| User | Host      | Password                                  |
+------+-----------+-------------------------------------------+
| root | localhost | *0AFF2E05C6A513A4FF86D9EBE1D7F8C4C53366A1 |
| root | %         | *0AFF2E05C6A513A4FF86D9EBE1D7F8C4C53366A1 |
+------+-----------+-------------------------------------------+
2 rows in set (0.00 sec)
```

WARNING The CREATE USER and GRANT USER commands (covered in the next section) can both be used to create users without passwords. This is very insecure and should be avoided! Always use the IDENTIFIED BY clause when using these commands.

Dropping the user removes all their privileges. Even if you recreate the exact same username and host the new user does not retain the privileges of the previous user. You are starting from scratch. Here is an example showing this:

```
mysql> CREATE USER 'ops'@'192.168.%' IDENTIFIED BY 'password';
Query OK, 0 rows affected (0.00 sec)

mysql> GRANT ALL PRIVILEGES ON test.* TO 'ops'@'192.168.%';
Query OK, 0 rows affected (0.00 sec)

mysql> DROP USER 'ops'@'192.168.%';
Query OK, 0 rows affected (0.00 sec)

mysql> SELECT user,host,password FROM mysql.user;
+------+-----------+-------------------------------------------+
| user | host      | password                                  |
+------+-----------+-------------------------------------------+
| root | localhost | *0AFF2E05C6A513A4FF86D9EBE1D7F8C4C53366A1 |
| root | %         | *0AFF2E05C6A513A4FF86D9EBE1D7F8C4C53366A1 |
+------+-----------+-------------------------------------------+
2 rows in set (0.00 sec)

mysql> CREATE USER 'ops'@'192.168.%' IDENTIFIED BY 'password';
Query OK, 0 rows affected (0.00 sec)

mysql> SHOW GRANTS FOR 'ops'@'192.168.%';
+-------------------------------------------+
| Grants for ops@192.168.%                  |
+-------------------------------------------+
| GRANT USAGE ON *.* TO 'ops'@'192.168.%'   |
+-------------------------------------------+
1 row in set (0.00 sec)
```

The RENAME USER command renames an existing account. The RENAME COMMAND will return an error if the new user already exists.

```
mysql> CREATE USER 'ops'@'192.168.%' IDENTIFIED BY 'password';
Query OK, 0 rows affected (0.00 sec)

mysql> SELECT user,host,password FROM mysql.user;
+------+-----------+-------------------------------------------+
| user | host      | password                                  |
+------+-----------+-------------------------------------------+
| root | localhost | *0AFF2E05C6A513A4FF86D9EBE1D7F8C4C53366A1 |
| ops  | 192.168.% | *2470C0C06DEE42FD1618BB99005ADCA2EC9D1E19 |
| root | %         | *0AFF2E05C6A513A4FF86D9EBE1D7F8C4C53366A1 |
+------+-----------+-------------------------------------------+
3 rows in set (0.00 sec)

mysql> CREATE USER 'support'@'192.168.%';
Query OK, 0 rows affected (0.00 sec)

mysql> SELECT user,host,password FROM mysql.user;
+---------+-----------+-------------------------------------------+
| user    | host      | password                                  |
+---------+-----------+-------------------------------------------+
| root    | localhost | *0AFF2E05C6A513A4FF86D9EBE1D7F8C4C53366A1 |
| ops     | 192.168.% | *2470C0C06DEE42FD1618BB99005ADCA2EC9D1E19 |
| root    | %         | *0AFF2E05C6A513A4FF86D9EBE1D7F8C4C53366A1 |
| support | 192.168.% | *2470C0C06DEE42FD1618BB99005ADCA2EC9D1E19 |
+---------+-----------+-------------------------------------------+
4 rows in set (0.00 sec)

mysql> RENAME USER 'ops'@'192.168.%' TO 'support'@'192.168.%';
ERROR 1396 (HY000): Operation RENAME USER failed for 'ops'@
  '192.168.%'
mysql> RENAME USER 'ops'@'192.168.%' TO 'over_lords'@'192.168.%';
Query OK, 0 rows affected (0.00 sec)

mysql> SELECT user,host,password FROM mysql.user;
+------------+-----------+-----------------------------------+
| user       | host      | password                          |
+------------+-----------+-----------------------------------+
| root       | localhost | *0AFF2E05C6A513A4FF86D9EBE1D7F8C4C |
|            |           | 53366A1                           |
| over_lords | 192.168.% | *2470C0C06DEE42FD1618BB99005ADCA2 |
|            |           | EC9D1E19                          |
| root       | %         | *0AFF2E05C6A513A4FF86D9EBE1D7F8C4C |
|            |           | 53366A1                           |
| support    | 192.168.% | *2470C0C06DEE42FD1618BB99005ADCA2 |
|            |           | EC9D1E19                          |
+------------+-----------+-----------------------------------+
4 rows in set (0.00 sec)
```

When a user is renamed, the password is retained by the new user. The user privileges are not migrated. Also RENAME USER does not change any database object properties (tables, views, stored routines, and triggers) that the user created.

GRANT and REVOKE commands

There are two commands that are used to control a user's privileges. The GRANT command is used to give an existing user privileges, and REVOKE is used to remove privileges. If a user does not exist, GRANT will create a new user at the same time you are giving them privileges.

WARNING It is not recommended that you use GRANT to create a user, because it is too easy to forget to specify a password when using the GRANT syntax. Users should be created with CREATE USER first, then given permissions with GRANT.

There are five levels that privileges can be granted.

Global

Global privileges apply to all databases on a MySQL server. These privileges are stored in the mysql.user table. You use the GRANT privilege_list ON *.* and REVOKE privilege_list ON *.* statements to grant and revoke only global level privileges.

The following example will grant all privileges (except the GRANT PRIVILEGES privilege) to the 'ops'@'192.168.%' user. These privileges apply for all databases on the server:

```
GRANT RELOAD,SHUTDOWN ON *.* TO 'ops'@'192.168.%';
```

The next example will grant only SELECT, INSERT, UPDATE, and DELETE privileges to the user 'ops'@'192.168.%' on all databases on the server:

```
GRANT SELECT, INSERT, UPDATE, DELETE ON *.* TO 'ops'@'192.168.%';
```

TIP The users with username of root created by default is only special because of the permissions it has. The root username has no significance and can be deleted from a fresh installation with no issues (servers currently in use may be depending on the root user for backups or some other important task). To create a new user with all privileges:

```
CREATE USER superuser@localhost IDENTIFIED BY 'superpass';
GRANT ALL ON *.* TO superuser@localhost;
```

Database

Database privileges apply to all objects of a specified database. These privileges are stored in the mysql.db and mysql.host tables. The GRANT ALL ON db_name.* and REVOKE ALL ON db_name.* commands grant and revoke only database level privileges.

The following example will grant all privileges (except the GRANT PRIVILEGES privilege) to the 'ops'@'192.168.%' user. These privileges apply only to the database user_db:

```
GRANT ALL ON user_db.* TO 'ops'@'192.168.%';
```

The next example will grant only SELECT, INSERT, UPDATE, and DELETE privileges to the user 'ops'@'192.168.%' on the database user_db:

```
GRANT SELECT, INSERT, UPDATE, DELETE ON user_db.* TO 'ops'
    @'192.168.%';
```

Table

Table privileges apply to all columns in a given table. These privileges are stored in the mysql.tables_priv table. The GRANT ALL ON db_name.table_name and REVOKE ALL ON db_name.table_name commands grant and revoke only table level privileges.

The following example will grant all privileges (except the GRANT PRIVILEGES privilege) to the 'ops'@'192.168.%' user. These privileges apply only to the table table_name of the database user_db:

```
GRANT ALL ON user_db.table_name TO 'ops'@'192.168.%';
```

The next example will grant only SELECT, INSERT, UPDATE, and DELETE privileges to the user 'ops'@'192.168.%' on to the table table_name of the database user_db:

```
GRANT SELECT, INSERT, UPDATE, DELETE ON user_db.table_name TO
    'ops'@'192.168.%';
```

If you had only specified table_name rather than db_name.table_name, the GRANT or REVOKE statement applies to the table table_name in the default database. To keep from having unexpected results, we would recommend you use the "full" database_name.table_name format instead.

Column

Column level privileges apply to one or more columns in a given table. These privileges are stored in the mysql.columns_priv table. When using the REVOKE command to remove column level privileges, you must specify the same columns that were granted. The column or columns for which the privileges are to be granted are enclosed within parentheses.

The following example will grant SELECT, INSERT, and UPDATE privileges to the user 'ops'@'192.168.%' on the columns col1 and col2 of the table table_name located in the database user_db:

```
GRANT SELECT (col1,col2), INSERT (col1,col2), UPDATE (col1,col2)
    ON user_db.table_name TO 'ops'@'192.168.%';
```

Routine

The CREATE ROUTINE, ALTER ROUTINE, EXECUTE, and GRANT privileges apply to stored routines (functions and procedures). They can be granted at the global and database levels. Also, except for CREATE ROUTINE, these privileges can be granted at the routine level for individual routines. The privileges are stored in the mysql.procs_priv table.

```
GRANT CREATE ROUTINE ON database.* TO 'ops'@'192.168.2.%';
GRANT EXECUTE ON PROCEDURE database.backup_proc TO 'backup'@
    '192.168.2.%';
```

Table 14-1 lists all of the privilege options available.

TABLE 14-1

MySQL User Privileges

Privilege	Description
ALL	Grants all privileges to specified user except the GRANT OPTION.
ALTER	Allows user to ALTER TABLE.
ALTER ROUTINE	Allows user to alter or drop stored routines.
CREATE	Allows user to execute the CREATE TABLE command.
CREATE ROUTINE	Allows user to create stored routines.
CREATE TEMPORARY TABLES	Allows user to execute the CREATE TEMPORARY TABLE command.
CREATE USER	Allows user to execute CREATE USER, DROP USER, RENAME USER and REVOKE ALL PRIVILEGES statements for user creation.
CREATE VIEW	Allows user to execute the CREATE VIEW command to create views.
DELETE	Allows user to execute the DELETE command.
DROP	Allows user to execute the DROP command.
EXECUTE	Allows user to run stored routines.
FILE	Allows user to execute both SELECT INTO OUTFILE and LOAD DATA INFILE.
GRANT OPTION	Allows user to grant other users privileges.
INDEX	Allows user to execute CREATE INDEX and DROP INDEX.

continued

TABLE 14-1   *(continued)*

Privilege	Description
INSERT	Allows user to execute the INSERT command.
LOCK TABLES	Allows user to execute LOCK TABLES (user must also have SELECT privileges on the table).
PROCESS	Allows user to see all processes when executing SHOW PROCESSLIST.
REFERENCES	This privilege is not currently implemented.
RELOAD	Allows user to execute FLUSH.
REPLICATION CLIENT	Allows user to execute both SHOW MASTER STATUS and SHOW SLAVE STATUS commands.
REPLICATION SLAVE	Needed by the replication slave to read binary logs from the master.
SELECT	Allows users to execute SELECT statement.
SHOW DATABASES	When user executes SHOW DATABASES command will return a list of all databases.
SHOW VIEW	Allows user to execute the SHOW CREATE VIEW command.
SHUTDOWN	Allows user to execute 'mysqladmin shutdown'.
SUPER	Allows user to execute CHANGE MASTER, KILL, PURGE MASTER LOGS, and SET GLOBAL commands. Also will allow user to always connect even if max_connections has been reached.
UPDATE	Allows user to execute UPDATE command
USAGE	Allows user to connect.

As you can see there are quite a few allowable privileges. This, in combination with the five privilege levels (global, database, table, column, and routine), allow for any level of granularity needed by a database administrator. This granularity creates complexity, but the end result is a more controllable and secure system.

TIP   Privileges are checked until either access is allowed or the end of the ACL is reached. If you want to query the table production.employee, then MySQL server first checks to see if you have global access privileges. If so, the query is executed. If you do not have global access then MySQL server checks for privileges at the database level (production). If you do not have privileges at the database level, then the table level (employee) privileges are checked. If this fails the column level privileges are checked and if this fails the user is denied access. If a check returns positive at any level mysqld stops checking privileges.

REVOKE

The REVOKE statement is used to remove privileges from a user account. Just as with the GRANT statement there are five levels that you can revoke privileges from: global, database, table, column, and routine.

The following example would revoke all privileges for the user 'ops'@'localhost':

```
mysql> REVOKE ALL PRIVILEGES, GRANT OPTION FROM 'ops'@'localhost';
```

NOTE Even if you revoke all privileges, the user is not dropped (they are still visible in the mysql.user system table). At this point, the user has the USAGE privilege, which means they can still connect to the server and execute a few commands such as SHOW VARIABLES and SELECT NOW(). To drop a user, you must use the DROP USER. It is a best practice to always drop users after revoking all their privileges.

What if the 'ops'@'localhost' had global SELECT, INSERT, UPDATE, DELETE, and DROP privileges but you wanted to only remove the DROP privilege? The following would accomplish this:

```
mysql> REVOKE DROP ON *.* FROM 'ops'@'localhost';
```

If the user 'ops'localhost' had SELECT, INSERT, UPDATE, and DELETE privileges on the table user_accounts of the database production, you could revoke the DELETE privileges on this one table like this:

```
mysql> REVOKE DELETE ON production.user_accounts FROM
'ops'@'localhost';
```

As you have probably noticed the REVOKE command very similar of the GRANT command.

SHOW GRANTS and mk-show-grants

The SHOW GRANTS command is used to show a user's privileges. This is done by displaying a list of all the GRANT statement(s) that could then be used to duplicate the privileges of a user. If the user has the GRANT PRIVILEGES privilege, then the user can also view the grants of other users.

Here is a simple example which shows the grants for the current user:

```
mysql> SHOW GRANTS\G
*************************** 1. row ***************************
Grants for root@localhost: GRANT ALL PRIVILEGES ON *.* TO 'root'@
'localhost' IDENTIFIED BY PASSWORD '*3800D13EE735ED411CBC3F23B2
A2E19C63CE0BEC' WITH GRANT OPTION
1 row in set (0.00 sec)
```

This was done with the root user who has all privileges, including the GRANT OPTION. Because this user has the GRANT OPTION, it can grant privileges to other users, and use the SHOW GRANTS command to display grants for other users.

 Remember, if you need to see a list of users on the server SELECT user,host FROM mysql.user will return all users.

Now to take a look at the privileges for 'over_lords'@'%':

```
mysql> SHOW GRANTS FOR 'over_lords'@'%'\G
*************************** 1. row ***************************
Grants for over_lords@'%': GRANT USAGE ON *.* TO 'over_lords'@'%'
IDENTIFIED BY PASSWORD '*2470C0C06DEE42FD1618BB99005ADCA2EC9D1E19'
```

This user has no privileges. If you are running Unix-based servers the Maatkit toolkit (http://www.maatkit.org) has a very useful command for systems that have more than a few users. The mk-show-grants command allows you display a list of all the users on the system. In addition, it is very easy to pipe the output to a file and then store the file in a version control system or use just simply copy it to another server and use the file to set up the same permissions on another server.

Here is a sample of the mk-show-grants command on a system with more users. Password hashes have been removed:

```
shell> ./mk-show-grants -u root -ppassword
-- Grants dumped by mk-show-grants @VERSION@
-- Dumped from server Localhost via UNIX socket, MySQL 6.0.8-alpha at
   2009-01-06 01:48:50
-- Grants for 'monitoring'@'10.%'
GRANT REPLICATION SLAVE ON *.* TO 'monitoring'@'10.%' IDENTI-
FIED BY PASSWORD 'PASSWORD_HASH';
-- Grants for 'monitoring'@'localhost'
GRANT ALL PRIVILEGES ON *.* TO 'monitoring'@'localhost' IDENTI-
FIED BY PASSWORD 'PASSWORD_HASH';
GRANT USAGE ON *.* TO 'company'@'%.company.com' IDENTIFIED BY
   PASSWORD 'PASSWORD_HASH';
GRANT ALL PRIVILEGES ON `company_production`.* TO 'company'@'%.
   company.com' WITH GRANT OPTION;
-- Grants for 'webuser'@'10.%'
GRANT USAGE ON *.* TO 'webuser'@'10.%' IDENTIFIED BY PASSWORD
   'PASSWORD_HASH';
GRANT ALL PRIVILEGES ON `company_production`.* TO 'webuser'@'10.%'
   WITH GRANT OPTION;
-- Grants for 'webuser'@'localhost'
GRANT USAGE ON *.* TO 'webuser'@'localhost' IDENTIFIED BY
   PASSWORD 'PASSWORD_HASH';
GRANT ALL PRIVILEGES ON `webuser_load_test`.* TO 'webuser'@
```

```
      'localhost';
   GRANT ALL PRIVILEGES ON `webuser_production`.* TO 'webuser'@
      'localhost' WITH GRANT OPTION;
   -- Grants for 'production_slave'@'8.%'
   GRANT REPLICATION CLIENT, REPLICATION SLAVE ON *.* TO
      'production_slave'@'8.%' IDENTIFIED BY PASSWORD 'PASSWORD_HASH';
   -- Grants for 'production_slave'@'192.168.1.191'
   GRANT REPLICATION SLAVE ON *.* TO 'production_slave'@'192.168.1.191'
      IDENTIFIED BY PASSWORD 'PASSWORD_HASH';
   -- Grants for 'production_slave'@'preview.company.com'
   GRANT REPLICATION SLAVE ON *.* TO 'production_slave'@
      'preview.company.com' IDENTIFIED BY PASSWORD 'PASSWORD_HASH';
   -- Grants for 'root'@'localhost'
   GRANT ALL PRIVILEGES ON *.* TO 'root'@'localhost' IDENTIFIED BY
      PASSWORD 'PASSWORD_HASH' WITH GRANT OPTION;
   -- Grants for 'tempuser'@'%'
   GRANT ALL PRIVILEGES ON *.* TO 'tempuser'@'%' IDENTIFIED BY
      PASSWORD 'PASSWORD_HASH';

   ahell>
```

To send this output to a file:

```
shell> ./mk-show-grants -u root -ppassword > grants.sql
```

Resetting the Root Password

There are times when the password for the root user is lost. It is not a trivial matter to reset the password and requires a server restart. However, there are times when this proves necessary. There are two methods for recovering the password. Both have their benefits and drawbacks.

A simple recovery method that works on any server platform uses the 'skip-grants-table' option in your configuration file. When the server is restarted with this option it starts "wide open" with anyone able to log in with all privileges without even specifying a username. This is a huge security risk and must be carefully considered on production system. We would recommend that when you add 'skip-grants-table' that you also add the 'bind-address=127.0.0.1' option, which does not allow remote network connections to the MySQL server. This minimizes the risk somewhat.

Here is the procedure:

1. Edit the configuration file and add the skip-grant-tables and (optionally) the bind-address option to the mysqld section.

2. Restart the MySQL server

487

3. Connect to the mysqld server using the mysql client. No password or user needs to be specified. If you also used the skip-networking option, you must run the mysql client from the server itself.

```
shell> mysql
```

4. Issue the following statements, replacing New_Password with the password that you want to update the root users to have.

```
mysql> UPDATE mysql.user SET Password=PASSWORD('New_Password')
  WHERE User='root';
mysql> FLUSH PRIVILEGES;
```

What happens here is that the UPDATE statement resets the password for all existing root accounts and the FLUSH PRIVILEGES statement tells the server to reload the grant tables into memory.

5. Exit the mysql client and test your new password. If everything works correctly, remove skip-grants-table and skip-networking from the configuration file, and restart the MySQL server.

This is a straightforward procedure and in an emergency might be the only method you have time to perform. However, as pointed out, it is not inherently secure.

The second method of resetting the root password is more secure. The basis for this recovery method is using an initialization file at server startup to execute the same UPDATE and FLUSH PRIVILEGES commands we used in the previous example. It varies somewhat from Windows servers to Unix-based servers, so approaches for both will be outlined.

Windows server

1. Log on to your system as a user with Administrator privileges.

2. Stop the MySQL server if it is currently running.

   If MySQL is running as a Windows service, click on Start Menu ➤ Settings ➤ Control Panel ➤ Administrative Tools ➤ Services. Then find the MySQL service in the list, right click on it, and then left-click on Stop.

   If your MySQL server is not running as a service, you may need to use the Task Manager to force it to stop.

3. With your favorite text editor, create a text file, and place the following statements in it:

```
UPDATE mysql.user SET Password=PASSWORD('New_Password') WHERE
User='root';
FLUSH PRIVILEGES;
```

Replace New_Password with the password that you want to use (but leave the quotation marks). Each of the statements must be written on a single line.

4. Save the file. For this example, the filename will be C:\reset_pass.txt.

5. Open a console window to get to the command prompt. Click on Start Menu ➤ Run and then type cmd.

6. Start the MySQL server with the --init-file option. It might look something like this:

```
C:\> C:\Program Files\MySQL\MySQL Server 5.1\bin\mysqld --console
  --init-file=C:\reset_pass.txt
```

If you installed MySQL to another location adjust the directory accordingly.

The server executes the contents of the file named by the --init-file option at startup while displaying any output to the console.

If you installed MySQL using the MySQL Installation Wizard, you also may need to specify a --defaults-file option. The appropriate --defaults-file setting can be found using the Services Manager:

Click Start Menu ➤ Control Panel ➤ Administrative Tools ➤ Services

Find the MySQL service in the list, right-click on it, and choose the Properties option. The Path to executable field contains the --defaults-file setting.

If you can not get the MySQL server to start from the command line, you can edit the server configuration file and add the init-file option in your mysqld section and then restart the server using the Services manager.

7. After the server has started successfully and you have confirmed the new password work, delete the initialization file C:\reset_pass.txt, and remove the init-file option from your configuration file if necessary and restart it in the normal manner.

Unix-based server

You can use the following procedure for resetting the password for any MySQL root accounts on a Unix-based sever:

1. Create a text file and place the following statements in it. Replace the password with the password that you want to use.

```
UPDATE mysql.user SET Password=PASSWORD('MyNewPass') WHERE
  User='root';
FLUSH PRIVILEGES;
```

The UPDATE and FLUSH statements each must be written on a single line. The UPDATE statement resets the password for all existing root accounts, and the FLUSH statement tells the server to reload the grant tables into memory.

2. Save the file. For this example, the file will be named /home/kmurphy/mysql-init. The file contains the root user password. Be certain that it cannot be read by other users.

Edit your /etc/my.cnf file. Under [myqld] add init-file=/home/kmurphy/ mysql-init.

3. Shut down the MySQL server in your normal manner.

4. Start the MySQL server in your normal manner.

   The server executes the contents of the file named by the init-file option at startup, changing each root account password to the new password specified.

5. After the server has started successfully and you have verified the new password works, delete the initialization file and edit my.cnf file to remove the init-file line.

Debugging User Account Problems

There are times when users will come to the database administrator with complaints that a newly created account isn't working. When this happens, there are some common issues you can look for to help when troubleshooting.

Bad password

A common problem is that the account does not work because of an improperly keyed password or a miscommunication in what the password should be. Here is the GRANT statement for a user:

```
mysql> SHOW GRANTS FOR 'ops'@'localhost';
+-------------------------------------------------------------------+
| Grants for ops@localhost                                          |
+-------------------------------------------------------------------+
| GRANT ALL PRIVILEGES ON *.* TO 'ops'@'localhost' IDENTIFIED BY    |
|    PASSWORD 'password_hash'                                        |
+-------------------------------------------------------------------+
1 row in set (0.00 sec)
```

The user comes to you and says their new account is not working. You check the error they are seeing:

```
shell> mysql -u ops -p
Enter password:
ERROR 1045 (28000): Access denied for user 'ops'@'localhost' (using
   password: YES)
shell>
```

This means that the privileges do not match the grants tables. The user is either typing in an incorrect password or the account has no password and the user is trying to specify a password. It could also be that the host they are coming from is not specified in a user@host string, or that they spelled the username wrong.

In this case, if there was not a miscommunication about what the password should be and you need to reset the password, then log in as a user who has GRANT privileges and do the following:

```
mysql> SET PASSWORD FOR ops@'192.168.%' = PASSWORD('New_Password');
Query OK, 0 rows affected (0.00 sec)
```

And now the user can log in with the new password:

```
shell> mysql -u ops -p
Enter password: ************
Welcome to the MySQL monitor.  Commands end with ; or \g.
Your MySQL connection id is 8
Server version: 6.0.8-alpha MySQL Community Server (GPL)

Type 'help;' or '\h' for help. Type '\c' to clear the buffer.

mysql>
```

Access issues

A more subtle issue is that of access. The user has the right username and password, but the host is either set incorrectly or there are multiple hosts listed with the same username and the "wrong" host is being used in authentication. You saw this issue earlier with the admin@127.0.0.1 and admin@localhost users.

If a user does not have the expected permissions, check SHOW GRANTS with no arguments to see what user and permissions the server is using. Also both SELECT USER(), CURRENT_USER(), and SELECT user, host, password FROM mysql.user WHERE user='<username>'; are useful to help troubleshoot issues where the permissions are not as they are expected.

Client does not support authentication protocol

Back in mysqld version 4.1 a new authentication protocol was used by default. This protocol is more secure and should be used if possible. The problem is that some clients only support the older protocol. For example, older Perl libraries can only support the older protocol, and at the time of this book's writing, PHP did not support the new protocol.

To fix the problem, run mysql and log in as user with the SUPER privilege. Then use following command which will change the password of the user to the old format:

```
mysql> SET PASSWORD FOR ops@'192.168.%' = OLD_PASSWORD('
My_Password');
```

This sets the password to format of the older authentication protocols. Then exit mysql and test your client connection. You can see the difference in the password hash using the SHOW GRANTS statement. Here is a hash using the new authentication protocol:

```
'*2470C0C06DEE42FD1618BB99005ADCA2EC9D1E19'
```

Here is a hash from after the password has been set with the OLD_PASSWORD format:

```
'5d2e19393cc5ef67'
```

If at all possible, you should use the newer authentication protocol as it is much more secure.

Can't connect to local mysqld through socket '/path/to/mysqld.sock'

This shows up quite frequently. This is only an issue on Unix-based servers. There are several things to check when you come across this problem.

Check to make sure that the MySQL server is actually running. From a command prompt, issue a ps aux | grep mysql command and see if you get any results back. If there are no results returned, then you need to start the server.

If the MySQL server is running then you need to make certain that your my.cnf file has the same location for the socket file, if there is more than one listing for it. If you are specifying the socket file on the command line, make sure it is exactly the same as the one in the my.cnf file.

Make certain that the directory that the socket file located in has the proper permissions. Assuming /var/lib/mysql is the directory of the mysqld.sock file do the following:

```
/home/kmurphy> ls -lh /var/lib
drwxr-x--- 5 mysql mysql 4096 Sep 06 18:33 mysql
```

This is the proper permissions, owned by the mysql user who is the user used to run the mysqld daemon. If it is owned by the root user this would cause a problem:

```
/home/kmurphy> ls -lh /var/lib
drwxr-x--- 5 root root 4096 Sep 06 18:33 mysql
```

In this case, the root user owns the directory and no one else has read or write permissions to it. To resolve the problem, you use the chown (change owner) command as root:

```
# chown -R mysql:mysql /var/lib/mysql
```

I do not have the right permissions!

There are times when users will connect and authenticate themselves, but it turns out that they do not have the proper permissions that were defined for their account. The problem here is usually the matching characteristics of user accounts.

In the following example the user attempted to connect as admin_account@localhost but actually logged in as the anonymous user and does not realize it.

```
mysql> SELECT USER();
+-------------------------+
| USER()                  |
+-------------------------+
| admin_account@localhost |
+-------------------------+
1 row in set (0.00 sec)
```

The user has connected to mysqld, and the USER() function even shows that they are connected as the admin_account@localhost user. However, when they attempt to do some work, they discover that permissions are not as they should be:

```
ERROR 1044 (42000): Access denied for user ''@'localhost' to
    database 'secret'
```

As you can see, the user information returned by mysqld (''@localhost) does not match the account the user logged in under. In this situation the user is logged in as an anonymous account (username is blank). To provide further confirmation, you can run the following:

```
mysql> SELECT current_user();
+---------------+
| current_user()|
+---------------+
| ''@localhost  |
+---------------+
1 row in set (0.00 sec)
```

The problem is that the USER() function returns the user that attempted to connect to the MySQL server. The CURRENT_USER() function shows the user that actually authenticated. The return from CURRENT_USER() can always be used in a SHOW GRANTS FOR statement, but the value returned from user USER() does not necessarily represent a user in the grant tables.

In this case, the anonymous account was enabled and it is a catch-all account with no password. If admin_account@locahost was removed (as in this case) and the user attempts to connect with the removed account they succeed but only because of the anonymous account was enabled. This is another reason to remove anonymous accounts from your systems. Without the anonymous account, the user would have received something similar to the following, which makes it much easier to understand what is happening:

```
shell > mysql -u admin_account
ERROR 1045 (28000): Access denied for user 'admin_account'@
  'localhost' (using password: NO)
```

Summary

Managing users is one of the more common database administration tasks. With MySQL server, the granularity of the permissions does provide a level of complexity that requires understanding by the administrator beyond surface-level knowledge in order to really understand what is happening.

In this chapter we covered the following topics:

- Access Control Lists
- The CREATE USER, DROP USER, and RENAME USER commands
- The GRANT and REVOKE commands
- Debugging user account problems

Chapter 15

Partitioning

artitioning is dividing up data in a database into distinct independent elements. Partitioning has three main purposes: to provide data manageability, performance, and availability. Partitioning is not part of relational database theory; it is a practical detail to help queries perform better. There are several methods of implementing partitioning with MySQL.

Learning about Partitioning

There are two ways to partition database tables:

IN THIS CHAPTER

Learning about partitioning

Partitioning tables

Using MERGE tables

Partitioning with MySQL cluster

Programmatic partitioning

- **Horizontal partitioning** — In *horizontal partitioning*, different rows are stored in different tables. Perhaps customers with IDs less than 500,000 are stored in customers1, while customers with IDs greater than or equal to 500,000 are stored in customers2. These two tables now horizontally partition the data set of customers. In horizontal partitioning, the table schemas are exactly the same (i.e., customers1 and customers2 have the same schema). It is as if a table were cut into parts using a horizontal line.

  Archiving older data is a commonly used example of horizontal partitioning. Another technique using horizontal partitioning is *sharding*, which involves using separate servers to host similar types of data. For example, customers with IDs less than 500,000 are stored in the customers table on server1, and customers with IDs greater than or equal to 500,000 are stored in the customers table on server2.

There are different criteria used to split the table or database. Horizontal partitioning is accomplished manually with MERGE tables, as MERGE tables do not automatically assign data to different underlying tables. Internal partitioning assigns records to a partition based on certain criteria.

■ **Vertical partitioning** — In *vertical partitioning*, different fields are stored in different tables. For example, customer names and e-mail addresses might be stored in `customers` and customer address might be stored in `address`. Often, normalization involves vertical partitioning. However, vertical partitioning usually means splitting up otherwise normalized data. For example, a customer may be allowed only one picture, but the picture may be stored in a `customer_pics` table separate from the `customers` table.

In vertical partitioning, the table schemas are different, although they contain similar records. In the example, the `customers` table and the `customer_pics` table have different schemas, but both have a primary key of `customer_id`, and so both may contain records for the same customer. It is as if a table were cut into parts using a vertical line. This type of partitioning is also called *row splitting*, because a row is being split up into more than one table.

Different physical storage could be used with vertical partitioning as well. As an example, store infrequently used or very wide fields in a table on a different hard drive. Storing pictures and documents on a file system instead of inside the database is a classic example of vertical partitioning using different physical storage.

A common form of vertical partitioning is splitting dynamic data from static data. A table with static data can make better use of the query cache (see Chapter 12), which in turn makes static data quicker to retrieve than dynamic data. This type of partitioning may be hidden from a developer by using a view to see a table all the rows. Performance will be better when accessing the static data, although the full table view has a performance penalty. See Chapter 8 for more information about views.

Partitioning Tables

Internal partitioning in `mysqld` was a huge improvement for MySQL, as previous to this, partitioning could only be done at the application level or through the use of MERGE tables (both are discussed later in this chapter). Using the table-level partitioning commands, `mysqld` uses a *partition key* and a *partitioning algorithm* to determine the division of data among the partitions. The partitioning algorithms are:

■ RANGE — Selects a partition by determining if the partition key is inside a range of values. An example is a partition for all rows based on customer ID; values less than 500,000 can go into one partition, and values greater than or equal to 500,000 can go into another.

■ LIST — A partition is assigned based on a list of integer values. If the partition key has one of these values, the partition is chosen. For example, all rows where the field `city_id` contains integers that reference Miami, Orlando, Jacksonville, Gainesville, Tallahassee, or Pensacola could form one partition for Florida cities, and another partition could contain `city_id` values for cities in Massachusetts such as Boston, Cambridge, Amherst, and Northampton.

■ HASH — The value of a hash function determines membership in a partition. If there are 10 partitions, the hash function returns a value from 0 to 9.

■ KEY — An internal algorithm is used by `mysqld` to try to evenly distribute the data across the partitions. A field, called the *key column*, is used for the determination of data distribution.

RANGE and LIST partitions can be subpartitioned using HASH or KEY partitioning. This is known as *composite partitioning*.

Each of these partitioning algorithms utilizes a partition key for determining in which partition the data is stored. This partition key is defined when creating the partition and must be an integer. Additionally, if the table has a primary key, the primary key must include all the fields in the partition key. If the table has no primary key but has a unique key, the unique key must include all the fields in the partition key. However, a table can use partitioning if it has no primary and unique keys specified.

No matter what the partition algorithm is, the advantage of using partitioning is *partition pruning*. If the field used in the partition key is part of a join or a filter (i.e., in the JOIN or WHERE clauses), the query optimizer will know which partition(s) it needs to search. Thus, the list of partitions to search is pruned, and query execution is faster. Horizontal partitioning makes data more manageable, and partition pruning can make queries on partitioned data much faster.

RANGE partitioning

Using partitioning to split data based on a range is a common form of partitioning used with MySQL. Suppose that Ziesel had a table of employee information for a large retail chain with 300 stores:

```
CREATE TABLE employees (
    emp_id INT NOT NULL,
    f_name VARCHAR(30) NOT NULL,
    l_name VARCHAR(30) NOT NULL,
    start_date DATE NOT NULL DEFAULT '2000-01-01',
    release_date DATE DEFAULT NULL,
    salary DECIMAL (8,2) NOT NULL,
    job_code INT NOT NULL,
    store_id INT NOT NULL
);
```

Because the employees table is getting too large, Ziesel decides to implement partitioning to improve manageability and performance. Each partition will contain 100 stores for a total of

300 stores. To add partitioning, she specifies the algorithm (RANGE), the partition key (the value of the store_id field), the names of the partitions (p0, p1, p2, etc.), and the data ranges:

```
ALTER TABLE employees
PARTITION BY RANGE (store_id) (
PARTITION p0 VALUES LESS THAN (101),
PARTITION p1 VALUES LESS THAN (201),
PARTITION p2 VALUES LESS THAN (301)
);
```

Creating partitions with CREATE TABLE uses the same syntax as the preceding ALTER TABLE statement. For example, if Ziesel realized ahead of time that she would have so many employees, she could have created the employees table with partitioning, using the following statement:

```
CREATE TABLE employees (
    emp_id INT NOT NULL,
    f_name VARCHAR(30) NOT NULL,
    l_name VARCHAR(30) NOT NULL,
    start_date DATE NOT NULL DEFAULT '2000-01-01',
    release_date DATE DEFAULT NULL,
    salary DECIMAL (8,2) NOT NULL,
    job_code INT NOT NULL,
    store_id INT NOT NULL
)
PARTITION BY RANGE (store_id) (
PARTITION p0 VALUES LESS THAN (101),
PARTITION p1 VALUES LESS THAN (201),
PARTITION p2 VALUES LESS THAN (301)
);
```

WARNING   With the range partition type, partitions must be defined in order from lowest to highest; otherwise, an error occurs:

```
mysql> CREATE TABLE out_of_order (id INT)
    -> PARTITION BY RANGE (id) (
    -> PARTITION not_first VALUES LESS THAN (20),
    -> PARTITION should_be_first VALUES LESS THAN (10)
    -> );
ERROR 1493 (HY000): VALUES LESS THAN value must be strictly increas-
ing for each partition
```

One problem with the partitioning of employees is that there is no room for growth. What happens when Ziesel adds store 701 and hires employees for it?

```
mysql> INSERT INTO employees
    -> SET f_name='Ziesel', l_name='Skelley',
    -> start_date='2009-01-01', salary='50000.00',
```

```
    -> job_code=5, store_id=301;
ERROR 1526 (HY000): Table has no partition for value 301
```

The solution is to create a final partition that is able to handle a higher range of values. This could be done in two ways — either specifying an explicit value or using MAXVALUE. Specifying an explicit larger value is not recommended, because at some point the partition key may increase above that value as well. It is not likely that Ziesel will have over a million stores, but it is possible, and using MAXVALUE provides a better solution.

MAXVALUE represents an integer value that is always greater than the largest possible integer value. A partition specifying VALUES LESS THAN MAXVALUE is a *catch-all* partition, to get all other values that do not fall into other partitions. Ziesel can use change the partitioning with:

```
ALTER TABLE employees
PARTITION BY RANGE (store_id) (
PARTITION p0 VALUES LESS THAN (101),
PARTITION p1 VALUES LESS THAN (201),
PARTITION p3 VALUES LESS THAN (301),
PARTITION pfinal VALUES LESS THAN MAXVALUE
);
```

NOTE The catch-all partition can be defined using either of the following syntaxes:

```
VALUES LESS THAN MAXVALUE
VALUES LESS THAN (MAXVALUE)
```

You may want to use the second syntax to keep the syntax consistent, always placing the range ceiling in parentheses.

Often a temporal field such as DATE, DATETIME or TIMESTAMP is used for range partitioning. A table used to store invoice data is often a good candidate for this type of partitioning. The following is a CREATE TABLE statement partitioning by the year of invoice entry:

```
CREATE TABLE invoices (
    customer_id INT NOT NULL,
    product_id INT NOT NULL,
    amount DECIMAL (8,2) NOT NULL,
    entry_date DATE NOT NULL DEFAULT '2006-01-01',
    store_id INT NOT NULL
)
PARTITION BY RANGE (YEAR(entry_date) ) (
PARTITION p0 VALUES LESS THAN (2008),
PARTITION p1 VALUES LESS THAN (2009),
PARTITION p2 VALUES LESS THAN (2010),
PARTITION p3 VALUES LESS THAN (2011),
PARTITION plast VALUES LESS THAN MAXVALUE
);
```

The partition key for partitions using the RANGE algorithm can be a field (as in employees) or an expression (as in invoices). Ordinarily, the MySQL optimizer cannot use an index on a field if there is a function modifying that field. For example, if there was an index on entry_date, partition pruning can not be used in the following query:

```
SELECT customer_id, amount FROM invoices
WHERE MONTH(entry_date)=2010;
```

However, mysqld has optimized the use of two date-based functions to be able to provide partition pruning: YEAR() and TO_DAYS().

WARNING Partition pruning is where the database server only references the partitions needed to fulfill the query. Partition pruning is how partitioning increases query performance with large data sets. Do not use partition keys involving functions to modify fields unless the function is YEAR() or TO_DAYS(). Otherwise, you will not realize the full performance improvements of partitioning.

If you use these two functions in converting a date to an integer for use as a partition key, partition pruning should occur during query execution. An example of the use of the TO_DAYS() function to have a new partition every month:

```
mysql> CREATE TABLE invoices_by_month (
    -> customer_id INT NOT NULL,
    -> product_id INT NOT NULL,
    -> amount DECIMAL (8,2) NOT NULL,
    -> entry_date DATETIME NOT NULL DEFAULT '2009-01-01 00:00:00',
    -> store_id INT NOT NULL )
    -> PARTITION BY RANGE (TO_DAYS(entry_date)) (
    -> PARTITION p0 VALUES LESS THAN (TO_DAYS('2009-01-01')),
    -> PARTITION p1 VALUES LESS THAN (TO_DAYS('2009-02-01')),
    -> PARTITION p2 VALUES LESS THAN (TO_DAYS('2009-03-01')),
    -> PARTITION p3 VALUES LESS THAN (TO_DAYS('2009-04-01')),
    -> PARTITION p4 VALUES LESS THAN (TO_DAYS('2009-05-01')),
    -> PARTITION p5 VALUES LESS THAN (TO_DAYS('2009-06-01')),
    -> PARTITION p6 VALUES LESS THAN (TO_DAYS('2009-07-01')),
    -> PARTITION p7 VALUES LESS THAN (TO_DAYS('2009-08-01')),
    -> PARTITION p8 VALUES LESS THAN (TO_DAYS('2009-09-01')),
    -> PARTITION p9 VALUES LESS THAN (TO_DAYS('2009-10-01')),
    -> PARTITION p10 VALUES LESS THAN (TO_DAYS('2009-11-01')),
    -> PARTITION p11 VALUES LESS THAN (TO_DAYS('2009-12-01')),
    -> PARTITION p12 VALUES LESS THAN MAXVALUE
    -> );
Query OK, 0 rows affected (0.39 sec)

mysql> INSERT INTO invoices_by_month (customer_id, product_id,
    -> amount, entry_date, store_id) VALUES
    -> (1,1,10.00,'2009-01-20',1), (65,2,152.98,'2009-06-03',1),
    -> (3,10,578.20,'2009-06-27',7), (105,1,9.99,'2009-07-01',10);
Query OK, 4 rows affected (0.00 sec)
Records: 4  Duplicates: 0  Warnings: 0
```

In this code, a partition is defined for any values less than 2009 and then a partition for each month of 2009. Finally, a partition is defined for any value larger than the 2009 values.

When using the TO_DAYS() function for partitioning in a CREATE TABLE statement it is a good idea to save a copy of the CREATE TABLE statement. The server stores the partitioning values internally as an integer, so when running SHOW CREATE TABLE, the partitioning information is very difficult to read:

```
mysql> SHOW CREATE TABLE invoices_by_month\G
*************************** 1. row ***************************
Table: invoices_by_month
Create Table: CREATE TABLE `invoices_by_month` (
  `customer_id` int(11) NOT NULL,
  `product_id` int(11) NOT NULL,
  `amount` decimal(8,2) DEFAULT NULL,
  `entry_date` datetime NOT NULL DEFAULT '2009-01-01 00:00:00',
  `store_id` int(11) NOT NULL
) ENGINE=MyISAM DEFAULT CHARSET=latin1 /*!50100 PARTITION BY RANGE
(TO_DAYS(entry_date)) (PARTITION p0 VALUES LESS THAN (733773) ENGINE
= MyISAM,
PARTITION p1 VALUES LESS THAN (733804) ENGINE = MyISAM, PARTITION p2
VALUES LESS THAN (733832) ENGINE = MyISAM, PARTITION p3 VALUES LESS
THAN (733863) ENGINE = MyISAM, PARTITION p4 VALUES LESS THAN (733893)
ENGINE = MyISAM, PARTITION p5 VALUES LESS THAN (733924) ENGINE =
MyISAM, PARTITION p6 VALUES LESS THAN (733954) ENGINE = MyISAM,
PARTITION p7 VALUES LESS THAN (733985) ENGINE = MyISAM, PARTITION p8
VALUES LESS THAN (734016) ENGINE = MyISAM, PARTITION p9 VALUES LESS
THAN (734046) ENGINE = MyISAM, PARTITION p10 VALUES LESS THAN
(734077) ENGINE = MyISAM, PARTITION p11 VALUES LESS THAN (734107)
ENGINE = MyISAM, PARTITION p13 VALUES LESS THAN MAXVALUE ENGINE =
MyISAM) */
```

Querying a partitioned table is no different from querying any other table. To get information about invoices entered in June 2009 a simple select will work:

```
SELECT customer_id,amount FROM invoices_by_month
WHERE entry_date >= '2009-06-01 00:00:00'
AND entry_date < '2009-07-01 00:00:00';
```

The query optimizer will use partition pruning to discard the 13 partitions that do not contain the data and work only with the one partition (p6) that does contain the needed data. Depending on the amount of data and other factors, this can provide for quite a dramatic increase in query execution speed.

To see what partitions are being used by a query, use the EXPLAIN PARTITIONS command:

```
mysql> EXPLAIN PARTITIONS SELECT customer_id,amount
    -> FROM invoices_by_month
```

```
    -> WHERE entry_date >= '2009-06-01 00:00:00'
    -> AND entry_date < '2009-07-01 00:00:00'\G
*************************** 1. row ***************************
          id: 1
  select_type: SIMPLE
        table: invoices_by_month
   partitions: p5,p6,p7
         type: ALL
possible_keys: NULL
          key: NULL
      key_len: NULL
          ref: NULL
         rows: 3
        Extra: Using where
1 row in set (0.00 sec)
```

The EXPLAIN PARTITIONS command outputs the same information as the EXPLAIN command, with one additional field. The extra field, partitions, shows a comma-separated list of partition names (i.e., p5,p6,p7) that will be searched during query execution. See Chapter 18 for more details on the EXPLAIN statement.

Range partitioning can help solve some many problems. For example, periodically purging older data is easy when range partitioning uses a partition key based on date. In the previous example of the invoices table, a simple ALTER TABLE invoices DROP PARTITION p0 would drop all invoices from before 2009. This is much quicker than running the following over a large number of rows:

```
DELETE FROM invoices
WHERE entry_date < '2008-12-31 23:59:59'
```

See the "Partition Management Commands" section later in this chapter for information on DROP PARTITION and other partition management commands.

LIST partitioning

The LIST partitioning algorithm assigns data to partitions based on a list of values. As with the range partitioning function, the values must be an integer. Instead of partitioning her employees by store, Ziesel decides to partition the data based on geographic region of the store.

Here is new CREATE TABLE statement she develops:

```
CREATE TABLE employees_by_region (
    emp_id INT NOT NULL,
    f_name VARCHAR(30) NOT NULL,
    l_name VARCHAR(30) NOT NULL,
    start_date DATE NOT NULL DEFAULT '2000-01-01',
    release_date DATE,
    salary DECIMAL (8,2) NOT NULL,
```

```
     job_code INT NOT NULL,
     store_id INT NOT NULL
)
PARTITION BY LIST (store_id) (
PARTITION Southeast VALUES IN (1,2,3,4,5,6,7,8,9,10,15,17,18,20,21,24),
PARTITION Midatlantic VALUES IN (11,12,13,14,16,19,22,23,25,26,27,28),
PARTITION Northeast VALUES IN (29,30,33,38,40,41,50,56,64,65,75),
PARTITION Midwest VALUES IN (32,34,35,42,43,49,51,61,62,63,71),
PARTITION Southwest VALUES IN (36,37,44,45,48,54,57,60,66,70),
PARTITION Northwest VALUES IN (46,53,58,67,68,69,72,74),
PARTITION Canada VALUES IN (31,47,52,59,73),
PARTITION England VALUES IN (39,55)
);
```

Unlike the range partitioning function with the list partitioning function, there is no catch-all value like MAXVALUE. All expected values should be covered in the PARTITION...VALUES IN (...) clauses. An INSERT statement containing a partition key that does not match any partition list will fail with an error.

> **TIP** The best LIST partition keys are ones in which there is a finite set of all of the possible values are known. For example, a partition key of num % 3 is excellent, because there is a finite set of possible values — for any value of num, the partition key is going to be evaluated as either 0, 1, or 2.

HASH partitioning

HASH partitions evenly distribute data across a predetermined number of partition tables. HASH partitioning uses the modulus operator (%) to distribute the data across these partitions. Unlike RANGE and LIST partitioning, partition names and matching criteria for the partition key are not user-defined. To create a table for employees partitioned into 16 partitions, Ziesel runs:

```
CREATE TABLE employees_hash (
    emp_id INT NOT NULL,
    f_name VARCHAR(30) NOT NULL,
    l_name VARCHAR(30) NOT NULL,
    start_date DATE NOT NULL DEFAULT '2000-01-01',
    release_date DATE DEFAULT NULL,
    salary DECIMAL (8,2) NOT NULL,
    job_code INT NOT NULL,
    store_id INT NOT NULL
)
PARTITION BY HASH (store_id)
PARTITIONS 16;
```

The first line of the partition definition looks very similar to previous partitioning examples. The rest of the partition definition is much simpler than those of RANGE and LIST partitioning. Instead of describing each partition in a long list surrounded by parentheses, there is only the

PARTITIONS clause, which specifies how many partitions to create. In the preceding example, Ziesel created a table that uses a partitioning key equivalent to store_id % 16 to partition the data across 16 partitions.

> **NOTE** LINEAR HASH can be specified instead of HASH. LINEAR HASH uses a linear powers-of-two algorithm instead of the modulus function used by HASH. For more information, including the algorithm, see the MySQL manual page on LINEAR HASH at http://dev.mysql.com/doc/refman/6.0/en/partitioning-linear-hash.html.

KEY partitioning

KEY partitioning is similar to hash partitioning. The difference is that the KEY partitioning algorithm uses a different partitioning function. HASH partitioning uses %, and KEY partitioning uses an algorithm similar to the algorithm used in the PASSWORD() function.

> **NOTE** The NDB storage engine uses the MD5() function for KEY partitioning.

To create a table of employees using KEY partitioning, Ziesel runs:

```
CREATE TABLE employees_key (
    emp_id INT NOT NULL,
    f_name VARCHAR(30) NOT NULL,
    l_name VARCHAR(30) NOT NULL,
    start_date DATE NOT NULL DEFAULT '2000-01-01',
    release_date DATE DEFAULT NULL,
    salary DECIMAL (8,2) NOT NULL,
    job_code INT NOT NULL,
    store_id INT NOT NULL
)
PARTITION BY KEY (store_id)
PARTITIONS 16;
```

> **NOTE** LINEAR KEY can be specified instead of KEY. LINEAR KEY uses a linear powers-of-two algorithm instead of the function used by KEY. The algorithm is the same as for LINEAR HASH.

Composite partitioning

A composite partition is a partition that is itself partitioned. Partitions of the RANGE and LIST types can be divided into HASH or KEY subpartitions.

Here is the table Ziesel used previously for a RANGE partition (if you tested the previous ALTER TABLE...DROP PARTITION statement, your table may look different):

```
CREATE TABLE invoices (
    customer_id INT NOT NULL,
```

```
        product_id INT NOT NULL,
        amount DECIMAL(8,2) NOT NULL,
        entry_date DATE NOT NULL DEFAULT '2006-01-01',
        store_id INT NOT NULL
)
PARTITION BY RANGE (YEAR(entry_date)) (
PARTITION p0 VALUES LESS THAN (2008),
PARTITION p1 VALUES LESS THAN (2009),
PARTITION p2 VALUES LESS THAN (2010),
PARTITION p3 VALUES LESS THAN (2011),
PARTITION plast VALUES LESS THAN MAXVALUE
);
```

Because the data set has grown too large for the four partitions, the decision is made to subpartition this table using a hash of the customer ID. Here is how Ziesel changes the table:

```
ALTER TABLE invoices
PARTITION BY RANGE (YEAR(entry_date))
SUBPARTITION BY HASH (customer_id)
SUBPARTITIONS 4 (
PARTITION p0 VALUES LESS THAN (2008),
PARTITION p1 VALUES LESS THAN (2009),
PARTITION p2 VALUES LESS THAN (2010),
PARTITION p3 VALUES LESS THAN (2011),
PARTITION plast VALUES LESS THAN MAXVALUE
);
```

There is a second method for specifying the subpartitions. This is through the use of the SUBPARTITIONS clause. Taking the previous example and rewriting it with the SUBPARTITIONS clause yields:

```
ALTER TABLE invoices
PARTITION BY RANGE (YEAR(entry_date))
SUBPARTITION BY HASH (customer_id) (
PARTITION p0 VALUES LESS THAN (2008) (
SUBPARTITION s0,
SUBPARTITION s1,
SUBPARTITION s2,
SUBPARTITION s3),
PARTITION p1 VALUES LESS THAN (2009) (
SUBPARTITION s4,
SUBPARTITION s5,
SUBPARTITION s6,
SUBPARTITION s7),
PARTITION p2 VALUES LESS THAN (2010) (
SUBPARTITION s8,
SUBPARTITION s9,
SUBPARTITION s10,
SUBPARTITION s11),
```

```
PARTITION p3 VALUES LESS THAN (2011) (
SUBPARTITION s12,
SUBPARTITION s13,
SUBPARTITION s14,
SUBPARTITION s15),
PARTITION plast VALUES LESS THAN MAXVALUE (
SUBPARTITION s16,
SUBPARTITION s17,
SUBPARTITION s18,
SUBPARTITION s19)

);
```

This syntax is much longer and helps to show exactly what is going on. In this syntax, the subpartitions must be given at minimum a name.

Two very important options to SUBPARTITION are DATA DIRECTORY and INDEX DIRECTORY. Subpartitioning can yield much improved performance, manageability, and availability by distributing data and indexes across more than one hard drive. Ziesel wants the invoices table to be spread across four hard drives, mounted on /invoices1, /invoices2, /invoices3, and /invoices4.

Here is the code for partition p0:

```
PARTITION p0 VALUES LESS THAN (2008) (
SUBPARTITION s0a
DATA DIRECTORY = '/invoices1/data'
INDEX DIRECTORY = '/invoices1/index',
SUBPARTITION s1a
DATA DIRECTORY = '/invoices2/data'
INDEX DIRECTORY = '/invoices2/index',
SUBPARTITION s2a
DATA DIRECTORY = '/invoices3/data'
INDEX DIRECTORY = '/invoices3/index',
SUBPARTITION s3a
DATA DIRECTORY = '/invoices4/data'
INDEX DIRECTORY = '/invoices4/index'
),
```

Figure 15-1 shows the final layout of the subpartitions on the hard drives.

FIGURE 15-1

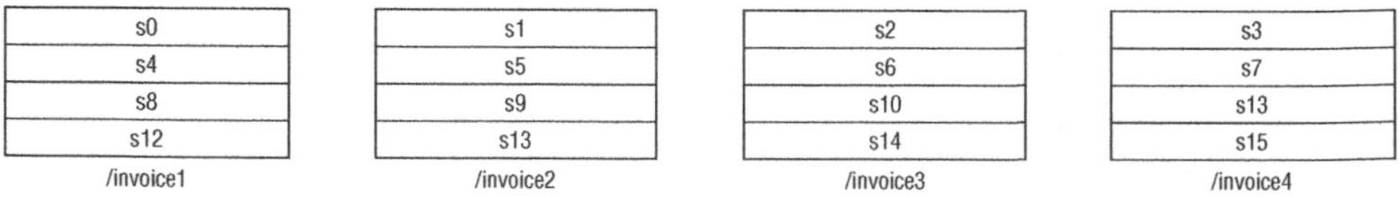

s0		s1		s2		s3
s4		s5		s6		s7
s8		s9		s10		s13
s12		s13		s14		s15
/invoice1		/invoice2		/invoice3		/invoice4

The four main partitions are striped evenly across the four drives. Theoretically, this would quadruple the available I/O bandwidth for the `invoices` table. In reality, there is less than a fourfold improvement. Nonetheless, striping across multiple drives is a significant performance improvement.

> **NOTE** The INDEX DIRECTORY and DATA DIRECTORY options can be used as part of the SUB-PARTITION command or the PARTITION command.

Partition management commands

There are a number of ALTER TABLE options used to manage, maintain and repair partitions:

- ADD PARTITION
- DROP PARTITION
- COALESCE PARTITION
- REORGANIZE PARTITION
- ANALYZE PARTITION
- CHECK PARTITION
- OPTIMIZE PARTITION
- REBUILD PARTITION

Adding and dropping partitions

There are some differences in the management of partitioning depending on the type of partitioning used. For partition types of RANGE and LIST, adding and dropping of partitions to a table is relatively straightforward. To add new partitions to the `employees_by_region` table Ziesel uses the ALTER TABLE...ADD PARTITION command:

```
ALTER TABLE employees_by_region ADD PARTITION (
PARTITION Australia VALUES IN (76, 77),
PARTITION Sweden VALUES IN (78, 79)
);
```

> **NOTE** For RANGE partitioned tables ADD PARTITION can be used to add a new range to the end of the existing partitions. If you specified a partition with VALUES LESS THAN MAXVALUE you will have to change your partitioning layout. Part of the employees partition definition is:

```
PARTITION p3 VALUES LESS THAN (301),
PARTITION pfinal VALUES LESS THAN MAXVALUE
```

If Ziesel tries to add a partition p4:

```
mysql> ALTER TABLE employees ADD PARTITION (
    -> PARTITION p4 VALUES LESS THAN (401));
```

```
ERROR 1481 (HY000): MAXVALUE can only be used in last partition
definition
```

To change the partition layout without deleting any data, Ziesel needs to redefine the entire partition layout:

```
mysql> ALTER TABLE employees
    -> PARTITION BY RANGE (store_id) (
    -> PARTITION p0 VALUES LESS THAN (101),
    -> PARTITION p1 VALUES LESS THAN (201),
    -> PARTITION p3 VALUES LESS THAN (301),
    -> PARTITION p4 VALUES LESS THAN (401),
     -> PARTITION pfinal VALUES LESS THAN MAXVALUE
    -> );
Query OK, 0 rows affected (0.36 sec)
Records: 0  Duplicates: 0  Warnings: 0
```

Dropping a partition is very simple:

```
ALTER TABLE employees_by_region DROP PARTITION Australia;
```

WARNING When a partition is dropped, all data stored on that partition is deleted.

Partitions using the HASH or KEY partition types can not use the ALTER TABLE...
DROP PARTITION command. Instead partitions must be combined using the ALTER TABLE
COALESCE PARTITION command. To reduce the number of partitions for the employees_hash
table from 16 to 12:

In order to delete four partitions run the following command:

```
mysql> ALTER TABLE employees_hash COALESCE PARTITION 4;
Query OK, 0 rows affected (6.05 sec)
Records: 0  Duplicates: 0  Warnings: 0

mysql> SHOW CREATE TABLE employees_hash\G
*************************** 1. row ***************************
       Table: employees_hash
Create Table: CREATE TABLE `employees_hash` (
  `emp_id` int(11) NOT NULL,
  `f_name` varchar(30) NOT NULL,
  `l_name` varchar(30) NOT NULL,
  `start_date` date NOT NULL DEFAULT '2000-01-01',
  `release_date` date DEFAULT NULL,
  `salary` decimal(8,2) NOT NULL,
  `job_code` int(11) NOT NULL,
  `store_id` int(11) NOT NULL
) ENGINE=MyISAM DEFAULT CHARSET=latin1 /*!50100 PARTITION BY HASH
(store_id) PARTITIONS 12  */
1 row in set (0.00 sec)
```

To add the three partitions back, use the ALTER TABLE command:

```
mysql> ALTER TABLE employees_hash ADD PARTITION PARTITIONS 4;
Query OK, 0 rows affected (2.19 sec)
Records: 0  Duplicates: 0  Warnings: 0
```

Partition table maintenance

The CHECK TABLE, OPTIMIZE TABLE, ANALYZE TABLE or REPAIR TABLE statements maintain and repair tables. However, these table-level commands are not allowed to be used on partitioned tables. Fortunately, there are alternative commands to work with partitioned tables.

A partition can be fragmented in the same way that any other table or index becomes fragmented. If a partition has a large number of rows deleted or if a partitioned table with variable-length rows (VARCHAR, BLOB or TEXT fields) has many updates, the ALTER TABLE...OPTIMIZE PARTITION statement will reclaim any unused space and defragment the partition data file.

Example:

```
ALTER TABLE employees OPTIMIZE PARTITION p0, p1;
```

Like ANALYZE TABLE, ALTER TABLE ... ANALYZE PARTITION reads the current index distribution of the partition and then updates the metadata so the query optimizer has more accurate information for building queries.

Example:

```
ALTER TABLE employees ANALYZE PARTITION p3;
```

The ALTER TABLE table_name REBUILD PARTITION p1 statement will rebuild the p1 partition. As with the OPTIMIZE TABLE command, it can be useful to defragment tables. In addition it will recalculate statistics for the query optimizer. More than one partition at a time can be rebuilt by specifying a comma-separated list of partition names. The following will rebuild the p0 and p1 partitions of the employee table.

```
ALTER TABLE employees REBUILD PARTITION p0,p1;
```

As with tables, it is a good idea to periodically check partitions for errors. The ALTER TABLE table_name CHECK PARTITION partition_name command will indicate if the data or indexes are corrupt on the specified partition.

Example:

```
ALTER TABLE employees CHECK PARTITION p1;
```

More than one partition can be checked by specifying a comma-separated list of partition names. If a partition is found to be corrupt, use ALTER TABLE...REPAIR PARTITION to repair the partition.

The `ALTER TABLE...REPAIR PARTITION` command repairs corrupted data and index partitions. More than one partition can be specified using a comma-separated list.

Example:

```
ALTER TABLE employees REPAIR PARTITION p0,p1;
```

Restrictions of partitioning

There are some limitations when using partitioning in `mysqld`:

- All partitions of the same partitioned table must use the same storage engine. It is not possible to use a MyISAM table for one partition of a table and InnoDB for a second partition. However, different tables can use different storage engines, partitioned or not. In other words, one partitioned table could consist of MyISAM partitions while a different partitioned table consists of InnoDB partitions.

- The maximum number of partitions possible for a table is 1024. This includes subpartitions.

- Foreign keys are not supported. If you try to add a partition to an existing table with a foreign key, the `ALTER TABLE` will fail with an error:

```
ERROR 1217 (23000): Cannot delete or update a parent row: a
foreign key constraint fails
```

- If you try to create a table with both a foreign key and a partition, the `CREATE TABLE` will fail with an error:

```
ERROR 1215 (HY000): Cannot add foreign key constraint
```

- All user-defined partitioning functions must evaluate to an integer (key partitioning does not use integers, but the partitioning function is also not user-defined). Partition pruning can be performed on date fields if the `TO_DAYS()` or `YEAR()` functions are used in the partitioning function, though other functions cannot use partition pruning.

- If a table contains a unique or primary key, the fields in the partition key must be part of the primary key.

It can be very advantageous to use MySQL partitioning to manage larger tables. The performance improvements and maintenance advantages are both reasons to use MySQL partitioning instead of more traditional forms of partitioning with MySQL.

MERGE Tables

The MERGE table storage engine was first implemented in `mysqld` 3.23.25. A MERGE table is a table structure with no data, which specifies a set of identically structured MyISAM tables. All tables must have exactly the same indexes and fields, in the same order. The MERGE table structure also specifies a table where new data should be inserted. A MERGE table does not have automatic data partitioning.

Creating a MERGE table

Before creating a MERGE table, Ziesel creates the identical underlying MyISAM tables first:

```
CREATE TABLE employees_1 (
    emp_id INT NOT NULL AUTO_INCREMENT PRIMARY KEY,
    f_name VARCHAR(30) NOT NULL,
    l_name VARCHAR(30) NOT NULL,
    start_date DATE NOT NULL DEFAULT '2000-01-01',
    release_date DATE DEFAULT NULL,
    salary DECIMAL (8,2) NOT NULL,
    job_code INT NOT NULL,
    store_id INT NOT NULL
) ENGINE = MyISAM;

CREATE TABLE employees_2 (
    emp_id INT NOT NULL AUTO_INCREMENT PRIMARY KEY,
    f_name VARCHAR(30) NOT NULL,
    l_name VARCHAR(30) NOT NULL,
    start_date DATE NOT NULL DEFAULT '2000-01-01',
    release_date DATE DEFAULT NULL,
    salary DECIMAL (8,2) NOT NULL,
    job_code INT NOT NULL,
    store_id INT NOT NULL
) ENGINE = MyISAM;
CREATE TABLE employees_3 (
    emp_id INT NOT NULL AUTO_INCREMENT PRIMARY KEY,
    f_name VARCHAR(30) NOT NULL,
    l_name VARCHAR(30) NOT NULL,
    start_date DATE NOT NULL DEFAULT '2000-01-01',
    release_date DATE DEFAULT NULL,
    salary DECIMAL (8,2) NOT NULL,
    job_code INT NOT NULL,
    store_id INT NOT NULL
) ENGINE = MyISAM;
```

Then she creates the MERGE table itself, specifying that new data should be inserted into employees_3:

```
CREATE TABLE all_employees (
    emp_id INT NOT NULL AUTO_INCREMENT,
```

511

```
        f_name VARCHAR(30) NOT NULL,
        l_name VARCHAR(30) NOT NULL,
        start_date DATE NOT NULL DEFAULT '2000-01-01',
        release_date DATE DEFAULT NULL,
        salary DECIMAL (8,2) NOT NULL,
        job_code INT NOT NULL,
        store_id INT NOT NULL,
        INDEX (emp_id)
) ENGINE=MERGE UNION=(employees_1,employees_2,employees_3)
INSERT_METHOD=LAST;
```

A couple of items here are different. The engine type is now MERGE. In addition there are two clauses to the ENGINE = MERGE statement that are required. The UNION clause determines what tables will be included in the merge table.

WARNING These MyISAM tables should already be created before creating the MERGE table itself. While mysqld does not return an error when creating a MERGE table first, it will error when trying to perform any operation on the MERGE table if the underlying MyISAM tables are not all created. Similarly, changing the structure of an underlying MyISAM table completes successfully with no warnings or errors but will affect the MERGE table.

In addition to the UNION clause there is an optional INSERT_METHOD clause. It specifies where inserts to the merge table actually go. Possible values are FIRST, LAST or NO. If INSERT_METHOD=FIRST, then inserts are performed on the first underlying MyISAM table. If INSERT_METHOD=LAST, then inserts are performed on the last underlying table. If no value is specified or if NO is specified then any attempt to insert into the merge table itself will result in an error.

One final note about merge table creation: though merge tables support unique/primary indexes on the underlying tables (as on the emp_id field in the example MyISAM tables), the merge table cannot enforce uniqueness over the set of underlying tables. Notice in the CREATE TABLE merge_employees statement that the PRIMARY KEY constraint on emp_id was removed and INDEX (emp_id) added. The underlying table will still enforce the primary index on itself.

Queries can be issued against the MERGE table or any of the underlying tables. All of these are valid queries for the tables created in the previous examples:

```
SELECT emp_id, f_name, l_name FROM all_employees;
SELECT f_name, l_name, salary FROM employees_1;
DLEETE FROM employees_2 WHERE emp_id = 10;
SELECT emp_id,store_id FROM employees_3;
```

Changing a MERGE table

When it becomes necessary to add or remove underlying tables from a MERGE table there are two available methods. The first method is to DROP the merge table and then recreate it with the new list of underlying tables. The second method is to use the ALTER TABLE table_name

UNION=(table_one,table_two,...) to change which tables are the underlying MyISAM tables. If an empty UNION clause is specified, the MERGE table will not reference any underlying tables.

> **NOTE** The MERGE table is a structure that has no data inside it, so there is no data lost when it is dropped. Dropping a merge table only drops the merge table definition. It does not drop the underlying tables.

Advantages of MERGE tables

Merge tables has the same basic advantages as the built-in partitioning. Merge tables provide for speed increases for large data sets and also for easier maintenance of the underlying tables. While there is no partition pruning, queries that rely on table indexes quickly see which underlying tables have no values.

Consider a MERGE table called English_dictionary. Its UNION clause references underlying tables called words_in_a, words_in_b, words_in_c, and so on for every letter of the alphabet. The MERGE and all underlying tables have an index on the word field. The INSERT_METHOD is specified as NO. A query that retrieved data using the filter WHERE word="merge" would:

- Go to the first table in the UNION definition (words_in_a).
- Scan the index to see if the word appears.
- When the word does not appear in this index, go to the second table in the UNION definition (words_in_b).

A MERGE table has better performance than an equivalent table with all of the data in it. However, a partitioned table performs much better — if English_dictionary was a table partitioned with a LIST algorithm, where a=1, b=2, c=3 and so on, a query looking up the word "merge" would only search the words_in_m partition.

A classic example for merge tables would be using a merge table to manage log tables. You could put a month of data in a table. If your volume of logged data is higher, make a new table each week, or each day. A MERGE table could then be used to query the data from all the tables. This is certainly easier than querying individual tables and provides for easy maintenance. When it is time to retire log data, simply ALTER TABLE table_name UNION=(...) and specify the new list of tables. Once the table is removed from the merge table, the underlying table can be moved, dropped, or even still used without affecting the performance of the merge table.

Partitioning with MySQL Cluster

MySQL Cluster began as the NDB storage engine inside mysqld. MySQL Cluster has grown greatly, and currently it is a product separate from mysqld. When using NDB, partitioning is *transparent* — by default, partitioning is done automatically across all the data nodes in the system. The automatic partitioning uses a hash algorithm based on the primary key of the table. The same table partitioning in mysqld is available in MySQL Cluster, so NDB tables can be manually partitioned if the automatic partitioning is not desired.

Because the partitioning is transparent, database developers and administrators often do not realize that they can take advantage of the benefits of table-level partitioning. The horizontal partitioning of NDB can provide dramatic speed increases for data retrieval on large tables. It does this just like the internal partitioning of mysqld by partition pruning.

Programmatic Partitioning

Partitioning can be achieved from an application level also. One common way of partitioning at this level is what is called functional partitioning. With functional partitioning different servers are dedicated to different parts of the application. One way of doing this is splitting a database up into several parts and having each part on its own dedicated server. An example would be a news website that functionally partitions data across three databases: news, forums, and archives. How much of an increase in performance and capacity this would provide varies depending on the application. Frequently, it can prove to be a significant amount as large data sets are moved to their own dedicated hardware.

This is the most common form of functional partitioning. However, it is possible to perform functional partitioning by simply determining which tables are either never or infrequently joined for querying purposes and then moving those tables to separate servers. If joins are necessary, they could be done at the application code level or even through federated tables. This is far more complex than the previous methods and rarely done.

Sharding provides almost linear scaling to websites that need to be able to handle large numbers of users and grow easily and quickly. Sites like MySpace and Google use sharding to provide a high-quality experience for millions of end users. Sharding is horizontal partitioning across multiple database servers — as such, it must be done from outside any one particular mysqld instance. Thus, it is done programmatically, for example using an algorithm in the application code, using a centralized database to look up information, or even by programming MySQL Proxy to do it (see Appendix A for more information on MySQL Proxy).

Summary

Partitioning is a good method of managing very large tables with MySQL. While it is a relatively new technology, there can be significant benefits to using partitions. Remember, always test before putting a new feature into production.

This chapter covered the following topics:

- Automatic table partitioning in `mysqld` using RANGE, LIST, HASH, and KEY algorithms.
- Composite partitioning
- Striping partitions across multiple disk drives
- Partition management commands
- Using the MERGE storage engine for partitioning
- Using the NDB storage engine (MySQL Cluster) for partitioning
- Programmatic data sharding

Chapter 16

Logging and Replication

IN THIS CHAPTER

Logging in MySQL

Configuring replication

Replication topologies

Correcting data

When changes are made to the database `mysqld` writes to *binary logs*, which are used in the replication process. Much of this chapter concerns configuration options that are used to manage both logging and replication. These options can be configured from server startup using the command line or set in the configuration file. Unless the material specifically says that an option can only be configured from the command line or the configuration file, either method is possible. In addition, many of the configuration options can be controlled at server runtime.

Log Files

Four log files are used by `mysqld`: the error log, the binary log, the general query log, and the slow query log. A fifth log type, the relay log, is used by a slave server. If the logs are enabled, `mysqld` writes them to the data directory unless otherwise specified. By default, no logging is enabled.

> **NOTE**   If you find that an error log is being written to when the configuration file does not enable the error log, there is no need to worry. Some startup scripts specify error log files. These startup scripts are dependent upon the installation.

Error log

The *error log* contains entries for when the `mysqld` daemon started and stopped and also any critical errors that occur while the server is running.

Information such as when the event scheduler executes an event and when replication starts and stops is also written to the error log. On some operating systems the error log additionally will write a stack trace if `mysqld` dies. This stack trace can be very useful for troubleshooting system failures. The error log is a plain text file.

To enable the error log, specify the `log-error` option. The error log will be written to the data directory using the format `host_name.err`. To customize the filename, give the `log-error` option a filename, such as:

```
log-error=/var/log/mysqld.err
```

The `log_warnings` option is used to control whether or not warning messages are logged to the error log. The default value is 1 (enabled). If the value is greater than 1, aborted connections are written to the error log. Warning logging can be disabled using a value of 0.

If you do not specify `log-error`, or if you use the `--console` option on Windows, errors are written to `stderr`, the standard error output. Even though you are not required to have an error log, it is extremely useful to help troubleshoot issues.

Binary logs

The *binary logs* are used for several reasons. They can be used to perform a point-in-time recovery during a recovery process. How this is done is detailed in Chapter 13. Another function of the binary log is to enable replication. This is covered later in this chapter.

The contents of the binary log are any statements that occur in the server that could potentially modify the databases. Non-modifying statements such as `SELECT` are not logged. However, a non-modifying statement will be logged if it is part of a transaction that modifies data, because the entire transaction will be logged.

To enable binary logging, use the `log-bin` option. The *binary log index file* is a plain text file that keeps track of the current binary logs. By default, its name is `mysql-bin.index`. To set the filename and path of the binary logs and binary log index file, specify the following options:

```
log-bin = /data/logs/binary/changelog
log-bin-index = /data/logs/relay/binarylog.index
```

Binary log data is stored in a binary format. This means you can not just open the file with a text editor and read it. To display the binary logs in text/readable format you must use the `mysqlbinlog` tool. The operation of the `mysqlbinlog` tool is pretty straightforward.

In the following example the entire contents of the `mysql-bin.00001` binary log are converted into text format and copied into a new file called `output.sql`:

```
shell> mysqlbinlog mysql-bin.00001 > output.sql
```

If you leave off the > `output.sql` the contents will be sent to the console.

Numerous options can be used with `mysqlbinlog`. Table 16-1 lists the frequently used `mysqlbinlog` options. The standard options for command-line programs that interact with `mysqld`, such as `-u`, `-h`, `-p`, and `-P`, are not listed

TABLE 16-1

Frequently used mysqlbinlog Options

Option	Description
read-from-remote-server	Used to read the binary log from a remote server.
start-position	Determines the position in the binary log where `mysqlbinlog` begins reading data.
end-position	Determines the position in the binary log where `mysqlbinlog` stops reading data.
start-datetime	Begins reading from the binary log at the first event with a timestamp equal to or greater than the specified datetime.
end-datetime	Stops reading from the binary log at the first event with a timestamp equal to or greater than the specified datetime.

The following is a more complicated example, reading from a remote server:

```
shell> mysqlbinlog --read-from-remote-server -uuser -p \
mysql-bin.000001 -h 192.168.2.65 -P 3306 \
--start-position=932 --stop-position=1132 > remote000001.sql
```

Here is an example showing how to use the time-based parameters:

```
shell> mysqlbinlog  mysql-bin.000001 \
--start-datetime="2009-02-15 17:34:40" \
--stop-datetime="2009-02-15 17:34:56" > sixteensecs.sql
```

This is a good way to extract a smaller log if you know approximately what time an event happened.

NOTE `mysqlbinlog` does not change the original binary log.

Relay logs

Relay logs are used by a replication slave to record events received from the master server before execution on the slave server. They utilize the same binary format as the binary logs and, like the binary logs, can be viewed using the `mysqlbinlog` tool. By default a slave server stores the relay logs in `datadir`. In addition to the relay logs there is the `relay-log.index` file, which is used to keep track of the currently used relay log. Also, the `relay-log.info` file documents the currently used relay log file and position, plus the position in the master binary log.

If you want to change the location for the relay logs, there are three configuration values you will want to add to the configuration file. These values are `relay-log`, `relay-log-index`, and `relay-log-info`. If you wanted to store all these logs in the directory `/data/logs/relay` you would need to add this to your MySQL configuration file:

```
relay-log = /data/logs/relay/relay-bin
relay-log-index = /data/logs/relay/relay-bin.index
relay-log-info-file = /data/logs/relay/relay-bin.info
```

As you can see, you can specify filenames in addition to directories. Relay logs are automatically deleted by the SQL thread of the slave server when it has executed all events in the log and it is no longer needed.

General and slow query logs

The general query and slow query log files are used to log the activities occurring in the database. If the general query log is enabled it logs all activity on the server. In addition to the actual SQL statements being executed it logs information such as when clients both connect and disconnect. It can be a very useful tool when troubleshooting issues.

The general log writes statements as they are sent to `mysqld`, including ones that result in errors.

WARNING It is not advisable to turn on the general query log on a production machine unless it is really necessary. Because it logs all server activity it can be quite a detriment to performance. The general query log can be turned on and off while the server is still running, so if a general log is needed for debugging purposes it can be enabled for a short period of time.

Beginning in MySQL Server 5.1 general and slow queries can be logged to either a log file or a table in the `mysql` database. The general queries are logged to the `general_log` table and the slow queries are logged to the `slow_log` table.

Why would you want to log this information to a database table? If all log statements are stored in a table rather than in a text file, you can use a simple `SELECT` statement to query the data — speeding up the information search of your logs.

To set the location of both the slow and general query log output, set the server variable log_output. Possible values for log_output are:

- FILE
- TABLE
- NONE
- FILE,TABLE

The default value is FILE.

> **TIP**   The log_output server variable is an example of a *dynamic variable*. That means that it can be set while the server is running. As an example, to set log_output to NONE (turning off both general and slow query logs), execute the following using mysql:

```
mysql> SET GLOBAL log_output=NONE;
```

Table 16-2 lists the server variables used to manage the general and slow query logs.

TABLE 16-2

Server Variables Used to Manage General and Slow Query Logs

Server Variable	Description
log_output=[NONE | FILE | TABLE | FILE,TABLE]	Determines where both general query and slow query logs are stored.
general_log= [ON|OFF]	Used to turn on or off the general query log. Possible values are ON and OFF.
general_log_file [=filename]	Specifies the location of the general query log file. The default location is the data directory.
slow_query_log	Possible values are ON and OFF.
slow_query_log_file [=filename]	Specifies the location of the slow query log file. The default location is the data directory.
long_query_time=num	Queries that take longer than num seconds are logged in the slow query log. Defaults to 10.
log-queries-not-using-indexes	Queries that do a full table scan will be logged.
min_examined_row_limits=num	Only logs queries in slow query log that examine at least num specified rows. Defaults to 0. This option is usually used in conjunction with log-queries-not-using-indexes, to log queries on large tables that do not use indexes.

The slow query log is similar to the general query log but only logs queries that take more than the number of seconds specified by the server variable long_query_time. The long_query_time server variable is used to control the granularity of the logging of slow queries. Up until mysqld version 5.1.21 you could only log queries that took a minimum of two seconds to execute (it would log queries greater than the minimum of one second). Beginning with version 5.1.21 you can specify the minimum query execution time in fractions of a second. For example, you could set long_query_time = .05 (fifty milliseconds). In all versions of mysqld, the long_query_time option defaults to 10 (seconds).

Like the error log, in almost every situation it will make sense to have the slow query log enabled. In fact, you should determine what amount of time it takes before you consider a query slow. For a web application, 4–5 seconds is the maximum most people will wait for a regular page to load. It is quite common to see a 2-second limit or even smaller.

Because it logs the time a query took, the slow query log does not write a statement until after it has finished. It will write statements that have failed, so long as they have taken more than long_query_time seconds.

To enable the general_log you have to set general_log = ON and, in a similar way, to enable slow_log you have to set log_slow_queries = ON. After logging is enabled you can choose log_output but, whereas there are two separate variables for enabling the general and slow query log, there is only one variable related to log output. So you can have the general_log enabled and the slow_log disabled, but if you choose an output (and both logs are enabled) that output (FILE, TABLE, or FILE,TABLE) applies to both the logs.

If the logs are disabled, no logging occurs regardless of the value of log_output. This is why no logging occurs by default, because the logs are disabled, even though the default for log_output is FILE.

Rotating logs

Log files can consume large amounts of disk space quickly and if they are rotated they can be compressed for archival purposes or deleted if not needed. Even if you have plenty of disk space, log files that become too large make it difficult to work with when troubleshooting and performing general monitoring. The most common methods of log file rotation are covered in the following sections.

flush logs

You can manually rotate the binary logs and error log by issuing a FLUSH LOGS command from mysql. When this is done the server closes the binary log currently in use and creates a new binary log by incrementing the sequence number of the file by one (in relation to the previous log). With the flushing of the error log the server:

- Closes the current file
- Creates a new error log
- Renames the old error log with a suffix of -old

For the other log files, FLUSH LOGS only closes and then reopens the log file. However, this means that other log files can be rotated by moving the original file, creating a blank file to replace the original, and performing a FLUSH LOGS statement.

The mysqladmin utility can perform a FLUSH LOGS from the shell. Here is an example of this type of usage:

```
shell> mysqladmin flush-logs
```

max_binlog_size

The max_binlog_size option automatically rotates the binary log after it reaches a certain size. The option name is a bit of a misnomer because the binary logs are rotated after the size is reached, so the size of the file may be slightly larger than max_binlog_size. Values can be specified as integers (which indicate bytes) or using K, M, or G to specify kilobytes, megabytes, or gigabytes. For example, to set mysqld to rotate binary logs after they reach 512 MB in size:

```
max_binlog_size=512M
```

purge binary logs

The PURGE BINARY LOGS command is another manual method of log management that is specifically designed for the binary logs. Unlike FLUSH LOGS, it deletes logs instead of saving them. There are two methods of purging: by filename and by timestamp.

For example to purge all binary logs older than 'mysql-bin.00987':

```
mysql> PURGE BINARY LOGS TO 'mysql-bin.00987';
```

To purge all logs older than December 13, 2008 at 11:00 PM:

```
mysql> PURGE BINARY LOGS BEFORE '2008-12-13 23:00:00';
```

The MASTER keyword is an alias for BINARY; this command is also called PURGE MASTER LOGS.

expire_logs_days

The expire_logs_days option purges binary logs after a configured number of days. Something to keep in mind is that if your slave servers fall behind the master it is possible to have the master delete old binary logs and ruin slave replication because it deleted data that had not been replicated to the slave server yet!

Other methods of rotating

With the Red Hat rpm installations of mysqld there should be a mysql-log-rotate script that can be used to rotate your log file. If you are using a non–Red Hat system you can create your own script and run it from `cron` for log rotation. Unfortunately, `FLUSH` statements cannot be used inside an event in `mysqld`.

Some operating system distributions, such as Debian, include a general script for log rotation called `logrotate`. Some specific hooks for the MySQL logs are included with the Debian MySQL packages. If you are using Debian this will almost certainly take care of any log rotation needs you have.

Various home-grown scripts are also available on the Internet and if none of these suit your purposes it would certainly be feasible to write you own without much difficulty.

Replication

Replication is the ability to keep distributed databases synchronized by copying either executed statements or data set changes from a *master* server to one or more *slave* servers. It is the primary method of keeping two `mysqld` instances synchronized. This could be done for a number reasons including:

- Failover requirements — high availability
- Load balancing and scale out
- Off-site processing — backups, running reporting queries, and so on

See Chapter 22 for more information on using replication to achieve scalability and high availability. With `mysqld` a slave can have only a single master. However, a master can have any number of slaves. In addition, it is possible for a master server to be a slave of another master. This allows you to build some fairly complicated replication topologies.

MySQL replication is *asynchronous*. This means that the master does not wait for slaves to acknowledge receiving the data before committing any changes. The master simply writes events to the binary log with no regard to the status of any slave servers. This means there is no guarantee that replication is actually synchronizing data appropriately. This is in contrast to *semisynchronous* replication, where a thread that performs a transaction commit on the master blocks after the commit is done and waits until at least one semisynchronous slave acknowledges that it has either received all events for the transaction or a timeout occurs. The benefit to this is immediately apparent — because both servers are always synchronized there is no chance of losing committed data. Even if your master server experienced a catastrophic hardware failure the slave would be guaranteed to have any committed changes.

This guarantee comes at a price. Semisynchronous replication does have a performance impact because commits are slower due to the need to wait for slaves. The amount of slowdown is at least the amount of time it takes the TCP/IP packet to go from the master to the slave and back. This is needed to send the commit to the slave and wait for the acknowledgment of receipt by the slave. This is the tradeoff for increased data integrity. This means that semisynchronous replication works best for close servers communicating over fast networks. You probably should not use it for situations where servers are not on the same network.

This capability was not included prior to mysqld version 6.0. Several patches are available that allow this capability in previous versions of mysqld.

With mysqld version 6.0 Sun has created the capability for semisynchronous replication using a plugin-based system. This will allow for a great deal of flexibility in the future. The actual code is based on code developed at Google by Mark Callaghan and Wei Li. It was ported to version 6.0 of the server as plugin components. Though the addition of semisynchronous replication is a great option, moving replication to a plugin-based system is far more exciting. This allows a great deal of flexibility. Several plugins are already being developed, including one for delayed replication.

> **TIP** Semisynchronous replication differs from true synchronous replication in that the master server does not wait for all slaves to acknowledge receipt of events. In addition, the master requires only acknowledgment of receipt, not that the events have been both fully executed and committed on the slave side. Synchronous replication is not available in mysqld. MySQL Cluster uses synchronous replication.

In a replication setup the data is written by the master server to the binary log. Any slave servers connect to the master server using what is called an *I/O thread*. This process writes the statements or data received from the master into the relay log. The *SQL thread* is the process that reads from the relay log and then replays the statements or data changes for the MySQL process on the slave server.

The end result of this process is that the slave server has executed the same statements or data changes that the master server executed.

If a slave server is also configured as a master server of other slaves, it simply writes its own binary logs and the *secondary* slaves read from that binary log using their I/O threads.

Setting up semisynchronous replication

When you set up replication it is configured by default to be asynchronous. Some extra steps are involved in configuring replication to be semisynchronous. To begin using semisyncronous replication the master server and one or more slave servers must be configured for semisynchronous replication. If you do not do this replication will default to asynchronous replication. In addition, asynchronous replication must already be running.

Semisynchronous replication is implemented using plugins. These plugins are not distributed with the server code itself and must be downloaded separately. The semisynchronous replication plugins are available at http://downloads.mysql.com/forge/replication_preview and work only on Linux.

A single file contains the plugins for both master and slave servers. You need to install the libsemisync_master* files in the plugin directory of the master server and the libsemisync_slave* files in the plugin directory of each slave server. If you do not know the location of the plugin directory, the command SHOW GLOBAL VARIABLES LIKE 'plug% should tell the location of the plugin directory. The plugins are available from http://downloads.mysql.com. After a plugin has been installed on a server, you control it by modifying the system variables associated with it. Until a plugin is installed these system variables are not available. To load a plugin you should use the INSTALL PLUGIN statement on the master and on each slave that is to be configured with semisynchronous replication.

On the master:

```
mysql> INSTALL PLUGIN rpl_semi_sync_master SONAME
'libsemisync_master.so';
```

On each slave:

```
mysql> INSTALL PLUGIN rpl_semi_sync_slave SONAME
'libsemisync_slave.so';
```

The preceding commands use a plugin filename suffix of .so. A different suffix might apply on your system. If you are not sure about the plugin filename, look for the plugins in the server's plugin directory.

Two simple methods exist for determining which plugins are installed on a running server:

- Use the SHOW PLUGINS statement
- Query the INFORMATION_SCHEMA.PLUGINS table

Installing the semisynchronous replication plugin will enable it by default. To use semisynchronous replication you must have the plugins enabled both on the master server and at least one slave server. If only one side is enabled any replication that occurs will be asynchronous.

To control an installed plugin you must set the appropriate system variables. You can set these variables at runtime using SET GLOBAL, or at server startup on the command line or in an option file.

At runtime, these master server system variables are available:

```
mysql> SET GLOBAL rpl_semi_sync_master_enabled = {0|1};
mysql> SET GLOBAL rpl_semi_sync_master_timeout = N;
```

On the slave side, this system variable is available:

```
mysql> SET GLOBAL rpl_semi_sync_slave_enabled = {0|1};
```

For rpl_semi_sync_master_enabled or rpl_semi_sync_slave_enabled, the value should be 1 to enable semisynchronous replication or 0 to disable it. By default, these variables are set to 1.

For rpl_semi_sync_master_timeout, the value N is given in seconds. The default value is 10.

If you enable semisynchronous replication on a slave at runtime, you must also start the slave I/O thread (stopping it first if it is already running) to cause the slave to connect to the master and register as a semisynchronous slave:

```
mysql> STOP SLAVE IO_THREAD;
mysql> START SLAVE IO_THREAD;
```

If the I/O thread is already running and you do not restart it, the slave continues to use asynchronous replication.

At server startup, the variables that control semisynchronous replication can be set as command-line options or in an option file. Typically, you set the variables in the my.cnf or my.ini files on the master and slave servers.

On the master:

```
[mysqld]
rpl_semi_sync_master_enabled=1
rpl_semi_sync_master_timeout=10
```

On each slave:

```
[mysqld]
rpl_semi_sync_slave_enabled=1
```

At this point you how have semisynchronous replication enabled and running.

Statement-based, row-based, and mixed-based replication

You have three methods of logging the data for replication:

- Statement-based replication (SBR) replicates SQL statements that modify data.
- Row-based replication (RBR) replicates only the changed rows.
- Mixed-based replication (MBR) is comprised of a combination of statement-based replication and row-based replication.

Currently for all versions of mysqld, statement-based replication is the default method of logging. Most storage engines support all three methods of logging data. The two exceptions are that Blackhole does not support row-based replication and Falcon does not support statement-based replication.

If mixed-based replication is in use it will utilize statement-based replication by default but will switch to row-based replication when needed. The reasons that RBR will be used are the following:

- When a function is called that contains the UUID() function.
- When two or more tables containing AUTO_INCREMENT fields are updated.

- Upon execution of the INSERT DELAYED statement.
- When a UDF is called.
- When the following functions are used:
    - FOUND_ROWS()
    - ROW_COUNT
    - USER()
    - CURRENT_USER()
    - CURRENT_USER

The use of row-based replication definitely resolves some issues with statement-based replication that are difficult, if not impossible, to fix otherwise. However, the relative newness of RBR means that it is not as widely deployed and is not as well understood by MySQL administrators. As well, a very small statement can change a very large amount of data, so RBR may be more bandwidth-intensive than SBR.

The mysqlbinlog tool has been updated to support RBR, but the output can still be somewhat difficult to decipher. If you just run the mysqlbinlog tool without special options

```
shell> mysqlbinlog mysql-bin.00001
# at 238
#081213 13:14:29 server id 1   end_log_pos 1278        Write_rows:
table id 17 flags: STMT_END_F

BINLOG '
fAS3SBMBAAAALAAAANoAAAAAABEAAAAAAAAABHRlc3QAAXQAAwMPCgIUAAQ=
fAS3SBcBAAAAKAAAAIBAAAQABEAAAAAAAEAA//8AQAAAAVhcHBsZ==
'/*!*/;
```

you will have binary data where the row-based events are in the log. Using the -v (verbose) option will enable to you to view the statements that made the data changes:

```
shell> mysqlbinlog -v mysql-bin.00001

# at 238
#081213 13:14:29 server id 1   end_log_pos 1278        Write_rows:
table id 17 flags: STMT_END_F

BINLOG '
fAS3SBMBAAAALAAAANoAAAAAABEAAAAAAAAABHRlc3QAAXQAAwMPCgIUAAQ=
fAS3SBcBAAAAKAAAAIBAAAQABEAAAAAAAEAA//8AQAAAAVhcHBsZ==
'/*!*/;
### INSERT INTO test.a
### SET
###   @1=1
###   @2='testing'
```

```
###    @3=NULL
...
# at 1298
#081213 13:14:29 server id 1  end_log_pos 1326        Update_rows:
table id 17 flags: STMT_END_F
```

Your output will now contain pseudo SQL statements that are commented out that represent the row-based events. This output is much better than the default, but if you look closely you will see that the INSERT statement does not include field names — only placeholders (@1, @2, @3). To be clear, the necessary data for replication and point-in-time recovery is stored in the binary log, but it just is not as easy to decipher as with statement-based replication logs.

Replication Configurations

Replication setup can be as simple as a master and a slave server. It can be as complex as what is called circular replication, where the servers form a ring with each master also being a slave of another master.

Simple replication

The simplest replication setup is a single master with a single slave. We will use this example to show the basics of replication setup. Figure 16-1 shows a simple master/slave configuration.

FIGURE 16-1

To begin with you need to edit the configuration file on both servers. On the master server in the [mysqld] directive you need to add:

```
server-id= X
log-bin = mysql-bin
sync_binlog= 1
```

The `server-id` value of X needs to be a positive integer that is unique among all your database servers. Often administrators will use the last octet of the server's IP address because this will typically be unique from server to server. For example, if the server's IP address was 192.168.2.100 you would use 100 as the `server-id`. To use more unique integers, the serial number of the system or the entire IP address could be used, such as 192168002100, or even the IP address plus the port, such as 1921680021003306.

If you do not use unique values of `server-id` among your replication servers unpredictable results will occur. Quite often if two slaves have the same `server-id` a master will send some data to one slave, then send different data to another slave, leaving both with an incomplete set of data changes.

After the configuration changes are made you must restart `mysqld`.

> **TIP** You must restart `mysqld` anytime changes are made to the configuration file for the changes to take effect.

Once this is done you must create a replication user on the master server. To do this, log in to `mysqld` and issue the following command:

```
mysql> CREATE USER 'username'@'host' IDENTIFIED BY 'password';
mysql> GRANT REPLICATION SLAVE ON *.*
    -> TO 'user'@'host' IDENTIFIED BY 'password';
```

You will need to replace `host` with the hostname or IP address of the slave server.

At this point you are done on the master server setup. You must now edit the configuration file on the slave server. In the `[mysqld]` section you need to add:

```
server-id = X
```

As before, for the `server-id` line, X should to be a unique positive integer that is different than any other `server-id` entries on other database servers. Most of the configuration on a slave server is done dynamically using the `CHANGE MASTER` command.

After this change is made you need to restart `mysqld` on the slave.

It is important to understand that in order to utilize replication you must have the same data sets on both servers. If your master server has no data this is simple; if this is not the case it is more difficult. You have multiple ways of ensuring you have the same data set on both servers. We cover the details of backing up and restoring in Chapter 13. The basic idea is that you need to take a consistent backup of the master, noting down at what point in the master binary logs the backup was taken.

The `--master-data` option to `mysqldump` will automatically store a `CHANGE MASTER TO` statement at the end of the export. On import, the slave information will already be set up. In a physical backup, copying the `master.info` file is all that is needed.

After the backup is restored on the slave, log in and execute a START SLAVE command and then the SHOW SLAVE STATUS command:

```
mysql> START SLAVE;
mysql> SHOW SLAVE STATUS;
*************************** 1. row ***************************
               Slave_IO_State: Waiting for master to send event
                  Master_Host: 192.168.16.4
                  Master_User: replica
                  Master_Port: 3306
                Connect_Retry: 60
              Master_Log_File: mysql-bin.000001
          Read_Master_Log_Pos: 548
               Relay_Log_File: mysql-relay-bin.000001
                Relay_Log_Pos: 600
        Relay_Master_Log_File: mysql-bin.000001
             Slave_IO_Running: Yes
            Slave_SQL_Running: Yes
              Replicate_Do_DB:
          Replicate_Ignore_DB:
           Replicate_Do_Table:
       Replicate_Ignore_Table:
      Replicate_Wild_Do_Table:
  Replicate_Wild_Ignore_Table:
                   Last_Errno: 0
                   Last_Error:
                 Skip_Counter: 0
          Exec_Master_Log_Pos: 4
              Relay_Log_Space: 3630
              Until_Condition: None
               Until_Log_File:
                Until_Log_Pos: 0
           Master_SSL_Allowed: No
           Master_SSL_CA_File:
           Master_SSL_CA_Path:
              Master_SSL_Cert:
            Master_SSL_Cipher:
               Master_SSL_Key:
        Seconds_Behind_Master: 0
Master_SSL_Verify_Server_Cert: No
                Last_IO_Errno: 0
                Last_IO_Error:
               Last_SQL_Errno: 0
               Last_SQL_Error:
1 row in set (0.00 sec)
```

Both Slave_IO_Running and Slave_SQL_Running must show YES for the slave to be running correctly.

Table 16-3 lists each field from the SHOW SLAVE STATUS command and a brief description.

TABLE 16-3

SHOW SLAVE STATUS Field Descriptions

Field Name	Description
Master_Host	The hostname or IP address of the master server.
Master_User	User used to establish the connection to the master host.
Master_Port	The TCP/IP port to connect to on the master host.
Connect_Retry	The amount of time that the slave waits before attempting to reconnect to the master server after a connection failure. The default value is 60 (seconds).
Master_Log_File	The master binary log file that the slave I/O thread is reading from.
Read_Master_Log_Pos	The position in the master binary log that the I/O thread is currently reading from.
Relay_Log_File	The relay log file on the slave from which the SQL thread is reading.
Relay_Log_Pos	The current position of the SQL thread in the relay log.
Slave_IO_Running	If this has a value of YES the I/O thread has started and connected successfully to the master host. If NO it has stopped running; for example, if the network connection is lost.
Slave_SQL_Running	If this has a value of YES the SQL thread is running. If it has a value of NO the SQL thread is not running. A statement causing an error can cause the SQL thread to stop running.
Replicate_Do_DB	Specifies a database which will be replicated. There can multiple entries for Replicate_Do_DB in a comma-separated list.
Replicate_Ignore_DB	Specifies a database that will not be replicated. There can be multiple entries for Replicate_Ignore_DB in a comma-separated list.
Replicate_Do_Table	Specifies a table that will be replicated. There can be multiple entries for Replicate_Do_Table in a comma-separated list.
Replicate_ Ignore_Table	Specifies a table that will not be replicated. There can be multiple entries for Replicate_Ignore_Table in a comma-separated list.
Replicate_Wild_ Do_Table	A "wildcard" entry specifying databases that will be replicated.

TABLE 16-3 (continued)	
Field Name	**Description**
Replicated_Wild_Ignore_Table	A "wildcard" entry specifying databases that will not be replicated.
Last_Errno	The error number of the last replication error that occurred.
Last_Error	A description of the last replication error that occurred. This may include an SQL statement that caused the SQL thread to stop.
Skip_Counter	The last value of num used when executing SET GLOBAL SQL_SLAVE_SKIP_COUNTER=num.
Exec_Master_Log_Pos	The position of the last event executed by the SQL thread from the master binary log.
Relay_Log_Space	The total size of all relay logs.
Seconds_Behind_Master	Shows how far the SQL thread is behind the IO thread in execution of the relay logs. This is calculated by taking the last timestamp value in the relay log and subtracting the timestamp value for the current event that the SQL thread is executing. Seconds_Behind_Master does not give any indication of how long the slave will take to become up-to-date. If the IO thread is not able to keep the relay logs current with the master binary logs, Seconds_Behind_Master can be falsely reassuring. If the IO thread cannot keep up with the volume of master binary logs, but the SQL thread can keep up with the IO thread, the value of Seconds_Behind_Master can be 0 even though the slave is lagging — potentially far behind.
Master_SSL_Verify_Server_Cert	Possible values are 0 (do not verify that the Common Name of the server certificate matches the hostname that the client connected to) or 1 (perform the verification, valid only when encrypted connections are in use). The default value is 0.
Last_IO_Errno	The last error number encountered by the IO thread.
Last_IO_Error	A description of the last error encountered by the IO thread.
Last_SQL_Errno	The last error number encountered by the SQL thread.
Last_SQL_Error	A description of the last error encountered by the SQL thread.

CHANGE MASTER statement

If your master server information was not stored in the backup or if you are configuring a slave of a master server with an empty data set, you will need to configure the connection information using the CHANGE MASTER command. The CHANGE MASTER command can also be used to change the slave information after the first slave configuration; for example, when you are promoting a slave to be a new master and want to change other slaves to stop replicating the old master and start replicating the new master (see Chapter 22 for examples of slave promotion).

To do this, log in to mysqld, and execute the following command while replication is stopped:

```
CHANGE MASTER TO
MASTER_HOST='host_name',
MASTER_USER='user',
MASTER_PASSWORD='password',
MASTER_LOG_FILE='mysql-bin.000001',
MASTER_LOG_POS=98;
```

The five fields listed here are the minimum data that mysqld needs to be able to configure replication. Almost all of the fields listed in Table 16-3 can be used in the CHANGE MASTER TO statement; for example, MASTER_PORT and MASTER_CONNECT_RETRY can be set. Once this has been executed, you can then execute a START SLAVE statement and finally the SHOW SLAVE STATUS command. If replication is not working smoothly, check the error log for more information.

More complex setups

It is possible to build more complicated replication setups than the simple master-slave setup. Each of the following sections briefly describes an elaborate setup you can use as needed.

Single master and multiple slaves

You can set up as many slaves as needed. Figure 16-2 illustrates a master server with data changes being replicated to three slaves.

FIGURE 16-2

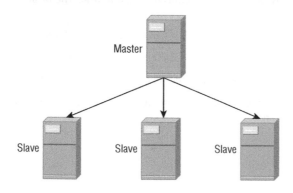

One common reason for a setup like this is to help alleviate the load on the master database. The application can read from any slave and receive data that is frequently as up-to-date as needed (replication is asynchronous by default, so the data may be out of date).

There is no difference in the previous configurations discussed for the master or the additional slave servers in this setup. As pointed out before, each server must have a unique `server-id` entry in the `[mysqld]` directive of the configuration file.

You should understand when working with multiple slaves that each slave causes a small amount of overhead on the master server. Even on busy servers this is not very much until you begin adding a large number of slaves directly to a master.

Master and relay slave

If you need more slaves than a master can comfortably manage, it is time to introduce a *relay server*. The sole function of this server is to relay the binary logs from the master to all the slaves. Figure 16-3 shows this type of setup.

FIGURE 16-3

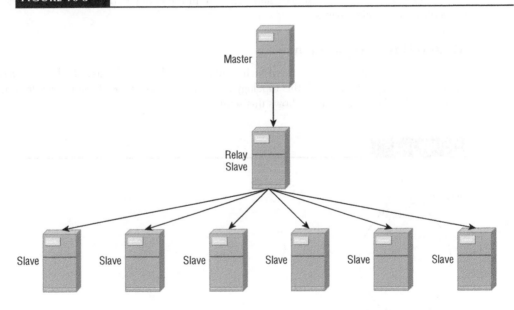

This will reduce the load on the master server. The configuration for this setup will need to be slightly different than before. The relay slave will need a specific configuration.

In the `[mysqld]` section you will need to have:

```
server-id = X
log-bin = mysql-bin
log-slave-updates
```

The difference between this configuration and the standard configuration is the addition of the `log-slave-updates` and `log-bin` statements. This tells the server that it should write binary logs and include the changes it receives from the master. Otherwise this cascading replication configuration will not work. The six slaves on the bottom level of our example do not need to have `log-slave-updates` or `log-bin` configured. There are other reasons to enable the binary logs, including incremental backup, point-in-time recovery, and consistent configuration setups in the event that one of the slaves on the bottom is promoted to be a relay slave.

Though not necessary, it can be useful to use the Blackhole storage engine on the relay slave. With the Blackhole storage engine the data is not actually stored in a table. All changes are written to the binary logs, which then enable the changes to propagate to the lower-level slaves. Because tables are not actually maintained the I/O demands on the server are typically much less. This will improve the overall performance of the server. You can find more details on the Blackhole storage engine in Chapter 11.

A final note about this: you could of course add another level of slaves below these six slaves if needed. As with the relay slave in the example you would have to make sure the `log-slave-updates` and `log-bin` statements are in the configuration file for the slaves that are replicating to other slaves.

Master-Master replication

A common way of providing a form of high availability is through the use of what is called master-master replication. With this topology there are two servers, each both a master and a slave of each other. Figure 16-4 shows this setup.

FIGURE 16-4

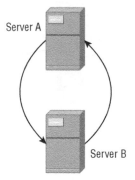

Server A

Server B

This setup might seem simple enough, but actually introduces some subtle issues that the database administrator needs to be aware of when working with master-master replication.

The primary issue is that both servers could potentially be simultaneously inserting a row into the same table with an auto-increment field. At this point replication will break on one of the servers because it can not insert a row with the same ID.

Two entries in the [mysqld] section of the configuration file are needed to resolve this issue:

```
auto_increment_increment
auto_increment_offset
```

These should each have an integer value. The auto_increment_increment value determines the increment amount between successive auto_increment values and should be the same for each server in the replication ring. It must be at least as large as the number of servers in the replication ring. The auto_increment_offset value should be different for each server. It is the offset used in combination with the auto_increment_increment value to get a final unique value.

Let's say you had the following auto_increment settings for Server A and Server B:

```
# Server A
auto_incremenent_increment = 10
auto_increment_offset = 1
# Server B
auto_incremenent_increment = 10
auto_increment_offset = 2
```

In this case any table with an auto_increment field would increment in amounts of 10. With Server A, the initial insert into a table (with an auto_increment field) will be with a value of 1. Server B will begin with 2. The next values would be 11 on Server A and 12 on Server B.

WARNING It is not wise to have your application write to both servers at the same time. Writing to both servers at the same time makes a reasonably durable fast failover for high availability but has no performance gains. Both servers have to execute all write statements, whether the write statements come directly from clients or come via replication.

For any replication setup, after a while the data gets out of sync. This causes a large problem on master-master replication architectures — if Server A has a certain value for a field and Server B has a different value, which is the right value? In a master-slave setup, you would say the master has the correct data set, because all data changes should happen there — no data changes should occur directly on the slave. But if there is more than one server on which a change is allowed to happen, which has the complete, true data set?

If you set up master-master replication in your environment, be prepared to run into this issue.

Circular replication

A final configuration that is an extension of master-master replication is called circular replication or *multi-master* replication. With this setup there are two or more servers in a ring formation. Figure 16-5 illustrates this arrangement with four servers:

FIGURE 16-5

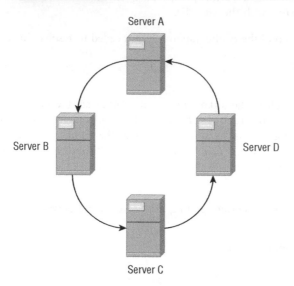

Server A

Server B

Server D

Server C

Like master-master replication, circular replication offers no performance gains for writes — even though the writes can be balanced among three or more servers, each server will have to perform all of the writes eventually, because the writes will come through replication. In addition, circular replication also has the problem of figuring out which server has the correct data set when the data becomes out of sync.

However, unlike master-master replication, circular replication cannot be used for high availability.

Circular replication introduces a very large problem: A problem with one server can affect the rest of the servers. For example, in the circular replication setup shown in Figure 16-5, Server A replicates to Server B, which replicates to Server C, which replicates to Server D, which replicates to Server A. If a write occurs on Server C, Server A does not receive it until after Server D receives it, executes it, and then saves it in its binary logs.

This means that if a problem occurs — for example, a network issue causes Server A not to be able to connect to Server D to read the binary logs — the rest of the servers are affected. Though statements from Server A can make it to Servers B, C, and D, statements from Server B go through Server C and Server D, but because Server A cannot connect to Server D, Server A never receives the statements from Server B. Statements from Server C only get to Server D and not Server A and B, and statements from Server D are only applied on Server D.

Circular replication is useful only in the rare cases when it is acceptable to have the data out of sync on the machines for long periods. However, most database administrators need replication to be synchronous — the only reason mysqld has lasted so long without synchronous replication is that ordinarily statements are processed very quickly. Most of the time, there is very little delay from the time a statement is executed on the master to the time it is executed on the slave.

If, after all these warnings, you still want to set up circular replication — perhaps to test its failure modes — it is very similar to setting up master-master replication. As with master-master replication, each server is both a master and a slave, and as such some additional entries are needed for the configuration file in order to operate properly.

In the [mysqld] section you will need to have:

```
server-id = X
log-bin = mysql-bin
log-slave-updates
```

You will also need auto_increment settings. Remember, only one of these sections is needed for a server.

```
# Server A
auto_incremenent_increment = 10
auto_increment_offset = 1

# Server B
auto_incremenent_increment = 10
auto_increment_offset = 2

# Server C
auto_incremenent_increment = 10
auto_increment_offset = 3

# Server D
auto_incremenent_increment = 10
auto_increment_offset = 4
```

Additional replication configuration options

Several configuration options are not mandatory but can be very beneficial. In particular, to help ensure a slave's data is kept in sync with the master, it is useful to include the read-only option in the slave's configuration file. This ensures that the only changes to the data will come through replication or from a user with SUPER privileges. The read-only option is a dynamic variable so it is very easy to change when promoting a slave to a master.

By default, replication attempts to start when mysqld is started up. If you do not want replication to begin on server start, you can use the skip-slave-start option in the [mysqld] directive of your configuration file. To begin replication you must log in to mysqld and execute a START SLAVE command.

Correcting Data Drift

If you work with replication setups for very long you will run across situations where the data sets differ on the master and slave. This is often referred to as data drift. This problem can arise for several reasons including the use of non-deterministic functions and allowing write access to a slave server.

Though it is possible to resolve data drift problems by hand, it is often highly impractical. Fortunately, Baron Schwartz recognized the problem and provided a solution in the Maatkit toolkit, available at `www.maatkit.org`. All the tools are programmed in Perl with minimal prerequisites. Maatkit includes one tool, `mk-table-checksum`, which you can use to uncover data drift problems. A second tool, `mk-table-sync`, is used to actually resolve these issues.

mk-table-checksum overview

The premise of the `mk-table-checksum` tool is that it should calculate checksums for tables on both the master and slave servers. It then compares checksums telling you if a slave's table is out of sync with the corresponding master's table. Several algorithms can be used to calculate checksums with the default being to use the `CHECKSUM` function. You can read about other algorithms and their strengths and weaknesses in the tool's documentation. To access the `mk-table-checksum` documentation just execute `perldoc mk-table-checksum` to get an overview of all functions and options.

The `--replicate` option is used to check if a master and its slaves are in sync. In this case `mk-table-checksum` is run on the master server and all calculations are replicated on slaves. The tool gets the master and slave information from the configuration files. In general command line looks like this:

```
shell> perl mk-table-checksum --replicate=test.checksum \
       --algorithm=BIT_XOR localhost --user=backup_user --askpass
```

Let's have a look at each of these options.

`--replicate=test.checksum` tells `mk-table-checksum` to use replication to compare master and slave. In general it is the most efficient way to do this. To use this method some preparations have to be made. A `test.checksum` table with the following structure has to be created:

```
CREATE TABLE checksum (
           db          char(64)    NOT NULL,
           tbl         char(64)    NOT NULL,
           chunk       int         NOT NULL,
           boundaries  char(64)    NOT NULL,
           this_crc    char(40)    NOT NULL,
           this_cnt    int         NOT NULL,
           master_crc  char(40)        NULL,
           master_cnt  int             NULL,
```

```
        ts            timestamp   NOT NULL,
    PRIMARY KEY (db, tbl, chunk)
) ENGINE=InnoDB;
```

The ENGINE=InnoDB option is optional, but it is highly recommended. A deadlock will break replication if the checksum table is non-transactional. The checksum table does not need to be created in the test database; it can be created in any database as long as it is being replicated.

The mk-table-checksum tool will insert at least one row into the checksum table for each table it calculates a checksum for. All the calculations will be replicated to the slave(s). Once this is done a simple query on the slave will show differences. The checksum table should be passed to the --replicate option using dot notation (that is, test.checksum) to specify the database in which it has been created.

--algorithm=BIT_XOR specifies what algorithm will be used to calculate table checksums. You can find detailed description in mk-table-checksum documentation. In general, two things you should remember are: the default algorithm uses the CHECKSUM function and is *order dependent*, and the BIT_XOR algorithm is order independent and sometimes is preferred.

host is the master's host server, where the utility is being run. The host option is specified with nothing introducing it. In the preceding example, the value of host is localhost.

--user and --askpass are credentials used to connect to mysqld. When using --askpass the script will ask for the password immediately after starting. If mk-table-checksum is being launched from a script, it is possible to use the option --password=password so it does not ask for a password.

For big tables (larger than a million rows) it is advisable to use the --chunksize option and specify a number of rows to divide the tables in smaller portions. This allows for better concurrency with the mk-table-checksum program. When specified, the tool will try to divide the table into segments with a number of rows as close as possible to this number. It will use table keys to determine the ranges for each portion. In this case test.checksum will hold one row per chunk. Using a smaller chunksize may improve concurrency because less of the table is locked, but actually ends up slowing the process down.

When the mk-table-checksum program starts it displays checksums for each table or chunk as it processes the table. When it is finished the following query can be used to check which tables/chunks differ on the slave(s):

```
SELECT db, tbl, chunk, this_cnt-master_cnt AS cnt_diff,
this_crc <> master_crc
 OR ISNULL(master_crc) <> ISNULL(this_crc) AS crc_diff
FROM checksum
WHERE master_cnt <> this_cnt OR master_crc <> this_crc
 OR ISNULL(master_crc) <> ISNULL(this_crc);
```

This will show which tables (or chunks) differ on the master and slave servers.

When running mk-table-checksum you should remember that the checksum process may be slow on large tables and can often cause slave servers to lag. The use of the checksum table does help to minimize these effects.

mk-table-sync overview

The mk-table-sync tool is used to synchronize tables. Once you have run mk-table-checksum and determined the databases and tables that need to be synchronized you can plug this information into mk-table-sync. If you built the test.checksum table as outlined earlier you can execute this on the master server and have it sync all slaves:

```
mk-table-sync --execute --replicate test.checksum master_host_name
```

If you have a master-master replication setup the recommended method of resolving synchronization issues is:

```
mk-table-sync --execute --synctomaster \
h=host2,u=backup_user,p=passwd,D=db_name,t=table_name
```

This should be run on the server (host2 in this case) with out-of-sync data.

There are three common command options:

- --execute: Runs the synchronization process
- --test: Tells what synchronization algorithm will be used but does not perform any actual changes
- --print: Prints the queries that could be run to resolve differences, instead of running the synchronization process.

As with all Maatkit tools, the documentation is available through perldoc: perldoc mk-table-sync.

Before running mk-table-sync to actually synchronize your data it would always be wise to run mk-table-sync with the --print option to see what it will actually be changing.

Putting this together

Using both of these tools together will give you a semi-automated process for master/slave synchronization. The process is simply this:

- Run mk-table-checksum to identify which tables have differences.
- Run mk-table-sync to synchronize tables.
- Run CHECKSUM TABLE on synchronized tables to ensure changes were properly made. Note that MyISAM tables can store a constantly updated CHECKSUM value in metadata. If a MyISAM table has the CHECKSUM option enabled, it is not necessary to run a CHECKSUM TABLE command — simply query the INFORMATION_SCHEMA.TABLES system view

or use SHOW TABLE STATUS to see the CHECKSUM value for the table. The "Table Definitions Extension" section of Chapter 4 has more information on the CHECKSUM option in MyISAM tables.

Summary

Both logging and replication are critical areas for a database administrator to understand. This chapter taught the tools and techniques used to work with replication and ensure it runs reliably. The following topics were covered:

- Logging in MySQL
  - Binary log
  - Relay log
  - Error log
  - General query log
  - Slow query log
- Replication setup in MySQL
  - Replication topologies
- Dealing with data drift

Chapter 17

Measuring Performance

Determining how well your systems are performing and where improvements can be made is an important part of a database administrator's job. The best way to determine this is through benchmarking and profiling. *Benchmarking* is the execution of a standard suite of programs in order to assess the performance of the system or systems being tested in a methodical manner relative to performance of other systems. *Profiling* is a methodical way of collecting metrics about systems you are testing. These systems can be in active testing or even in production if the profiling methods used do not generate a large load. Together, they can be used for capacity planning purposes. Each of these topics will be discussed in this chapter.

Benchmarks answer the question, "Will my application work faster when configured in this way, or in that way?" By measuring a set of activities, benchmarks can be used to compare how a database responds under varying conditions. You can create as many different test scenarios as you can imagine. Possible scenarios might include testing your database performance with server configuration changes, testing your database for deadlock handling, testing different methods of loading data, and testing new application code releases.

Through planning and benchmarking, you can become more aware of when a system is approaching the limits of its capabilities. You can then plan to either upgrade the server, replace the server, or add another server if the application supports this capability. Starting with a baseline of how a current system performs, benchmarks allow the QA and testing cycles in the development process to work better and get more done in the same amount of time. In the end, using benchmarks provides a better experience for the end user of the application.

Profiling is used to reveal characteristics about your system, whether good or bad. For example, profiling can show that a query cache is being used effectively, or it can lead to pinpointing specific bottlenecks such as too much disk I/O. Profiling is accomplished in a number of ways. It can be as simple as running the SHOW GLOBAL STATUS command. It could be as complicated as having code in your application that collects metrics and generates statistics about system use on a real-time basis.

Profiling is a used in benchmarking — benchmarking without measurements is just running the same set of actions. Many of the same techniques used to profile a server are used in benchmarking.

Benchmarking

Some of the tools that can be used to benchmark mysqld include mysqlslap, downloadable from http://dev.mysql.com/doc/refman/6.0/en/mysqlslap.html and sysbench, downloadable from http://sysbench.sourceforge.net.

There is a BENCHMARK function in mysqld that allows you to see the execution time of an expression. The BENCHMARK function takes two arguments — a number for how many times to evaluate the expression, and an expression. In this way, BENCHMARK can be used to compare queries. For example:

```
mysql> SELECT BENCHMARK(10000000, 1+1);
+--------------------------+
| BENCHMARK(10000000, 1+1) |
+--------------------------+
|                        0 |
+--------------------------+
1 row in set (0.46 sec)

mysql> SELECT BENCHMARK(1000000, 1/1);
+-------------------------+
| BENCHMARK(1000000, 1/1) |
+-------------------------+
|                       0 |
+-------------------------+
1 row in set (0.54 sec)
```

So, the divide operation takes about 10 times as long as an addition operation!

We can compare how long different functions that return the same result take. For example, to extract the date from a DATETIME field, we can use the appropriate DATE() function, or we can use the idea that a date is a string, and use the LEFT() function to retrieve the date:

```
mysql> SELECT LEFT('2009-05-01 00:00:00',10),
    -> DATE('2009-05-01 00:00:00');
+--------------------------------+-----------------------------+
| LEFT('2009-05-01 00:00:00',10) | DATE('2009-05-01 00:00:00') |
+--------------------------------+-----------------------------+
| 2009-05-01                     | 2009-05-01                  |
+--------------------------------+-----------------------------+
1 row in set (0.00 sec)
```

Indeed, these return the same result. But which is quicker?

```
mysql> SELECT BENCHMARK(10000000, LEFT('2009-05-01 00:00:00',10));
+----------------------------------------------------+
| BENCHMARK(10000000, LEFT('2009-05-01 00:00:00',10)) |
+----------------------------------------------------+
|                                                  0 |
+----------------------------------------------------+
1 row in set (0.68 sec)

mysql> SELECT BENCHMARK(10000000, DATE('2009-05-01 00:00:00'));
+-------------------------------------------------+
| BENCHMARK(10000000, DATE('2009-05-01 00:00:00')) |
+-------------------------------------------------+
|                                               0 |
+-------------------------------------------------+
1 row in set (12.41 sec)
```

The LEFT() function is almost 20 times faster!

mysqlslap

The mysqlslap program will emulate client load on mysqld. It executes an arbitrary number of SQL statements contained in a text file. It is included with MySQL Server running on Unix-based systems. Part of a general or (converted) binary log can be used with mysqlslap. With its ability to auto-generate data the mysqlslap program provides a quick way to benchmark mysqld.

Table 17-1 lists all the options available for mysqlslap.

TABLE 17-1

mysqlslap Options

Option	Description
`--auto-generate-sql`	Automatically generate SQL statements.
`--auto-generate-sql-add-auto-increment`	Automatically generated tables will contain an `AUTO_INCREMENT` field.
`--auto-generate-sql-execute-number=num`	Automatically generate and execute `num` statements.
`--auto-generate-sql-guid-primary`	Automatically generated tables will contain a GUID-based primary key.
`--auto-generate-sql-load-type=load_type`	When using automatically generated SQL queries, this option determines the type of SQL statements: read (scan tables), write (inserts), key (read primary keys), update (update primary keys), and mixed (half inserts, half scanning selects).
`--auto-generate-sql-secondary-indexes=num`	Add `num` secondary indexes to the automatically generated tables.
`--auto-generate-sql-unique-query-number=num`	Automatically generate `num` unique statements. When using automatically generated SQL queries, this option specifies how many unique queries are generated for `--auto-generate-sql-write-number`.
`--auto-generate-sql-write-number=num--auto-generate-sql-unique-write-number=num`	Each thread executes `num1` inserts. Automatically generate `num2` unique inserts for each thread.
`--burnin`	Runs the test suite in burn-in mode (looping continuously). This was added in MySQL Server 6.0.
`--commit`	Determines how many queries `mysqlslap` executes before a commit is performed.
`--compress`	All data traveling between the client and server is compressed.
`--concurrency=num_of_clients`	Determines the number of clients that `mysqlslap` simulates during program execution.
`--create=value`	Specifies either the file or string with the `CREATE TABLE` statement used for table creation.
`--create-schema=value`	This option specifies the database to be created by `mysqlslap` where the tests are run.

TABLE 17-1	*(continued)*
Option	**Description**
`--csv=file_name`	The output of `mysqlslap` is stored in CSV format in the specified file.
`--debug`	When `mysqlslap` is run, it will generate a debugging log.
`--debug-check`	When `mysqlslap` exits, it prints debugging information.
`--debug-info`	When `mysqlslap` exits, it prints debugging information plus additional CPU and memory usage statistics.
`--delayed-start=num`	Each thread start is delayed by a random number of microseconds up to the value specified by `num`. This was added in MySQL Server 6.0.
`--delimiter=string`	Determines what delimiter is used for SQL statements stored in an external file.
`--detach=num`	Each of the connections closes and reopens after execution of `num` statements.
`--engine=engine_type`	Determines the storage engine used for table creation.
`--help`	When used `mysqlslap` generates help message and exits.
`--host=name`	Specifies the hostname (`name`) of the `mysqld` that `mysqlslap` connects to for conducting test runs.
`--ignore-sql-errors`	When using this option, `mysqlslap` will ignore SQL errors. This was added in MySQL Server 6.0.
`--iterations=num`	This option specifies the number of test runs executed by `mysqlslap`.
`--label=value`	Specifies the label used during generation of printed and CVS output. This was added in MySQL Server 6.0.
`--number-blob-cols=num`	Determines the number of `BLOB` fields used for automatically generated tables. This was added in MySQL Server 6.0.
`--number-char-cols=num`	Determines the number of `VARCHAR` fields used for automatically generated tables.
`--number-int-cols=num`	Determines the number of `INT` fields used for automatically generated tables.
`--number-of-queries=num`	Each client will execute approximately this number of queries.
`--only-print`	Performs a dry run showing what `mysqlslap` would have done. The `mysqlslap` program does not connect to the database.

continued

TABLE 17-1	(continued)
Option	**Description**
`--password[=password]`	The password used by `mysqlslap` for establishing a connection with the server.
`--pipe`	On Windows servers uses a named pipe to connect to `mysqld.exe`.
`--port=port_number`	Specifies the TCP/IP port number used by `mysqlslap` for connecting to the database server.
`--post-query=value`	Specifies the file or string containing statements executed after the tests are finished.
`--post-system=value`	After `mysqlslap` finishes, this string is executed via a `system()` call.
`--pre-query=value`	Prior to `mysqlslap` beginning a test run the statement in the file or string specified is executed.
`--pre-system=value`	The specified string is executed by a `system()` call before `mysqlslap` begins.
`--preserve-schema`	The database from the test run is retained for later analysis.
`--protocol=protocol_type`	Specifies the protocol used for connection to `mysqld`. Possible values include: `TCP`, `SOCKET`, `PIPE`, and `MEMORY`.
`--query`	This option specifies a custom query string or file containing multiple queries that `mysqlslap` will run.
`--silent`	Suppresses output.
`--socket=path_to_socket_file`	Used for `localhost` connections to the database on Unix-based systems.
`--ssl-ca=file_name`	Specifies the directory path to a file of trusted SSL CAs.
`--ssl-capath=directory`	Specifies the path to the directory that has the trusted SSL CA certificates. These certificates must be in PEM format.
`--ssl-cert=file_name`	The filename of the SSL certificate used for SSL-based connections.
`--ssl-cipher=values`	Specifies the allowable ciphers for SSL encryption.
`--ssl-key=file_name`	The filename of the SSL key file used for SSL-based connections.
`--ssl-verify-server-cert`	When using this option `mysqlslap` verifies that the Common Name value of the server's certificate is verified against the hostname when connecting to the server.

TABLE 17-1	(continued)
Option	Description
`--timer-length=num_of_seconds`	Specifies the number of seconds to run each test. (added in 6.0)
`--user=username`	The username used by `mysqlslap` when connecting to `mysqld`.
`--verbose`	Turns on verbose mode. If specified more than once there is more output.
`--version`	When run `mysqlslap` will display version information and exit.

As you can see there are many options for `mysqlslap`. Here is an example of using `mysqlslap` with auto-generated data:

```
shell> mysqlslap --user=qa_user --password --auto-generate-sql
Enter password:
Benchmark
        Average number of seconds to run all queries: 0.035 seconds
        Minimum number of seconds to run all queries: 0.035 seconds
        Maximum number of seconds to run all queries: 0.035 seconds
        Number of clients running queries: 1
        Average number of queries per client: 0
```

A more complex example looks like this:

```
shell> mysqlslap --user=qa_user --password --concurrency=5 \
--auto-generate-sql --auto-generate-sql-execute-number=1000 \
--auto-generate-sql-unique-query-number=1000
Enter password:
Benchmark
        Average number of seconds to run all queries: 28.550 seconds
        Minimum number of seconds to run all queries: 28.550 seconds
        Maximum number of seconds to run all queries: 28.550 seconds
        Number of clients running queries: 5
        Average number of queries per client: 1000
```

In this case `mysqlslap` generates five threads on the server and executes 1000 auto-generated queries on each one of those threads.

The `mysqlslap` program also has the ability to use custom tables and queries when running benchmarks. You can use this to perform a custom benchmark that most accurately reflects your production environment. In this example, we use the files `queries.sql` for SQL queries and `create_table.sql` for the table creation.

```
shell> cat create_table.sql
CREATE TABLE benchmarking (a int)
CREATE TABLE benchmarking_two (b int)
INSERT INTO benchmarking (a) VALUES (23)
INSERT INTO benchmarking_two (b) VALUE (45)

shell> cat queries.sql
SELECT * from benchmarking
SELECT * from benchmarking_two

shell> mysqlslap --user=qa_user --password \
--concurrency=100 --iterations=10 \
--create=/home/bmurphy/create_table.sql \
--query=/home/bmurphy/queries.sql
Enter password:
Benchmark
        Average number of seconds to run all queries: 0.125 seconds
        Minimum number of seconds to run all queries: 0.124 seconds
        Maximum number of seconds to run all queries: 0.127 seconds
        Number of clients running queries: 100
        Average number of queries per client: 2
```

Of course, these queries could be much more complicated. In the previous example, we also use the `iterations` option to run the test ten times and the concurrency option to simulate 100 client connections. When run `mysqlslap` then displays the average time for a test run execution and the minimum and maximum time required for run execution. When performing any kind of benchmarking, it is important that you execute multiple test runs and then average the runs. This will help to ensure high-quality results.

One nice feature of `mysqlslap` is that it does not have to be run on the same computer as `mysqld`. This is an important consideration, as it will allow for a more accurate view of the server's actual ability. The `mysqlslap` tool is one of the most flexible (and easiest to use) tools available for benchmarking servers.

SysBench

The SysBench program was written to provide a more general system-level view of a server running `mysqld`. There are separate test modes for CPU performance, I/O performance, mutex contention, memory speed, thread performance, and database performance.

The syntax for `sysbench` execution is:

```
sysbench [common-options] --test=name [test-options] command
```

There are four possible command options with `sysbench`.

- ■ **Prepare** — Performs preparation for tests which need them (`fileio` and `oltp` tests).
- ■ **Run** — Executes the specified test
- ■ **Cleanup** — Removes temporary data after the test run (`fileio` and `oltp` tests).
- ■ **Help** — Displays usage information for the specified test

There are numerous options for SysBench. However, they can be broken down into common options for all the test modes and then options for each specific test mode.

Table 17-2 lists common options for all tests.

TABLE 17-2

SysBench Common Options

Option	Description	Default
`--debug`	Prints debugging output.	off
`--help={on	off}`	Prints help message and exits.	off
`--init-rng`	Initializes a random number generator before testing begins.	off
`--max-requests`	Limits the total number of requests. A value of zero means unlimited.	10000
`--max-time=seconds`	Limits the total execution time to specified seconds. The default of zero means unlimited time.	0
`--num-threads`	Determines the total number of threads created.	1
`--percentile`	Display the average execution time of some percentile of the requests. With the default of 95%, `sysbench` will drop 5 percent of the longest-running queries.	95
`--test`	Specifies which test to run during program execution.	
`--thread-stack-size`	Specifies the stack size for each thread.	32k
`--validate={on	off}`	`sysbench` performs validation of results when it is possible.	off
`--verbosity=num`	Sets the verbosity level of `sysbench` output. This can range from 0 (critical messages only) to 5 (debugging output)	4

There are six possible test modes with SysBench. Each test mode covers different aspects of server operation. Each test mode has different possible options, which will be covered in the following sections.

CPU test mode

The CPU test mode runs a calculation of the prime numbers up to the value specified by the `--cpu-max-prime` options. This test focuses on the speed of the CPU and is useful for comparing different processors. Table 17-3 lists the options for CPU test mode.

TABLE 17-3

CPU Test Mode Options

Option	Description	Default
`--cpu-max-prime=num`	The `cpu` test calculates prime numbers up to this limit.	10000

The following example shows a run of the `cpu` test with a maximum prime number calculated of 20000:

```
shell> sysbench --test=cpu --cpu-max-prime=20000 run
sysbench v0.4.8:  multi-threaded system evaluation benchmark

Running the test with following options:
Number of threads: 1

Doing CPU performance benchmark

Threads started!
Done.

Maximum prime number checked in CPU test: 20000


Test execution summary:
    total time:                          119.8476s
    total number of events:              10000
    total time taken by event execution: 119.8215
    per-request statistics:
         min:                            0.0118s
         avg:                            0.0120s
         max:                            0.0198s
         approx.  95 percentile:         0.0124s

Threads fairness:
    events (avg/stddev):           10000.0000/0.00
    execution time (avg/stddev):   119.8215/0.00
```

I/O test mode

The I/O performance test mode is one of the most complex and comprehensive test modes available in SysBench. It can be used to test the file system of a server in multiple ways that can very closely reflect your server's actual usage. Table 17-4 lists the options for the I/O test mode.

TABLE 17-4

I/O Test Mode Options

Option	Description	Default
--file-async-backlog	If --file-io-mode=asynce this determines the number of asynchronous operations that will be queued for each thread.	128
--file-block-size	Determines the block size for all I/O operations.	16k
--file-extra-flags=value	Specifies flags for use when opening files. Possible values are sync, dsync, and direct.	
--file-fsync-all	Performs a fsync() call after each write operation.	no
--file-fsync-end	Performs a fsync() call at the end of the test.	yes
--file-fsycnc-freq=num	Performs a fsync() call after specified number of requests.	100
--file-fsync-mode=value	Determines which method of file synchronization to perform during testing, Possible values are fsync and fdatasync.	fsync
--file-io-mode=value	Determines the I/O mode used for testing. Possible values are async, sync, fastmmap, and slowmmap.	sync
--file-merged-requests=num	Merges up to this number of I/O requests.	0
--file-num=num	Specifies the number of files created for the test run.	128
--file-rw-ratio	Specifies the ratio of reads to writes for tests using both read and write subtests.	1.5
--file-test-mode=value	Specifies the type of test to run. Values can be seqwr, seqrewr, seqrd, rndrd, rndr, rndwr.	
--file-total-size=value	Determines the total size of the files generated for the test run.	2G

There are six types of files test available. Table 17-5 shows the possible values used for the `--file-test-mode` option and the type of test the value specifies.

TABLE 17-5

File Tests

File test	Description
seqwr	Sequential write test
seqrewr	Sequential rewrite test
seqrd	Sequential read test
rndrd	Random read test
rndwr	Random write test
rndrw	Random read/write test

With using the I/O test mode, there are three steps to perform. First you prepare the data, then you run the test, and finally you clean up the data after the test run.

Here is an example of a complete random read/write test including preparation, running, and cleanup:

```
shell> sysbench --num-threads=16 --test=fileio --file-total-size=1G
--file-test-mode=rndrw prepare
sysbench v0.4.8:  multi-threaded system evaluation benchmark

128 files, 8192Kb each, 1024Mb total
Creating files for the test...

shell> sysbench --num-threads=16 --test=fileio --file-total-size=1G
--file-test-mode=rndrw run
sysbench v0.4.8:  multi-threaded system evaluation benchmark

Running the test with following options:
Number of threads: 16

Extra file open flags: 0
128 files, 8Mb each
1Gb total file size
Block size 16Kb
Number of random requests for random IO: 10000
Read/Write ratio for combined random IO test: 1.50
Periodic FSYNC enabled, calling fsync() each 100 requests.
Calling fsync() at the end of test, Enabled.
```

```
Using synchronous I/O mode
Doing random r/w test
Threads started!
Done.

Operations performed:  6006 Read, 3994 Write, 12800 Other = 22800
Total
Read 93.844Mb  Written 62.406Mb  Total transferred 156.25Mb
  (5.0737Mb/sec)  324.72 Requests/sec executed

Test execution summary:
    total time:                      30.7961s
    total number of events:          10000
    total time taken by event execution: 150.6302
    per-request statistics:
        min:                         0.0000s
        avg:                         0.0151s
        max:                         0.4560s
        approx. 95 percentile:       0.0956s

Threads fairness:
    events (avg/stddev):             625.0000/89.43
    execution time (avg/stddev):     9.4144/1.41

shell> sysbench --num-threads=16 --test=fileio \
  --file-total-size=1G --file-test-mode=rndrw cleanup
sysbench v0.4.8:  multi-threaded system evaluation benchmark

Removing test files...
```

mutex contention test mode

The mutex test mode is designed to examine the performance of mutex implementation.
Table 17-6 lists the options for the mutex test mode.

TABLE 17-6

mutext Test Mode Options

Option	Description	Default
--mutex-locks=num	The number of mutex locks to acquire with each request	50000
--mutex-loops=num	The number of times an empty loop operation is performed before a mutex lock is acquired	10000
--mutex-num=num	The number of mutexes to create	4096

In the following two runs of SysBench the settings are the same except the number of threads. Clearly, the increased number of threads on this system (a Ubuntu GNU/Linux VM running on a dual-core Windows laptop) is impacting mutex performance:

```
shell> sysbench --num-threads=2 --mutex-locks=100000 --mutex-
num=10000 --test=mutex run
sysbench v0.4.8:  multi-threaded system evaluation benchmark

Running the test with following options:
Number of threads: 2

Doing mutex performance test
Threads started!
Done.


Test execution summary:
    total time:                          0.0842s
    total number of events:              2
    total time taken by event execution: 0.1388
    per-request statistics:
         min:                            0.0557s
         avg:                            0.0694s
         max:                            0.0831s
         approx. 95 percentile:          10000.0000s

Threads fairness:
    events (avg/stddev):           1.0000/0.00
    execution time (avg/stddev):   0.0694/0.01

shell> sysbench --num-threads=32 --mutex-locks=100000 --mutex-
num=10000 --test=mutex run
sysbench v0.4.8:  multi-threaded system evaluation benchmark

Running the test with following options:
Number of threads: 32

Doing mutex performance test
Threads started!
Done.


Test execution summary:
    total time:                          1.1898s
    total number of events:              32
    total time taken by event execution: 29.9150
    per-request statistics:
         min:                            0.4712s
         avg:                            0.9348s
```

```
      max:                        1.1457s
      approx. 95 percentile:      1.1302s

Threads fairness:
    events (avg/stddev):        1.0000/0.00
    execution time (avg/stddev): 0.9348/0.20
```

Memory test mode

The memory test mode is used to test sequential reads and writes to and from system memory. Table 17-7 lists the options for memory test mode.

TABLE 17-7

memory Test Mode Options

Option	Description	Default
--memory-access-mode=value	Determines the memory access method used for test. Possible values are seq and rnd.	seq
--memory-block-size=value	Determines the size of the memory block to use for test.	1k
--memory-oper=value	Determines which memory operation to run. Possible values are read, write, and none.	write
--memory-scope=value	Determines if each thread uses a globally allocated memory block or a local memory block. Possible values are global and local.	global
--memory-total-size=value	The total amount of data transferred during test.	100G

Here is an example of a memory test:

```
shell> sysbench --num-threads=64 --test=memory run
sysbench v0.4.8:  multi-threaded system evaluation benchmark

Running the test with following options:
Number of threads: 64

Doing memory operations speed test
Memory block size: 1K

Memory transfer size: 102400M

Memory operations type: write
Memory scope type: global
```

```
Threads started!
Done.

Operations performed: 104857600 (111087.89 ops/sec)

102400.00 MB transferred (108.48 MB/sec)


Test execution summary:
    total time:                        943.9156s
    total number of events:            104857600
    total time taken by event execution: 44706.7730
    per-request statistics:
        min:                           0.0000s
        avg:                           0.0004s
        max:                           1.8700s
        approx. 95 percentile:         0.0000s

Threads fairness:
    events (avg/stddev):               1638400.0000/13527.29
    execution time (avg/stddev):       698.5433/10.92thread test mode
```

The thread test mode is designed to benchmark the server scheduler performance. Server performance can often be impaired when there are large numbers of threads competing for a set of mutexes. Table 17-8 lists the options for thread test mode.

TABLE 17-8

thread Test Mode Options

Option	Description	Default
--thread-locks=num	Specifies the number of locks for each thread.	8
--thread-yields=num	Specifies the number of lock/yield/unlock loops to execute per request.	1000

Here is an example using two threads:

```
shell> sysbench --num-threads=2 --test=threads run
sysbench v0.4.8:  multi-threaded system evaluation benchmark

Running the test with following options:
Number of threads: 2
```

```
Doing thread subsystem performance test
Thread yields per test: 1000 Locks used: 8
Threads started!
Done.


Test execution summary:
    total time:                          104.9172s
    total number of events:              10000
    total time taken by event execution: 209.7935
    per-request statistics:
        min:                             0.0024s
        avg:                             0.0210s
        max:                             0.0681s
        approx. 95 percentile:           0.0227s

Threads fairness:
    events (avg/stddev):                 5000.0000/23.00
    execution time (avg/stddev):         104.8967/0.01
```

OLTP test mode

The OLTP (online transaction processing) test mode is targeted at benchmarking RDMS. Currently mysqld is the only supported database. As with the I/O test mode the OLTP test mode requires three stages: preparation, the test run, and cleanup. Table 17-9 lists the options for the OLTP test mode.

TABLE 17-9

OLTP Test Mode Options

Option	Description	Default
--db-ps-mode=value	SysBench uses server-side prepared statement for any possible query if the database drive supports the Prepared Statements API. If it is not possible to use server-side prepared statements client-side prepared statements are used. Possible values are disable and auto, and you can force client-side prepared statements.	auto
--myisam-max-rows=value	Specifies the max_rows options for MyISAM tables.	1000000
--mysql-db=value	Specifies the MySQL database used for the test. This database must already be created.	sbtest

continued

561

TABLE 17-9 *(continued)*

Option	Description	Default
--mysql-host=value	Specifies the mysqld hostname(s) used to run the test. You can specify more than hostname (separated by commas) and SysBench will distribute connections between the servers with a round-robin method.	localhost
--mysql-password= value	The password used to connect to mysqld.	
--mysql-port=num	The TCP/IP port used by mysqld.	3306
--mysql-socket=value	Determine the Unix socket file use to establish a connection to mysqld.	
--mysql-table- engine=value	Determines the table engine type. Possible options are myisam, innodb, heap, ndbcluster, and bdb.	innodb
--mysql-user=value	The username used to connect to mysqld.	user
--oltp-connect- delay=value	Specifies the time (in microseconds) SysBench sleeps after each connection to the database.	10000
--oltp-dist-pct=num	Determines the percentage of values treated as special.	1
--oltp-dist-res=num	Determines the percentage of cases were special values are generated.	75
--oltp-dist- type=value	Determines the distribution of random numbers. The three possible values are uniform (uniform distribution), gauss (gaussian distribution) and special. With a value of special there are a specified percentage of number (--oltp-dist-pct) in a specified percentage of cases (--oltp-dist-res).	special
--oltp-distinct- ranges=num	Specifies the number of DISTINCT range queries in a transaction.	1
--oltp-index- updates=num	Specifies the number of UPDATE queries using an index in a transaction.	1
--oltp-nontrx- mode=num	Determines the queries used for nontransactional mode. Possible values are select, insert, delete, update_key, and update_nonkey.	select
--oltp-non-index- updates=num	Specifies the number of UPDATE queries that do not use indexes in a transaction.	1

TABLE 17-9	(continued)	
Option	Description	Default
`--oltp-order-ranges=num`	Specifies the number of `ORDER` range queries in transaction.	1
`--oltp-point-selects=num`	Specifies the number of point select queries in a transaction.	1
`--oltp-range-size=num`	Determines the range size for range queries.	100
`--oltp-read-only=value`	No `DELETE`, `UPDATE`, or `INSERT` queries will be used in test.	off
`--oltp-simple-ranges`	Specifies the number of range queries in a transaction.	1
`--oltp-sp-name=value`	Specifies the name of the stored procedure `sysbench` should use when called in sp test mode.	
`--oltp-sum-ranges=num`	Specifies the number of `SUM` range queries in a transaction.	1
`--oltp-table-name=value`	Determines the name of the table used by `sysbench`.	sbtest
`--oltp-table-size=num`	Determines the number of rows in the test table.	10000
`--oltp-test-mode=value`	Determines execution mode used by `sysbench`. The possible values are simple, `complex`, `nontrx` (nontransactional), and `sp` (stored procedure).	complex
`--oltp-user-delay-max=num`	Specifies the maximum amount of time (in microseconds) to sleep after each client request.	0
`--oltp-user-delay-min=num`	Specifies the minimum amount of time (in microseconds) to sleep after each client request.	0

Following is an example of an OLTP test mode being prepared, run and cleaned up:

```
shell> sysbench --num-threads=16 --max-requests=100000 \
--mysql-user=qa_user --mysql-password=rach123el --test=oltp \
--oltp-table-size=1000000 prepare
sysbench v0.4.8: multi-threaded system evaluation benchmark

No DB drivers specified, using mysql
```

```
Creating table 'sbtest'...
Creating 1000000 records in table 'sbtest'...

shell> sysbench --num-threads=16 --max-requests=100000 \
--mysql-user=qa_user --mysql-password=rach123el --test=oltp \
--oltp-table-size=1000000 run
sysbench v0.4.8:  multi-threaded system evaluation benchmark

No DB drivers specified, using mysql
WARNING: Preparing of "BEGIN" is unsupported, using emulation
(last message repeated 15 times)
Running the test with following options:
Number of threads: 16

Doing OLTP test.
Running mixed OLTP test
Using Special distribution (12 iterations,  1 pct of values are
returned in 75 pct cases)
Using "BEGIN" for starting transactions
Using auto_inc on the id column
Maximum number of requests for OLTP test is limited to 100000
Threads started!
Done.

OLTP test statistics:
    queries performed:
        read:                            1400000
        write:                           500000
        other:                           200000
        total:                           2100000
    transactions:                        100000 (55.88 per sec.)
    deadlocks:                           0      (0.00 per sec.)
    read/write requests:                 1900000 (1061.64 per sec.)
    other operations:                    200000 (111.75 per sec.)

Test execution summary:
    total time:                          1789.6849s
    total number of events:              100000
    total time taken by event execution: 28631.5237
    per-request statistics:
        min:                             0.0083s
        avg:                             0.2863s
        max:                             2.5081s
        approx. 95 percentile:           0.7151s

Threads fairness:
    events (avg/stddev):           6250.0000/34.52
    execution time (avg/stddev):   1789.4702/0.05
```

```
shell> sysbench --num-threads=16 --max-requests=100000 \
--mysql-user=qa_user --mysql-password=rach123el --test=oltp \
--oltp-table-size=1000000 cleanup
sysbench v0.4.8:  multi-threaded system evaluation benchmark

No DB drivers specified, using mysql
Dropping table 'sbtest'...
Done.
```

During the preparation stage SysBench creates a table in the database server you specify. If you do not specify a server, it defaults to a database called sbtest. Regardless of the database you choose to use, it must already be created before the test run begins and the user must have the appropriate permissions on the database. If this is not the case SysBench will not be able to run.

The table created is called sbtest and has the following structure:

```
CREATE TABLE `sbtest` (
        `id` int(10) unsigned NOT NULL auto_increment,
        `k` int(10) unsigned NOT NULL default '0',
        `c` char(120) NOT NULL default '',
        `pad` char(60) NOT NULL default '',
        PRIMARY KEY  (`id`),
        KEY `k` (`k`));
```

Compiling SysBench

While the SysBench program is only available as source code, it has a straightforward compile process:

```
$ ./configure
$ make
# make install
```

The last step must done using the root account. On Ubuntu, we needed the build-essential package (which installs a number of programs) and the libmysqclient15-dev package.

The SysBench program is available at http://sysbench.sf.net.

Benchmarking recommendations

When performing benchmarks, regardless of the program used there are several principles that you should keep in mind. If at all possible do not change more than one variable at a time. A variable might be an actual mysqld configuration value, or a hardware variable such as the type of RAID used or the amount of RAM in the server. If you change two variables at the same time, then you do not know what is happening. One variable change could be causing a decrease in performance and one might be causing an increase. The changes, in effect, cancel each other out. Alternatively, if the performance is severely impacted or gets a lot better, you have no idea if it was because one variable, the other, or the combination of the two.

It is important that you perform multiple benchmarking test runs. That way it is much more likely that any testing aberrations will be discovered. A background process kicking off during the middle of a test run can skew your results and if you only run the test once you will have no other results to make comparisons against.

When running benchmarks you should always try and run the tool that generates the test load on another computer and not the server being tested. As with background processes, running a client load generator program on the same computer as mysqld will skew the results, unless, of course, you are attempting to benchmark the benchmarking program.

Consider that other factors other than mysqld might affect benchmarking results (and ultimately server performance). For example, using a RAID controller with a RAID 10 configuration might provide better performance than a RAID 5 configuration. Enabling a writeback cache on the controller will almost certainly dramatically improve performance. Networking configurations (MTU settings for example) can be benchmarked.

Profiling

Profiling gathers information that can be later compared to determine if there were any changes in behavior. Just as mysqld has a BENCHMARK() function that can benchmark based on one expression, there is a SHOW PROFILE statement that gives a description of the profile of a particular query. See the section on The SHOW extension in Chapter 4 for more details on how to use this command.

Another simple method of profiling is to use another SQL extension. The SHOW GLOBAL STATUS command displays approximately 300 status variables that MySQL keeps track of. Comparing SHOW GLOBAL STATUS output can be very time-consuming and tedious. There are open source third-party tools that do some analysis for you; we will discuss mysqltuner, mysqlreport and mk-query-profiler. In addition, the MySQL Enterprise Monitor, covered in Chapter 19, can help assess the overall health of mysqld.

SHOW GLOBAL STATUS

The server status variables in SHOW GLOBAL STATUS output are system counters. Their values are the current values of the system counter for each variable. For more information about SHOW GLOBAL STATUS, see Chapter 4.

TIP   The best place to find a list of all the status variables and whether they are on a GLOBAL or SESSION level is at the official MySQL manual page at: http://dev.mysql.com/doc/refman/6.0/en/server-status-variables.html.

For some status variables, such as `Slave_running`, the current output is enough information — either the slave is running or it is not. The `Threads_connected` status variable shows how many threads are currently connected. However, for many status variables, there is more to be done than simply looking at the value of each variable. For example, the `Slow_queries` status variable provides a count of how many slow queries the system has logged:

```
mysql> SHOW GLOBAL STATUS LIKE 'Slow_queries';
+---------------+-------+
| Variable_name | Value |
+---------------+-------+
| Slow_queries  | 1073  |
+---------------+-------+
1 row in set (0.00 sec)
```

Is it good or bad that there have been 1073 slow queries? You should investigate and optimize all the slow queries that are logged — see the `mysqldumpslow` and `mysqlsla` tools discussed later in this chapter for how to find slow queries, and see Chapter 18 for how to analyze queries.

When determining the health of a system, the important data is how frequently slow queries are happening. The `Uptime` status variable shows how long, in seconds, that particular `mysqld` has been running:

```
mysql> SHOW GLOBAL STATUS WHERE Variable_name='Slow_queries'
    -> OR Variable_name='uptime';
+---------------+-------+
| Variable_name | Value |
+---------------+-------+
| Slow_queries  | 1073  |
| Uptime        | 10906 |
+---------------+-------+
2 rows in set (0.08 sec)
```

The server has been up for 10906 seconds (or roughly seven and a half days);

The rate of slow queries is an average of about one slow query every 10 seconds. Ideally, you would like to be able to see the rate of change over time. For example, the slow query information you saw earlier would indicate a problem in a database that usually has one slow query every hour; the database administrator would be celebrated in a database that usually has one slow query every second. Establishing a baseline for a system's status and comparing over time will make patterns evident and shows where problems may lurk.

One way to establish a baseline is to compare the status variables over a short period of time. To get an average of status variables in an hour, you can compare the output of SHOW GLOBAL STATUS taken from a server at 1 pm to the output of SHOW GLOBAL STATUS taken from the same server at 2 pm. Instead of comparing variables to `Uptime`, variables are compared to each other. We may find that from 1–2 PM, there are only two slow queries, but from 2-3 PM, there are ten slow queries.

With about 300 status variables, manual analysis is tedious. However, no automated tool can take into consideration the specifics of your system, and what is acceptable to your users. There is a tradeoff to using automated tools, which may be acceptable. Even if you use an automated tool or tools, knowing how to use SHOW GLOBAL STATUS is a key skill for a database administrator working with mysqld.

mysqltuner

The open source program mysqltuner is a Perl script that is a part of the default package distribution for some operating systems. If it is not part of your operating system, you can download it at www.mysqltuner.com. It can be run with no options — by default, mysqltuner.pl connects to mysqld on localhost port 3306, and prompts for a username and password:

```
shell>  ./mysqltuner.pl

 >>  MySQLTuner 0.9.9 - Major Hayden <major@mhtx.net>
 >>  Bug reports, feature requests, and downloads at http://
mysqltuner.com/
 >>  Run with '--help' for additional options and output
filtering
Please enter your MySQL administrative login: username
Please enter your MySQL administrative password:
```

You do not need SUPER privileges in order to run the script. After entering your password, mysqltuner analyzes mysqld and outputs four sections:

- General Statistics
- Storage Engine Statistics
- Performance Metrics
- Recommendations

Each line of information is prefixed with a code that indicates whether the check is positive, neutral, or negative:

- Check neutral or skipped [--]
- Check OK [OK]
- Warning, check not OK [!!]

Before the first section, mysqltuner will output a problem if the password provided is blank:

```
[!!] Successfully authenticated with no password - SECURITY RISK!
```

General Statistics

There are three checks in the General Statistics section. The first is whether or not there is a new version of mysqltuner. This is skipped by default, but can be turned on by giving the --checkversion flag to mysqltuner. The second check determines which version of mysqld you are running, and whether or not that version is supported by mysqld. If you are running a version that has been marked as *end of life* by Sun Microsystems, a warning will be issued. The final check is whether or not the operating system is 64 bit.

```
-------- General Statistics ---------------------------------------
[--] Skipped version check for MySQLTuner script
[!!] Currently running unsupported MySQL version 6.0.6-alpha-
community-log
[OK] Operating on 64-bit architecture
```

If the system is running a 32-bit architecture with 2 GB of RAM or less, mysqltuner notes:

```
[OK]  Operating on 32-bit architecture with less than 2GB RAM
```

Otherwise, you get a warning:

```
[!!] Switch to 64-bit OS - MySQL cannot currenty use all of your RAM
```

Storage engine statistics

This section analyzes the sizes and storage engines of tables, except for tables in the mysql and information_schema databases. At the time of this writing, mysqltuner does not give any details about the Falcon or Maria storage engines. mysqltuner uses SHOW TABLE STATUS in pre-5.0 database servers to determine the size of each table and whether or not the table is fragmented. With MySQL 5.0 and above, it uses the information_schema database to gather the same information. It prints out a list of the total data stored in each table type and ends with a count of fragmented tables.

```
-------- Storage Engine Statistics ----------------------------
[--] Status: +Archive -BDB -Federated +InnoDB -ISAM -NDBCluster
[--] Data in MyISAM tables: 6G (Tables: 128)
[--] Data in InnoDB tables: 21G (Tables: 44)
[--] Data in MEMORY tables: 0B (Tables: 1)
[!!] Total fragmented tables: 7
```

It is important to note that the size of Data_length in SHOW TABLE STATUS or the information_schema database is not always accurate. For storage engines that estimate the size of their data the size shown will be an approximation. Also, the size of indexes is not taken into consideration, so this information cannot be used to figure out how much space the database is using.

The Data_free field of either SHOW TABLE STATUS or the information schema. The TABLES database is used to determine whether a table is fragmented or not. If Data_free is greater than zero, mysqltuner considers the table fragmented. This may lead to false warnings when using global InnoDB data files (i.e., not using innodb_file_per_table), as Data_free shows the amount of data left in the global InnoDB data files.

If a storage engine is enabled, but there are no tables that are defined with that storage engine, mysqltuner will issue a warning such as:

```
[!!] InnoDB is enabled but isn't being used
```

A false positive may arise if you run mysqltuner with a user that cannot see all the tables within mysqld, as the storage engine may actually be in use by a table that the user does not have permissions to see.

Performance Metrics

The Performance Metrics section uses the output from SHOW GLOBAL STATUS and performs the tedious calculations you would ordinarily do by hand. The first line gives a general overview of mysqld:

```
-------- Performance Metrics ------------------------------------
Up for:116d 21h 10m 14s (338M q[33.501 qps],39M conn,TX:174B,RX: 28B)
```

The values in the first line are simply the status variables from SHOW GLOBAL STATUS with some formatting for better readability, as shown in Table 17-10:

TABLE 17-10

Relationships between Variables in Performance Metrics and SHOW GLOBAL STATUS

Performance Metrics Variable	Status Variable from SHOW GLOBAL STATUS
Up for	Uptime
q	Questions
qps	qps (queries per second)
conn	Connections
TX	Bytes Sent
RX	Bytes Received

The next line gives the percentage of reads and writes, using the Com_select status variable as the number of reads, and the sum of the Com_delete, Com_insert, Com_update, Com_replace status variables as the writes. The percentage given is a percentage of the total reads and writes (all five Com variables added together) and does not include administrative commands like SHOW. Because of this, these percentages may be misleading.

```
[--] Reads / Writes: 32% / 68%
```

The next two lines relate to memory usage:

```
[--] Total buffers: 1.9G global + 12.2M per thread (300 max threads)
[!!] Maximum possible memory usage: 5.5G (91% of installed RAM)
```

Information for these lines comes from the system variables that are the output of SHOW GLOBAL VARIABLES.

The global buffer formula that mysqltuner uses is:

```
key_buffer_size + max_tmp_table_size + innodb_buffer_pool_size +
innodb_additional_mem_pool_size + innodb_log_buffer_size +
query_cache_size
```

The per thread buffer formula that mysqltuner uses is:

```
read_buffer_size + read_rnd_buffer_size + sort_buffer_size +
thread_stack + join_buffer_size
```

The max_threads comes from the system variable max_connections.

The Maximum possible memory usage is calculated by:

```
global + max_connections * (per thread)
```

The global and per thread buffers in mysqltuner are not a complete picture of how much memory is allocated for global use; they do not take into account any of the memory settings for the BDB, Falcon, and Maria storage engines. Thus, the Maximum possible memory usage is inaccurate.

The Maximum possible memory usage in our example is a large percentage of available memory. In some cases, it may exceed the memory available. This may or may not be a problem; in many cases, there will not be max_connections number of connections that are all using the maximum per thread memory allocation. In fact, there may be a few queries that require high values for some of the per thread memory variables. The max_connections variable is useful to reduce the number of connections, so that mysqld does not crash by trying to allocate more memory than is available. However, there are many cases in which both a high number of max_connections and a high number of per thread memory variables are needed. This is one of the reasons that automated tuning is not always useful.

The values in the rest of the Performance Metrics section are simple calculations involving system and status variables from SHOW GLOBAL VARIABLES and SHOW GLOBAL STATUS:

```
[OK] Slow queries: 0% (4K/338M)
[OK] Highest usage of available connections: 34% (102/300)
[OK] Key buffer size / total MyISAM indexes: 350.0M/13.7G
[OK] Key buffer hit rate: 97.2% (368M cached / 10M reads)
[!!] Query cache efficiency: 14.1% (12M cached / 90M selects)
[!!] Query cache prunes per day: 246
[OK] Sorts requiring temporary tables: 8% (1M temp sorts / 19M sorts)
[OK] Temporary tables created on disk: 12% (162K on disk / 1M total)
[OK] Thread cache hit rate: 99% (102 created / 39M connections)
[OK] Table cache hit rate: 53% (358 open / 675 opened)
```

```
[OK] Open file limit used: 1% (310/25K)
[OK] Table locks acquired immediately: 100% (236M immediate /
236M locks)
[!!] InnoDB data size / buffer pool: 21.3G/1.5G

Recommendations



-------- Recommendations -----------------------------------------
General recommendations:
    Run OPTIMIZE TABLE to defragment tables for better performance
Variables to adjust:
  *** MySQL's maximum memory usage exceeds your installed memory ***
  *** Add more RAM before increasing any MySQL buffer variables  ***
    query_cache_limit (> 2M, or use smaller result sets)
    query_cache_size (> 64M)
    innodb_buffer_pool_size (>= 21G)



    Performance and Reporting Options
    --skipsize          Don't enumerate tables and their types/sizes
    --checkversion      Check for updates to MySQLTuner
    --forcemem <size>   Amount of RAM installed in megabytes
    --forceswap <size>  Amount of swap memory configured in MB

    Output Options:
        --nogood        Remove OK responses
        --nobad         Remove negative/suggestion responses
        --noinfo        Remove informational responses
        --nocolor       Don't print output in color
```

As you can see, the information provided by mysqltuner can be quite valuable. However, any recommendations from this (or other) profiling programs should be taken with some caution. It is very easy to make changes just based on the recommendations of mysqltuner, without understanding what is really happening, and have a system that does not perform as optimally as possible.

mysqlreport

The mysqlreport program is similar in scope to mysqltuner. Like mysqltuner it is a Perl program that uses the SHOW STATUS command to gather an overall picture of a server's health. Unlike mysqltuner, the mysqlreport program does not provide any recommendations. However, it does provide a more in-depth analysis of your system that you can use to determine where changes need to be made. The program is available at http://hackmysql.com/mysqlreport.

Running the program is not difficult:

```
shell> ./mysqlreport --user qa_user --password
```

After you are prompted for the password, the report is generated. While this is the simplest way to run mysqlreport, there are a number of options used for connecting to mysqld and managing the mysqlreport program run. Table 17-11 lists the available options.

TABLE 17-11

Available Options For mysqlreport

Option	Description
--user username	Specifies the username used by mysqlreport to for connection to mysqld.
--password password	Specifies the password used by mysqlreport to connect to mysqld.
--host address	Specifies an address of mysqld to connect and gather data from.
--port tcpip_port	The TCP/IP port used for connection to mysqld.
--socket socket_file_location	Specifies the socket file used for local connections on a Unix-based server.
--infile file_name	Reads status information from file_name instead of connecting to a server and running SHOW STATUS and SHOW VARIABLES commands.
--outfile file_name	Writes report to both the file named file_name and the screen.
--email email_address	On Unix-based systems emails report to email_address.
--flush-status	After gathering the current values issues a FLUSH STATUS command.
--relative value	By default, mysqlreport generates a report based on the status of the server since it began operation. The --relative option can be used to generate reports that are based on the values from previous reports. If value is an integer the reports are generated live from mysqld every num seconds. The option value can also be a list of input files (generated by running mysqlreport with the --report-count option), and the relative report is generated from these input files in the order specified.
--report-count num	Collects num number of reports for use as input files for the --relative option.
--detach	Runs the mysqlreport program in the background.
--help	Prints help information and exits.
--debug	Prints debugging information and exits.

As with `mysqltuner`, the `mysqlreport` program generates a report with sections devoted to various aspects of `mysqld` being analyzed. The header section provides some general information about what version of MySQL is running, how long the server has been running and the time the report was generated.

```
shell> ./mysqlreport --user qa_user --password
Password for database user qa_user:
MySQL 5.0.45-Debian_1ub  uptime 27 22:47:2        Tue Sep 23
23:56:20 2008
```

The next section is the Key section and covers information about the key buffer usage. The key buffer is the buffer used to store MyISAM indexes.

```
__ Key _____
Buffer used     13.08M of  16.00M  %Used:  81.76
   Current      16.00M              %Usage: 100.00
Write hit       96.88%
Read hit        99.22%
```

The first line of the Key section should be ignored. Buffer used is suppose to show the highest ever level of buffer usage. However, it is very often inaccurate. In this example, it shows a maximum of 13.08 megabytes used. The Current line shows the buffer amount currently being utilized. In this case, the entire 16 MB is being utilized.

The `Write hit` value can vary quite a lot, depending on your overall server usage. If `mysqld` has a lot of write activity that primarily executes `INSERT` and `UPDATE` statements, then `Write hit` may be very low. If your server has a high percentage of `SELECT` statement execution, then the key `Write hit` may be close to 100 percent. However, a negative key `Write hit` indicates that MySQL is writing keys to hard disk more frequently than the key buffer in RAM. This is going to be slow.

The `Read hit` value shows the ratio of key reads from hard disk to key reads from memory. This percentage should be very high — near 100 percent. Having your MyISAM table indexes stored in the key buffer is going to provide for much faster updating than having the indexes stored on disk. If this value is not very close to 100 percent, you should see a performance increase by allocating more memory to the key buffer.

The next section, Questions, includes information about both SQL queries being executed and the MySQL protocol communications:

```
__ Questions _____
Total        14.20M      5.9/s
   DMS        8.20M      3.4/s  %Total:  57.73
   Com_       5.68M      2.4/s           40.02
   COM_QUIT   346.13k    0.1/s            2.44
  -Unknown    340.18k    0.1/s            2.39
   QC Hits    313.62k    0.1/s            2.21
Slow 10 s        492    0.0/s            0.00  %DMS: 0.01  Log:  ON
```

The Total line shows how many total questions were processed by the server. It is simply a summation of the two fields of data. While it is somewhat disingenuous, you can say that the second field of the Total line is your server's query per second average. In the case of the server being profiled, it doesn't execute very many queries per second.

After the Total line, all of the lines following are sorted based upon frequency. In the case of the server being profiled, the DMS statements were the majority of the total questions executed by the server. The DMS line shows statistics about Data Manipulation Statements (SELECT, INSERT, UPDATE, and DELETE queries). The majority of the server processing should be DML statements, and if it is not, it probably indicates a problem. The Com_ line displays the server communication commands, and the QC Hits line shows how many query result sets were served from the query cache. In the case of the profile server, it is not a significant percentage (2.21%). There is a significant amount of data about the query cache later in the report, so it will be examined more closely at that point. The Unknown line should be fairly small. Unknown questions are the questions that MySQL handles and increments the total questions counter but does not have a separate status value to increment. The Slow line shows how many queries took longer than the server variable long_query_time to return a result. With the server being profiled the long_query_time is 10 s (seconds).

In addition to these lines showing general information, the Questions section provides a separate subsection for each line. With the server being profiled for the example, the most activity occurred with data manipulation statements, so it is the first subsection.

```
DMS              8.20M      3.4/s          57.73
    INSERT       7.17M      3.0/s          50.51         87.49
    UPDATE     752.84k      0.3/s           5.30          9.18
    DELETE     219.20k      0.1/s           1.54          2.67
    SELECT      53.88k      0.0/s           0.38          0.66
    REPLACE          0        0/s           0.00          0.00
```

This subsection can tell you at a glance how read or write heavy the application is. In this case, it is almost entirely writes (99.34%). This is *very* unusual. This also explains why the earlier percentage for queries served out of the query cache is so low.

For the profiled server, the next subsection is the Com_ subsection:

```
Com_              5.68M      2.4/s          40.02
    begin         3.86M      1.6/s          27.16
    show_status 517.09k      0.2/s           3.64
    set_option  352.17k      0.1/s           2.48
```

The Com_ subsection shows the values for the most used Com_ commands on the profiled server. If you have some very unusual activity, it might show up here.

```
__ SELECT and Sort _____
Scan           758.38k      0.3/s  %SELECT: 1407.6
Range              559      0.0/s              1.04
```

```
Full join            4     0.0/s          0.01
Range check          0      0/s           0.00
Full rng join        0      0/s           0.00
Sort scan          182     0.0/s
Sort range           6     0.0/s
Sort mrg pass      152     0.0/s
```

The SELECT and Sort subsection provides information about the Select_status values. These values can help you pinpoint issues with selects. For example, the Scan line indicates how full table scans were performed. This could indicate that indexes might be needed to use these tables effectively. A Full join is when full table scans are performed on tables being joined in a multi-table queries. Both of these values should be as low as possible.

The other values tend not to impact performance. If you want more information about them, complete documentation is available online at http://hackmysql.com.

Notice that the Scan line has a percentage value of 1407.6. Since the total for all these values should add up to 100 percent, this is clearly incorrect. Be careful when going through this report, as there are occasional glitches.

```
__ Query Cache _____
Memory usage  361.34k of  32.00M  %Used:     1.10
Block Fragmnt  11.36%
Hits           313.62k    0.1/s
Inserts         42.09k    0.0/s
Insrt:Prune  42.09k:1     0.0/s
Hit:Insert      7.45:1
```

As stated earlier, this server is very heavy on writes. Because of this the query cache is not used very much. The Memory usage line shows the amount of memory actually being used out of the total memory allocated to the Query Cache. In this case, it is 361.34k out of 32 MB. The Block Fragment percentage should be somewhere between 10 and 20 percent. It indicates the amount of fragmentation in the query cache. The Hits line indicates the number of query result data sets actually served from the query cache. This should be as high as possible. For additional details one query cache optimization, see Chapter 12.

The next two lines are ratios that indicate the general effectiveness of your query cache. The first line, Insert:Prune, is the ratio of inserts (into the query cache) to prunes. A *prune* is when a query is removed from the query cache. In this case, the ratio is very heavy on inserts because prunes are not really happening. If the amount of prunes is very large, it might be beneficial to increase the size of the query cache. The Hit:Insert ratio shows the number of hits (results) returned from the query cache versus the number of inserts into the query cache. The higher this ratio is the better your server performance. For additional details on query cache optimization, see Chapter 12.

```
__ Table Locks _____
Waited             6     0.0/s  %Total:    0.00
Immediate       8.33M    3.4/s
```

The Table Locks subsection shows how often the database had to wait to obtain a lock on a table (Waited) and how often the lock was granted immediately (Immediate). If the database had to wait for table locks very often, this indicates there often a problem with MyISAM contention.

```
__ Tables _____
Open                    467 of 1024      %Cache:   45.61
Opened          13.23k          0.0/s
```

The Tables subsection Open line indicates the number of tables that were open when the report was ran, the total number of open tables allowed in the table cache, and the percentage of table cache used. The Opened line indicates the total number of tables opened since mysqld started up and the average number opened per second.

If the number of open tables is equal to the table cache, it could possibly indicate a problem. You might want to increase the size of the table cache.

```
__ Connections _____
Max used                 19 of  500     %Max:    3.80
Total           346.36k          0.1/s
```

The connections subsection is straightforward. The Max used line indicates the maximum number of connections every used out of the total possible. If the Max used is approaching the maximum number you might need to raise the max_connections variable. The Total line indicates the total number of connections and the average number being made per second.

```
__ Created Temp _____
Disk table      159.56k          0.1/s
Table           745.02k          0.3/s    Size: 128.0M
File                 45          0.0/s
```

The Created Temp subsection is very important. The Disk table line shows the total number of temporary tables that were created on disk. When temporary tables are created on disk instead of remaining in memory, it is a big performance hit. It happens because some of the temporary tables created in memory exceed the maximum size configured with the max_tmp_tables variable. If you have a significant quantity of these, it would be best to increase the size of max_tmp_tables. Assuming, of course, that your server has enough RAM to increase this value. The next line shows the number of temporary tables created in memory, the average per second, and the maximum allowable size before they are converted to disk-based temporary tables.

```
__ Threads _____
Running          1 of    2
Cached           7 of    8      %Hit:  99.99
Created         37          0.0/s
Slow             0           0/s
```

The Threads subsection details information about the threads used for each connection to the server. The most important line in this subsection is Cached. It shows the number of threads that are stored in the thread cache ready for reuse. This keeps the server from having to create a new thread for a new connection. The cache hit rate of 99.99 percent is excellent. If it is not very high, it indicates that the server has to continually create and destroy new threads, which can impact performance. If this is the case, you should probably increase the size of the thread cache.

```
__ Aborted _____
Clients             451      0.0/s
Connects             50      0.0/s
```

The Aborted subsection show statistics about connections to the server that have been dropped. If this number is very high in relation to the amount of uptime, it can indicated a problem. The Clients line shows connections that are closed because of three possibilities:

- The client program did not call mysql_close() before exiting.
- The client has been sleeping more seconds than the values of either of the two system variables wait_timeout or interactive_time.
- The client program ended in the middle of a data transfer.

The Connects line is incremented when one of four things happens:

- The client does not the required privileges to connect to the database.
- The client used an incorrect password.
- A connection packed is malformed or doesn't contain the proper information.
- It takes the server more than connect_timeout seconds to get a connection packet form the client.

```
__ Bytes _____
Sent          121.68G      50.4k/s
Received        8.78G       3.6k/s
```

The Bytes subsection shows the number of bytes sent from and received by the server:

```
__ InnoDB Buffer Pool _____
Usage          511.98M of 512.00M   %Used: 100.00
Read hit        99.94%
Pages
  Free               1            %Total:    0.00
  Data          32.28k                      98.51 %Drty:    0.03
  Misc             486                       1.48
  Latched            0                       0.00
Reads         501.12M     207.5/s
  From file    320.24k       0.1/s
```

```
   Ahead Rnd        12536      0.0/s
   Ahead Sql         3729      0.0/s
   Writes         104.87M     43.4/s
   Flushes          8.93M      3.7/s
   Wait Free            0        0/s
```

The InnoDB Buffer Pool section details information about the InnoDB buffer pool. The Usage line shows you the total amount of RAM dedicated to the InnoDB buffer pool and how much of it is actually being used. The Read hit line indicates the percentage of buffer pool page hits from RAM instead of the much slower hard disks. Ideally, this percentage should be very near 100 percent.

The Pages subsection provides a breakdown of how the buffer pool pages are being used. The Free pages are buffer pages that not allocated to any data at the time mysqlreport is run. The Data pages are the buffer pages that currently contain data. The %Drty statistic shows the quantity of the Data pages that have been modified in RAM but whose changes have not yet been flushed to disk. The Misc pages are pages in the buffer allocated for administrative overhead. Latched pages are pages that cannot be flushed or removed from the buffer pool because they are being written to or read from at the time the report is run.

The Reads subsection shows the read activity of the buffer pool. The Reads line shows the total read activity both in number of reads and the average amount of reads per second. The From file line shows the number of reads of InnoDB pages that were served from hard disk instead of memory. A high number here is an indication of poor performance. Reads from memory are always going to be faster than reads from storage. The two Ahead lines detail the number of read ahead requests that are random (Rnd) or Sequential (Sql). These sequential read-ahead reads indicate full table scans, which are a performance issue.

The Write lines describe the total number and average rate of writes to the buffer pool. This system is quite busy with write activity, and it is shown here. The Flushes line indicates the total and per second average number of flushes (writing data changes from the buffer pool to disk). The Wait Free line indicates the number of times and the average that when the buffer pool attempts to create a new page and there are no clean pages available. When this happens, it is necessary to wait for the dirty pages to be flushed. This number should be low when compared to the total read numbers.

```
 __ InnoDB Lock _____
Waits                0          0/s
Current              0
Time acquiring
    Total            0 ms
    Average          0 ms
    Max              0 ms
```

The InnoDB Lock subsection details information about the row-level locks for InnoDB tables. Ideally, these statistics will be at or near zero. The Waits line shows the total and average number of times the server had to wait for the release of a lock on an InnoDB row. The Current line shows the number of locks the server is waiting for at the time the report is run. The Time acquiring section shows the total, average, and maximum amount of time (in milliseconds) the server waited for rows locks.

```
__ InnoDB Data, Pages, Rows _____
Data
  Reads        482.10k      0.2/s
  Writes        16.53M      6.8/s
  fsync          9.17M      3.8/s
  Pending
    Reads            0
    Writes           0
    fsync            0

Pages
  Created       85.23k      0.0/s
  Read         947.16k      0.4/s
  Written        8.93M      3.7/s

Rows
  Deleted      609.09k      0.3/s
  Inserted       5.86M      2.4/s
  Read         529.57M    219.3/s
  Updated       10.08M      4.2/s
```

The InnoDB Data, Pages, Rows subsection provides very general information about InnoDB activity. It can be used as a quick overview before moving to the appropriate subsection for more detailed information.

Overall the mysqlreport program provides very good information about the activity of your server. You can use it to provide a profile of your operational servers and see potential trouble spots or places for improvement.

mk-query-profiler

The mk-query-profiler script reads a file containing SQL statements or shell commands, executes them, and performs analysis of the output of SHOW STATUS. At the end of program execution, it displays statistics about query performance.

If the batch file contains multiple queries, it is necessary to separate the queries by blank lines. If the queries are not separated, then query execution on mysqld will fail because mk-query-profiler can not split the individual queries apart. Table 17-12 lists the options available for mk-query-profiler.

TABLE 17-12

mk-query-profiler Options

Option	Description
--allowcache or -a	Uses the MySQL query cache during query execution. Defaults to no caching.
--askpass	Will ask for a password when connecting to mysqld.
--[no]calibrate or -c	The script attempts to compensate for the SHOW STATUS query execution. Defaults to yes.
--charset or -A	Determines the default character set.
--database or -D	Determines the database used for query execution.
--defaults-file or -F	The script read mysql options from the specified files, which must have an absolute pathname.
--external or -e	The script calibrates and then pauses while you run an external program. When your external program is finished, you must press the Enter key again to resume execution.
--port or -P	TCP/IP port used for connection.
--socket or -S	Socket file used for connection.
--flush or -f	Performs FLUSH TABLES before profiling begins. If you specify --flush twice while also specifying a batch file of queries, FLUSH TABLES will be performed after each query.
--help	Displays help information and exits.
--host or -h	Specifies the hostname of mysqld used for query execution.
--[no]innodb or -i	Displays InnoDB table information. Defaults to yes.
--only or -n	Only shows statistics for a list of queries or commands (separated by commas).
--password or -p	The password used for connection to mysqld.
--port or -P	The TCP/IP port used for connections to mysqld.
--separate or -s	The script will print separate statistics for each query.
--session	The script uses SHOW SESSION STATUS and SHOW SESSION VARIABLES.
--setvars	Used to set MySQL variables. You can specify any variable you want configured before query execution begins.
--socket or -S	Determines the Unix socket file used for a local connection.

continued

TABLE 17-12 *(continued)*	
Option	**Description**
--tab or -t	Output is displayed with tab-separated values.
--user or -u	Username that is used for connection to mysqld.
--verbose or -v	Determines the verbosity of the output. If you specify multiple times the output is more detailed.
--verify or -r	Verifies that nothing else is accessing mysqld.
--version	Outputs version information and exits.

Here is an example run of mk-query-profiler with very simple queries:

```
shell> mk-query-profiler --askpass --user=qa_user --database=sbtest
--socket=/var/run/mysqld/mysqld.sock /home/bmurphy/queries.sql
Enter password:


+------------------------------------------------------------+
|                      3 (0.0008 sec)                        |
+------------------------------------------------------------+


__ Overall stats _____ Value _____
    Total elapsed time                     6.423
    Questions                              3
      COMMIT                               0
      DELETE                               0
      DELETE MULTI                         0
      INSERT                               0
      INSERT SELECT                        0
      REPLACE                              0
      REPLACE SELECT                       0
      SELECT                               3
      UPDATE                               0
      UPDATE MULTI                         0
    Data into server                       110
    Data out of server                     64889279
    Optimizer cost                         212982.199

__ Table and index accesses _____ Value _____
    Table locks acquired                   3
    Table scans                            1
      Join                                 0
    Index range scans                      0
      Join without check                   0
      Join with check                      0
    Rows sorted                            0
```

Range sorts	0
Merge passes	0
Table scans	0
Potential filesorts	0

You can see that mk-query-profiler can return a great deal of information about your queries. While these queries were very simple and did not return much data, it could be useful to determine what some of your application's potential "trouble queries" are; use mk-query-profiler to analyze them.

The maatkit toolkit (which includes the mk-query-profiler) is available at www.maatkit.org.

mysqldumpslow

When profiling a server to determine bottlenecks, the slow query log provides a very useful way to see which queries are causing problems and could possibly be optimized to improve query execution time. While there are a modest number of programs available on the Internet to help with analyzing the slow query log, a script called mysqldumpslow, which can be used for this analysis, is included in MySQL Server. Table 17-13 lists the options for mysqldumpslow.

TABLE 17-13

mysqldumpslow Options

Option	Description
-a	Does not abstract all numbers to 'N' and strings to 'S'.
-d or --debug	Runs in debug mode.
-g STRING	Performs a grep of the dump only including statements with string STRING.
-h HOSTNAME	Hostname of database server. This is used to determine the name of the slow query log (hostname-slow.log format).
--help	Displays help message and exits.
-i NAME	Specifies the server instance name.
-l	Includes lock time in the total query time.
-n NUM	Abstracts all numbers in queries with at least NUM digits.
-r	Reverses the sort order listing longest query run last instead of first.
-s ORDER	Determines the sort order of the queries.
-t NUM	Displays the top NUM queries.
-v or --verbose	Raises the verbosity level of output.

With the -s (sort order) option there six possible values: t, at, l, r, c, and s.

- The t value sorts the query output by total execution time. Total execution time is the average query execution time × the number of times the query was executed.

- The at value sorts the query output by the average query execution time. It is the default sorting method.

- The l value sorts the query output by lock time.

- The al value sorts the query output by lock time average.

- The r value sorts the query output by total rows.

- The ar value sorts the query output by average rows sent.

- The c value sorts the query output by count.

Here is an example of performing the sort by total execution time of the top five queries:

```
$ mysqldumpslow -s t -t 5 /mnt/mysql/logs/slowquery.log

Reading mysql slow query log from /mnt/mysql/logs/slowquery.log
Count: 3324  Time=9.79s (32533s)  Lock=0.00s (0s)  Rows=1.0 (3324),
username@hostname
  SELECT count(*) AS count_all FROM table_one WHERE (sweepstake_id =
N and user_id is null)

Count: 1957  Time=11.26s (22028s)  Lock=0.00s (0s)  Rows=1.0 (1955),
username@hostname
  SELECT * FROM table_one WHERE (sweepstake_id = N and user_id is
null)  LIMIT N

Count: 279  Time=30.27s (8446s)  Lock=0.00s (0s)  Rows=0.6 (163),
username@hostname
  SELECT * FROM table_two WHERE (table_two.`id` = N)  FOR UPDATE

Count: 132  Time=43.59s (5754s)  Lock=0.00s (0s)  Rows=0.2 (23),
username@hostname
  SELECT * FROM table_one WHERE (table_one.`id` = N)  FOR UPDATE

Count: 901  Time=5.41s (4872s)  Lock=0.02s (14s)  Rows=1.0 (897),
username@hostname
  SELECT * FROM table_three WHERE (table_three.`value`='S')  LIMIT N
```

Knowing that these five queries spent more time executing (total execution time) than all the other queries, you can concentrate your time on optimizing these queries. Query optimization is covered in detail in Chapter 18.

Capacity Planning

Capacity planning, as it relates to information technology, is the process of determining the computing infrastructure requirements needed by a company to meet changing demands for products or services. The ultimate goal of benchmarking and profiling is to measure the capacity of a server. If you know through benchmarking that a server can operate at a peak capacity of X performance units and you know through profiling that a production server is operating at a level of Y performance units, then you know that you have a current excess capacity level of $X - Y$ performance units. When the production server is operating at a level of X production units, then you have no more room for growth.

If you have been profiling production servers over a period of time, you can develop trending patterns and, through simple extrapolation, know how much time you have before a production server reaches full capacity. In many cases, this is all the capacity planning needed (at least when it comes to database servers!). If you know that your current servers will reach capacity in 9 to 12 months, it will be much easier to plan for increased capacity by adding more servers or upgrading the current servers, rather than being surprised when your servers suddenly *bogs down* and performs extremely poorly because it is overloaded.

Unfortunately, many database administrators feel that they are too busy to either measure the performance of servers or do any type of capacity planning. In the end, this costs you more time and effort when you have to reacting to a situation where your servers reach capacity instead of planning ahead.

Summary

The skills to perform benchmarking and profiling on database servers are some of the skills that differentiate beginner database administrators from their more experienced colleagues. It is invaluable to be able to perform both benchmarking and profiling and use the data gathered to have optimally running database servers. This saves organizations money and provides for a better experience for the end users of the application who rely on the database servers.

In this chapter, we covered the following topics:

- Benchmarking `mysqld`
- `mysqlslap`
- MyBench
- SysBench

- Profiling `mysqld`
  - `mysqltuner`
  - `mysqlreport`
  - `mk-query-profiler`
  - `mysqldumpslow`
- Capacity planning for your organization

Part IV

Extending Your Skills

Chapter 18

Query Analysis and Index Tuning

"The database is slow!"

A DBA will hear this over and over during his or her career. Although there are times when performance can be tuned best by changing server parameters, most of the time database slowness, it is because the:

- The query cache is not being utilized properly (see Chapter 12 for troubleshooting).

- The query contains subqueries (MySQL Server 5.1) or unoptimized subqueries (MySQL Server 6.0). See the companion website at www.wiley.com/go/mysqladminbible for information about how to avoid subqueries.

- The table contains a large amount of unnecessary data.

- The table is fragmented.

- The schema was not designed for the queries being run.

- The queries being run do not take into consideration the schema design.

- Tables have no indexes that are appropriate for the query.

The reason for the disparity between the schema and queries may be that a developer is not familiar with MySQL, a DBA made assumptions about database usage, or the schema and queries were in sync at one point, but the data and/or application has grown.

A database schema is always a work in progress; as long as different queries are being written or the data inside a schema is changing, it is necessary to reanalyze both the schema and queries.

The larger issues of benchmarking and profiling are covered in Chapter 17, "Measuring Performance"; these techniques are used to identify the queries you need to analyze. Once you have identified queries causing problems, the information in this chapter will help you analyze and tune queries and, where appropriate, the database schema.

While there can be performance improvements done by tuning a server (Chapter 10), particularly to the needs of your storage engine (Chapter 11), overwhelmingly the reason that a query is slow is because of the data in the table, the schema, and the query itself.

Using EXPLAIN

The most widely used query analysis tool is EXPLAIN, an SQL extension. EXPLAIN select_statement shows information about how select_statement will likely be executed.

This information includes:

- How many tables are involved
- How the tables are joined
- How the data is looked up
- If there are subqueries
- If there are unions
- If DISTINCT is used
- If a WHERE clause is used
- If a temporary table is used
- Possible indexes used
- Actual indexes used
- Length of actual indexes used
- Approximate number of records returned
- If sorting requires an extra pass through the data

The information is known as the query execution plan, and is also referred to as the EXPLAIN plan.

EXPLAIN plan basics

EXPLAIN is used in front of a SELECT statement, and returns 10 fields:

```
mysql> EXPLAIN SELECT return_date
    -> FROM rental WHERE rental_id = 13534\G
```

```
*************************** 1. row ***************************
           id: 1
  select_type: SIMPLE
        table: rental
         type: const
possible_keys: PRIMARY
          key: PRIMARY
      key_len: 4
          ref: const
         rows: 1
        Extra:
1 row in set (0.00 sec)
```

The first field, id, is a sequential identifier, which is different for each row. Each row represents a physical table, subquery, temporary table, or derived table. In this simple example, there is only one table being queried, so there is only one row, with an id of 1. Tables are returned in join queue order, which means that a table in row 1 is used first, then joined to the table in row 2, and so on.

NOTE When EXPLAIN involves a view, returned rows correspond to the tables, subqueries, unions, and temporary tables used in the view definition. There is no row returned for the view itself.

The second field, select_type, is the type of SELECT represented by the row. The third field, table, shows the table alias that the row refers to. Often, the select_type will be SIMPLE, as it is in our example. When using EXPLAIN on a UNION query, the select_type of the first row is PRIMARY. Other rows have a select_type of UNION, and there is a final row representing the action of performing the UNION on the result sets of the previous queries. For example, here is an EXPLAIN plan for a simple UNION, getting the first names for all staff and customers:

```
mysql> EXPLAIN SELECT first_name FROM staff UNION SELECT first_name
FROM customer\G
*************************** 1. row ***************************
           id: 1
  select_type: PRIMARY
        table: staff
         type: ALL
possible_keys: NULL
          key: NULL
      key_len: NULL
          ref: NULL
         rows: 1
        Extra:
*************************** 2. row ***************************
           id: 2
  select_type: UNION
        table: customer
         type: ALL
```

```
      possible_keys: NULL
                key: NULL
            key_len: NULL
                ref: NULL
               rows: 541
              Extra:
*************************** 3. row ***************************
                 id: NULL
        select_type: UNION RESULT
              table: <union1,2>
               type: ALL
      possible_keys: NULL
                key: NULL
            key_len: NULL
                ref: NULL
               rows: NULL
              Extra:
3 rows in set (0.00 sec)
```

The first row returned refers to the staff table and shows a select_type of PRIMARY because it is used first. The second row returned refers to the customer table and shows a select_type of UNION because it is not the first table in the UNION. The final row represents the actual union of the result sets — the select_type is UNION_RESULT and the table alias (table) is <union1,2>.

There are other select_type values, which are used when subqueries are present. EXPLAIN statements involving subqueries are described in "Subqueries and EXPLAIN."

Note that table refers to the table alias. When a table is not explicitly aliased, the alias is the table name. For example, using a table alias in our simplest example:

```
mysql> EXPLAIN SELECT return_date FROM rental AS r WHERE rental_id =
13534\G
*************************** 1. row ***************************
                 id: 1
        select_type: SIMPLE
              table: r
               type: const
      possible_keys: PRIMARY
                key: PRIMARY
            key_len: 4
                ref: const
               rows: 1
              Extra:
1 row in set (0.09 sec)
```

Table aliases are sometimes necessary — when doing a self-join, for example. However, they are often used when they are not necessary, for convenience. When fields need to be qualified with their table names (i.e., rental.return_date), it is much shorter to alias the table and qualify the field name with the table alias (i.e., r.return_date). However, an EXPLAIN plan can be somewhat confusing when there are many rows that have a `table` value that is hard to decipher. For example, an `EXPLAIN` on the `sakila` view `sales_by_store` returns four rows:

```
mysql> EXPLAIN SELECT name, address FROM staff_list\G
*************************** 1. row ***************************
           id: 1
  select_type: SIMPLE
        table: s
         type: ALL
possible_keys: idx_fk_address_id
          key: NULL
      key_len: NULL
          ref: NULL
         rows: 1
        Extra:
*************************** 2. row ***************************
           id: 1
  select_type: SIMPLE
        table: a
         type: eq_ref
possible_keys: PRIMARY,idx_fk_city_id
          key: PRIMARY
      key_len: 2
          ref: sakila.s.address_id
         rows: 1
        Extra:
*************************** 3. row ***************************
           id: 1
  select_type: SIMPLE
        table: city
         type: eq_ref
possible_keys: PRIMARY,idx_fk_country_id
          key: PRIMARY
      key_len: 2
          ref: sakila.a.city_id
         rows: 1
        Extra:
*************************** 4. row ***************************
           id: 1
  select_type: SIMPLE
        table: country
         type: eq_ref
possible_keys: PRIMARY
          key: PRIMARY
      key_len: 2
          ref: sakila.city.country_id
         rows: 1
        Extra: Using index
4 rows in set (0.00 sec)
```

The last two rows refer to the city and country tables, but what do the first two rows refer to? You have to go back to the view definition to find out. The point of this example is to show that short table aliases can be confusing in an EXPLAIN. Keep that in mind if you consider setting a policy of always aliasing tables, or using software that always aliases tables in queries.

> **NOTE** The table field of the EXPLAIN plan is always the table alias. It is possible to alias a table as the name of another table. To see this for yourself, use the sakila database and compare the output for the following EXPLAIN statements:

```
EXPLAIN SELECT country,city
FROM country INNER JOIN city USING (country_id)
WHERE city='Brockton'\G
```

and

```
EXPLAIN SELECT country,city
FROM country AS city INNER JOIN city AS country USING (country_id)
WHERE city='Brockton'\G
```

It is a good idea to *always* verify which tables the table aliases refer to in an EXPLAIN plan.

A NULL value for table means that there is no table alias used for that row. An example of an EXPLAIN plan that does not use a table is:

```
mysql> EXPLAIN SELECT 1+2\G
*************************** 1. row ***************************
           id: 1
  select_type: SIMPLE
        table: NULL
         type: NULL
possible_keys: NULL
          key: NULL
      key_len: NULL
          ref: NULL
         rows: NULL
        Extra: No tables used
1 row in set (0.00 sec)
```

Another reason that an EXPLAIN plan may not use a table is if the optimizer notices that a condition will always be false. For example, the rental_id field of the rental table is an INT NOT NULL AUTO_INCREMENT. If we try to get the query execution plan for a rental_id that is not an INT, the query optimizer will realize that the WHERE condition will never be met:

```
mysql> EXPLAIN SELECT return_date FROM rental WHERE rental_id='a'\G
*************************** 1. row ***************************
           id: 1
  select_type: SIMPLE
```

```
        table: NULL
         type: NULL
possible_keys: NULL
          key: NULL
      key_len: NULL
          ref: NULL
         rows: NULL
        Extra: Impossible WHERE noticed after reading const tables
1 row in set (0.02 sec)
```

The query optimizer uses some parts of the schema definition to come up with query execution plans. The reason that the EXPLAIN plan comes back impossible is not because 1.5 is not an INT — to prove this, note that inventory_id is defined as a MEDIUMINT UNSIGNED NOT NULL, and see what happens when you run:

```
EXPLAIN SELECT return_date FROM rental WHERE inventory_id='a'\G
```

Other metadata used includes data ranges. For example, with the knowledge that:

- The data values for rental_id are between 1 and 16049, with no duplicates, and there are gaps in the sequence.

- There is no data for rental_id=321.

- The data values for inventory_id are between 1 and 4581, and there are duplicates and gaps in the sequence.

- There is no data for inventory_id=5.

The following queries should give you an interesting look at what types of metadata are taken into consideration when the query optimizer forms an execution plan:

```
EXPLAIN SELECT return_date FROM rental WHERE rental_id=0\G
EXPLAIN SELECT return_date FROM rental WHERE inventory_id=0\G

EXPLAIN SELECT return_date FROM rental WHERE inventory_id < 10\G
EXPLAIN SELECT return_date FROM rental WHERE inventory_id > 10\G

EXPLAIN SELECT return_date FROM rental WHERE rental_id=17000\G
EXPLAIN SELECT return_date FROM rental WHERE inventory_id=5000\G

EXPLAIN SELECT return_date FROM rental WHERE rental_id=321\G
EXPLAIN SELECT return_date FROM rental WHERE inventory_id=5\G

EXPLAIN SELECT return_date FROM rental WHERE rental_id=1.5\G
EXPLAIN SELECT return_date FROM rental WHERE inventory_id=1.5\G
-- Not getting what you expected?  See what is really happening
by running:
SELECT inventory_id, return_date FROM rental WHERE inventory_id=1.5;
```

Data access strategy

The data access strategy is in the `type` field of the `EXPLAIN` plan. Table 18-1 summarizes `type` values and their meanings. The table is organized in the order of the slowest data access strategy to the fastest.

Full table scan

Usually, the slowest data access method is to access each record in `table`. This happens when there is no suitable index that can make data retrieval faster. In the `EXPLAIN` plan, rows that use the slowest data access method have a `type` of `ALL`. When executing the query, MySQL will perform a full table scan:

```
mysql> EXPLAIN SELECT return_date FROM rental\G
*************************** 1. row ***************************
           id: 1
  select_type: SIMPLE
        table: rental
         type: ALL
possible_keys: NULL
          key: NULL
      key_len: NULL
          ref: NULL
         rows: 15616
        Extra:
1 row in set (0.00 sec)
```

MySQL will scan each record in the `rental` table to retrieve the `return_date`. A full table scan is done in this example because there is no `WHERE` clause, and no index on `return_date`. There are other reasons (besides this example's lack of `WHERE` clause and index on `return_date`) that cause there to be no suitable index that can make data retrieval faster. Adding an index on `return_date` would make this use a full index scan instead.

Full index scan

A data access method that is usually slightly faster is when the query execution plan scans each index record for a table. This is known as a full index scan, and is shown in an `EXPLAIN` plan by a `type` of `index`:

```
mysql> EXPLAIN SELECT rental_date FROM rental\G
*************************** 1. row ***************************
           id: 1
  select_type: SIMPLE
        table: rental
         type: index
possible_keys: NULL
          key: rental_date
      key_len: 13
          ref: NULL
         rows: 15616
        Extra: Using index
1 row in set (0.00 sec)
```

TABLE 18-1

Values for type

Value of type	Data Access Strategy	See Subheading
ALL	Full scan of the entire table structure.	Full table scan
index	Full scan of the entire index structure.	Full index scan
range	Partial scan of the index structure.	Partial index scan
index_subquery	Subquery using a nonunique index.	Subqueries and EXPLAIN
unique_subquery	Subquery using a unique index.	Subqueries and EXPLAIN
index_merge	More than one of the indexes are used to perform multiple scans.	Using more than one index
ref_or_null	More than one record may be looked up for each set of results from previous records in the EXPLAIN plan. These records may be null.	Looking up nonunique, nullable index values
fulltext	Use MySQL's FULLTEXT search	Data access strategy for fulltext searching
ref	More than one record may looked up for each record being joined, or for each set of results from previous records in the EXPLAIN plan.	Joining and looking up nonunique index values
eq_ref	Fewer than two records are looked up for each record being joined from previous records in the EXPLAIN plan.	Joins and unique index values
Const	Fewer than two records are looked up from a nonsystem table.	Looking up unique index values
System	Fewer than two records are looked up from a system table.	
NULL	The data is not looked up using a table.	

There is an index on `rental_date`, but the lack of WHERE clause means that every index record must be read and returned. In order for the data access method to be set as a full index scan, there must be a suitable index, and the query optimizer must decide whether using the index will make the data lookup faster.

Partial index scan

In a partial index scan, only a part of the index is scanned. A partial index scan has a `type` of `range`, because most often it is caused by a query searching for records in a certain range.

```
mysql> EXPLAIN SELECT rental_id
    -> FROM rental
    -> WHERE rental_date BETWEEN
    -> '2006-02-14 00:00:00' and '2006-02-14 23:59:59'\G
*************************** 1. row ***************************
           id: 1
  select_type: SIMPLE
        table: rental
         type: range
possible_keys: rental_date
          key: rental_date
      key_len: 8
          ref: NULL
         rows: 2614
        Extra: Using where; Using index
1 row in set (0.00 sec)
```

You could have guessed that the `type` of `range` would be returned as the data access method; you know that there is an index on `rental_date`, and BETWEEN indicates that you want to look up index values within a certain range. Operators other than BETWEEN that may indicate a partial index scan are: <, <=, > and >=.

There are several hundred values of `rental_id` that have a `rental_date` meeting the filter criteria:

```
ysql> SELECT COUNT(rental_id)
    -> FROM rental
    -> WHERE rental_date BETWEEN
    -> '2006-02-14 00:00:00' and '2006-02-14 23:59:59';
+------------------+
| COUNT(rental_id) |
+------------------+
|              182 |
+------------------+
1 row in set (0.00 sec)
```

Notice that the COUNT() returned from this query is actually 182 rows. The EXPLAIN output includes a `rows` field showing 2614. The row count in EXPLAIN is an estimate of how many rows the query optimizer will need to examine. This is based on table statistics and is an estimate only. See the subsection "Rows" later in this chapter.

The `rental` table has many thousands of records:

```
mysql> SELECT COUNT(rental_id) FROM rental;
+------------------+
| COUNT(rental_id) |
+------------------+
|            16044 |
+------------------+
1 row in set (0.01 sec)
```

Scanning part of an index is the fastest way to look for a few hundred values within many thousands of records. An `EXPLAIN` plan can return a row with the `type` of `range` only if a suitable index exists, and only if the query optimizer decides that using the index will make the data lookup faster.

Using more than one index

The `type` of `index_merge` is very special — it is the only data access strategy that can utilize more than one index. The query optimizer will decide the best plan involves using more than one index if the `WHERE` clause involves conditions that, when examined separately, have a data access strategy of either a partial or a full index scan. This means that the `WHERE` clause must involve more than one condition, that at least two of the conditions have suitable indexes, and that the index appropriate for one condition is not appropriate for another.

An example is the best way to show this data access strategy:

```
mysql> EXPLAIN SELECT customer_id
    -> FROM customer
    -> WHERE last_name LIKE "Hill%" OR customer_id<10\G
*************************** 1. row ***************************
           id: 1
  select_type: SIMPLE
        table: customer
         type: index_merge
possible_keys: PRIMARY,idx_last_name
          key: idx_last_name,PRIMARY
      key_len: 182,2
          ref: NULL
         rows: 10
        Extra: Using sort_union(idx_last_name,PRIMARY); Using where
1 row in set (0.00 sec)
```

The query that this `EXPLAIN` plan was generated for has conditions on the `last_name` and `customer_id` fields. The `customer` table has a nonunique index on `last_name` and a unique index on `customer_id`. Either the condition on `last_name` must be met, or the condition on `customer` must be met. There is not one ideal index to use — the ideal indexing strategy would be to use one index to find the records that meet the condition on `last_name`, and another index to find the records that meet the condition on `customer_id`, and then merge the two result sets.

The `last_name` index cannot help with the `customer_id` condition, and the `customer_id` index cannot help with the `last_name` index. This is important because, if there is one index appropriate for both conditions, the query optimizer will choose that index for its execution plan — even if the data access strategy is slower than `index_merge`.

An `EXPLAIN` plan will also show a data access strategy of `range` when it determines `range` is actually better. In these cases, although the data access strategy is slower, the execution is most likely faster. For example, let's take our query that has a `type` of `index_merge` and add a condition on `store_id`:

```
mysql> EXPLAIN SELECT customer_id
    -> FROM customer
    -> WHERE (last_name LIKE "Hill%" OR customer_id<10) AND
       store_id>2\G
*************************** 1. row ***************************
           id: 1
  select_type: SIMPLE
        table: customer
         type: range
possible_keys: PRIMARY,idx_fk_store_id,idx_last_name
          key: idx_fk_store_id
      key_len: 1
          ref: NULL
         rows: 1
        Extra: Using index condition; Using where; Using MRR
1 row in set (0.00 sec)
```

There is a nonunique index on `store_id`. In this query, the `store_id` condition must always be met, and thus the index on `store_id` is sufficient for the query optimizer. The general rule is that if there is a single index `mysqld` can use, it prefers that over using more than one index and the `index_merge` data access strategy.

Looking up nonunique, nullable index values

See the section "Joining and looking up nonunique index values," which explains the data access strategy `ref`. For looking up nonunique index values that are nullable, the `EXPLAIN` plan may show `ref_or_null`. The possibility of a `NULL` value is the only difference between `ref` and `ref_or_null`.

Data access strategy for fulltext searching

The data access strategy for a fulltext search is a type of `fulltext`:

```
mysql> EXPLAIN SELECT film_id, title
    -> FROM film_text
    -> WHERE MATCH (title,description) AGAINST ('storm')\G
*************************** 1. row ***************************
           id: 1
  select_type: SIMPLE
        table: film_text
         type: fulltext
possible_keys: idx_title_description
          key: idx_title_description
      key_len: 0
          ref:
         rows: 1
        Extra: Using where
1 row in set (0.00 sec)
```

For more information about fulltext searching, see Chapter 6.

Joining and looking up nonunique index values

When searching an index over a range of values, the `range` data access strategy is used. However, if you are searching a nonunique index for an *exact* match, MySQL does not need to access a range of values. The query optimizer can search the index for one value and find all of the records that match. This data access strategy will return a `type` of `ref` in the EXPLAIN plan:

```
mysql> EXPLAIN SELECT rental_id
    -> FROM rental
    -> WHERE customer_id=75\G
*************************** 1. row ***************************
           id: 1
  select_type: SIMPLE
        table: rental
         type: ref
possible_keys: idx_fk_customer_id
          key: idx_fk_customer_id
      key_len: 2
          ref: const
         rows: 40
        Extra: Using index
1 row in set (0.00 sec)
```

This query is looking for instances where customer_id exactly matches the constant 75. The rental table includes an index for the field customer_id, but the index is not unique. If the index were unique, the definition would include UNIQUE or PRIMARY.

The ref data access strategy means that MySQL will go to the index and retrieve records that match the constant value given. This is faster than the range data access strategy, because only one value in the index table needs to be looked up, instead of doing a partial scan of the index table. However, once the value is found in the index table, all the records that match will need to be retrieved.

The ref data access strategy is also used when a table is joined using a nonunique index. The same process applies — each record that matches the index value is retrieved.

Joins and unique index values

When a join uses a unique index — that is, the index is specified as UNIQUE or PRIMARY — the data access strategy is eq_ref. The data is accessed like ref, except that there will be at most one matching record.

```
mysql> EXPLAIN SELECT first_name,last_name
    -> FROM rental
    -> INNER JOIN customer USING (customer_id)
    -> WHERE rental_date BETWEEN '2006-02-14 00:00:00'
    -> AND '2006-02-14 23:59:59'\G
*************************** 1. row ***************************
           id: 1
  select_type: SIMPLE
        table: rental
         type: range
possible_keys: rental_date,idx_fk_customer_id
          key: rental_date
      key_len: 8
          ref: NULL
         rows: 2614
        Extra: Using where; Using index
*************************** 2. row ***************************
           id: 1
  select_type: SIMPLE
        table: customer
         type: eq_ref
possible_keys: PRIMARY
          key: PRIMARY
      key_len: 2
          ref: sakila.rental.customer_id
         rows: 1
        Extra:
2 rows in set (0.03 sec)
```

The eq_ref data access strategy appears when one table has a unique index, and the other table in a join does not. In this case, customer_id is a PRIMARY KEY on the customer table, and a nonunique index on the rental table.

Looking up unique index values

An index lookup on a unique value is very fast — MySQL only needs to go to the specified value in the index and retrieve the one record associated with that index value. In these cases, the query optimizer determines there will be fewer than two records looked up. In the EXPLAIN plan, a type of const is returned, reflecting that at most there is one record that will need to be retrieved:

```
mysql> EXPLAIN SELECT return_date FROM rental AS r WHERE rental_id =
13534\G
*************************** 1. row ***************************
           id: 1
  select_type: SIMPLE
        table: r
         type: const
possible_keys: PRIMARY
          key: PRIMARY
      key_len: 4
          ref: const
         rows: 1
        Extra:
1 row in set (0.09 sec)
```

The query optimizer sees that rental_id is an index marked as UNIQUE and NOT NULL, and that the WHERE clause is testing for when rental_id equals a constant. A row will have a type of const when the WHERE clause uses a constant and an equality operator on a field defined as UNIQUE and NOT NULL. In other words, the type is const when the WHERE clause looks like:

- WHERE unique_key=const — unique_key is a unique, not null, single-field key.
- WHERE unique_key_part1=const AND unique_key_part2 — (unique_key_part1,unique_key_part2) is a unique, not null, two-field key.

Constant propagation

The query optimizer can use deductions to make better query execution plans. For example, the query:

```
SELECT return_date, first_name, last_name
FROM rental INNER JOIN customer USING (customer_id)
WHERE rental_id = 13534\G
```

references two tables — rental and customer. In an EXPLAIN plan, the rental row should have a type of const, because of the WHERE clause. But what does the customer row look like?

```
mysql> EXPLAIN SELECT return_date, first_name, last_name
    -> FROM rental INNER JOIN customer USING (customer_id)
    -> WHERE rental_id = 13534\G
*************************** 1. row ***************************
           id: 1
  select_type: SIMPLE
        table: rental
```

```
              type: const
      possible_keys: PRIMARY,idx_fk_customer_id
                key: PRIMARY
            key_len: 4
                ref: const
               rows: 1
              Extra:
*************************** 2. row ***************************
                 id: 1
        select_type: SIMPLE
              table: customer
               type: const
      possible_keys: PRIMARY
                key: PRIMARY
            key_len: 2
                ref: const
               rows: 1
              Extra:
2 rows in set (0.00 sec)
```

The customer row also has a type of const! The query optimizer deduced that the customer table will have at most one record returned using the following facts:

- The rental row has a type of const and thus will return at most one record.
- The rental and customer tables are joined with an INNER JOIN using customer_id.
- There is at most one value for customer_id, because the rental row has a type of const.
- The customer_id field is defined as a key that is unique and specified as NOT NULL.

This set of deductions is called *constant propagation*. The constant, which causes the rental row to have a type of const, is propagated through the join in the following manner:

1. The values for the SELECT fields and customer_id are retrieved from the rental table:

   ```
   mysql> SELECT return_date, customer_id FROM rental WHERE rental_
   id=13534;
   +-------------+-------------+
   | return_date | customer_id |
   +-------------+-------------+
   | NULL        |          75 |
   +-------------+-------------+
   1 row in set (0.00 sec)
   ```

2. The JOIN is replaced — instead of joining two tables, the constant is propagated as a query on the customer table, using the filter WHERE customer_id=75:

```
mysql> SELECT NULL, first_name, last_name FROM customer WHERE
customer_id=75;
+------+------------+-----------+
| NULL | first_name | last_name |
+------+------------+-----------+
| NULL | TAMMY      | SANDERS   |
+------+------------+-----------+
1 row in set (0.01 sec)
```

This is why the eq_ref data access strategy shows up when only one table in a join joins on a unique index. When both tables in the join are joining on a unique index, constant propagation can occur.

Retrieve at most one record from a system table

MySQL defines a system table as any MyISAM table in the mysql database. A special data access strategy exists for retrieving information from a system table that contains fewer than two records — a type of system:

```
mysql> EXPLAIN SELECT Time_zone_id, Use_leap_seconds FROM mysql.
time_zone\G
*************************** 1. row ***************************
           id: 1
  select_type: SIMPLE
        table: time_zone
         type: system
possible_keys: NULL
          key: NULL
      key_len: NULL
          ref: NULL
         rows: 0
        Extra: const row not found
1 row in set (0.00 sec)
```

No data accesss strategy

The type is always NULL when the table is NULL. This is the fastest data access method because the data is not looked up using a table. If the table is NULL because the WHERE clause is not possible, the optimizer will immediately return the empty set without attempting to access the data from any tables. If the `table` is NULL because the query does not refer to a table, then it also does not access the data from any tables, although it may access sources such as variables in memory.

EXPLAIN plan indexes

The fields `possible_keys`, `key`, `key_len` and `ref` in the EXPLAIN plan relate to indexes.

The `possible_keys` field shows which indexes the query optimizer considers using to satisfy data filters — that is, the WHERE clause and join conditions. If there are no indexes that can be used for this purpose, the value of `possible_keys` is NULL.

The `key` field shows which index the query optimizer actually uses. In the case of an `index_merge` strategy, the `key` field is a comma-delimited list of indexes used. The `key` field sometimes shows an index that was not listed in `possible_keys`. The list of `possible_keys` only considers filters; however, if all of the fields retrieved are part of an index, the query optimizer will decide that it is faster to do a full index scan than a full data scan. Thus, it will use an access strategy of `index` with a `key` that was not listed in `possible_keys`.

The `key_len` field shows the length of the key used, in bytes. Queries that use indexes can be further optimized by making the length of the index smaller.

The `ref` field shows what is compared to the index. For a range of values or a full table scan, `ref` is NULL.

In a join, a field is compared to the index, and the field name is shown as the `ref` field.

```
mysql> EXPLAIN SELECT first_name,last_name FROM rental
    -> INNER JOIN customer USING (customer_id)
    -> WHERE rental_date BETWEEN '2006-02-14 00:00:00'
    -> AND '2006-02-14 23:59:59'\G
*************************** 1. row ***************************
           id: 1
  select_type: SIMPLE
        table: rental
         type: range
possible_keys: rental_date,idx_fk_customer_id
          key: rental_date
      key_len: 8
          ref: NULL
         rows: 2614
        Extra: Using where; Using index
*************************** 2. row ***************************
           id: 1
  select_type: SIMPLE
        table: customer
         type: eq_ref
possible_keys: PRIMARY
          key: PRIMARY
      key_len: 2
```

```
              ref: sakila.rental.customer_id
             rows: 1
            Extra:
2 rows in set (0.03 sec)
```

If a constant is compared, the ref field is const:

```
mysql> EXPLAIN SELECT return_date FROM rental WHERE rental_id =
13534\G
*************************** 1. row ***************************
              id: 1
     select_type: SIMPLE
           table: rental
            type: const
   possible_keys: PRIMARY
             key: PRIMARY
         key_len: 4
             ref: const
            rows: 1
           Extra:
1 row in set (0.09 sec)
```

A type of fulltext has a ref field that is blank:

```
mysql> EXPLAIN SELECT film_id, title
    -> FROM film_text
    -> WHERE MATCH (title,description) AGAINST ('storm')\G
*************************** 1. row ***************************
              id: 1
     select_type: SIMPLE
           table: film_text
            type: fulltext
   possible_keys: idx_title_description
             key: idx_title_description
         key_len: 0
             ref:
            rows: 1
           Extra: Using where
1 row in set (0.00 sec)
```

Rows

The rows field in an EXPLAIN plan is the approximate number of records examined for this row. This number is based on metadata, and metadata may or may not be accurate, depending on the storage engine. In addition, LIMIT is not considered in this approximation:

```
mysql> EXPLAIN SELECT first_name,last_name FROM customer LIMIT 10\G
*************************** 1. row ***************************
              id: 1
     select_type: SIMPLE
```

```
            table: customer
             type: ALL
    possible_keys: NULL
              key: NULL
          key_len: NULL
              ref: NULL
             rows: 541
            Extra:
1 row in set (0.00 sec)
```

If LIMIT were considered, rows would be 10.

The more data in the database, the longer it will take to run a query. Even optimized queries take longer to examine more data. One way to make your tables smaller is by partitioning — see Chapter 15, "Partitioning," for more information. Chapter 22, "Scaling and High Availability Solutions," has some introductory information about MySQL Cluster, which distributes data among servers.

Another way to make the amount of data smaller is by purging data — after archiving to a different table, different server, or backup. Making data smaller is often the key to a smoothly running database. See the section "Batching expensive operations" later in this chapter for an example of purging data.

Of course, the easiest way to make data smaller is to actually make the data types themselves smaller. Are you storing a user ID AUTO_INCREMENT field in a BIGINT? Most likely, there is no need to have capacity for over four billion users — at the time of this writing, that amount is more than half the population of the entire planet.

Even though VARCHAR values are variable in length, they convert to fixed-length fields when they are stored in memory or in a memory-backed temporary table. Therefore, it is useful to use a reasonable length for VARCHAR, instead of just using VARCHAR(255) or VARCHAR(100) for everything.

Use the PROCEDURE ANALYSE() statement to find the best value type and size for existing data. See Chapter 5 for more information on PROCEDURE ANALYSE().

Extra

The last field in the EXPLAIN plan is Extra. This is a catch-all field that shows good, neutral, and bad information about a query plan. Table 18-2 shows the most common Extra types, their meaning, and their ramifications:

TABLE 18-2

EXPLAIN Plan Extra Values

Extra value	Meaning	Ramifications
No tables used	No table, temporary table, view, or derived table will be used.	None; this is neutral.
Impossible WHERE noticed after reading const tables	There is no possible satisfactory value.	There is probably is a false assumption in the query (i.e., WHERE numfield='a').
const row not found	There is no possible satisfactory value.	Either a false assumption or a system table contains no records.
Using where	There is a filter for comparison or joining.	If this does not exist, the data access strategy is either at the slow extreme (ALL, index) or the fast extreme (NULL, system, const, eq_ref). Desirable — this means that some second stage filtering is being applied on the examined rows before joining on the next table. So you may be doing fewer nested loop joins than you think, which is faster.
Using intersection	Examines indexes in parallel in an index_merge data access strategy, then performs an intersection of the result sets.	Examining indexes in parallel is faster than the alternative.
Using union	Examines indexes in parallel in an index_merge data access strategy, then performs a union of the result sets.	Examining indexes in parallel is faster than the alternative.
Using sort_union	Examines indexes in an index_merge data access strategy by fetching all record IDs, sorting them, then performing a union of the result sets.	Undesirable; this requires an extra pass through the data for sorting.
Using index	Only data from the index is needed; there is no need to retrieve a data record.	Desirable; this uses a covering index. See REFERENCE for more about covering indexes.
Using index for group-by	Only data from the index is needed to satisfy a GROUP BY or DISTINCT; there is no need to retrieve a data record.	Desirable; this uses a covering index. See REFERENCE for more about covering indexes.

continued

TABLE 18-2   *(continued)*

Extra value	Meaning	Ramifications
`Using index condition` (Not found in versions < 6.0.4)	Accesses an index value, testing the part of the filter that involves the index. If the index matches, then retrieves the full data record and tests the rest of the filter. Applies to the data access strategies `range`, `ref_or_null`, `ref`, and `eq_ref`.	This is more desirable than the default, which is to retrieve the index value and the full data record, and then test both at once.
`Using MRR` (Not found in versions < 6.0.4)	Uses the Multi Read Range optimization — accesses the index values and sorts them in the order the records appear on disk.	This makes retrieval of the data records on disk faster, and is more desirable than the default.
`Using join buffer`	Table records are put into the join buffer, then the buffer is used for joining.	Desirable; without using this buffer, extra passes through the data are needed.
`Distinct`	Stops looking after the first matched record for this row.	Desirable; stops looking after first matched record.
`Not exists`	Used in outer joins where one lookup is sufficient for each record being joined.	Desirable; stops looking after first lookup.
`Range checked for each record (index map: N)`	No index could be found, but there might be a good one after some other rows (tables) have values. *N* is a bitmask value of the index number on the table; if a table has indexes, 0xB = 1101, so the first, second, and fourth indexes are considered.	Faster than the data access strategy `ALL` but slower than `index`.
`Select tables optimized away`	Metadata or an index can be used, so no tables are necessary; one record is returned.	Desirable; used with aggregate functions.
`Using where with pushed condition`	The cluster "pushes" the condition from the SQL nodes down to the data nodes. `Using where with pushed condition` is desirable; it makes the query faster.	Desirable; faster than `ALL`. Only seen on `NDBCLUSTER` tables when a non-indexed field is compared to a constant.
`Using temporary`	Needs to use a temporary table for intermediate values.	Undesirable.
`Using filesort`	Needs to pass through the result set an extra time for sorting.	Undesirable.

In addition to Table 18-2, there are five additional Extra values. One of these is used in subqueries (see "Subqueries and EXPLAIN"), and the other four are used when querying the INFORMATION_SCHEMA database:

- Scanned N databases — N is 0, 1 or all. The fewer databases scanned, the better.
- Skip_open_table — No table files need to be opened. Fastest.
- Open_frm_only — Only open the .frm file.
- Open_trigger_only — Only open the .TRG file.
- Open_full_table — Open all the table files. Slowest.

Subqueries and EXPLAIN

MySQL handles subqueries very differently than it handles queries. The EXPLAIN plans show these differences. The biggest difference is in the number of select_type values that are used to describe subqueries. Table 18-3 shows the different select_type values used in subqueries:

TABLE 18-3

Subquery Values for select_type

If the select_type is:	Then the row is the:
PRIMARY	Outermost query when using subqueries.
DERIVED	SELECT subquery in FROM clause
SUBQUERY	First SELECT in a subquery
DEPENDENT SUBQUERY	First SELECT in a dependent subquery
UNCACHEABLE SUBQUERY	Subquery result cannot be cached; must be evaluated for every record.
DEPENDENT UNION	Second or later SELECT statements in a UNION and is used in a dependent subquery
UNCACHEABLE UNION	Second or later SELECT statements in a UNION and is used in a dependent subquery; cannot be cached and must be evaluated for every record

The other big difference in the EXPLAIN plan is an additional Extra value — Full scan on NULL key. This indicates a slow subquery and is undesirable.

```
mysql> EXPLAIN SELECT first_name,last_name,email
    -> IN (SELECT customer_id FROM rental AS rental_subquery WHERE
       return_date IS NULL)
    -> FROM customer AS customer_outer\G
```

```
*************************** 1. row ***************************
           id: 1
  select_type: PRIMARY
        table: customer_outer
         type: ALL
possible_keys: NULL
          key: NULL
      key_len: NULL
          ref: NULL
         rows: 541
        Extra:
*************************** 2. row ***************************
           id: 2
  select_type: DEPENDENT SUBQUERY
        table: rental_subquery
         type: index_subquery
possible_keys: idx_fk_customer_id
          key: idx_fk_customer_id
      key_len: 2
          ref: func
         rows: 13
        Extra: Using where; Full scan on NULL key
2 rows in set (0.00 sec)
```

ON the WEBSITE More information on how to avoid the use of unoptimized subqueries can be found on the accompanying website for this book at www.wiley.com/go/ mysqladminbible.

EXPLAIN EXTENDED

The EXPLAIN statement can be modified with the EXTENDED keyword to provide two sets of additional information. One of these is the filtered field in the EXPLAIN EXTENDED output:

```
mysql> EXPLAIN EXTENDED SELECT customer_id
    -> FROM rental
    -> WHERE staff_id=2 AND inventory_id<100\G
*************************** 1. row ***************************
           id: 1
  select_type: SIMPLE
        table: rental
         type: range
possible_keys: idx_fk_inventory_id,idx_fk_staff_id
          key: idx_fk_inventory_id
      key_len: 3
          ref: NULL
         rows: 326
     filtered: 75.15
        Extra: Using index condition; Using where; Using MRR
1 row in set, 1 warning (0.00 sec)
```

The filtered field is an approximate percentage of how many rows examined (the rows field) will be returned after the table conditions are all applied. In this example, the query optimizer approximates that 75.15 percent of the 326 rows examined will be returned after the staff_id condition is applied. The number of rows examined is estimated using statistics about the inventory_id index, so the only condition left to apply is the staff_id condition.

You can calculate how accurate the optimizer's estimate was by calculating how many rows the optimizer thinks will be returned and comparing to the actual number of rows returned:

```
mysql> SELECT 326*75.15/100 AS optimizer_estimate;
+--------------------+
| optimizer_estimate |
+--------------------+
|         244.989000 |
+--------------------+
1 row in set (0.00 sec)

mysql> SELECT COUNT(customer_id) AS actual
    -> FROM rental
    -> WHERE staff_id=2 AND inventory_id<100;
+--------+
| actual |
+--------+
|    151 |
+--------+
1 row in set (0.00 sec)
```

The optimizer is not very accurate in this example.

The second set of information that EXPLAIN EXTENDED provides can be seen by issuing SHOW WARNINGS after the EXPLAIN EXTENDED statement — the EXPLAIN EXTENDED output shown above shows that there was a warning thrown. Had we issued SHOW WARNINGS at that time, you would have seen:

```
mysql> SHOW WARNINGS\G
*************************** 1. row ***************************
  Level: Note
   Code: 1003
Message: select `sakila`.`rental`.`customer_id` AS `customer_id`
from `sakila`.`rental` where ((`sakila`.`rental`.`staff_id` =
2) and (`sakila`.`rental`.`inventory_id` < 100))
1 row in set (0.00 sec)
```

The Message field shows the query after the optimizer is finished. Field names are qualified with database and table names. Table names are qualified with database names. Object names are escaped. Sometimes the Message field contains a viable SQL statement, as our example does. Other times, there is advanced information in the Message field that is not valid SQL syntax. This most often occurs in subqueries, and because the information does not help optimize the query, we will not explain the advanced information.

EXPLAIN on Non-SELECT Statements

EXPLAIN cannot be used in front of data manipulation statements such as UPDATE, INSERT, REPLACE, or DELETE statements. However, DML can be transformed into a corresponding SELECT statement.

For example, a clerk processes movie rental returns for Tammy Sanders. The following query sets the return_date to NOW() for all of Tammy's movies:

```
UPDATE customer INNER JOIN rental USING (customer_id)
INNER JOIN inventory USING (inventory_id)
INNER JOIN film USING (film_id)
SET return_date=NOW()
WHERE email='TAMMY.SANDERS@sakilacustomer.org'
AND return_date IS NULL
```

To see a corresponding EXPLAIN plan, you can convert an UPDATE to a SELECT query. Use the fields in the SET clause(s) as the SELECT fields, and keep the rest of the query intact. Then prepend EXPLAIN:

```
EXPLAIN SELECT return_date FROM
customer INNER JOIN rental USING (customer_id)
INNER JOIN inventory USING (inventory_id)
INNER JOIN film USING (film_id)
WHERE email='TAMMY.SANDERS@sakilacustomer.org'
AND return_date IS NULL\G
```

Converting DML to a SELECT query and running an EXPLAIN in this manner can help determine if a DML statement is slow because of retrieval issues. There are many other reasons DML may be slow, including heavy disk I/O, the need to update many indexes, table fragmentation, and statistics calculation.

Other Query Analysis Tools

While EXPLAIN is the most widely used tool to analyze queries, it is not comprehensive. Other tools are needed to give a full overview of how fast a query runs:

- Tools to reveal the schema and/or indexes
    - SHOW CREATE TABLE...
    - SHOW INDEXES FROM...
    - Querying the INFORMATION_SCHEMA tables that provide information about indexes (see Chapter 21, "MySQL Data Dictionary")
- PROCEDURE ANALYSE() to estimate cardinality and optimal data type/size (see Chapter 5, "MySQL Data Types")

While not strictly query analysis tools, the following tools can help optimize queries:

- ANALYZE TABLE — To recalculate statistics for a more accurate query plan (see Chapter 4, "How MySQL Extends and Deviates from SQL")
- OPTIMIZE TABLE — Defragments a table for faster access and recalculates statistics for a more accurate query plan (see Chapter 4, "How MySQL Extends and Deviates from SQL")

Optimizing Queries

The real benefit of EXPLAIN is not in analyzing queries but in using that analysis to make queries faster. The first two EXPLAIN fields to consider when optimizing queries are the data access strategy (type) and Extra fields.

Earlier in this chapter, Table 18-1 listed the values of type in order from slowest to fastest. To optimize a query, examine the data access strategy and attempt to use a faster data access strategy. Table 18-2 listed the values of Extra, including meanings and ramifications; optimizing means trying to get rid of the Extra values that indicate slowness and trying to add the Extra values that indicate better optimization.

Factors affecting key usage

Most of the data access strategies involve using an index. Obviously, in order to be used, an index must exist. However, there are reasons why an index may not be used. One such reason is that the query uses a function on one or more of the fields in the index. See the section "Using an index by eliminating functions" later in this chapter for ways to use an index.

Another time that a full table scan may be done is when the result set of the query includes fields not in the index and a significant percentage of rows. The exact percentage differs, although it is typically around 20–30 percent of rows and depends on many factors, including the size of the index and the size of the non-index fields. This percentage can be influenced by optimizer hints. See the next section on optimizer hints.

This percentage is also influenced by the cardinality of the data. The cardinality of a field or index is the number of unique values for that field or index. If cardinality is high, as is the case with UNIQUE and PRIMARY KEY fields and indexes, it is more likely that a query filtering on those fields and returning other fields will use an index. However, if cardinality is low, it is more likely that a query filtering on those fields and returning other fields will use a full table scan to return many rows. An example of a low-cardinality field is a flag such as *account status* or *active*. Selecting all the usernames from a table named user where the value of a field named active is 1 will most likely not use an index on only the active field, because most likely 20–30 percent or more of the rows in the user table have an active value of 1. A low-cardinality field can be used in an index, but it is not recommended that it occur after a field with higher cardinality, if you want to get the most benefit from the index.

Data changes, whether by INSERT, UPDATE, or DELETE, can affect the cardinality of nonunique fields and indexes.

Optimizer hints

Optimizer hints include:

- Specifying the join order of tables with STRAIGHT_JOIN
- Specifying indexes to ignore with IGNORE INDEX or IGNORE KEY
- Giving extra weight to indexes with USE INDEX or USE KEY
- Specifying indexes to use with FORCE INDEX or FORCE KEY
- Changing the value of optimizer_prune_level, a dynamic variable in the GLOBAL and SESSION scopes. The default value of 1 will limit the number of query plans examined based on the number of rows retrieved. A value of 0 does not limit the number of query plans examined.
- Changing the value of optimizer_search_depth, a dynamic variable in the GLOBAL and SESSION scopes. This variable controls how many data access plans the optimizer considers. A lower value means that less time is spent by the query optimizer, usually producing a suboptimal query. A larger value means that more data access plans are examined. A value of 0 means that mysqld chooses the depth. The default value is 62.
- Changing the value of optimizer_use_mrr, a dynamic variable in the GLOBAL and SESSION scopes. The default value is force, which will use the Multi-Read-Range Access method (MRR) when possible. One possible value is disable, which will never use MRR. The other possible value is auto, which calculates whether or not to use MRR based on cost — however, this value is not recommended by Sun Microsystems.
- Setting a low value for max_seeks_for_key, a dynamic variable in the GLOBAL and SESSION scopes. The default value is 4294967295 (2^32-1). This value is the maximum number of seeks the query optimizer assumes an index search will have. The default is large to allow the query optimizer uses index cardinality statistics to estimate the number of seeks. If you make the value small (for example, 100), the query optimizer may disregard seek estimates based on index cardinality statistics.

Traditionally, the advice has been to use optimizer hints when the optimizer is not using the best plan. In practice, many optimizer hints provide immediate solutions while creating future problems. These future problems are a result of the query optimizer using the hint even when the hint is no longer valid. To avoid this situation, document and periodically reanalyze queries in which you have used optimizer hints. Changes in the amount of data, the cardinality of data, and the schema will change what the optimal query plan is, so if you must use optimizer hints, review the validity of the hint by reanalyzing queries every few months and when there are complaints of the database being slow.

Adding an Index

The query used as an example of a full table scan was SELECT return_date FROM rental. Is there a faster data access strategy for this query?

The reason this is a full table scan is that there are no suitable indexes to use. We can use the INFORMATION_SCHEMA table STATISTICS to show all the indexes on the rental table:

```
mysql> SELECT COLUMN_NAME, INDEX_NAME, SEQ_IN_INDEX AS pos
    -> FROM INFORMATION_SCHEMA.STATISTICS
    -> WHERE TABLE_SCHEMA='sakila' AND TABLE_NAME='rental';
+--------------+----------------------+-----+
| COLUMN_NAME  | INDEX_NAME           | pos |
+--------------+----------------------+-----+
| rental_id    | PRIMARY              |   1 |
| rental_date  | rental_date          |   1 |
| inventory_id | rental_date          |   2 |
| customer_id  | rental_date          |   3 |
| inventory_id | idx_fk_inventory_id  |   1 |
| customer_id  | idx_fk_customer_id   |   1 |
| staff_id     | idx_fk_staff_id      |   1 |
+--------------+----------------------+-----+
7 rows in set (0.11 sec)
```

There is no index that includes the return_date field, so add an index to optimize this query:

```
mysql> USE sakila;
Database changed
mysql> ALTER TABLE rental ADD INDEX (return_date);
Query OK, 16044 rows affected (12.08 sec)
Records: 16044  Duplicates: 0  Warnings: 0

mysql> EXPLAIN SELECT return_date FROM rental\G
*************************** 1. row ***************************
           id: 1
  select_type: SIMPLE
        table: rental
         type: index
possible_keys: NULL
          key: return_date
      key_len: 9
          ref: NULL
         rows: 16249
        Extra: Using index
1 row in set (0.00 sec)
```

Now the type is index, which means a full scan of an index is being done. The index being scanned is the return_date index (key), which we just created, with a length (key_len) of 9. Is there a way to further optimize this query?

Looking at Table 18-1, data access strategy types below index involve using only parts of an index. The query we are analyzing returns every value of the return_date field. Therefore, there is no way to avoid accessing every value in the return_date index. mysqld needs to access a value in order to return it, and every value is returned, so every value must be accessed. This need to access every value is also shown by the lack of `Using where` in the `Extra` field.

Index consequences

In Chapter 6, we explained how indexes work. Indexes can make data retrieval faster because they are ordered subsets of data, and can be searched faster than the entire set of data, which may be ordered differently than an index. There is a cost to maintaining indexes. Data changes are slower because the data needs to be inserted into the table and any appropriate indexes need to be updated. An index needs uses disk space, memory, and processing power to stay up to date.

When analyzing queries, remember that there are tradeoffs for actions. Many times, adding an index will make an application run faster because the query runs faster. However, there are times when adding an index makes an application run more slowly, because although the `SELECT` query runs faster, the `INSERT`, `UPDATE`, and `DELETE` queries run more slowly.

It helps to be familiar with the nature of all the queries against the database. If you find that selecting a field from a table that stores user session information is slow, adding an index may make the application slower because there are many changes to user session information. From time to time, you may want to reexamine indexes to ensure that they are being used. An index that is not being used is a waste of resources.

Optimizing away Using filesort

The `Extra` value `Using filesort` is not desirable; it means that `mysqld` has to pass through the data an extra time in order to sort it. If the `Extra` value `Using filesort` shows up in a subquery, it is best to optimize the query by eliminating the subquery. In queries that do not involve subqueries, the `Extra` value `Using filesort` may occur in the `EXPLAIN` plan for queries that use `ORDER BY`, `DISTINCT`, and `GROUP BY`.

ON the WEBSITE   More information on how to create and use subqueries can be found on the accompanying website for this book at www.wiley.com/go/mysqladminbible.

For example, the following `EXPLAIN` plan is for a query to find the customer name and active status based on an e-mail lookup, sorted by last name:

```
mysql> EXPLAIN SELECT first_name, last_name, active
    -> FROM customer WHERE email='barbara.jones@sakilacustomer.org'
    -> ORDER BY last_name\G
*************************** 1. row ***************************
           id: 1
    select_type: SIMPLE
```

```
          table: customer
           type: ALL
  possible_keys: NULL
            key: NULL
        key_len: NULL
            ref: NULL
           rows: 541
          Extra: Using where; Using filesort
1 row in set (0.00 sec)
```

In order to optimize away the Using filesort, you need to have an index that
mysqld can use instead of sorting. In most cases, mysqld can only use one index, so
you will need to have an index that handles both the sorting and the filter of WHERE
email='barbara.jones@sakilacustomer.org':

```
mysql> ALTER TABLE customer ADD INDEX (email, last_name);
Query OK, 599 rows affected (0.56 sec)
Records: 599  Duplicates: 0  Warnings: 0

mysql> EXPLAIN SELECT first_name, last_name, active
    -> FROM customer WHERE email='barbara.jones@sakilacustomer.org'
    -> ORDER BY last_name\G
*************************** 1. row ***************************
             id: 1
    select_type: SIMPLE
          table: customer
           type: ref
  possible_keys: email
            key: email
        key_len: 203
            ref: const
           rows: 1
          Extra: Using index condition; Using where
1 row in set (0.00 sec)
```

You have removed the undesirable Extra value Using filesort, and added the desirable
Using index condition. You have also gone from a data access strategy (type) of full table
scan (ALL) to one of looking up a nonunique index value (ref).

Often, first instincts may not fully optimize a query. For example, your first instinct in optimizing this query might have been to add an index on only the email field. This would have
optimized the data access strategy, but the query would still have an Extra value of Using
filesort. Having one index for both fields allows mysqld to use that index to optimize
the data access strategy and the filesort. It is always a good idea to test as many optimization
solutions as possible see the sidebar "Testing ideas."

Testing ideas

In the example from the section "Optimizing away Using filesort," you might have tried to see if mysqld would use an index on last_name only; if that was your first instinct, you can try out the following commands to see if the index would work:

```
ALTER TABLE customer DROP KEY email;

ALTER TABLE customer ADD INDEX (last_name);

EXPLAIN SELECT first_name, last_name, active
FROM customer WHERE email='barbara.jones@sakilacustomer.org'
ORDER BY last_name\G
```

Sometimes, the first idea you have to optimize a query will not actually optimize the query. In this case, the index on last_name does not help because mysqld needs to filter for the WHERE clause first, before ordering. If mysqld was to use the index on last_name, it would have to go through the entire index, and for each row in the index, look up the email field from the data to see if it matched. If there were a match, the last_name would be put in the result set, and the first_name and active field would be looked up and also put in the result set. Those lookups are a lot of extra work, and the query optimizer rightfully uses a full table scan, even with an index on last_name.

There will be other times when the best solution for optimization is not the best solution overall for the application. In this example, an index was added on (email, last_name) and the EXPLAIN plan showed a key length (key_len) of 203. That is a very large key to keep up to date, and if it slows down the application, it may be more beneficial to use an index with a shorter length, even if it means mysqld has to do a filesort.

Optimizing away Range checked for each record

As shown in Table 18-2, the Extra value Range checked for each record is faster than a full table scan (type: ALL) but slower than a full index scan (type: index). To optimize queries with this Extra value, create or modify an index so that the query optimizer has a good index to use. Often, optimizing queries to get rid of Range checked for each record results in a data access strategy (type) of range, ref or eq_ref.

Optimizing away Using temporary

Unlike in previous discussions, optimizing away an Extra value of Using temporary cannot be done by adding an index. Using temporary is undesirable, as it means that a temporary table must be used to store intermediate results. There are several ways to optimize this, depending on why a temporary table is used:

- If ORDER BY and GROUP BY are both present, and use different fields and/or ordering, the way to optimize this is to get rid of either the ORDER BY or the GROUP BY. This may be done by splitting the query into two queries. It may be possible to combine the two queries by using UNION so that intermediate results do not need to be stored in a temporary table.

■ The presence of ORDER BY and DISTINCT may cause a temporary table to be used. The way to optimize this is to get rid of either the ORDER BY or the DISTINCT. This may be done by splitting the query into two queries. It may be possible to combine the two queries by using UNION so that intermediate results do not need to be stored in a temporary table.

■ If the SQL_CALC_FOUND_ROWS keyword is used, the number of rows is stored in a temporary table, which can be retrieved by issuing SELECT FOUND ROWS(). To optimize, get rid of SQL_CALC_FOUND_ROWS. Depending on what you are counting, you might count results periodically and have an estimate for a time period (i.e., run a query every 10 minutes to put the number into table and read the table, doing one count every 10 minutes instead of one count every time the query is issued).

■ The SQL_SMALL_RESULT keyword is used in a SELECT statement with DISTINCT or GROUP BY. The SQL_SMALL_RESULT keyword is a hint to the optimizer that the result is small, and thus it should use a temporary table instead of a filesort. To optimize, get rid of SQL_SMALL_RESULT. If you need the SQL_SMALL_RESULT keyword because a temporary table is more desirable than a filesort, then you cannot optimize Using temporary away.

If you use optimizer hints, be sure to run periodic testing. Only through periodic testing can you determine whether a temporary table or a filesort is better for your particular situation.

■ ORDER BY or GROUP BY is used on a field that is not the first table in the join queue (the first row returned in the EXPLAIN plan). One way to optimize this query is to change or eliminate the ORDER BY clause. Another way would be to change the filter so that the table order changes.

For example, the following query uses the customer table first in the join queue, but is sorting based on rental_date, a field in the rental table:

```
mysql> EXPLAIN SELECT first_name, last_name FROM rental
    -> INNER JOIN customer USING (customer_id)
    -> ORDER BY rental_date\G
*************************** 1. row ***************************
           id: 1
  select_type: SIMPLE
        table: customer
         type: ALL
possible_keys: PRIMARY
          key: NULL
      key_len: NULL
          ref: NULL
         rows: 591
        Extra: Using temporary; Using filesort
```

```
*************************** 2. row ***************************
           id: 1
  select_type: SIMPLE
        table: rental
         type: ref
possible_keys: idx_fk_customer_id
          key: idx_fk_customer_id
      key_len: 2
          ref: sakila.customer.customer_id
         rows: 13
        Extra:
2 rows in set (0.00 sec)
```

To optimize this query, we could change the ORDER BY to use a field in the customer table, or we could change the query to use the rental table first in the join queue. Join table order can be forced by using a join type of STRAIGHT_JOIN (which cannot use the USING syntax):

```
mysql> EXPLAIN SELECT first_name, last_name FROM rental
    -> STRAIGHT_JOIN customer ON rental.customer_id=customer.
       customer_id
    -> ORDER BY rental_date\G
*************************** 1. row ***************************
           id: 1
  select_type: SIMPLE
        table: rental
         type: index
possible_keys: idx_fk_customer_id
          key: rental_date
      key_len: 13
          ref: NULL
         rows: 16291
        Extra: Using index
*************************** 2. row ***************************
           id: 1
  select_type: SIMPLE
        table: customer
         type: eq_ref
possible_keys: PRIMARY
          key: PRIMARY
      key_len: 2
          ref: sakila.rental.customer_id
         rows: 1
        Extra:
2 rows in set (0.00 sec)
```

However, this may or may not actually make the query better — Using filesort is gone, but the data access strategy for the rental table is much slower. In general, using techniques like index hints and STRAIGHT_JOIN are dangerous query optimization strategies, because changes in the amount of data, the cardinality of data, and the schema may change the optimal query plan. If you must use these techniques, reassess their validity every few months and whenever complaints of database slowness arise.

A better way to change the order of the join queue is to limit the rows examined in the desired table. For example, you can limit the rows examined in rental table to a certain range:

```
mysql> EXPLAIN SELECT first_name, last_name FROM rental
    -> INNER JOIN customer USING (customer_id)
    -> WHERE rental_date BETWEEN '2005-01-01 00:00:00' AND
    -> '2005-01-31 00:00:00' ORDER BY rental_date\G
*************************** 1. row ***************************
          id: 1
 select_type: SIMPLE
       table: rental
        type: range
possible_keys: rental_date,idx_fk_customer_id
         key: rental_date
     key_len: 8
         ref: NULL
        rows: 1
       Extra: Using where; Using index
*************************** 2. row ***************************
          id: 1
 select_type: SIMPLE
       table: customer
        type: eq_ref
possible_keys: PRIMARY
         key: PRIMARY
     key_len: 2
         ref: sakila.rental.customer_id
        rows: 1
       Extra:
2 rows in set (0.00 sec)
```

It is beneficial to optimize away Using temporary because in certain cases, temporary tables will be written to disk. These situations include: when a temporary table exceeds the smaller of tmp_table_size and max_heap_table_size, when a temporary table includes BLOB or TEXT data types, when DISTINCT or GROUP BY clauses contain fields that use more than 512 bytes, and when any field is more than 512 bytes in a UNION or UNION ALL query.

Using an index by eliminating functions

Sometimes, an index exists but is not being used. For example, the film table has the following indexes:

```
mysql> SELECT COLUMN_NAME, INDEX_NAME, SEQ_IN_INDEX AS pos
    -> FROM INFORMATION_SCHEMA.STATISTICS
    -> WHERE TABLE_SCHEMA='sakila' AND TABLE_NAME='film';
```

```
+---------------------+------------------------------+-----+
| COLUMN_NAME         | INDEX_NAME                   | pos |
+---------------------+------------------------------+-----+
| film_id             | PRIMARY                      | 1   |
| title               | idx_title                    | 1   |
| language_id         | idx_fk_language_id           | 1   |
| original_language_id| idx_fk_original_language_id  | 1   |
+---------------------+------------------------------+-----+
4 rows in set (0.01 sec)
```

However, the following query does not use the index on title, as you might expect it would:

```
mysql> EXPLAIN SELECT title FROM film WHERE LEFT(title,2)='Tr'\G
*************************** 1. row ***************************
           id: 1
  select_type: SIMPLE
        table: film
         type: ALL
possible_keys: NULL
          key: NULL
      key_len: NULL
          ref: NULL
         rows: 953
        Extra: Using where
1 row in set (0.00 sec)
```

The reason for this is that there is an index on title, but the WHERE clause is filtering based on a function of the title field. Values (such as 'Tr') cannot be compared to a function (LEFT(title,2)) using an index in mysqld, unless the index is on the function itself. Unfortunately, mysqld does not support an index on functions, and so it is not possible to define an index on LEFT(title,2) even if you had the desire.

To optimize this type of query, see if you can take away the function. In this case, you can replace LEFT(title,2)='Tr' with title LIKE 'Tr%' to get rid of the function on title. Just by changing the query to get rid of the function, you can change your data access strategy from a type of ALL to a type of range:

```
mysql> EXPLAIN SELECT title FROM film WHERE title LIKE 'Tr%'\G
*************************** 1. row ***************************
           id: 1
  select_type: SIMPLE
        table: film
         type: range
possible_keys: idx_title
          key: idx_title
      key_len: 766
          ref: NULL
         rows: 15
        Extra: Using where
1 row in set (0.00 sec)
```

This type of optimization is done most frequently to queries involving date ranges.

Compare:

```
EXPLAIN SELECT inventory_id, customer_id FROM rental
WHERE DATE(return_date)='2005-05-30'\G
```

with:

```
EXPLAIN SELECT return_date FROM rental
WHERE return_date BETWEEN '2005-05-30 00:00:00' and '2005-05-30
23:59:59'
```

However, there are other ways in which functions can be optimized out of a query. Table 18-4 shows some common optimizations:

TABLE 18-4

Common Ways to Optimize by Eliminating Functions

WHERE clause Function	Optimization
LEFT(stringfield) = 'Tr'	stringfield LIKE 'Tr%'
DATE(datefield) = '2005-05-30' --or LAST_DAY(field)='2005-05-30' --or LEFT(datefield, 10) = '2005-05-30' SUBSTRING_INDEX(datefield,' ') = '2005-05-30'	field BETWEEN '2005-05-30 00:00:00' AND '2005-05-30 23:59:59'
ABS(field) > 20	field > 20 or field < -20
field + 1 > 20	field > 19
FLOOR(field)=1	field >= 1 AND field < 2
CONCAT(field,'day')='Saturday'	field='Satur'
FROM_UNIXTIME(field)='2005-05-30 00:00:00'	field= 1117425600
LEFT(INET_NTOA(field),10)='192.168.1.'	field BETWEEN 3232235777 AND 3232236031

You may be wondering why anyone would ever create WHERE clauses like the ones in Table 18-4. Most of the time it happens because of the way the developer is thinking. Developers write queries to answer questions, so these types of WHERE clauses happen when the developer writes a query to "find sales on May 30" or to "find distances greater than 20". In an ideal world, no query would be saved to code unless it were optimized. In practice, developers write queries, and DBAs optimize queries — if the developer writes a suboptimal query, in many organizations the DBA will find it only when it slows down the application.

Optimizing the last two queries in Table 18-4 requires some work to retrieve the numerical values. To optimize FROM_UNIXTIME(field)='2005-05-30 00:00:00', you have to find the UNIX timestamp value for the datetime. There is a function to do that:

```
mysql> SELECT UNIX_TIMESTAMP('2005-05-30 00:00:00');
+---------------------------------------+
| UNIX_TIMESTAMP('2005-05-30 00:00:00') |
+---------------------------------------+
|                            1117425600 |
+---------------------------------------+
1 row in set (0.05 sec)
```

To optimize LEFT(INET_NTOA(field),10)='192.168.1.', you first have to figure out what the query is looking for. This filter finds rows that have field with the numerical equivalent of an IP address whose left 10 characters are '192.168.1.'. Another way to look at the filter is that it finds rows that have field with the numerical equivalent of an IP address between 192.168.1.1 and 192.168.1.255.

This new way to look at the data presents you with a way to eliminate the function from the WHERE clause. If you find the numerical equivalent of the boundary IPs, you can use those in the BETWEEN comparison shown in Table 18-4. Again, mysqld has a function that will let you look those values up:

```
mysql> select INET_ATON('192.168.1.1'), INET_ATON('192.168.1.255');
+--------------------------+----------------------------+
| INET_ATON('192.168.1.1') | INET_ATON('192.168.1.255') |
+--------------------------+----------------------------+
|               3232235777 |                 3232236031 |
+--------------------------+----------------------------+
1 row in set (0.00 sec)
```

There are functions that simply cannot be eliminated. For example, it is difficult to eliminate WHERE clauses such as MOD(field,10)=2 and LENGTH(field)<5.

Non-index schema changes

Sometimes the best way to optimize a query is to change the data structure. Consider the following query:

```
mysql> EXPLAIN SELECT first_name, last_name, email
    -> FROM staff
    -> WHERE email LIKE '%sakilastaff.com'\G
*************************** 1. row ***************************
           id: 1
  select_type: SIMPLE
```

```
        table: staff
         type: ALL
possible_keys: NULL
          key: NULL
      key_len: NULL
          ref: NULL
         rows: 1
        Extra: Using where
1 row in set (0.00 sec)
```

An index on staff would not help, because text indexes work from the beginning of the word (see Chapter 6). Much like a dictionary, an index is set up to look for words that begin a certain way, not words that end a certain way. The way to optimize this query would be to have an index that could look up words that end a certain way.

Such an index does not exist. However, what you can do is add a field to the table that contains the text reversed, with a regular index on that. For example:

```
mysql> ALTER TABLE staff ADD COLUMN revemail VARCHAR(50) DEFAULT
        NULL,
    -> ADD INDEX (revemail);
Query OK, 2 rows affected (0.38 sec)
Records: 2  Duplicates: 0  Warnings: 0

mysql> UPDATE staff SET revemail=REVERSE(email);
Query OK, 2 rows affected (0.08 sec)
Rows matched: 2  Changed: 2  Warnings: 0

mysql> SELECT email, revemail FROM staff;
+-------------------------------+-------------------------------+
| email                         | revemail                      |
+-------------------------------+-------------------------------+
| Mike.Hillyer@sakilastaff.com  | moc.ffatsalikas@reylliH.ekiM  |
| Jon.Stephens@sakilastaff.com  | moc.ffatsalikas@snehpetS.noJ  |
+-------------------------------+-------------------------------+
2 rows in set (0.03 sec)
mysql> EXPLAIN SELECT first_name, last_name, email
    -> FROM staff
    -> WHERE email LIKE '%sakilastaff.com'\G
```

You can use the REVERSE() function to show you what the comparison string should be, and then run an EXPLAIN to see if the new field and index help:

```
mysql> SELECT REVERSE('%sakilastaff.com');
+-----------------------------+
| REVERSE('%sakilastaff.com') |
+-----------------------------+
| moc.ffatsalikas%            |
+-----------------------------+
1 row in set (0.00 sec)
```

```
mysql> EXPLAIN SELECT first_name, last_name, email
    -> FROM staff
    -> WHERE revemail LIKE 'moc.ffatsalikas%'\G
*************************** 1. row ***************************
           id: 1
  select_type: SIMPLE
        table: staff
         type: range
possible_keys: revemail
          key: revemail
      key_len: 203
          ref: NULL
         rows: 1
        Extra: Using index condition; Using MRR
1 row in set (0.00 sec)
```

You have optimized the query to have a data access strategy (type) of range. You also have the desirable Extra values Using index condition and Using MRR — see Table 18-2 for details.

Note that having an extra field also means upkeep of the field. The best way to upkeep the field would be to have any code that inserts or updates the email field also update the new revemail field. Another option is to create triggers to update the revemail field when the email field is changed. See Chapter 7 for more information about triggers.

Batching expensive operations

INSERT and DELETE operations need to update indexes, and DELETE operations can cause fragmentation. These operations are particularly expensive on MyISAM tables, as the table blocks all other reads and writes until the INSERT and DELETE operations are complete. One way to optimize INSERT queries on MyISAM is to use the system variable concurrent_insert, which allows some nonblocking INSERT operations. Another way to optimize these queries, regardless of storage engine, is to batch expensive INSERT and DELETE operations.

INSERT operations can be batched by using the INSERT DELAYED syntax. For more information on INSERT DELAYED, see Chapter 4.

To batch DELETE operations and reduce fragmentation, use a table for deleted records:

```
CREATE TABLE deleted_customer (
customer_id smallint(5) unsigned NOT NULL PRIMARY KEY
ENGINE=InnoDB DEFAULT CHARSET=utf8;
```

When a customer is deleted, they are flagged for deletion by inserting their customer_id into the deleted_customer table. When a query looks for nondeleted customers, it can use a very fast join with the desirable Not exists value for Extra:

```
mysql> EXPLAIN SELECT first_name, last_name
    -> FROM customer LEFT JOIN deleted_customer USING (customer_id)
    -> WHERE deleted_customer.customer_id IS NULL\G
```

```
*************************** 1. row ***************************
           id: 1
  select_type: SIMPLE
        table: customer
         type: ALL
possible_keys: NULL
          key: NULL
      key_len: NULL
          ref: NULL
         rows: 579
        Extra:
*************************** 2. row ***************************
           id: 1
  select_type: SIMPLE
        table: deleted_customer
         type: eq_ref
possible_keys: PRIMARY
          key: PRIMARY
      key_len: 2
          ref: sakila.customer.customer_id
         rows: 1
        Extra: Using where; Using index; Not exists
2 rows in set (0.02 sec)
```

Because DELETE operations are expensive, a batch DELETE should be scheduled for nonpeak times. After deleting rows from the customer table, defragment the table. Table defragmentation will lock the table with a write lock, blocking all reads and writes, but that is another reason to perform batch deletions during nonpeak times. The batch deletion is done by running:

```
DELETE customer.* FROM customer
INNER JOIN deleted_customer USING (customer_id);

TRUNCATE TABLE deleted_customer;

OPTIMIZE TABLE;
```

Even though the table join when retrieving nondeleted customer information is fast, it is more overhead. However, because expensive DELETE operations are batched, overall the application will run much faster if problems are caused by having many DELETE operations.

Optimizing frequent operations

There may be a database query that is run extremely frequently. Even if it is not a particularly slow or expensive query, it is contributing to load on your servers. Example queries retrieve information such as:

- The number of currently online customers
- The total number of active customers

629

- Rankings
- Tag clouds
- How many articles or other resources appear on the site
- How many comments an article has
- Up-to-the-second calculations of account balances

These queries can often be batched. For example, do your customers need the exact up-to-the-second number of logged-in customers? This may be a number displayed on every web page, including pre-login pages, to get people to log in and stay logged in. It may be sufficient in these cases to calculate the number of logged-in customers once every 5 minutes.

Depending on the usage of your application, calculating rankings, number of comments on an article, and account balances may make more sense to be denormalized instead of calculated on the fly. For example, the following query lists customers in order from those who have paid the most to those who have paid the least:

```
mysql> EXPLAIN SELECT first_name, last_name, SUM(amount) AS
       total_paid
    -> FROM customer INNER JOIN payment USING (customer_id)
    -> GROUP BY customer_id ORDER BY total_paid DESC\G
*************************** 1. row ***************************
           id: 1
  select_type: SIMPLE
        table: customer
         type: ALL
possible_keys: PRIMARY
          key: NULL
      key_len: NULL
          ref: NULL
         rows: 591
        Extra: Using temporary; Using filesort
*************************** 2. row ***************************
           id: 1
  select_type: SIMPLE
        table: payment
         type: ref
possible_keys: idx_fk_customer_id
          key: idx_fk_customer_id
      key_len: 2
          ref: sakila.customer.customer_id
         rows: 14
        Extra:
2 rows in set (0.00 sec)
```

If this query is run every time a report is accessed, it may be running quite often, depending on who can access the reports! Rankings, number of comments per article, and tag cloud calculations are frequently run at a rate higher than the data actually changes.

One way to optimize reporting queries and other calculations that are run more frequently than the data changes is to denormalize the data, using new field(s) or table(s) to store the relevant calculations. When the data is changed, the denormalized field(s) must also be updated. This can be done by changing your application code or by adding a trigger. For more on triggers, see Chapter 7.

Another way to optimize these types of queries is to run them periodically, storing the results in the database, file, or globally accessible application-wide variable. This can pose problems if users are expected to seeing up-to-the-second current results, so try to train your customers to expect recent, but not necessarily up-to-the-second, results. If there is resistance to changing user expectations, calculating features such as rankings periodically can be a great marketing tool. Customers will likely log in more often if their rankings change every 4–6 hours, instead of immediately after each action they take.

Summary

In this chapter, you have learned how to use EXPLAIN to generate a query plan. How data and data changes over time can affect the query plans has been discussed. You have explored how to make a query plan better by:

- Adding indexes
- Changing the size and type of data fields
- Adding new data fields
- Moving indexed fields out of functions
- Limiting the use of temporary tables
- Batching expensive and/or frequent queries
- Periodically calculating frequent queries

Chapter 19

Monitoring Your Systems

I n Chapter 17, we discussed how to measure database performance. By taking regular measurements of the health of your systems, you can learn about database problems before they are happening, send a message as they are happening, and have information to help debug after they happen. This type of automated monitoring can make your job easier, whether monitoring alerts you when a system is down, or gives you the information necessary for capacity planning.

It is surprising how many organizations do not have any automated alerting, because "when the database is down, we know because users call us." Alerting frameworks are easy to set up and use and can let you know not only about current problems, but alert you to what may be a problem in the future. For example, a full disk will cause `mysqld` to hang and may cause corrupt data and log files. Alerting when a disk is approaching capacity can save a lot of problems — you can clear out some space and make sure the disk does not become full.

Sending an alert is as easy as sending an e-mail; most pagers and cell phones have e-mail addresses that can be set up to send the device a message. It may be tempting to schedule scripts that, when they fail, send an e-mail. However, there is a lot more flexibility in alerting systems that do not take much time to set up. Alerting systems come bundled with basic checks, and the best ones are ones where you can write your own checks and easily integrate them into the alerting framework.

Even in organizations that have alerting, graphing trends and patterns ends up being a low priority. However, organizations that graph data are better able to handle alerts, find the root causes of problems, and predict when future problems may occur. Though graphs are not necessarily examined daily, they are an immense help when they are examined.

IN THIS CHAPTER

Deciding what to monitor

Examining open source monitoring

Examining commercial monitoring

> **TIP** It should be pointed out when examining the output of whatever program that you use for monitoring that, as an example, just because your systems are operating at an average of 10% of resource utilization that you expect the systems to be able to operate with 10 times that load. The reason why is that systems scaling is never a linear issue. When you hit 20% utilization you might uncover a bottleneck that keeps your systems from working well until you resolve the problem.

We will discuss some of the widely-used open source monitoring tools, as well as the MySQL Enterprise Monitor that is part of paid support for MySQL, and MONyog, another commercially available monitoring tool. While all of the solutions presented in this chapter are suitable for production use in an enterprise environment, you may find that some are more suitable than others for your environment. For example, many of the tools depend heavily on SNMP (the Simple Network Management Protocol), which some organizations deem unsecure. Other organizations may require an agent-less protocol, or that the monitoring tool(s) run on the Windows operating system. The many solutions provided in this chapter reflect the needs of different organizations.

Deciding What to Monitor

Monitoring, like documentation, is an ongoing process. New features in mysqld and changes in database use may require changing what is monitored. Monitoring adds overhead to your systems and takes time to implement and maintain, so *monitor everything* is not always desirable.

Exactly what you should monitor is different for different environments. Each item you monitor must have a purpose for monitoring — for example, you may monitor replication lag to be able to see trends in how far behind replication lags. You may also monitor replication lag to alert you when replication lags beyond a certain point, as that may indicate a bigger problem.

Thinking of the reasons for monitoring can help you figure out what you need to monitor. Some reasons for monitoring are:

- Alerting when:
  - The database is unavailable
  - A database error occurs
  - InnoDB tablespaces are running out of space
  - The file system is running out of space (mysqld hangs when it cannot write to a log or data file)
  - The file system is running out of memory
  - A query has been running for a long time
  - There are many connections, approaching max_connections
  - The database response time is unacceptable

- Replication is lagging behind
- Temporary disk tables get very large
- Slow query rate is high
- Number of sleeping queries is high

- Graphing and seeing trends/patterns for:

  - Database/system uptime
  - InnoDB buffer pool efficiency
  - Query cache efficiency
  - How much disk space the database uses
  - How many users your application has
  - Table locks
  - How often tables in a database are changed
  - File I/O caused by the database
  - Number and size of reads/writes/transactions
  - Replication lag
  - Table cache efficiency
  - Number of connections and their states (sleeping, copying to temp table, query)
  - Frequency of query joins, sorts, full table scans, range scans
  - Temporary table and temporary disk table usage

This list is not exhaustive, but it is a good start to thinking about what you might want to monitor. Note that the items on the list above point to more than simply monitoring database parameters. The best monitoring solutions take into account the database, the server, the application, and other architectural pieces of the system such as load balancers and switches.

Many organizations run an excellent alerting solution (such as Nagios) and an excellent graphing solution (such as Cacti), though this has the overhead and duplication that information about what hosts and services to monitor is in more than one place. However, the alternative is an all-in-one solution that is not as strong in both alerting and graphing.

When deciding what to use for your monitoring needs, consider how the organization as a whole can benefit from your choices. It is not uncommon for a DBA to install monitoring on their systems, and have a systems administrator say "can you just monitor Apache on the webservers, too?" Small projects can grow, and with the right technologies in place, you can start the ball rolling on a monitoring system that will be able to see details such as whether or not a server is running, as well as overall pictures such as how many concurrent users your application can withstand.

Monitoring systems can be divided into two groups: agent-based and agentless. With an agent-based system a program (*agent*) is installed on the host server being monitored that is continually running as a service (on Windows) or a daemon (on Unix-based servers). This agent monitors the local system and communicates back to a central server. Agentless monitoring, on the other hand, does not require an additional agent to be running on the local server. Monitoring may be done remotely through protocols such as SSH and SNMP, or locally via a scheduled task or cronjob.

An agent can often give more visibility of the inner workings of the monitored server. However, an agent requires maintenance of a distributed program, and may use more system resources on the monitored server than agentless monitoring. If there are hundreds of servers, installation and upgrades can be quite time consuming. With agentless monitoring, you can have a very quick rollout of monitoring services for even large numbers of servers.

Examining Open Source Monitoring

The most popular monitoring systems are open source frameworks. Though Nagios is the most popular alerting system and Cacti is the most popular graphing system, there are other monitoring systems that are good enough to deserve mention. This section will discuss the following monitoring frameworks:

- Nagios
- Cacti
- Hyperic HQ
- OpenNMS
- Zenoss core
- Munin
- Monit

Nagios

One of the most widely used open source alerting systems is Nagios (pronounced "NAH-ghee-ose"). Nagios was originally developed for use under Linux, though it can be used under other variants of Unix, including BSD systems, Solaris and Mac OS X. Nagios can monitor Windows servers, but the centralized Nagios server does not run natively on Windows. Nagios does not do graphing or trending very well. The web interface is written in PHP, and the checks are mostly Perl and shell scripts, though checks can be a script in any language that can run from the command line.

Many operating system distributions include Nagios; if yours does not, it can be downloaded at www.nagios.org, where there is also extensive documentation. The main features of Nagios are:

- Graphical web-based user interface
- Convenient dashboard overview for overall health at-a-glance
- Supports host, service and network monitoring

- Supports agent-less checks and client-server agents (a daemon running on each client machine checked sends information back to the centralized server)

- Supports agent-less checking of cloud computing environments. Supports agent-based checking if the agent is installed in the cloud computing environment.

- Text file based configuration (there is a separate nagiosql package that makes the configuration web-based)

- Extensive user community, including many free third-party plugins (www. nagiosexchange.org)

- Define custom alerting scripts, with four possible statuses

- Define custom actions based on status

- Extremely customizable user permissions

- Web interface authorization for security

- Servers can be easily grouped

- History and basic reporting of alert status

- Which machines are checked, when they are checked, who is notified and what actions are taken are all configurable in almost any way possible — you can specify that a machine is not checked Sundays from 3 pm to 4 pm, or a group of machines should e-mail alerts from 6 pm to 8 am and send pages from 8 am to 6 pm.

- One-off downtimes can be scheduled

- Custom paging escalations

- Acknowledgement of a problem can be optional or required

- Dependencies can be set up, reducing pager storms when a parent service goes down.

- Very basic network topology map

- Screenshots of Nagios are available at www.nagios.org/about/screenshots.php

- Virtual appliance for VMWare are available at www.vmware.com/appliances/directory/372

All this flexibility and customizability comes with a learning curve. However, it is not a large learning curve, and there is a "quickstart" guide to setting up Nagios in 15 minutes at http://nagios.sourceforge.net/docs/3_0/quickstart.html. There is also a large user community available to help.

Cacti

Cacti is a widely-used PHP time-series graphing tool with a centralized server that can be installed on Unix, Mac OS X and Windows. Data is gathered via SNMP. Cacti is available from www.cacti.net.

The main features of Cacti are:

- Graphical web-based user interface

- Convenient dashboard overview for overall health at-a-glance

- Supports host, service and network monitoring
- Agent-less monitoring
- Due to agent-less monitoring, implicitly supports checking of cloud computing environments
- Web-based configuration management
- Extensive user community, including many free templates (`http://forums.cacti.net/about15067.html`)
- Define custom data-gathering scripts
- Define custom graphs
- Extremely customizable user permissions
- Web interface authorization for security
- User-defined preferences
- History and extensive reporting of data gathered
- Servers can be easily grouped
- View many graphs at once
- View multiple servers on a graph
- View multiple services on a graph
- Customizable graph type (line, area, stack, etc) and graph order
- Easy drag-and-drop to zoom on any graph
- View/edit raw data
- Screenshots of cacti are available at `www.cacti.net/screenshots.php`
- Virtual appliances for VMWare, Parallels, Qemu, KVM, VirtualIron and Microsoft Virtual PC are available at `http://virtualappliances.net/products/cacti.php`

There are plugins to Cacti which give basic alerting functionality, but nowhere near the flexibility of Nagios. However, Cacti is the most comprehensive open source graphing tool available. There is also no way to define a custom set of times for when to gather data for graphing with Cacti.

Baron Schwartz, MySQL community member and co-author of *High Performance MySQL, 2nd edition*, developed a set of Cacti templates for monitoring MySQL (`www.xaprb.com/blog/tag/cacti-templates/`).

Hyperic HQ

Hyperic HQ is a Java-based comprehensive graphing solution, with some alerting features. It is available for download from `www.hyperic.com`. Binaries for Windows, Solaris and Linux are available, and there is also a platform-independent version, which uses the Java Runtime Environment (JRE) already installed on your system. Hyperic HQ can run SNMP checks, but is not dependent on SNMP.

The main features of Hyperic HQ are:

- Graphical web-based user interface
- Convenient dashboard overview for overall health at-a-glance
- Supports host, service and network monitoring
- Supports client-server agents (a daemon running on each client machine checked sends information back to the centralized server)
- Explicitly supports checking of cloud computing environments including Amazon Web Services and Google App Engine.
- Auto-discovery of services on a host (once an agent is deployed)
- Web-based configuration management
- Many built-in checks, including hundreds of MySQL checks. See `www.hyperic.com/products/managed/mysql-management.htm` for the impressive list of metrics on reliability, transactions, connections, SQL commands, configuration changes, resource utilization, queries, I/O, and tables.
- Define custom alerting scripts
- Manually perform `ANALYZE TABLE`, `CHECK TABLE`, `OPTIMIZE TABLE` and `REPAIR TABLE` from the Hyperic HQ interface
- History and extensive reporting of data gathered
- Define custom data-gathering scripts
- Define custom graphs
- Servers can be easily grouped
- View multiple servers on a graph
- View multiple services on a graph
- Custom paging escalations
- Acknowledgement of a problem can be optional or required
- Dependencies can be set up, reducing pager storms in the event that a parent service goes down
- Screenshots available at `www.hyperic.com/demo/gallery.html`
- VMWare virtual appliance version

Hyperic does have a user community and user-contributed plugins, though the user community is not as large as that of Nagios. There are not many user-contributed plugins, but that is likely due to the comprehensive nature of Hyperic's built-in checks. There is an Enterprise edition for purchase that adds in many features including automated failover, more flexible alerting, automated corrective actions, scheduled maintenance, and role-based access control.

Hyperic HQ is an appropriate solution for an organization that requires graphing and alerting to be a part of the same application. Although the alerting functionality in the non-Enterprise version is similar to that of Cacti's capabilities, Hyperic HQ has more out-of-the-box graphs for MySQL.

OpenNMS

The open network management system, or OpenNMS, is a distributed graphing and alerting system. Written in Java, XML and XSL, it is available from www.opennms.org for Linux, Solaris, BSD, Mac OS X, and Windows. OpenNMS checks a number of protocols, though it is dependent on SNMP for many checks.

The main features of OpenNMS are:

- Graphical web-based user interface
- Convenient dashboard overview for overall health at-a-glance
- Supports host, service and network monitoring
- Auto-discovery of services on a host or IP address range
- Web-based configuration management
- Agent-less monitoring
- Define custom data-gathering scripts
- Define custom graphs
- Define custom alerting scripts
- Define custom actions based on status
- Extremely customizable user permissions
- Web interface authorization for security
- User-defined preferences
- History and extensive reporting of data gathered
- Servers can be easily grouped
- View many graphs at once
- Zoom by time-period on any graph
- Active user community
- Custom paging escalations
- Acknowledgement of a problem can be optional or required

- Dependencies can be set up, reducing pager storms in the event that a parent service goes down

- Extensive network topology map

- Official demo available from `http://demo.opennms.org/opennms/` (username: demo, password: demo)

OpenNMS does not seem to have many custom checks, and it is unclear whether that is because SNMP can handle most of the checks, or if there is no easy way such as a script, plug-in or template to share a check.

Zenoss Core

Zenoss Core is a Python-based monitoring system that runs on Linux, Solaris, BSD and Mac OS X environments. Data can be gathered via SNMP or via the Zenoss Plugins, platform-specific python monitoring scripts. Zenoss Core can be downloaded at `www.zenoss.com/download/links`.

The main features of Zenoss Core are:

- Graphical web-based user interface

- Convenient dashboard overview for overall health at-a-glance

- Supports host, service and network monitoring

- Supports agentless checks and client-server agents (a daemon running on each client machine checked sends information back to the centralized server)

- Supports agent-less checking of cloud computing environments. Supports agent-based checking if the agent is installed in the cloud computing environment.

- Auto-discovery of services on a host

- Web-based configuration management

- Very active user community, with many user-contributed customizations (`www.zenoss.com/community/wiki/tips-and-tricks/`)

- Define custom data-gathering scripts

- Define custom graphs

- Define custom alerting scripts

- Define custom actions based on status

- Extremely customizable user permissions

- Web interface authorization for security

- History and extensive reporting of data gathered

- Servers can be easily grouped

- View many graphs at once

641

- View multiple servers on a graph

- View multiple services on a graph

- Customizable graph type (line, area, stack, etc.) and graph order

- Easy zooming on any graph using scrolling and enlarge/reduce functionality

- Which machines are checked, when they are checked, who is notified and what actions are taken are all configurable in almost any way possible — you can specify that a machine is not checked Sundays from 3 pm to 4 pm, or a group of machines should e-mail alerts from 6 pm to 8 am and send pages from 8 am to 6 pm

- One-off downtimes can be scheduled

- Custom paging escalations

- Acknowledgement of a problem can be optional or required

- Advanced network topology and geography maps

- Screenshots available at `www.zenoss.com/product/screenshots`

- Virtual appliance for VMware available at `www.zenoss.com/download/links`

Like Hyperic HQ, Zenoss Core has an enterprise product. Zenoss Enterprise adds in support and more features, including predictive thresholds, finer-grained access control, report libraries and advanced checks such as web, email and database transactions. One of the bigger downsides of Zenoss is a lack of ability to set up dependencies.

Munin

Munin is a Perl-based graphing tool with basic alerting capability. It can be installed on any platform that Perl can be run on, though there are no official Windows installation instructions. Checks can be written in any language, as long as the script runs on command-line. Munin is downloadable from `http://sourceforge.net/projects/munin/`.

The main features of Munin are:

- Graphical web-based user interface

- Supports host, service and network monitoring

- Supports agent-less checks and client-server agents (a daemon running on each client machine checked sends information back to the centralized server)

- Supports agent-less checking of cloud computing environments. Supports agent-based checking if the agent is installed in the cloud computing environment.

- Web-based configuration management

- Extensive user community, including many free third-party plugins (`http://muninexchange.projects.linpro.no/`)

- Define custom data-gathering scripts

- Basic alerting capabilities

- Define custom actions based on status
- History and extensive reporting of data gathered
- Multiple services per graph
- View many graphs at once
- Very active user community
- Demo site at `http://munin.ping.uio.no/`
- Virtual appliance

Unfortunately, Munin is limited to server per graph, and there are no zooming capabilities. There is also no dashboard overview, and no built-in user authentication. Other desirable features are very basic or lacking, such as server grouping, scheduled maintenance windows and one-off downtimes. In addition, the monitoring capabilities are limited. Munin is a good choice for organizations that prefer not to use SNMP.

Monit

Monit is a Unix-based tool to perform custom actions based on the output of a check. Though it is not strictly designed as an alerting framework, many organizations use Monit to e-mail or page when a check has a certain output. Unlike all of the other frameworks in this chapter, Monit has no centralized server to gather data. Instead, it is installed on each server that requires alerting. This can be beneficial, as there is no loss of data if there is a network disconnect. However, this can also create a lot of overhead. Also, Monit requires that each server be able to e-mail or page if there is a problem — which means both that each server must be able to access resources such as an SMTP server to send mail, and that a network problem could get in the way of important e-mails and pages being sent.

Monit is designed for Unix platforms, and can be run on Linux, Solaris, BSD and Mac OS X. It can be downloaded at `www.tildeslash.com/monit/download/`.

The main features of Monit are:

- Graphical web-based user interface
- Convenient dashboard overview for overall health at-a-glance
- Supports host, service and network monitoring
- Monitoring is done via separate daemons on each machine to be monitored, and each instance is separate. It is possible to check remote hosts, but Monit is not designed to be a remote monitoring framework.
- Text file based configuration
- Define custom alerting scripts, limited to checking processes on the process list and file checks for: file permissions, checksum, timestamp, and size
- Define custom actions based on status

- Services can be stopped, started and restarted manually via the web interface

- Dependencies can be set up, reducing pager storms in the event that a parent service goes down

- Screenshots are available at `www.tildeslash.com/monit/doc/screen.php`

- Virtual appliance for VMWare (note that this is a virtual appliance with many programs, not just Monit) is available at `www.vmware.com/appliances/directory/342`

Monit is a very lightweight solution, suitable for environments with automated setups and configuration. The tradeoff is that functionality is limited — there are no user/role based permissions, no acknowledgement procedures and no historical reports.

Examining Commercial Monitoring

There are many commercial monitoring solutions, but we will focus on two in particular: MySQL Enterprise Monitor, developed by the same company that brings us MySQL, and MONyog, a MySQL monitoring tool from `www.webyog.com`, the same folks who brought us SQLyog, a popular MySQL GUI client access tool which we discussed in Chapter 3.

MySQL enterprise monitor

The MySQL Enterprise Monitoring is a tool developed by Sun/MySQL specifically for monitoring MySQL. It is available with a paid support contract, although there is a 30-day free trial.

Though it is not a full database, server and network alerting and graphing framework, it does provide comprehensive alerting and graphing of MySQL systems.

The main features of MySQL Enterprise Monitor include:

- Graphical web-based user interface

- Convenient dashboard overview for overall health at-a-glance

- Supports full MySQL and some host monitoring

- Supports client-server agents (a daemon running on each client machine checked sends information back to the centralized server)

- Supports agent-based checking if the agent is installed in the cloud computing environment.

- Replication auto-discovery

- Web-based configuration management

- Supported by Sun/MySQL

- Define custom data-gathering scripts

- Over 600 MySQL and operating system parameters checked

- Over 100 advisors to warn of security risks and possible poor query and replication performance
- Define custom graphs
- Define custom alerting thresholds
- Extremely customizable user permissions
- Web interface authorization for security
- User-defined preferences
- History and extensive reporting of data gathered
- Servers can be easily grouped
- View many graphs at once
- View multiple servers on a graph
- Maintenance windows can be scheduled
- English and Japanese language versions
- Screenshots are available along the right-hand side of `www.mysql.com/products/enterprise/demo.html`
- Demo videos available at: `www.mysql.com/products/enterprise/demo.html` (requires login)

There is more information on the MySQL Enterprise Monitor on MySQL's website at: `www.mysql.com/products/enterprise/monitor.html`. The MySQL Enterprise Monitor is an extremely useful tool for a MySQL database administrator. Its main detractors are the fact that it is not open source, it costs money, and it is limited to database and some operating system parameters, so it is not a comprehensive monitoring solution for an entire application. However, it is an exceptionally good tool for graphing, alerting and advising of both current and potential problems.

MONyog

MONyog is a MySQL Monitor and Advisor sold by Webyog Softworks Private, Ltd. It is a full-featured MySQL alerting and graphing tool, which can also monitor some Linux parameters. It is a closed-source commercial offering, though the price is moderate and there is a 30-day free trial.

The main features of MONyog include:

- Graphical web-based user interface
- Convenient dashboard overview for overall health at-a-glance
- Supports full MySQL and some host monitoring
- Log analyzer for the general and slow query logs
- Real-time, interactive `SHOW PROCESSLIST` monitoring

- Advisors to warn of security risks and possible poor query and replication performance
- Agent-less monitoring (without the use of SNMP; ssh tunnels are used)
- Define custom data-gathering scripts
- Supports agent-less checking of cloud computing environments
- Web-based configuration management
- Web interface authorization for security
- User-defined preferences
- History and extensive reporting of data gathered
- View many graphs at once
- Screenshots available at www.webyog.com/en/screenshots_monyog.php
- Trial version available at www.webyog.com/en/downloads.php

MONyog lacks the ability to see multiple servers on a graph, and multiple services on a graph. Though it provides both graphs and alerts, the alerting capability is basic — there are no acknowledgements, escalations, scheduled maintenance windows nor one-off downtimes. However, the graphing capabilities are excellent, and it is the only tool with out-of-the-box monitoring of the MySQL process list and logs. Being able to remotely view these, and even view more than one server side-by-side, comes in very handy when trying to troubleshoot more than one database server having a problem. Instead of logging into each server and monitoring the process list and slow query logs, it can be done from one centralized server.

> **NOTE**   A full, independent review of MONyog by one of the authors of this book is available at www.pythian.com/blogs/1086/reviewing-monyog.

Summary

In this chapter, we reviewed nine different software tools that can monitor MySQL systems. We discussed why both alerting and graphing are important and the many parameters that can be monitored. After reading this chapter, you should be able to choose one or more tools that are appropriate for alerting and graphing MySQL in your environment.

This chapter covered the following topics:

- Monitoring system background
  - Agent vs agentless monitoring
- Deciding what to monitor
- Open source monitoring systems

- Nagios
- Cacit
- Hyperic HQ
- OpenVMS
- Zenoss Core
- Munin
- Monit
- Closed source monitoring tools
  - MySQL Enterprise Monintor
  - MONyog

Chapter 20

Securing MySQL

Databases contain critical data about a company's operations, customers, and history. Most companies would have a difficult time surviving a data loss or data theft. This chapter reviews the various features of MySQL that can be used to secure MySQL databases.

One of the worst assumptions a developer or administrator can make is "At this point, trust is assumed." Allowing an anonymous user, allowing a specific user from any machine, and trusting data that was verified in a previous step are examples of assuming trust. These assumptions result in security breaches when it is possible to subvert the reason trust is allowed.

Having many different layers of security is called *defense in depth*. It is a critical strategy that is often overlooked. It is all too easy to believe that there are no vulnerabilities and no ways to bypass security measures on operating systems, databases, application code, web servers, application servers, and firewalls. Unfortunately, it is possible that one or more of the security mechanisms in place may fail. With defense in depth, a failure of one layer need not result in a security incident.

Access Control Lists

An *access control list* (ACL) is a list of associated permissions. This list specifies which users are allowed to perform operations on an object. In MySQL, the object can be global or tied to a specific database, event, routine, table, or even field. For example, a user such as developer@dev.company.com can have a SELECT privilege on a table, and a user such as admin@localhost can have the SHUTDOWN global privilege to stop mysqld. For more information on how to create these users and privileges, see Chapter 14.

Wildcards and blank values

SQL wildcard values (% and _) are allowed in the host string part of a user, and are a tradeoff between security and convenience. Wildcards pose security risks, but without wildcards, allowing usage from many hosts would make the access control list very large and hard to manage.

MySQL allows `%` to be specified as the entire host string, which allows a username and password to connect from any host. In our experience we have never found it necessary to specify `%` as a host string.

> **NOTE** Even when access to the host is restricted by a firewall, we recommend limiting host string values.

Organizations that have the need for many hosts to connect to a database can be more secure by using wildcards in part of the host string. Table 20-1 shows the use of wildcards in part of the host string.

TABLE 20-1

Use of Wildcards in Host Strings

Host String	Description
192.168.1.%	Matches 192.168.1.[0-255]
192.168._.%	Matches 192.168.[0-9].[0-255]
192.168.%	Matches 192.168.[0-255].[0-255]
%.web.hostname.com	Matches any host ending in ".web.hostname.com"
%.hostname.com	Matches any host ending in ".hostname.com"

A blank value (' ') in a host string acts the same as a host string of '%'. A blank value for a username means that any user can connect from the host string specified, with the password specified. A blank username is called the "anonymous" user. A blank value for a password means that the user can connect from the host string specified and must not specify a password.

Blank values for host strings, usernames, and passwords are not appropriate. By default a mysqld binary installation will create a root@localhost user with a blank password, and an anonymous user. On a non-Windows system, these can be fixed by running the mysql_secure_installation program. The Windows installer asks if an anonymous user should be created, and prompts for a root password.

Privilege and privilege levels

The GRANT statement syntax allows privileges to be applied on a global, database, table, column, and routine level (see Chapter 14 for more information). Determining appropriate privilege levels depends on what the user's role is and the structure of your schema. For example, a backup user has the need for read privileges on the structures it needs to back up; however, there is no need for a backup user to be able to bulk load data or execute stored routines related to the application. A monitoring application that only needs to connect to the database to see if it is working needs only the USAGE privilege at the global level. Table 20-2 lists the various privileges available.

TABLE 20-2

Privilege and Privilege Levels

Privilege	Allows	Global	Db	Table	Column	Routine
ALL	All privileges for the level	Yes	Yes	Yes	No	No
ALL PRIVILEGES	Same as ALL	Yes	Yes	Yes	No	No
ALTER	ALTER TABLE	Yes	Yes	Yes	No	No
ALTER ROUTINE	ALTER and DROP stored routines	Yes	Yes	No	No	No
CREATE	CREATE TABLE	Yes	Yes	Yes	No	Yes
CREATE ROUTINE	Create stored routines	Yes	Yes	No	No	No
CREATE TEMPORARY TABLES	CREATE TEMPORARY TABLES	Yes	Yes	No	No	No
CREATE USER	CREATE USER, DROP USER, RENAME USER, REVOKE ALL PRIVILEGES	Yes	No	No	No	No
CREATE VIEW	CREATE VIEW	Yes	Yes	Yes	No	No
DELETE	DELETE	Yes	Yes	Yes	No	No
DROP	DROP TABLE	Yes	Yes	Yes	No	No
EVENT	Event creation	Yes	Yes	No	No	No
EXECUTE	Run stored routines	Yes	Yes	No	No	No
FILE	SELECT ... .INTO OUTFILE and LOAD DATA INFILE	Yes	No	No	No	No

continued

TABLE 20-2   *(continued)*

Privilege	Allows	Global	Db	Table	Column	Routine
INDEX	CREATE INDEX, DROP INDEX	Yes	Yes	Yes	No	No
INSERT	INSERT	Yes	Yes	Yes	No	No
LOCK TABLES	LOCK TABLES on all tables the user is allowed the SELECT privilege	Yes	Yes	No	No	No
PROCESS	SHOW PROCESSLIST shows all users' processes	Yes	No	No	No	No
REFERENCES	[currently a placeholder, unused]	Yes	Yes	Yes	Yes	No
RELOAD	FLUSH	Yes	No	No	No	No
REPLICATION CLIENT	Can determine master and slave hosts	Yes	No	No	No	No
REPLICATION SLAVE	Reading binary log events	Yes	No	No	No	No
SELECT	SELECT	Yes	Yes	Yes	Yes	No
SHOW DATABASES	Shows all databases, including those the user has no privileges for	Yes	No	No	No	No
SHOW VIEW	SHOW CREATE VIEW	Yes	Yes	Yes	No	No
SHUTDOWN	mysqladmin shutdown	Yes	No	No	No	No
SUPER	CHANGE MASTER, KILL, PURGE MASTER LOGS, SET GLOBAL, mysqladmin debug, one connection even if there are already max_connections	Yes	No	No	No	No
TRIGGER	CREATE TRIGGER, DROP TRIGGER	Yes	Yes	Yes	No	No
UPDATE	UPDATE	Yes	Yes	Yes	Yes	No
USAGE	Authentication only	Yes	Yes	Yes	No	No
WITH GRANT OPTION	GRANT for the privileges specified	Yes	Yes	Yes	Yes	Yes

The GRANT ALL ON *.* command gives a broad range of privileges, which are usually unnecessary. Does the user actually need to KILL threads, bulk load data, perform FLUSH commands, and be able to DROP any table? For all databases and tables, including the ones for mysqld internal use? Table 20-3 lists examples of appropriate privileges.

TABLE 20-3

Sample Permissions Based on User Role

User Role	Privilege
Application, read-only	SELECT
Application, read/write	DELETE, EXECUTE, INSERT, SELECT, UPDATE
Monitoring	USAGE
Replication monitoring	REPLICATION CLIENT
Replication slave	REPLICATION SLAVE
Schema Administrator	ALTER, ALTER ROUTINE, CREATE, CREATE ROUTINE, CREATE VIEW, DROP, EVENT, EXECUTE, INDEX, SHOW DATABASES, TRIGGER
Developer	FILE
DBA	CREATE USER, EVENT, FILE, LOCK TABLES, PROCESS, FLUSH, REPLICATION CLIENT, SHOW DATABASES, SHUTDOWN, SUPER, WITH GRANT OPTION

Note that an actual developer will likely need more privileges than just FILE. However, most of the time when a developer is using a database, the actual role being used is the application. Therefore, a developer might actually have two roles: Developer and Application, read/write. It is important to point out that the FILE privilege is used for operations such as LOAD DATA INFILE and as such, are usually not appropriate for a user role within an application, but loading data certainly is something appropriate for a developer. The preceding table is merely an example of possible recommendations; roles can be changed and combined to fit your needs. For example, if your application allows end users to upload files to be loaded into the database, it would be completely appropriate for the Application role to have the FILE privilege.

In many organizations multiple roles are combined. It can be appropriate for a DBA who also debugs an application and administers the application schema to have ALL PRIVILEGES. However, there is very little reason a web-based application needs to be able to create a VIEW or drop a routine. Assigning appropriate privileges helps prevent user compromise as well as limits disaster when a user is compromised.

Accessing the Operating System

When considering the security of a database it is important to remember that the database server runs on a host server. This host server has security measures that need to be in place also to help ensure the security of the entire system.

Database access

To store to and retrieve from a database, an application needs access to the database. Traditionally this is done by allowing inbound TCP/IP connections on port 3306, the default port `mysqld` runs on. The weakest security is no security at all, meaning that the database port is open to the world. In the previous section we said allowing access from every host was a bad idea. Similarly, to have defense in depth, there should be some sort of firewall to limit database access on the `mysqld` host server.

Only the machines expected to connect to the database should be allowed that privilege. The firewall should deny access to all incoming traffic on the database port and then have rules to open up access to just the machines or subdomains that may access the database directly.

NOTE   Unfortunately, `mysqld` does not log attempted or successful logins to the database. This is one of the most often lamented inabilities of `mysqld`. `mysql-proxy` can be used for this; see Appendix A for more information on `mysql-proxy`.

Changing MySQL connectivity defaults

The `mysqld` daemon, by default, listens for TCP/IP traffic on port 3306 on all the interfaces of a server. On Unix systems, `mysqld` also accepts local connections by default, using a socket. On Windows servers, only TCP/IP is enabled by default. Accessing MySQL on a Windows server through shared memory or named pipes is possible, but needs to be configured explicitly.

Table 20-4 shows the options to `mysqld` that can be used to change the default MySQL connectivity settings.

NOTE   In MySQL version 5.1.20 and earlier, named pipes are not supported in `mysqld`. The `mysqld-nt` package has support for named pipes and enables them by default. In MySQL version 5.1.21 and higher, there is no `mysqld-nt` package; the `mysqld` package has support for named pipes but they are not enabled by default.

Operating system login

Not many roles require a login to the operating system that `mysqld` is running on. Database names, table definitions, data, indexes, and logs are stored by `mysqld` on the file system. Backups and data dumps may also be stored on the file system. The configuration file and `mysqld` running process are also available on the operating system. The operating system itself may keep logs with information about `mysqld`.

TABLE 20-4

Connectivity Options

Option	Example Usage	Description
bind-address	bind-address= 192.168.1.1	Binds the mysqld server to the specified IP address. Only one address may be specified. mysqld only accepts connections made directly to this interface.
enable-named-pipe	enable-named-pipe	Enables connectivity to mysqld on Windows via named pipes.
port	port=3307	Specifies the port mysqld listens on.
shared-memory	shared-memory	Enabled connectivity to mysqld on Windows via shared memory. To connect via shared memory, the client will have to connect specifying protocol=memory.
skip-name-resolve	skip-name-resolve	mysqld will not do a DNS lookup of hostnames (it will not resolve the names to IP addresses). This option is off by default. Turning this option on makes mysqld somewhat less secure; however, if DNS is slow and lookups are taking a long time, it may be necessary to turn this option on.
skip-networking	skip-networking	mysqld will not listen on a TCP/IP port.
socket	socket=/tmp/ mysqld.sock	Specifies the location of the mysqld socket.

Access to all that information should be as limited as possible. For example, the configuration file should have restricted permissions so that only the logins that need to read or write the file have permissions to do so. The mysqld process should not be able to be killed by anyone who is not a database administrator. Having permission to start mysqld means someone might start it with the skip-grant-tables option, which allows everyone to have full permissions across the entire schema — including the system tables.

Startup and shutdown scripts, data and log directories and files, backups, and any other information about the database should have appropriate read, write, and execute permissions so only those that are supposed to may perform actions that access, change, run, and kill.

WARNING Eliminate as many possible ways for your system to be compromised as you can. A database system should have very few entry methods exposed. Many database systems only allow machines on the local network, behind a firewall, to access two ports: the port mysqld is listening on (by default 3306) and a port that a login application is listening on (usually SSH, by default port 22).

Other open ports give other ways for access — unauthorized and authorized. As discussed in Chapter 10, running other server daemons such as the Apache web server can greatly reduce performance. However, server daemons that require more ports to be open (the Apache web server, mail transfer agent such as `sendmail`) reduce the security of the system. In addition, a security breach in another server daemon can lead to unauthorized access to the operating system. Web and mail servers in particular are a threat because they are designed to receive traffic from everywhere, and are often not behind a firewall.

To avoid this, do not install other server daemons on machines with `mysqld` installed for production use.

Securing Backups and Logs

In the previous section we mentioned that backups and logs should be secured. The processes for backups and logging also need to be secured. Taking a backup requires database access; a disk snapshot requires access to the directories and files, a logical backup requires a database login, and a cold backup requires access to the directories and files as well as the power to stop and start the database. Backups are often copied to another server in case of disaster. Logging and backups can be done from a centralized server.

The importance of this is to get you to think about where crucial information might be seen, and secure every path the information takes. A database server may be secured, but if it uses a plaintext protocol like FTP to copy logs or backups to another location, anyone who can sniff the network traffic can get a copy of the logs or backups. Even using a secure protocol to pass information back and forth, you may want to consider encrypting the information.

Similarly, remote backups and remote logging tools need to pass information back and forth through a secured protocol. Do not use a wireless network to send and receive information and if possible, use a private wired network when passing information back and forth.

Data Security

You cannot have a security breach on data you do not store. Do you need to store credit card information or national identification numbers in the database? Do you need to store them indefinitely? If your application uses authentication, is the password stored in plain text?

If you need to store and retrieve sensitive information, you can limit exposure by encrypting the data. If you are storing sensitive data for comparison, you can choose an encryption method that does not have a way to decrypt the data. This is called a *one-way hash*. A desirable feature of a one-way hash is that even if the data is compromised, the one-way encryption would have to be broken to figure out the sensitive data.

As an example, passwords are often encrypted with a one-way hash. When users try to authenticate with their password, the user-supplied password will be encrypted with the one-way hash and then compared to the stored, encrypted password. If they match, authentication is allowed.

Not all data can use a one-way hash. Storing credit card data for recurring purchases requires that the credit card information be decrypted so it can be used to process a payment. In this case you would need an encryption algorithm that has a corresponding decryption algorithm.

Data flow

Data flow is one of the most important aspects of data security. Very often there are a few places where data is checked and secured, and after that point the data is assumed to be trustworthy. Here is a sample data flow:

1. User enters text into a field on an HTML form and clicks a Submit button.
2. JavaScript verifies the text to ensure it has only valid characters.
3. The text gets sent to the next page, which performs an SQL query using that text.

This data flow shows one way to limit SQL injection. This method does not avoid all SQL injection, however. The page performing the SQL query assumes that the text is valid and does not check to make sure the previous page verified the text. A malicious user could bypass the HTML form, sending HTML POST or GET requests to the page performing the SQL query. Because the page performing the SQL query assumes the data has already been validated, SQL injection can occur.

SQL Injection

SQL injection occurs when a query is injected into another query. This occurs when the trusted data contains characters that form an unwanted subquery, UNION query, or query separator (semicolon is the most common). On a registration form users may be prompted to enter in their first and last names, which will then be inserted to the database. In the code, a query might be defined as:

```
INSERT INTO customer (first_name, last_name) VALUES ($first_name, $last_name);
```

When a user inserts the expected values into the form, the variables are populated and the query expands:

```
INSERT INTO customer (first_name, last_name) VALUES ('Sheeri', `Cabral');
```

What if a malicious user typed the following into the first name field instead of "Sheeri"?

```
Sheeri', (SELECT last_name FROM staff limit 1));  SELECT CONCAT('
```

Then the INSERT statement would expand to:

```
INSERT INTO customer (first_name, last_name) VALUES ('Sheeri',
(SELECT last_name FROM staff limit 1));  SELECT CONCAT('', `Cabral');
```

continued

continued

This is a valid INSERT statement, but not what the application developers intended. The malicious user has been able to access the database. This example may seem innocent, but it shows how allowing characters like quotes, semicolons, and parentheses can lead to compromised data.

Using SQL injection, a malicious user can do anything the application user can, including reading, changing, and deleting data. If the application user has DROP DATABASE permissions, the risk is much greater.

Programming languages have ways to escape and replace text to avoid SQL injection. Most programming languages also have ways of disallowing multiple SQL queries in one statement, which is another way to help avoid SQL injection. MySQL allows prepared statements, which escape text in a similar way that parameterized statements do in a programming language.

TIP   For information about prepared statements in MySQL, see the accompanying website to this book at www.wiley.com/go/mysqladminbible.

Another example of a data flow that could use more securing is when using encryption. MySQL comes with functions to encrypt and decrypt data; however, encryption can also happen at the client's machine or in the application code. Here is an example data flow:

1. User enters a credit card number into a field on an HTML form and clicks a "Submit" button.

2. A web server or application server runs application code to generate an SQL query, which includes a MySQL function call for encryption.

3. The query gets sent to MySQL.

4. MySQL encrypts the data before storage.

Anyone who can see the traffic along the path before the last step will be able to sniff the credit card number. The most common method of securing this type of issue is to use a secure protocol such as https to send traffic.

For each path that sensitive data can take, write down the data flow and note where the data is at risk. The only way to be 100% secure is not to take any user input and not to store any sensitive information. Because this is not possible, the best method is to find all the places where a data compromise is possible and perform a risk assessment analysis. For instance, users' credit card information may be stolen if they type it into a form when there is a keystroke logger installed on their computer. However, this most likely does not fall under the scope of a problem you have to plan for. You will likely accept that it is a risk, but conclude the cost of ensuring it does not exist is too great. It is useful to show coworkers within IT and the management hierarchy that some safeguards are in place to mitigate the most likely attacks, and note where the vulnerabilities are that may need further research.

Encrypted connectivity

One way to achieve encrypted connectivity to mysqld is to set up an SSH tunnel. You can do this using SSH itself or through some MySQL clients, as discussed in Chapter 3. Another way is to use the internal encryption connectivity settings in mysqld.

Encrypting connectivity to mysqld is not difficult to achieve. As with all encryption, though, encrypted connectivity adds computing overhead, so that factor should be taken into account when deciding whether or not to use encrypted connectivity. Other programs use an encrypted protocol, which would require that all traffic using that protocol be encrypted. Though this makes sense for some protocols (such as SFTP and HTTPS), mysqld uses the TCP/IP protocol to connect, and thus can support encrypted and non-encrypted traffic on the same port.

Encrypted connectivity is managed on a per-user basis. By default, a user is created with no connectivity requirements — the user may connect via an unencrypted or encrypted connection. The REQUIRE option to the GRANT statement is used to require the user to use encrypted connectivity. Its usage and options are explained later in this section.

Confirming encrypted connectivity support

To set up encrypted connectivity support in mysqld, the first step is to see if you have a version that is compiled with the appropriate libraries (SSL support):

```
mysql> SHOW GLOBAL VARIABLES LIKE `%ssl';
+---------------+----------+
| Variable_name | Value    |
+---------------+----------+
| have_openssl  | DISABLED |
| have_ssl      | DISABLED |
+---------------+----------+
2 rows in set (0.01 sec)
```

If the values are DISABLED, mysqld has SSL support compiled, but is not configured to support encrypted connections yet. YES values indicate that mysqld is configured to support encrypted connections. The MySQL manual at http://dev.mysql.com/doc/refman/6.0/en/secure-using-ssl.html has information on what to do if you do not have a version compiled with the appropriate SSL libraries.

Because encrypted connectivity is specified on a per-user basis, make sure that your grant tables can support setting encryption requirements for users. Query the INFORMATION_SCHEMA database to see if the necessary fields are present in the mysql.user system table:

```
mysql> SELECT COLUMN_NAME FROM INFORMATION_SCHEMA.COLUMNS
    -> WHERE TABLE_SCHEMA='mysql' AND TABLE_NAME='user'
    -> AND (COLUMN_NAME LIKE `ssl%` OR COLUMN_NAME LIKE `x509%');
+-------------+
| COLUMN_NAME |
+-------------+
```

```
| ssl_type      |
| ssl_cipher    |
| x509_issuer   |
| x509_subject  |
+---------------+
4 rows in set (0.09 sec)
```

If you do not see these fields, it means that at some point an upgrade was done but the mysql_upgrade script was not used. In that case, you must run mysql_upgrade to update your grant tables and do everything else that may have been missed previously.

WARNING Running mysql_upgrade will check all tables, which may take some time. In addition, it may change tables, including system tables. It is a good idea to have a physical backup of your database files before you begin. See Chapter 13 for more information on physical backups.

The operating system user that runs mysql_upgrade must have permissions to update the mysql_upgrade.info file in the datadir, otherwise at the end of the output you will see the following error:

```
Could not create the upgrade info file `/usr/local/mysql/data/
mysql_upgrade_info' in the MySQL Servers datadir, errno: 13
```

By default, mysql_upgrade will try to connect as the root@localhost user. You will need to specify the password. Alternatively, you can specify any other user with the SUPER privilege to run mysql_upgrade:

```
shell> mysql_upgrade -u adminuser -ppassword
Looking for `mysql' as: mysql
Looking for `mysqlcheck' as: mysqlcheck
Running `mysqlcheck'...
mysql.backup_history
Error    : You can't use locks with log tables.
status   : OK
mysql.backup_progress
Error    : You can't use locks with log tables.
status   : OK
mysql.columns_priv                                      OK
mysql.db                                                OK
mysql.event                                             OK
mysql.func                                              OK
mysql.general_log
Error    : You can't use locks with log tables.
status   : OK
mysql.help_category                                     OK
mysql.help_keyword                                      OK
mysql.help_relation                                     OK
mysql.help_topic                                        OK
mysql.host                                              OK
```

```
mysql.ndb_binlog_index                              OK
mysql.plugin                                        OK
mysql.proc                                          OK
mysql.procs_priv                                    OK
mysql.servers                                       OK
mysql.slow_log
Error    : You can't use locks with log tables.
status   : OK
mysql.tables_priv                                   OK
mysql.time_zone                                     OK
mysql.time_zone_leap_second                         OK
mysql.time_zone_name                                OK
mysql.time_zone_transition                          OK
mysql.time_zone_transition_type                     OK
mysql.user                                          OK
sakila.actor                                        OK
sakila.address                                      OK
sakila.category                                     OK
sakila.city                                         OK
sakila.country                                      OK
sakila.customer                                     OK
sakila.film                                         OK
sakila.film_actor                                   OK
sakila.film_category                                OK
sakila.film_text                                    OK
sakila.inventory                                    OK
sakila.language                                     OK
sakila.payment                                      OK
sakila.rental                                       OK
sakila.staff                                        OK
sakila.store                                        OK
Running `mysql_fix_privilege_tables'...
OK
shell>
```

After `mysql_upgrade` has finished, you should be able to re-issue the previous query on `INFORMATION_SCHEMA.COLUMNS` and see the necessary fields in the `mysql.user` table.

Creating the mysqld certificate

An encrypted connection requires a public key and a private key. The public key is stored in a *certificate file*, and the private key is stored in a *key file*. The following example uses `openssl` to create the key and certificate files; if you are using a different method of creating key and certificate files, use the files you create when configuring and using encrypted connections.

First a key file and certificate signing request must be created, and then the request must be signed by a certificate authority to create a certificate file. Generating a request involves putting in some information. The most important field is `Common name`, in which you should put the hostname of the database that users will be connecting to with encrypted connections (the following example uses `db.company.com` for the `Common` name).

The following example generates a certificate signing request and a key file, writing the key file to `mysql-server.key` and the certificate signing request to `mysql-server.csr`. The request should be valid for 10 years and the `-nodes` option specifies that no DES encryption should be used:

```
shell> openssl req -nodes -new -out mysql-server.csr \
        -days 3650 -keyout mysql-server.key
Generating a 1024 bit RSA private key
.......................++++++
...........................++++++
writing new private key to `mysql-server.key'
-----
You are about to be asked to enter information that will be incorpo-
rated
into your certificate request.
What you are about to enter is what is called a Distinguished Name
or a DN.
There are quite a few fields but you can leave some blank
For some fields there will be a default value,
If you enter `.', the field will be left blank.
-----
Country Name (2 letter code) [AU]:US
State or Province Name (full name) [Some-State]:Florida
Locality Name (eg, city) []:Pensacola
Organization Name (eg, company) [Internet Widgits Pty Ltd]:Company,
Inc.
Organizational Unit Name (eg, section) []:IT department
Common Name (eg, YOUR name) []:db.company.com
Email Address []:

Please enter the following `extra' attributes
to be sent with your certificate request
A challenge password []:
An optional company name []:
shell>
```

The certificate signing request must be signed by a Certificate Authority (CA). There is no need to pay money for a third-party Certificate Authority to sign this request. If your organization does not have a local Certificate Authority, you can set up your own using the instructions in the MySQL manual at `http://dev.mysql.com/doc/refman/6.0/en/secure-create-certs.html`. Once the certificate is signed, you will have a certificate file containing the public key. In our example this file is named `mysql-server.crt`.

Configure mysqld to enable encrypted connections

To configure mysqld to enable encrypted connections, use the certificate file, key file, and local CA certificate file to set the following options in the [mysqld] directive of your configuration file:

```
ssl-ca=/path/to/cacert.pem
ssl-cert=/path/to/mysql-server.crt
ssl-key=/path/to/mysql-server.key
```

Restart mysqld for the changes to take effect. Once mysqld is restarted, confirm that the encrypted connections are enabled:

```
mysql> SHOW GLOBAL VARIABLES LIKE `%ssl';
+---------------+-------+
| Variable_name | Value |
+---------------+-------+
| have_openssl  | YES   |
| have_ssl      | YES   |
+---------------+-------+
2 rows in set (0.00 sec)
```

At this point, any user can create an encrypted connection to mysqld if he has access to the same CA certificate file. To open an encrypted connection with mysql:

```
shell> mysql -u username -p --ssl-ca=/path/to/cacert.pem
```

The connection looks the same. To ensure that the connection is encrypted:

```
mysql> SHOW SESSION STATUS LIKE `ssl_cipher';
+---------------+--------------------+
| Variable_name | Value              |
+---------------+--------------------+
| Ssl_cipher    | DHE-RSA-AES256-SHA |
+---------------+--------------------+
1 row in set (0.01 sec)
```

If the connection is not encrypted, you will see:

```
mysql> SHOW SESSION STATUS LIKE `ssl_cipher';
+---------------+-------+
| Variable_name | Value |
+---------------+-------+
| Ssl_cipher    |       |
+---------------+-------+
1 row in set (0.00 sec)
```

Requiring encrypted connections

The GRANT statement can be used to require that a user can only connect via an encrypted connection. By default, users are created with the REQUIRE NONE option, which means that no encryption is required — users can connect via an unencrypted connection, or via an encrypted connection. To require that a user can only connect via an encrypted connection, specify the REQUIRE SSL option:

```
mysql> CREATE USER read_secure@localhost IDENTIFIED BY `rs_pass';
Query OK, 0 rows affected (0.00 sec)

mysql> GRANT SELECT ON sakila.* TO read_secure@localhost REQUIRE SSL;
Query OK, 0 rows affected (0.00 sec)
```

If read_secure@localhost tries to connect without specifying the CA certificate (mysql uses the --ssl-ca option for this), or tries to connect using a different CA certificate as the server, access will be denied, just as if the username or password had been incorrectly typed:

```
ERROR 1045 (28000): Access denied for user `read_secure'@'localhost'
(using password: YES)
```

A user can also be required to connect with a client certificate, which is signed by the CA certificate used by the client and server. Encrypted connections can be further restricted by only allowing use of a client certificate that meets certain requirements. The many levels of encryption granularity that can be applied to users is a mature, yet little-used feature of mysqld. You can see more information about all of the restrictions that can be applied to a user on the MySQL manual page at http://dev.mysql.com/doc/refman/6.0/en/grant.html.

Data security using MySQL objects

MySQL has several different ways to store SQL code. Events, views, stored routines, and triggers can be used to allow very specific actions to be taken without giving more granular permissions. For example, using a stored routine a user can be given permission to update particular fields of a table without having to know the actual structure of the table itself. Routine events scheduled inside mysqld reduce the need for storing authentication credentials in a script. Stored routines, triggers, and events are discussed in detail in Chapter 7. Using views for security purposes is discussed in detail in the section on security and privacy in Chapter 8.

Triggers are often used for recording what actions are taken, by which user, and when — for more information on how to create triggers, see Chapter 7. This type of auditing seems like a good idea. However, there are two major faults with trigger-based auditing, both stemming from the fact that trigger-based auditing is not independent of the system it is auditing.

The first major fault is that trigger-based auditing is a performance nightmare. A trigger is invoked when a data change from an INSERT, UPDATE, or DELETE statement occurs. Trigger-based auditing adds the overhead of a write to an auditing table. This means that instead of one write, a data change will now cost an overhead of two writes — or more, if the trigger has more than one DML statement.

The second major fault is that trigger-based auditing is still controlled by a database administrator. One major purpose of an audit trail is to hold everyone accountable for their actions, including the administrator of the system. Trigger-based auditing allows database administrators to hide their actions by dropping triggers, running statements, and re-creating triggers. A database administrator can hide suspicious activities by modifying the data in an auditing table.

The third major fault is that trigger-based auditing can only be used to track INSERT, UPDATE, and DELETE statements. Statements such as TRUNCATE TABLE or DROP TABLE remove data but do not use the DELETE statement to do so. GRANT and REVOKE statements are also not caught by trigger-based auditing.

Triggers are often not the right answer to create a true independent auditing trail suitable to comply with governmental regulations, or even most companies' internal policies. However, trigger-based auditing can still be a valuable tool when applied correctly to a problem. For instance, trigger-based auditing can help form an application debug log. Though trigger-based auditing is not appropriate for database system auditing, it is a good tool to audit user actions.

Creating Security Policies

If your organization already has security policies in place, you should review them and add to the policies as necessary. Security breaches can be caused by miscommunication about how the environment is secured. Specifically, security policies should address the following issues:

- Where are database user passwords allowed to be stored? Should periodic jobs be required to be stored as MySQL events?
- Who knows the database user passwords?
- Who has access to where the database user passwords are stored?
- Who has administrative access to the database?
- Who creates database users and creates new passwords if a password is forgotten?
- What happens to application, database, and operating system account passwords when an employee leaves?
- What kind of penetration testing is done, and how frequently, to test security?
- When and with whom is confidential data shared? Often governments may require confidential data to be reported. Should information be given to a lawyer/barrister? Police officer? What documentation needs to be verified before sharing private information?

Summary

The issue of database security often receives little attention. However, when you consider the value of the data stored in the database it should be one of the most important aspects of a database administrator's job. After reading this chapter you should understand the following topics:

- How access control lists work
- MySQL privileges
- Controlling host server access
- Managing backups
- Data security
- Encrypted connections
- Security policies

Chapter 21

The MySQL Data Dictionary

MySQL stores information about the data in the databases; this is called metadata. Much of this information is stored in the INFORMATION_SCHEMA database, following the SQL 2003 standard.

Tables in the INFORMATION_SCHEMA database are read-only, in-memory, and show data from various sources.

SHOW CREATE TABLE will show the tables as TEMPORARY, because they reside in memory and do not persist between mysqld restarts. INFORMATION_SCHEMA tables are called *system views* and they may be of different storage engine types. At the time of this writing all the system views are either the MEMORY, MyISAM, or Maria storage engine.

Regular SQL statements can be used to query them, though they have some special properties that other views do not have:

- mysqldump will not export any information (data, schema) from INFORMATION_SCHEMA system views

- There is no data directory for the INFORMATION_SCHEMA database

- There is no .frm file associated with the INFORMATION_SCHEMA views. The definitions are hard-coded into the database.

The table definitions for the data dictionary are hard-coded into the source code, and loaded when mysqld starts. Unlike other databases, there is no directory in the datadir for the INFORMATION_SCHEMA database. All users have permission to see the INFORMATION_SCHEMA database; however, they can only see the objects they have permission to see. For example, table details in the TABLES system view are limited to the tables that the user has permission to see.

Some of the metadata provided by the INFORMATION_SCHEMA database is also provided by various SHOW commands (see Chapter 4). The INFORMATION_SCHEMA database is a more complete data dictionary than using SHOW commands. Also, standard SQL statements can be used to query the system views to retrieve metadata.

The INFORMATION_SCHEMA database contains more than 40 system views. They can be informally categorized as:

- Object catalog (databases, tables, columns, and so on)
- System information (variables, statistics, available options)
- Permissions
- Storage engine-specific metadata

Querying metadata is a powerful tool for a database administrator, answering simple questions such as "how many tables of each storage engine type exist?" and "which tables have columns using the DECIMAL type?" and "how many foreign key constraints exist?" and even "how much space does a certain group of three tables use?" Querying metadata provides a way to retrieve information about the system that can be used to track and tune performance. Any tool that performs queries can retrieve metadata by querying the INFORMATION_SCHEMA database, exactly the same way it queries any other database.

Object Catalog

The INFORMATION_SCHEMA database contains system views with metadata about objects such as databases, tables, views, columns, indexes, partitions, stored routines, triggers, and events.

SCHEMATA

"Schema" is another name for a database, and "schemata" is the plural of schema. The SCHEMATA system view in the INFORMATION_SCHEMA database provides information about all the databases, including the mysql system database and the INFORMATION_SCHEMA database itself. The fields in the SCHEMATA system view are:

- CATALOG_NAME — Provided for standards compliance. However, because MySQL does not have catalogs, this value is always NULL.
- SCHEMA_NAME — The name of the database, such as sakila.
- DEFAULT_CHARACTER_SET_NAME — The default character set of the database. If no default character set is assigned by a CREATE DATABASE or ALTER DATABASE command, the default character set for the system is stored. Thus, the DEFAULT_CHARACTER_SET_NAME field always has a non-NULL value, and defaults to the character set of the system at the time of database creation.

- `DEFAULT_COLLATION_NAME` — The default collation of the database. If no default collation is assigned by a `CREATE DATABASE` or `ALTER DATABASE` command, the default collation for the system is stored. Thus, the `DEFAULT_CHARACTER_SET_NAME` field always has a non-`NULL` value, and defaults to the collation of the system at the time of database creation.

- `SQL_PATH` — Provided for standards compliance, this field is usually used to find files related to the database. However, MySQL does not support this field, so it is always `NULL`.

The `SHOW DATABASES` command is a shorter way to find the names of existing databases than running `SELECT SCHEMA_NAME FROM SCHEMATA`. To show a subset of all databases, it is easier to use the `SCHEMATA` system view. The `SHOW DATABASES` command returns a result set where the field name is `Database`. Because `Database` is a reserved word, in order to use the `WHERE` extension to `SHOW DATABASES`, the `Database` field must be quoted:

```
mysql> SHOW DATABASES WHERE Database NOT IN ('mysql','information_
schema');
ERROR 1064 (42000): You have an error in your SQL syntax; check the
manual that corresponds to your MySQL server version for the right
syntax to use near 'NOT IN ('mysql','information_schema')' at line 1
mysql> SHOW DATABASES WHERE `Database` NOT IN ('mysql','information_
schema');
+----------+
| Database |
+----------+
| sakila   |
| test     |
+----------+
2 rows in set (0.02 sec)
```

See Chapter 4 for more information about using the backtick (`` ` ``) to quote identifiers.

The field name in the `SCHEMATA` system view is `SCHEMA_NAME`, which is not a reserved word, and does not need to be escaped:

```
mysql> USE INFORMATION_SCHEMA;
Database changed
mysql> SELECT SCHEMA_NAME FROM SCHEMATA WHERE SCHEMA_NAME
NOT IN ('mysql','information_schema');
+-------------+
| SCHEMA_NAME |
+-------------+
| sakila      |
| test        |
+-------------+
2 rows in set (0.02 sec)
```

The `SHOW DATABASES` command also accepts the `LIKE` extension. The `SHOW SCHEMAS` command behaves the same way as the `SHOW DATABASES` command, and outputs the same information — `SCHEMAS` is an alias for `DATABASES`.

The SHOW CREATE DATABASE command returns two fields: Database, which is equivalent to SCHEMA_NAME, and Create Database, which does not have an exact equivalent but contains the value of DEFAULT_CHARACTER_SET_NAME. SCHEMA is an alias for DATABASE, so SHOW CREATE SCHEMA returns the same information as SHOW CREATE DATABASE does.

TABLES

Metadata about non-temporary tables is available in the TABLES system view. The fields in the TABLES system view are:

- TABLE_CATALOG — Provided for standards compliance. However, because MySQL does not have catalogs, this value is always NULL.

- TABLE_SCHEMA — The name of the database, such as sakila.

- TABLE_NAME — The name of the table.

- TABLE_TYPE — Whether the table is a base table, view, or system view. Only the INFOR-MATION_SCHEMA views are system views.

- ENGINE — The storage engine of the table, such as InnoDB. To find out which tables, if any, in the INFORMATION_SCHEMA database do not use the MEMORY storage engine:

```
mysql> SELECT TABLE_NAME,ENGINE FROM TABLES WHERE TABLE_
SCHEMA='INFORMATION_SCHEMA' AND ENGINE!='MEMORY';
+-------------+--------+
| TABLE_NAME  | ENGINE |
+-------------+--------+
| COLUMNS     | MARIA  |
| EVENTS      | MARIA  |
| PARAMETERS  | MARIA  |
| PARTITIONS  | MARIA  |
| PLUGINS     | MARIA  |
| PROCESSLIST | MARIA  |
| ROUTINES    | MARIA  |
| TRIGGERS    | MARIA  |
| VIEWS       | MARIA  |
+-------------+--------+
9 rows in set (0.56 sec)
```

- From this query we see that most system views in the INFORMATION_SCHEMA database are the MEMORY storage engine, but there are some that use the Maria storage engine.

- VERSION — The version of the .frm file, currently 10. The VERSION is NULL for table objects that do not have .frm files, such as views. The exception to this rule is system views, which have a VERSION of 10 — even though there are no .frm files, system views have hard-coded definitions, and thus have versions.

- ROW_FORMAT — Different storage engines allow the row storage to vary. Fixed-width rows are a fixed size, which minimizes fragmentation. Dynamic rows are a variable size, which are good for variable-length data, such as VARCHAR, TEXT, and BLOB. InnoDB has a compact row format by default, which eliminates some redundant data. When an InnoDB table has a redundant format, there is less CPU work needed at the cost of additional storage space. MyISAM has a compressed format, obtained by packing the data with the myisampack tool. See Chapter 11 for more details on myisampack.

- TABLE_ROWS — The number of rows this table contains. This value may be an estimate, depending on the storage engine. The value is NULL for views and system views (INFORMATION_SCHEMA tables).

- AVG_ROW_LENGTH — The average size in bytes of rows this table contains. This value may be an estimate, depending on the storage engine. The value is NULL for views, but has a value for system views. If there are no rows, the value will be 0.

- DATA_LENGTH — The size in bytes of rows this table contains. This value may be an estimate, depending on the storage engine. The value is NULL for views and 0 for MEMORY tables. System views that are not MEMORY tables have a value for DATA_LENGTH.

- MAX_DATA_LENGTH — The maximum size in bytes that this table may contain. The value is NULL for views, because there is no data stored. The value is 0 for storage engines that do not populate this field, such as Falcon and CSV.

- INDEX_LENGTH — The size in bytes of the indexes for this table. This value may be an estimate, depending on the storage engine. The value is NULL for views and 0 for MEMORY tables. System views that are not MEMORY tables have a value for DATA_LENGTH.

- DATA_FREE — The size in bytes of the free space allocated for this table, and still available. This value may be an estimate, depending on the storage engine. The value is NULL for views and 0 for system views. Many tables have a DATA_FREE value of 0 because there is not space allocated for them, though there may be plenty of free space available to them. For example, CSV tables simply use available disk space, without needing MySQL to allocate space for rows. In some storage engines such as MyISAM, this might indicate fragmentation and that the table needs to be rebuilt with an OPTIMIZE command. See Chapter 4 for more information about OPTIMIZE.

- AUTO_INCREMENT — The next AUTO_INCREMENT value to be used. If the maximum AUTO_INCREMENT value for a table is 100, the value of AUTO_INCREMENT is 101. If a table has an AUTO_INCREMENT value and no rows have ever been stored in the table, the value of AUTO_INCREMENT is 1.

- CREATE_TIME — The DATETIME the table was created. The value is NULL for views and MEMORY tables. System views that use storage engines other than MEMORY have a proper DATETIME value. FEDERATED tables have a value of NULL.

- UPDATE_TIME — The most recent DATETIME that an ALTER TABLE was performed on the table. The value is NULL for views, CSV, and MEMORY tables. MyISAM, Archive, and Maria tables that have never had ALTER TABLE performed on them have an UPDATE_TIME equivalent to their CREATE_TIME. InnoDB and Falcon tables that have never had ALTER TABLE performed on them have a NULL value. System views that use storage engines other than MEMORY have a proper DATETIME value. FEDERATED tables have a value of NULL.

671

- CHECK_TIME — The most recent DATETIME the table was checked with CHECK TABLE. The value is NULL for views, system views, and tables that have never been checked or do not support the check function.

- TABLE_COLLATION — The character set and collation of the table, for example utf8_bin utf8_general_ci, or latin1_swedish_ci. The value is NULL for views. If no default character set and collation is assigned by a CREATE TABLE or ALTER TABLE command, the default character set and collation are stored. Thus, this field always has a non-NULL value for base tables and system views.

- CHECKSUM — Live checksums can be maintained for MyISAM tables (see Chapter 11). If this table is a MyISAM table with CHECKSUM=1, the live checksum value is displayed. For all other tables, the value is NULL.

- CREATE_OPTIONS — CREATE TABLE has many different options. The options that are not shown in other fields (such as TABLE_COLLATION) are shown in this field, separated by a space. Sample values are partitioned and max_rows=10000 checksum=1. If there are no relevant options to CREATE TABLE, the value is the empty string ("). The value is NULL for views.

- TABLE_COMMENT — The COMMENT option to CREATE TABLE and ALTER TABLE can be used to provide information about a table. If there was no comment specified, the value is the empty string ("). The value is VIEW for views. Most of the tables in the mysql system database have comments:

```
mysql> SELECT TABLE_NAME, TABLE_COMMENT FROM TABLES WHERE
TABLE_SCHEMA='mysql'\G
*************************** 1. row ***************************
    TABLE_NAME: backup_history
TABLE_COMMENT:
*************************** 2. row ***************************
    TABLE_NAME: backup_progress
TABLE_COMMENT:
*************************** 3. row ***************************
    TABLE_NAME: columns_priv
TABLE_COMMENT: Column privileges
*************************** 4. row ***************************
    TABLE_NAME: db
TABLE_COMMENT: Database privileges
*************************** 5. row ***************************
    TABLE_NAME: event
TABLE_COMMENT: Events
*************************** 6. row ***************************
    TABLE_NAME: func
TABLE_COMMENT: User defined functions
*************************** 7. row ***************************
    TABLE_NAME: general_log
TABLE_COMMENT: General log
*************************** 8. row ***************************
    TABLE_NAME: help_category
```

```
TABLE_COMMENT: help categories
*************************** 9. row ***************************
    TABLE_NAME: help_keyword
TABLE_COMMENT: help keywords
*************************** 10. row ***************************
    TABLE_NAME: help_relation
TABLE_COMMENT: keyword-topic relation
*************************** 11. row ***************************
    TABLE_NAME: help_topic
TABLE_COMMENT: help topics
*************************** 12. row ***************************
    TABLE_NAME: host
TABLE_COMMENT: Host privileges;  Merged with database privileges
*************************** 13. row ***************************
    TABLE_NAME: ndb_binlog_index
TABLE_COMMENT:
*************************** 14. row ***************************
    TABLE_NAME: plugin
TABLE_COMMENT: MySQL plugins
*************************** 15. row ***************************
    TABLE_NAME: proc
TABLE_COMMENT: Stored Procedures
*************************** 16. row ***************************
    TABLE_NAME: procs_priv
TABLE_COMMENT: Procedure privileges
*************************** 17. row ***************************
    TABLE_NAME: servers
TABLE_COMMENT: MySQL Foreign Servers table
*************************** 18. row ***************************
    TABLE_NAME: slow_log
TABLE_COMMENT: Slow log
*************************** 19. row ***************************
    TABLE_NAME: tables_priv
TABLE_COMMENT: Table privileges
*************************** 20. row ***************************
    TABLE_NAME: time_zone
TABLE_COMMENT: Time zones
*************************** 21. row ***************************
    TABLE_NAME: time_zone_leap_second
TABLE_COMMENT: Leap seconds information for time zones
*************************** 22. row ***************************
    TABLE_NAME: time_zone_name
TABLE_COMMENT: Time zone names
*************************** 23. row ***************************
    TABLE_NAME: time_zone_transition
TABLE_COMMENT: Time zone transitions
*************************** 24. row ***************************
    TABLE_NAME: time_zone_transition_type
TABLE_COMMENT: Time zone transition types
```

```
*************************** 25. row ***************************
    TABLE_NAME: user
 TABLE_COMMENT: Users and global privileges
25 rows in set (0.00 sec)
```

There are a few SHOW commands that show table information. SHOW TABLES returns one field, the equivalent of TABLE_NAME. SHOW FULL TABLES adds another field, Table_type, which is the equivalent of TABLE_TYPE.

The SHOW CREATE TABLE command returns two fields: Table, which is the equivalent of TABLE_NAME, and Create Table, which is the full CREATE TABLE statement. There is no equivalent in the TABLES system view, though it includes the information in ENGINE, AUTO_INCREMENT, CREATE_OPTIONS, and TABLE_COMMENT.

SHOW TABLE STATUS returns many fields:

- Name — Equivalent to TABLE_NAME.

- Engine, Version, and Row_format — Equivalent to ENGINE, VERSION, and ROW_FORMAT.

- Rows — Equivalent to TABLE_ROWS.

- Avg_row_length, Data_length, Max_data_length, Index_length, Data_free, Auto_increment, Create_time, Update_time, and Check_time — Equivalent to AVG_ROW_LENGTH, DATA_LENGTH, MAX_DATA_LENGTH, INDEX_LENGTH, DATA_FREE, AUTO_INCREMENT, CREATE_TIME, UPDATE_TIME, and CHECK_TIME.

- Collation — Equivalent to TABLE_COLLATION.

- Checksum, Create_options — Equivalent to CHECKSUM and CREATE_OPTIONS.

- Comment — Equivalent to TABLE_COMMENT.

VIEWS

The TABLES system view includes rows for views. However, many of the fields in TABLES are NULL for views, and some features specific to views are not encompassed in the TABLES system view. So MySQL provides the VIEWS system view, with the following fields:

- TABLE_CATALOG — Provided for standards compliance. However, because MySQL does not have catalogs, this value is always NULL.

- TABLE_SCHEMA — The name of the database, such as sakila.

- TABLE_NAME — The name of the view.

- VIEW_DEFINITION — The SELECT statement that defines the view. If the current user is not the definer, the value will be blank, even if the current user has permissions to see the view definition:

```
mysql> SELECT DEFINER,VIEW_DEFINITION,CURRENT_USER()
    ->   FROM VIEWS
    ->   WHERE TABLE_NAME='staff_list';
```

```
+-----------------+-----------------+-----------------+
| DEFINER         | VIEW_DEFINITION | CURRENT_USER() |
+-----------------+-----------------+-----------------+
| root@localhost  |                 | root@127.0.0.1 |
+-----------------+-----------------+-----------------+
1 row in set (0.03 sec)

mysql> SHOW GRANTS;
+----------------------------------------------------------------+
| Grants for root@127.0.0.1                                      |
+----------------------------------------------------------------+
| GRANT ALL PRIVILEGES ON *.* TO 'root'@'127.0.0.1' WITH GRANT|
|                                                        OPTION |
+----------------------------------------------------------------+
1 row in set (0.00 sec)

mysql> SHOW CREATE VIEW sakila.staff_list\G
*************************** 1. row ***************************
               View: staff_list
        Create View: CREATE ALGORITHM=UNDEFINED DEFINER=root@
localhost SQL SECURITY DEFINER VIEW sakila.staff_list AS select
s.staff_id AS ID,concat(s.first_name,_utf8' ',s.last_name) AS name,
a.address AS address,a.postal_code AS zip code,a.phone AS phone,
sakila.city.city AS city,sakila.country.country AS country,s.
store_id AS SID from (((sakila.staff s join sakila.address a
on((s.address_id = a.address_id))) join sakila.city on((a.city_id
= sakila.city.city_id))) join sakila.country on((sakila.city.
country_id = sakila.country.country_id)))
character_set_client: utf8mb3
collation_connection: utf8mb3_general_ci
1 row in set (0.00 sec)
```

- In this example, the user root@127.0.0.1 saw a blank view definition for the staff_list view, because the DEFINER is root@localhost.

- CHECK_OPTION — This value is NONE if the view definition has no WITH CHECK OPTION clause; CASCADED if the view definition contains WITH [CASCADED] CHECK OPTION, and LOCAL if the view definition contains WITH LOCAL CHECK OPTION.

- IS_UPDATABLE — YES if the view is updatable, NO if the view is not updatable. See Chapter 8, subsection "Updatable Views," for more information on updatable views.

- DEFINER — The view definer, in the MySQL user@host format.

- SECURITY_TYPE — DEFINER if the view definition was specified with the SQL SECURITY DEFINER option or did not contain an SQL SECURITY option. The value is INVOKER if the view definition was specified with the SQL SECURITY INVOKER option.

- CHARACTER_SET_CLIENT — Stores the environmental character set as it was when the view was created.

■ COLLATION_CONNECTION — Stores the environmental collation as it was when the view was created.

SHOW CREATE VIEW is the SHOW command that shares the most information with the VIEWS system view. The fields of SHOW CREATE VIEW are:

■ View — Equivalent to TABLE_NAME.

■ Create View — No exact equivalent. This is the full CREATE VIEW statement, and has elements from TABLE_NAME, VIEW_DEFINITION, CHECK_OPTION, IS_UPDATABLE, DEFINER, and SECURITY_TYPE.

■ character_set_client — Equivalent to CHARACTER_SET_CLIENT.

■ collation_connection — Equivalent to COLLATION_CONNECTION.

COLUMNS

The COLUMNS system view contains information about table fields. This system view contains information about the fields from every table, view, and system view.

■ TABLE_CATALOG — Provided for standards compliance. However, because MySQL does not have catalogs, this value is always NULL.

■ TABLE_SCHEMA — The name of the database, such as sakila.

■ TABLE_NAME — The name of the table.

■ COLUMN_NAME — The name of the field.

■ ORDINAL_POSITION — The number representing the order of the field. The first field has a value of 1, the third field has a value of 3, and so on. The value is never NULL.

■ COLUMN_DEFAULT — The default value of the field. If the default is not specified or specified as NULL, the value is NULL.

■ IS_NULLABLE — Whether or not the field is allowed to be null. If the field is specified as NOT NULL, the value is NO. Otherwise, the value is YES. Note that it is possible to have a table where the value of IS_NULLABLE is NO and the COLUMN_DEFAULT is NULL:

```
mysql> USE test;
Database changed
mysql> CREATE TABLE paradox (numfield INT NOT NULL);
Query OK, 0 rows affected (0.11 sec)
mysql> SELECT IS_NULLABLE,COLUMN_DEFAULT
    -> FROM INFORMATION_SCHEMA.COLUMNS
    -> WHERE TABLE_NAME='paradox' AND TABLE_SCHEMA='test';
+-------------+----------------+
| IS_NULLABLE | COLUMN_DEFAULT |
+-------------+----------------+
| NO          | NULL           |
+-------------+----------------+
1 row in set (0.00 sec)
```

- DATA_TYPE — The data type of the field, such as INT, CHAR, or ENUM.

- CHARACTER_MAXIMUM_LENGTH — The maximum number of characters allowed by the field definition. For example, a field defined as VARCHAR(64) has a CHARAC-TER_MAXIMUM_LENGTH of 64. This is only valid for string data, which includes CHAR, VARCHAR, TEXT, BLOB, SET, and ENUM types.

- CHARACTER_OCTET_LENGTH — Maximum octet (byte) size allowed by the field definition. CHARACTER_OCTET_LENGTH is the same as CHARACTER_MAXIMUM_LENGTH except when multi-byte character sets are used (such as utf8).

- NUMERIC_PRECISION — Mathematically, *precision* is the number of digits used to define a number, for example 10 for an INT and 5 for a SMALLINT. This is only valid for numeric data types, including INT, DECIMAL, and FLOAT. For all other data types, the value is NULL.

- NUMERIC_SCALE — This is only valid for numeric data types, including INT, DECIMAL, and FLOAT. For all other data types, the value is NULL. This value is equivalent to the number of digits after the decimal point, which is 0 for data types that are integers.

- CHARACTER_SET_NAME — The default character set for this column. This is only valid for non-binary string data, which includes CHAR, VARCHAR, TEXT, SET, and ENUM types.

- COLLATION_NAME — The default collation for this column. This is only valid for non-binary string data, which includes CHAR, VARCHAR, TEXT, SET, and ENUM types. Sample values are utf8_general_ci, latin1_bin, and latin1_swedish_ci.

- COLUMN_TYPE — The entire data type part of the column definition, without any NULL or DEFAULT definers. For example, varchar(64), bigint(21) unsigned, enum('N','Y'), or year(4).

- COLUMN_KEY — If the column is not part of an index, this field contains the empty string ("). Otherwise, the value is the type of index the columns is a part of:
  - PRI — Primary key
  - UNI — Unique, non-primary key
  - MUL — Non-unique key

- EXTRA — This field stores extra information about the column that does not have a place in another field. If there is no such extra information, the value is the empty string ("). Example values are on update CURRENT_TIMESTAMP and auto_increment.

- PRIVILEGES — The privileges the querying user has for use with this column. If the user has no privileges for a column, there is no row returned for that column. Therefore, the field always contains at least the select privilege. Privileges are separated by a comma, for example select,insert,update.

- COLUMN_COMMENT — The COMMENT option to a column definition within CREATE TABLE and ALTER TABLE can be used to provide information about a column. If there was no comment specified, the value is the empty string (").

- STORAGE — Indicates whether the column is stored in memory or on disk. These only apply to columns in NDB tables. The value for all other tables is Default.

- FORMAT — Indicates whether the column storage format is fixed, dynamic, or default. Fixed and dynamic storage formats only apply to columns in NDB tables. The value for all other tables is Default.

The SHOW COLUMNS command is the SHOW command that shares the most information with the COLUMNS system view. It accepts the LIKE and WHERE extensions, and will show three extra fields when the SHOW FULL COLUMNS syntax is used:

```
mysql> SHOW COLUMNS FROM sakila.staff LIKE 's%'\G
*************************** 1. row ***************************
  Field: staff_id
   Type: tinyint(3) unsigned
   Null: NO
    Key: PRI
Default: NULL
  Extra: auto_increment
*************************** 2. row ***************************
  Field: store_id
   Type: tinyint(3) unsigned
   Null: NO
    Key: MUL
Default: NULL
  Extra:
2 rows in set (0.00 sec)


mysql> SHOW FULL COLUMNS FROM sakila.staff LIKE 's%'\G
*************************** 1. row ***************************
     Field: staff_id
      Type: tinyint(3) unsigned
 Collation: NULL
      Null: NO
       Key: PRI
   Default: NULL
     Extra: auto_increment
Privileges: select,insert,update,references
   Comment:
*************************** 2. row ***************************
     Field: store_id
      Type: tinyint(3) unsigned
 Collation: NULL
      Null: NO
       Key: MUL
   Default: NULL
     Extra:
```

```
   Privileges: select,insert,update,references
      Comment:
2 rows in set (0.00 sec)
```

The fields from SHOW COLUMNS and SHOW FULL COLUMNS are:

- Field — Equivalent to COLUMN_NAME.
- Type — Equivalent to COLUMN_TYPE.
- Collation — Equivalent to COLLATION_NAME. SHOW FULL COLUMNS only.
- Null — Equivalent to IS_NULLABLE.
- Key — Equivalent to COLUMN_KEY.
- Default — Equivalent to COLUMN_DEFAULT.
- Extra — Equivalent to EXTRA.
- Privileges — Equivalent to PRIVILEGES. SHOW FULL COLUMNS only.
- Comment — Equivalent to COLUMN_COMMENT. SHOW FULL COLUMNS only.

SHOW COLUMNS returns the fields in the order in which they appear in the table. To guarantee that ordering with the COLUMNS system view, add ORDER BY ORDINAL_POSITION to queries.

STATISTICS

Information about indexes is stored in the STATISTICS system view, which has one row for each field in an index. STATISTICS has the following fields:

- TABLE_CATALOG — Provided for standards compliance. However, because MySQL does not have catalogs, this value is always NULL.
- TABLE_SCHEMA — The name of the database that contains the table that is associated with this index, such as sakila.
- TABLE_NAME — The name of the table that is associated with this index.
- NON_UNIQUE — Whether or not the index is unique. The value is 0 for unique indexes and 1 for non-unique indexes.
- INDEX_SCHEMA — The name of the database that contains this index. This is always the same as TABLE_SCHEMA.
- INDEX_NAME — The name of the index.
- SEQ_IN_INDEX — The position of this field in the index. The first field in an index has a value of 1, the second field in an index has a value of 2, and so on. For example, the sakila.rental table has an index defined as:

```
UNIQUE KEY `rental_date` (`rental_date`,`inventory_id`,
`customer_id`),
```

This index is represented by three rows in the STATISTICS system view:

```
mysql> SELECT SEQ_IN_INDEX, COLUMN_NAME
    -> FROM STATISTICS
    -> WHERE TABLE_SCHEMA='sakila'
    -> AND TABLE_NAME='rental'
    -> AND INDEX_NAME='rental_date';
+--------------+--------------+
| SEQ_IN_INDEX | COLUMN_NAME  |
+--------------+--------------+
|            1 | rental_date  |
|            2 | inventory_id |
|            3 | customer_id  |
+--------------+--------------+
3 rows in set (0.00 sec)
```

- COLUMN_NAME — The name of the field.

- COLLATION — The collation for this field. Currently all records have NULL values. However, in the future, when mysqld supports ascending and descending collations, the value will be A for ascending collations and D for descending collations.

- CARDINALITY — The cardinality of this field. The cardinality of a field is the number of unique values in that field. This value may be an estimation, depending on the storage engine of the table. If the cardinality is small compared to the number of rows in the table, it means that there are many repeating values. This means a query will return multiple values for a field when searching on a value that is indexed, but repeating.

  When the field cardinality is large, approaching the value of the number of rows, it means that there are very few repeating values. Fields in a unique index have a cardinality equal to the number of rows in the table.

- SUB_PART — The number of characters in the prefix of the index for this field. If the index does not contain a prefix for this field, the value is NULL. For example, the sakila.film table has the following index defined:

```
KEY `idx_title` (`title`(191)),
```

And the value of SUB_PART is 191:

```
mysql> SELECT INDEX_NAME, COLUMN_NAME, SUB_PART
    -> FROM STATISTICS
    -> WHERE TABLE_SCHEMA='sakila'
    -> AND TABLE_NAME='film'
    -> AND INDEX_NAME='idx_title';
+------------+-------------+----------+
| INDEX_NAME | COLUMN_NAME | SUB_PART |
+------------+-------------+----------+
| idx_title  | title       |      191 |
+------------+-------------+----------+
1 row in set (0.00 sec)
```

- PACKED — Whether or not the index is packed. This only applies to MyISAM tables. If the index is not packed, the value is NULL. If the index is packed, the value is 0 (nothing packed), 1 (strings and integers are packed), or DEFAULT (only strings are packed).

- NULLABLE — Whether or not the field can contain NULL values. If the field can contain NULL values, the value is YES. If the field cannot contain NULL values, the value is the empty string ('').

- INDEX_TYPE — The type of index. Example values are BTREE, FULLTEXT, HASH, and RTREE.

- COMMENT — Always the empty string ('').

- INDEX_COMMENT — The comment defined by the index_comment option when creating or changing an index.

The output of SHOW INDEX is very similar to the fields in the STATISTICS system view:

- Table — Equivalent to TABLE_NAME.

- Non_unique — Equivalent to NON_UNIQUE.

- Key_name — Equivalent to INDEX_NAME.

- Seq_in_index, Column_name, Collation, Cardinality, Sub_part, Packed, Null, Index_type, Comment, and Index_Comment — Equivalent to SEQ_IN_INDEX, COLUMN_NAME, COLLATION, CARDINALITY, SUB_PART, PACKED, NULLABLE, INDEX_TYPE, COMMENT, and INDEX_COMMENT.

TABLE_CONSTRAINTS

Unique and primary keys restrict data values in a table, only allowing one set of values for the fields in those indexes. A foreign key restricts the allowable data for fields in a table by only allowing values from another set of fields. The restrictions that unique, primary, and foreign keys place on tables are referred to as table constraints. The TABLE_CONSTRAINTS system view has information about unique keys, primary keys, and foreign keys in the following fields:

- CONSTRAINT_CATALOG — Provided for standards compliance. However, because MySQL does not have catalogs, this value is always NULL.

- CONSTRAINT_SCHEMA — The name of the database that the constraint belongs to, such as sakila. This is the same as the TABLE_SCHEMA field.

- CONSTRAINT_NAME — The name of the index. The value is PRIMARY for a primary key. Unique keys and foreign keys have names that can be set when an index is created or changed. The default name for foreign keys starts with fk_.

- TABLE_SCHEMA — The name of the database that the constrained table belongs to.

- TABLE_NAME — The name of the table constrained.

- CONSTRAINT_TYPE — The type of constraint. Either PRIMARY KEY, UNIQUE, or FOREIGN KEY.

There is no equivalent SHOW statement for the data in TABLE_CONSTRAINTS, but the output of SHOW INDEX has some of the same fields:

- Table — Equivalent to TABLE_NAME.

- Key_name — Equivalent to CONSTRAINT_NAME for unique and primary keys. For foreign keys, the Key_name is the name of the index on the field, and the CONSTRAINT_NAME is the name of the foreign key constraint.

As an example, in the sakila.staff table, the address_id field is a foreign key, defined with:

```
KEY idx_fk_address_id (address_id),
CONSTRAINT fk_staff_address FOREIGN KEY (address_id) REFERENCES
address (address_id) ON UPDATE CASCADE,
```

The Key_name from SHOW INDEX is idx_fk_address_id, and the CONSTRAINT_NAME that appears in the TABLE_CONSTRAINTS system view is fk_staff_address.

- Column_name — Equivalent to COLUMN_NAME.

Note that SHOW INDEX shows all indexes and TABLE_CONSTRAINTS has information only for unique, primary, and foreign keys.

KEY_COLUMN_USAGE

Like the TABLE_CONSTRAINTS system view, the KEY_COLUMN_USAGE system view only shows information about unique keys, primary keys, and foreign keys. The fields in KEY_COLUMN_USAGE are:

- CONSTRAINT_CATALOG — Provided for standards compliance. However, because MySQL does not have catalogs, this value is always NULL.

- CONSTRAINT_SCHEMA — The name of the database that the constraint belongs to, such as sakila. This is the same as the TABLE_SCHEMA field.

- CONSTRAINT_NAME — The name of the index. The value is PRIMARY for a primary key. Unique keys and foreign keys have names that can be set when an index is created or changed. The default name for foreign keys starts with fk_.

- TABLE_CATALOG — Provided for standards compliance. However, because MySQL does not have catalogs, this value is always NULL.

- TABLE_SCHEMA — The name of the database that the constrained table belongs to.

- TABLE_NAME — The name of the table constrained.

- COLUMN_NAME — The name of the field constrained.

- ORDINAL_POSITION — The constrained field's position in the index. The first field in an index has a value of 1, the second field has a value of 2, and so on. For example, the sakila.rental table has a composite unique index (a unique index with more than one field):

```
UNIQUE KEY rental_date (rental_date, inventory_id, customer_id)
```

The ORDINAL_POSITION of rental_date is 1, of inventory_id is 2, and of customer_id is 3.

■ POSITION_IN_UNIQUE_CONSTRAINT — NULL for keys that are not foreign keys. For foreign keys, the value is the referenced field's position in the foreign key.

As an example, the foreign key fk_staff_address on the sakila.staff table is defined as:

```
CONSTRAINT fk_staff_address FOREIGN KEY (address_id) REFERENCES
address (address_id) ON UPDATE CASCADE
```

The value of POSITION_IN_UNIQUE_CONSTRAINT is 1, referring to the fact that the address_id field is the first referenced field. Foreign keys are usually defined as:

```
FOREIGN KEY (fld1,fld2) REFERENCES reftbl (reffld1,reffld2)
```

Thus, the POSITION_IN_UNIQUE_CONSTRAINT is the same as ORDINAL_POSITION.

■ REFERENCED_TABLE_SCHEMA — NULL for keys that are not foreign keys. For foreign keys, the database name of the referenced table. As an example, the foreign key fk_staff_address on the sakila.staff table is defined as:

```
CONSTRAINT fk_staff_address FOREIGN KEY (address_id) REFERENCES
address (address_id) ON UPDATE CASCADE
```

The REFERENCED_TABLE_SCHEMA is sakila, which is the database containing the address table.

■ REFERENCED_TABLE_NAME — NULL for keys that are not foreign keys. For foreign keys, the name of the referenced table. In the previous example, the value is address.

■ REFERENCED_COLUMN_NAME — NULL for keys that are not foreign keys. For foreign keys, the name of the referenced field. In the previous example, the value is address_id.

There is no equivalent SHOW statement for the data in KEY_COLUMN_USAGE, but the output of SHOW INDEX has some of the same fields:

■ Table — Equivalent to TABLE_NAME.

■ Key_name — Equivalent to CONSTRAINT_NAME for unique and primary keys. For foreign keys, the Key_name is the name of the index on the field, and the CONSTRAINT_NAME is the name of the foreign key constraint.

As an example, in the sakila.staff table, the address_id field is a foreign key, defined with:

```
KEY idx_fk_address_id (address_id),
CONSTRAINT fk_staff_address FOREIGN KEY (address_id) REFERENCES
address (address_id) ON UPDATE CASCADE,
```

The Key_name from SHOW INDEX is idx_fk_address_id, and the CONSTRAINT_NAME that appears in the TABLE_CONSTRAINTS system view is fk_staff_address.

■ Column_name — Equivalent to COLUMN_NAME.

Note that SHOW INDEX shows all indexes and KEY_COLUMN_USAGE has information only for unique, primary, and foreign keys.

REFERENTIAL_CONSTRAINTS

There is more information about foreign keys than the KEY_COLUMN_USAGE and TABLE_CONSTRAINTS system views show. The REFERENTIAL_CONSTRAINTS system view shows the behavior of a foreign key during updates and deletes. These behaviors are defined in the foreign key constraint with the ON UPDATE and ON DELETE clauses. The REFERENTIAL_CONSTRAINTS system view also repeats the constraint and referenced constraint:

- CONSTRAINT_CATALOG — Provided for standards compliance. However, because MySQL does not have catalogs, this value is always NULL.

- CONSTRAINT_SCHEMA — The name of the database that the constraint belongs to, such as sakila.

- CONSTRAINT_NAME — The name of the index. The value is PRIMARY for a primary key. Unique keys and foreign keys have names that can be set when an index is created or changed. The default name for foreign keys starts with fk_.

- UNIQUE_CONSTRAINT_CATALOG — Provided for standards compliance. However, because MySQL does not have catalogs, this value is always NULL.

- UNIQUE_CONSTRAINT_SCHEMA — The database name of the referenced table. This is equivalent to the REFERENCED_TABLE_SCHEMA in the KEY_COLUMN_USAGE system view.

- UNIQUE_CONSTRAINT_NAME — The name of the referenced constraint. Similar to the CONSTRAINT_NAME field of the KEY_COLUMN_USAGE system view, this value is PRIMARY for a primary key or the name of the index for non-primary keys.

- MATCH_OPTION — This feature has not been implemented yet, so the value is always NONE.

- UPDATE_RULE — The update behavior of the foreign key, as set by the foreign key definition. Possible values are CASCADE, NO ACTION, RESTRICT, SET NULL, SET DEFAULT. See Chapter 6 for more information on defining foreign keys.

- DELETE_RULE — The delete behavior of the foreign key, as set by the foreign key definition. Possible values are CASCADE, NO ACTION, RESTRICT, SET NULL, SET DEFAULT. See Chapter 6 for more information on defining foreign keys.

- TABLE_NAME — The table name that the foreign key constraint belongs to.

- REFERENCED_TABLE_NAME — The table name of the referenced table.

There is no complete SHOW statement for the fields in REFERENTIAL_CONSTRAINTS, but the Key_name field from the output of SHOW INDEX is equivalent to CONSTRAINT_NAME.

TRIGGERS

Triggers are user-defined stored SQL that get run when data changes. Triggers are defined on a per-table basis, and can occur before and after inserts, updates, and deletes. The fields in the TRIGGERS system view are:

- TRIGGER_CATALOG — Provided for standards compliance. However, because MySQL does not have catalogs, this value is always NULL.

- TRIGGER_SCHEMA — The name of the database that the trigger belongs to, such as sakila.

- TRIGGER_NAME — The name of the trigger.

- EVENT_MANIPULATION — The name of the action that calls this trigger. Possible values are INSERT, DELETE, or UPDATE.

- EVENT_OBJECT_CATALOG — Provided for standards compliance. However, because MySQL does not have catalogs, this value is always NULL.

- EVENT_OBJECT_SCHEMA — The name of the database that the table associated with the trigger belongs to, such as sakila.

- EVENT_OBJECT_TABLE — The name of the table associated with the trigger.

- ACTION_ORDER — The order the trigger is run in. This value is always 0 because MySQL only supports one trigger per set of ACTION_TIMING and EVENT_MANIPULATION.

- ACTION_CONDITION — Always NULL.

- ACTION_STATEMENT — The SQL that is run by the trigger.

- ACTION_ORIENTATION — Always ROW.

- ACTION_TIMING — When the trigger occurs. Possible values are BEFORE or AFTER.

- ACTION_REFERENCE_OLD_TABLE — Always NULL.

- ACTION_REFERENCE_NEW_TABLE — Always NULL.

- ACTION_REFERENCE_OLD_ROW — How the trigger references the row prior to the data change. This is not settable by the user, and is always OLD.

- ACTION_REFERENCE_NEW_ROW — How the trigger references the row after the data is changed. This is not settable by the user, and is always NEW.

- CREATED — Always NULL.

- SQL_MODE — Stores the environmental sql_mode as it was when the trigger was created. This is also the sql_mode that is used when the trigger is invoked.

- DEFINER — The trigger definer, in the MySQL user@host format.

- CHARACTER_SET_CLIENT — Stores the environmental character set as it was when the trigger was created. This is also the character_set_client that is used when the trigger is invoked.

- COLLATION_CONNECTION — Stores the environmental collation as it was when the trigger was created. This is also the collation_connection that is used when the trigger is invoked.

- DATABASE_COLLATION — The default collation of the database associated with the trigger.

For more information on triggers, see Chapter 7.

The SHOW TRIGGERS statement outputs some of the same information in the TRIGGERS system view. The equivalent fields are:

- Trigger — Equivalent to TRIGGER_NAME.

- Event — Equivalent to EVENT_MANIPULATION.

- Table — Equivalent to EVENT_OBJECT_TABLE.

- Statement — Equivalent to ACTION_STATEMENT.

- Timing — Equivalent to ACTION_TIMING.

- Created, sql_mode, Definer, character_set_client, collation connection — Equivalent to CREATED, SQL_MODE, DEFINER, CHARACTER_SET_CLIENT, COLLATION_CONNECTION.

The SHOW CREATE TRIGGER statement outputs the following fields, which are similar to fields in the TRIGGERS system view:

- Trigger — Equivalent to TRIGGER_NAME.

- sql_mode — Equivalent to SQL_MODE.

- SQL Original Statement — This is the entire CREATE TRIGGER statement, which includes the information shown in the EVENT_MANIPULATION, ACTION_ORDER, ACTION_STATEMENT, ACTION_TIMING, and DEFINER fields.

- character_set_client, collation connection, Database Collation — Equivalent to CHARACTER_SET_CLIENT, COLLATION_CONNECTION, and DATABASE_COLLATION.

ROUTINES

The ROUTINES system view stores metadata about stored procedures and stored routines. For more information on stored routines, see Chapter 7. The fields in the ROUTINES system view are:

- SPECIFIC_NAME — The name of the stored routine.

- ROUTINE_CATALOG — Provided for standards compliance. However, because MySQL does not have catalogs, this value is always NULL.

- ROUTINE_SCHEMA — The name of the database that the stored routine belongs to, such as sakila.

- ROUTINE_NAME — The name of the stored routine. This is equivalent to the SPECIFIC_NAME.

- ROUTINE_TYPE — The type of stored routine, either FUNCTION or PROCEDURE.

- DATA_TYPE — For a stored procedure, this value is the empty string ("). For a stored function, the data type of the return value, such as INT, CHAR, or ENUM.

- CHARACTER_MAXIMUM_LENGTH — For a stored procedure, this value is NULL. For a stored function, this value is the maximum number of characters allowed by the data type of the return value. For example, a return data type defined as VARCHAR(64) has a CHARACTER_MAXIMUM_LENGTH of 64. This is only valid for string data, which includes CHAR, VARCHAR, TEXT, BLOB, SET, and ENUM types.

- CHARACTER_OCTET_LENGTH — For a stored procedure, this value is NULL. For a stored function, this value is the maximum octet size allowed by the data type of the return value. CHARACTER_OCTET_LENGTH is the same as CHARACTER_MAXIMUM_LENGTH except when multi-byte character sets are used (such as utf8).

- NUMERIC_PRECISION — For a stored procedure, this value is NULL. For a stored function, the number of digits used to define the data type of the return value. Example values are 10 for an INT and 5 for a SMALLINT. This is only valid for numeric data types, including INT, DECIMAL, and FLOAT. For non-numeric data types, the value is NULL.

- NUMERIC_SCALE — For a stored procedure, this value is NULL. For a stored function, this value is NULL for non-numeric data types. For numeric data types including INT, DECIMAL, and FLOAT, this value is equivalent to the number of digits after the decimal point, which is 0 for data types that are integers.

- CHARACTER_SET_NAME — For a stored procedure, this value is NULL. For a stored function, this value is the default character set for the return value. This is only valid for non-binary string data, which includes CHAR, VARCHAR, TEXT, SET, and ENUM types.

- COLLATION_NAME — For a stored procedure, this value is NULL. For a stored function, this value is the default collation for the return value. This is only valid for non-binary string data, which includes CHAR, VARCHAR, TEXT, SET, and ENUM types. Sample values are utf8_general_ci, latin1_bin, and latin1_swedish_ci.

- DTD_IDENTIFIER — For a stored procedure, this value is NULL. For a stored function, this value is the definition of the return value. For example, a function that defines the return value as RETURNS decimal(5,2) has a DTD_IDENTIFIER of decimal(5,2).

> **NOTE** The DATA_TYPE, CHARACTER_MAXIMUM_LENGTH, CHARACTER_OCTET_LENGTH, NUMERIC_PRECISION, NUMERIC_SCALE, CHARACTER_SET_NAME, COLLATION_NAME, and DTD_IDENTIFIER fields were added in version 6.0.

- ROUTINE_BODY — The language that the body of the stored routine is written in. Currently MySQL only allows SQL, so the value will always be SQL.

- ROUTINE_DEFINITION — The stored routine SQL statement. For multi-statement routines, this field will start with BEGIN and the last part of the field will be END.

- EXTERNAL_NAME — The name of the stored routine if it is stored externally. Because all MySQL stored routines are stored internally, this value is always NULL.

- EXTERNAL_LANGUAGE — The name of the language the stored routine is written in if it is stored externally. Because all MySQL stored routines are stored internally, this value is always NULL.

- PARAMETER_STYLE — The style of parameters that are used in this stored routine. Currently MySQL only allows SQL, so the value will always be SQL.

- IS_DETERMINISTIC — Whether or not the stored routine is deterministic. See "Deterministic vs. Not Deterministic Routines in MySQL" in Chapter 7 for more information.

- SQL_DATA_ACCESS — The nature of the SQL that the stored routine contains. Possible values are MODIFIES SQL DATA, READS SQL DATA, CONTAINS SQL, and NO SQL.

- SQL_PATH — Provided for standards compliance, this field is usually used to find files related to the stored routine. However, MySQL does not support this field, so it is always NULL.

- SECURITY_TYPE — DEFINER if the routine definition was specified with the SQL SECURITY DEFINER option or did not contain an SQL SECURITY option. The value is INVOKER if the routine definition was specified with the SQL SECURITY INVOKER option.

- CREATED — The datetime of the stored routine creation.

- LAST_ALTERED — The datetime the stored routine was last changed. If the stored routine has not changed since it was created, the LAST_ALTERED time is equivalent to CREATED.

- SQL_MODE — Stores the environmental sql_mode as it was when the stored routine was created. This is also the sql_mode that is used when the stored routine is invoked.

- ROUTINE_COMMENT — The COMMENT option to CREATE and ALTER statements for stored routines can be used to provide user-defined information. If there was no comment specified, the value is the empty string (").

- DEFINER — The stored routine definer, in the MySQL user@host format.

- CHARACTER_SET_CLIENT — Stores the environmental character set as it was when the stored routine was created. This is also the character_set_client that is used when the stored routine is invoked.

- COLLATION_CONNECTION — Stores the environmental collation as it was when the stored routine was created. This is also the collation_connection that is used when the stored routine is invoked.

- DATABASE_COLLATION — the default collation of the database associated with the stored routine.

The SHOW PROCEDURE STATUS and SHOW FUNCTION STATUS statements output some information that is stored in the ROUTINES system view:

- `Db` — Equivalent to ROUTINE_SCHEMA.
- `Name` — Equivalent to ROUTINE_NAME.
- `Type` — Equivalent to ROUTINE_TYPE.
- `Definer` — Equivalent to DEFINER.
- `Modified` — Equivalent to LAST_ALTERED.
- `Created` — Equivalent to CREATED.
- `Security_type` — Equivalent to SECURITY_TYPE.
- `Comment` — Equivalent to ROUTINE_COMMENT.
- `character_set_client, collation connection, Database Collation` — Equivalent to CHARACTER_SET_CLIENT, COLLATION_CONNECTION, and DATABASE_COLLATION.

The fields in the ROUTINES system view are similar to the output of the SHOW CREATE PROCEDURE and SHOW CREATE FUNCTION statements:

- `Procedure (SHOW CREATE PROCEDURE)` — Equivalent to ROUTINE_NAME for stored procedures.
- `Function (SHOW CREATE FUNCTION)` — Equivalent to ROUTINE_NAME for stored functions.
- `sql_mode` — Equivalent to SQL_MODE.
- `Create Procedure (SHOW CREATE PROCEDURE)` — The entire CREATE PROCEDURE statement, which includes the information shown in the ROUTINE_DEFINITION, IS_DETERMINISTIC, SQL_DATA_ACCESS, SECURITY_TYPE, ROUTINE_COMMENT, and DEFINER fields for stored procedures.
- `Create Function (SHOW CREATE FUNCTION)` — The entire CREATE FUNCTION statement, which includes the information shown in the DATA_TYPE, CHARACTER_MAXIMUM_LENGTH, CHARACTER_OCTET_LENGTH, NUMERIC_PRECISION, NUMERIC_SCALE, CHARACTER_SET_NAME, COLLATION_NAME, DTD_IDENTIFIER, ROUTINE_DEFINITION, IS_DETERMINISTIC, SQL_DATA_ACCESS, SECURITY_TYPE, ROUTINE_COMMENT, and DEFINER fields for stored functions.
- `character_set_client, collation connection, Database Collation` — Equivalent to CHARACTER_SET_CLIENT, COLLATION_CONNECTION, and DATABASE_COLLATION.

Stored routines are stored in the mysql.proc table, so some of the metadata in ROUTINES is similar to fields in the mysql.proc table:

- `db` — Equivalent to ROUTINE_SCHEMA.
- `name` — Equivalent to ROUTINE_NAME.
- `type` — Equivalent to ROUTINE_TYPE.

- `specific_name`, `language`, `sql_data_access`, `is_deterministic`, and `security_type` — Equivalent to `SPECIFIC_NAME`, `LANGUAGE`, `SQL_DATA_ACCESS`, `IS_DETERMINISTIC`, and `SECURITY_TYPE`.

- `returns` — Equivalent to `DTD_IDENTIFIER` for stored functions. For stored procedures, `returns` is the empty string (""), while `DTD_IDENTIFIER` is NULL.

- `body` — Equivalent to `ROUTINE_DEFINITION`.

- `definer` — Equivalent to `DEFINER`.

- `created` — Equivalent to `CREATED`.

- `modified` — Equivalent to `LAST_ALTERED`.

- `sql_mode` — Equivalent to `SQL_MODE`.

- `comment` — Equivalent to `ROUTINE_COMMENT`.

- `character_set_client` — Equivalent to `CHARACTER_SET_CLIENT`.

- `collation_connection` — Equivalent to `COLLATION_CONNECTION`.

- `db_collation` — Equivalent to `DATABASE_COLLATION`.

PARAMETERS

The `ROUTINES` system view has a lot of information about stored routines. It contains many fields with information about the return value of a stored function, however there is no information about input parameters to stored functions, nor is there any information about the `IN`, `OUT`, and `INOUT` parameters in a stored procedure.

The `PARAMETERS` system view, added in MySQL version 6.0, contains information about stored routine parameters. Each parameter in a stored routine is represented by a row in the `PARAMETERS` system view, with the following fields:

- `SPECIFIC_CATALOG` — Provided for standards compliance. However, because MySQL does not have catalogs, this value is always `NULL`.

- `SPECIFIC_SCHEMA` — The name of the database that the stored routine containing this parameter. For example, if a parameter was stored in a routine associated with the `sakila` database, the value of `SPECIFIC_SCHEMA` would be `sakila`.

- `SPECIFIC_NAME` — The name of the stored routine containing this parameter.

- `ORDINAL_POSITION` — The position of the parameter in the parameter list for the stored routine. The first parameter has a value of 1, the second has a value of 2, and so on. The return value of a stored function has a value of 0.

- `PARAMETER_MODE` — This value is `NULL` for the return value of a stored function, `IN` for an input parameter of a stored routine, `OUT` for an output parameter of a stored procedure, and `INOUT` for a parameter that is used for both input and output.

- `PARAMETER_NAME` — The name of the parameter. The value is `NULL` for the return value of a stored function.

- `DATA_TYPE` — The data type of the parameter, such as `INT`, `CHAR`, or `ENUM`.

- `CHARACTER_MAXIMUM_LENGTH` — The maximum number of characters allowed by the data type of the parameter. For example, a parameter data type defined as `VARCHAR(64)` has a `CHARACTER_MAXIMUM_LENGTH` of 64. This is only valid for string data, which includes `CHAR`, `VARCHAR`, `TEXT`, `BLOB`, `SET`, and `ENUM` types.

- `CHARACTER_OCTET_LENGTH` — The maximum octet size allowed by the data type of the parameter. `CHARACTER_OCTET_LENGTH` is the same as `CHARACTER_MAXIMUM_LENGTH` except when multi-byte character sets are used (such as `utf8`).

- `NUMERIC_PRECISION` — The number of digits used to define the data type of the parameter. Example values are 10 for an `INT` and 5 for a `SMALLINT`. This is only valid for numeric data types, including `INT`, `DECIMAL`, and `FLOAT`. For non-numeric data types, the value is `NULL`.

- `NUMERIC_SCALE` — This value is `NULL` for non-numeric data types. For numeric data types including `INT`, `DECIMAL`, and `FLOAT`, this value is equivalent to the number of digits after the decimal point, which is 0 for data types that are integers.

- `CHARACTER_SET_NAME` — The default character set for this parameter. This is only valid for non-binary string data, which includes `CHAR`, `VARCHAR`, `TEXT`, `SET`, and `ENUM` types.

- `COLLATION_NAME` — The default collation for this parameter. This is only valid for non-binary string data, which includes `CHAR`, `VARCHAR`, `TEXT`, `SET`, and `ENUM` types. Sample values are `utf8_general_ci`, `latin1_bin`, and `latin1_swedish_ci`.

- `DTD_IDENTIFIER` — The definition of the parameter. For example, a function that defines the return value as `RETURNS decimal(5,2)` has a `DTD_IDENTIFIER` of `decimal(5,2)`.

- `ROUTINE_TYPE` — The type of stored routine, either `FUNCTION` or `PROCEDURE`. Added in MySQL version 6.0.5.

The `SHOW CREATE PROCEDURE`, `SHOW CREATE FUNCTION` statements, and the `mysql.proc` system table have some details about stored routine parameters. The `SHOW CREATE` statements contain the definition of the parameters, and the `mysql.proc` table has the `param_list` field, which contains the part of the routine definition that defines the parameters. The `mysql.proc` table contains one row per stored routine, so the `PARAMETERS` system view is the only way to get information about an individual parameter.

EVENTS

The `EVENTS` system view stores metadata about events. For more information on events, see Chapter 7. The fields in the `EVENTS` system view are:

- `EVENT_CATALOG` — Provided for standards compliance. However, because MySQL does not have catalogs, this value is always `NULL`.

- `EVENT_SCHEMA` — The name of the database that the event belongs to, such as `sakila`.

- `EVENT_NAME` — The name of this event.

- DEFINER — The event definer, in the MySQL user@host format.

- TIME_ZONE — The time zone associated with the event. See Chapter 4 for more information on time zones. Ordinarily this value is SYSTEM.

- EVENT_BODY — The language that the body of the event is written in. Currently MySQL only allows SQL, so the value will always be SQL.

- EVENT_DEFINITION — The event SQL statement. For multi-statement events, this field will start with BEGIN and the last part of the field will be END.

- EVENT_TYPE — Either RECURRING or ONE TIME.

- EXECUTE_AT — The date and time a ONE TIME event will execute at. NULL if the EVENT_TYPE is RECURRING.

- INTERVAL_VALUE — Together with INTERVAL_FIELD, the frequency at which RECURRING event will execute at. For example, if an event was defined as running EVERY 1 HOUR, the value of INTERVAL_VALUE is 1. NULL if the EVENT_TYPE is ONE TIME.

- INTERVAL_FIELD — Together with INTERVAL_VALUE, the frequency at which a RECURRING event will execute at. For example, if an event was defined as running EVERY 1 HOUR, the value of INTERVAL_FIELD is HOUR. NULL if the EVENT_TYPE is ONE TIME.

- SQL_MODE — Stores the environmental sql_mode as it was when the stored routine was created. This is also the sql_mode that is used when the stored routine is invoked.

- STARTS — The date and time a RECURRING event will start recurring. NULL if the EVENT_TYPE is ONE TIME.

- ENDS — The date and time a RECURRING event will stop recurring. NULL if the EVENT_TYPE is ONE TIME.

- STATUS — One of ENABLED, DISABLED, or DISABLED ON SLAVE.

- ON_COMPLETION — One of PRESERVE or NOT PRESERVE.

- CREATED — The date and time of the event creation.

- LAST_ALTERED — The date and time the event was last changed. If the event has not changed since it was created, the LAST_ALTERED time is equivalent to CREATED.

- LAST_EXECUTED — The date and time the event was last executed. NULL if the event has never been executed.

- EVENT_COMMENT — The COMMENT option to CREATE and ALTER statements for events can be used to provide user-defined information. If there was no comment specified, the value is the empty string (").

- ORIGINATOR — The value of ORIGINATOR is always 0.

- CHARACTER_SET_CLIENT — Stores the environmental character set as it was when the event was created. This is also the character_set_client that is used when the event is executed.

- COLLATION_CONNECTION — Stores the environmental collation as it was when the event was created. This is also the collation_connection that is used when the event is invoked.
- DATABASE_COLLATION — The default collation of the database associated with the event.

The SHOW EVENTS statement outputs some information that is stored in the EVENTS system view:

- Db — Equivalent to EVENT_SCHEMA.
- Name — Equivalent to EVENT_NAME.
- Definer — Equivalent to DEFINER.
- Time Zone — Equivalent to TIME_ZONE.
- Type — Equivalent to EVENT_TYPE.
- Execute at — Equivalent to EXECUTE_AT.
- Interval value — Equivalent to INTERVAL_VALUE.
- Interval field — Equivalent to INTERVAL_FIELD.
- Starts — Equivalent to STARTS.
- Ends — Equivalent to ENDS.
- Status — Equivalent to STATUS.
- Originator — Equivalent to ORIGINATOR.
- character_set_client, collation connection, Database Collation — Equivalent to CHARACTER_SET_CLIENT, COLLATION_CONNECTION, and DATABASE_COLLATION.

The SHOW CREATE EVENT statement and mysql.event system table have similar details about events. The SHOW CREATE statement contains the event definition.

PARTITIONS

The PARTITIONS system view stores metadata about partitions and subpartitions. For more information on partitioning, see Chapter 15. Each table and system view has at least one record in the PARTITIONS system view. The fields in the PARTITIONS system view are:

- TABLE_CATALOG — Provided for standards compliance. However, because MySQL does not have catalogs, this value is always NULL.
- TABLE_SCHEMA — The name of the database that this table belongs to, such as sakila.
- TABLE_NAME — The name of the table.

- PARTITION_NAME — The name of this partition. If the table is not partitioned, this value is NULL.

- SUBPARTITION_NAME — The name of this subpartition. If the table is not partitioned, this value is NULL.

- PARTITION_ORDINAL_POSITION — The position of the partition. The first partition has an ordinal position of 1. If the table is not partitioned, this value is NULL.

- SUBPARTITION_ORDINAL_POSITION — The position of the subpartition. The first subpartition has an ordinal position of 1. If the table is not subpartitioned, this value is NULL.

- PARTITION_METHOD — The partition algorithm. One of RANGE, LIST, KEY, LINEAR KEY, HASH, LINEAR HASH, or NULL if the table is not partitioned.

- SUBPARTITION_METHOD — The subpartition algorithm. One of KEY, LINEAR KEY, HASH, LINEAR HASH, or NULL if the table is not subpartitioned.

- PARTITION_EXPRESSION — The partitioning field and function, such as TO_DAYS(entry_date) or store_id. This function must evaluate to an integer. If the table is partitioned but does not use a RANGE or LIST algorithm, this value is the partitioning field (such as store_id). If the table is not partitioned, this value is NULL.

- SUBPARTITION_EXPRESSION — The subpartitioning field, such as id. If the table is not subpartitioned, this value is NULL.

- PARTITION_DESCRIPTION — The partition key values when PARTITION_METHOD is LIST. The partition key maximum value when PARTITION_METHOD is RANGE. If the table is not partitioned using a RANGE or LIST algorithm, this value is NULL.

- TABLE_ROWS — Same as the TABLE_ROWS field of the TABLES system view, but only for this partition. If the table is not partitioned, this field is exactly the same as in the TABLES system view.

- AVG_ROW_LENGTH — Same as the AVG_ROW_LENGTH field of the TABLES system view, but only for this partition. If the table is not partitioned, this field is exactly the same as in the TABLES system view.

- DATA_LENGTH — Same as the DATA_LENGTH field of the TABLES system view, but only for this partition. If the table is not partitioned, this field is exactly the same as in the TABLES system view.

- MAX_DATA_LENGTH — Same as the MAX_DATA_LENGTH field of the TABLES system view, but only for this partition. If the table is not partitioned, this field is exactly the same as in the TABLES system view.

- INDEX_LENGTH — Same as the INDEX_LENGTH field of the TABLES system view, but only for this partition. If the table is not partitioned, this field is exactly the same as in the TABLES system view.

- DATA_FREE — Same as the DATA_FREE field of the TABLES system view, but only for this partition. If the table is not partitioned, this field is exactly the same as in the TABLES system view.

- CREATE_TIME — Same as the CREATE_TIME field of the TABLES system view, but only for this partition. If the table is not partitioned, this field is exactly the same as in the TABLES system view.

- UPDATE_TIME — Same as the UPDATE_TIME field of the TABLES system view, but only for this partition. If the table is not partitioned, this field is exactly the same as in the TABLES system view.

- CHECK_TIME — Same as the CHECK_TIME field of the TABLES system view, but only for this partition. If the table is not partitioned, this field is exactly the same as in the TABLES system view.

- CHECKSUM — Same as the CHECKSUM field of the TABLES system view, but only for this partition. If the table is not partitioned, this field is exactly the same as in the TABLES system view.

- PARTITION_COMMENT — The COMMENT option for partitions can be used to provide user-defined information. If there was no comment specified, the value is the empty string (").

- NODEGROUP — If the table is partitioned, the value is default, otherwise the value is the empty string ("). There are different values when using MySQL Cluster.

- TABLESPACE_NAME — Always NULL.

System Information

The INFORMATION_SCHEMA database has system views relating to server information such as available character sets, collations, storage engines, plugins, and system variable values. There is also runtime information about status variable values, processes, and profiling information.

CHARACTER_SETS

Each character set available in mysqld is represented by a row in the CHARACTER_SETS system view. The fields in CHARACTER_SETS are:

- CHARACTER_SET_NAME — The name of the character set, such as utf8.
- DEFAULT_COLLATE_NAME — The name of the default collation for this character set, such as utf8_general_ci.
- DESCRIPTION — A description of the character set, such as UTF-8 Unicode.
- MAXLEN — The number of bytes a single character is stored in.

The SHOW CHARACTER SET statement returns the same information as the CHARACTER_SETS system view:

- Charset — Equivalent to CHARACTER_SET_NAME.
- Description — Equivalent to DESCRIPTION.

- Default collation — Equivalent to DEFAULT_COLLATE_NAME.

- Maxlen — Equivalent to MAXLEN.

COLLATIONS

Each collation available to the current user is represented by a row in the COLLATIONS system view. The fields in COLLATIONS are:

- COLLATION_NAME — The name of the collation.

- CHARACTER_SET_NAME — The name of the character set associated with the collation.

- ID — The integer identifier of the collation.

- IS_DEFAULT — If this collation is the default mysqld collation for CHARAC-TER_SET_NAME, this value is Yes. Otherwise, the value is the empty string (").

- IS_COMPILED — If this collation has been compiled into mysqld, the value is Yes. Otherwise the value is the empty string ("). If your server has collations that are not compiled into mysqld, the collations are loaded from XML files in the directory specified by the system variable character_sets_dir:

```
mysql> SHOW VARIABLES LIKE 'character_sets_dir';
+--------------------+---------------------------+
| Variable_name      | Value                     |
+--------------------+---------------------------+
| character_sets_dir | /usr/share/mysql/charsets/ |
+--------------------+---------------------------+
1 row in set (0.02 sec)
```

- SORTLEN — The number of bytes needed in memory to sort using the collation.

The SHOW COLLATION statement returns the same information as the CHARACTER_SETS system view:

- Collation — Equivalent to COLLATION.

- Charset — Equivalent to CHARACTER_SET_NAME.

- Id — Equivalent to ID.

- Default — Equivalent to IS_DEFAULT.

- Compiled — Equivalent to IS_COMPILED.

- Sortlen — Equivalent to SORTLEN.

COLLATION_CHARACTER_SET_APPLICABILITY

The COLLATION_CHARACTER_SET_APPLICABILITY system view is a join table for CHARAC-TER_SETS and COLLATIONS. Each collation has a row in this view. The fields are:

- COLLATION_NAME — The collation name.

- CHARACTER_SET_NAME — The character set this collation is associated with.

This INFORMATION_SCHEMA system view is part of the SQL standard. MySQL extended the SQL standard for the COLLATIONS system view to include the associated character set, so there is no reason to use this system view instead of the first two fields of the COLLATIONS system view.

ENGINES

The ENGINES system view shows metadata about the available storage engines. The fields are:

- ENGINE — The name of the storage engine.
- SUPPORT — If the storage engine can be used, the value is YES. If the storage engine has not been compiled in or plugged into mysqld, the value is NO. The value is DEFAULT for the default storage engine for mysqld, and DISABLED if the storage engine is available in mysqld but unusable.
- A storage engine may be DISABLED if mysqld was started with an option to skip the storage engine, such as --skip-bdb, or if the storage engine cannot be used for some other reason. For example, if InnoDB cannot open its data or log files at server startup, InnoDB will be DISABLED.
- The MyISAM and Maria storage engines are used by mysqld and cannot be disabled.
- COMMENT — A short description of the storage engine.
- TRANSACTIONS — YES if the storage engine supports transactions, NO if it does not.
- XA — YES if the storage engine supports XA transactions, NO if it does not.
- SAVEPOINTS — YES if the storage engine supports savepoints, NO if it does not.

The SHOW [STORAGE] ENGINES statement returns the same information as the ENGINES system view:

- Engine — Equivalent to ENGINE.
- Support — Equivalent to SUPPORT.
- Comment — Equivalent to COMMENT.
- Transactions — Equivalent to TRANSACTIONS.
- XA — Equivalent to XA.
- Savepoints — Equivalent to SAVEPOINTS.

PLUGINS

Extensions to mysqld can be written as plugins. There are some plugins that are bundled with a new installation, third-party plugins, and you can write your own user-defined plugins. Metadata about plugins is stored in the PLUGINS system view, in the following fields:

- PLUGIN_NAME — The name of the plugin.
- PLUGIN_VERSION — The version of the plugin, as defined by the plugin author(s).
- PLUGIN_STATUS — The status of the plugin. Currently the only supported value is ACTIVE.

697

- PLUGIN_TYPE — The plugin type, such as INFORMATION SCHEMA for a plugin that extends the data dictionary, or STORAGE ENGINE for a plugin that adds a new storage engine.

- PLUGIN_TYPE_VERSION — The version of the plugin type. This corresponds to the mysqld version; mysqld version 6.0.6 has a value of 60006.0, and mysqld version 5.1.22 has a value of 50122.0.

- PLUGIN_LIBRARY — The filename of the plugin library. This value is NULL for the built-in plugins such as storage engines that do not have a library file in the plugin directory (defined by the system variable plugin_dir).

- PLUGIN_LIBRARY_VERSION — The library version of the plugin. This value is NULL for the built-in plugins such as storage engines that do not have a library file in the plugin directory (defined by the system variable plugin_dir).

- PLUGIN_AUTHOR — The organization, individual, or people who wrote the plugin.

- PLUGIN_DESCRIPTION — A description of the plugin.

- PLUGIN_LICENSE — The license applied to the plugin. The plugins provided with mysqld use the GPL2 license and have a value of GPL. Other possible values are BSD and Proprietary.

The SHOW PLUGINS statement outputs some of the same information as the PLUGINS system view:

- Name — Equivalent to PLUGIN_NAME.
- Status — Equivalent to PLUGIN_STATUS.
- Type — Equivalent to PLUGIN_TYPE.
- Library — Equivalent to PLUGIN_LIBRARY.
- License — Equivalent to PLUGIN_LICENSE.

The mysql.plugin system table lists the installed plugins that have library files associated with them. The fields in the mysql.plugin system table are:

- name — Equivalent to PLUGIN_NAME.
- dl — Equivalent to PLUGIN_LIBRARY.

PROCESSLIST

The PROCESSLIST system view contains information about the processes currently running in mysqld. The SHOW [FULL] PROCESSLIST statement outputs the exact same information as the PROCESSLIST system view, but cannot be queried to filter results like the system view can. Each process in mysqld has a row in the PROCESSLIST system view, and the fields are:

- ID — The id of the connection that is running this process.

- USER — The username that the thread running this process authenticated with, such as root. The value is system_user for internal tasks such as reading and applying logs during replication. The value is event_scheduler for the system event scheduler. The value is unauthenticated user for the short time a thread has connected but not authenticated yet.

- Many rows with a USER of unauthenticated user may indicate that it is taking a long time to authenticate a user. This can be indicative of a DNS problem.

- HOST — The host and port that the thread running this process authenticated from, such as localhost:3058. If the user is system user or event_scheduler, the host value is the empty string (").

- DB — The database in use by the thread, such as sakila. If the thread connected without specifying a database and no USE statements have been issued to change the database, the value is NULL.

- COMMAND — The type of command the thread is running. Possible values and their corresponding meanings are shown in Table 21-1.

TABLE 21-1

Values and Meanings of COMMAND in the PROCESSLIST System View

Value General Commands	Meaning
Change user	Changing user
Create DB	Creating a new database
Daemon	Used by an internal thread only
Delayed insert	Handling delayed inserts to a table
Debug	Creating debugging information
Drop DB	Dropping a database
Error	Though the authors have not seen this value of COMMAND, it is likely used while a thread is throwing an error, and only can be seen for a split second before the COMMAND changes again or the connection is stopped.
Field List	Getting field information
Init DB	Changing to a new database
Kill	Killing a thread
Long Data	Getting long data
Ping	Handling a ping request

continued

TABLE 21-1 *(continued)*

Value General Commands	Meaning
Query	Executing a statement
Quit	Quitting
Refresh	Running a FLUSH command
Set option	Setting an option
Shutdown	Shutting down mysqld
Sleep	Waiting for a statement to be sent from the client
Statistics	Obtaining server status information
Prepared Statement Commands	
Close stmt	Closing a prepared statement
Execute	Executing a prepared statement
Fetch	Fetching prepared statement results
Prepare	Preparing a prepared statement
Reset stmt	Resetting a prepared statement
Replication Commands	
Binlog Dump	On a master server, the process that sends logs to a slave. There is one thread running a COMMAND of Binlog Dump for each slave connected to the master.
Connect	On a slave server, the slave is connected to the master.
Connect Out	On a slave server, the slave is attempting to connect to the master.
Register Slave	On a master server, registering a slave server.
Table Dump	On a master server, sending table contents to a slave server, such as when LOAD DATA FROM MASTER or LOAD TABLE FROM MASTER is executed on a slave.

- TIME — The number of seconds the process has been in STATE.

- STATE — The current state of the process. Possible values and their meanings are shown in Table 21-2.

- INFO — The statement being executed by the process. The value is NULL if the thread is not executing a statement, which can occur if a thread is in a STATE of Sleep.

TABLE 21-2

Values and Meanings of STATE in the PROCESSLIST System View

Value General States (in alphabetical order)	Meaning
After create	The end of a table creation, whether it was from a CREATE TABLE statement or an internal temporary table creation. This state appears whether or not the table creation was successful.
Analyzing	Calculating index distributions for a MyISAM table.
Checking table	Checking a table, as with CHECK TABLE.
cleaning up	Preparing to free memory and reset some state variables after processing a command.
closing tables	Closing tables and flushing changed data to disk.
converting HEAP to MyISAM	An internal, in-memory table became too large and is being converted to an on-disk MyISAM table.
copy to tmp table	Copying information to a temporary table during an ALTER TABLE, after creating a new structure. Note that this is different from Copying to tmp table.
Copying to group table	During a query that has an ORDER BY different from its GROUP BY clause, after rows are sorted into by group they are copied to a temporary table.
Copying to tmp table	Copying to a temporary in-memory table. Note that this is different from copy to tmp table.
Copying to tmp table on disk	Copying to an on-disk temporary table.
Creating index	On a MyISAM table, creating an index, such as with ALTER TABLE tblname ENABLE KEYS.
Creating sort index	Resolving a SELECT statement with an internal temporary table. For a non-temporary internal table, the state is Sorting result.
creating table	Creating a table, including a temporary table.
Creating tmp table	Creating an in-memory or on-disk temporary table.
deleting from main table	Deleting from the first table in a multi-table delete, saving data to be used when deleting from the other tables, called reference tables.

continued

TABLE 21-2 *(continued)*

Value General States (in alphabetical order)	Meaning
deleting from reference tables	Deleting matched rows from the rest of the tables in a multi-table delete.
discard_or_import_ tablespace	Discarding a table space, such as with ALTER TABLE tblname DISCARD TABLESPACE, or importing a tablespace, such as with ALTER TABLE tblname IMPORT TABLESPACE.
end	The end of ALTER TABLE, CREATE VIEW, SELECT, INSERT, UPDATE, and DELETE statements. The end state occurs just before the cleaning up state.
Execution of init_command	The init_command system variable allows you to specify a command that gets run whenever a user connects. For example, init_command="SET AUTOCOMMIT=0".
freeing items	Freeing items after a command has finished executing; usually followed by a state of cleaning up.
Flushing tables	Waiting for threads to close tables while executing a FLUSH TABLES.
FULLTEXT initialization	Preparing a FULLTEXT search.
init	Initializing ALTER TABLE, SELECT, INSERT, UPDATE, and DELETE statements.
Killed	Kill flag has been set, waiting for the thread to abort.
Locked	Waiting for another query to finish.
logging slow query	Writing to the slow query log.
login	Waiting for successful authentication.
NULL	The state of a SHOW PROCESSLIST statement.
Opening table[s]	Attempting to open a table, most often seen when a table is locked and cannot be opened.
preparing	Preparing a query during query optimization.
Purging old relay logs	On a slave, purging relay logs after they have been applied.
query end	Query processing completed; followed by the freeing items state.
Reading from net	Reading a packet from the network.

TABLE 21-2 *(continued)*

Value General States (in alphabetical order)	Meaning
Removing duplicates	Removing duplicate rows, such as during a SELECT DISTINCT. This may not appear if the DISTINCT operation was optimized out in an earlier step.
removing tmp table	Removing an internal temporary table after a SELECT statement requiring the internal temporary table has been processed.
rename	Renaming a table.
rename result table	Replacing an old table with a new one via renaming during an ALTER TABLE statement.
Reopen tables	Trying to re-open a table after initially getting a lock, realizing the table structure changed, releasing the lock, and closing the table.
Repair by sorting	Sorting to create indexes during a REPAIR TABLE.
Repair done	Multi-threaded repair for a MyISAM table has completed.
Repair with keycache	Using the key cache to create indexes one row at a time. Slower than Repair by sorting.
Rolling back	Rolling back a transaction, as with ROLLBACK.
Saving state	Saving table state information such as row count, AUTO_INCREMENT value, and key distributions to the .MYI file (MyISAM tables only). This occurs during statements such as REPAIR TABLE or ANALYZE TABLE.
Searching rows for update	Finding all matching rows. This occurs when the rows must be found first, as when an UPDATE is changing an index used to find the rows. Note that changing the row data may change the index values for that row, so this can occur when an UPDATE changes data used in an index.
Sending data	Returning data from a SELECT statement to the client program.
setup	Starting an ALTER TABLE.
Sorting for group	Sorting due to a GROUP BY clause.
Sorting for order	Sorting due to an ORDER BY clause.
Sorting index	Sorting index pages to be more efficient during a MyISAM table defragmentation, such as with OPTIMIZE TABLE.

continued

TABLE 21-2   *(continued)*

Value General States (in alphabetical order)	Meaning
Sorting result	Resolving a SELECT statement with an internal table. If the internal table is temporary, the state is Creating sort index.
statistics	Calculating statistics to help the query optimizer find a query execution plan.
System lock	Waiting for an external system table lock. External system locks are disabled by default and only needed if there is more than one program accessing the table, such as if there are multiple mysqld servers accessing the same tables.
Table lock	Waiting for an internal table lock, after getting an external system table lock.
Updating	Updating rows or searching for rows to update.
updating main table	Updating the first table in a multi-table update, saving data to be used when updating the other tables, called reference tables.
updating reference tables	Updating matched rows from the rest of the tables in a multi-table update.
User lock	Waiting for a lock requested by a GET_LOCK() statement.
Waiting for table[s]	Waiting for other threads to close a table so it can reopen the table after realizing the table structure changed.
Waiting on cond	The generic state when there is no available state information.
Writing to net	Writing a packet to the network.

States Related to INSERT DELAYED (in order of operation)

Creating delayed handler	Creating a delayed insert handler.
waiting for handler open	Waiting for the handler initialization and the table to open.
got old table	End of initialization phase after table has been opened.
waiting for INSERT	Delayed insert handler is waiting for a row to be added to the batch.

TABLE 21-2   *(continued)*

Value General States	Meaning
waiting for delay_list	Waiting to receive the list of delayed insert handler threads.
waiting for handler lock	Waiting for access to the delayed insert handler.
got handler lock	Access to the delayed insert handler has been acquired.
allocating local table	Preparing to send rows to the delayed insert handler.
storing row into queue	Adding a row to the batch that the delayed handler insert will process.
Upgrading lock	Delayed insert handler is waiting for a lock on the table to insert rows.
insert	Delayed insert handler is inserting rows into the table.
reschedule	Delayed insert handler is inserting is sleeping after processing a batch and before processing another, so other threads can access the table.
waiting for handler insert	Delayed insert handler is waiting for new inserts after processing all batches.
update	There is no information on what this status indicates.

States Related to Replication (in order of operation)

Sending binlog event to slave	Master is sending a binary log event to a slave.
Finished reading one binlog; switching to next binlog	Master is opening the next binlog to send more events to a slave.
Has sent all binlog to slave; waiting for binlog to be updated	Master is waiting for more updates after all updates have been sent to a slave.
waiting to finalize termination	Master is waiting for the thread on the master that sends events to the slave to stop.
Waiting for master update	Slave I/O is initializing.
Connecting to master	Slave I/O thread is trying to connect to master.

continued

TABLE 21-2   *(continued)*

Value General States	Meaning
Checking master version	Slave I/O thread is checking the mysqld version of the master.
Registering slave on master	Slave I/O thread is registering this slave server with the master.
Requesting binlog dump	Slave I/O thread is requesting the contents of the binary logs.
Waiting to reconnect after a failed binlog dump request	Slave I/O thread is sleeping after a binary log dump request failed. The amount of sleep time is determined by the MASTER_CONNECT_RETRY option, which can be set in the CHANGE MASTER TO statement or at startup using the --master-connect-retry option.
Reconnecting after a failed binlog dump request	Slave I/O thread is reconnecting to the master after a binary log dump request failed.
Waiting for master to send event	Slave I/O thread is waiting for a binary log event to be sent from the master. The slave server has connected successfully to the master.
Queueing master event to the relay log	Slave I/O thread is copying binlog event from master to the relay log.
Waiting to reconnect after a failed master event read	Slave I/O thread is sleeping after an event read from the master failed. The amount of sleep time is determined by the MASTER_CONNECT_RETRY option, which can be set in the CHANGE MASTER TO statement or at startup using the --master-connect-retry option.
Reconnecting after a failed master event read	Slave I/O thread is reconnecting to the master after an event read from the master failed.
Waiting for the SQL thread to free enough relay log space	Slave I/O thread is waiting for the slave SQL thread to process events from the relay log. The relay logs have filled due to exceeding the relay_log_space_limit value. The default value is a value of 0, meaning unlimited.
Waiting for the next event in relay log	Slave SQL thread is waiting for the first event to appear in the relay log after the slave SQL thread has been initialized.
Reading event from the relay log	Slave SQL thread is reading an event from the relay log.

TABLE 21-2   *(continued)*

Value General States	Meaning
Has read all relay log; waiting for the slave I/O thread to update it.	Slave SQL thread is waiting for a new event to appear in the relay log.
Making temp file	Slave SQL thread is creating a temporary file to read in rows for a LOAD DATA INFILE statement.
Waiting for slave mutex on exit	Slave I/O thread or SQL thread is stopping.
Changing master	Applying a CHANGE MASTER statement.
Creating table from master dump	Creating a table from a master dump, such as when executing LOAD DATA FROM MASTER or LOAD TABLE FROM MASTER.
Opening master dump table	Opening a table to receive table contents from a master dump, such as when executing LOAD DATA FROM MASTER or LOAD TABLE FROM MASTER.
Reading master dump table data	Receiving table data from a master dump, such as when executing LOAD DATA FROM MASTER or LOAD TABLE FROM MASTER.
Rebuilding the index on master dump table	Rebuilding the index on a table after data from a table dump has been received, such as when executing LOAD DATA FROM MASTER or LOAD TABLE FROM MASTER.
starting slave	Starting the slave I/O and slave SQL threads after a table dump has completed.
Killing slave	Applying a SLAVE STOP or STOP SLAVE statement.

States Related to MySQL Cluster (in order of operation)

Processing events	Processing events to write to the binary log.
Committing events to binlog	Writing events to the binary log.
Syncing ndb table schema operation and binlog	Syncing the schema and binary log before replicating the schema.
Processing events from schema table	Replicating the schema.

continued

TABLE 21-2 *(continued)*

Value General States	Meaning
Shutting down	Shutting down.
Waiting for event from ndbcluster	An SQL node connected to a cluster management node is waiting for an event.
Waiting for first event from ndbcluster	An SQL node connected to a cluster management node is waiting for the first event.
Waiting for ndbcluster binlog update to reach current position	A node is waiting for the binary logs to become current.
Waiting for ndbcluster to start	A node is waiting for MySQL Cluster to start.
Waiting for schema epoch	Waiting for a global checkpoint for the schema.
Opening mysql.ndb_apply_status	A node is waiting for a system table to be opened.

States Related to the Event Scheduler (in order of operation)

Initialized	Event scheduler or event execution thread has been initialized.
Waiting on empty queue	Waiting; event queue is empty.
Waiting for next activation	Waiting; event queue has items but the next activation will happen later.
Waiting for scheduler to stop	Waiting for the scheduler to stop; this occurs after a SET GLOBAL event_scheduler=OFF statement has been issued.
Clearing	Event scheduler or event execution thread is ending.

Being able to query the PROCESSLIST system view is a large advantage over using the SHOW [FULL] PROCESSLIST statement. With SHOW [FULL] PROCESSLIST, all of the fields are shown, with no filtering. For example, the following query shows information about queries running longer than one minute:

```
SELECT ID, USER, HOST, DB, COMMAND, TIME, STATE, INFO
FROM PROCESSLIST
WHERE TIME>60;
```

You can also find out how many processes a certain username is running, and from what hosts:

```
SELECT ID, USER, HOST, DB, COMMAND, TIME, STATE, INFO
FROM PROCESSLIST
WHERE USER=some_user ORDER BY HOST;
```

PROFILING

As of MySQL version 6.0.5, query profiling can be done on a session-level basis. By default, the profiling session variable is set to 0 and the PROFILING system view has no rows. If it is set to 1, the PROFILING system view populates the following fields:

- QUERY_ID — The integer identifier of the query.
- SEQ — The sequence number, showing the display order for rows with the same QUERY_ID.
- STATE — The state the query was in. See Table 21-2 for the list of possible values.
- DURATION — How long the query stayed in STATE.
- CPU_USER — Seconds of user CPU use during STATE.
- CPU_SYSTEM — Seconds of system CPU use during STATE.
- CONTEXT_VOLUNTARY — The number of voluntary context switches that occurred during STATE.
- CONTEXT_INVOLUNTARY — The number of involuntary context switches that occurred during STATE.
- BLOCK_OPS_IN — The number of block input operations during STATE.
- BLOCK_OPS_OUT — The number of block output operations during STATE.
- MESSAGES_SENT — The number of communication messages sent during STATE.
- MESSAGES_RECEIVED — The number of communication messages received during STATE.
- PAGE_FAULTS_MAJOR — The number of major page faults that occurred during STATE.
- PAGE_FAULTS_MINOR — The number of minor page faults that occurred during STATE.
- SWAPS — The number of swaps that occurred during STATE.
- SOURCE_FUNCTION — The function in the source code where STATE executed.
- SOURCE_FILE — The source code file where STATE executed.
- SOURCE_LINE — The line number in SOURCE_FILE where STATE executed.

The SHOW PROFILE statement output information contains some of the same fields as the PROFILING system view. Just like the PROFILING system view, the SHOW PROFILE statement outputs one row per query state. However, the SHOW PROFILE statement only shows profiling information for one query. The information in the SHOW PROFILE output is:

- Status — Equivalent to STATE in the PROFILING system view.
- Duration — Equivalent to DURATION in the PROFILING system view.

See Chapter 4 for more information on using SHOW PROFILE. The SHOW PROFILES statement is very different from the SHOW PROFILE statement — it outputs profiling information for the most recent queries. There is one query per row, and the maximum number of queries shown is determined by the profiling_history_size session variable. This session variable also restricts the number of queries that are saved in the PROFILING system view. The information in the SHOW PROFILES output is:

- Query_ID — Equivalent to QUERY_ID in the PROFILING system view.
- Duration — The total amount of time spent on the query. Equivalent to:

  SELECT SUM(DURATION) FROM PROFILING WHERE QUERY_ID=num;

- Query — The text of the query that was executed. There is no equivalent in the PROFIL-ING system view.

See Chapter 4 for more information on using SHOW PROFILES.

GLOBAL_VARIABLES

The GLOBAL_VARIABLES system view contains information about the global server variables in mysqld. The SHOW GLOBAL VARIABLES command contains the same information as the GLOBAL_VARIABLES system view, using similar field names:

- VARIABLE_NAME — The name of the global system variable. Variable_name in SHOW GLOBAL VARIABLES is equivalent.
- VARIABLE_VALUE — The value of the global system variable. Value in SHOW GLOBAL VARIABLES is equivalent.

SESSION_VARIABLES

The SESSION_VARIABLES system view contains information about the session server variables in mysqld. The SHOW SESSION VARIABLES command contains the same information as the SESSION_VARIABLES system view, using similar field names:

- VARIABLE_NAME — The name of the session system variable. Variable_name in SHOW SESSION VARIABLES is equivalent.
- VARIABLE_VALUE — The value of the session system variable. Variable_name in SHOW SESSION VARIABLES is equivalent.

GLOBAL_STATUS

The GLOBAL_STATUS system view contains information about the global server status in mysqld. The SHOW GLOBAL STATUS command contains the same information as the GLOBAL_STATUS system view, using similar field names:

- ■ VARIABLE_NAME — The name of the global status variable. Variable_name in SHOW GLOBAL STATUS is equivalent.

- ■ VARIABLE_VALUE — The value of the global status variable. Value in SHOW GLOBAL STATUS is equivalent.

SESSION_STATUS

The SESSION_STATUS system view contains information about the session server status in mysqld. The SHOW SESSION STATUS command contains the same information as the SESSION_STATUS system view, using similar field names:

- ■ VARIABLE_NAME — The name of the session system variable. Variable_name in SHOW SESSION STATUS is equivalent.

- ■ VARIABLE_VALUE — The value of the session system variable. Variable_name in SHOW SESSION STATUS is equivalent.

Displaying Permissions

The preferred method of changing permissions is by using the GRANT and REVOKE statements. However, viewing permissions can be difficult. SHOW GRANTS can be used to see the grant statement for the current user, and SHOW GRANTS FOR user@host can be used to see the GRANT statements for user@host. In order to run the SHOW GRANTS statement to see permissions for other users, you must know the user@host. This may seem obvious, but it is a tricky problem to solve — for example, finding all the users who have permissions to write to a specific table.

Four INFORMATION_SCHEMA system views make retrieving permissions easier. The COLUMN_PRIVILEGES and TABLE_PRIVILEGES are SQL standard system views that show permission information at the column and table levels, respectively. The SCHEMA_PRIVILEGES and USER_PRIVILEGES system views are MySQL extensions to the data dictionary, which contain information about permissions at the database and global levels, respectively.

Unlike the mysql system tables, the INFORMATION_SCHEMA system views show the full user. The mysql system tables contain separate fields for User and Host, and the INFORMATION_SCHEMA system views contain one field called GRANTEE, in the user@host format.

If a user has certain permissions for a database, those permissions will show up only on the database level — the SCHEMA_PRIVILEGES system view and the mysql.db system table.

This means that there is no trickle down of permissions, thus to get all the users with permissions for a single column you need to write a query that retrieves:

- The users with permissions on that column
- The users with table-level permissions on the table containing the column
- The users with database-level permissions on the database with the table containing the column
- The users with global permissions on all databases.

The SHOW PRIVILEGES statement returns all of the permissions that mysqld supports. There are three fields in the result of SHOW PRIVILEGES:

- Privilege — The name of the permission. Possible values are Alter, Alter routine, Create, Create routine, Create temporary tables, Create user, Create view, Delete, Drop, Event, Execute, File, Grant, Index, Insert, Lock tables, Process, References, Reload, Replication client, Replication slave, Select, Show databases, Show view, Shutdown, Super, Trigger, and Update.

- Context — A comma-separated list of contexts of the permission. Possible contexts are Databases, File access on server, Functions, Indexes, Procedures, Server Admin, and Tables.

- Comment — A short description of the permission.

COLUMN_PRIVILEGES

The COLUMN_PRIVILEGES system view contains the same information as the columns_priv system table in the mysql database. The COLUMN_PRIVILEGES system view contains one row per privilege per user — this means there are separate rows for a SELECT and an INSERT on a column for a user. In the columns_priv system table, there is one row per column per user, and a field with a SET data type to store all of the privileges for that user on that column.

The fields in the COLUMN_PRIVILEGES system view and their equivalences in the columns_priv system table are:

- GRANTEE — The user for which this permission is granted, in user@host format. The User and Host fields in mysql.columns_priv contain the same information.

- TABLE_CATALOG — Provided for standards compliance. However, because MySQL does not have catalogs, this value is always NULL. There is no equivalent in mysql.columns_priv.

- TABLE_SCHEMA — The name of the database, such as sakila. The Db field in mysql.columns_priv is equivalent.

- TABLE_NAME — The name of the table containing the field associated with this permission. The Table_name field in mysql.columns_priv is equivalent.

■ COLUMN_NAME — The name of the field associated with this permission. The Column_name field in mysql.columns_priv is equivalent.

■ PRIVILEGE_TYPE — The type of privilege. Possible values are SELECT, INSERT, UPDATE, and REFERENCES. The Column_priv field in mysql.columns_priv contains the same information. However, the Column_priv field is a SET data type, and the COLUMN_PRIVILEGES system view has one row per privilege.

To get the equivalent of the Column_priv field, query the COLUMN_PRIVILEGES system view with:

```
SELECT GROUP_CONCAT(PRIVILEGE_TYPE)
FROM COLUMN_PRIVILEGES
WHERE GRANTEE="'user'@'host'"
AND TABLE_NAME=tblname
AND COLUMN_NAME=fldname;
```

■ IS_GRANTABLE — Whether or not the user can grant this permission to another user. If the user can grant this permission to another user, the value is YES; otherwise the value is NO. There is no equivalent in mysql.columns_priv.

TABLE_PRIVILEGES

The TABLE_PRIVILEGES system view contains the same information as the tables_priv system table in the mysql database. The TABLE_PRIVILEGES system view contains one row per privilege per user — this means there are separate rows for a SELECT and an INSERT on a table for a user. In the tables_priv system table, there is one row per table per user, and a field with a SET data type to store all of the privileges for that user on that table.

The fields in the TABLE_PRIVILEGES system view and their equivalences in the tables_priv system table are:

■ GRANTEE — The user for which this permission is granted, in user@host format. The User and Host fields in mysql.tables_priv contain the same information.

■ TABLE_CATALOG — Provided for standards compliance. However, because MySQL does not have catalogs, this value is always NULL. There is no equivalent in mysql.tables_priv.

■ TABLE_SCHEMA — The name of the database, such as sakila. The Db field in mysql.tables_priv is equivalent.

■ TABLE_NAME — The name of the table associated with this permission. The Table_name field in mysql.tables_priv is equivalent.

■ PRIVILEGE_TYPE — The type of privilege. Possible values are SELECT, INSERT, UPDATE, DELETE, CREATE, DROP, GRANT, REFERENCES, INDEX, ALTER, CREATE VIEW, SHOW VIEW, and TRIGGER. The Table_priv field in mysql.tables_priv contains the same information. However, the Table_priv field is a SET data type, and the TABLE_PRIVILEGES system view has one row per privilege.

To get the equivalent of the `Table_priv` field, query the `TABLE_PRIVILEGES` system view with:

```
SELECT GROUP_CONCAT(PRIVILEGE_TYPE)
FROM TABLE_PRIVILEGES
WHERE GRANTEE="'user'@'host'"
AND TABLE_NAME=tblname;
```

■ `IS_GRANTABLE` — Whether or not the user can grant this permission to another user. If the user can grant this permission to another user, the value is `YES`; otherwise the value is `NO`. There is no equivalent in `mysql.tables_priv`.

SCHEMA_PRIVILEGES

The `SCHEMA_PRIVILEGES` system view contains the same information as the db system table in the `mysql` database. The `SCHEMA_PRIVILEGES` system view contains one row per privilege per user — this means there are separate rows for `SELECT` and `INSERT` permissions on a database for a user. In the db system table, there is one row per table per user, with many fields storing the permissions.

The fields in the `SCHEMA_PRIVILEGES` system view and their equivalences in the db system table are:

■ `GRANTEE` — The user for which this permission is granted, in `user@host` format. The `User` and `Host` fields in `mysql.db` contain the same information.

■ `TABLE_CATALOG` — Provided for standards compliance. However, because MySQL does not have catalogs, this value is always `NULL`. There is no equivalent in `mysql.db`.

■ `TABLE_SCHEMA` — The name of the database associated with this permission, such as `sakila`. The `Db` field in `mysql.db` is equivalent.

■ `PRIVILEGE_TYPE` — The type of privilege. Possible values are `SELECT`, `INSERT`, `UPDATE`, `DELETE`, `CREATE`, `DROP`, `GRANT`, `REFERENCES`, `INDEX`, `ALTER`, `CREATE TEMPORARY TABLES`, `LOCK TABLES`, `CREATE VIEW`, `SHOW VIEW`, `CREATE ROUTINE`, `ALTER ROUTINE`, `EXECUTE`, `EVENT`, and `TRIGGER`. The `mysql.db` system table contains the same information. However, the db system table contains one row for each table, with separate `ENUM` fields for each permission. The `ENUM` fields have a value of `Y` or `N`, indicating whether or not the user has that permission. The `SCHEMA_PRIVILEGES` system view has one row per privilege.

■ To find out which users have `SELECT` permissions for the `sakila` database, the `mysql.db` table can be queried with:

```
SELECT User,Host FROM mysql.db
WHERE Select_priv='Y'
AND Db='sakila';
```

- To get the same result from the SCHEMA_PRIVILEGES system view, the query is:

```
SELECT GRANTEE FROM SCHEMA_PRIVILEGES
WHERE PRIVILEGE_TYPE='SELECT'
AND TABLE_SCHEMA=sakila';
```

- IS_GRANTABLE — Whether or not the user can grant this permission to another user. If the user can grant this permission to another user, the value is YES; otherwise the value is NO. There is no equivalent in mysql.tables_priv.

USER_PRIVILEGES

The USER_PRIVILEGES system view contains the same information as the user system table in the mysql database. The USER_PRIVILEGES system view contains one row per privilege per user — this means there are separate rows for the global SUPER and FILE permissions for a user. In the user system table, there is one row per user, with many fields storing the permissions.

The fields in the USER_PRIVILEGES system view and their equivalences in the user system table are:

- GRANTEE — The user for which this permission is granted, in user@host format. The User and Host fields in mysql.db contain the same information.

- TABLE_CATALOG — Provided for standards compliance. However, because MySQL does not have catalogs, this value is always NULL. There is no equivalent in mysql.user.

- PRIVILEGE_TYPE — The type of privilege. Possible values are all of the Privilege values except Grant from the output of SHOW PRIVILEGES. There is no need for a GRANT privilege type because the USER_PRIVILEGES system view stores whether or not a user has grant permission in the IS_GRANTABLE field.

  The mysql.user system table contains the same information. However, the user system table contains one row for each user, with separate ENUM fields for each permission. The ENUM fields have a value of Y or N, indicating whether or not the user has that permission. The USER_PRIVILEGES system view has one row per privilege.

  To find out which users have SUPER permissions, the mysql.user table can be queried with:

```
SELECT User,Host FROM mysql.user
WHERE Super_priv='Y';
```

  To get the same result from the USER_PRIVILEGES system view, the query is:

```
SELECT GRANTEE FROM USER_PRIVILEGES
WHERE PRIVILEGE_TYPE='SUPER';
```

■ IS_GRANTABLE — Whether or not the user can grant this permission to another user. If the user can grant this permission to another user, the value is YES; otherwise the value is NO. There is no equivalent in mysql.user.

Storage Engine-Specific Metadata

Storage engine authors are increasingly adding system views to the INFORMATION_SCHEMA database. At the time of this writing, the only storage engine–specific system views that ship with mysqld are Falcon system views. However, because Falcon is not yet complete at the time this book was written, the Falcon system views are being changed regularly. Therefore, we will not review any of the storage-engine–specific system views here.

Custom Metadata

The powerful plugin feature in MySQL allows server components to be loaded and unloaded without restarting mysqld. Plugins can be thought of as shared libraries that can be dynamically loaded.

At the time of this writing, there is no support for plugins in MySQL on Windows. Plugins are written in any language that can use C calling conventions, such as C or C++. Plugins can only be used on an operating system that supports dynamic loading with a version of mysqld that has been dynamically linked. You will need to compile your plugin with a C++ compiler (such as g++, the GNU C/C++ compiler) and some of the MySQL header files.

To obtain the header files, download the source package from the official website at http://dev.mysql.com/downloads/mysql/6.0.html. You can download either the rpm package or the tar archive. If you are using the rpm package, install it; if you are using the tar archive, extract the files from it.

Defining the plugin

For this example, we will use Roland Bouman's sample plugin "Hello, Information Schema." You can find the original article and code source online at http://www.oreillynet.com/databases/blog/2008/02/mysql_information_schema_plugi.html.

The includes you will need are follow; note that the numbers are not part of the code:

```
1.      #include <mysql_priv.h>
2.      #include <stdlib.h>
3.      #include <ctype.h>
4.      #include <mysql_version.h>
5.      #include <mysql/plugin.h>
6.      #include <my_global.h>
7.      #include <my_dir.h>
```

> **NOTE** `mysql_version.h` is **not in the** source **package, but it is in the** `mysql-devel` **package (the compilation process creates** `mysql_version.h` **later on). Unfortunately** `mysql_priv.h` **is only in the** source **package, not the** `mysql-devel` **package, so you need to download both the** source **and the** `mysql-devel` **packages.**

On an abstract level, making a custom system view in the INFORMATION_SCHEMA database requires:

- The field definitions of the system view (that is, the structure of the system view). In our example, we define a system view named MYSQL_HELLO with a field defined as HELLO VARCHAR(64) NOT NULL DEFAULT `'`.

- The function that populates the system view upon request (that is, the values in the system view). We will define a function to store the string `plugin: hello,` `information_schema!!!` into the HELLO field of our MYSQL_HELLO system view.

On a more technical level, to create the custom system view, you need to instantiate the ST_SCHEMA_TABLE struct and define two members. One member, `field_info`, is an array of ST_FIELD_INFO structures, which define the fields in your system view. The values in the ST_FIELD_INFO structure are defined in the source code in the `sql/table.h` header file and explained in Table 21-3.

TABLE 21-3

ST_FIELD_INFO Structure

Code	Explanation	Example Value
`const char*` `field_name;`	Field name	"HELLO"
`uint field_length;`	In string-type fields, the maximum number of characters. In other fields, the display length.	64 in our example, a string-type field
`enum enum_field_types` `field_type;`	Field data type	MYSQL_TYPE_VARCHAR
`int value;`	Field value	0
`uint field_flags;`	0 means NOT NULL and SIGNED. It can be overridden by MY_I_S_MAYBE_NULL, MY_I_S_UNSIGNED, or both constants, separated by | (bitwise or).	0
`const char* old_name;`	Old field name	"Hello"
`uint open_method;`	How the table is opened. One of SKIP_OPEN_TABLE, OPEN_FRM_ONLY, or OPEN_FULL_TABLE.	SKIP_OPEN_TABLE

Our example contains the following code to define the custom system view:

```
8.     static ST_FIELD_INFO mysql_is_hello_field_info[]=
9.     {
10.            {"HELLO", 64, MYSQL_TYPE_VARCHAR, 0, 0, "Hello",
SKIP_OPEN_TABLE},
11.            {NULL, 0, MYSQL_TYPE_NULL, 0, 0, NULL, 0}
12.     };
```

The first structure in the array is the field we are creating. The last structure is an indication that the array is complete, and must be present. We named the array mysql_is_hello_field_info, which stands for "the field information of the hello system view in the mysql information schema."

The next line of code is:

```
13.    int schema_table_store_record(THD *thd, TABLE *table);
```

This line declares the schema_table_store_record function, which we will use later to store a row in a system view.

The second member of ST_SCHEMA_TABLE that we need to define is the function that populates the system view, called the fill_table:

```
14.    int mysql_is_hello_fill_table(
15.       THD *thd
16.       , TABLE_LIST *tables
17.       , COND *cond
18.       )
19.       {
20.          int status;
21.          CHARSET_INFO *scs= system_charset_info;
22.          TABLE *table= (TABLE *)tables->table;
23.          const char *str = "plugin: hello, information_schema!!!";
24.          table->field[0]->store(
25.             str
26.             , strlen(str)
27.             , scs
28.             );
29.          status = schema_table_store_record(
30.             thd
31.             , table
32.             );
33.          return status;
34.       }
```

In lines 15–17 we see THD *thd again, pointing to the current session, and TABLE_LIST *tables, which is an array of table instantiations of our "Hello" system view. COND *cond is a condition that could be used by our plugin for filtering or optimization, though we will not use it in this example.

The status variable is initialized as an int on line 20. At the end of the function (line 33), status is returned; a value of 1 indicates an error, and a value of 0 indicates success. Then on line 21, CHARSET_INFO *scs is initialized with the character set information. This is needed to properly store the field of our system view.

On line 22, TABLE *table is set as the handler to the instantiation of our system view. We initialize the char *str on line 23 with the string we will store in our system view. This means that when we finally install the plugin, we will see str in our system view:

```
mysql> SELECT * FROM INFORMATION_SCHEMA.MYSQL_HELLO;
+-------------------------------------+
| HELLO                               |
+-------------------------------------+
| plugin: hello, information_schema!!! |
+-------------------------------------+
1 row in set (0.00 sec)
```

Lines 24–28 store the string str, its length, and the character set scs (defined on line 21) into the first field (field[0]) of the row. Lines 29–32 store the row into the instantiation of our system view for the current session. If the function that stores the row is successful, status gets a value of 0. If there was an error, status gets a value of 1. status is returned on line 33, thus giving the mysql_is_hello_fill_table function a return value of 0 if it is successful and 1 if there was an error.

So far we have defined a system view in an ST_FIELD_INFO array and a fill_table function to populate the system view. We now need to create a plugin function to use these:

```
35.    static int mysql_is_hello_plugin_init(void *p)
36.    {
37.      ST_SCHEMA_TABLE *schema= (ST_SCHEMA_TABLE *)p;
38.      schema->fields_info= mysql_is_hello_field_info;
39.      schema->fill_table= mysql_is_hello_fill_table;
40.      return 0;
41.    }
```

The plugin_init function initializes the plugin as an INFORMATION SCHEMA plugin with the fields_info and fill_table we defined previously. Because we have a simple plugin_init function, we have a simple plugin_deinit function as well:

```
42.    static int mysql_is_hello_plugin_deinit(void *p)
43.    {
44.         return 0;
45.    }
```

In our example there is nothing that needs to be done during the plugin_deinit, so we simply return 0, indicating the function was successful. In a more complex example, there may be memory or other resources allocated in the plugin_init function that should be deallocated in the plugin_deinit function.

At this point, we still have not created the plugin. However, we have most of the parts we need to make an INFORMATION_SCHEMA plugin, and can now create the code to define the plugin itself:

```
46.     struct st_mysql_information_schema mysql_is_hello_plugin=
47.     { MYSQL_INFORMATION_SCHEMA_INTERFACE_VERSION };
48.     mysql_declare_plugin(mysql_is_hello)
49.     {
50.       MYSQL_INFORMATION_SCHEMA_
                      PLUGIN,                 /* type constant    */
51.       &mysql_is_hello_plugin,
                                              /* type descriptor  */
52.       "MYSQL_HELLO",
                                              /* Name             */
53.       "Roland Bouman (http://
                  rpbouman.blogspot.com/)", /* Author           */
54.       "Says hello.",
                                              /* Description      */
55.       PLUGIN_LICENSE_GPL,
                                              /* License          */
56.       mysql_is_hello_plugin_init,
                                              /* Init function    */
57.       mysql_is_hello_plugin_deinit,
                                              /* Deinit function  */
58.       0x0010,                            /* Version (1.0)     */
59.       NULL,                              /* status variables  */
60.       NULL,                              /* system variables  */
61.       NULL                               /* config options    */
62.     }
63.     mysql_declare_plugin_end;
```

Lines 46–47 define the type descriptor for the plugin, which is set as part of the plugin in line 51. Line 50 defines the type of plugin as an INFORMATION_SCHEMA plugin. Lines 52–55 define metadata that appear after plugin installation in the PLUGINS system view as the PLUGIN_NAME, PLUGIN_AUTHOR, PLUGIN_DESCRIPTION, and PLUGIN_LICENSE fields, respectively.

Lines 56–57 point to the previously created plugin_init and plugin_deinit functions, and line 58 defines the version metadata, which corresponds to the value of PLUGIN_VERSION in the PLUGINS system view. Lines 59–61 are pointers to structures containing the status variables, system variables, and configuration options. Our plugin does not have any of these, so we define them as NULL.

The entirety of the code is:

```
#include <mysql_priv.h>
#include <stdlib.h>
#include <ctype.h>
```

```c
#include <mysql_version.h>
#include <mysql/plugin.h>
#include <my_global.h>
#include <my_dir.h>

static ST_FIELD_INFO mysql_is_hello_field_info[]=
{
  {"HELLO", 64, MYSQL_TYPE_VARCHAR, 0, 0, "Hello", SKIP_OPEN_TABLE},
  {NULL, 0, MYSQL_TYPE_NULL, 0, 0, NULL, 0}
};

int schema_table_store_record(THD *thd, TABLE *table);

int mysql_is_hello_fill_table(
  THD *thd
, TABLE_LIST *tables
, COND *cond
)
{
  int status;
  CHARSET_INFO *scs= system_charset_info;
  TABLE *table= (TABLE *)tables->table;
  const char *str = "plugin: hello, information_schema!!!";
  table->field[0]->store(
    str
  , strlen(str)
  , scs
  );
  status = schema_table_store_record(
    thd
  , table
  );
  return status;
}

static int mysql_is_hello_plugin_init(void *p)
{
  ST_SCHEMA_TABLE *schema= (ST_SCHEMA_TABLE *)p;

  schema->fields_info= mysql_is_hello_field_info;
  schema->fill_table= mysql_is_hello_fill_table;

  return 0;
}

static int mysql_is_hello_plugin_deinit(void *p)
{
  return 0;
}
```

```
struct st_mysql_information_schema mysql_is_hello_plugin=
{ MYSQL_INFORMATION_SCHEMA_INTERFACE_VERSION };

mysql_declare_plugin(mysql_is_hello)
{
  MYSQL_INFORMATION_SCHEMA_
                     PLUGIN,                    /* type constant    */
  &mysql_is_hello_plugin,
                                                /* type descriptor  */
  "MYSQL_HELLO",
                                                /* Name             */
  "Roland Bouman (http://
                  rpbouman.blogspot.com/)",  /* Author           */
  "Says hello.",                                /* Description      */
  PLUGIN_LICENSE_GPL,                           /* License          */
  mysql_is_hello_plugin_init,                   /* Init function    */
  mysql_is_hello_plugin_deinit,                 /* Deinit function  */
  0x0010,                                       /* Version (1.0)    */
  NULL,                                         /* status variables */
  NULL,                                         /* system variables */
  NULL                                          /* config options   */
}
mysql_declare_plugin_end;
```

Compiling the plugin

Now that the code has been created, we need to compile the plugin as a dynamic shared object and then load it into mysqld. In our example we will save the source code in a file named mysql_is_hello.cc, and use g++ to compile the source. Table 21-4 shows the compile flags we will use and their meanings.

So the complete compile statement is:

```
shell> g++ -DMYSQL_DYNAMIC_PLUGIN -Wall -shared \
-I/path/to/mysql-6.0.x-source/include \
-I/path/to/mysql-6.0.x-source/sql \
-I/usr/include/mysql \
-o mysql_is_hello.so mysql_is_hello.cc
```

> **NOTE** The include paths were not specified for stdlib.h and ctype.h, because they are likely in your default include path. On our machines, we found these files in /usr/include, which was in the default include path. If you get errors such as:

```
error: stdlib.h: No such file or directory
error: ctype.h: No such file or directory
```

you should specify the include path for stdlib.h and ctype.h with another -I flag.

Some architectures, such as AMD64, require shared libraries to be compiled with the -fPIC flag. If your architecture requires this, you will see output similar to the following when you try to compile:

```
/usr/bin/ld: /tmp/ccNXOEqH.o: relocation R_X86_64_32S against `a
    local symbol' can not be used when making a shared object;
recompile with -fPIC /tmp/ccNXOEqH.o: could not read symbols:
    Bad value
collect2: ld returned 1 exit status
```

In this case, simply add -fPIC to the list of compile flags and try to compile again.

TABLE 21-4

g++ Compile Flags for Compiling a Plugin as a Dynamic Shared Object

Compile Flag	Meaning
-DMYSQL_DYNAMIC_ PLUGIN	-D indicates a constant; the constant is MYSQL_DYNAMIC_PLUGIN, which is required to compile the plugin as a dynamic shared object for mysqld.
-Wall	-W indicates warnings should be shown; all specifies showing all warnings.
-shared	Compile as a shared, dynamically linked library.
-I/path/to/mysql- 6.0.x-source/include	The include path for the my_global.h, my_dir.h, and mysql/plugin.h header files.
-I/path/to/mysql- 6.0.x-source/sql	The include path for the mysql_priv.h header file.
-I/usr/include/mysql	The include path for the mysql_version.h header file.
-o mysql_is_hello.so	The output file. The extension .so is traditionally used for shared objects.

If all goes well, a dynamic shared plugin will be created with a filename of mysql_is_ hello.so.

Installing the plugin

MySQL plugins are installed in `mysqld` using a MySQL extension to SQL. Thus, `mysqld` must be running, and no downtime is required to install a plugin. For security purposes, `mysqld` only looks for plugin libraries in the directory specified by the system variable `plugin_dir`:

```
mysql> SHOW VARIABLES LIKE 'plugin_dir';
+---------------+------------------------+
| Variable_name | Value                  |
+---------------+------------------------+
| plugin_dir    | /usr/lib64/mysql/plugin |
+---------------+------------------------+
1 row in set (0.01 sec)
```

For our example, we make sure the plugin directory exists, copy the plugin to the `mysqld` plugin directory, and ensure that the directory and plugin have appropriate permissions so `mysqld` can load the plugin:

```
shell> mkdir /usr/lib64/mysql/plugin/
shell> cp mysql_is_hello.so /usr/lib64/mysql/plugin
shell> sudo chown -R mysql:mysql /usr/lib64/mysql/plugin/
```

Now we use the `INSTALL PLUGIN` statement to install our plugin. The syntax of `INSTALL PLUGIN` is:

```
INSTALL PLUGIN plugin_name SONAME 'plugin_library';
```

The `plugin_name` was set in the plugin metadata (on line 52 of our code). The `plugin_library` is the name of the compiled plugin file (the complete path to the plugin file is plugin_dir/plugin_library):

```
mysql> INSTALL PLUGIN MYSQL_HELLO SONAME 'mysql_is_hello.so';
Query OK, 0 rows affected (0.00 sec)
```

And our plugin has successfully been installed:

```
mysql> SELECT * FROM INFORMATION_SCHEMA.MYSQL_HELLO;
+------------------------------------+
| HELLO                              |
+------------------------------------+
| plugin: hello, information_schema!!! |
+------------------------------------+
1 row in set (0.00 sec)
```

We can now see our plugin in the `mysql.plugin` system table and the `INFORMATION_SCHEMA.PLUGINS` system view:

```
mysql> SELECT * FROM mysql.plugin
    -> WHERE name='MYSQL_HELLO'\G
```

```
*************************** 1. row ***************************
name: MYSQL_HELLO
  dl: mysql_is_hello.so
1 row in set (0.00 sec)

mysql> SELECT * FROM INFORMATION_SCHEMA.PLUGINS
    -> WHERE PLUGIN_NAME='MYSQL_HELLO'\G
*************************** 1. row ***************************
           PLUGIN_NAME: MYSQL_HELLO
        PLUGIN_VERSION: 0.21
         PLUGIN_STATUS: ACTIVE
           PLUGIN_TYPE: INFORMATION SCHEMA
   PLUGIN_TYPE_VERSION: 60006.0
        PLUGIN_LIBRARY: mysql_is_hello.so
PLUGIN_LIBRARY_VERSION: 1.0
         PLUGIN_AUTHOR: Roland Bouman (http://rpbouman.blogspot.com/)
    PLUGIN_DESCRIPTION: Says hello.
        PLUGIN_LICENSE: GPL
1 row in set (0.00 sec)
```

To uninstall the plugin, run UNINSTALL PLUGIN plugin_name:

```
mysql> UNINSTALL PLUGIN MYSQL_HELLO;
Query OK, 0 rows affected (0.00 sec)
```

The plugin is loaded when the INSTALL PLUGIN is run. If you want to change the plugin you have to uninstall the plugin, change the plugin file, and re-install the plugin. If the plugin file changes or is removed while installed on a running server, mysqld will most likely crash.

Summary

This chapter described the information contained in the MySQL data dictionary, including:

- All of the metadata in the system views of the INFORMATION_SCHEMA database
- Many SHOW statements (see Chapter 4 for the remainder of the SHOW statements that show metadata)
- Many of the system tables in the mysql database
- Creating custom metadata as INFORMATION_SCHEMA plugins

Chapter 22

Scaling and High Availability Architectures

I
n these days of an online world where applications need to run all the
time, and need to run quickly, scaling and high availability are very
important. MySQL's cost and three basic tenets of *fast*, *reliable*, and
easy-to-use have redefined the database market. These days, those without
advanced training and large amounts of money can create successful applications with database backends. In many ways, you can scale more and
have a higher availability just by using MySQL instead of another database
product.

Scaling and high availability are both very important to a successful application. *Scaling* means an application works with acceptable speed when
there are one hundred users or one hundred million users. *High availability* means that the application is up and running for much of the time. Not
all architectures that provide scaling will provide high availability, and vice
versa.

A simple way to scale is to upgrade your hardware to a configuration
with faster CPUs and disk, and more CPUs and RAM. This is costly, and
only scales to a certain point. This is called *scaling up*, or *vertical scaling*,
because you are upgrading the hardware. *Horizontal scaling*, or *scaling out*,
increases the maximum capacity of your database architecture by adding
more database servers.

One of the best ways to scale is to make sure your queries are running as
quickly as possible. If a database can handle 2,000 writes per second, there
is no architectural solution that will allow the database to handle more
than that. If a write query can run faster, the same database will be able to
handle more writes per second. Query optimization, schema optimization,

data reduction, and server tuning are ways to make a query run faster. We cover data reduction and query and schema optimization in Chapter 18. Server tuning is covered in Chapter 10. If your queries are running as fast as they possibly can, but there is a large amount of data to wade through, you may want to partition your data. We discuss different ways to partition in Chapter 15.

This chapter goes through a number of technologies, which can be used for high availability or scalability:

- Scalability
  - Replication
  - MySQL Proxy
  - MySQL Cluster
  - Connection pooling
  - memcached
- High Availability (Data Synchronization)
  - Replication
  - SAN
  - DRBD
  - MySQL Cluster
- High Availability (Automated Failover)
  - MySQL Proxy
  - Linux-HA Heartbeat
  - MySQL Cluster

As with all difficult problems, there is no easy solution that will solve every different type of scaling and high availability issue for most people. Many web-based application administrators have found that users are using the application differently than they had anticipated. Changing schema and adding features causes the architecture design to change, so even if you plan the best solution for your application, the requirements may change based on how the application is used. Through measurement, planning, flexibility, and risk assessment, high availability and scalability can be achieved and maintained.

Replication

The basics of replication, and how to set up replication, are discussed in detail in Chapter 16. Replication allows copies of data to be kept asynchronously on different servers. In traditional master/slave replication, where a master database server replicates to a slave database server, all writes must occur on the master database server. A write to a master server needs to propagate to any slaves, so there is no real way to reduce the number of writes to a machine using replication. However, reads can be done on either the master or the slave, and because no data is changed, nothing needs to propagate.

If your application has a high ratio of reads to writes, you can move some or all of the load generated by reads a different server. Thus, replication can be a scaling technique.

Replication can also be a technique for high availability. If a master server cannot be reached, a slave can be promoted to be a master server. The slave is already loaded with the data, so there is no need to spend time restoring from a backup.

One read slave

A machine can have many slaves, but a machine can have only one master. The traditional master/slave replication architecture can be represented by Figure 22-1.

FIGURE 22-1

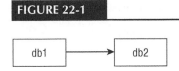

If db1 cannot be accessed, an administrator will promote db2 to a master server. This is often called *failover* — a server failed, so the slave will be promoted. Some administrators use the term *switchover* when they are promoting a slave when the master has not failed, for instance if the master needs to be taken offline for maintenance. Unfortunately, MySQL does not ship with a tool to automate slave promotion; however, automation is possible using scripts and heartbeat tools. MySQL Proxy or Linux-HA Heartbeat (described later in this chapter) can be used with replication to achieve an automated failover solution.

Promoting a new master

Promoting a slave is not a difficult task, though many steps are involved.

Gather information

- Determine if the slave to be promoted is read-only
- Determine if the slave to be promoted has binary logging enabled
- Decide if you want to reset the binary logs on the slave to be promoted — this will delete any previous binary logs and reset the binary log to the first binary log (default is `mysql-bin.000001`)
- Check for other slaves that will need to be changed to replicate the new master

Make sure the slave is caught up applying its relay logs

When the information has been gathered, make sure the slave's SQL thread has caught up to the slave's I/O thread. That is, make sure all the statements in the relay logs have been applied. Compare the parameters Read_Master_Log_Pos, the position at which the I/O thread has read from the master's binary logs, and Exec_Master_Log_Pos, which is the position at which the SQL thread has finished applying the logs:

```
mysql> show slave status\G
*************************** 1. row ***************************
               Slave_IO_State: Reconnecting after a failed
master event read
                  Master_Host: 192.168.1.1
                  Master_User: master_user
                  Master_Port: 3306
                Connect_Retry: 60
              Master_Log_File: mysql-bin.000051
          Read_Master_Log_Pos: 3253467
               Relay_Log_File: slave-relay-bin.000072
                Relay_Log_Pos: 3253613
        Relay_Master_Log_File: mysql-bin.000051
             Slave_IO_Running: No
            Slave_SQL_Running: Yes
              Replicate_Do_DB:
          Replicate_Ignore_DB:
           Replicate_Do_Table:
       Replicate_Ignore_Table:
      Replicate_Wild_Do_Table:
  Replicate_Wild_Ignore_Table:
                   Last_Errno: 0
                   Last_Error:
                 Skip_Counter: 0
          Exec_Master_Log_Pos: 3253467
              Relay_Log_Space: 3253782
              Until_Condition: None
               Until_Log_File:
                Until_Log_Pos: 0
            Master_SSL_Allowed: No
            Master_SSL_CA_File:
            Master_SSL_CA_Path:
               Master_SSL_Cert:
             Master_SSL_Cipher:
                Master_SSL_Key:
        Seconds_Behind_Master: NULL
Master_SSL_Verify_Server_Cert: No
                Last_IO_Errno: 2013
                Last_IO_Error: error reconnecting to master
'master_user@192.168.1.1:3306' - retry-time: 60  retries: 86400
```

```
                   Last_SQL_Errno: 0
                   Last_SQL_Error:
    1 row in set (0.00 sec)
```

In this sample, Read_Master_Log_Pos and Exec_Master_Log_Pos are the same value (3253467). This shows that the slave has applied all of the logs it has read from the master, and is ready to become a master. If the Exec_Master_Log_Pos is less than the Read_Master_Log_Pos, you will need to wait until the slave SQL thread catches up before you promote the slave to a master; otherwise there will have been transactions that completed on the old master that do not appear on the new master.

Stop and reset the slave process

Stop the slave with the STOP SLAVE command, and then ensure the slave will not accidentally become re-enabled and try to read from the master by clearing out the slave information. You can do this with the RESET SLAVE command:

```
mysql> RESET SLAVE;
Query OK, 0 rows affected (0.52 sec)

mysql> show slave status\G
*************************** 1. row ***************************
               Slave_IO_State:
                  Master_Host: 192.168.1.1
                  Master_User: master_user
                  Master_Port: 3306
                Connect_Retry: 60
              Master_Log_File:
          Read_Master_Log_Pos: 4
               Relay_Log_File: slave-relay-bin.000001
                Relay_Log_Pos: 4
        Relay_Master_Log_File:
             Slave_IO_Running: No
            Slave_SQL_Running: No
              Replicate_Do_DB:
          Replicate_Ignore_DB:
           Replicate_Do_Table:
       Replicate_Ignore_Table:
      Replicate_Wild_Do_Table:
  Replicate_Wild_Ignore_Table:
                   Last_Errno: 0
                   Last_Error:
                 Skip_Counter: 0
          Exec_Master_Log_Pos: 0
              Relay_Log_Space: 126
              Until_Condition: None
               Until_Log_File:
```

```
                Until_Log_Pos: 0
            Master_SSL_Allowed: No
            Master_SSL_CA_File:
            Master_SSL_CA_Path:
               Master_SSL_Cert:
             Master_SSL_Cipher:
                Master_SSL_Key:
         Seconds_Behind_Master: NULL
Master_SSL_Verify_Server_Cert: No
                 Last_IO_Errno: 2013
                 Last_IO_Error: error reconnecting to master
'master_user@192.168.1.1:3306' - retry-time: 60  retries: 86400
                Last_SQL_Errno: 0
                Last_SQL_Error:
1 row in set (0.00 sec)
```

Note that though the connection parameters (Master_Host, Master_User, and Master_Port) have not changed, the Slave_IO_State has been reset, and so have the master log and relay log parameters (Master_Log_File, Read_Master_Log_Pos, Relay_Log_File, Relay_Log_Pos, Relay_Master_Log_File, Exec_Master_Log_Pos, and Relay_Log_Space). If you look at the data directory, you will note that the master.info file has disappeared, and if you search where the relay logs are kept, you will note that the relay-log.info file and relay logs are gone. Although those files have been deleted, MySQL has the connection information cached in memory. To make the slave information truly disappear, the mysqld process needs to be restarted.

TIP You can find more information on the how the master.info and relay-log.info files relate to replication in Chapter 16.

Change configuration parameters

If the slave is set as read_only, you will want to change that so writes can occur once it is promoted to be the new master. If the slave does not have binary logging enabled, you will need to enable it with the bin-log parameter. Though you can change the read_only system variable dynamically, changing the bin-log parameter requires a mysqld restart after updating the my.cnf or my.ini configuration file.

WARNING The read_only parameter is global, so only a user with the SUPER privilege can modify it. If there are transactions that have locked tables (explicit locks or implicit locks because they are changing data or schema), setting read_only dynamically will wait until the locks are released before it is successful. If you hold a table lock and try to set the read_only parameter, an error will occur.

Restart

If necessary, restart the mysqld process, checking the error logs to ensure the process starts without any problems. Note that the slave configuration is truly gone now:

```
mysql> show slave status\G
Empty set (0.00 sec)
```

RESET MASTER

If you prefer, you can reset the binary logs for your new master. This deletes all current and previous binary logs, and resets the binary log to the first binary log (default is `mysql-bin.000001`), log position 4.

Change any remaining slaves to replicate off the new master

Any other slaves that were replicating the old master now need to be changed to replicate the new master. This involves a `STOP SLAVE` and `CHANGE MASTER TO` command. In the event that the logs have been reset, the `MASTER_LOG_FILE` and `MASTER_LOG_POS` variables are already known as the first binary log file, log position 4. In the event that the logs have not been reset, run the `SHOW MASTER STATUS` command on the new master:

```
mysql> SHOW MASTER STATUS;
+------------------+----------+--------------+------------------+
| File             | Position | Binlog_Do_DB | Binlog_Ignore_DB |
+------------------+----------+--------------+------------------+
| mysql-bin.000235 |        4 |              |                  |
+------------------+----------+--------------+------------------+
1 row in set (0.00 sec)
```

In this case, the value of `MASTER_LOG_FILE` is `mysql-bin.000235` and the value of `MASTER_LOG_POS` is 4. The log position value should be fairly low, because the `mysqld` process on the new master was just restarted, which rotates the binary logs.

You may also choose to have the old master replicate the new master. In this case, the same procedure applies: use the `CHANGE MASTER TO` command to replicate off the new master. Chapter 16 has more information about setting up replication.

Slave promotion summary

To promote a slave to a master:

1. Gather information.
2. Make sure the slave is caught up applying its relay logs.
3. Stop the slave process with `STOP SLAVE`.
4. Ensure the old slave is no longer a slave by issuing `RESET SLAVE`.
5. If necessary: Remove the `read_only` restriction and enable `log-bin` in the configuration file.
6. If necessary: Restart the `mysqld` process and double-check that the slave parameters have disappeared.

7. If desired: RESET MASTER.

8. Change any remaining slaves to replicate off the new master (if using many read slaves).

Many read slaves

With only one slave, there is a decision to be made. Is db2 meant for scaling, or for high availability? If db2 is meant for high availability, it should be unused by the application until it is time to be promoted to be the master. If db2 is meant for scalability, there is no failover server, because both the master and slave are necessary to handle the volume of read queries. As well, there may be so many read queries that one slave cannot process them all. For these cases, more than one read slave can be defined.

One master database server can have many slaves replicating directly from it, as in Figure 22-2.

FIGURE 22-2

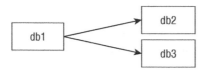

This is the simplest method for having more than one slave of a master. Read queries can go to either db1, db2, or db3, whereas write queries remain on db1 and propagate to db2 and db3. There are no tricks to setting up this sort of replication architecture; merely go through the process of creating db2 as a slave of db1 as described in Chapter 17, and then repeat the process to create db3 as a slave of db1.

Perhaps db2 and db3 are both for scalability, accepting many read queries to take the load off db1. Alternatively, db2 could be for scalability, accepting read queries, and db3 could be for high availability, ready to be promoted to the master should the need arise.

Some applications use a replication relay slave, as in Figure 22-3.

FIGURE 22-3

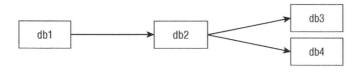

One reason for using this architecture is that if there are 10 or more slaves, it can be easier to have the slaves connect to a non-master server to avoid the small extra bit of load that each slave produces. For large setups with hundreds of slaves in a *replication farm*, replication relay slaves are needed. Another reason for this type of setup is that if something happens to db1, and db2 is promoted to be a master, there is no need to change the replication setup for db3 and db4, because they are already replicating db2. One of the biggest drawbacks of this architecture is that problems with slave lag may be compounded.

For this setup, db3 and db4 are set up as slaves of db2 in the usual way. To set up db2 as a relay slave, it is set up as a slave of db1 in the usual way, with one addition in the configuration setup: `log-slave-updates`. This will ensure that the binary logs for db2 contain the changes that replicate from db1.

Master/master replication

Master/master replication, also called dual-master replication, is a way to scale reads. As with all replication architectures, it is not a way to scale writes. However, with master/master replication, either of the `mysqld` processes can accept writes, which will propagate to the other master. Figure 22-4 shows what a master/master replication architecture looks like.

FIGURE 22-4

You set up master/master replication by setting up db1 to be a slave of db2, and setting up db2 to be a slave of db1. In addition, some extra parameters need to be set to ensure data integrity:

- `auto_increment_offset`
- `auto_increment_increment`

Having writes to more than one server can cause problems with `auto_increment` fields. If an `auto_increment` field has used up to number 100, and there's a write to db1 and db2 at the same time, both will use 101 as the field value. Replication will break on both servers because of duplicate key errors. The `auto_increment_offset` parameter is set with a number indicating at what number the `auto_increment` field should start. The `auto_increment_increment` is set with a number indicating by how much the `auto_increment` value should be incremented.

For example, if db1 is configured with:

```
auto_increment_offset=1
auto_increment_increment=10
```

and db2 is configured with:

```
auto_increment_offset=2
auto_increment_increment=10
```

the first five consecutive inserts into `auto_increment` fields on db1 will have the values 1, 11, 21, 31, 41, and the first five consecutive inserts into `auto_increment` fields on db1 will have the values 2, 12, 22, 32, 42.

The advantage of this setup is that a load balancing solution can point to both db1 and db2, and if one of the servers is unavailable, the other can be used with no change in setup. However, the biggest disadvantage of this is that replication can get out of sync — that is, the data on a slave may not match its master. If there are writes to both db1 and db2, and they are out of sync with each other, which has the "correct" data set? It is very likely that neither data set is complete and correct.

The safest way to use this setup is to have one database be the primary database, and the other to be a failover server. This is still not completely safe — as long as writes are allowed on the failover server when the primary server is running, there is the possibility of having different data sets that cannot be resolved with each other (the "which has the correct data set?" problem).

To get around this, put the `read_only` parameter on the failover database. However, this turns the property of "using the failover with no change in setup" to "using the failover but having to change a server variable." In general, the only savings in a master/master replication setup are that both servers are set up appropriately to be a master and a slave — for example, both servers already have binary logging enabled and are already replicating each other.

> **TIP** We recommend having a master/slave setup where binary logging is enabled on both the master and slave — by doing that, the only additional step in a master/slave setup (instead of a master/master setup) is having to run the CHANGE MASTER TO command. This extra step is well worth it to know which data set is the correct data set in case the two machines have different data.

Circular replication

In circular replication, you have a ring of master/slave connections, as in Figure 22-5.

FIGURE 22-5

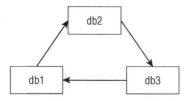

Again, though it does allow the ability to write to more than one server, it does not scale writes — remember, eventually all writes will have to be done on all servers. Reads can be scaled this way.

Although circular replication offers the capability of having a load balancing solution point to more than two servers, it has the same major issue as master/master replication — that if more than one server accepts writes, it can be impossible to tell which server has the "correct" data set. In addition, circular replication is not fault-tolerant — if db1 is unavailable, updates from db3 will not reach db2 even though they are both available.

WARNING Circular replication is not recommended; instead, use a master with more than one slave.

SAN

A SAN is a *storage-area network*. It is a shared disk solution, similar to Oracle RAC. A SAN is a high availability technology; in the event that a database server is unavailable, another database server can be attached to the SAN to read the data and logs for the mysqld process. Figure 22-6 shows a high availability architecture using a SAN.

FIGURE 22-6

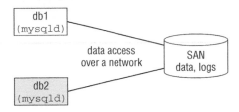

An advantage of using a SAN instead of replication is that replication is asynchronous; SAN is a shared disk solution, so you never have to worry that a transaction occurred on the primary server that did not make it to the secondary server. As Figure 22-6 shows, though, the data access occurs over a network, which is slower than reading from a local disk. Another advantage is that a shared disk means that only one copy of the data is kept, which can be critical for large databases.

NOTE A SAN contains shared disk partitions that can be mounted on more than one machine. A partition is mounted over a network — the network used depends on how a machine is connected to the SAN. The network might be a standard TCP/IP network if Ethernet cables are used for connection or if the SAN is mounted across an existing Ethernet network such as a LAN. A SAN can also be accessed via other means such as SCSI cables from the SAN to the machine(s) mounting partitions from the SAN. Regardless of what type of network is used to access a SAN, SAN access is slower than local disk access.

One of the biggest drawbacks of a SAN is that it is expensive, and may be prohibitively so. One of the biggest benefits of a SAN is unrelated to high availability or scaling — most SANs come with disk snapshot software, which makes consistent backups very quick with minimal locking (see the discussion of snapshots in Chapter 13).

Replication can be used with a SAN to provide read scalability. MySQL Proxy or Linux-HA Heartbeat can be used with a SAN for automated failover.

DRBD

DRBD stands for "distributed replicated block device." A block device is what an operating system reads blocks from and writes blocks to; it is a storage system. DRBD can perform synchronous replication ("replicated") of a storage system ("block device) across two nodes ("distributed"). It is a free and open source Linux kernel module that is not maintained by Sun. DRBD information and downloads are available at www.drbd.org.

Sun does not develop DRBD, but support for DRBD can be purchased as an add-on to a MySQL Enterprise subscription. This is a very convenient option for many organizations, because they can get support for MySQL and a third-party high availability solution from the same place.

A sample high availability architecture using DRBD is depicted in Figure 22-7.

FIGURE 22-7

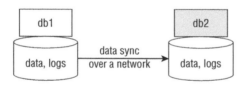

The advantage of using DRBD instead of a SAN is that storage access is local to the server. However, as with replication, it takes time for the request to travel across the network from one machine to another. The advantage of using DRBD instead of replication for high availability is that DRBD is synchronous. One drawback of using DRBD instead of replication is that DRBD does not allow read scalability — the secondary node cannot use the DRBD device. Having a primary and secondary mysqld instance using DRBD is very much like Oracle replication.

MySQL and DRBD setup

These instructions are intended to show how MySQL and DRBD work together. They are not step-by-step technical instructions.

NOTE The MySQL manual has good step-by-step instructions at http://dev.mysql.com/doc/refman/6.0/en/ha-drbd.html.

1. Install DRBD each machine.

2. Configure DRBD on each machine. You must choose which machine (*node*) will be the primary and which will be the secondary (failover). You must also physically configure how the machines will synchronize; if they synchronize over a regular network connection, they must be able to reach each other under normal circumstances.

3. Create a DRBD block device, and mount it as a partition.

4. Configure mysqld to put its data and log files on the DRBD partition.

Getting these four steps to work is not simple. There is plenty of system and network administration overhead in setting up DRBD. However, synchronous data sync without the expense of a SAN is usually worth the time invested.

Though mysqld needs to be installed and configured on both nodes, the data files from the primary node will be replicated synchronously to the secondary node.

Replication can be used with DRBD to provide read scalability.

MySQL Proxy

MySQL Proxy is a technology that can be used for scaling or high availability. It is a proxy server that is transparent; there is not a way for an application or user to tell they are connected to a mysql-proxy process instead of directly to a mysqld process. It is written and maintained by MySQL developers, including Jan Kneschke.

MySQL Proxy is very powerful and flexible due to its simplicity. It allows you to intercept queries and results, adding functionality and changing which mysqld process to send information to, what is sent to mysqld, and what is received from mysqld. This is all done via a Lua script and a configuration file. For step-by-step instructions on how to install and configure MySQL Proxy and a primer on Lua, see Appendix A. We will go over the configuration parameters necessary to achieve scalability and high availability.

Figure 22-8 shows how MySQL Proxy can fit into an architecture for high availability or scalability.

FIGURE 22-8

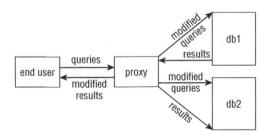

The end user connects to `mysql-proxy`, which may modify a query and send it to any of the backend addresses specified (in this example, db1 or db2). The database server then sends the results, which may be modified by the proxy before being sent back to the end user.

Scaling read queries

The easiest task to perform with the `mysql-proxy` process is load balancing. You do this by simply setting the `proxy-backend-addresses` parameter(s). Like `mysqld`, `mysql-proxy` can take parameters on the command line or in a configuration file. To configure `mysql-proxy` to do load balancing of `db1.company.com` and `db2.company.com`:

```
shell> mysql-proxy --proxy-backend-addresses=db1.company.com:3306 \
--proxy-backend-addresses=db2.company.com:3306 \
--proxy-address=localhost:3306
```

A thread that connects to port 3306 on the server running the `mysql-proxy` process will be sent to `db1.company.com`. If a second thread connects while the first is still running, it will be sent to `db2.company.com`. If the first thread is finished, the second thread will be send to `db1.company.com`. There is no Lua script needed for this type of load balancing.

Load balancing in this way, by number of threads connecting via `mysql-proxy`, is useful for scaling reads. If you are using a technology like replication to make slave servers that can process read queries, you can point the application at the server running `mysql-proxy` and your read queries are now load-balanced. Adding and removing servers means that application code does not need to change; the number of `proxy-backend-addresses` specified can be one server, two servers (as in our example), or more than two servers. Note that adding or removing a server from the proxy requires `mysql-proxy` to be restarted.

Automated failover

The `mysql-proxy` process can be used to automate failover. To do this, there must be a failover server that is active (able to be used without any changes) and has the same data the primary does. Master/slave, master/master, and SAN architectures all would be appropriate. The `mysql-proxy` configuration is similar to the previous one, except we add a Lua script:

```
shell> mysql-proxy --proxy-backend-addresses=db1.company.com:3306 \
--proxy-backend-addresses=db2.company.com:3306 \
--proxy-address=localhost:3306 \
--proxy-lua-script=/path/to/luascript.lua
```

The Lua script we use (saved at `/path/to/luascript.lua`) will intercept the initial connection and any queries sent, and send the connection and queries to the first backend that is up. Do not worry about understanding the code exactly, but you will likely be able to follow along with what is going on:

```
function connect_server()
  for i = 1, #proxy.backends do
```

```
        local s = proxy.backends[i]

        if s.state ~= proxy.BACKEND_STATE_DOWN then
          proxy.connection.backend_ndx = i
          return
        end
      end
    end
  end

  function read_query(packet)
    for i = 1, #proxy.backends do
      local s = proxy.backends[i]

      if s.state ~= proxy.BACKEND_STATE_DOWN then
        proxy.connection.backend_ndx = i
        return
      end
    end
  end
```

(You can find this Lua script on the MySQL Forge at `http://forge.mysql.com/tools/tool.php?id=125`).

The Lua script is what makes `mysql-proxy` handle automated failover. However, it also handles automated failback — that is, when db1 is available again, all connections and queries will go through db1. Note that this is not desired behavior with a master/slave architecture, because when the master is unavailable, `mysql-proxy` will failover to the slave, but if the master is available again, `mysql-proxy` will failback to the master — and now the slave may have updates that the master does not. As well, even if you are using master/master replication or a SAN, you may not want automated failback.

Lua

Lua is a lightweight programming language that has been around since 1993. As of the time of this writing, it is in version 6.0. The entire language is less than 200 kilobytes compiled, so it is very small and very fast. It is used by big applications such as Adobe Photoshop Lightroom. Lua is also used in a web server that has become very popular specifically because it is lightweight and fast — `lighttpd`. It is probably more famous for being used in the popular online game World of Warcraft.

The fact that it is used in such a popular online game speaks of the ease-of-use of the syntax. For use in a proxy, it has everything we need — from the basics such as array data structures to more complex features like string manipulation to the holy grail of I/O (logging, anyone?). For more information about using Lua in the MySQL Proxy, see Appendix A. You can find information about Lua and the Lua community at `http://www.lua.org` and `http://www.lua-users.org`.

Read/write splitting

Using Lua you can write a script that will intercept an incoming query, determine if it changes data or is a read-only query, and send the query to the appropriate backend, a master (for writes) or a slave (for reads). Actually, `mysql-proxy` comes with many sample scripts, and there is a script that does this read/write splitting, called `rw-splitting.lua`. You can find it in the `share/mysql-proxy` directory of the MySQL Proxy package.

Sharding

Similar to read/write splitting, MySQL Proxy can use a script that intercepts incoming queries, and determines somehow which database backend to send queries to. Perhaps the criteria that chooses which backend is used involves tables — in this way, sharding your application is possible without having to change application code. There is no sample script for this, because it is highly application-dependent. However, it is certainly possible.

Linux-HA Heartbeat

Linux-HA is the High Availability Linux Project with a third-party tool that can be used with MySQL to automate failover. Though it is called Linux-HA, the software actually runs on other operating systems such as Solaris, FreeBSD, OpenBSD, and has been known to work on Mac OS X. The Linux-HA `heartbeat` program can determine if a resource (such as a database or file system) is available, change virtual IPs, and run scripts. Combined together in `heartbeat`, these features make automated failover possible, and can be used to automate failover of any of the high availability architectures we have discussed. Automated failback is configurable in `heartbeat`. You can decide whether or not to enable it, which will depend on the behavior you want.

We will not give an in-depth technical look at how to install and configure heartbeat, but we will give some of the basics so you can get a sense of how to use it. For a good configuration guide, see the MySQL manual at `http://dev.mysql.com/doc/refman/6.0/en/ha-heart beat.html`.

The `heartbeat` daemon is installed on all the machines you want to include in the failover architecture. This group of machines is called a "heartbeat cluster," and each machine is a "node." Each node sends out a signal ("heartbeat") to the other nodes in the heartbeat cluster. Each node also contains a list of the other nodes in the heartbeat cluster. If n1 (a node) fails to see a heartbeat from n2 (another node), n1 will mark n2 as disabled, and run some processes to enable n1 if necessary.

You can use `heartbeat` to configure db1.company.com as your primary database server and db2.company.com as your failover database server, and failover automatically. Part of the configuration involves specifying a virtual IP address to point to the enabled resource. This virtual IP address is configured in the `haresources` configuration file. To disable and enable services when a node is disabled or enabled, there must be a script in `/etc/init.d/`

or /etc/ha.d/resource.d/, and the haresources configuration file contains which scripts and arguments should be run when a resource is enabled, and which scripts and arguments should be run when a resource is disabled. An example might be the /etc/init.d/mysql script — for a resource that is enabled, you would specify the mysql script with the start argument, and for a resource that is disabled, you would specify the mysql script with the stop argument.

The following is sufficient for automating failover of a DRBD high availability architecture:

- A heartbeat cluster with a virtual IP pointing to a primary and failover server
- On resource disable, stop mysqld
- On resource enable, start mysqld

For a SAN high availability architecture, it is slightly more complex:

- A heartbeat cluster with a virtual IP pointing to a primary and failover server
- On resource disable, stop mysqld and switch the DRBD device into secondary mode
- On resource enable, start mysqld and switch the DRBD device into primary mode

It gets even more complicated when using a master/slave or master/master architecture:

- A heartbeat cluster with a virtual IP pointing to a primary and failover server
- On resource disable, stop mysqld
- On resource enable, run a script or series of scripts that do the following:
  - Ensure the Master_Log_File is the same as the Relay_Master_Log_File. If not, wait for replication to catch up. If the Master_Log_File and Relay_Master_Log_File do not exist, this is a new master (not a slave promotion), so the next step can proceed.
  - Ensure the Read_Master_Log_Pos is the same as the Exec_Master_Log_Pos. If not, wait for replication to catch up. If the Read_Master_Log_Pos and Exec_Master_Log_Pos do not exist, this is a new master (not a slave promotion), so the next step can proceed.
  - If this is a slave promotion, run STOP SLAVE and RESET SLAVE on the resource to be enabled. If the configuration file (my.cnf) contains a line with read_only (and the line is not commented out), comment out read_only.
  - If the configuration file (my.cnf) does not contain a line with log-bin, insert that line into the file under the [mysqld] configuration directive.
  - Restart the mysqld process.
  - Optionally you can script a CHANGE MASTER command to run on a list of machines that should be slaves of the new master. This is a bit more difficult to script.

The power and flexibility of heartbeat is due to the fact that if an action can be scripted, it can be performed when a resource is enabled or disabled. The heartbeat daemon also allows for manual failover, in case you want to take a server offline on purpose (say, for upgrade or database maintenance).

MySQL Cluster

MySQL Cluster is a great tool for copies of data to be partitioned and kept synchronously on different servers. It is a separate version of MySQL. MySQL Cluster is freely available, but there is not a version yet for Windows. Because it is a very complex and separate product from the standard MySQL server, we will not delve into how to set up a MySQL Cluster. We will provide information for you to determine whether MySQL Cluster is an appropriate solution for your needs.

 MySQL Cluster is being changed at a very fast rate. You can find the most up-to-date information in the Cluster manual at MySQL's website at http://mysql.com/cluster**. The complete documentation is linked from the Cluster Resources page at** http://mysql.com/products/database/cluster/resources.html**. Currently, the best in-print book about MySQL Cluster is** *MySQL 5.1 Cluster DBA Certification Study Guide* **by Jon Stephens, Mike Kruckenberg, Roland Bouman, and Stewart Smith.**

Historically, MySQL Cluster was developed for the telecom industry to be highly available and very fast. It was designed with a *shared nothing* architecture in mind, with every part being redundant.

In the standard version of MySQL, a server runs mysqld, data is stored on the server, and clients connect to the server to run SQL commands. In MySQL Cluster, only the SQL nodes run mysqld. The data is stored only on data nodes, which run ndbd. Clients connect to any of the SQL nodes to run a query; the SQL node will connect to the data nodes to store and retrieve the data necessary. There is also a management node, which runs ndb_mgmd.

NOTE ndb **stands for "network database"**

ndbd **stands for "network database daemon"**

ndb_mgmd **stands for "network database management daemon"**

As Figure 22-9 shows, the SQL nodes are redundant. A client can connect to any one of the SQL nodes to run queries that access the data. A client cannot connect directly to the data nodes to access the data.

Each SQL node in the diagram points to a node group. A node group is one or more data nodes that store identical data. In the figure, there are four data nodes each in two node groups. The data is partitioned — half the data goes to one node group, where four identical copies are stored. The other half of the data goes to the other node group, where four identical copies of that data are stored. The data nodes are redundant: if one data node is not functional, there are still three other data nodes that the SQL node can access for data.

FIGURE 22-9

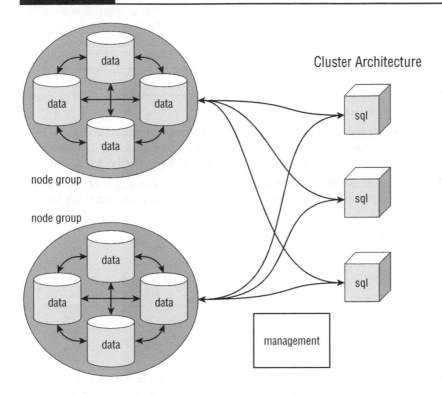

The management node is only needed during cluster startup. It can be made redundant by having more than one machine running the ndb_mgmd process.

The data is split by how many node groups there are. With two node groups, each data node in a node group holds 50% of the data. If you have four node groups, each data node in the node group would hold 25% of the data.

MySQL Cluster is a good solution for both scalability and high availability. The redundancy of each part addresses the issue of high availability. Both the partitioning and the separation of SQL node and data node address scalability. However, MySQL Cluster is not the appropriate solution for many applications. MySQL Cluster was designed for telecom, to store and retrieve a lot of small data quickly with very little downtime, failure, and corruption. This is accomplished by storing most or all of the data in memory.

MySQL Cluster allows tables to be stored on disk. However, any data fields that are a part of an index, and the indexes themselves, are stored in memory. This means that large tables stored in MySQL Cluster will require a lot of memory. The amount of memory needed per data node is equivalent to the total amount of memory needed to be split among the node groups. Figure 22-9 showed a sample architecture with two node groups and four data nodes per node group. If the sample application has 10 Gb of indexes and data fields that are part of indexes, each data node would need to allocate 5 Gb of memory just for the indexes and data fields.

The following list is just a few of the limitations MySQL Cluster has, which should be helpful in determining whether or not MySQL Cluster is appropriate for your environment:

- The data must have a primary key. If there is none, a primary key will be made with an AUTOINCREMENT value.

- When data is deleted in a table, memory is freed up for that table only. To free up the memory for any table to use, a rolling data node restart is needed. This limitation is acceptable if tables have a proportional amount of data inserted and deleted.

- There is a non-configurable limit of 20,320 for the total number of "metadata objects." There is no public exact formula to calculate this. It includes, but is not limited to, the number of:

  - Logical databases
  - Tables
  - Columns
  - Indexes
  - Views
  - Triggers
  - Stored procedures

- MySQL Cluster is transaction-aware, though the online manual spells out many limitations. The larger a transaction becomes, the more memory it uses, and the risk involved increases. Many parameters for many transaction-related operations are complex and confusing.

MySQL Cluster is not a broad solution that most people can use; it a solution for only a small number of applications. Data that is appropriate for use in a MySQL Cluster architecture is small, mostly fixed-width. An example of an excellent data set for use in MySQL Cluster is a table of user sessions.

Connection Pooling

Connection pooling is a scalability technology. When a query is sent to the mysqld process, it has to connect, authenticate, send the query, retrieve the results, and disconnect. A connection pool saves the time it takes to connect to and disconnect from the `mysqld` process by having a pool of connections that an application can use, without needing to connect or disconnect.

In general, connection setup and break down is not an expensive process with MySQL. Other database software products may see very large performance increases with a connection pool, whereas an application with a MySQL backend may not see a similar increase. Those that see the most performance gain are those that have a slow network connection to MySQL, and therefore benefit greatly from not having to go across the network an extra time to initialize a connection.

A reused connection retains its state, which may lead to problems with user-defined variables, temporary tables, and other settings that assume connections are independent. Another problem with connection pooling is that `mysqld` will kill idle processes after a configurable timeout, so a connection pool either must be able to handle stale connections, or have the ability to automatically reconnect a disconnected connection.

memcached

Without a doubt, the fastest way to get data is to not have to connect to `mysqld` at all. Having a cache outside the database for application data is the best scalability solution aside from actually optimizing queries. `memcached` is the best and most widely used distributed in-memory cache program.

The distributed nature of `memcached` makes it better than a local cache; local caches (whether on an application server, web server, or database server) may have a different cached data set, because the data set is dependent on what has been run on the server. For instance, two `mysqld` servers running different queries at different times will likely have different data in their query caches. Even if the caches are the same, they are redundant; storing 50 Mb of data in the local cache of two different servers requires 50 Mb per server, or double the size of the data.

On the other hand, `memcached` is a shared, key-based cache. When a client requests data from the cache, it uses a key to specify the data it wants. A hash is performed on this key, and the hash result determines which `memcached` server the client will access. The client in this case is the application code, via a web or application server. Thus, the application code needs to be changed in order to take advantage of `memcached`. This may not fall under the domain of administration tasks for a database administrator, but it is well worth learning about the technology, because it greatly speeds up applications that use a database backend.

You can find more information on using `memcached` with MySQL in Chapter 12. There is also information in the MySQL Manual at `http://dev.mysql.com/doc/refman/6.0/en/ha-memcached.html` and at the `memcached` website at `http://www.danga.com/memcached/`.

Summary

This chapter discussed different ways to scale MySQL and make it highly available. The technologies discussed were:

- MySQL Cluster for scaling, automated failover, and data synchronization
- Replication for data synchronization and scaling
- MySQL Proxy for scaling and automated failover
- Connection pooling for scaling
- memcached for scaling
- Using a SAN for data synchronization
- DRBD for data synchronization
- Linux-HA Heartbeat for automated failover

You can find more information on MySQL Proxy in Appendix A, and more information on memcached in Chapter 12.

Appendix A

MySQL Proxy

I n a simple client/server model, a client sends a request to a server, which will then send results back. This is true for all sorts of servers — including web servers, e-mail servers, and database servers. A proxy sits in between the client and server, intercepting traffic that travels back and forth. MySQL Proxy is a proxy tool that sits between a client and `mysqld` instance, intercepting client traffic to the server and server traffic from the server.

MySQL Proxy runs on most operating systems: Linux, Windows, Solaris, Mac OS X, and more. Using MySQL Proxy, you can:

- Load balance queries to `mysqld`:
  - In a round-robin fashion
  - By function (read/write)
  - By table/database
  - To share data
- Perform custom caching
- Create and utilize connection pools
- Create macros and extend the commands `mysqld` understands
- Filter queries
- Enforce permissions based on username or hostname
- Transform queries
- Perform custom logging
  - Turn logs on and off on the fly
  - Log specific queries

IN THIS APPENDIX

Understanding MySQL proxy

Learning Lua basics

Changing the query backend

Changing and injecting queries

Understanding MySQL proxy internals

    ▩ Log queries based on tables/databases/columns accessed

    ▩ To share data

■ Analyze queries and gather statistics

MySQL Proxy is an open source tool that is simple and powerful; Sun Microsystems, Inc. is using it to create products for sale such as their query analyzer. As of the time this book was written, MySQL Proxy was in alpha status, and our examples use version 0.6.0. However, many organizations have used MySQL Proxy in production enterprise settings.

> **NOTE** Since the time this was written, version 0.7.0 was released. Throughout this appendix, we have added notes to highlight the major differences between 0.6.0 and 0.7.0.

Understanding MySQL Proxy

MySQL Proxy is a daemon that listens on a port and forwards traffic to one or more `mysqld` servers. The `mysql-proxy` daemon can also be scripted, which is where its power and extensibility comes in. `mysql-proxy` accepts scripts written in Lua, a lightweight scripting language used by many applications, including Adobe Photoshop Lightroom, Wireshark, Snort, lighttpd, PlayStation Home, and the popular online game World of Warcraft.

Installing mysql-proxy

MySQL Proxy is not included in any distributions of MySQL. There are three different ways to install `mysql-proxy`:

■ From a binary distribution

■ From a source distribution

■ From a third-party package repository

The binary and source distributions can be freely downloaded at `http://dev.mysql.com/downloads/mysql-proxy`. Binary distributions need only to be extracted and copied to your desired location. For Windows, this means extracting from a `.zip` file and moving the resulting directory. This directory contains some dynamic linked libraries (`.dll` files), the `mysql-proxy.exe` binary, an `examples` directory with tutorials, and a `share` directory with ready-to-use code.

For all other operating systems, installing from a binary distribution means extracting from a `.tar.gz` file and moving the resulting directory, such as:

```
tar -zxvf mysql-proxy-0.6.0-linux-rhas3-x86_64.tar.gz
sudo mv mysql-proxy-0.6.0-linux-rhas3-x86_64 /usr/local/share/
```

There are two directories that are unpacked: the sbin directory contains the mysql-proxy executable, and the share directory contains tutorials and ready-to-use code. This package is a standalone binary — no other MySQL package needs to be installed, nor does Lua need to be installed.

To install from a source distribution, you will have to extract the source code from the .tar.gz file and compile the binary yourself. Instructions for compilation are included in the source code package and are also in the manual at http://dev.mysql.com/doc/refman/6.0/en/mysql-proxy-install-source.html.

Many operating system distributions, such as Red Hat and Debian, have compiled and packaged mysql-proxy. Installing these versions is like installing anything else from your distributions' package repositories, for example:

```
redhat shell> yum install mysql-proxy
debian shell> apt-get install mysql-proxy
```

Proxy backends

In the examples we use, we will use the binary mysql-proxy, as if we were on a non-Windows system. All the examples will work on a Windows system — the only difference is that the binary name is mysql-proxy.exe.

The minimum configuration mysql-proxy needs is specifying on which port the mysql-proxy daemon will listen, and where mysql-proxy will send requests. This is achieved with two options:

```
mysql-proxy --proxy-address=host:port --proxy-backend-
addresses=host:port
```

The proxy-address option specifies where the mysql-proxy listens. The default value is :4040, which is the same as localhost:4040. The proxy-backend-addresses option specifies the server(s) where mysql-proxy might send traffic. The default value is 127.0.0.1:3306. Because there are only two required parameters, and both have default values, starting mysql-proxy with no options is equivalent to:

```
mysql-proxy --proxy-address=:4040 --proxy-backend-addresses=
127.0.0.1:3306
```

This means that mysql-proxy will listen on localhost port 4040, and forward traffic to 127.0.0.1 port 3306. Connecting to a mysqld instance via mysql-proxy is transparent to the user. In the following example, we will first connect directly to the database, and then connect via the proxy while the first connection is still open:

```
shell> mysql -u root -p -h 127.0.0.1 -P3306
Password:
Welcome to the MySQL monitor. Commands end with ; or \g.
Your MySQL connection id is 2
```

```
Server version: 6.0.8-alpha-community-log MySQL Community
    Server (GPL)

Type 'help;' or '\h' for help. Type '\c' to clear the buffer.

mysql> show processlist\G
*************************** 1. row ***************************
      Id: 2
    User: root
    Host: localhost:1583
      db: NULL
 Command: Query
    Time: 0
   State: NULL
    Info: show processlist
1 row in set (0.00 sec)

mysql>

shell> mysql -u root -p -h 127.0.0.1 -P4040
Password:
Welcome to the MySQL monitor. Commands end with ; or \g.
Your MySQL connection id is 3
Server version: 6.0.8-alpha-community-log MySQL Community
  Server (GPL)

Type 'help;' or '\h' for help. Type '\c' to clear the buffer.

mysql> show processlist\G
*************************** 1. row ***************************
      Id: 2
    User: root
    Host: localhost:1583
      db: NULL
 Command: Sleep
    Time: 58
   State:
    Info: NULL
*************************** 2. row ***************************
      Id: 3
    User: root
    Host: localhost:1588
      db: NULL
 Command: Query
    Time: 0
   State: NULL
    Info: show processlist
2 rows in set (0.00 sec)
```

There is no way for a user to tell whether or not they connected via mysql-proxy or directly to the mysqld instance.

Multiple backends can be specified by using more than one `proxy-backend-addresses` option. In a real load-balancing example, you would specify that `mysql-proxy` should listen on localhost port 3306 and forward traffic to databases on `server1.company.com` port 3306, `server2.company.com` port 3306, and `server3.company.com` port 3306:

```
mysql-proxy --proxy-address=localhost:3306 \
--proxy-backend-addresses=server1.company.com:3306 \
--proxy-backend-addresses=server2.company.com:3306 \
-backend-addresses=server3.company.com:3306
```

In this setup, `mysql-proxy` will serve the connections in a round-robin fashion. When a connection exits, the server it was connected to automatically becomes the next server to receive a connection. The preceding setup will produce the results summarized in Table A-1.

TABLE A-1

Simple Round-Robin Behavior of mysql-proxy with Multiple Backends

Action Sequence	Backend Connection
Connect to localhost:3306	server1.company.com:3306
Exit server1 connection	server1.company.com:3306
Connect to localhost:3306	server1.company.com:3306
Connect to localhost:3306	server2.company.com:3306
Connect to localhost:3306	server1.company.com:3306
Exit server1 connection	server1.company.com:3306
Connect to localhost:3306	server2.company.com:3306
Connect to localhost:3306	server2.company.com:3306
Connect to localhost:3306	server1.company.com:3306
Exit server2 connection	server2.company.com:3306
Reconnect to localhost:3306	server3.company.com:3306
Connect to localhost:3306	server1.company.com:3306
Connect to localhost:3306	server2.company.com:3306
Connect to localhost:3306	server3.company.com:3306
Connect to localhost:3306	server1.company.com:3306
Connect to localhost:3306	
Connect to localhost:3306	
Connect to localhost:3306	

The mysql-proxy daemon does take into consideration whether previous connections via mysql-proxy are still alive, as shown in Table A-2. The columns at the right of the table show how many connections there are to each server after the action is taken.

TABLE A-2

More Complex Round-robin Behavior of mysql-proxy with Multiple Backends

Action Sequence	Backend Connection	# server1 cxns	# server2 cxns	# server3 cxns
Connect to localhost:3306	server1.company.com:3306	1	0	0
Exit server1 connection	server1.company.com:3306	0	0	0
Connect to localhost:3306	server2.company.com:3306	1	0	0
Connect to localhost:3306	server1.company.com:3306	1	1	0
Exit server1 connection	server2.company.com:3306	0	1	0
Connect to localhost:3306	server3.company.com:3306	1	1	0
Exit server2 connection	server2.company.com:3306	1	0	0
Connect to localhost:3306	server1.company.com:3306	1	1	0
Connect to localhost:3306	server3.company.com:3306	1	1	1
Exit server2 and server3	server1.company.com:3306	1	0	0
Connect to localhost:3306	server2.company.com:3306	1	1	0
Exit server1 connection	server2.company.com:3306	0	1	0
Connect to localhost:3306	server3.company.com:3306	1	1	0
Connect to localhost:3306		1	1	1

TABLE A-2	(continued)			
Action Sequence	Backend Connection	# server1 cxns	# server2 cxns	# server3 cxns
Connect to localhost:3306		2	1	1
Exit server2 connection		2	0	1
Connect to localhost:3306		2	1	1
Connect to localhost:3306		2	2	1
Connect to localhost:3306		2	2	2

Scripting

Using mysql-proxy without a script allows load-balancing queries in a round-robin fashion. This is useful for sending read queries to many slaves, where the slaves may or may not be up. However, much of the power of mysql-proxy comes from being able to program functionality with a Lua script.

Lua is an interpreted language like Perl, and as such, scripts do not need to be compiled. Scripts can be easily edited, and mysql-proxy will re-read its script for every new connection. To call mysql-proxy with a script, use the proxy-lua-script option:

```
mysql-proxy --proxy-address=localhost:3306 \
--proxy-backend-addresses=server1.company.com:3306 \
--proxy-backend-addresses=server2.company.com:3306 \
--proxy-lua-script=/usr/local/mysql-proxy/running.lua
```

NOTE   In mysql-proxy version 0.7.0, the proxy-lua-script is cached and mysql-proxy will re-read the script when the script changes.

Programming mysql-proxy consists of overriding one or more of six functions:

- connect_server()
- read_handshake()
- read_auth()
- read_auth_result()
- read_query()
- read_query_result()

A client attempting to log in to `mysqld` first tries to connect to the server. By overriding the `connect_server()` function, you can change the way `mysql-proxy` passes connections to backend servers. Once `mysql-proxy` sends passes the connection attempt to a backend server, the backend server sends handshake information back. Overriding the `read_handshake()` function in `mysql-proxy` will give access to this information, which contains the version of `mysqld`, the `thread_id` that `mysqld` assigns this connection, the host and port of the client and server, and a password scramble.

After these first two steps in the handshake, the client then sends authentication information. Overriding the `mysql-proxy` function `read_auth()` gives access to the username, salted password, and default database the client sends. The server attempts to authenticate the client login, sending back success or failure, which can be accessed by overriding the `read_auth_result()` function of `mysql-proxy`.

The previous four functions deal with the initial client connection. The remaining two functions allow queries and results to be changed — these functions are `read_query()` and `read_query_result()`.

Running MySQL proxy

If you start `mysql-proxy` as described previously and there is no script in `/usr/local/mysql-proxy/running.lua`, clients will be able to form connections to the backend servers; however, `mysql-proxy` will contain the following warning on each connection and for each query sent by a client:

```
lua_loadfile(/usr/local/mysql-proxy/running.lua) failed: cannot
open /usr/local/mysql-proxy/running.lua: No such file or directory
```

If the script exists but is empty, the client will be able to connect and no errors or warnings will occur.

Errors and warnings from `mysql-proxy` are directed to standard output. Thus far you have only seen how to run `mysql-proxy` as an active process in the foreground. It is possible to run `mysql-proxy` as a daemon, optionally specifying a filename where the process ID can be stored:

```
mysql-proxy --proxy-address=localhost:3306 \
--proxy-backend-addresses=server1.company.com:3306 \
--proxy-backend-addresses=server2.company.com:3306 \
--proxy-lua-script=/usr/local/mysql-proxy/running.lua \
--daemon --pid-file=/var/run/mysql-proxy.pid
```

NOTE   In versions 0.7.0 and later, `mysql-proxy` outputs nothing to standard output by default. Output only occurs when the log level is set using the following option:

```
--log-level=(error|warning|info|message|debug)
```

Only one log level can be set, but the subsequent log levels are cumulative. For example, the `info` level contains all errors, warnings, and informational notes.

Learning Lua Basics

The first thing to note is that comments in Lua are of the form:

```
-- a single line comment
--[[ a comment
that spans
multiple lines ]]
```

There are no other acceptable characters to indicate a comment, and attempting to use any others (such as #, //, /* */) will generate a warning, such as the following warning when # appears at the beginning of a line:

```
lua_loadfile(/usr/local/mysql-proxy/running.lua) failed: /usr/
local/mysql-proxy/running.lua:1: unexpected symbol near '#'
```

To print out strings, the print() function is used in combination with (the concatenation function):

```
print("Hello, " .. "World!")
```

To assign variables, the assignment operator = is used. The local keyword can be used to set the scope of a variable. To test values, the syntax if ... then ... elseif ... end is used, and == is the operator to test for equality:

```
local numval=2
if numval>1 then
  print(numval .. " is greater than 1")
elseif numval<1 then
  print(numval .. " is less than 1")
elseif numval==1 then
  print (numval .. " is equal to 1")
else print (numval .. " is not less than, equal to or greater
  than 1.")
end
```

A function is defined as:

```
function func_name( args )
  code here
end
```

For example:

```
function compare_to_one(numval)
  if numval>1 then
    print(numval .. " is greater than 1")
  elseif numval<1 then
    print(numval .. " is less than 1")
  elseif numval==1 then
    print (numval .. " is equal to 1")
```

```
    else print (numval .. " is not less than, equal to or greater
       than 1.")
    end
end
```

To call this function:

```
compare_to_one(2)
```

Note that there are no special identifiers (such as @, $, or func) required to use variables and functions.

Basic script functionality

In order to change the behavior of mysql-proxy, override one of the six mysql-proxy functions. Tutorials are stored in the examples directory on Windows, and in the share directory on other operating systems. In the tutorial-basic.lua file, the read_query() function is overridden, and prints out all queries that are sent through the proxy:

```
function read_query( packet )
    if string.byte(packet) == proxy.COM_QUERY then
       print("we got a normal query: " .. string.sub(packet, 2))
    end
end
```

The packet argument is the input to the function. The string.byte() function is a function that returns the numerical representation of a substring. It takes three arguments — the first argument is mandatory and the last two are optional arguments:

```
string.byte(s [, i [, j]])
```

The first argument, s, specifies a string. The second argument, i, specifies an index to start at and the third argument, j, specifies an index to stop at. String indexes start at 1, not 0. The default value for i is 1, and the default value for j is i. So:

```
string.byte(packet)
```

is equivalent to:

```
string.byte(packet, 1, 1)
```

and returns the numerical representation first character of the string represented by packet.

> **NOTE** In mysql-proxy version 0.7.0 and greater, string.byte(packet) has been replaced with packet:byte. The meaning is the same, but the syntax is a bit shorter and easier to read, and lends to a more object oriented view. The same goes for string.sub(mystring,x,y) — in examples in mysql-proxy 0.7.0 and greater, mystring:sub(x,y) is used.

The string.sub() function is a substring function that takes three arguments, similar to string.byte(). However, the first two arguments are mandatory in string.sub():

```
string.sub(s, i [, j)
```

The arguments in string.sub() have the same meaning as the arguments in string.byte(). However, there is no default for i, and j defaults to -1, which is the end of the string.

Finally, proxy.COM_QUERY is a mysql-proxy internal constant. Taking tutorial-basic.lua line by line:

```
1   function read_query( packet )
2     if string.byte(packet) == proxy.COM_QUERY then
3       print("we got a normal query: " .. string.sub(packet, 2))
4     end
5   end
```

Line 1 defines the function — in this case, we are actually defining a function that already exists, thus overriding the mysql-proxy function read_query(). The argument to read_query is packet.

On line 2, we compare the numerical representation of the first byte of packet to the proxy.COM_QUERY constant. If they are the same, line 3 is executed and the query is printed out prepended with "we got a normal query:" The query is the rest of packet, without the first character. Line 4 ends the if statement, and line 5 ends the function.

If these five lines are saved to a script, and that script is used as the proxy-lua-script to mysql-proxy, the behavior will be as shown in Table A-3.

TABLE A-3

Basic Proxy Script Behavior

Client Command Line	mysql-proxy Output
Shell> mysql -h 127.0.0.1 -P3306	we got a normal query: select @@version_comment limit 1
Mysql> SHOW DATABASES;	we got a normal query: SHOW DATABASES
Mysql> USE sakila;	we got a normal query: SELECT DATABASE() we got a normal query: show databases we got a normal query: show tables
mysql> SELECT COUNT(*) FROM staff;	we got a normal query: SELECT COUNT(*) FROM staff

This example is very interesting — the client sees the normal heading, such as:

```
Welcome to the MySQL monitor. Commands end with ; or \g.
Your MySQL connection id is 1
```

```
Server version: 6.0.8-alpha-community-log MySQL Community
  Server (GPL)

Type 'help;' or '\h' for help. Type '\c' to clear the buffer.

mysql>
```

No queries were issued, and yet `mysql-proxy` shows that the client sent a query. That query actually does the following:

```
mysql> select @@version_comment limit 1;
+-------------------------------+
| @@version_comment             |
+-------------------------------+
| MySQL Community Edition (GPL) |
+-------------------------------+
1 row in set (0.00 sec)
```

So, the comment after the server version in the header is actually derived from the result of a query sent from the client to `mysqld`. In a similar manner, the output of `SHOW DATABASES` and the last query in the example are expected. However, the `mysql-proxy` output from the client sending `USE sakila` is not expected. `SELECT DATABASE()` is sent by the client to change the active database. A client issuing `USE sakila` sees:

```
mysql> USE sakila;
Reading table information for completion of table and column names
You can turn off this feature to get a quicker startup with -A

Database changed
mysql>
```

The table and column name completions are a feature on non-Windows clients. The feature enables tab completion of table and column names. The way the client *knows* the table and column names for tab completing is simple: it queries the server every time the active database is changed.

The proxy tokenizer

It would be very tedious to decode all the packets sent back and forth by using string manipulation. For an advanced use case such as auditing, it would be necessary to match each word to particular statements and keywords, including `SELECT`, `INSERT IGNORE INTO`, `SHOW`, `SET` and individual table and column names. Luckily, the developers of `mysql-proxy` have created packages that make this job much simpler.

These packages live in the `share/mysql-proxy/proxy` directory (on Windows, `share/proxy`). These packages are Lua scripts containing modularized functions that can be used by other scripts. For example, the `commands.lua` script defines a `parse()` function, which takes in an argument, and returns a Lua table structure with the following fields:

- `type`
- `type_name`

- query (when `type` is `proxy.COM_QUERY` and `proxy.COM_STMT_PREPARE`)
- schema (when `type` is `proxy.COM_INIT_DB`)

Instead of the previous example, the input to `read_query()` was manipulated by using substrings, take advantage of the `parse()` function:

```
1  local commands = require("commands")
2  function read_query(packet)
3    local cmd = commands.parse(packet)
4    if cmd.type == proxy.COM_QUERY then
5      print("we got a normal query: " .. cmd.query)
6    end
7  end
```

Line 1 requires the `commands.lua` file and assigns the contents to an object called `commands`. Line 2 defines the function we are overriding. Line 3 assigns the object `cmd` as the output of `commands.parse(packet)`, which is a Lua table structure. Line 4 uses the `type` field to check what type of statement the client sent. Previously, the awkward `string.byte(packet)` was used to retrieve the type of statement; now you can use the cleaner and more intuitive `cmd.type`. Similarly, line 5 uses `cmd.query` instead of `string.sub(packet, 2)` in the print statement. Lines 6 and 7 end the `if` statement and the function definition, respectively.

Lua Packages

Modular code is extremely useful. Lua has a `package.path` structure that stores the paths to check when using packaged code. If `mysql-proxy` outputs errors starting with:

```
/usr/local/mysql-proxy/running.lua:1: module 'proxy.commands' not found:
    no field package.preload['proxy.commands']
    no file './proxy/commands.lua'
```

you may need to change the `package.path` value. For example, if your installation is in `/usr/local/mysql-proxy`, and `commands.lua` is in `/usr/local/mysql-proxy/share/mysql-proxy/proxy/commands.lua`, add this to the top of your Lua script:

```
package.path = package.path .. ";/usr/local/mysql-proxy/share/mysql-proxy/?.
lua" local commands = require("proxy.commands")
```

The first line assigns `package.path` to be the old value of `package.path` concatenated with another path. As you may have guessed, the ? in the `package.path` string is a substitution operator. This is why the second line requires `commands` instead of `commands.lua`. The other reason for this is that the . character is used as a directory indicator. If you had specified:

```
package.path = package.path .. ";/usr/local/mysql-proxy/share/mysql-proxy/
proxy" local commands = require("commands.lua")
```

you would have seen errors that there is no such file as `commands/lua`.

Getting the command type is one useful task; being able to figure out which tables are being used, what kind of query (SELECT, INSERT, UPDATE, DELETE, SHOW, etc.) is another large task. The developers of mysql-proxy built in a tokenizer that divides a packet into its keywords and parts.

To see the tokenizer in action, run mysql-proxy with the Lua script tutorial-tokenize.lua. The read_query() function override calls the tokenize(packet) function. The function returns a hash of tokens, which read_query() goes through, printing out the token name and text.

WARNING   In order to use the tokenize() function, you must load the tokenizer package first with require first (see the sidebar on Lua packages for more information). For example:

```
local tk = require("proxy.tokenizer")
local tokens = tk.tokenize(query)
```

For example, the query:

```
SELECT COUNT(*) FROM sakila.staff WHERE email LIKE "%sakila%com";
```

becomes tokenized as seen in Table A-4.

TABLE A-4

Sample Tokenized Query

Token Name	Token Value
TK_SQL_SELECT	SELECT
TK_FUNCTION	COUNT
TK_OBRACE	(
TK_STAR	*
TK_CBRACE	)
TK_SQL_FROM	FROM
TK_LITERAL	sakila
TK_DOT	.
TK_LITERAL	staff
TK_SQL_WHERE	WHERE
TK_LITERAL	Email
TK_SQL_LIKE	LIKE
TK_STRING	"%sakila%com"

For the full list of tokens and their meanings, see the "MySQL Proxy Tokens" section later in this appendix.

Changing the Query Backend

The backend mysqld server that mysql-proxy sends information to can be changed in the connect_server() function override and the read_query() function override. The connect_server() function happens once per connection, and the read_query() function happens every time a query is sent. The following is simple code to change the backend connection to the first mysqld backend in the list of proxy backends that is not in a *down* state:

```
1   function connect_server()
2     for i = 1, #proxy.backends do
3       local s = proxy.backends[i]
4
5       if s.state ~= proxy.BACKEND_STATE_DOWN then
6         proxy.connection.backend_ndx = i
7         return
8       end
9     end
10  end
11
12  function read_query(packet)
13    for i = 1, #proxy.backends do
14      local s = proxy.backends[i]
15
16      if s.state ~= proxy.BACKEND_STATE_DOWN then
17        proxy.connection.backend_ndx = i
18        return
19      end
20    end
21  end
```

Note that both functions contain the same code. Both of these function overrides may or may not be necessary, depending on your application. In cases where neither persistent connections nor connection pools are being used, the ratio of queries:connection is 1:1. When the number of queries is greater than the number of connections, you are in a scenario where there is a query sent to an existing connection. It is in this case that you want to override both the connect_server() function and the read_query() function.

In lines 2 and 13, #proxy.backends is the length of the proxy.backends array. This is the number of backends that were specified by the --backend-proxy-addresses in the mysql-proxy configuration. Lua starts numbering its indexes at 1, not 0, so the for loop starts at 1 and continues until i has the value of the length of the array.

For each backend, lines 5 and 16 evaluate whether or not that backend is in a *down* state (unreachable). The *not equals* operator in Lua is ~=. If the backend is not down, this connection's backend is set to that backend, and the function returns. Otherwise, the for loop continues.

Setting the proxy backend for a connection is as simple as the assignment on lines 6 and 17:

```
proxy.connection.backend_ndx = i
```

Using more complicated Lua scripts, the read_query() function can be overridden, starting with a query tokenizer, using some part of the query to decide which backend the query should go to, and ending with setting the backend of the connection. This is how read/write splitting and arbitrary partitioning can be achieved with mysql-proxy.

Changing and Injecting Queries

By overriding the functions read_query() and read_query_result(), the queries sent to the mysqld backend server and the output that is returned can be examined and modified, if desired. A sample Lua script to perform query injection with mysql-proxy overrides the read_query() function:

```
1   local commands = require("commands")
2   function read_query(packet)
3     local cmd = commands.parse(packet)
4     if cmd.type == proxy.COM_QUERY then
5       print("we got a normal query: " .. cmd.query)
6       proxy.queries:append(1, packet)
7       proxy.queries:append(2, string.char(proxy.COM_QUERY) ..
"SELECT NOW()" )
8       return proxy.PROXY_SEND_QUERY
9     end
10  end
```

NOTE   In mysql-proxy versions 0.7.0 and greater, the append() and prepend() syntax has been changed. Instead of:

```
proxy.queries:prepend(num,packet)
proxy.queries:append(num,packet)
```

a third argument has been added to improve performance. The syntax now is:

```
proxy.queries:prepend(num, packet, {resultset_is_needed = true })
proxy.queries:append(num, packet, {resultset_is_needed = true })
```

This third argument is needed to send the result set back.

Lines 1–5 are familiar; they were explained in "The Proxy Tokenizer" section earlier in this appendix. Lines 6 through 8, however, are new. Lines 6 and 7 add values to the proxy.queries array. The proxy.queries array is the array of queries that mysql-proxy sends to the backend. Line 6 pushes the id value 1 and the existing query packet as the first item in the proxy.queries array. Line 7 pushes the id value 2 and a new query as the second item in the proxy.queries array. Line 8 sends the modified proxy.queries array to the backend mysqld server.

Note that the id values can be any number you choose. The order of proxy.queries is determined by the order in which items are appended to the array (or prepended with the proxy.queries:prepend function). If lines 6 and 7 had been:

```
6        proxy.queries:append(2, packet)
7        proxy.queries:append(1, string.char(proxy.COM_QUERY) ..
"SELECT NOW()" )
```

the order of the queries in proxy.queries would still have been the same — the original query would still be first, and the new query, SELECT NOW(), would be second. The first query has an id value of 2, and the second query has an id value of 1, but the id values are not what determine the order of the queries. This can be confusing!

So at this point, two queries were sent to mysqld instead of one, for each COM_QUERY type of statement sent through mysql-proxy. The results still have to be handled on the way back — the client only sent one query, so it only expects one result. The result must be intercepted to make sure that the client only receives one result set back, instead of two result sets. To intercept the query results, override the read_query_result() function:

```
11  function read_query_result(inj)
12     print("injected result-set: id = " .. inj.id)
13
14     if (inj.id == 2) then
15        for row in inj.resultset.rows do
16           print("injected query returned: " .. row[0])
17        end
18        return proxy.PROXY_IGNORE_RESULT
19     end
20  end
```

The read_query_result() function is called for each result set that is sent back by the server. In this example, the read_query() function was called once, the read_query_result() function will be called twice — first, for the result of the original query, and second, for the result of the injected query.

On line 12, you print the id value that you assigned when appending the queries. Again, this is just the id value and has no bearing on the order of the results. The order of the results is determined by the order of the queries in the proxy.queries array, not by the id values of the queries. On line 14, the script starts to deal with the case that your query is the injected query, whose id is 2.

On lines 15 through 17, the first field of each row in the result set is printed. On line 18, `mysql-proxy` is told not to send along this result set; this is still part of the case where the query has an `id` of 2. Line 19 closes the case that this query has an `id` of 2. Line 20 ends the `read_query_result()` function — the result set is sent by default if there is no `proxy.PROXY_IGNORE_RESULT` value returned.

Overriding `read_query()` allows us to change the queries sent. Lua can change the query that is sent — change the original query itself or add more queries to be sent. Overriding `read_query_result()` allows the results sent to be changed, which can be used in conjunction with injected queries to handle multiple results. However, `read_query_result()` can also be overridden without having changed the query sent to the `mysqld` backend. Thus, the result(s) sent back to the client can be changed even if the original query sent was not changed.

Understanding MySQL Proxy Internals

There are several internal structures that `mysql-proxy` has control over. Using a Lua script to read, and in some cases write to, these internal structures is what allows you to change `mysql-proxy` default behavior. For example, to change `mysql-proxy` from its default round-robin load-balancing behavior, you would use a Lua script to override the `connect_server()` function, and use the internal structure `proxy.connection.backend_ndx` to change the backend server that `mysql-proxy` will forward the connection to.

The top-level internal structure is `proxy`, which is a container for all the internal structures used by `mysql-proxy`. The second-level internal structures are `backends`, `connection`, `servers`, `queries`, and `global`.

The second level also contains many constants used for comparison, as shown in Table A-5.

TABLE A-5

MySQL Proxy Constants

Constant Name	Context	Meaning
BACKEND_STATE_DOWN	proxy.backends [x].state	The backend server is down.
BACKEND_STATE_UNKNOWN	proxy.backends [x].state	The backend server is in an unknown state.
BACKEND_STATE_UP	proxy.backends [x].state	The backend server is up.
BACKEND_TYPE_RO	proxy.backends [x].type	The backend server was defined with `--proxy-read-only-address`.

TABLE A-5	*(continued)*	
Constant Name	**Context**	**Meaning**
`BACKEND_TYPE_RW`	`proxy.backends` `[x].type`	The backend server was defined with `--proxy-backend -address`.
`MYSQLD_PACKET_ERR`	`auth.packet:byte()` `proxy.response.type`	This packet contains an error.
`MYSQLD_PACKET_OK`	`auth.packet:byte()` `proxy.response.type`	This packet was successful.
`MYSQLD_PACKET_RAW`	`proxy.response.type`	This packet contains raw data.
`PROXY_IGNORE_RESULT`	`Return`	Do not send the results to the client.
`PROXY_SEND_QUERY`	`Return`	Send the query queue to the server.
`PROXY_SEND_RESULT`	`Return`	Send the results to the client.
`PROXY_VERSION`	`N/A`	Returns the proxy version, in hex. 0x00700 corresponds to version 0.7.0
`COM_SLEEP`	`string.byte(packet)`	This packet contains a sleep command.
`COM_QUIT`	`string.byte(packet)`	This packet contains a quit command.
`COM_INIT_DB`	`string.byte(packet)`	This packet contains a init db command.
`COM_QUERY`	`string.byte(packet)`	This packet contains a query command.
`COM_FIELD_LIST`	`string.byte(packet)`	This packet contains a field list command.
`COM_CREATE_DB`	`string.byte(packet)`	This packet contains a create db command.
`COM_DROP_DB`	`string.byte(packet)`	This packet contains a drop db command.
`COM_REFRESH`	`string.byte(packet)`	This packet contains a refresh command.
`COM_SHUTDOWN`	`string.byte(packet)`	This packet contains a shutdown command.

continued

TABLE A-5   *(continued)*

Constant Name	Context	Meaning
COM_STATISTICS	string.byte(packet)	This packet contains a statistics command.
COM_PROCESS_INFO	string.byte(packet)	This packet contains a process info command.
COM_CONNECT	string.byte(packet)	This packet contains a connect command.
COM_PROCESS_KILL	string.byte(packet)	This packet contains a kill command.
COM_DEBUG	string.byte(packet)	This packet contains a debug command.
COM_PING	string.byte(packet)	This packet contains a ping command.
COM_TIME	string.byte(packet)	This packet contains a time command.
COM_DELAYED_INSERT	string.byte(packet)	This packet contains a delayed insert command.
COM_CHANGE_USER	string.byte(packet)	This packet contains a change user command.
COM_BINLOG_DUMP	string.byte(packet)	This packet contains a binlog dump command.
COM_TABLE_DUMP	string.byte(packet)	This packet contains a table dump command.
COM_CONNECT_OUT	string.byte(packet)	This packet contains a connect out command.
COM_REGISTER_SLAVE	string.byte(packet)	This packet contains a register slave command.
COM_STMT_CLOSE	string.byte(packet)	This packet contains a close command.
COM_STMT_EXECUTE	string.byte(packet)	This packet contains a execute command.
COM_STMT_PREPARE	string.byte(packet)	This packet contains a prepare command.
COM_STMT_SEND_LONG_DATA	string.byte(packet)	This packet contains a send long data command.
COM_STMT_RESET	string.byte(packet)	This packet contains a reset command.

TABLE A-5	*(continued)*	
Constant Name	**Context**	**Meaning**
COM_SET_OPTION	string.byte(packet)	This packet contains a set command.
MYSQL_TYPE_NEWDECIMAL	proxy.response. resultset { field {{type,name}} }	This field has a type of DECIMAL.
MYSQL_TYPE_TINY	proxy.response. resultset { field {{type,name}} }	This field has a type of TINY.
MYSQL_TYPE_SHORT	proxy.response. resultset { field {{type,name}} }	This field has a type of SHORT.
MYSQL_TYPE_LONG	proxy.response. resultset { field {{type,name}} }	This field has a type of LONG.
MYSQL_TYPE_FLOAT	proxy.response. resultset { field {{type,name}} }	This field has a type of FLOAT.
MYSQL_TYPE_DOUBLE	proxy.response. resultset { field {{type,name}} }	This field has a type of DOUBLE.
MYSQL_TYPE_NULL	proxy.response. resultset { field {{type,name}} }	This field has a type of NULL.
MYSQL_TYPE_TIMESTAMP	proxy.response. resultset { field {{type,name}} }	This field has a type of TIMESTAMP.
MYSQL_TYPE_LONGLONG	proxy.response. resultset { field {{type,name}} }	This field has a type of LONGLONG.
MYSQL_TYPE_INT24	proxy.response. resultset { field {{type,name}} }	This field has a type of INT.
MYSQL_TYPE_DATE	proxy.response. resultset { field {{type,name}} }	This field has a type of DATE.
MYSQL_TYPE_TIME	proxy.response. resultset { field {{type,name}} }	This field has a type of TIME.

continued

TABLE A-5   *(continued)*

Constant Name	Context	Meaning
MYSQL_TYPE_DATETIME	proxy.response. resultset { field {{type,name}} }	This field has a type of DATETIME.
MYSQL_TYPE_YEAR	proxy.response. resultset { field {{type,name}} }	This field has a type of YEAR.
MYSQL_TYPE_NEWDATE	proxy.response. resultset { field {{type,name}} }	This field has a type of NEWDATE.
MYSQL_TYPE_ENUM	proxy.response. resultset { field {{type,name}} }	This field has a type of ENUM.
MYSQL_TYPE_SET	proxy.response. resultset { field {{type,name}} }	This field has a type of SET.
MYSQL_TYPE_TINY_BLOB	proxy.response. resultset { field {{type,name}} }	This field has a type of TINY_BLOB.
MYSQL_TYPE_ MEDIUM_BLOB	proxy.response. resultset { field {{type,name}} }	This field has a type of MEDIUM_BLOB.
MYSQL_TYPE_LONG_BLOB	proxy.response. resultset { field {{type,name}} }	This field has a type of LONG_BLOB.
MYSQL_TYPE_BLOB	proxy.response. resultset { field {{type,name}} }	This field has a type of BLOB.
MYSQL_TYPE_VAR_STRING	proxy.response. resultset { field {{type,name}} }	This field has a type of VAR_STRING.
MYSQL_TYPE_STRING	proxy.response. resultset { field {{type,name}} }	This field has a type of STRING.
MYSQL_TYPE_GEOMETRY	proxy.response. resultset { field {{type,name}} }	This field has a type of GEOMETRY.
MYSQL_TYPE_BIT	proxy.response. resultset { field {{type,name}} }	This field has a type of BIT.

Further layers in the internal structures are shown in Table A-6. Note that the first five rows correspond to the internal structures:

- `proxy.socket.client.server`
- `proxy.socket.socket.server`
- `proxy.connection.backend_ndx`
- `proxy.connection.client.default_db`
- `proxy.connection.client.send_queue`

TABLE A-6

MySQL Proxy Internal Structures

Level 1	Level 2	Level 3	Level 4	Level 5
proxy	socket	client	server	
		socket	server	
	connection	backend_ndx		
		client	default_db	
			send_queue	
			username	
			address	
			scrambled_password	
		server	thread_id	
			mysqld_version	
			scramble_buffer	
	backends	connected_clients		
		address		
		state		
		type		
	backends	pool	queue	
			users	
	servers			
	queue			
	queries	type		

continued

TABLE A-6	(continued)			
Level 1	Level 2	Level 3	Level 4	Level 5
		query		
	response			
		type		
		resultset	fields	
			rows	
		rrrmsg		
		packet		
	tokens	pdata		
		text		
		token_id		
		token_name		
	global	config	proxy	lua_script

The `proxy.global.config` structure can be extended to store user-defined variables. For example, the `rw-splitting.lua` sample script extends the `proxy.global.config` structure to include:

- `proxy.global.config.rwsplit`
- `proxy.global.config.rwsplit.min_idle_connections`
- `proxy.global.config.rwsplit.max_idle_connections`

MySQL proxy tokens

The proxy tokenizer has a set of tokens that it uses to define parts of a statement. The "Proxy Tokenizer" section earlier showed a few such tokens, including ones for punctuation (TK_OBRACE, TK_CBRACE, TK_DOT, TK_STAR), type (TK_LITERAL, TK_STRING), and SQL keywords (TK_SQL_SELECT, TK_SQL_FROM, TK_SQL_WHERE, TK_SQL_LIKE).

The tokens in `mysql-proxy` 0.6 .0 that are not SQL statement keywords can be found in the source code file `sql-tokenizer.c` and are listed in Table A-7.

The SQL keyword tokens in `mysql-proxy` 0.6.0 are also found in the source code file `sql-tokenizer.c` and are listed in Table A-8. There are no examples given, because each token name is the keyword with TK_SQL_ appended. For example, the token TK_SQL_ALTER corresponds to the SQL keyword ALTER.

TABLE A-7

MySQL Proxy Tokens

Token Name	Example
Punctuation	
TK_DOT	.
TK_COMMA	,
TK_OBRACE	(
TK_CBACE	)
TK_SEMICOLON	;
TK_STAR	*
Arithmetic	
TK_PLUS	+
TK_MINUS	-
TK_DIV	/
TK_LE	<=
TK_GE	>=
TK_LT	<
TK_GT	>
TK_EQ	=
TK_NE	!=
Data Types	
TK_STRING	''foo''
TK_INTEGER	6
TK_FLOAT	1.2
TK_FUNCTION	NOW (as in SELECT NOW())
TK_COMMENT	/* comment in here */
TK_LITERAL	The word after SHOW (as in SHOW TABLES, SHOW VARIABLES, etc.) @ and @@ variables Database, table, and column names

continued

773

TABLE A-7   *(continued)*

Token Name	Example
	Functions
TK_BITWISE_AND	&
TK_BITWISE_OR	|
TK_BITWISE_XOR	^
TK_LOGICAL_AND	&&
TK_LOGICAL_OR	||
TK_ASSIGN	:=
	Other
TK_COMMENT_MYSQL	'A MySQL Comment'
TK_UNKNOWN	[ ] { }

TABLE A-8

MySQL Proxy SQL Keyword Tokens

SQL Statement Keywords
TK_SQL_ACCESSIBLE
TK_SQL_ACTION
TK_SQL_ADD
TK_SQL_ALL
TK_SQL_ALTER
TK_SQL_ANALYZE
TK_SQL_AND
TK_SQL_AS
TK_SQL_ASC
TK_SQL_ASENSITIVE
TK_SQL_BEFORE
TK_SQL_BETWEEN
TK_SQL_BIGINT

TABLE A-8	(continued)
SQL Statement Keywords	
TK_SQL_BINARY	
TK_SQL_BIT	
TK_SQL_BLOB	
TK_SQL_BOTH	
TK_SQL_BY	
TK_SQL_CALL	
TK_SQL_CASCADE	
TK_SQL_CASE	
TK_SQL_CHANGE	
TK_SQL_CHAR	
TK_SQL_CHARACTER	
TK_SQL_CHECK	
TK_SQL_COLLATE	
TK_SQL_COLUMN	
TK_SQL_CONDITION	
TK_SQL_CONSTRAINT	
TK_SQL_CONTINUE	
TK_SQL_CONVERT	
TK_SQL_CREATE	
TK_SQL_CROSS	
TK_SQL_CURRENT_DATE	
TK_SQL_CURRENT_TIME	
TK_SQL_CURRENT_TIMESTAMP	
TK_SQL_CURRENT_USER	
TK_SQL_CURSOR	
TK_SQL_DATABASE	
TK_SQL_DATABASES	
TK_SQL_DATE	

continued

TABLE A-8 *(continued)*

SQL Statement Keywords
TK_SQL_DAY_HOUR
TK_SQL_DAY_MICROSECOND
TK_SQL_DAY_MINUTE
TK_SQL_DAY_SECOND
TK_SQL_DEC
TK_SQL_DECIMAL
TK_SQL_DECLARE
TK_SQL_DEFAULT
TK_SQL_DELAYED
TK_SQL_DELETE
TK_SQL_DESC
TK_SQL_DESCRIBE
TK_SQL_DETERMINISTIC
TK_SQL_DISTINCT
TK_SQL_DISTINCTROW
TK_SQL_DIV
TK_SQL_DOUBLE
TK_SQL_DROP
TK_SQL_DUAL
TK_SQL_EACH
TK_SQL_ELSE
TK_SQL_ELSEIF
TK_SQL_ENCLOSED
TK_SQL_ENUM
TK_SQL_ESCAPED
TK_SQL_EXISTS
TK_SQL_EXIT
TK_SQL_EXPLAIN
TK_SQL_FALSE

TABLE A-8	*(continued)*
SQL Statement Keywords	
TK_SQL_FETCH	
TK_SQL_FLOAT	
TK_SQL_FLOAT4	
TK_SQL_FLOAT8	
TK_SQL_FOR	
TK_SQL_FORCE	
TK_SQL_FOREIGN	
TK_SQL_FROM	
TK_SQL_FULLTEXT	
TK_SQL_GRANT	
TK_SQL_GROUP	
TK_SQL_HAVING	
TK_SQL_HIGH_PRIORITY	
TK_SQL_HOUR_MICROSECOND	
TK_SQL_HOUR_MINUTE	
TK_SQL_HOUR_SECOND	
TK_SQL_IF	
TK_SQL_IGNORE	
TK_SQL_IN	
TK_SQL_INDEX	
TK_SQL_INFILE	
TK_SQL_INNER	
TK_SQL_INOUT	
TK_SQL_INSENSITIVE	
TK_SQL_INSERT	
TK_SQL_INT	
TK_SQL_INT1	
TK_SQL_INT2	

continued

TABLE A-8   *(continued)*

SQL Statement Keywords

TK_SQL_INT3

TK_SQL_INT4

TK_SQL_INT8

TK_SQL_INTEGER

TK_SQL_INTERVAL

TK_SQL_INTO

TK_SQL_IS

TK_SQL_ITERATE

TK_SQL_JOIN

TK_SQL_KEY

TK_SQL_KEYS

TK_SQL_KILL

TK_SQL_LEADING

TK_SQL_LEAVE

TK_SQL_LEFT

TK_SQL_LIKE

TK_SQL_LIMIT

TK_SQL_LINEAR

TK_SQL_LINES

TK_SQL_LOAD

TK_SQL_LOCALTIME

TK_SQL_LOCALTIMESTAMP

TK_SQL_LOCK

TK_SQL_LONG

TK_SQL_LONGBLOB

TK_SQL_LONGTEXT

TK_SQL_LOOP

TK_SQL_LOW_PRIORITY

TK_SQL_MASTER_SSL_VERIFY_SERVER_CERT

TABLE A-8	*(continued)*
SQL Statement Keywords	
TK_SQL_MATCH	
TK_SQL_MEDIUMBLOB	
TK_SQL_MEDIUMINT	
TK_SQL_MIDDLEINT	
TK_SQL_MINUTE_MICROSECOND	
TK_SQL_MINUTE_SECOND	
TK_SQL_MOD	
TK_SQL_MODIFIES	
TK_SQL_NATURAL	
TK_SQL_NO	
TK_SQL_NOT	
TK_SQL_NO_WRITE_TO_BINLOG	
TK_SQL_NULL	
TK_SQL_NUMERIC	
TK_SQL_ON	
TK_SQL_OPTIMIZE	
TK_SQL_OPTION	
TK_SQL_OPTIONALLY	
TK_SQL_OR	
TK_SQL_ORDER	
TK_SQL_OUT	
TK_SQL_OUTER	
TK_SQL_OUTFILE	
TK_SQL_PRECISION	
TK_SQL_PRIMARY	
TK_SQL_PROCEDURE	
TK_SQL_PURGE	
TK_SQL_RANGE	

continued

TABLE A-8   (continued)

SQL Statement Keywords
TK_SQL_READ
TK_SQL_READ_ONLY
TK_SQL_READS
TK_SQL_READ_WRITE
TK_SQL_REAL
TK_SQL_REFERENCES
TK_SQL_REGEXP
TK_SQL_RELEASE
TK_SQL_RENAME
TK_SQL_REPEAT
TK_SQL_REPLACE
TK_SQL_REQUIRE
TK_SQL_RESTRICT
TK_SQL_RETURN
TK_SQL_REVOKE
TK_SQL_RIGHT
TK_SQL_RLIKE
TK_SQL_SCHEMA
TK_SQL_SCHEMAS
TK_SQL_SECOND_MICROSECOND
TK_SQL_SELECT
TK_SQL_SENSITIVE
TK_SQL_SEPARATOR
TK_SQL_SET
TK_SQL_SHOW
TK_SQL_SMALLINT
TK_SQL_SPATIAL
TK_SQL_SPECIFIC
TK_SQL_SQL

TABLE A-8	*(continued)*
SQL Statement Keywords	
TK_SQL_SQL_BIG_RESULT	
TK_SQL_SQL_CALC_FOUND_ROWS	
TK_SQL_SQLEXCEPTION	
TK_SQL_SQL_SMALL_RESULT	
TK_SQL_SQLSTATE	
TK_SQL_SQLWARNING	
TK_SQL_SSL	
TK_SQL_STARTING	
TK_SQL_STRAIGHT_JOIN	
TK_SQL_TABLE	
TK_SQL_TERMINTED	
TK_SQL_TEXT	
TK_SQL_THEN	
TK_SQL_TIME	
TK_SQL_TIMESTAMP	
TK_SQL_TINYBLOB	
TK_SQL_TINYINT	
TK_SQL_TINYTEXT	
TK_SQL_TO	
TK_SQL_TRAILING	
TK_SQL_TRIGGER	
TK_SQL_TRUE	
TK_SQL_UNDO	
TK_SQL_UNION	
TK_SQL_UNIQUE	
TK_SQL_UNLOCK	
TK_SQL_UNSIGNED	
TK_SQL_UPDATE	

continued

TABLE A-8   (continued)
SQL Statement Keywords
TK_SQL_USAGE
TK_SQL_USE
TK_SQL_USING
TK_SQL_UTC_DATE
TK_SQL_UTC_TIME
TK_SQL_UTC_TIMESTAMP
TK_SQL_VALUES
TK_SQL_VARBINARY
TK_SQL_VARCHAR
TK_SQL_VARCHARACTER
TK_SQL_VARYING
TK_SQL_WHEN
TK_SQL_WHERE
TK_SQL_WHILE
TK_SQL_WITH
TK_SQL_WRITE
TK_SQL_X509
TK_SQL_XOR
TK_SQL_YEAR_MONTH
TK_SQL_ZEROFILL

Summary

In this appendix you have learned how to use the MySQL Proxy, including:

- Using multiple backends with MySQL Proxy
- How MySQL Proxy's default round-robin connection logic works
- A brief Lua tutorial
- How MySQL Proxy tokenizes queries
- Query injection with MySQL Proxy
- Reference material for more advanced MySQL Proxy scripting

Appendix B

Functions and Operators

This appendix contains the functions and operators available in MySQL, including whether they are an SQL Standard or a MySQL Extension.

Using Aggregation Functions

Aggregation functions take a single expression as an argument but may take input from many rows; they are *row-wise* functions. For example, the AVG(expr) function takes a simple average (the sum divided by the count):

```
mysql> CREATE TABLE nums (num TINYINT);
Query OK, 0 rows affected (0.09 sec)

mysql> INSERT INTO nums (num) VALUES (1),(2),(3);
Query OK, 3 rows affected (0.48 sec)
Records: 3 Duplicates: 0 Warnings: 0

mysql> select AVG(num) FROM nums;
+----------+
| AVG(num) |
+----------+
| 2.0000   |
+----------+
1 row in set (0.03 sec)
```

Although aggregate functions work on expressions that encompass one or more rows, they only take one expression as an argument. For example, the syntax of AVG(expr) does not allow for the following:

IN THIS APPENDIX

Using aggregation functions

Using bitwise operators

Compressing and encrypting data

Testing, logic, and control flow

Using server-level functions

Working with data types

```
mysql> SELECT AVG(1,2,3);
ERROR 1064 (42000): You have an error in your SQL syntax; check the
manual that corresponds to your MySQL server version for the
right syntax to use near '2,3)' at line 1
```

WARNING One exception to this rule is that COUNT(DISTINCT expr) can take multiple arguments.

When expr evaluates as NULL, for example when there are no rows that match, most aggregation functions return NULL. Functions that return 0 when expr evaluates as NULL are COUNT(*), COUNT(expr), COUNT(DISTINCT expr), BIT_OR, and BIT_XOR.

Bug

There is one function that returns an unexpected result: BIT_AND(NULL):

```
mysql> SELECT BIT_AND(NULL);
+----------------------+
| BIT_AND(NULL)        |
+----------------------+
| 18446744073709551615 |
+----------------------+
1 row in set (0.00 sec)
```

For the curious, 18446744073709551615 is a 63-bit string where each bit is 1. This has been reported as MySQL bug 37754 and can be seen at: http://bugs.mysql.com/bug.php?id=37754.

Table B-1 lists the aggregate functions and a brief description of each one.

Using Bitwise Operators

MySQL extends standard SQL with special functions for bits. Bitwise operators implicitly cast arguments to UNSIGNED BIGINT. This has the most noticeable effect on bit inversion (~):

```
mysql> SELECT 5,~5,BIN(5),BIN(~5)\G
*************************** 1. row ***************************
       5: 5
      ~5: 18446744073709551610
  BIN(5): 101
 BIN(~5): 111111111111111111111111111111111111111111111111111111111111
    11010
1 row in set (0.00 sec)
```

Aggregation functions for bits are listed in Table B-1.

TABLE B-1

Aggregation Functions

Function Syntax	Standard SQL?	Description
AVG(expr)	Yes	Simple average; SUM/COUNT.
BIT_AND(expr)	No	Bitwise AND; returns true if all rows are true and false if any rows are false.
BIT_OR(expr)	No	Bitwise OR; returns true if any row is true; returns false if all rows are false.
BIT_XOR(expr)	No	Bitwise XOR; a pair where exactly one value is true returns true; all other pairs will return false. More than 2 rows are done commutatively.
COUNT(expr) COUNT(*) COUNT(DISTINCT expr)	Yes Yes Yes	Returns a count of all non-NULL values of expr. COUNT(*) returns a count of all rows. COUNT(DISTINCT expr) returns a count of how many rows contain different values for expr.
GROUP_CONCAT(expr)	No	Concatenates non-NULL values, separated by a comma by default.
MAX(expr)	Yes	Returns the maximum value of expr.
MIN(expr)	Yes	Returns the minimum value of expr.
STD(expr)	No	Nonstandard SQL equivalent to STDDEV_POP(expr).
STDDEV_POP(expr)	Yes	Population standard deviation. Same as SQRT(VAR_POP(expr)).
STDDEV_SAMP(expr)	Yes	Sample standard deviation. Same as SQRT(VAR_SAMP(expr)).
STDDEV(expr)	No	Nonstandard SQL equivalent to STDDEV_POP(expr).
SUM(expr)	Yes	Returns the sum of all values of expr.
VAR_POP(expr)	Yes	Population standard variance. This is calculated by taking the average of the square of the differences between each value and the average value.
VAR_SAMP(expr)	Yes	Population standard variance. This is calculated by taking the sum of the square of the differences between each value and the average value, and dividing by the number of values (rows) minus one.
VARIANCE(expr)	No	Nonstandard SQL equivalent to VAR_POP(expr).

Table B-2 lists the bit functions and their descriptions.

TABLE B-2

Bit Functions

Function Syntax	Standard SQL?	Description
&	No	Bitwise AND, returns true when both bit positions are true
~	No	Bit inversion (unary operator)
|	No	Bitwise OR, returns true when either or both bit positions are true
^	No	Bitwise XOR, returns true when exactly one bit position is true
<<	No	Shifts to the left
>>	No	Shifts to the right
BIT_COUNT	No	Returns the number of bits that are set

Combining multiple statements

Much like basic arithmetic operators (such as + - * /), these bitwise operators can be combined into longer statements, which are then parsed using precedence rules.

Precedence from highest to least is shown in Table B-3.

TABLE B-3

Bit Operator Precedence

Operator(s)	Level of Precedence
~	Highest
^	
<< >>	
&	
|	Lowest

Let's walk through an example:

```
mysql> SELECT 5 | 2 ^ 7 << 3 | 4 & 6;
+-----------------------+
```

```
| 5 | 2 ^ 7 << 3 | 4 & 6 |
+------------------------+
|                     45 |
+------------------------+
1 row in set (0.02 sec)
```

Using parentheses to make the order of operations clear, the expression translates to:

```
5 | ((2 ^ 7) << 3) | (4 & 6)
```

It would be easier to evaluate the bitwise operators by changing the numbers to be in binary instead of base 10. A simple MySQL query can act as a reference chart:

```
mysql> SELECT BIN(2), BIN(3), BIN(4), BIN(5), BIN(6), BIN(7)\G
*************************** 1. row ***************************
BIN(2): 10
BIN(3): 11
BIN(4): 100
BIN(5): 101
BIN(6): 110
BIN(7): 111
1 row in set (0.00 sec)
```

The expression is now:

```
101 | ((10 ^ 111) << 11) | (100 & 110)
```

The first operation is 10 ^ 111, which evaluates to 101, or 5 in base 10.

```
101 | (101 << 11) | (100 & 110)
```

101 << 11 shifts the bits in 101 to the left by three positions to produce 101000, or 40 in base 10.

```
101 | 101000 | (100 & 110)
```

Evaluating the remaining expression in parenthesis, 100 & 110 equates to 100, or 4 in base 10.

```
101 | 101000 | 100
```

Just like arithmetic operators, it is standard to evaluate from left to right when all the operators have the same precedence. 101 | 101000 evaluates to 101101, or 45 in base 10, which leaves the expression as:

```
101 | 101101
```

The remaining expression 101 | 101101 evaluates to 101101 for a final result of 45.

Compressing and Encrypting Data

The binaries from MySQL are compiled with compression libraries. If MySQL is not compiled with a compression library, compression functions will return NULL. Table B-4 lists the compression functions and a brief description of each one.

Compression Functions

Function Syntax	Standard SQL?	Description
COMPRESS(expr)	No	Returns the compressed value of expr
UNCOMPRESS(expr)	No	Returns the uncompressed value of expr. Returns NULL if expr is not a compressed value.
UNCOMPRESSED_LENGTH(expr)	No	Returns the length of expr before compression. UNCOMPRESSED_LENGTH(COMPRESS(expr)) is equivalent to LENGTH(expr).

Cryptographic

Security is a critical aspect of database systems; MySQL provides several cryptographic functions. Table B-5 lists the encryption functions along with a brief description.

Encryption Functions

Function Syntax	Standard SQL?	Description
AES_DECRYPT (str,key)	No	Returns the result of AES decryption of str using key. AES_DECRYPT(AES_ENCRYPT(x,y),y) is equivalent to x.
AES_ENCRYPT (str,key)	No	Returns the AES encryption of str using key. Returns NULL if either str or key is NULL. Uses 128-bit keys by default; this can be increased to 256-bit keys by modifying the source code.
DECODE (str,pass)	No	Returns the result of decoding str using a password of pass. DECODE(ENCODE(x,y),y) is equivalent to x.
DES_DECRYPT (str[,key])	No	Returns the result of decoding str using key. See DES_ENCRYPT() for a description of how key is used as the key string or key number.

TABLE B-5	*(continued)*	
Function Syntax	**Standard SQL?**	**Description**
DES_ENCRYPT (str[,key])	No	Returns the Triple-DES encryption of str. If key is a string, key is used as the key string. If key is a number from 0–9, the key string is the key number from the DES key file. If key is not specified, the first key number from the DES key file is used for encryption.
ENCODE (str,pass)	No	Returns the result of encoding str with a password of pass.
ENCRYPT (str[,pass])	No	Returns the encryption of str with a salt of pass, using the UNIX function crypt(). Returns NULL on systems that do not have crypt(), including Windows.
MD5(str)	No	Returns the 32-character hex string representing the 128-bit MD5 checksum of str, for non-NULL values of str. Returns NULL if str is equivalent to NULL.
OLD_PASSWORD (str)	No	Returns the old, pre-MySQL 4.1 of the PASSWORD function applied to str. Used to generate password hashes on newer database servers that need to support older clients/client libraries. See PASSWORD.
PASSWORD(str)	No	Returns the one-way password hash of str. Used in the MySQL privilege system. Pre-MySQL 4.1, the encryption is weaker (see the OLD_PASSWORD).
SHA1(str), SHA(str)	No	Returns the 40-character hex string representing the 160-bit SHA1 checksum of str, for non-NULL values of str. Returns NULL if str is equivalent to NULL.
SHA2(str, bit_length)	No	Added in MySQL version 6.0.5. Acceptable values for the required bit_length field are 224, 256, 384 and 512, which will return the 224-bit, 256-bit, 384-bit and 512-bit SHA2 checksums for non-NULL values of str, respectively. Returns NULL if str is equivalent to NULL.

Testing, Logic, and Control Flow

SQL would be much less powerful without the filtering power of comparison operators and the ability to test and control procedural flow. Table B-6 lists the comparison functions and a brief description of each one.

Comparison Functions

Function Syntax	Standard SQL?	Description
expr1 BETWEEN expr2 AND expr3	No	Equivalent to expr1>=expr2 AND expr1<=expr3
COALESCE(list)	Yes	Returns the first non-null value in a list containing one or more expressions
expr1 <=> expr2	No	Returns true if expr1 equals expr2, including if they are both NULL (NULL-safe)
expr1 = expr2	Yes	Returns true if expr1 equals expr2; not NULL-safe
expr1 >= expr2	Yes	Returns true if expr1 is greater than or equal to expr2; not NULL-safe
expr1 > expr2	Yes	Returns true if expr1 is greater than expr2
GREATEST(list)	No	Returns the greatest value of a list containing two or more expressions
expr1 IN(list)	No	Returns true if the value of expr1 is contained in a list of one or more expressions
INTERVAL(list)	No	The list argument is two or more integer values separated by commas. When INTERVAL is called it returns a count the number of integers in the list that are smaller in value than the initial integer. If there are no smaller integers in the list than the first value a 0 is returned.
expr IS NOT NULL	Yes	Returns true if expr is not equivalent to NULL
expr IS NOT bool	Yes	Returns true if the Boolean value of expr is equivalent to bool
expr IS NULL	Yes	Returns true if expr is equivalent to NULL
expr IS bool	Yes	Returns true if the Boolean value of expr is equivalent to bool
ISNULL(expr)	No	Returns true if expr is equivalent to NULL. Nonstandard SQL equivalent to expr IS NULL
LEAST(list)	No	Returns the least value of a list containing two or more expressions
expr1 <= expr2	Yes	Returns true if expr1 is less than or equal to expr2; not NULL-safe
expr1 < expr2	Yes	Returns true if expr1 is less than expr2

TABLE B-6	*(continued)*	
Function Syntax	**Standard SQL?**	**Description**
expr LIKE pattern [ESCAPE 'char']	Yes	Returns true if expr matches pattern; pattern uses SQL regular expressions. The default escape character is "\", used to match the literal values of the wildcard characters "%" and "_". The optional ESCAPE parameter sets the escape character to char.
expr1 != expr2 expr1 <> expr2	No Yes	Returns true if expr1 is not equivalent to expr2
expr1 SOUNDS LIKE expr2	No	Equivalent to SOUNDEX(expr1) = SOUNDEX(expr2) (see Table B-16)

Control Flow

Even though SQL is a declarative query language, like all database vendors MySQL has added control flow functions. Table B-7 lists each control flow function and a brief description.

TABLE B-7		

Control Flow Functions

Function Syntax	**Standard SQL?**	**Description**
CASE val WHEN test1 THEN expr1 [WHEN test2 THEN expr2 ...] [ELSE exprN] END CASE WHEN test1 THEN expr1 [WHEN test2 THEN expr2 ...] [ELSE exprN] END	No	Returns the exprX of the first testX that matches val. If no testX matches and an optional ELSE statement is defined, returns exprN. If no testX matches and no ELSE statement is defined, returns NULL. Returns the exprX of the first testX that evaluates as true. If no testX evaluates to true and an optional ELSE statement is defined, returns exprN. If no testX evaluates to true and no ELSE statement is defined, returns NULL.
IF(expr1,expr2, expr3)	No	Returns expr2 when expr1 evaluates as true. Returns expr3 when expr1 evaluates as false or NULL.
IFNULL(expr1, expr2)	No	Returns expr2 if expr1 is equivalent to NULL. Returns expr1 if expr1 is not equivalent to NULL. Equivalent to IF(ISNULL(expr1),expr2,expr1).
NULLIF(expr1, expr2)	Yes	Returns expr1 if expr1 does not equal expr2. Returns NULL if expr1 equals expr2.

Logical

Logical operators are a mainstay of computer science. MySQL has extended the SQL standards to provide database developers with a more familiar syntax. Logical values are expressed by MySQL as 1 (true), 0 (false) or NULL.

Table B-8 lists the logical functions and a brief description of each function.

TABLE B-8

Logical Functions

Function Syntax	Standard SQL?	Description
expr1 AND expr2 expr1 && expr2	Yes No	Returns true if expr1 and expr2 are both true; returns NULL if either expr1 or expr2 is NULL; returns false if either expr1 or expr2 is false and neither expression is NULL
NOT expr1! expr1	Yes No	Returns true if expr1 is false; returns false if expr1 is true; returns NULL if expr1 is NULL
expr1 OR expr2 expr1 || expr2	Yes No	Returns true if either expr1 or expr2 are true; returns false if expr1 and expr2 are both false; returns NULL if either expr1 or expr2 is NULL and the other expression is not true
expr1 XOR expr2	No	Returns true if only one of expr1 and expr2 is true; returns false if expr1 and expr2 are the same Boolean value; returns NULL if either expr1 or expr2 is NULL

Using Server-Level Functions

The MySQL server contains metadata that can be seen by using server functions. Table B-9 contains a list of the available functions that retrieve this metadata from the server.

Keyword locking

MySQL provides a way to lock a keyword. One use of this meta-locking is for distributed code to have a centralized database location where application or database locks are managed. Note that neither data nor schemas are locked in this manner.

Table B-10 lists the locking functions available and a brief description of each one.

TABLE B-9

Server Functions

Function Syntax	Standard SQL?	Description
BENCHMARK (num,expr)	No	Execute expr num times. Always returns 0. Can be used to compare test results, thus benchmarking expr.
CONNECTION_ID()	No	Returns the ID of the current thread
CURRENT_USER()	Yes	Returns the current user@host as specified in MySQL's grant tables
DATABASE()	No	Returns the current working database name; returns NULL if no default database is defined. If USE sakila is specified, then SELECT DATABASE(), the result is sakila.
DEFAULT(col)	No	Returns the default value for the column col. If col does not have a default value, throws ERROR 1364 (HY000): Field col doesn't have a default value.
FOUND_ROWS()	No	Returns the number of rows selected by the previous SELECT or SHOW statement. Returns true for all INSERT, UPDATE, and DELETE statements and all errors. Returns the total number of rows that would have been returned in a nonlimited query when the previous SELECT statement used LIMIT and included the keyword SQL_CALC_FOUND_ROWS.
LAST_INSERT_ID()	No	Returns the first AUTO_INCREMENT value of the latest query that was the inserted successfully.
MASTER_POS_WAIT (log_file, log_pos [,num])	No	Returns the number of queries from the logs that ran on a slave in order to update to the log position log_pos of the log file named log_file. Returns NULL when there is no slave SQL thread running. Returns an error when the SQL threads stops running while MASTER_POS_WAIT is running. Returns -1 if the timeout has been exceeded; the number of seconds to timeout after is specified by num.
NAME_CONST(name, value)	No	Returns value; sets the internal variable called name to value. Used for nondeterministic functions in replication. This statement may be seen in the binary logs if stored procedures are used. This is not a function that is used by the end user.

continued

TABLE B-9	*(continued)*	
Function Syntax	**Standard SQL?**	**Description**
ROW_COUNT()	Yes	Returns the number of rows inserted, updated, or deleted in the previous statement; returns -1 if the last statement was not an INSERT, UPDATE, or DELETE statement
SCHEMA()	No	Equivalent to DATABASE()
SESSION_USER()	Yes	Returns the username and hostname of the current connection. Equivalent to USER() and SYSTEM_USER().
SLEEP(num)	No	Sleep for num seconds. Returns a result set of 0.
SYSTEM_USER()	Yes	Returns the username and hostname of the current connection. Equivalent to SESSION_USER() and USER().
USER()	No	Equivalent to SYSTEM_USER() and SESSION_USER()
VALUES()	No	Defines INSERT values
VERSION()	No	Returns the current MySQL server version

TABLE B-10

Locking Functions

Function Syntax	**Standard SQL?**	**Description**
GET_LOCK(str,num)	No	Obtains lock and returns true if a lock named str can be obtained within num seconds. Returns false if a lock named str cannot be obtained within num seconds.
IS_FREE_LOCK(str)	No	Returns true if there is no lock named str. Returns false if str is locked.
IS_USED_LOCK(str)	No	Returns the thread id of the process that holds a lock named str; returns NULL if there is no lock named str.
RELEASE_LOCK(str)	No	Returns true if a lock named str can be released; returns false if a lock named str cannot be released; returns NULL if there is no lock named str.

Working with Data Types

Chapter 5 discussed the different types of data supported by mysqld. This section will discuss functions appropriate to different data types:

- Mathematical functions and numbers
- Date and time functions
- String functions on text types
- Data type conversion
- Working with XML

Mathematical functions and numbers

Mathematics and databases go hand in hand; SQL is based on a mathematical model for processing relational data. There are many numeric functions and operators available in MySQL.

Table B-11 lists the numeric functions and operators with a brief description of each.

| TABLE B-11 |

Numeric Functions and Operators

Function Syntax	Standard SQL?	Description
ABS(expr)	Yes	Returns the absolute value of expr
ACOS(expr)	No	Returns the arc cosine of expr
ASIN(expr)	No	Returns the arc sine of expr
ATAN(expr) ATAN2(expr)	No No	Returns the arc tangent of expr Equivalent to ATAN(expr)
CEILING(expr) CEIL(expr)	Yes No	Returns the smallest integer less than expr; returns expr if expr is an integer Equivalent to CEILING(expr)
CONV(num,base_from, base_to)	No	Converts num from base_from to base_to. For example, to change 100 from binary to decimal: ```mysql> SELECT CONV(100,2,10);
+----------------+
CONV(100,2,10)
+----------------+
| 4 |
+----------------+
1 row in set (0.00 sec)``` |

continued

TABLE B-11	(continued)	
Function Syntax	**Standard SQL?**	**Description**
COS(expr)	No	Returns the cosine of expr
COT(expr)	No	Returns the cotangent of expr
CRC32(expr)	No	Returns the 32-bit unsigned cyclic redundancy check value of expr. Returns NULL if expr is NULL.
DEGREES(expr)	No	Returns the value of expr radians converted to degrees
expr1 DIV expr2	No	Returns the integer value of expr1 divided by expr2; equivalent to FLOOR(expr1/expr2). Returns NULL if expr2 is 0.
expr1 / expr2	Yes	Returns expr1 divided by expr2. Returns NULL if expr2 is 0.
EXP(expr)	No	Returns e^expr. e is the base for natural logarithms. LN(EXP(expr)) and EXP(LN(expr)) are equivalent to expr.
FLOOR(expr)	No	Returns the greatest integer less than expr; returns expr if expr is an integer
FORMAT(num [,dec])	No	Returns a pretty-print string of num using the thousands separator, rounded to dec decimal places. If dec is unspecified, num is rounded to 0 decimal places. If dec is negative, num is rounded to a multiple of 10.
HEX(num)	No	Returns the value of expr converted to hexadecimal. Equivalent to CONV(expr,10,16). Note that there is a HEX(str) function in the "Type Conversion Functions" section.
INET_ATON(str)	No	Returns the value of a string representing an IP address converted to an UNSIGNED INT.
INET_NTOA(num)	No	Returns the value of an UNSIGNED INT converted to a string representing an IP address
LN(expr)	Yes	Returns the natural log of expr. LN(EXP(expr)) and EXP(LN(expr)) are equivalent to expr
LOG10(expr)	No	Returns the base-10 log of expr
LOG2(expr)	No	Returns the base-2 log of expr
LOG(expr)	No	Equivalent to LN(expr)
LOG(num_base,expr)	No	Returns the log of expr using base num_base
expr1 - expr2	Yes	Returns expr2 subtracted from expr1

TABLE B-11	*(continued)*	
Function Syntax	**Standard SQL?**	**Description**
MOD(expr1,expr2)	Yes	Returns the remainder of expr1 divided by expr2
expr1 MOD expr2	No	Equivalent to MOD(expr1,expr2)
expr1 % expr2	No	Equivalent to MOD(expr1,expr2)
PI()	No	Returns the value of pi
expr1 + expr2	Yes	Returns the value of expr1 plus expr2
POW(expr1, expr2)	No	Returns the value of expr1 raised to the power of expr2
POWER(expr1, expr2)	Yes	Equivalent to POW(expr1,expr2)
RADIANS(expr)	No	Returns the value of expr degrees converted to radians
RAND([num])	No	Returns a random, floating point number between 0 and 1, using the optional num as a seed
ROUND(num[,dec])	Yes	Returns the value of num rounded to dec decimal places. If dec is unspecified, num is rounded to 0 decimal places. If dec is negative, num is rounded to a multiple of 10.
SIGN(expr)	No	Returns 1 if expr is positive; returns 0 if expr is 0; returns -1 if expr is negative
SIN(expr)	No	Returns the sine of expr
SQRT(expr)	Yes	Returns the square root of expr; returns NULL if expr is negative
TAN(expr)	No	Returns the tangent of expr
expr1 * expr2	Yes	Returns expr1 multiplied by expr2
TRUNCATE (expr,dec)	No	Returns the value of num truncated to dec decimal places. If dec is 0, num is truncated to an integer. If dec is negative, num is truncated to a multiple of 10.

Date and time functions

MySQL has many functions to manipulate dates and times, including one to specify how to display dates and times. The DATE_FORMAT() function has an extremely flexible formatting structure. The structure is made of building blocks called *specifiers*, which are marked by starting with %. The building blocks can be separated by whitespace or other characters by adding to the specifier string in the appropriate place:

```
mysql> SELECT DATE_FORMAT('2009-04-03 07:05:01.975468' ,
    -> '** %W, %m %D %Y %% %H-%i-%S**') as PrintedDate;
```

```
+------------------------------------+
| PrintedDate                        |
+------------------------------------+
| ** Friday, 04 3rd 2009 % 07-05-01** |
+------------------------------------+
1 row in set (0.00 sec)
```

Table B-12 lists the specifiers used by the DATE_FORMAT() function.

TABLE B-12

DATE_FORMAT() Specifiers

Specifier	Description	Sample Output DATE_FORMAT ('2009-04-03 07:05:01.975468', specifier)	Sample Output DATE_FORMAT ('2009-04-03 20:05:01', specifier)
%a	Short day of the week	Fri	Fri
%b	Short month name	Apr	Apr
%c	Numeric month, no leading zero	4	4
%D	Ordinal day of the month	3rd	3rd
%d	Numeric day of the month	03	03
%e	Numeric day of the month, no leading zero	3	3
%f	Microseconds	975468	000000
%H	Hour, 24-hour time	07	20
%h	Hour, 12-hour time	07	08
%I	Hour, 12-hour time	07	08
%i	Minutes	05	05
%j	Numeric day of the year	093	093
%k	Hour, 24-hour time, no leading zero	7	20
%l	Hour, 12-hour time, no leading zero	7	8
%M	Month Name	April	April

TABLE B-12	(continued)		
Specifier	**Description**	**Sample Output DATE_FORMAT ('2009-04-03 07:05:01.975468', specifier)**	**Sample Output DATE_FORMAT ('2009-04-03 20:05:01', specifier)**
%m	Numeric month	04	04
%p	AM or PM	AM	PM
%r	12-hour time	07:05:01 AM	08:05:01 PM
%S	Seconds	01	01
%s	Seconds	01	01
%T	24-hour time	07:05:01	20:05:01
%U	Numeric week of the year, week starts on Sunday, week numbering starts at 0	13	13
%u	Numeric week of the year, week starts on Monday, week numbering starts at 0	14	14
%V	Numeric week of the year, week starts on Sunday, week numbering starts at 1 (use with %X)	13	13
%v	Numeric week of the year, week starts on Monday, week numbering starts at 1 (use with %v)	14	14
%W	Weekday name	Friday	Friday
%w	Numeric day of the week, week starts on Sunday, day numbering starts at 0	5	5
%X	Year, week starts on Sunday	2009	2009
%x	Year, week starts on Monday	2009	2009
%Y	Year	2009	2009
%y	Year, two digits	09	09

The INTERVAL keyword defines custom, relative periods of time using different units. The simple units are shown in Table B-13.

Simple INTERVAL Units

Unit	Sample	Description
MICROSECOND	INTERVAL num MICROSECOND	Defines a period of num microseconds
SECOND	INTERVAL num SECOND	Defines a period of num seconds
MINUTE	INTERVAL num MINUTE	Defines a period of num minutes
HOUR	INTERVAL num HOUR	Defines a period of num hours
DAY	INTERVAL num DAY	Defines a period of num days
WEEK	INTERVAL num WEEK	Defines a period of num weeks
MONTH	INTERVAL num MONTH	Defines a period of num months
QUARTER	INTERVAL num QUARTER	Defines a period of num quarters
YEAR	INTERVAL num YEAR	Defines a period of num years

Microseconds

Before MySQL 6.0.5, the MICROSECOND unit for the INTERVAL keyword did not exist. Instead, the FRAC_SECOND unit was used. The use of FRAC_SECOND is deprecated and will cause errors when used in a time expressions using INTERVAL or within functions such as DATE_ADD(). The only functions that do not give an error when using FRAC_SECOND are TIMESTAMPADD() and TIMESTAMPDIFF().

Composite INTERVAL units define one or more simple unit(s). Table B-14 shows how simple unit values can be joined by either : or . to make composite INTERVAL values in mysqld.

The rest of the date and time functions are useful for obtaining dates and times and performing mathematical, and other operations on dates and times. Many functions use the INTERVAL expr unit syntax described in Table B-13.

Some functions make use of time zones; by default, MySQL will use the system time zone (see the "Time zones" section of Chapter 4 for more information). To use time zone names, you need to populate the appropriate system table. The operating system's list of time zones is a set of files and may be found in a directory such as /usr/share/zoneinfo — check your operating system's manuals for the correct location. The mysql_tzinfo_to_sql script takes in the zoneinfo directory as an input and outputs SQL that populates the appropriate mysql system tables.

TABLE B-14

Composite INTERVAL Units

Unit Sample	Allowable str Values	Simple Unit Equivalence
SECOND_MICROSECOND INTERVAL str SECOND_MICROSECOND	5 or '5' 4.5, '4.5' or 4:5	INTERVAL 5 MICROSECOND INTERVAL 4 SECOND + INTERVAL 5 MICROSECOND
MINUTE_MICROSECOND INTERVAL str MINUTE_MICROSECOND	Same as SECOND_MICROSECOND '3.4.5' or '3:4:5'	Same as SECOND_MICROSECOND INTERVAL 3 MINUTE + INTERVAL 4 SECOND + INTERVAL 5 MICROSECOND
MINUTE_SECOND INTERVAL str MINUTE_SECOND	4 or '4' 3.4, '3,.4' or '3:4'	INTERVAL 5 SECOND INTERVAL 3 MINUTE + INTERVAL 4 SECOND
HOUR_MICROSECOND INTERVAL str HOUR_MICROSECOND	Same as MINUTE_MICROSECOND '2.3.4.5' or '2:3:4:5'	Same as MINUTE_MICROSECOND INTERVAL 2 HOUR + INTERVAL 3 MINUTE + INTERVAL 4 SECOND + INTERVAL 5 MICROSECOND
HOUR_SECOND INTERVAL str HOUR_SECOND	Same as MINUTE_SECOND '2.3.4' or '2:3:4'	Same as MINUTE_SECOND INTERVAL 2 HOUR + INTERVAL 3 MINUTE + INTERVAL 4 SECOND
HOUR_MINUTE INTERVAL str HOUR_MINUTE	3 2.3, '2:3' or '2:3'	INTERVAL 3 MINUTE INTERVAL 2 HOUR + INTERVAL 3 MINUTE
DAY_MICROSECOND INTERVAL str DAY_MICROSECOND	Same as HOUR_MICROSECOND '1.2.3.4.5','1:2:3:4:5'	Same as HOUR_MICROSECOND INTERVAL 1 DAY + INTERVAL 2 HOUR + INTERVAL 3 MINUTE + INTERVAL 4 SECOND + INTERVAL 5 MICROSECOND
DAY_SECOND INTERVAL str DAY_SECOND	Same as HOUR_SECOND '1.2.3.4','1:2:3:4'	Same as HOUR_MICROSECOND INTERVAL 1 DAY + INTERVAL 2 HOUR + INTERVAL 3 MINUTE + INTERVAL 4 SECOND + INTERVAL 5 MICROSECOND

continued

TABLE B-14	(continued)	
Unit Sample	**Allowable str Values**	**Simple Unit Equivalence**
DAY_MINUTE INTERVAL str DAY_MINUTE	Same as HOUR_MINUTE '1.2.3','1:2:3'	Same as HOUR_MICROSECOND INTERVAL 1 DAY + INTERVAL 2 HOUR + INTERVAL 3 MINUTE
DAY_HOUR INTERVAL str DAY_HOUR	2 1.2, '1.2' or '1:2'	INTERVAL 2 HOUR INTERVAL 1 DAY + INTERVAL 2 HOUR
YEAR_MONTH INTERVAL str YEAR_MONTH	6 7.6, '7.6' OR '7:6'	INTERVAL 6 MONTH INTERVAL 7 YEAR + 6 MONTH

If you need to populate the mysql internal system tables on a Windows machine or other operating system that do not have a list of time zones, you can do so by downloading a prebuilt package from MySQL's website at http://dev.mysql.com/downloads/timezones.html.

Table B-15 shows the available data and time functions along with a brief description of each one.

TABLE B-15

Date and Time Functions

Function Syntax	Standard SQL?	Description
ADDDATE(dt, INTERVAL expr unit) ADDDATE(dt,num)	No No	Returns a DATE that is dt plus the period defined by the INTERVAL expression. Returns a DATE that is dt plus num days.
ADDTIME(dtq, time_expr)	No	Returns a time that is expr1 plus time_expr; dtq is either a DATE or DATETIME data type.
CONVERT_TZ(dtm, tz_from, tz_to)	No	Returns a DATETIME data type resulting from converting the time zone associated with dtm from tz_from to tz_to.
CURDATE()	No	Equivalent to CURRENT_DATE().
CURRENT_DATE()	Yes	Returns the current date.
CURRENT_TIME()	Yes	Returns the current time.
CURRENT_TIMESTAMP()	Yes	Returns the current date and time. This function is safe for replication. NOW() is an alias for CURRENT_TIMESTAMP().

TABLE B-15	*(continued)*	

Function Syntax	Standard SQL?	Description
CURTIME()	No	Equivalent to CURRENT_TIME().
DATE_ADD(dt, INTERVAL expr unit)	No	Equivalent to ADDDATE(dt, INTERVAL expr unit).
DATE_FORMAT(dtm, specifier)	No	Format datetime dtm using specifier. For a complete listing of specifiers, see Table B-12.
DATE_SUB(dt, INTERVAL expr unit)	No	Equivalent to SUBDATE(dt, INTERVAL expr unit).
DATE(dtq)	No	Returns the date part of dtq in %Y-%m-%d format; dtq is a DATE or DATETIME data type.
DATEDIFF(dtq1, dtq2)	No	Return the result of subtracting DATE(dtq2) from DATE(dtq1). dtq1 and dtq2 are DATE or DATETIME data types.
DAY(dtq)	No	Returns the day part of dtq; format defaults to %e; dtq is a DATE or DATETIME data type.
DAYNAME(dtq)	No	Returns the weekday name part of dtq; format defaults to %W; dtq is a DATE or DATETIME data type.
DAYOFMONTH(dtq)	No	Same as DAY(dtq).
DAYOFWEEK(dtq)	No	Returns the numeric day of the week part of dtq; format defaults to %w; dtq is a DATE or DATETIME data type.
DAYOFYEAR(dtq)	No	Returns the day of the year part of dtq; format defaults to %h; dtq is a DATE or DATETIME data type.
EXTRACT(unit FROM dtq)	Yes	Returns the value of the specified unit of dtq; dtq is a DATE or DATETIME data type. EXTRACT uses the same units as INTERVAL.
FROM_DAYS(num)	No	Returns the date calculated by num days in %Y-%m-%d format. Returns 0000-00-00 when num is less than 366; returns 0001-01-01 when num is 366. FROM_DAYS should not be used for values of num less than 578,101 (October 15th, 1582, when the Gregorian calendar usage began).

continued

TABLE B-15	*(continued)*	
Function Syntax	**Standard SQL?**	**Description**
FROM_UNIXTIME(uts [,specifier])	No	Returns a DATETIME that corresponds to the UNIX timestamp uts. When the specifier string (see Table B-12) is not defined, the format defaults to %Y-%m-%d %H:%i:%s.
GET_FORMAT(dta,fmt)	No	Returns a specifier string (See Table B-12); fmt is one of 'EUR', 'INTERNAL', 'ISO', 'JIS', 'USA'; dta is one of DATE, DATETIME, or TIME.
HOUR(dtq)	No	Returns the hour part of dtq in %l format; dtq is a DATE or DATETIME data type.
LAST_DAY(dtq)	No	Returns the date in %Y-%m-%d format of the last day of the month dtq is in; dtq is a DATE or DATETIME data type.
LOCALTIME()	Yes	Equivalent to CURRENT_TIMESTAMP().
LOCALTIMESTAMP()	Yes	Equivalent to CURRENT_TIMESTAMP().
MAKEDATE(yr,num)	No	Returns a day corresponding to the num day of the year yr.
MAKETIME(hr,min,sec)	No	Returns a time corresponding to hr:min:sec.
MICROSECOND(dtq)	No	Returns the microsecond part of dtq in %f format; dtq is a DATE or DATETIME data type.
MINUTE(dtq)	No	Returns the minute part of dtq in %i format; dtq is a DATE or DATETIME data type.
MONTH(dtq)	No	Returns the numeric month part of dtq in %c format; dtq is a DATE or DATETIME data type.
MONTHNAME(dtq)	No	Returns the month part of dtq in %M format; dtq is a DATE or DATETIME data type.
NOW()	No	Equivalent to CURRENT_TIMESTAMP(), which is safe to use for replication.
PERIOD_ADD(per,num)	No	Return a period of per plus num months. Periods are of the format %Y%m or %y%m.
PERIOD_DIFF(per1,per2)	No	Returns the number of months between per1 and per2; per1 and per2 are periods of the format %Y%m or %y%m.
QUARTER(dtq)	No	Returns a number between 1 and 4 that represents which quarter dtq is in; dtq is a DATE or DATETIME data type.
SEC_TO_TIME(num)	No	Returns a time corresponding to num seconds; in %H:%i:%s format.

TABLE B-15 *(continued)*		
Function Syntax	**Standard SQL?**	**Description**
SECOND(dtq)	No	Returns the second part of dtq in %s format; dtq is a DATE or DATETIME data type.
STR_TO_DATE(dta, specifier)	No	Returns a DATE, DATETIME or TIME value that corresponds to the mapping of dta to the specifier (see Table B-12). dta is a nonstandard date string representing a DATE, DATETIME, or TIME value. This function is used to translate a nonstandard date string to standard form: STR_TO_DATE('20 2009 04','%d %Y %m') returns '2009-04-20'.
SUBDATE(dt, INTERVAL expr unit) SUBDATE(dt, num)	No No	Returns a date that is dt minus the period defined by the INTERVAL expression. Returns a date that is dt minus num days.
SUBTIME(dtq, time_expr)	No	Returns a time that is expr1 minus time_expr in %H:%i:%s format. dtq is a DATE or DATETIME data type.
SYSDATE()	Yes	Returns the current date and time in %Y-%m-%d %H:%i:%s format. SYSDATE() is not safe for replication unless mysqld is started with the sysdate-is-now option. CURRENT_TIMESTAMP() and the NOW() alias are safe for replication.
TIME_FORMAT(ttm, specifier)	No	Format time ttm using specifier. For a complete listing of specifiers, see Table B-12.
TIME_TO_SEC(tm)	No	Returns the number of seconds corresponding to tm.
TIME(ttq)	Yes	Returns the time part of dtq in %H:%i:%s format, unless microseconds are >0. Then the format returned is %H:%i:%s.%f; ttq is a either a TIME or DATETIME data type.
TIMEDIFF(ttq1, ttq2)	No	Returns the result of subtracting TIME(ttq2) from TIME(ttq1). ttq1 and ttq2 are DATE or DATETIME data types.
TIMESTAMP(dtq) TIMESTAMP (dtq,time_expr)	Yes No	Returns the date and time of dtq in %Y-%m-%d %H:%i:%s format. Equivalent to ADDTIME(dtq, time_expr). In both usage cases, dtq is a DATE or DATETIME data type.
TIMESTAMPADD(specifier, num,dtq)	No	Equivalent of TIMESTAMP(dtq,INTERVAL num specifier). See Table B-12 for a list of specifiers.

continued

Function Syntax	Standard SQL?	Description
TIMESTAMPDIFF (specifier,dtq1,dtq2)	No	Returns the result of dtq2 minus dtq1 with respect to specifier. See Table B-12 for a list of specifiers. TIMESTAMPDIFF(MONTH,'2008-06-01', '2009-04-20') returns 10.
TO_DAYS(dtm)	No	Returns the number of days since day 0.
UNIX_TIMESTAMP([dtm])	No	Returns a number of seconds that corresponds to the UNIX timestamp for dtm. When dtm is not defined, it uses CURRENT_TIMESTAMP().
UTC_DATE()	No	Returns a DATE in %Y-%m-%d format corresponding to the current date in the UTC time zone.
UTC_TIME()	No	Returns a TIME in %H:%i:%s format corresponding to the current time in the UTC time zone.
UTC_TIMESTAMP()	No	Returns a DATETIME in %Y-%m-%d %H:%i:%s format corresponding to the current date and time in the UTC time zone.
WEEK(dtm[,mode])	No	Returns a number corresponding to the numeric week of the year; the value relies on the mode, or the default mode if unspecified.
WEEKDAY()	No	Returns a number corresponding to the numeric day of the week; format is %w (week starts on Sunday, day numbering starts at 0).
WEEKOFYEAR()	No	Equivalent to WEEK(date,3).
YEAR(dtq)	No	Returns the YEAR part of dtq in %Y format. dtq is either a DATE or DATETIME data type.
YEARWEEK(date[,mode])	No	Returns a six-digit number corresponding to the year and week of the year; the value relies on the mode, or the default mode if unspecified.

String functions on TEXT types

The string functions that MySQL provides are quite extensive. Table B-16 shows all functions that are used when working with strings along with a brief description of each one.

TABLE B-16

String Functions

Function Syntax	Standard SQL?	Description
ASCII(expr)	No	Returns the numeric ASCII value of the first character in expr. Not multi-byte-character safe, see ORD(str) for the multi-byte-character safe version.
BIT_LENGTH(expr)	No	Returns the number of bits in expr
CHAR_LENGTH(expr)	Yes	Returns the number of characters in expr
CHAR(list)	No	Returns the character represented by each number in list
CHARACTER_LENGTH(expr)	Yes	Same as CHAR_LENGTH(expr)
CHARSET(expr)	No	Returns the character set of expr. See Chapter 21 for how to find the character sets supported by your instance of mysqld.
COERCIBILITY(expr)	No	Returns the coercibility of expr. See Table B-17.
COLLATION(expr)	No	Returns the collation of expr. See Chapter 21 for how to find the collations supported by your instance of mysqld.
CONCAT_WS(sep,list)	No	Returns a string of all items in a comma-separated list separated by sep. Ignores NULL values in list. Returns NULL if the separator is NULL.
CONCAT(list)	No	Returns a string of all items in list; returns NULL if any item in list is NULL
ELT(num,list)	No	Returns the num item in list; returns NULL if num<1 or num > list length.
EXPORT_SET(bt, on_val,off_val [,sep [,num_bits]])	No	Returns a string consisting of the on_val and off_val characters separated by sep; the pattern of on_val and off_val corresponds to the order of bits set in bt; sep defaults to ',' and num_bits defaults to 64
FIELD(expr,list)	No	Returns the position of the first occurrence of expr in list
FIND_IN_SET(expr, str)	No	Returns the position of the first occurrence of expr in str; str is a comma-separated list of expressions

continued

TABLE B-16   *(continued)*

Function Syntax	Standard SQL?	Description
HEX(str)	No	Returns the value of each character in str converted to a hexadecimal value
INSERT(str,pos, len, add_str)	No	Returns a string that is str with len characters replaced by add_str, starting at pos. If pos is not within the length of str, return str.
INSTR(str,find_me)	No	Returns the position of the first occurrence of find_me in str
LCASE(str)	No	Equivalent to LOWER(str)
LEFT(str,num)	No	Returns a string corresponding to the leftmost num characters of str
LENGTH(str)	No	Equivalent to OCTET_LENGTH(str)
LOAD_FILE(file_name)	No	Loads the file named file_name and returns the contents as a string. For example:INSERT INTO tbl SET txt_field = LOAD_FILE(info.txt);
LOCATE(str_find, str [,st_pos])	No	Returns the position of the first occurrence of str_find in str starting from st_pos; st_pos defaults to 0
LOWER(str)	Yes	Returns str with all characters converted to lowercase
LPAD(str, num, pad_str)	No	Returns a string where the first num characters are pad_str, and str is appended to the end
LTRIM(str)	No	Returns str with the leading whitespace trimmed off
MAKE_SET(bt,list)	No	Returns a SET of the expressions in list that have the same bits set as in bt
MID(str,pos,num)	No	Equivalent to SUBSTRING(str,pos,num)
OCTET_LENGTH(str)	Yes	Returns the length of str in bytes
ORD(str)	No	Equivalent to ASCII(str) but ORD(str) can be used for multi-byte characters
POSITION(find_me IN str)	No	Equivalent to LOCATE(find_me,str)

TABLE B-16	*(continued)*	

Function Syntax	Standard SQL?	Description
QUOTE(str)	No	Returns a string that is `str` quoted. See Chapter 4 for more details on quoting: `mysql> SELECT QUOTE("hi!"), QUOTE('hi');` `+--------------+-------------+` `| QUOTE("hi!")	QUOTE('hi') |` `+--------------+-------------+` `| 'hi!'	'hi' |` `+--------------+-------------+` `1 row in set (0.00 sec)`

REPEAT(char,num)	No	Repeats `char` character `num` times:
		
		`mysql> SELECT REPEAT('#', 5);`
		`+----------------+`
		`| REPEAT('#', 5) |`
		`+----------------+`
		`| #####          |`
		`+----------------+`
		`1 row in set (0.00 sec)`

REPLACE(str, old, new)	No	Returns the string that corresponds to `str` with `old` replaced by `new`
REVERSE(str)	No	Reverse the order of characters in `str`
RIGHT(str,num)	No	Returns a string corresponding to the rightmost num characters of `str`
RPAD(str, num, pad_str)	No	Returns a string with `str` at the beginning, and the last num characters are `pad_str`
RTRIM(str)	No	Returns `str` with the trailing whitespace trimmed off
SOUNDEX(str)	No	Returns the SOUNDEX of `str`
SPACE(num)	No	Returns a string with num spaces
STRCMP(expr1,expr2)	No	Returns 1 if `expr1` is lexically greater than `expr2`; returns 0 if `expr1` is lexically equal to `expr2`; returns -1 if `expr1` is lexically less than `expr2`
SUBSTR(str,pos,num)	Yes	Equivalent to SUBSTRING(str,pos,num)
SUBSTRING_INDEX (str,sep,num)	No	If num is positive, returns `str` before the num occurrence of `sep`. If num is negative, returns `str` after the occurrence of `sep` that is num counting from the right.

continued

TABLE B-16 *(continued)*		
Function Syntax	**Standard SQL?**	**Description**
SUBSTRING(str,pos [,num])SUBSTRING(str FROM pos[FOR num])	Yes Yes	For both forms, returns a string starting from pos, ending after num characters; num defaults to -1 (the end of the string)
TRIM([trim_str FROM] str)TRIM([{BOTH | LEADING | TRAILING} [trim_str] FROM] str)	No Yes	Returns a string with all leading and trailing values of trim_str removed from str. If trim_str is not defined, trims spaces. Returns a string with values of trim_str removed from str; if LEADING is specified, trims the leading values; if TRAILING is specified, removes the trailing values; if unspecified or BOTH is specified, trims the leading and trailing values. If trim_str is not defined, trim spaces.
UCASE(str)	No	Equivalent to UPPER(str)
UPPER(str)	Yes	Returns str with all characters converted to uppercase
UUID()	No	Returns a UUID (Universal Unique Identifier)
WEIGHT_STRING(str)	No	Returns a weight string. This function is only available in MySQL server 6.0.

Character sets and collations

Character sets and collations are described in detail in Chapter 4. How to find out the character sets and collations supported by a running version of mysqld can be found in Chapter 21.

Coercibility

The return value of the COERCIBILITY() function is called *coercibility*. The coercibility of a string specifies how likely it is that mysqld can determine the collation of the input value. A coercibility of 0 means mysqld can definitely determine the collation of the input value, because the input value has a COLLATE clause. There is no guesswork involved; mysqld just looks at the COLLATE clause. A coercibility of 5 means mysqld cannot determine the collation of the input value at all, because the input value is NULL.

The values returned by the COERCIBILITY() function have the meanings shown in Table B-17. Lower values have higher precedence.

Data type conversions

Data flow from a web browser to a web server to a database is handled by the end user's web browser, the programs that form the interface into the database, and the database itself. Each of these technologies defines data types in different ways; utilizing more than one technology for data storage and processing will likely require the use of type conversion. Data types are not standard, which is where type conversion is useful.

TABLE B-17

Coercibility values

Coercibility	Meaning	Example
0	Explicit collation	Value with COLLATE clause
1	No collation	Concatenation of strings with different collations
2	Implicit collation	Column value, stored routine parameter or local variable
3	System constant	USER() return value
4	Coercible	Literal string
5	Ignorable	NULL or an expression derived from NULL

Table B-18 lists the data types that are available for conversion in MySQL.

TABLE B-18

Data Types for the CAST() and CONVERT() Functions

Type	Notes
BINARY[(N)]	Convert to BINARY; if N is specified, do not use more than N bytes.
CHAR[(N)]	Convert to a CHAR; if N is specified, do not use more than N characters.
DATE	Returns a DATE
DATETIME	Returns a DATETIME
DECIMAL[(M[,D])]	Returns a DECIMAL value; if M is specified, do not use more than M digits. If D is also specified, do not use more than D digits after the decimal point.
SIGNED [INTEGER]	Returns a signed INTEGER
TIME	Returns a TIME
UNSIGNED [INTEGER]	Returns an unsigned INTEGER

The functions used for the type conversion are listed in Table B-19.

TABLE B-19

Type Conversion Functions

Function Syntax	Standard SQL?	Description
CAST(expr AS type)	Yes	Equivalent to CONVERT(expr,type)
BIN(expr)	No	Returns the binary representation of expr
BINARY(expr)	No	Returns the binary string of expr
CONVERT(expr,type) CONVERT(expr USING type)	Yes	For both forms, returns a type value of expr. See Table B-18 for data types.
OCT(expr)	No	Returns the value of expr converted to octal
UNHEX(num)	No	Returns the value of the characters represented by each pair of numbers in num

Working with XML

MySQL includes several functions for use when manipulating XML. Table B-20 lists these functions.

TABLE B-20

XML Functions

Function Syntax	Standard SQL?	Description
ExtractValue (frag, expr)	No	Returns a string of the first text node that is a child of the elements matched by expr; expr is an XPath expression
UpdateXML (target, expr,xml)	No	Returns a string that is target with expr replaced with XML; expr is an XPath expression. If expr does not appear exactly once in target, returns target.

Appendix C

Resources

MySQL has a large user base and a very helpful community. There are many resources available for database administrators who need help or want to learn more.

MySQL maintains a website at `http://dev.mysql.com/tech-resources` that contains a list of technical resources; it is a good place to start, although many of those resources are, at the time of this writing, listed here as well.

The resources in this chapter are loosely grouped. Although it may be appropriate to ask a question as a reply to a blog post, most blogs are meant to be informative. Thus, blogs are categorized as *Learning more*, even though they might be considered appropriate in the *Asking questions* category. People often share solutions on forums, though the MySQL forums are not categorized under *Sharing solutions*. In this way, the categories are guidelines, not hard-and-fast rules.

Finding Paid Support

Sun/MySQL offers paid support in the form of their MySQL Enterprise offering. The most current details of the support offerings can be found online at `www.mysql.com/support/`; current pricing can be found at `https://shop.mysql.com/enterprise`.

A paid subscription to MySQL Enterprise gives you access to:

- **Problem Resolution Support** — Traditional incident response model; allows a customer to contact Sun/MySQL with a specific incident

- **Online Knowledge Base** — Allows a customer to search a special Enterprise-only knowledge base containing solutions
- **Software** — The MySQL Enterprise binary, the MySQL Enterprise Monitor, and the MySQL Query Analzyer
- **Consultative Support** — Traditional consulting model; Sun/MySQL employees can support remote troubleshooting, remote maintenance, replication review, schema review, query review, performance tuning, and customer code review

There are many third-party consulting companies that offer paid support and/or training options. Sun/MySQL maintains a list of partners at `http://solutions.mysql.com/solutions/partners/consulting`.

Asking Questions

The best resource for asking questions is a colleague. However, many organizations do not have more than one person filling the role of a MySQL DBA. You may find yourself in this position, or you may ask colleagues and still want more information. In those cases, the following resources are available:

- MySQL Forums
- MySQL Lists
- Bug Reports

Conferences and user group meetings (see the section "Learning more" in this chapter) also provide a place to ask questions. Many user groups have forums associated with them. There is a worldwide MySQL User Group message board at `http://mysql.meetup.com/boards`.

MySQL forums

Official web-based MySQL forums can be found at `http://forums.mysql.com`. There are over 100 forums, categorized as:

- **Forums** — A forum devoted to announcements such as new releases
- **MySQL Usage** — Several forums devoted to general usage, such as building from source, installing, and configuring, and the *Newbie* forum
- **Migration** — Over 10 forums devoted to the free MySQL Migration Toolkit, migrating from Oracle, Microsoft SQL Server, PostgreSQL, SQLite, and more
- **MySQL Enterprise** — Several forums devoted to MySQL Enterprise offerings. Some forums, such as the MySQL Monitor forum or the MySQL Query Analyzer forum, relate to tools that are only available to paid subscribers of MySQL Enterprise. Others, such as the MySQL Proxy forum, are about tools available to anyone. All forums are freely available, even if the tools they relate to are not.

- **MySQL Workbench** — Several forums devoted to features in the MySQL Workbench GUI tool

- **MySQL Tools** — A few forums devoted to the MySQL Query Browser, MySQL Administrator GUI Tools, and general database administration issues

- **3rd Party Applications** — A forum devoted to third-party applications such as reporting and business intelligence tools

- **MySQL Connectors** — A few forums devoted to MySQL connectors such as ODBC, .NET, Connector/J, and Connector/C++

- **Computer Languages** — Several forums devoted to using MySQL with programming languages. There are forums for languages with growing usage such as Ruby and Python, popular languages such as Java, Perl, and PHP, and even a Delphi forum!

- **MySQL Storage Engines** — Over 10 forums devoted to the different storage engines, including standards such as MyISAM and InnoDB, newer storage engines such as Falcon and Maria, custom storage engines and a forum for using memcached as a storage engine

- **Systems** — A few forums devoted to using MySQL on virtual systems, using MySQL on Amazon EC2, and using MySQL on different storage systems such as SANs.

- **SQL Standards** — Over 10 forums devoted to SQL such as Transactions, Constraints, Cursors, Events, Stored Procedures, UDFs, and character sets

- **MySQL Technology** — Over 15 forums devoted to general MySQL areas such as the optimizer, replication, high availability (HA), embedded MySQL, MySQL Cluster, backup, and the catch-all General forum

- **Business** — Several forums devoted to business issues such as licensing, hosting, certification, jobs, and partners

- **International** — Over 10 forums for asking MySQL questions in different languages such as French, Portuguese, Russian, Turkish, Chinese, Japanese, and more

MySQL lists

Information about official MySQL mailing lists can be found at http://lists.mysql.com, which includes links to subscribe to each list, unsubscribe from each list, and the archives for each list. There is a low-volume general announcements list. There are more than 40 other lists, categorized as:

- **Server** — Contains lists relating to the mysqld server, including lists for storage engines, replication, cluster, and the General Discussion list

- **Connectors** — Contains lists relating to MySQL connectors such as Connector/C++, Connector/J, .NET, PHP, the NDB Connectors, and the Message API

- **Internals** — Contains lists relating to MySQL internals such as bugs, documentation, benchmarks, and commits

- **Eventum** — Contains lists for users and developers of the Eventum issue tracking tool, developed by MySQL and available for free at `http://dev.mysql.com/downloads/other/eventum`

- **Community** — Contains lists for the community, such as the Google Summer of Code, the MySQL Conference and Expo, and community contributions

- **Non-English** — Contains lists for non-English-speaking users of MySQL, including general lists in German, Spanish, and Japanese

- **User Groups** — Discussion lists for some of the user groups. A full list of the MySQL User Groups, many of which have third-party sites containing lists and message boards, can be found at `http://forge.mysql.com/wiki/List_of_MySQL_User_Groups`.

Bug reports

If a MySQL component is acting in a way that is not documented, you may need to ask or inform the developers of this behavior by filing a bug report. Visit `http://bugs.mysql.com` to report a bug or search the bug system for existing bugs. There are tips on how to report a bug at `http://bugs.mysql.com/how-to-report.php` — a detailed bug report involves stating your assumptions, what you have done, what you expect to happen and what actually happens. This process, combined with searching the existing bug reports before starting to create a new one, often causes DBAs to realize that what they thought was a bug was actually caused by a misunderstanding or mistake — and they realize they can fix the issue without actually creating a bug report. Of course, there are times when an issue is a bug, and in those cases, a bug report is appropriate.

Sharing Solutions

The centralized source for shared MySQL solutions is on the MySQL Forge at `http://forge.mysql.com`. The MySQL Forge contains the following sections:

- **Projects** (`http://forge.mysql.com/projects`) — Community contributed projects relating to MySQL, such as sample databases, `memcached` functions for MySQL, and the MySQL Sandbox. Projects can be tagged and rated.

- **Tools & Code** (`http://forge.mysql.com/tools`) — Community contributed solutions, ranging from code snippets to storage engines to user-defined functions (UDFs)

- Software Preview (`http://forge.mysql.com/wiki/Category:Software_Preview`) — Sneek peaks at unofficial distributions containing new features

- **Worklog** (`http://forge.mysql.com/worklog/`) — Tasks that MySQL engineers are working on or requesting feedback from. There is more information about the Forge Worklog at `http://forge.mysql.com/wiki/WorkLog`.

- **Contribute** (`http://forge.mysql.com/wiki/Community_Contributions`) — The MySQL Community Development Program, including how to contribute, coding standards and guidelines, and the Sun Contributor Agreement

- **Wiki** (http://forge.mysql.com/wiki/Main_Page) — Anyone can create and edit pages to share knowledge. Current information on the wiki includes conference presentations, user-contributed documentation, articles, tutorials, and specifications.

Getting Documentation

The official documentation for MySQL is online at http://dev.mysql.com/doc. It includes links to:

- The comprehensive *MySQL Reference Manual*, for downloading or online viewing. The reference manuals for MySQL 5.0 and 5.1 have been translated into several different formats and languages. Visit http://dev.mysql.com/doc/#refman to see a matrix of the documentation available.
- MySQL GUI Tools documentation
- Expert Guides for internals, the Cluster API, and the test framework
- The sakila, world, employee, and menagerie example databases
- Community contributed documentation
- Documentation about the MySQL documentation

> **TIP**   At the time of this writing, the official reference manual for MySQL 6.0 is only available in English, and can be viewed online at http://dev.mysql.com/doc/refman/6.0/en/index.html or downloaded from the main documentation site at http://dev.mysql.com/doc/#refman.

Cheat sheets and quick references

- **MySQL 6.0 function and statement cheat sheets** (www.visibone.com/sql/) — From VisiBone, full-color quick-reference guides to all of the MySQL functions and statements. Available for free download or purchase laminated pages or posters. Indicates whether a function or statement is part of the ISO/ANSI SQL:2003 standard.
- EXPLAIN **cheat sheet** (http://www.pythian.com/blogs/960/explain-cheatsheet) — Developed by author Sheeri K. Cabral with formatting help from Dave Edwards, the EXPLAIN cheat sheet is a freely downloadable reference for quick or offline lookup of what the different fields of output from EXPLAIN means
- **Common DBA tasks cheat sheet** (http://en.wikibooks.org/wiki/MySQL/CheatSheet) — From Wikibooks, a cheat sheet containing commands for sample queries, metadata access, privilege administration, data types, resetting the root password, and more.
- **Metadata access comparison** (http://sqlzoo.net/howto/source/z.dir/i12meta.xml) — Shows how to access metadata such as table names, column names, and the software version in many vendors' DBMS, including MySQL. A similar cheat

sheet, formatted for printing, is available at `http://mentalaxis.com/ref/mysql cheatsheet.pdf`.

Learning More

There are many resources for further education about MySQL. The most recent and up-to-date learning opportunities can be found online or in person, in the form of articles and presentations.

Articles

- **Planet MySQL** (`www.planetmysql.org`) — An aggregated feed of blog posts from the MySQL Community. The top 30 most active contributors are highlighted, so if you prefer you can follow the links and choose to follow a few individual blogs.

- *MySQL Magazine* (`www.mysqlzine.net`) — Edited by Keith Murphy, *MySQL Magazine*'s inaugural issue appeared in the summer of 2007. *MySQL Magazine* is produced four times annually, with current and back issues freely available online as printable PDFs.

- **MySQL Developer Zone articles** (`http://dev.mysql.com/tech-resources/articles`) and news (`http://dev.mysql.com/tech-resources/news`) — Collections of tech news and articles from and for MySQL developers

- *MySQL Newsletter* (`www.mysql.com/news-and-events/newsletter`) — The monthly newsletter "with articles about new products, new features, training, security issues, known bugs, and events of interest to the MySQL community." Current and back issues are freely available online.

- **MySQL White Papers** (`www.mysql.com/why-mysql/white-papers`) — White papers about MySQL.

- **Sun's list of MySQL Resources for System Administrators** (`www.sun.com/bigadmin/topics/mysql`) — Sun's BigAdmin System Administration Portal contains a section on MySQL resources for system administrators.

- **HowToForge articles** (`www.howtoforge.com/howtos/mysql`) — How To articles for MySQL tasks.

Presentations

There are many resources for seeing presentation slides and videos available:

- **MySQL presentations from before 2007** (`http://dev.mysql.com/tech-resources/presentations/`) — Presentations from conferences before 2007

- **Presentations from the 2007 MySQL User Conference and Expo** (`www.technocation.org/content/2007-mysql-user-conference-and-expo-presentations-and-videos`) — A comprehensive list of presentations, slides, notes, and videos from the 2007 MySQL User Conference and Expo

- **Presentations from the 2008 MySQL User Conference and Expo** (http://forge.mysql.com/wiki/MySQLConf2008Notes)—A comprehensive list of presentations, slides, notes, and videos from the 2008 MySQL User Conference and Expo

- **Presentations from the 2009 MySQL User Conference and Expo** (http://forge.mysql.com/wiki/MySQLConf2009Notes)—A comprehensive list of presentations, slides, notes, and videos from the 2009 MySQL User Conference and Expo

> **TIP** The MySQL Forge Wiki (http://forge.mysql.com/wiki) will link to future conferences, so make sure to look there.

- **MySQL live webinars** (www.mysql.com/news-and-events/web-seminars)— MySQL offers free live Webex webinars containing technology overviews

- **MySQL on-demand webinars** (www.mysql.com/news-and-events/on-demand-webinars/)— MySQL makes the most popular live webinars available for playback any time

- **MySQL University** (http://forge.mysql.com/wiki/MySQL_University)— In-depth technical sessions given by leading MySQL developers and community members

- **MySQL presentations at Technocation** (http://technocation.org/category/areas/presentationsvideos)— Technocation, Inc. is a not-for-profit organization providing educational resources for IT professionals. They host many video presentations and provide slides that can be freely downloaded or streamed for viewing online.

- **Popular video hosting sites** — YouTube and Google Video are the most popular video sharing sites in the United States. However, there are many more video-sharing sites, and most have search capabilities. Simply searching for "mysql" on a video-sharing site can turn up presentations and video tutorials about MySQL.

  - **YouTube MySQL videos** (www.youtube.com/results?search_query=mysql) — YouTube limits video uploads to 10 minutes, so the videos returned by this search are usually short. The exception is videos on YouTube that come from Google Video.

  - **Google Video MySQL presentations** (http://video.google.com/video search?q=mysql)— Do a basic search for videos containing the keyword "mysql".

User group meetings

There are MySQL user groups throughout the world. Information about starting a user group as well as what user groups currently exist can be found at http://forge.mysql.com/wiki/Category:MySQLUserGroups.

Conferences

Conferences are an excellent place to see live presentations about MySQL and provide opportunities to meet other MySQL DBAs while learning.

819

- **MySQL Conference and Expo** (www.mysqlconf.com) — Traditionally held in April in Santa Clara, California, the MySQL Conference and Expo is the premier conference for learning about MySQL and networking with other MySQL users.

- **OSCon** (http://conferences.oreillynet.com/oscon/) — OSCon, or the Open Source Convention, is traditionally held during July in Portland, Oregon. There are usually several MySQL-related presentations.

- **Various camps** — MySQL Camp is a free *unconference* for MySQL, held annually. As MySQL Camp is organized by the MySQL Community and is not a commercial event, the date and location changes often. MySQL Camp dates will be announced in many places, including Planet MySQL blogs (http://planetmysql.org). OpenSQL Camp (www.opensqlcamp.org) is a free unconference for open source databases, including MySQL.

Training/certification

The training and certification opportunities that MySQL offers are listed at www.mysql.com/training. MySQL maintains a list of third-party partners offering training at http://solutions.mysql.com/solutions/partners/training.

Index

Index

Symbols

-- (double dash), 88
\# (pound), 89–90
% (modulus operator), 503–504
|| (string concatenation)
   MySQL support, 107
   SQL mode definitions, 210
\ (backslash)
   escape characters, 91–93
   naming limitations and quoting, 93–94
. (dot), 95–97
" (double quotation mark)
   naming limitations and, 93
   SQL mode definitions, 204
! (exclamation point), 89
? (question mark), 49
; (semi-colons), 60
' (single quotation mark), 93
\. (source), 54–55
32-bit systems
   vs. 64-bit systems, 12
   choosing hardware, 349–350
\! command, 62
64-bit systems
   vs. 32-bit systems, 12
   choosing hardware, 349–350
   OS architecture, 352

A

abstraction, view, 307–308
access. *See also* security
   data access strategy, 596–606
   database, 654
   user account problems, 491
Access Control Lists (ACLs). *See* ACLs (Access Control Lists)
accessing MySQL
   Administrator, 74–80
   command-line client tool, 52–62
   with command-line tools, 49–52
   mysqladmin, 62–66
   phpMyAdmin, 69–71
   Query Browser, 71–74
   SQLyog, 66–69
   summary, 83–84
   Workbench, 80–83
accounts, user
   debugging problems, 490–494
   managing, 478–487
ACID (atomicity, consistency, isolation and durability) compliance
   defined, 319–320
   PBXT, 410
   understanding, 320–322
ACLs (Access Control Lists)
   defined, 474–475
   securing MySQL, 649–653
   security with stored routines, 256
activity logging, 520–522
administration
   Administrator tool, 74–80
   log. *See* logs
   measuring performance. *See* performance measurement
   with mysqladmin, 62–66
   server tuning. *See* MySQL server tuning
   storage engine. *See* storage engines
   user management. *See* user management
agent-based systems, 635–636
agentless systems, 635–636
aggregate functions
   NULL values and, 211
   overview, 783–784
alerts, monitoring. *See* monitoring systems
algorithms
   MyISAM index buffer, 366
   partitioning, 496–497
   view, 309–310
aliases
   creating trigger, 244
   extension, 115
   table, 592–594
ALLOW_INVALID_DATES, 204

The books you read to succeed.

Get the most out of the latest software and leading-edge technologies with a Wiley Bible—your one-stop reference.

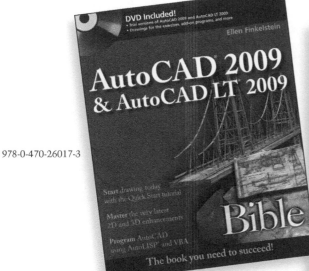

Printed and bound by CPI Group (UK) Ltd, Croydon, CR0 4YY

27/10/2024

14580185-0001